DIVORCES and SEPARATIONS

from

Petitions

to the

North Carolina
General Assembly

1779–1837

Abstracted by
Janet and Ransom McBride

HERITAGE BOOKS
2019

HERITAGE BOOKS
AN IMPRINT OF HERITAGE BOOKS, INC.

Books, CDs, and more—Worldwide

For our listing of thousands of titles see our website
at
www.HeritageBooks.com

Published 2019 by
HERITAGE BOOKS, INC.
Publishing Division
5810 Ruatan Street
Berwyn Heights, Md. 20740

Copyright © 2009
North Carolina Genealogical Society
P.O. Box 30815
Raleigh, North Carolina 27622-0815

Edited by Amy Moore

All rights reserved. No part of this book may be reproduced or transmitted in any form or by any means, electronic or mechanical, including photocopying, recording or by any information storage and retrieval system without written permission from the author, except for the inclusion of brief quotations in a review.

International Standard Book Number
Paperbound: 978-0-936370-20-0

INTRODUCTION

Divorces and separations from the bonds of matrimony are never pleasant subjects to discuss, however the Petitions and Memorials which request that such steps be approved on the part of parties involved often contain genealogical information that cannot be obtained in any other way. The very fact that injured parties petition for a separation or a divorce presumes that a legal marriage took place, and this presumption may complement or supplement marriage information from another source. The names of children and parents are sometimes revealed in such petitions as well as previous residences. Reasons given in a petition requesting a divorce or separation are always subjective and should be viewed in that light. Complete details or both sides of the argument are rarely provided in early petitions.

The North Carolina Genealogical Society Journal has published two articles on divorces and separations both of them addressing only those cases which were approved by act of the North Carolina Assembly (NCGSJ, Vol III, No. 1 (Feb. 1977), pp. 43-47; and NCGSJ, Vol. IX, No. 1 (Feb. 1983), pp. 43-46). Background to the handling of divorce and separation in early North Carolina may be found in these articles. The purpose of this book is to abstract the genealogical information found in surviving petitions addressed to the North Carolina General Assembly requesting relief from the bond of matrimony. Until 1808, only the General Assembly had jurisdiction over these matters, but in that year a complete divorce could be obtained for impotency or adultery by having the injured party address the county superior courts. For other than complete divorces, the following provisions prevailed:

If any husband shall maliciously either abandon his family or turn his wife out of doors, or by cruel and barbarous treatment endanger her life or offer such indignities to her person as to render her condition intolerable or life burthensome, and thereby force her to withdraw from his house and family...A Superior Court may grant a divorce from bed and board and allow her such alimony as her husband's circumstances will admit...not to exceed one-third of the annual profits or income of his estate, occupation or labors...

A divorce of "Bed and Board" did not dissolve the marriage bond, but suspended the effect of marriage as to cohabitation. Following such authorization, an act would be passed to secure the injured party such estate or property as might be acquired after the separation as if there had been no marriage.

Each article in this series will list the involved parties as if there had been no marriage.

Divorces and Separations from Petitions to the North Carolina General Assembly from 1779

Each article in this series will list the involved parties in alphabetical order. Source identification for each petition will be shown in parentheses according to the following abbreviations:

    GASR - General Assembly Session Records
    HCR - House Committee Reports
    HM - House Messages
    HR - House Resolutions
    JCR - Joint Committee Reports
    Pet. - Petitions
    SCR - Senate Committee Reports
    SM - Senate Messages
    SR - Senate Resolutions
    HB - House Bill
    SB - Senate Bill

All of these sources are filed at the North Carolina State Archives in Raleigh, North Carolina.

1784-1799

1.   **Bell, Ruth.** Memorial of Ruth Bell, wife of William Bell of Currituck Co., NC, no date. Memorialist married William Bell about three years ago, but after twelve months, he left your memorialist with one child but did not contribute to their support. The father of your memorialist took both her and her child into his house and supported them. Her father would like her to share in his property with his other children, but believes that said William's creditors would seize any such share given to said Ruth. Prays for an act to grant relief. (GASR, Nov.-Dec. 1798, Box 3: Folder - "Petitions, Divorce & Inheritance). Ruth Bell, wife of William of Currituck Co., NC, is entitled to possess and enjoy sole right to all estate she may hereafter acquire, as if she had never been married. (GASR, Nov.-Dec. 1798, Box 1: Folder "House Bills, 13 Dec.").

2.   **Bostick, Ezra.** The Committee of Propositions and Grievances No. 2, to whom was referred the Petition of Ezra Bostick praying for a divorcement, report that after taking into consideration the allegations set forth in the petition, conceive the subject improper for the investigation of the Legislature… [and] do unanimously reject the same. (GASR, Dec. 1791-Jan. 1792, Box 2: Folder "JCR- Propositions and Grievances"). Petition of Ezra Bostick of Anson Co., NC, no date, states that Sarah, the petitioner's wife, withdrew from him in 1782 and took up with one Timothy Haney. She has remained with said Haney as his wife ever since and has had several children by him. By the laws of North Carolina, these children are not excluded as heirs to the estate of the petitioner should he die intestate. A law of divorce in the petitioner's favor has never been passed. The petitioner requests that such a law be passed to exclude his former wife Sarah from her right of dower, and that her children by Timothy Haney be excluded from any right of inheritance of said petitioner's estate. [Below:] Statement signed by thirty-two petitioners on behalf of Ezra Bostick that said Bostick's wife Sarah made her elopement with Timothy Haney when Bostick was out in the defense and service of his country. Said Sarah had only one child by Bostick, and said child was amply provided for. Haney and Sarah have left the county. Ezra Bostick is a Justice of the Peace with a moderate estate. (GASR, Nov.-Dec. 1796, Box 3: Folder "Pet. - Divorce, inheritance").

3.   **Bowers, Mary.** Petition of Peter Brown and Mary Bowers of Rowan Co., NC, states that petitioner Mary Bowers, daughter of the other petitioner Peter Brown, married Barnabas Bowers in 1795 "at an age so young that it was almost impossible for her to judge the solemnity of the contract." They lived together only a short time before a separation took place owing "to the ill usage and cruelty" said Mary was obliged to bear from said Barnabas. The latter has abandoned said Mary as his wife and gone to some unknown place without making provision for her support. Petitioners pray for a law to secure said Mary any property she may hereafter acquire. Committee of Propositions and Grievances No. 1 recommend passage of such an act. In Senate, 17 Dec. 1799 and in House, 18 Dec. 1799. Concurrence. (GASR, Nov.-Dec. 1799, Box 3: Folder "JCR, Propositions & Grievances"). Bill passed Senate, 20 Dec. and House, 23 Dec. 1799 (Box 1: HB, 6 Dec.).

Divorces and Separations from Petitions to the North Carolina General Assembly from 1779

4.   **Braswell, Robin.** Petition of Robin Braswell declares that about thirteen years ago, he married Calley Powell. They lived together almost five years and had children, all of whom are now dead. At the end of this time frame, said Calley gave birth to a black child, and a separation of bed and board took place. Said Calley remained away for about eight years and gave birth to three more black children. About two years ago, she returned with the youngest child, which the petitioner thinks is an "unnecessary and at the same time an uncomfortable expense." There are no ties of friendship between them, and petitioner prays for a divorce. Committee of Propositions and Grievances recommends a bill be passed granting the divorce, but empowering commissioners to make an annual allowance to said Calley out of said Robin's estate. (GASR, Nov.-Dec. 1798, Box 1: Folder "House Bills, 4 Dec.").

5.   **Butler, Teresa.** (Also see number 9, "Davis, Teresa alias Butler"). Petition of Teresa Butler of Wilmington, NC, who states she was married to Henry L. Butler on 1 April 1786 as will appear by a certificate of James Parratt, Esq. (the magistrate by whom they were married) and by the affidavit of her father, Isaac Davis. About five months after the marriage, said Henry L. Butler, without any just cause of complaint or disaffection, left the house of your petitioner's father, the said Isaac Davis, where the couple had resided. Said Henry L. Butler has never since that time given your petitioner the least assistance nor even corresponded with her. He abandoned his wife and infant daughter, and if it were not for the paternal care of her father, your petitioner would have languished out her life in wretchedness and misery. Your petitioner has been credibly informed that prior to her marriage with the said Henry L. Butler, he had been married in Boston, and that since his marriage with your petitioner, has again married in the West Indies. Your petitioner requests relief to which she is entitled, viz., a divorce.

   [End:] Deposition of Isaac Davis of New Hanover Co., NC, 26 Nov. 1791, before J. Fergus, Justice of Peace, that on 1 Apr. 1786, his daughter Teresa was joined to Henry L. Butler in the Holy State of Matrimony by James Perrot, Esq., a Magistrate of the Town of Beaufort, NC. After living in the house of the deponent with his said wife for five months, the said Henry L. Butler left the deponent's house and said town of Beaufort. The said Teresa has resided in the deponent's house ever since, and neither the said Teresa or her infant daughter by said Henry L. Butler have received the least assistance from said Butler. [End:] Letter to Mrs. Teresa Butler, Bald Head, Cape Fear, from J. Parratt, no date: "Reed. a few lines from you requesting a Certificate of your marriage with Mr. Butler, which I with pleasure obey, as it may be satisfactory to you and your friends. The day & year has escaped my memory, but all the world may believe as fact, that you was lawfully married to Mr. Butler some time in the Spring of the Year 1786 I think - I guess by your request, you intend to make a second tryal of the matrimonial state, and I sincerely wish you may enjoy as much happiness as that state can afford..." In House and Senate, 10 Dec. 1791, and referred to Committee of Propositions and Grievances No. 1.

   (GASR, Dec. 1791-Jan. 1792, Box 3: Folder "Pet., divorce, name changes").

   The Committee of Propositions and Grievances No. 1, to whom the Petition of Teresa Butler was referred, reports that on considering the several circumstances stated in the petition, they are of opinion that should the Legislature enter into the business of granting divorces, it would be production of many dangerous and evil circumstances, therefore they reject the petition. In House, 29 Dec. 1791, and in Senate, 30 Dec. 1791, with concurrence in action of said Committee. Petition is rejected. (GASR, Dec. 1791-Jan. 1792, Box 2: Folder "JCR, Propositions & Grievances No. 1).

6.   **Byrum, James.** Petition of James Byrum of Bertie Co., NC, who states that he married Amelia Keen of the same county in August 1792. Soon after the marriage, he discovered "to his great sorrow and mortification that said Amelia was possessed of a most violent and ungovernable temper." Your petitioner tried for five years with kindness and attention to ameliorate this difficulty and bore with patience

her turbulent temper without being able to soften or render it more affable. In March 1796, she deserted him and went to reside in what was then called Cumberland, now Tennessee, and remained there. Your petitioner has been informed that his said wife was delivered of a child in January last. He prays for relief by means of a divorce. [Below:]] Endorsement of four subscribers attesting to the above to the best of their knowledge. [End:] Committee of Propositions and Grievances recommends a bill granting petitioner such relief as necessary. [End:] Draft bill grants petitioner, James Byrum, a divorce from his wife, Amelia. In Senate, 3 Dec. 1799, read 2nd time and passed. In House, 4 Dec. 1799, read 2nd time, and rejected. (GASR, Nov.-Dec. 1799, Box 1: Folder "Senate Bills, 22 Nov.").

7. **Carter, Elizabeth.** Petition of Elizabeth Carter, no date, no location, who states she married Benjamin Carter "several years past," but that said Benjamin left her with a "parcel of Suffering Children and has gone to Cumberland with Mr. Sowell who moved from Raleigh." Prays relief.

[Below:] Endorsed by twenty-one residents of [Nash] County, NC. Referred to Committee of Propisitions and Grievance #2. (GASR, Nov.-Dec. 1798, Box 3: Folder "Petitions - divorce & inheritance"), Committee to whom petition of Elizabeth Carter was referred states that said Elizabeth intermarried with Benjamin Carter, who a few years afterwards left her and now lives in Tennessee. Since said Benjamin has notified his wife by letter that he never will return or acknowledge her as his wife again, Committee recommends a bill be passed to provide relief to petitioner. In House, 13 Dec. 1798, which concurs with Committee. (GASR, Nov.-Dec. 1798, Box 2: Folder "HCR"), Act to secure to Elizabeth Carter, wife of Benjamin Carter, such estate as she may hereafter acquire. Said Benjamin has for several years past absented himself from his wife Elizabeth. (GASR, Nov.-Dec. 1798, Box 1: Folder "Senate Bills, 13 Dec."),

8. **Davis, Sarah.** Petition of Sarah Davis of Rebeson Co., NC, who states that in 1793 in Robeson County, she married Richard Child Davis, who continued to live with petitioner until the month of January following, when he left her after selling and disposing of all the property of which the petitioner was possessed before and during the marriage. Said husband was "a very extravagant man and immoral in his conduct. He has gone to some part of the world unknown to the petitioner. Prays for a law to secure to her all of her remaining property.

[Above petition enclosed in following bill:] Bill to secure Sarah Davis, wife of Richard Child Davis, such property as she may hereafter acquire as if she had never been married. Said Richard Child Davis for some considerable time past absented himself from his said wife with no expectation of a reconciliation. In Senate, 5 Dec. 1799, & in House, 6 Dec. 1799. Read third time and passed. (GASR, Nov.-Dec. 1799, Box 1: Folder "Senate Bill 22 Nov.").

9. **Davis, Teresa alias Butler.** Petition of Teresa Davis alias Butler, no date, no location, who states that by the advice of her parents and friends, she unfortunately contracted marriage with a certain person by the name of Butler, who appeared to be an honest, reputable man – but a few months after their marriage, the said Butler left her and married another woman in South Carolina & that she has neither seen nor heard from him for several years. She had the misfortune to find out that said Butler previous to his marriage with her had a wife & children in Philadelphia. In consequence she applied to the last Assembly for a divorce but failed to obtain same…she therefore petitions that her name be altered from Butler to Dunbar. (GASR, Nov. 1792-Jan. 1793, Box 3: Folder "Petitions - divorce, name changes"). Act granting Teresa Davis, alias Butler, of New Hanover Co., NC, to change her name to Teresa Dunbar passed. (NC Laws of North Carolina, 1792, p. 19).

Divorces and Separations from Petitions to the North Carolina General Assembly from 1779

---

10. **Dick, Catharina.** Petition of Catharina (x) Dick: "Having been so unfortunate to marry Joseph Dick, a Pedlar, from Canada and by Birth a Frenchman," petitioner prays to be secured in her small estate, free from all claims of her husband. Said Joseph Dick brought distress upon his family by foolish trading, everything being taken by the constables. Said husband deserted his wife, Catharina, first on 22 Dec. 1787, and the second time for good in April 1790. She did not further hear from him, so she made a resolution to begin anew to acquire a small maintenance for herself and her little son, John. [Below:] Endorsement by eight subscribers and dated 13 Nov. 1799, Montgomery Co., NC. Petition approved, and bill enacted to secure Catherine Dick, wife of Joseph Dick, such property as she may have acquired since her husband left her & such as she may hereafter acquire. (GASR, Nov.-Dec. 1799, Box 3: Folder "Petitions - miscellaneous"),

11. **Dickson, Alex.** Petition of Alex Dickson of Duplin Co., NC, who prays for a divorce from his wife Elizabeth. [House Minutes, Oct. 1779: Walter Clark, ed., The State Records of North Carolina [Winston and Goldsboro: State of North Carolina, 16 vols., numbered XI-XXVI, 1895-1907], XIII:932; original petition and outcome not found in GASR,)

12. **Dills, William.** Petition of William Dills states that about May 1791, his wife (unnamed) took advantage of the petitioner's absence on business by forsaking her family of three small children and absconding with a certain Bailey. Since that time, said Dills has not heard anything from his wife, and prays to be allowed to take another wife should he choose to do so without being liable to punishment under the law.
    [Below:] Endorsement of 98 residents of [Rowan] County, NC, before one Justice of Peace Bodenhamer that William Dills "has from character and appearance been a Loving and Indulgent Husband." In House & Senate, 21 Nov. 1791. Read and ordered to lie on the table. (GASR, Nov. 1792-Jan. 1793, Box 3: Folder "Petitions - divorce, name changes").

13. **Dowd, Mary.** "Whereas Conner Dowd, husband of Mary Dowd), attached himself in the Cause of the Revolutionary War to the British forces, whereby his property became forfeited to the State of North Carolina, but the Court of Chatham County in which county the said property chiefly lay was returned to and allotted for the maintenance of said Mary and her children, it is hereby enacted that the said Mary shall be in her own name and for her own use and the use of her children…all debts owing to said Conner Dowd and all things which said Conner Dowd ought lawfully sue for and recover were he a citizen of this state." (NC Session Laws, 19 Apr. 1784, p. 86).

14. **Ferguson, Malcolm.** Petition of Malcolm Ferguson of Robeson Co., NC, no date, states that in sometime past, the petitioner married a woman whose charms at that time have since excelled her virtues. Since the intermarriage, said woman (unnamed) made an elopement from him and has rendered life a discontentment and done "wrongs to his personal property." She has had several children by the other man with whom she lives. Petitioner prays for a divorce. In House, 4 Dec. 1795, and rejected. (GASR, Nov.-Dec. 1795, Box 2: Folder "Petitions - divorce").

15. **Hall, Priscilla.** Bill to secure Priscilla Hall of Randolph Co., NC, wife of Levi Hall, late one of the Constables for Guilford Co., NC, such property as she may hereafter acquire as if she had never been married. In House, 11 Dec. 1799, and Senate, 7 Dec. 1799. Read three times and passed. [Original petition of Priscilla Hall not found.] (GASR, Nov.-Dec. 1799, Box 1: Folder "House Bill, Nov. 23").

16. **Hare, Rachel.** Petition of Rachel Hare of Chowan Co., NC, who married Marmaduke Hare of Hertford Co., NC, in 1792. "She expected to Enjoy a life of felicity, but it too soon proved only an idea." Said Marmaduke became a debaucher, and soon spent what little property he and your petitioner possessed. After "living a life of disquietude together for three years and ten months, during which time your petitioner was often abused and beaten in a most cruel manner and her life threatened," she availed herself of going before Lemuel Creecy, Esq., and her said husband was committed to jail for some time, but at length he was discharged. The petitioner and her husband do not have any children and have been separated for three years and upwards without seeing each other. Your petitioner's aged and wealthy father wants your petitioner to share in his estate, but is concerned about said husband's rights to such estate. Petitioner asks for a divorce.

[Below:] Endorsement by 88 subscribers who request the NC Assembly grant her prayer.

[Above petition enclosed in following bill:] Bill to secure Rachel Hare, wife of Marmaduke Hare, such estate as she may hereafter acquire as if she were never married. Said Marmaduke shall not be answerable for any debts contracted by said Rachel, his wife.[1] In Senate, 18 Dec. 1799, and in House, 20 Dec. 1799. Read three times and passed. (GASR, Nov.-Dec. 1799, Box 1: Folder "Senate Bill 7 Dec.").

17. **Houser, Catherine.** Senate Bill, 17 Nov. 1795: Because Henry Houser of Rockingham Co., NC, has absented himself from his wife Catherine and intermarried with another woman [unnamed], an act is passed to secure such estate as may be acquired by said Catherine as if she had never been married to said Henry.[2] (NC Session Laws, 2 Nov. 1795, p.29 and GASR, Nov.-Dec. 1795, Box 1: Folder "Senate Bill, 17 Nov.")

18. **Naylor, John.** Petition of John Naylor of Fayetteville, NC, who married his present wife, Matilda, and lived with her for several years. The petitioner was "put to the severest trial by the misconduct of his said wife…incompatible with the marriage vows." There is no chance of a reconciliation, and petitioner prays that relief be granted through divorce. In House, 10 Jan. 1795, and in Senate, 12 Jan. 1795. Referred to Committee. (GASR, Dec. 1794-Feb. 1795, Box 3: Folder "Petitions - divorce"). Divorce granted by NC Session Law, 1 July 1794, p. 32.

19. **Patterson, Daniel.** Petition of Daniel Patterson, no location, no date, who states that he "had the misfortune to be married to a woman [unnamed] whose morality and conduct came far short of his Expectation." After living together a considerable time in the married state, she left the house of your petitioner without any provocation. She made an elopement with another man [unnamed] to the State of Georgia, and she has been there for two years. Petitioner prays for a divorce or other relief. In House and Senate, 29 Dec. 1791, and referred to Committee. (GASR, Dec. 1791-Jan. 1792, Box 3: Folder "Petitions - divorce, name changes").

The Committee of Propositions and Grievances No. 2, to whom was referred the Petition of Daniel Patterson, report that said petition praying a divorce be granted petitioner from his wife is a subject improper for the investigation of this or any other committee. Committee unanimously rejects same. In Senate, 3 Jan. 1792, and in House, 5 Jan. 1792. Committee's report concurred with. (GASR, Dec. 1791-Jan. 1792, Box 2: Folder "JCR - Propositions and Grievances, folder 2").

---

1 Divorce was not mentioned in this bill.
2 Original petition not found.

Divorces and Separations from Petitions to the North Carolina General Assembly from 1779

20.   **Perry, Eleanor.** Petition of twenty-two inhabitants of Orange Co., NC, no date, who remark on the unhappy circumstances of Eleanor Perry, wife of John Perry of Orange Co., NC. Said John and Eleanor married 2 March 1797.[3] Soon after the marriage, said John Perry took to card playing, wasting his property, and abusing his wife until they parted. Said Eleanor and her child went to her father's, the said John remaining in the neighbourhood, pretending to work. He sold a great part of the property he acquired through his wife and left with a huge debt remaining. Creditors executed the remainder of the property, including said Eleanor's riding saddle which she had purchased before marriage. Petitioners request that this woman's grievances be given relief. (GASR, Nov.-Dec. 1798, Box 3: Folder "Petitions - divorce, inheritance")

Joint Committee on Propositions and Grievances reports that John Perry has deserted his wife, Eleanor, and recommends that such property as she may hereafter acquire be secured to her for her sole benefit. In Senate, 15 Dec. 1798, and in House, 17 Dec. 1798. Committee's recommendation concurred with. Bill enacted. (GASR, Nov.-Dec. 1798, Box 2: Folder "JCR - Propositions and Grievances" and GASR, Nov.-Dec. 1798, Box 1: Folder "House Bill, 5 Dec.")

21.   **Powell, Nancy.** Bill enacted to secure Nancy Powell of Johnston Co., NC, wife of Nathan Powell, such estate as she may hereafter acquire as if she had never married. In Senate, 5 Dec. 1799, and in House, 6 Dec. 1799. Read third time and passed. (GASR, Nov.-Dec. 1799, Box 1: Folder "House Bill 23 Nov.").[4]

22.   **Rice, Abigail.** Petition of Abigail Rice and Joshua Sugg: In or about the year 1773, the petitioner, Abigail Rice, was married to John Rice. After eight or ten years, said John Rice left said Abigail with one child and took another woman with whom he continues to live. The petitioners pray that a law be passed to prevent said John Rice from taking anything that said Abigail has attained by her own industry or that has been bestowed on her by friends. "Your petitioners do affirm that they have no Intention to defraud any Person…But your Petitioner_ having but Two children desires to Bestow of the Blessing God has Bestowed on him, on them both [The above petition is enclosed in the following committee report:] The Committee to whom was referred the above petition reports that the prayer of the said petitioner ought to be granted and recommend a law be passed to entitle said Abigail Rice to enjoy all the estate that she may acquire independent of her husband, John Rice. In Senate, 21 Jan. 1795, and in House, 25 Jan. 1795. Concur with recommendation of Committee. (GASR, Dec. 1794-Feb. 1795, Box 2: Folder "HCR").

23.   **Sanders, Lemuel.** Petition of Lemuel Sanders states that in the year 1792, petitioner married his present wife, Sabra, and lived with her "in great harmony and domestic comfort until July 1793," when, without just cause, she eloped with another man [unnamed] and has since not returned. Prays for a bill to dissolve marriage. Said petitioner is "of Currituck Co., NC." In Senate, 27 Nov. 1795. Petition rejected. (GASR, Nov.-Dec. 1795, Box 1: Folder "Senate Bills, Nov. 18").

24.   **Shaver/Sheaver, George.** Petition of twenty-four inhabitants of Wilkes Co., NC, who say they have been well acquainted with George Shaver/Sheaver and his wife, Fanny, for several years. The conduct of said Fanny "is such that her husband cannot live in peace with her and has been under the necessity of putting her away from his house for near two years…" Petitioners pray that a divorce be granted

---

3   Marriage bond identifies bride as Eleanor Bunch and bondsman as Thomas Bunch
4   Original petition not found.

to said George Shaver/Sheaver from his wife, Fanny. Referred to Committee, 21 Nov. 1798.[5] (GASR, Nov.-Dec. 1798, Box 3: Folder "Petitions - divorce, inheritance").

25. **Smelley, Frances.** Bill to secure Francis Smelley, wife of John Smelley of Warren Co., NC, all estate she may acquire by purchase or descent as if she had never been married. Said John had for several years absented himself from his wife, and there is no expectation of a reconciliation. In Senate, 5 Dec. 1799, and in House, 6 Dec. 1799. Read third time and passed.[6] (GASR, Nov.-Dec. 1799, Box 1: Folder "Senate Bill 25 Nov.").

26. **Smith, Thomas & Sally (Dobson).** Petitioners Thomas Smith & Sally (Dobson) Smith of Burke Co., NC, state that early after their marriage, they found a dislike for each other that increased until they parted. They employed an attorney to draw up articles of separation, which is now nearly three years past. Petitioners pray that an act be passed to annul and make void their marriage and award a divorce. Dated 5 Nov. 1795. Committee recommends rejection of petition and notes that "marriage is a contract of the most solemn and important kind and ought not to be dissolved except for some very special cases..." In House and Senate, which concur with recommendation of Committee. Petition rejected. (GASR, Nov.-Dec. 1795, Box 2: Folder "JCR - Propositions and Grievances").

27. **Stanaland, Thomas.** Petition of Thomas Stanaland of Brunswick Co., NC, who states that he married Judah Robinson some years ago, but at the conclusion of the matrimonial ceremony, said Judah "took up and lived with another man [unnamed] some years by whom she had several children. The petitioner has not co-habited with the said Judah to the day of her Death. The petitioner lived ten years as a single person and then "married a second time by which wife he has several children..." The petitioner prays for a law to exclude the children of said Judah from all right of inheritance in his estate and make the children he has or will have by his present wife his lawful heirs.[7] (GASR, Nov.-Dec. 1796, Box 3: Folder "Petitions - divorce, inheritance").

28. **Thomas. Jenny Jarrit.** Petition of Jenny Jarrit Thomas, wife of Charles Thomas of Wake Co., NC. Petitioner married "some years past, at which time, in addition to property given her by her father, her said husband was possessed of a considerable estate, both real and personal. Her said husband, through mismanagement and neglect, has entirely wasted all the property he possessed. Said husband for "some years past" has been entirely regardless of your petitioner and has not made any provision for her support. She has been compelled to return to the house of her aged parents for the necessities of life. She has had one child by her said husband, and this child is with her. Her father desires to make a gift of some property to her, but fears that the husband of your petitioner would acquire ownership of such property. Petitioner prays relief to secure such property as she may acquire. Dated 28 Nov. 1799. [Below:]] Deposition of Nathaniel Jones "(C.T.)"). [Crab Tree] supports petitioner in her statements. Committee of Propositions & Grievances No. 2 recommends approval of petition. In Senate & House, 11-12 Dec. 1799 with concurrence of Committee recommendation. (GASR, Nov.-Dec. 1799, Box 3: Folder "JCR - Prop* & Grievances"). Bill to secure Jenny Jarrit Thomas, wife of Charles Thomas, in any estate she may hereafter acquire as if she had never been married. In Senate, 18 Dec. 1799, and in House, 19 Dec. 1799. Read third time and passed. (GASR, Nov.-Dec. 1799, Box 1: Folder "House Bill 2 Dec.").

---

5   No further action found.
6   Original petition not found.
7   No further action noted.

Divorces and Separations from Petitions to the North Carolina General Assembly from 1779

29. **Thompson, William.** Petition of William Thompson, no date, no location, states that his wife, Ann, "Left my Bed and Board this several years…& hath refused to live with me as a wife but is Trying to Destroy my property by Runing me in Debt…" Petitioner prays for divorce. In House & Senate, 7 Nov. 1795, and referred to Committee of Propositions and Grievances. (GASR, Nov.-Dec. 1795, Box 2: Folder "Petitions - divorce").[8]

30. **Torence, Elizabeth.** Petition of Elizabeth Torence, Dobbs Co., NC, 24 Oct. 1783, states that her husband, Thomas Torence, late resident of Dobbs Co., NC, and father to "seven helpless infants," left his family and connection by the instigation and perseverance of the enemies of this country. Said Thomas was but a passive offender against the laws of this country, and petitioner prays that said Thomas be permitted to remain with his distressed, and at present, unhappy family. In House and Senate, 14 May 1784. Petition rejected. (GASR, Apr.-June 1784, Box 1: Folder "JSC - Committee on Propositions and Grievances, 13-26 May 1784").

31. **Whidbee, Sarah.** Committee on Propositions & Grievances No. 1 recommends rejection of petition to secure Sarah Whidbee, wife of Robert Whidbee, such estate as she may acquire. On 3 Dec. 1798, Senate rejects petition and draft bill. (GASR, Nov.-Dec. 1798, Box 2: Folder "JCR - Prop. & Griev. #1 and GASR, Nov.-Dec. 1798, Box 1: Folder "Senate Bill, 3 Dec").

32. **Withrow, James & Sydney.** Memorial of James and Sydney Withrow of Rutherford Co., NC, who about ten years past mutually agreed to live separate and dissolve the bonds of matrimony, being formerly husband and wife. They have made an equitable division of property and have no expectation of coming together again as husband and wife. They pray for an act to divorce them. (GASR, Nov.-Dec. 1798, Box 1: Folder "Senate Bill, 8 Dec."). Committee on Propositions and Grievances reports that the petition of James and Sydney Withrow for a divorce shows that the aforesaid James Withrow and Sydney, his wife, have for many years been separated and lived apart and have mutually agreed to a division of their property. The Committee believes a legal separation should take place by means of a divorce. In Senate, 14 Dec. 1798, and concurred with. In House, 15 Dec. 1799, and petition and bill rejected. (GASR, Nov.-Dec. 1798, Box 2: Folder "JCR - Prop. & Griev. #1").

33. **Wood, Joseph.** Petition of Joseph Wood of Robeson Co., NC, who states that he married Elisabeth Wilkinson in the early part of his life, however "the harmony, between your petitioner & the said Elisabeth was destroyed…[and] a separation by mutual consent did take place…" The petitioner married a second time to Sarah Oliphant in 1782. Soon after this second marriage, the aforesaid Elisabeth, who had been subject to an incurable malady, died leaving no issue. Since that time, the petitioner has lived in the greatest harmony of happiness with his present wife by whom he has issue four children, viz., William, Ann, Joseph, and Sarah. Your petitioner has acquired property sufficient for the maintenance of his family as well as a handsome "Competent" when he can assist them no longer, but fears that his second marriage may be annulled and his children then be deprived of the enjoyment of his estate. He prays for relief.[9] (GASR, Dec. 1794-Feb. 1795, Box 3: Folder "Petitions - divorce").

---

8 No further action found.
9 No further action found

1800-1801

34. **Bostick, Mary.** Petition of Mary Bostick of Richmond Co., NC, states that she was married to Nathaniel Bostick about six years ago, but he left her, and she has been informed that he married another woman about two years ago. The said "Nathaniel has departed from this Country and is not to be heard of…" She prays that a law be passed "to prevent the said Nathaniel from having any claim to any property, personal or real, that shall fall to her by descent or that she may hereafter acquire by her own industry…" [Below:] Deposition of Arthur Robinson and William Hendley and deposition of Robert J. Steele, sworn to before Benjamin Powell, Justice of Peace for Richmond Co., NC, 27 Nov. 1801, which attest to the facts as stated by said Mary Bostick in her petition. (GASR, Nov.-Dec. 1801, Box 3: Folder "Petitions (Divorce, name changes))

Bill to secure Mary Bostick, wife of Nathaniel Bostick, such estate as she may hereafter acquire. In House (5 Dec. 1801) and Senate (7 Dec. 1801) and referred to Committee. (GASR, Nov.-Dec. 1801, Box 1: Folder "HB – 7 Dec."). No further action found.

35. **Brown, Bond V.** Petition of Bond V. Brown of Caswell Co., NC, states that on 27 January [1800], his wife eloped from his bed and board and went off with one Joshua Byron, leaving a suckling child. She took a horse worth $100 and $42 in cash, but he has never heard any account of them since they left. He prays for relief for his four children and himself. Petition is attested to by the signatures of 79 subscribers. Committee recommends rejection of petition. (GASR, Nov.-Dec. 1801, Box 2: Folder "SCR, Divorces and Alimony")

36. **Byrum, James.** Petition of James Byrum of Bertie Co., NC, states that he married Amelia Keen of said county of Bertie in August 1791. He discovered too late that he was united with one "whose violence of temper and inconstancy in bed rendered it barely possible for him to endure her ways." He lived with her four years and hoped for some change, but she removed herself to the State of Tennessee and has remained there ever since. During the petitioner's cohabitation with the said Amelia, one child was born to them which your petitioner means to provide for in the best manner. He has been informed that the said Amelia long since her residence in Tennessee has been delivered of another child, and he is bound by law to support as well the children born to his wife as long as the marriage continues. He prays an act to dissolve the marriage between him and the said Amelia. (GASR, Nov.-Dec. 1801, Box 3: Folder "Petitions, Divorce, name change").

House Bill: whereas Amelia Byrum, wife of James Byrum of Bertie Co., has left the house of her husband and removed to the State of Tennessee and given herself up to illicit practices of familiarity with other men, the said James Byrum shall not be answerable for any debt hereafter contracted by said Amelia his wife, nor shall said Amelia have any right of dower in any estate of said James nor shall said James be liable for the support of any children the said Amelia shall have delivered after the expiration of nine months from the time she left his house. In House and Senate, 26 Nov. 1801, and referred to Committee. (GASR, Nov.-Dec. 1801, Box 1: Folder "HB, 26 Nov").

37. **Candler, Zachariah.** Petition of Zachariah Candler of Buncombe Co., NC, attested to by 17 subscribers' signatures, prays for a divorce from his wife, Rhoday, dated 15 Oct. 1800. Said Zachariah and wife were resident in Buncombe County for eight years past. He is still a resident, but his wife Rhoday departed from her said husband nearly five years previous to the said date and has not returned. From other evidence- "we have been creaditly informed that the afore said Rhoday has been Marryed to another Man and has one child by him and we do believe that if any man on Earth is intitled to a Devorsment from his wife that the aforesaid Candler is justly intitled to one from his wife Rhoday…" In Senate, 21 Nov. 1800, and referred to Committee. (GASR, Nov.-Dec. 1800, Box 3: Folder "Petitions, Divorce, name change").

38. **Cazey [Casey?], William.** Petition of William (x) Cazey and wife Catharine (x) Cazey of Rowan Co., NC, that they married each other in 1793 and "continued together a great strife for the Term of six weeks, after which time Your Petitioners seperated themselves and have ever since continued seperated." They pray for an act to divorce them or to secure to each such property as they now possess or may hereafter acquire. In House and Senate, 20 Nov. 1801, and referred to Committee. (GASR, Nov.-Dec. 1801, Box 3: Folder "Petitions, Divorce, name change").

39. **Coakeley/Cokely, Sarah.** Petition of Sarah Cokeley, generally called Sarah Hawley, sheweth that in the Year 1780, your petitioner intermarried on the Island of St. Martins with a certain Benjamin Coakley with whom she lived in the habits of matrimony till sometime in the Year 1786. This union became intolerable, and the two partners agreed to separate. Said Benjamin delivered to your petitioner his written obligation, bearing date of 17 June 1788, in the sum of £5,000 "conditioned for his never thereafter intermeddling with or disturbing your Petitioner either on her person or her property." Your petitioner having then been but a short time resident in the State of North Carolina and being to a great measure ignorant of its laws, your petitioner erroneously considered that said Benjamin s written obligation amounted to a dissolution of the bonds of matrimony between said Benjamin and herself, and in the Year 1788, intermarried with William Hawley of Newbern. Your petitioner lived with said William "in a state of great conjugal happiness (having had by him several children) till the Fall of 1799, when the yellow fever raged with great violence in the Town of Newbern, and said William died intestate, leaving considerable property both real and personal. However, in consequence of her not being legally divorced from the said Benjamin Coakley (her first husband), she and her said children have been considered as having no claim upon the estate of said William. She prays for a law entitling her to the sole use of the property she now has or may hereafter acquire. In House and Senate, 24 Nov. 1800, and referred to Committee. Report of Committee of Propositions and Grievances recommends that her prayers be granted and a suitable bill be passed. In House and Senate, 29 Nov. 1800, and concurred with. (GASR, Nov.-Dec. 1800, Box 3: Folder "JCR, Prop. & Grievances #1").

Bill to secure to Sarah Cokely (alias Sarah Hawley, widow of William Hawley) of New Bern, formerly the wife of Benjamin Cokeley, such estate as she now has or hereafter may acquire. In House and Senate, 3 & 4 Dec. 1800, read 3d time, and passed. (GASR, Nov.-Dec. 1800, Box 1: Folder "HB – 29 Nov.").

40. **Easton, Samuel.** Report of Committee on Divorce and Alimony recommends rejection of the petition [not enclosed] of Samuel Easton and wife Zylpha. In House and Senate, 14 Dec. 1801, and concurred with. (GASR, Nov.-Dec. 1800, Box 1: Folder "HB 25 Nov.").

41. **Evans, Anna.** Petition of Anna Evans of Caswell Co., NC, sheweth that her husband, Zachariah Evans, because of debt and inability to satisfy his creditors, departed some years ago to the western parts of the country and left his family (wife and five children) in a low circumstance. The return of said husband is uncertain, and she prays for a law to secure to herself and children what may be acquired by their own labor and industry. Attested to by the signatures of twelve subscribers. In House and Senate, Nov. 1800, and passed. Referred to a committee to consolidate similar actions into one bill. (GASR, Nov.-Dec. 1800, Box 1: Folder "HB 25 Nov.").

42. **Farrow, John.** Petition of John Farrow of Currituck Co., NC, at Cape Hatteras states that he married Rebekah Tolson in the Year 1791. She became very discontented with him after the marriage and oftentimes absented herself from his bed and board for months at a time. She "also frequented the Company of wicked and Adulterous men and was so open and publick in her Lewd and Abominable actions that many Sponcible persons knew of a certainty that it was so; Finally took up with a Thomas Rolinson…then She Removed to the town of Washington and so from place to place Continuing in the Same Detestable practices Till this time…Your petitioner has remained in lonesome, melancholy circumstances for more than two years. He prays for a dissolution of the marriage. "She also joins me so far as to the prayer of the petition being granted." Attested to by the signatures of four subscribers. Petitioner Rebekah (x) Farrow also signs. In Senate, 22 Nov. 1800, and in House, 25 Nov. 1800, and referred to Committee. (GASR, Nov.-Dec. 1800, Box 3: Folder "Petitions-Divorce, name changes").

Second petition of John Farrow, dated 26 Aug. 1801, begins in the same manner as the one above but adds the following: "[She] finally took up with a Thomas Rolinson & removed to the Town of Washington and after some length of time forsook him and removed toward the town Beauford and continued there some months…& at Length Returnd again to the Aforesd. County & place and in a short time after Took up with a certain William O Neal & has been with him going on two years in which length of time she has had one child and at this period of time they are living together…Your Humble Petitioner has Remained in this Lonsom_ malancoly Circumstance for now more [than] Four Years…" He prays for a favorable consideration to "Finaly seperate Disolve and Nullify the afforesd. marriage For Ever. She also joins me so Far as to Prayer of the petition Being Granted." Attested to by the signatures of 27 subscribers. [On reverse;] Depositions of Elisabeth (x) Burket, Sarah (+) Midyett, and Christain (x) Jennett, dated 26 Aug. 1801, which state that they had seen the said Rebecca Farrow, wife of John Farrow, in bed with other men. (GASR, Nov.-Dec. 1801, Box 3: Folder "Petitions-Divorce, name change").

43. **Ferguson, Malcom.** [See also #18 in first article of this series.] Petition of Malcom Ferguson of Robeson Co., NC, dated 18 Nov. 1800, states that his wife Mary eloped sometime in the Year 1792 and forsook the petitioner's bed and board. Since that time, he has not seen nor heard of his aforesaid wife except that she is living with another man and has a family of children. The petitioner applied to the North Carolina Assembly at the November 1795 session but failed to obtain relief. He considers his circumstances to be a hardship and worries "that his hard earned labour should perhaps at some unforeseen period be subject to the caprice of an abandoned woman and her offspring." He prays for a divorce. In Senate, 26 Nov. 1800, and in House, 28 Nov. 1800. and referred to Committee. (GASR, Nov.-Dec. 1800, Box 3: Folder "Petitions-Divorce, name change").

Divorces and Separations from Petitions to the North Carolina General Assembly from 1779

44. **Ford, Susanna.** Petition of Susanna Ford of Bladen Co., NC, states that she married James Ford and lived with him for some time as a dutiful and affectionate wife. However, "owing to the evil inclinations and disposition of her said husband, a separation between them has taken place." She prays for relief to secure her as a feme sole in her future acquisitions. In House and Senate, 24 Nov. 1801, and referred to Committee. (GASR, Nov.-Dec. 1801, ox 3: Folder "Petitions-Divorce, name change").

45. **Garrett, Esther.** Senate Bill: to secure to Esther Garrett of Mecklenburg Co., wife of William Garrett, such estate as she may hereafter acquire. William Garrett has for several years past absented himself from his wife Esther with no expectations of a reconciliation. In House, 26 Nov. 1801, read first time, and passed. In Senate, read second time, and referred to Committee(GASR, Nov.-Dec. 1801, Box 1: Folder "SB 25 Nov.").

46. **Gregory, William.** Petition of William Gregory and wife Elizabeth of Chowan Co., NC, dated 8 May 1801. They were married in February 1799 and lived together in an unhappy state until 1800, during which time they had one child, since dead. They agreed to a separation and pray for an act to grant them a divorce. Committee Report recommends rejection of petition. (GASR, Nov.-Dec. 1801, Box 2: Folder "Petitions-Divorce & Alimony")

47. **Hawkins, James.** Petition of James (x) Hawkins and Mary Hawkins ("late the wife of said James") of Buncombe Co., NC, who state that they are desirous of being divorced. They have been apart many years and never expect to be together as husband and wife again. In Senate, 21 Nov. 1800, and referred to Committee. (GASR, Nov.-Dec. 1800, Box 3: Folder Petitions-Divorce, name changes").

48. **Hill, Isaac.** Petition of Isaac Hill of Carteret Co., NC, dated 15 Oct. 1801, states that it is his unhappy fate to be married to a woman [Mary Hill] near four years that he cannot live with. For the past two years, she has left his bed and mostly board, except that she has taken considerable money from him and claims that she found it hidden in the ground. She has applied many times to have your petitioner make over her property to her and "to retain my own to myself." He prays for relief by securing to his wife Mary the property she possessed at the time of marriage and all she shall accumulate by her own industry hereafter, but to be debarred from her right of dower in your petitioner's estate. [Below:]] Certificate attesting to the situation as described in the petition and signed by 42 subscribers. The Senate Committee rejects the prayer of the petitioner. (GASR, Nov.-Dec. 1801, Box 2: Folder "SCR, divorce & alimony").

49. **Hosea, Penelope.** Petition of Penelope (x) Hosea of Pasquotank Co., NC, states that she married Seth Hosea of the same county some years ago. At that time, he was possessed of a very considerable real and personal estate. However, he was reduced to a state of insolvency within two or three years through bad management and a fondness for spirituous liquors. At the end of this period, her said husband absconded himself from your petitioner. She prays for an act to authorize her to hold such property as she has acquired since the separation and all she may hereafter acquire, as if she had never been married to said Seth Hosia. The petition is certified by nine subscribers who attest to the facts presented in the petition. Dated 10 Nov. 1800. In House and Senate, 21 Nov. 1800, and referred to Committee. (GASR, Nov.-Dec. 1800, Box 3: Folder "Petitions-Divorce, name changes").

50. **Humphreys, Milley.** Petition of Milley Humphreys, wife of Finus (?) Humphreys of Wilkes Co., NC, claims that her said husband deserted her in the Year 1785 in very indigent circumstances. When

she married him, he was seized of a considerable estate, but he has gone out of the state and allegedly supports an immoral character. She prays that she be granted relief to secure to her as a feme sole such property as she may hereafter acquire. In Senate and House, 24 & 25 Nov. 1800, and referred to Committee. (GASR, Nov.-Dec. 1800, Box 3: Folder "Petitions- Divorce, name change"). North Carolina Act of 1800 grants relief to Milly Humphreys, wife of Spencer Humphreys.

51. **Johnson, Rachel.** Petition of Rachel Johnson, wife of Jacob Johnson of Rowan Co., NC. Her said husband left her in October 1794 with six small children and in low circumstances. She has since through honest industry acquired considerable property and prays for a bill to secure to her all the property she has acquired or may hereafter acquire for herself and her children, as if she and her husband had never been married. Ninety-one subscribers endorse her petition. [Attached:] Bill to secure to Rachel Johnson, wife of Jacob Johnson, of Rowan County such estate as she may hereafter acquire. In Senate and House, Nov. 1800, and referred to Committee to consolidate applications of this kind into one bill. (GASR, Nov.-Dec. 1800, Box 1: Folder "SB 21 Nov."). North Carolina Act of 1800 approves prayer in petition to secure such estate to Rachel Johnston.

52. **Jonston, Joel.** Petition of Joel Jonston of Lincoln Co., NC, states that said Joel married Mary Matox about seven years past. They lived together three years and had two children. Mareloped from his bed and board, leaving her two children with him, and the petitioner believes she now lives in the State of Georgia and understands she will never return. Petitioner prays relief for his two children and himself through divorce. [Below:] Certificate attests to facts in the petition and is signed by James (x) Ballard, Wiley (•<?) Ballard, and Nancy ("W) Ballard before John Moore, Justice of Peace for Lincoln Co., NC. Dated 7 Nov. 1801. Committee report rejects petition. (GASR, Nov.-Dec. 1801, Box 2: Folder "SCR, Divorce & Alimony").

53. **Keaton, Patrick.** Petition of Patrick Keaton of Camden Co., NC, which states that he married Elizabeth Meeds some thirteen or fourteen years ago and lived with her for six or seven years. Said Elizabeth was possessed "with a most wicked and diabolical temper" and rendered the existence of your petitioner miserable and wretched. Said Elizabeth gave herself to acts of lewdness and adultry and became a prostitute. She took up with one John Jennings with whom she still lives and has had several children. Your petitioner prays for relief. [Below:]] Deposition of four subscribers before J. Keaton, Justice of Peace for Pasquotank Co., who attest to the facts in the petition. Dated 31 Oct. 1801. Committee recommends rejection of petition. (GASR, Nov.-Dec. 1801, Box 2: Folder "SCR, Divorces & Alimony").

Bill to carry out the petition of Patrick Keaton for a divorce from his wife Elizabeth. It appears that Elizabeth Keaton, wife of Patrick Keaton, has absented herself from the said husband and cohabits with another man by whom she has had several children. In House and Senate, 25 & 26 Nov. 1800, and referred to Committee. In House, 17 Dec. 1800, read first time and rejected. (GASR, Nov.-Dec. 1800, Box 1: Folder "HB 25 Nov.").

54. **Knight, Nancy.** Bill to secure Nancy Knight, wife of Murfree Knight, such estate as she may hereafter acquire. Said parties have separated, and reconciliation is not expected. In House and Senate, 19 Dec. 1800, read 3d time and passed. (GASR, Nov.-Dec. 1800, Box 2: Folder "SB 6 Dec.").

55. **Lawwell, Elizabeth.** Petition of Elizabeth Lawwell, wife of Samuel Lawwell, of Warren Co. NC, which states that the petitioner married the said Samuel in July of 1797. In the month of September fol-

lowing, the said Samuel separated himself from the petitioner, but where he has gone she does not know. At the time of her marriage, she was in possession of some property, including a negro wench, who has been sold to pay said Samuel's debts. The petitioner prays for a law to secure to her such property as she may hereafter acquire, as she has expectations of inherit in property from her mother (now living) and of property acquired through her own industry. The petitioner is concerned that such property may be taken from her and her child to pay demand of the said Samuel Lawwell. Dated 17 Nov. 1800, Warrenton, NC. Facts subscribed to by signatures of 28 persons. In House, 4 Dec. 1800, and in Senate, 5 Dec. 1800, who refer it to the committee to consolidate with applications of a similar nature. (GASR, Nov.-Dec. 1800, Box 3: Folder "JCR Committee Reports (Prop. & Grievances #1) -Petitions (Divorce, etc.)").

56. **Mason, Hannah.** Petition of Hannah Mason states that she was joined in wedlock with Richard Mason about nine years past and has borne three children to the said Richard. He left her and has been gone five years. She prays a law to secure to her all such estate she now has and may acquire in the future-clear from any claims of said Richard Mason or his creditors. [Attached: Bill to secure to Hannah Mason, wife of Richard Mason, such estate as she may hereafter acquire. In House and Senate, 2 Dec. 1801, and referred to Committee. (GASR, Nov.-Dec. 1801, Box 1: Folder "HB 2 Dec.").

57. **Massongill. James.** Petition of James Massongill, planter, of Nash Co., NC, who states that about ten years ago, he married Amey Sanders, "then a widow, who lived with me eight years and then eloped, taking with her considerably more than I got with her when I had her. And as I am an old man myself, that is to say near Seventy years of age and but of Small property And havin worked hard for the little it has been pleased God To bless me with, And whereas in all probability I may die before my said wife Amey, and in such case considering it a hardship that she should enjoy any part of my estate…But rather that my children should reap the Benefits if any, in such manner as I may think proper to direct - And whereas I have no children by the last woman; or any other tie than that of matrimony-" therefore request an act to secure your petitioner his property free from any encumbrances on the score of his wife. In Senate, 20 Nov. 1801, and referred to Committee. Committee Report recommends rejection of said petition. In Senate and House, 14 Dec. 1801, and concurred with. (GASR, Nov.-Dec. 1801, Box 2: Folder "SCR, Divorce & Alimony").

58. **Moore, John.** Petition of John Moore of Bertie Co., NC, shows that he married Lovy Holten "about two years previous to May eighteen hundred…" In a short time after the marriage, "your petitioner had to buffet the most continued and violent torrent of invective that ever flowed from the mouth of a female within the bounds of the appearance of modesty…And she who during courtship was a lamb…after marriage was a violent scold…But the small semblance of virtue and modesty which yet remained was shortly to be removed." Suspicion on the petitioner's part became absolute certainty "by your Petitioner's arriving at home in an hour which at once put a period to the existence of his happiness, for with her was a man under such circumstances as chased every vestige of doubt…" The petitioner's "Neighbours were not backward in informing him that such things had long been well known to them…[but] they had declined communicating until he should first make the discovery himself…" The petitioner and said Hotlen came to an agreement in May 1800 of a separation from each other for matrimony.[10] Petitioner prays that a divorce be granted. [Below:] Depositions of two women before Thomas

---

10   Original agreement is enclosed with petition.

1800-1801 Session

Whitmell Pugh, Justice of Peace for Bertie Co., NC, who attest to seeing Lovey Moore, wife of John Moore, in bed with William White and Daniel Massingale on separate occasions. In House, 3 Dec. 1801, and rejected. (GASR, Nov.- Dec. 1801, Box 3: Folder "Pet., Divorce").

59. **Morgan, James**. Bill; Whereas James Morgan and his wife Rebeckah have agreed to part by mutual consent and divide their property, it is directed that any property that either of the parties is now possessed of or hereafter may acquire, shall be secured to the parties themselves. In Senate (3 Dec. 1801) and House (9 Dec. 1801) and referred to Committee. (GASR, Nov.-Dec. 1801, Box 1: Folder "SB 3 Dec.").

60. **Morrice, Rebekah**. Memorial of Rebekah Morrice, alias Davidson, of Buncombe Co., NC, which states that she "did (unfortunately) marry a geRfc-fcemaR [scratched out] man by the name of John G. Morrice the 5th day of September 1799 who came into the neighbourhood of your memorialist's Father about the first of June Preceding. About the first of October following…there was reports began to circulate purporting that my Husband had been guilty of a number of felonious actions, and in a short time he was taken with a State's warrant and committed to Jail…after sometime he found Security for his appearance at Court…on the day for his tryal he disappeared, and your memorialist has never seen him since. Your memorialist further informs your Honbl. Body that said Morrice (both from his own confession and Intelligence received from Major Evans of the State of Kentucky) had at the time of your Memorialist's marriage with him as wife and one or two children then alive. Major Evans I am Creditably informed was personally acquainted with said Morrice prior to my knowledge of him -" The memorialist prays for a divorce. In House and Senate, 25 Nov. 1800, and referred to Committee. (GASR, Nov.-Dec. 1800, Box 3: Folder "Petitions- Divorce, name changes").

61. **Query, Susanna.** Petition of Susanna Query of Mecklenburg Co., NC, sheweth that William Query, husband of the petitioner, has absented himself from the bed and board of said Susanna for more than five years and has left the petitioner with a family of small children and with little to support them. She "has been entirely strip[p]ed of all the property he left by the Creditors of the said William." She prays an act to secure to her cill such estate as she may hereafter acquire by her own industry. In House and Senate, 20 Nov. 1801, and referred to Committee. (GASR, Nov.-Dec. 1801, Box 3: Folder "Petitions- Divorce, name change").

62. **Record, Mary.** Petition of Mary Record of Chatham Co., NC, who states she was married to David Record and lived with him as an affectionate and dutiful wife for some time. However "owing to the evil disposition of said husband finds she can no longer suffer to be treated in the manner she hath bore…" They have agreed to live separate, and he has given your petitioner a part of his estate. She prays a law be passed to secure to her the estate granted by said husband and such as she may hereafter acquire. [Attached;] Bill to secure to Mary Record wife of David Record, such estate as she now has or may hereafter acquire. In House and Senate, 21 Nov. 1801, and referred to Committee. (GASR, Nov.-Dec. 1801, Box 1: Folder "HB 21 Nov.").

63. **Roan, Peggy.** Petition of Peggy Roan of Hertford Co., NC, states that she married Matthew Roan in Hertford Co., NC, in 1796. In a few months, after many instances of maltreatment by said Matthew, he absconded from the petitioner, and she has not heard from him since that time. She prays a law to secure her such property as she may acquire in the future by her own industry. (GASR, Nov.-Dec. 1800, Box 3: Folder "Petitions-Divorce, name change"), Bill to secure to Peggy Roan, wife of Matthew Roan

Divorces and Separations from Petitions to the North Carolina General Assembly from 1779

of Hertford Co. such estate as she may hereafter acquire. Matthew Roan has absented himself from his wife Peggy, and there is no expectation of a reconciliation. In House and Senate, Nov. 1800. Application to be consolidated into one bill with similar applications. (GASR, Nov.-Dec. 1800, Box 1: Folder "HB 21 Nov.").

64. **Rodgers/Roygers, Samuel.** Petition of Samuel Roygers states that he was lawfully married to Agatha Hulsenback on ^ July 1788 by the Rev. George Roberts. He lived in a conjugal manner with her for several years and had by her several children. After some time, however, his said wife Agatha cohabited with another man for these four years past and has had other children by this said person. Your petitioner has often entreated the said Agatha to return to him, and he would forgive her breach of fidelity, but she has refused such request. The petitioner prays that a divorce be granted him from the said Agatha. Certified and attested to by 29 subscribers, including R. Holdsonback "her brother." [Below:]] Deposition of James Hicks and John (9) Blalock before Robert Dickins, Justice of Peace for Person Co., NC, 13 Nov. 1800, that "they have good reason to believe…that what is set forth in this petition is True." In Senate (22 Nov. 1800) and in House (25 Nov. 1800) and referred to Committee. (GASR, Nov.-Dec. 1800, Box 3: Folder "Petitions -Divorce, name changes").

65. **Russell, Lizea.** Petition of Lizea (x) Russell states that she intermarried with Aaron Russell about eight years past and had by him two children. She lived with him about four years. By this time, his affections appeared to be alienated without just cause and placed on another woman, who he kept in his house for some time. At length, he left your petitioner, taking with him the eldest child but leaving the youngest one with the said Lizea. He declared his intention never to live with your petitioner, still keeps the other woman, and threatens to come and take what little property your petitioner has produced by her own industry. She prays a law be passed securing her what property she may have or hereafter acquire. [Attached:] Bill to secure rights of Lizea Russell to such estate as she may hereafter acquire. Read third time and passed in House and Senate, November 1800. (GASR, Nov.-Dec. 1800, Box 1: Folder "HB 20 Nov.").

66. **St. Lawrence, Elisabeth.** Bill to secure to Elisabeth ST. Lawrence of Chatham Co. such estate as she may hereafter acquire. Patrick St. Lawrence of Chatham Co. left his wife Elisabeth in 1797 and has not yet returned, and as such estate or property that his wife may acquire is liable to be sold for debts of her husband, this Bill is passed. In House and Senate, Nov. 1800. Application to be consolidated with other such applications into one bill. (GASR, Nov.-Dec. 1800, Box 1: Folder "HB 20 Nov.").

67. **Sawyer, Willis & Dinah.** Petition of Willis Sawyer and Dinah (+) Sawyer, his wife, inhabitants of Camden Co., NC, who state that they were married about four years ago, but "from mancauses which they will not trouble your honorable body with a recital of-they have separated and have not the smallest prospect of ever residing together again." They pray for an act to secure to them and their children separately the property they now possess and what they may hereafter acquire. Dated 7 Oct. 1800. In House and Senate, 21 Nov. 1800, and referred to Committee. (GASR, Nov.-Dec. 1800, Box 3: Folder "Petitions-Divorce, name changes").

Petition of Willis Sawyer and wife Dinah (+) Sawyer of Camden Co., NC, states that the petitioners have agreed to live separate and petitioned the last General Assembly to pass a law to secure to them separately the property they then had or might thereafter acquire. A law was passed, but it was not explicit enough. Said Dinah has had a child born since the petitioners separated. The wish that said child not inherit any part of the estate of petitioner Willis Sawyer and that petitioner Dinah Sawyer be excluded from her right of dower in the estate of said Willis. The petitioners pray reconsideration. Dated 3 June 1801. (GASR, Nov.-Dec. 1801, Box 3: Folder "Petitions -Divorce, name change").

Bill to amend act to secure to Dinah Sawyer, wife of Willis Sawyer of Camden Co., such propertas she may acquire. Said Willis Sawyer shall not be accountable to any debt hereafter contracted by said Dinah, his wife, nor shall said Dinah Sawyer have any right or title of dower in any estate of said Willis Sawyer. In Senate (24 Nov. 1801) and in House (25 Nov. 1801), read 3d time, and passed. (GASR, Nov.-Dec. 1801, Box 1: Folder "SB 19 Nov.").

68. **Spell, John.** Petition of John Spell prays to be divorced from his wife Celia. Senate Committee Report of Divorce and Alimony recommends prayer should be rejected. In Senate, 14 Dec. 1801, and concurred with. (GASR, Nov.-Dec. 1801, Box 2: Folder "SCR, Divorce & Alimony").

69. **Starr, Henry.** Petition of Henry Starr of Tyrrell Co., NC, states that he married Margaret Mewir/Muvir [Muir?] in 1791 and supported her, during which time she has had three children and is now pregnant with a fourth, "two of which she publicly says your petitioner is not the father of…She…has abandoned herself to drunkenness and the destruction of your petitioner's property and ruin of their children…" Petitioner prays the Legislature to grant a divorce. Enclosed with this petition are five depositions, including those of two women, who support the petitioner's statements, and the signatures of fifteen subscribers. In House and in Senate on 10 Dec. 1800, and referred to Committee. Report of Committee of Propositions and Grievances recommend approval of a divorce bill to grant relief to Henry Starr, who shall not be answerable for debts contracted by his wife Margaret, and that said Margaret shall not have any right or title of dower on the estate of said Henry Starr. In House and Senate, 15 Dec. 1800, read 3d time, amended and passed. (GASR, Nov.-Dec. 1800, Box 2: Folder "SB 1C Dec.").

Bill to repeal Act for relief of Henry Starr of Tyrrell Co. Further, that Margaret Starr, wife of said Henry Starr, shall be entitled to her dower and otherwise inherit all property which she would have entitled to by Law as though the repealed act had never been passed. In House (15 Dec. 1801) and in Senate (18 Dec. 1801), read 3d time, and ordered engrossed. (GASR, Nov.-Dec. 1801, Box 1: Folder "HB 28 Nov.").

70. **Sumner, Elizabeth.** Petition of Elizabeth Sumner, wife of James B. Sumner of Gates Co., NC states that prior to her marriage to said James in 1790, she possessed in her own right a number of valuable negro slaves, a large sum of money, and other valuable articles more than enough to support said Elizabeth in a decent and genteel manner. Subsequent to the said marriage, a handsome property came into the hands of said James by reason of the death of your petitioner's mother. Lately, by reason of the death of your petitioner's brother, a much larger estate has vested in the said James in right of your petitioner, in all amounting to a very ample fortune. Said James B. Sumner, however, has not only wasted and consumed what he originally acquired by his said marriage with your petitioner, but also that which has fallen to him by the death of your petitioner s relations. This has profoundly affected not only your petitioner, but the wants of four young and helpless children. Petitioner prays for a law vesting in your petitioner all such property as she may hereafter acquire. Dated 10 Nov. 1801, Gates Co., NC. (GASR, Nov.- Dec. 1801, Box 3: Folder "Petitions-Divorce, name change").

Bill to secure to Elizabeth Sumner, wife of James B. Sumner of Gates Co., such estate as she may hereafter acquire. In House and Senate, 19 Nov. 1801, and referred to Committee. (GASR, Nov. - Dec. 1801, Box 1: Folder "HB 19 Nov.").

Divorces and Separations from Petitions to the North Carolina General Assembly from 1779

71. **White, Thomas.** Petition of Thomas White of Northampton Co., NC, who states that sometime about 1778, he married his present wife Ann, and after living together several years, had two children. However, he experienced some uneasiness over her suspected conduct, which became confirmed. Within five months, she was delivered of a black child, which brought about a separation between the petitioner and his wife Ann, although the petitioner retained the two white infants. In this wretched situation, the petitioner continued for several years, but then took to his bed and board Esther Bittle, by whom he has had ten children. Only four of these children are now living, the names of which are Parthena, Achsa, Joseph, and Agatha Bittle, all of whom are carefully provided for. Your petitioner well knows that the laws of the state prevent his ever marrying again while his wife, Ann, is living. He humbly requests an act to divorce him from his said wife Ann, so that he may marry the said Esther with whom he has lived about 15 years in great harmony, peace and quietness. He also prays for the alteration of the last names of his said four living children to that of White from Bittle. He wishes that these four said children and the other two children born in wedlock by his said wife Ann be able to inherit from him as heirs at law.

[Attached:] Deposition of Henry Gotten, 5 Dec. 1800, attesting to facts in above petition.

[Enclosed:] Bill to divorce Thomas White of Northampton Co. from his wife Ann, and to alter the names of his illegitimate children [as stated in above petition] and for said children by wife Ann to be his heirs at law. In House and Senate, 4 Dec. 1800, and referred to Committee.

[Enclosed:] Report of Committee of Propositions and Grievances reports that so much of the petitioner's prayer as related to separation and divorce from his wife should be rejected, but that the legitimization of the names of the children should be put into the bill. Concurred with in House and Senate, 11 and 9 Dec. 1800. (GASR, Nov.-Dec. 1800, Box 1: Folder "HB 29 Nov.").

72. **Whitworth, Elizabeth.** Petition of Elizabeth Whitworth of Stokes Co., NC, who states that she married John Whitworth in the Year 1780. Previous to said marriage, she was a widow with two children and was in affluent circumstances. Immediately after the marriage with said John, he betook himself to gaming, drinking, and contracting debts. He brought himself, your petitioner, and family into indigent circumstances. In the Year 1796, said John deserted your petitioner and has not returned. It is currently reported that said John is living in adultery with a woman in the State of South Carolina. The petitioner prays that the property she may hereafter acquire shall not be subject to the debts of the said John, and that he not have the authority to sell or dispose of such property as your petitioner may acquire. In House and Senate, 29 Nov. 1800, and referred to Committee. (GASR, Nov.-Dec. 1800, Box 3: Folder "Petitions- Divorce, name changes").

Bill to secure Elizabeth Whitworth, wife of John Whitworth, such estate as she may hereafter acquire. Said John Whitworth has for several years absented himself from his wife Elizabeth, and there is no expectation of a reconciliation. (GASR, Nov.-Dec. 1800, Box 1: Folder "HB 29 Nov.").

73. **Wills, Mildred.** Petition of Mildred Wills of Raleigh, Wake Co., NC, who states that her husband, Nathaniel Wills/Wells, has been absent from his family for upwards of two years, except for a few days with them about a year ago. She is not certain if he is alive or dead, but in the absence of her husband, she has frequently been constrained to pay debts contracted by him to a greater value than the property which he left her possessed. She has difficulty discharging such debts, for she has a family of children to support. She prays for a law to secure her such property as she may hereafter possess, free from any claim of her said husband or his creditors. Dated 20 Nov. 1801, Raleigh, NC.

[Below:]] Attested to by B. Williams, a near neighbor to the petitioner, dated 17 Nov. 1801. In House and Senate, 20 Nov. 1801, and referred to Committee. (GASR, Nov.-Dec. 1801, Box 3: Folder "Petitions- Divorces, name change").

74.   **Winders, John.** A Senate Bill states that "Whereas Martha Winders, wife of John Winders of Duplin Co. has left her husband, said John Winders shall not be answerable for any debt contracted by said Martha, nor shall said Martha Winders have any right of dower in any estate of said John Winders. In Senate, 26 Nov. 1800, and in House, 27 Nov. 1801, and referred to Committee. [Attached:] Petition of John Winders of Duplin Co., NC, who states that he married Martha Turnage in August 1799 and lived with her until Dec. 1800, when his said wife left of her own free will without cause on his part, and they separated. Petitioner prays for a law to secure his property, which she is greatly lessening. (GASR, Nov.-Dec. 1801, Box 4: Folder "SB 26 Nov.").

75.   **Wingate, Dorcas.** Petition of Dorcas Wingate states that "She entered into Marriage With a certain Arthur Wingate, Who, has Since Separated himself from her, and there remains no hope of a reconciliation…" The petitioner prays that she be secured in her sole right to such estate as she may hereafter acquire. In House and in Senate on 24 Nov. 1801 and referred to Committee. (GASR, Nov.-Dec. 1801, Box 3: Folder "Petitions- Divorce, name change").

76.   **Young, Tabitha.** Petition of Tabitha Young of Stokes Co., NC, wife of Nathaniel Young, states that the said Nathaniel has willfully absented himself from her bed and board for five or six years and in his absence has intermarried with two or three other women. Petitioner prays for an act to secure to her all such estate as she may hereafter acquire. In House, 19 Nov. 1801, and referred to Committee. (GASR, Nov.-Dec. 1801, Box 3: Folder "Petitions (Divorce, etc.)").

77.   **Consolidated List of Separations and Divorces:** Abrams, Penelope…Roan, Peggy…Grant, Catherine…Johnston, Rachel…Evans, Anne…St. Lawrence, Elizabeth…Whitworth, Elizabeth…Hosea, Penelope. [End. "A":] - Lawwell, Elizabeth, wife of Samuel; Russell, Leziah, wife of Aaron; Sawyer, Dinah, wife of Willis; Humphreys, Milley of Wilkes Co., wife of Spencer; Allen, Elizabeth, wife of Micajah; Cratch, Mary, wife of John; Hill, Patsey, wife of Aaron; Hawkins, Mary, wife of James; Davidson, Rebeckah, otherwise Morris, who intermarried with John G. Morris of Buncombe Co., NC. (GASR, Nov.-Dec. 1800, Box 1: Folder "SB 9 Dec")

1802 - 1803

78.   **Allison, Jane/Jean and Andrew.** Petition of Jane Allison, formerly Jane Todd, states that her former husband, Thomas Todd, was killed by Indians sometime in the year 1780, leaving a considerable real and personal estate which was divided between petitioner and her children. About the year 1786, "your petitioner unfortunately intermarried with a certain Andrew Allison, who was not at that time worth any property either real or personal, but by the marriage to your petitioner became possessed of a comfortable living." The said Andrew "hath never behaved to her with that tenderness and affection as became a husband, nor to her surviving children, but has sold a part of the personal estate he got by your petitioner and has gone away from her." She prays for the Legislature to secure to her the separate use and occupance of her dower and such part of the personal property now remaining. "Your petitioner is the more emboldened to ask this, as she has no children by the said Andrew, and he has oftentimes threatened her that he would sell all she had and go away without making any provision for her support." /s/ Jean Alison [Below:] Statement by Thomas Todd the Younger, son & heir at law of the above mentioned Thomas Todd, consents to the above dower and other property to be secured to his mother, the said Jane, during her natural life. [Below:] Certificate of Theoph. Allison that "after a separation took place between Andrew Allison and his wife Jane, I applied to him Either to give her a reasonable maintenance or give her a part of the property, intimating that as he became possessed of the property through his intermarriage with her, that she was justly entitled to a part thereof, which he refused to do, saying that he would give what the Law would make him." [Enclosure:] Certificate of seventeen subscribers, residents of Rowan County, North Carolina, states that many of the subscribers have been personally acquainted with Jane Allison, formerly Jane Todd widow of Thomas Todd, for more than twenty years. Further statements confirm facts as noted in the above petition of Jane Allison. [Enclosure:] Report of Committee of Divorce and Alimony to whom was referred the petition of Jane Allison of Rowan County states that the Committee is of the opinion that the petition is not entitled to the clemency of the General Assembly and recommend the same be rejected. In Senate and House, 14-15 December 1803, and concurred with. (GASR, Nov.-Dec. 1803, Box 2: folder - "SCR - Divorces and Alimony" Nov.-Dec. 1803.)

79.   **Beeson, Elizabeth.** Report of Committee of Propositions and Grievances No. 1 to whom was referred the petition of Elizabeth Beeson of Randolph County, North Carolina, praying that what property she now has, or what she may hereafter acquire, may be secured to her, recommends that the Bill now on its passage, entitled "A Bill for the relief of certain persons therein mentioned" be amended "to secure to Elizabeth Beeson of Randolph Co. what property she now has and what she may hereafter acquire." In House, 19 December 1803, and concurred with. In Senate 19 December 1803, and rejected. (GASR, Nov.-Dec. 1803, Box 2: folder "JCR, Propositions & Grievances #1").

80.   **Bitting, Anthony and Ursilla.** Memorial of Anthony Bitting of Stokes County, North Carolina, states that he married Ursilla Ray sometime in the year 1793, and within the space of four or five weeks after said marriage, the said Ursilla absconded from the petitioner's bed and board and has never re-

turned. The petitioner states that he has never received any part of the Estate of said Ursilla by virtue of the marriage, she being possessed of considerable property at the time of the marriage. She had made over to her children some property of which your petitioner would not receive any benefit. He prays for an act to secure to him all said estate which he now has or may hereafter acquire, either real or personal, free from the claim of said Ursilla by virtue of the marriage, and also secure to said Ursilla all such property as she now has or may hereafter acquire. Referred to Committee of Propositions and Grievances No. 2. Report of Committee of Propositions and Grievances No. 2 to whom was referred above petition, states that such prayer should come under the consideration of the Committee of Divorce and Alimony. No further action found. (GASR, Nov.-Dec. 1802, Box 2: folder "JCR, Propositions & Grievances No. 2").

81. **Campbell, Elizabeth and Archibald.** Report of the Committee of Divorce and Alimony to whom was referred the petition of Elizabeth Campbell of Rowan County praying that a law might be passed to divorce her from her husband Archibald Campbell, states that the Committee is of the opinion that the petition should not be wholly rejected, but the bill amended so as to secure to the said Elizabeth such property as she now has or hereafter may acquire. Bill to secure to Elizabeth Campbell, wife of Archibald Campbell, such estate as she may hereafter acquire as if she had never been married to said Archibald. It is represented to the General Assembly that Archibald Campbell hath for several years past absented himself from his wife Elizabeth with no expectation of a reconciliation. In Senate, 17 December 1802, reconsidered, read third time and passed. Ordered to be engrossed. (GASR, Nov.-Dec. 1802, Box 1: folder "HB, 24 Nov.").

82. **Cowan, Isaac and Sarah.** Petition of Isaac Cowan of Rowan County, North Carolina, that he married Sarah Steward, now Sarah Cowan, and "lived in the utmost conjugal happiness with the said Sarah until sometime in the Year 1794 and had by her the said Sarah six children..." However, about this time the said Sarah was delivered of a child "which must have been the offspring of...a person of color." Being unwilling to separate from her and still entertaining hopes of her sincere repentance and a return to her former virtuous conduct, the petitioner felt disposed to pardon said Sarah's error. However, the birth of a second child of the same hue as the last one convinced him that he must abandon her to her vice and folly. Your petitioner has been constantly harassed by said Sarah's visits in his absence from home, and his desks are opened and the property therein taken. With malice and spite the said Sarah has required him to give security for the peace, pretending that she was in danger of her life, whereas your petitioner expressly states thai; he never offered or intended to use any violence against her. The petitioner prays the passage of a law divorcing him from the bonds of matrimony. Petition is subscribed to by some twenty-six names. In Senate, 24 November 1802, and referred to Committee of Divorce and Alimony. Committee of Divorce and Alimony to whom was referred the above petition reports that it is of the opinion that relief ought to be granted to the petitioner and that a complete divorce should be passed into law. Bill to divorce Isaac Cowan from his wife Sarah. In House and Senate, 17 December 1802, read third time and passed. Ordered to be engrossed. (GASR, Nov.-Dec. 1802, Box 1: folder "Senate Bills, 24 Nov.").

83. **Easton, Samuel and Zilphia.** Petition of Samuel Easton of Carteret County, North Carolina, sheweth that "in the year 1796 he was united in wedlock with Zilphia Guthrie, and for two years enjoyed uninterruptedly all that domestic comfort which flows from the interchange of kind offices..." In the year 1800, "he returned from a voyage to sea, and to his grievous disappointment and bitter mortification discovered that the wife for whom he had braved the dangers and suffered all the hardships of his oc-

Divorces and Separations from Petitions to the North Carolina General Assembly from 1779

cupation had fled from his house, taking with her whatever was valuable. Since that time "she has lived in a state of open adultery and has precluded all hope that she might return her steps to innocence…" Your petitioner prays for a dissolution of his said marriage. In House, 25 November 1803, and referred to Committee. (GASR, Nov.-Dec. 1803, Box 1: folder "Senate Bills, 1 Dec.").

Committee of Divorce and Alimony to whom was referred the petition of Samuel Easton of Carteret County praying to be divorced from his wife Zilphia believe "that a separation in this case is highly necessary and Just, and that it would only be common Justice to grant the prayer of the petitioner." The Committee therefore recommends the bill to divorce Samuel Easton from his wife Zilphia be passed into law. (GASR, Nov.-Dec. 1803, Box 2: folder "SCR, Divorce & Alimony"). Bill to divorce Samuel Easton and his wife Zilphia from the bonds of matrimony as if said marriage had never taken place. In Senate, 1 December 1803, read first time and rejected. (GASR, Nov.-Dec. 1803, Box 1: folder "Senate Bill, 1 Dec.").

84.　**Elrod, A. C. Barbara and Jeremiah Elrod.** Petition of A. C. Barbara Elrod states that she married Jeremiah Elrod by whom she had ten children, but unfortunately said Jeremiah took home a certain Mary Corner and since has sold his property and moved to the western countries taking said Mary with him. Petitioner prays for an Act vesting in her the sole and exclusive right of what property she now has or may hereafter acquire. Dated 1 December 1803. In House, 12 December 1803, and referred to Committee. In Senate, 13 December 1803, and ordered to be laid on table. (GASR, Nov.-Dec. 1803, Box 1: folder "Petitions, divorce"). Bill to secure A. C. Barbara Elrod [formerly of Stokes County, North Carolina] such property as she now has or may hereafter acquire, as if she had never been married to said Jeremiah. In House, 2 December 1802, read first time and passed.[11] (GASR, Nov.-Dec. 1802, Box 1: folder "House Bills, 2 Dec.").

85.　**Gregory, William and Elizabeth.** Petition of William Gregory and Elizabeth Gregory sheweth "that some time in the year [blank], your petitioners being then both single and promising to themselves all those felicities and comforts for the engagement of which the state of matrimony was ordained, did [intermarry] together and continued to live with each other for the space of about [blank] years…" On "finding themselves deceived in their expectations and instead of that happiness of which they had flattered themselves would result from their marriage, they discovered that they had formed a connection which would make the lives of both of them miserable on the extreme." They mutually agreed to separate and live apart and entered into articles of separation whereby petitioner Elizabeth Gregory was secured a certain portion of the estate to which she was entitled at the time of her marriage in her own right. Your petitioners now live separately and have not the distant hope of being able to live together. They pray for a divorce to enable them to intermarry with any person whatsoever. Referred to Committee, 8-9 December 1803.[12] Committee of Divorce and Alimony to whom was referred the petition of William Gregory and his wife Elizabeth Gregory are of opinion "that the object sought for by the petitioners is in its nature of the almost importance to society and ought to be acted on with the utmost caution and delicacy, and the Committee does not conceive the grievance complained of entitles the petitioners to the clemency of the General Assembly and therefore recommends the same be rejected. In Senate and House, 14-15 December 1803, and concurred with. (GASR, Nov.-Dec. 1803, Box 2: folder "SCR, Divorce and Alimony").

11　　Such bills must be read three times and passed before becoming law.

12　　Marriage Bond of William Gregory and Elizabeth Frazier, dated 11 February 1799 in Chowan County, North Carolina, may refer to this case.

86. **Harris, Amelia.** Petition of Amelia Harris of Gates County, North Carolina, states that Benjamin Norfleet of Edenton married her only daughter Peggy in or about the year 1789, and for causes unknown, their little property is entirely exhausted and the said Peggy is in indigent circumstances. The petitioner prays for a law investing some small property in said Peggy Norfleet as she may hereafter acquire by gift or otherwise. Referred to Committee, 26-28 November 1803. (GASR, Nov.-Dec. 1803, Box 2: folder "Petitions, Divorce"). Committee of Divorce and Alimony "to whom was referred the petition of Amelia Harris of Gates County" is of opinion "that the prayer of the petitioner is improperly extended to the relief of Peggy Norfleet, and they are further of opinion that the said Peggy's situation does not merit the clemency of this General Assembly and therefore recommend rejection." In Senate and House, 14-15 December 1803, and concurred with. (GASR, Nov.-Dec. 1803, Box 2: folder "Senate Committee Reports, Divorce and Alimony").

87. **Hoffler, James and Deborah.** Petition of James Hoffler of Gates County, North Carolina, states that he married Deborah Outlaw in September 1802, but in December 1802, she "quit the bed and board of your petitioner and took herself to her father's house, where she remains and denies ever living with your petitioner…" Petitioner prays a law be passed "vesting such property as he now hath or may hereafter acquire in him, free from any claim by dower or otherwise of the said Deborah…or passing some General Law for divorce…" Petition is endorsed by some twenty-five subscribers. In House and Senate, 29-30 November 1803, and referred to Committee on Divorce and Alimony. (GASR, Nov.-Dec. 1803, Box 2: folder "Petitions, Divorce"). Committee on Divorce and Alimony "to whom was referred the petition of James Hoffler of Gates County praying to be divorced from his wife Deborah" is of opinion the interference of the Legislature would be improper in this case and recommend that the same be rejected. In Senate and House, 14-15 December 1803, and concurred with. (GASR, Nov.-Dec. 1803, Box 2: folder "Senate Committee Reports, Divorce and Alimony").

88. **Hughes, Lydia and Francis.** Petition of Lydia Hughes of Mecklenburg County, North Carolina, states that she married "Francis Hughes sometime in October 1796, that they continued to live, altho' in a very disagreeable manner…until the 10th day of Jan'y. 1799 when they mutually agreed to separate & as far as in their power dissolve the marriage contract which will appear by the written contract…accompanying this petition. Your petitioner would have rested satisfied had Francis HUGHES abided by the said agreement, but lately he has refused to be bound thereby & has set up a claim for all property in the possession of your petitioner & for such as she has disposed of, notwithstanding that she was possessed of all such property before the intermarriage or had acquired the same by her own industry since the separation. Petitioner prays for a law to dissolve the marriage contract & grant your petitioner a Divorce from the said Francis Hughes. If the Legislature cannot divorce her from the tyranny & cruelty of her said husband, then she prays a law would be passed securing the property in her possession from her own industry and "for the support of her two children by a former husband." Subscribed to by twelve persons who "know the Petitioner to be a very industrious & well conducting woman." Referred to Committee. Committee of Divorce and Alimony to whom was referred the petition of Lydia Hughes is of the opinion "there is no sufficient grounds for granting the prayer of the petitioner and therefore recommend that the same be rejected." In Senate and House, 14-15 December 1803, and concurred with. (GASR, Nov.-Dec. 1803, Box 2: folder "SCR, Divorce & Alimony").

89. **McClure, John and Rachel.** Petition of John McClure of Lincoln County sheweth that "whereas Rachel McClure his wife hath elop'd from his bed and board without any just cause, he prays that an act be passed to empower her to hold a separate property from the said John and empower the County Court

Divorces and Separations from Petitions to the North Carolina General Assembly from 1779

of Lincoln to bind out the children of the said John to such fit persons as they may think proper. She hath stated that the said John wishes to bind them to persons of ill fame. Your petitioner sheweth that he & the said Rachel were married and lived together for a considerable time, during which they had four children, three of whom are now alive. Through misfortune, they were reduced to low circumstances, but with tlieir joint industry they were able to maintain their children free from want of the necessaries of life." The said Rachel "through persuasion of ill dispos'd persons left him & took away his children without his consent & he was refus'd liberty to visit them at any time." The petitioner has frequently attempted a reconciliation, but was refused this in a most obstinate manner, which encourages her hopes of a separation whereby she may be empowered to hold separate property. Petitioner prays that he is anxious to direct and educate his children but is interested in having them bound to some respectable persons to learn a trade. He has sincere parental affection toward his children and would not wish them to be bound to any person of ill fame. He prays that the "honorable Body will leave to him the Direction & Education of his children during their minority & that you would not interfere in the affair between him & his said wife Rachel..." Dated 16 November 1803. Subscribed to by the names of twenty-two persons. In House and Senate, 25 November 1803, and referred to Committee. Committee of Divorce and Alimony to whom was referred the above petition is of opinion that the evidence is not sufficient to cause the petition to call for and stand in need of the clemency of the legislature and therefore recommend the same be rejected. In Senate and Commons, 14-15 December 1803, and concurred with. (GASR, Nov.-Dec. 1803, Box 2: folder "SCR, Divorce and Alimony").

90.   **Rhodes, Arnold and Euphan.** Petition of Arnold Rhodes and of Uphan/Euphan A. Rhodes states that they have long since resolved mutually and deliberately to live separate and no more to cohabit with each other for two years by entering into a covenant of separation which bears date of 1 May 1803. Petitioners pray for act to dissolve the bonds of marriage between them and thereby fully divorce them from each other, leaving each free to intermarry again. [Below:] Deposition of John Alderson before Daniel Marsh, Justice of Peace for Beaufort County, North Carolina, 20 November 1803, that on 1 May 1803 at said Alderson's house in Washington, Capt. Arnold Rhodes subscribed the above petition and on 14 May 1803 at the house of Mrs. Fohey in Washington also, Mrs. Euphan Alston Rhodes subscribed the same. Referred to Committee, 29-30 November 1803. [Enclosure:] Petition of Mary Farris, Hellen Leroy, Margaret Fohey, and L. S. Leroy-respectively mother, sister, sister and brother of Mrs. Euphan A. Rhodes—which states that the said Euphan married Capt. Arnold Rhodes in 1795, she being then of the age of seventeen years, that she possessed at the time of her marriage a valuable estate in lands and a number of valuable slaves. Said Captain Rhodes has abandoned himself to illness, intoxication, gambling and the wasting of the said Euphan's estate. The husband and wife have mutually agreed to separate and have signed such an agreement. Petitioners pray for a dissolution of said marriage. In Senate, 29 November 1803, and referred to Committee. Committee on Divorce and Alimony "to whom was referred the petition of Arnold Rhodes and Uphan Alston Rhodes of Beaufort County praying to be divorced from each other" is of opinion that they do not meet the patronage of the legislature and recommend the same be rejected. In Senate and House, 14-15 December 1803, and concurred with. Committee of Divorce and Alimony to whom was referred the petition of Mary Farress and others of the County of Beaufort is unanimously of opinion that the interferences of the Legislature in the case would be improper and recommend the same be rejected. In Senate and House, 14-15 December 1803, and concurred with. (GASR, Nov.-Dec. 1803, Box 2: folders "SCR, Divorce and Alimony" and "Petitions, Divorce").

91. **Sawyer, Willis and Dinah.** Petition of Will is Sawyer of Camden County, North Carolina, that sometime in the month of July 1799, Dinah Sawyer, wife of the petitioner, "left him and took up with another man and had a child by him, whom she hath since quitted, and continues to live in an open and avowed state of adultery." Your petitioner states that he lived with the said Dinah nearly two years prior to her elopement, and much of the time [she] frequently cohabited with diverse persons. She has since removed into another county and lately had a child there. Petitioner prays for divorce. In House and Senate, 29-30 November 1803, and referred to Committee. [Enclosures:] Depositions taken in Camden County at request of Will is Sawyer of said County]

    (a). Deposition of David Etherage, 11 November 1799, states that Davis Etherage came to his house and asked him, said David, if a certain woman might tarry at his house that day. The woman was named as Dinah Sawyer who had runaway through the night, and said David "saw her go to bead and the sd. Davis beaded with her & the next morning they both continued in bead for some time."

    (b). Deposition of Solomon Grandy, 12 November 1799, who deposes that he was in company with David and Davis Etheridge, and the said Davis "said he was agoing of_ then with [Dinah Sawyer]. Said Davis being a married man I asked him if [he] Like", the said Dinah & he made answer he loved her better than any Woman in the world, this being near a place caled the Lake, several miles from their homes."

    (c). Deposition of James (x) Dowdy, 12 November 1799, that he saw Dinah Sawyer, wife of said Willis "on the bed with certain Davis Etheridge at the said deponent's own house on the 10th of August 1799. In September 1799, "the deponent and the said Dinah was talking together about her & the said Davis Etheridge agoing of_ together & the said Dinah said there was but one reason and that was for want of her man…"

    (d). Deposition of Mary (x) Dowdy, 12 November 1799, deposes statements similar to the above. Committee of Divorce and Alimony to whom was referred the petition of Willis Sawyer report that the prayer of the petitioner is not entitled to the patronage of the Legislature and recommend that the same be rejected. In Senate and House, 14-15 December 1803, and concurred with. (GASR, Nov.-Dec. 1803, Box 2-folder "Senate Committee Reports, Divorce and Alimony").

92. **Smith, Alexander and Sarah.** Petition of Alexander Smith of Ashe County, North Carolina, states that said Smith's wife Sarah eloped from his bed in the year 1800, and he has been informed that she has taken up with a young man of ill repute in the western country. The petitioner requests "relief by divorcing him from his wife Sarah and not let him…continue to be bound to raise any children that she the said Sarah may hereafter bare as she has left him with five daughters and the youngest but about three years of age…" Endorsed by County Clerk Jno. McMillan that "the facts contained in the above petition are known by the Court to be true." In House and Senate, 22-23 November 1802, and referred to Committee on Divorce. (GASR, Nov.-Dec. 1802, Box 2: folder "Petitions- Divorce, name changes").

Committee on Divorces and Alimony to whom was referred the petition of Alexander Smith praying to be divorced from his wife Sarah reports that after hearing the prayer of the petitioner and [having] considered the facts advanced, are induced to believe that they are not sufficiently substantiated and recommend the same be rejected. In House and Senate, 7-8 December 1802, and concur with said report. (GASR, Nov.-Dec. 1802, Box 2: folder "House Committee Reports, Miscellaneous").

Divorces and Separations from Petitions to the North Carolina General Assembly from 1779

93. **Spell, John and Celia.** Certificate of Thomas Guion, Justice of Peace, states that Joseph Morgan of [Edgecombe] County was present about 1 October last when John Spell gave notice to his wife, Celia Spell, that he should endeavour to obtain a divorce at the November Term, 1802, of the General Assembly. Draft Bill that John Spell of Edgecombe County is hereby divorced from his wife Celia and that the marriage tie between said John and Celia be annulled and dissolved as if they had never been married. In House, 8 December 1802, read third time and passed. In Senate, 11 December 1802, read third time, amended by striking out the words "had never been married," passed, and ordered to be engrossed. (GASR, Nov.-Dec. 1802, Box 1: folder "House Bills, 22 Nov.").

94. **Tillery, Ann and George.** Petition of Ann (0) Tillery states that she was lawfully married to George Tillery of Randolph County, North Carolina, and became his second wife. She bore him four children, but after then his cruel treatment and arbitrary measures caused her and the children to leave him. Said George was possessed of a tract of land which he sold and distributed the price thereof amongst the children of his former wife, all of whom had reached maturity. Said George died sometime afterwards, and William Barton of said County of Randolph administered upon his estate and paid the just debts of said estate, leaving in balance a sum of £15. Petitioner prays that the Legislature gives her said sum so she can raise her children. Referred to Committee of Propositions and Grievances. (GASR, Nov.-Dec. 1803, Box 2: folder "Petitions, Divorce").

1804-1805

95. **Abercrombie, Robert and Anne.** Petition of Robert Abercrombie sheweth that he married his wife, Anne, about thirty years past and at first enjoyed those comforts attached to the matrimonial life. About three years after the marriage, said Anne began to act with indecency owing to a deranged state of her mind. She has continued to act in this way ever since. Your petitioner cannot ascertain whether this conduct has proceeded from the depravity of her morality or from a state of lunacy. She appears not only to be lost to a due sense of shame to the preservation of her character in chastity but also to common reason. Your petitioner continues to find in her every comfortable enjoyment, but has taken bonds from persons having the charge of her person. He prays for an act dissolving the ties of matrimony between him and his wife Anne. [Attached:] Depositions taken in Wake Co., NC: Deposition of Mordecai Sutherland before Justice of Peace, John P. Rencher, 19 Nov. 1804, that the deponent is well acquainted with Robert Abercrombie, Esq., of Warren Co., Georgia, where said Abercrombie has moved from North Carolina. Deponent was first acquainted with said Abercrombie's wife, Anne, about twenty-one years ago, and she then had an imperious and turbulent disposition. She made use of every means in her power to injure her said husband by wasting and destroying his estate. Her husband at last came to be afraid to live with her, but still used every means to reclaim her. When Mr. Abercrombie moved to Georgia, his wife Anne would not consent to go with him, and this led to considerable expense to provide for her remaining in North Carolina. The deponent was employed by Mr. Abercrombie to keep her, and this was undertaken for three years and eight months. The longer she lived with the deponent, the worse she got, and as she had to be watched strictly, the deponent finally could not put up with her any longer. Deposition of John G. Rencher before Justice of Peace, Nathaniel Jones, 21 Nov. 1804, proceeds along the same line as the deposition above and also notes that Benjamin Rhodes of Orange Co., NC, had agreed to provide for the said Anne Abercrombie "in as genteel & comfortable manner as the nature of her situation will admit of during her life." Deposition of Benjamin Rhodes before Justice of Peace John G. Rencher, 24 Nov. 1804, notes that Robert Abercrombie of Warren Co., GA, has always been an honest, upright man. Deponent moved from the State of Georgia to North Carolina in 1793. Anne Abercrombie, wife of said Robert, was then living at Mordecai Sutherland's in Orange Co., NC, although she was much deranged in her reasonings. Deponent took her after said Sutherland and kept her four months, after which her half-sister took her, but then moved away and left said Anne to suffer. Deponent then moved to Georgia but returned and again took said Anne at her husband's request for the past two years. During this time, she has behaved as a person void of reason and incapable of acting for herself. She has gotten worse instead of better. Her husband employed the deponent to keep her during her life in as comfortable a manner as possible. Committee of Divorce and Alimony to whom was referred the petition of Robert Abercrombie believes that legislative interference in this case would be highly inexpedient, and therefore recommends rejection of petition. North Carolina Senate and House concur in committee's recommendation on 6-7 Dec. 1804. (GASR, Nov.-Dec. 1804, Box 2: folder "Petitions (Divorce, etc.)". and folder "Senate Cmte. Reports.")

Divorces and Separations from Petitions to the North Carolina General Assembly from 1779

96.   **Alexander, Fanny and Azariah.** Petition of Fanny Alexander states she was unmercifully driven from home by her husband, Azariah Alexander, without leaving her the least means of subsistence, and she is afraid to return home to live with him. She prays for assistance "to grant and secure to me and my Child, all such acquisitions of Property as I have made and may hereafter make…without molestation from him…" Act passed to secure Fanny Alexander, wife of Azariah, such property as she may hereafter acquire. (GASR, Nov.-Dec. 1805, Box 3: folder "Petitions (Divorce, name changes, etc.)"; GASR, Nov.-Dec. 1805, Box 2: folder "Senate Bill 7 Dec."; N.C. Laws, 1805, p. 42.)

97.   **Anderson, Charlotte and George.** Memorial of Charlotte (+) Anderson, wife of George Anderson of Wilkes Co., NC, states said George left her bed and board sometime in the year 1797 and is said to be residing at this time in a western state. He left your memorialist with four small children, but with no property to support them. Her husband's absence is going on eight years, and he has never contributed to the support of said children. Being desirous of raising her children in some kind of decency, and for fear the said George may deprive her of such necessaries as she has or may acquire, the memorialist prays for a law to rectify her situation. Act is passed to secure Charlotte Anderson of Wilkes Co., wife of George Anderson, such property as she may hereafter acquire. (GASR, Nov.-Dec, 1805, Box 3: folder "Petitions (Divorce, name changes, etc.)"; GASR, Nov.-Dec. 1805, Box 2: folder "Senate Bill 7 Dec."; N.C. Laws, 1805, p. 42.)

98.   **Armstrong, Martha (Crywell) and Archibald Armstrong.** Petition of Martha Armstrong (alias Crywell) of Iredell Co., NC, states she married Archibald Armstrong in November 1792. Said Archibald said he was from the State of New York. The couple lived together for ten years, when said husband "without any cause left said Martha in indigent circumstances, and she has not heard from her said husband for about twelve years." She prays a law to "grant her such property as she has since made or hereafter may acquire…" Senate Bill of 7 December 1805 passed to secure to persons named…, including Martha Armstrong, wife of Archibald Armstrong…such property as she may hereafter acquire. (GASR, Nov.-Dec. 1805, Box 3: folder "Petitions (Divorce, name changes, etc.)"; GASR, Nov.-Dec. 1805, Box 2: folder "Senate Bill 7 Dec."; N.C. Laws, 1805, p. 42.)

99.   **Badger, Temperance and Nathaniel.** Memorial of Temperance Badger of Wake Co., NC, wife of Nathaniel Badger, states that said Nathaniel set out from home with a few hogs to the State of Virginia about twelve months ago, but has never since returned. A few months after he left home, said Temperance heard that he was in the State of Georgia, and "from there he took a woman a Daughter of your memorialist, and has since heard that he is now living with her in the State of Maryland, where he the said Badger was raised, and there being no prospect, or expectation, of his ever returning to her again." The whole of the property left by said Nathaniel has been sold by his creditors. The memorialist prays that the General Assembly pass a law securing to her such property as she may hereafter acquire. North Carolina Laws, 1804, p. 54, secures to Temperance Badger, wife of Nathaniel, such property as she may hereafter acquire as if she had never been married. (GASR, Nov.-Dec. 1804, Box 2: folder "Petitions (Divorce, etc.)"; N.C. Laws, 1804, p. 54.)

100.   **Ball, Mourning and Spencer.** Petition of Mourning Ball of Edgecombe Co., NC, states that she was married to a certain Spencer Ball. He left her and several small children about eighteen years ago without common necessaries of life to support them. Her said husband has never since returned nor taken any charge of his children. Your petitioner has acquired through her own industry a small property,

and since her said husband can legally take such property from her at any time, she prays a law to secure to her such property as she has or may hereafter acquire. North Carolina Assembly concurs with her prayer. (GASR, Nov.-Dec. 1804, Box 2: folder "Petitions (Divorce, etc.)"; N.C. Laws, 1804, p. 54.).

101.   **Barker, Liney and John.** Petition of Liney Barker of Rockingham Co., NC, that she "was unfortunately married to John Barker on the 30th of March 1778, who cohabited with her as a husband until October the 16th day ensuing the Above date." During this time, said John Barker used no industry for the maintenance of his family, but resumed to himself all manner of vice & dissipation. After all his ill treatment and abuse, he absconded and left said Liney in a pregnant and distressed circumstance. He removed to the State of Virginia where he has taken up with, or married, another woman. Through her own industry, she has acquired a small estate since he left her and prays a law to redress her situation. North Carolina Assembly concurs in her prayer and passes law to secure her such property as she now has and may hereafter acquire. (GASR, Nov.-Dec. 1804, Box 2: folder "Petitions (Divorce, etc.)" and "House Bill 23 Nov."; N.C. Laws, 1804, p. 54.).

102.   **Beeson, Elizabeth and Azael.** Petition of Elizabeth Beeson of Randolph Co., NC, states she once had a husband [unnamed] who lived with her several years and bore him four children. He then deserted his family and removed to the State of South Carolina and married another woman. The petitioner has supported her said children for fourteen years through her own care and industry and has acquired some property which greatly assisted her in maintaining her family. She further stated that her age, hardships and infirmities made her unable to transact business as formerly, and she has had difficulty in recovering monies due her because she cannot bring suit in her situation. She prays the General Assembly to secure such property as she now has or may hereafter acquire and grant her the privilege in her own name to buy, sell, and sue as if she had never been married. Her prayer is granted, and the General Assembly passes an act in response. (GASR, Nov.-Dec. 1804, Box 2: folder "Petitions (Divorce, etc.)"; N.C. Laws, 1804, p. 54.)

103.   **Betz, George and Elizabeth (Barringer) Betz.** Petition of George Betz and Elizabeth, his wife, states that they intermarried in 1803, "and that a very short time afterwards, they discovered that they could not live together in the habits of mutual love and affection as man and wife ought to do." They agreed to part by mutual consent and entered into an agreement for that purpose and have been separated ever since. They have no hopes of reconciliation and pray for a law to separate them and secure to each such property as they now have or may hereafter respectively acquire, and that neither shall be responsible for the debts of the other. Bill referred to Committee on Divorce and Alimony, but apparently rejected. (GASR, Nov.-Dec. 1804, Box 1: folder "HB 27 Nov."; GASR, Nov.-Dec. 1804, Box 2: folder "SCR"). Petition of George Betz of Town of Salisbury states that he was united in the bond of matrimony with Elizabeth Barringer in March 1803, believing that his happiness would be promoted and usefulness in society extended. To his sad regret, a few months experience convinced him that he had mistaken the object of his happiness, for "her steady determinations appeared to be to wound his feelings by every mark of strident insult & disobedience and to ruin the little fortune which he had acquired by involving him expences which…his business as a mechanic could not afford…Your petitioner states that in her frequent fits of anger & rage, his person was not free from her violence, and his property threatened to be burnt by her. In this unpleasant situation they lived together until the latter part of June in the same year, when she voluntarily left his bed and board & hath ever since resided with her Father and utterly refused to return to him…" Your petitioner believes that if she were to return, her conduct would only involve him in greater misery, and as her father is a man of opulence, able and willing to support

her, your petitioner prays for a separation from bed and board. (GASR, Nov.-Dec. 1805, Box 3: folder "Petitions (Divorce, name changes, etc.)"). Bill to separate George Betts from his wife Elizabeth and to secure each of them such property as they now possess or may hereafter acquire. In Senate, 7 Dec. 1805, read 1st time and rejected. (GASR, Nov.-Dec. 1805, Box 2: folder "Senate Bill 7 Dec.")

104. **Blackman, Barzillai Jr. and Druzillai (Ganey) Blackman.** Petition of Barzillai Blackman, Jr., of Johnston Co., NC, that he married Druzillai Ganey of Sampson Co., NC, in 1803. He "anticipated that happiness which might reasonably be expected…[but] to the great mortification of your Petitioner…," his spouse disregarded her marriage vows. He is unable to live with her and prays a law "Disannulling the rights of Matrimony" between the said Druzillai and your petitioner. Subscribed to by ten signatures. The following depositions are enclosed: Deposition of Heroad Thornton before Bennitt Hill, J.P. for Sampson Co., NC, 15 Nov. 1805, that in September 1805 he was in the house of Barzillai Blackman, Jr., and heard the said Barzillai's wife, Druzillai, say to her husband: "I am now at peace with you as much as I shall Ever be for she never ment to Live with him another Day, and he said to her he woud. have the child…[S]he answered to him he should not hav_ the Child for he never Got such a one nor never woud. for she will be cusd. if She Didant believe he was a Moffarradite…[probably morphodlte, a corruption of hermaphrodite]" Deposition of Polley Lassiter before Bennitt Hill, J.P. for Sampson Co., NC, 15 Nov. 1805, that in September 1805, she heard Druzillai Blackman, wife of Barzillai Blackman, Jr., say in the house of William Ganey: "…if Barzillai did not mind she would make a fire two hot for him to warm by, for I will Burn Every house on that plantation - then said, Barzillai thought to keep her out of the houes but she said she woud. Brake open Locks & Doors when she pleasd and that she said she did Cut Down a garden of Collerds and Left them lying there & said they might Eat them if they Coud." This petition was probably rejected, as no concurring action was taken. (GASR, Nov.-Dec. 1805, Box 3: folder "Petitions (Divorce, name changes, etc.)").

105. **Bledsoe, Isaac and Elizabeth (Legget) Bledsoe.** Memorial of Isaac Bledsoe of Robeson Co., NC, that he married Elizabeth Legget in 1801, but she only stayed one night. The next morning, she eloped from his bed and board for unknown reasons and has never lived with your petitioner. She took up with another man and has had a child by him. Petitioner prays for a divorce from said wife, Elizabeth. This petition was rejected. (GASR, Nov.-Dec. 1805, Box 3: folder "Petitions (Divorce, name changes, etc.)").

106. **Brinson, Elizabeth and John.** Petition of Elizabeth Brinson of Brunswick Co., NC, states that she married John Brinson in 1796. Three years later, he left her and went to Duplin County, attached himself to another woman, and brought her home. After considerable abuse, said John Brinson turned your petitioner out of doors. He "wasted most of the little Property Her Father had given Her & then left the County abandoning her & carrying with him the said woman he had connected Himself Contrary to the laws of God & Man…" He has remained absent from her about five years and lives in the State of South Carolina in a state of adultery. Petitioner prays for a law divorcing her from said John Brinson. Petition is concurred in and alimony granted. (GASR, Nov.-Dec. 1804, Box 2: folder "Petitions (Divorce, etc.)"; N.C. Laws, 1804, p. 54.)

107. **Brown, Bonville and Susannah.** Petition of Bonville Brown of Caswell Co., NC, states that his wife, Susannah Brown, deserted from his home in January 1802, attached herself to a certain Joshua Pirant, and removed themselves to the State of Tennessee near Knoxville. Said Susannah has two children by the said Pirant. Petitioner further states that when his said wife, Susannah, left, "she took with her the

best Horse that your petitioner owned and about one hundred dollars in cash." Petitioner prays for a law to prevent his said wife, Susannah, or any of her children by said Pirant from having any demand on said Bonville or his heirs. (GASR, Nov.-Dec. 1804, Box 2: folder "Petitions (Divorce, etc.)"). Senate Committee of Divorce and Alimony notes that it is inexpedient to grant prayer of said petitioner and recommends rejection. Senate and House concur in recommendation. (GASR, Nov.-Dec. 1804, Box 2: folder "Senate Committee Reports").

108. **Brucks, Nancy and William.** Petition of Nancy Brucks of Burke Co., NC, sheweth that she married William Brucks in 1799, but said William left her "without any cause to her knowledge" about four or five months after the marriage. She has no expectation that he will ever come to live with her as a good husband ought to do. Petitioner prays for a divorce or a law to secure her the property she now has and what she may hereafter acquire. Subscribed to by eleven signatures. (GASR, Nov.-Dec. 1805, Box 3: folder "Petitions (Divorce, name changes, etc.)"). Bill to secure to persons named such property as they may hereafter acquire, includes name of Nancy Brinks of Burke Co., wife of William Brinks. (GASR, Nov.-Dec. 1805, Box 2: folder "Senate Bill 7 Dec."; read 3d time in Senate, 18 Dec. 1805 and passed; read 3d time in House, 19 Dec. 1805 and passed.) Passed into law. (N.C. Laws, 1805, p. 42, and listed as "Brucks").

109. **Buie, Margaret and Donald.** Bill passed to secure to persons named such property as they may hereafter acquire, includes "Margaret Buie of Cumberland Co., wife of Donald Buie." (GASR, Nov.-Dec. 1805, Box 2: folder "Senate Bill 7 Dec."). Passed into law. (N.C. Laws, 1805, p. 42.)

110. **Caldwell, Betsy and Thomas G.**[13] Petition of Betsy G. Caldwell and others (James Conner, JP; Archd. Cathey - Capt. & brother-in-law to Thomas G. Caldwell; Joseph Byars; Thomas Byars; Ephm. Davidson - Brig. Gen'l.; Henry Conner, JP; Reuben Emerson; Jonth. Potts, JP; and William Caldwell and James Caldwell - brothers of Thomas G. Caldwell) sheweth that said Betsy Caldwell intermarried with Thomas G. Caldwell on 2 May 1801. This couple lived together in perfect harmony for five weeks and two days, but after that time, said Thomas G. "joined himself to a certain Polly Hanna of the neighborhood & took her from the County of Mecklenburg in this State to the State of Tennessee as these petitioners are informed…, where he lives with the said Polly Hanna in a State of Adultery. These Petitioners are firmly of the opinion that the said Thomas never will return to live with his wife, your petitioner…Your Petitioners farther State that they have been acquainted with the said Betsy Caldwell for many years from her childhood, that she has supported a fair character at all times, & that she has been particularly circumspect since the Elopement of her Husband. These petitioners state from their own personal knowledge that the said Betsy Caldwell is a decent well conducting young woman and in their firm opinion a virtuous woman & that she has been treated extremely ill by her said husband &…she is well entitled to a Divorce…" (GASR, Nov.-Dec. 1805, Box 3: folder "Petitions (Divorce, name changes, etc.)"). Bill to divorce Betsey Caldwell of Mecklenburg Co., NC, from…husband Thomas Givens Caldwell…as if they had never been married. In House 10 Dec. 1805 and passed. In Senate 11 Dec. 1805 and rejected. (GASR, Nov.- Dec. 1805, Box 1: folder "House Bill 10 Dec."). Bill to secure to persons named such property as they may hereafter acquire, includes Betsy Caldwell, wife of Thomas G. Caldwell, and is passed on 18-19 Dec. 1805. (GASR, Nov.-Dec. 1805, Box 2: folder "Senate Bill 7 Dec."; N.C. Laws, 1805, p. 42.)

---

13 Betsy Caldwell's maiden name is Black according to deposition of James Caldwell, brother of her husband, Thomas G. See 1806 Session of North Carolina Assembly.

Divorces and Separations from Petitions to the North Carolina General Assembly from 1779

111.   **Carrick, Anne (Mills) and John Carrick.** Petition of Anne Carrick of Rutherford Co., NC, formerly Anne Mills and widow of Ambrose Mills, decd., states that she intermarried with John Carrick, but that said John frequently abused her for some years and then absconded and has remained absent for seven or eight years last past. By her industry, she has procured property sufficient for her needs, but has been informed that the said John Carrick may return and take possession of her property and reduce her and her children to poverty and indigent circumstances. Petitioner prays for an act to secure her the property she has acquired and what property she may hereafter acquire. (GASR, Nov.-Dec. 1804, Box 2: folder "Petitions (Divorce, etc.)"). Petition is concurred in and passed into law. (N.C. Laws, J804, p. 54.)

112.   **Deavon/Deavor, John and Elizabeth (Grey) Deavon/Deavor.** Petition of John Deavon/Deavor, 20 Nov. 1805, that he married Elizabeth Grey in September 1805, "expecting to receive all the blessings and benefits resulting from the connubial vow..." Unfortunately, for causes unknown, the said Elizabeth eloped from his bed and board. Petitioner prays for a divorce. Petition is rejected. (GASR, Nov.-Dec. 1805, Box 3: folder "Petitions (Divorce, name changes, etc.)").

113.   **Dennis, Francis and Nancy (Battee) Dennis.** Petition of Francis (F) Dennis, Carteret Co., NC, 3 Nov. 1803, states that he married Nancy Battee about three years or "upwards" ago. She resided with him about three or four months, after which she deserted him without provocation or ill usage on his part. Soon afterwards, she attached herself to Morris Greenwood of Brunswick Co., NC, married him, and had a child by him. Your petitioner has considerable estate, real and personal, whereas said Nancy had no property at all at the time of their marriage, nor has she acquired any since. He has been advised that in case of his death, said Nancy and her child aforesaid, and other children she may have by said Morris, would be entitled to a claim on his estate. The petitioner prays for an act to divorce him from said wife. Nancy, and to secure his estate from any claims that she or her children may make. [Below:] Indorsement of Nancy Greenwood, alias Dennis, at Smithsville, Brunswick Co., NC, 1803, that she is perfectly satisfied to be barred from all future claims to be made on the estate of the above petitioner in the event of his death, and she also approves of the divorce. Petition is rejected. (GASR, Nov.-Dec. 1805, Box 3: folder "Petitions (Divorce, name changes, etc.)").

114.   **Dillingham, Betsey Sally (Beaty) and Vechel Dillingham.** Petition of John Carruth, Peter Forney, Jno. Fulenwider and Thos. Wheeler at Lincolnton, 3 Oct. 1804, states that in March 1797, Betsey Sally Beaty married Vachel Dillingham, and she bore him twin children. In January 1798, said Vechel left his said wife without any known cause. She was then pregnant with the two said children. Said Vechel never returned nor even wrote his said wife, although she has often solicited him by letter to return and acquaint himself with his two lovely children. The said Vechel left this country, but left his wife in debt. She has acquired some property, and the petitioners pray that the Legislature relieve the said Betsey Sally of her aforementioned difficulties. A bill to secure to Betsey Sally Dillingham what property she now has or may hereafter acquire was referred to Committee on Divorce and Alimony along with the petition. (GASR, Nov.-Dec. 1804, Box 1: folder "House Bill 28 Nov."). Bill was enacted into law. (N.C. Laws, 1804, p. 54.)

115.   **Doak, Susannah [husband unnamed].** Bill to secure to persons named such property as they may hereafter acquire, includes Susannah Doak of Guilford Co. (GASR, Nov.-Dec. 1805, Box 2: folder "Senate Bill 7 Dec."). Bill passed into law. (N.C. Laws, 1805, p. 42.)

116. **Eisenhauer, Mary (Meyers) and Nicholas Eisenhauer.** Petition of Mary Eisenhauer of Cabarrus Co., NC, 12 Nov. 1805, states that her rude, lazy and misanthropic husband, Nicholas Eisenhauer, drove her from her home about twenty years ago without the slightest subsistence. He "made away with all we had" and abandoned your petitioner "for good and all," except once when he returned and tried to convince her to sell 200 acres of land that her father, Michael Meyers, bestowed upon her. "[H]e left me again under hundreds of bitter and cruel curses, and I truly have suffered since many times, although by the help of my children and God's blessings, I acquired a little again." The petitioner reflects upon the "nasty character" of the said Nicholas by including the following about him: "He got in an intimate understanding with a licentious widow. Some neighbors, mistrusting them, watched and catched them in fornication; took him out of the house, tarred and feathered him and exposed him in that figure to the public execration." Your petitioner prays for assistance to secure herself all such small acquisitions she has saved since her husband left her and what she may hereafter acquire. Signed by fifteen subscribers, most of them signing in German script. (GASR, Nov.-Dec. 1805, Box 3: folder "Petitions (Divorce, name changes, etc.)"). Bill to secure to persons named such property as they may hereafter acquire, includes Mary Eisenhauer, wife of Nicholas Eisenhauer, and is passed 18-19 Dec. 1805. (GASR, Nov.-Dec. 1805, Box 2: folder "Senate Bill 7 Dec.") Bill made into law. (N.C. Laws, 1805, p. 42.)

117. **Ellrod, Barbara (Vogler) and Jeremiah Ellrod.** Petition of Barbara Ellrod, alias Vogler, that her husband, Jeremiah Ellrod, has deserted her and married another woman. He moved with her several years ago and now lives in the State of Kentucky, "leaving your petitioner in the condition of a desolate widow without the legal Priviledges of Widows and yet liable by his capacity to loose all property she has since by her industry acquired." Petitioner prays a law to divorce her from said husband or to be relieved in some other manner. (GASR, Nov.-Dec. 1805, Box 3: folder "Petitions (Divorce, name changes, etc.)"). Bill to secure to persons named such property as they may hereafter acquire, includes Barbara Ellrod of Stokes Co., wife of Jeremiah Ellrod, and is passed into law. (GASR, Nov.-Dec. 1805, Box 2: folder "Senate Bill 7 Dec."; N.C. Laws, 1805, p. 42.)

118. **Fabre, Elizabeth and Peter, Jr.** Bill to divorce…Elizabeth Fabre of Newbern from…Peter Fabre as if they had never been married was passed in House, 10 Dec. 1805, but rejected by Senate, 11 Dec. 1805. (GASR, Nov.-Dec. 1805, Box 1: folder "House Bill 10 Dec.").

119. **Farrow, John and Rebekah (Foulson) Farrow.** Petition of John Farrow of Currituck Co., NC, 3 Oct. 1805, notes that he married Rebekah Foulson about fourteen years ago and lived with her about six years "in the most conjugal affection." However, "she gave herself up to Habitual Dissipation and Illicit Amours with Other men and Becom_ a prostitute to all who woud. partake on her wicked and lewd practice and has now for Eight year. last past Absconded & Elopd. from your Petitioners Bed and board and Still Continues to live in an open State of Adultery." She has removed from place to place, and at this time, "lives with a man and wife. She has had three children and is now pregnant again, which she has begotten in adultery…" Petitioner prays for a divorce. Signatures of 48 subscribers are appended in support of the petitioner. Petition for divorce is rejected. (GASR, Nov.-Dec. 1805, Box 3: folder "Petitions (Divorce, name changes, etc.)").

120. **Harris, William and Amelia (Odom) Harris.** Petition of William Harris sheweth that he intermarried with Amelia Odom about thirty years past and lived together until about seven years last past. At that time, said Amelia left your petitioner and has since lived with her friends and relatives. She recovered in the Court of Equity for the District of Edenton against your petitioner the sum of $200 to be paid

annually during her natural life. Your petitioner prays for a law "vesting your petitioner with full power to dispose of his Estate, So as to prevent the said Amelia from Heiring any part of your petitioner's Estate, or having any lawful Claim to any part thereof, save the two Hundred dollars annually, during her natural life…" Signed by eleven subscribers. Petitioner's prayer is rejected. (GASR, Nov.-Dec. 1805, Box 3: folder "Petitions (Divorce, name changes, etc.)").

121.   **Hinson, Joshua and Delilah**. Memorial of Joshua Hinson and Delilah Hinson of Anson Co., NC, states that they intermarried about eight years ago "under a full assurance of enjoying that felicity and happiness which is generally supposed to result from a union thus cemented by mutual or endearing affection." Unfortunately, in the course of six months, "they both experienced that the hopes of advancing and promoting each other's happiness was entirely blasted…" Your memorialists have been separated for six or seven years, and "during this period, both your petitioners have had children by Other persons, and that there is not the least hope or expectation of a reconciliation taking place between them." The memorialists pray for a law dissolving the bond of matrimony between them. The Committee of Divorce and Alimony to whom was referred the above memorial…report that it is their opinion that such prayers be rejected. Concurred in by Senate, 14 Dec. 1805, and by the House of Commons, 19 Dec. 1805. (GASR, Nov.-Dec. 1805, Box 2: folder "Senate Committee Reports").

122.   **Houston, Cassandra (Alexander) and James Houston.** Deposition of Cassandra Alexander, alias Houston, before Thomas Green and Geo. W. Smart, Justices of Peace for Mecklenburg Co., NC, 19 Oct. 1804, remarks that she intermarried with James Houston of said county on 4 Jan. 1803. Said Cassandra bedded with said James for about three weeks, and then one day, he directed questions to the deponent relative to the connubial pleasures as being rather futile, and expressed himself thusly: "I believe that the desires of one woman are so great as would require twenty men to gratify them." Whereupon the said deponent replied that if he thought so, he must have received his first impressions from very low bred people. After this altercation, said James appeared to be unhappy and shed tears frequently. He could not suffer her to be absent from him on any occasion until May or June following. At that time, her brother, Adam Alexander, returned from the westward, and from that time until July, several disputes between the deponent and her husband took place. In July, her said husband was disquieted to the extent that he could not follow his employment on the plantation or plow unless the deponent carried her spinning wheel to the field and sit down at the end of the corn row and spin. Your deponent denied this request, as she believed her said husband was jealous of the deponent's brothers and brother-in-law. This state of disquietude continued with direct and indirect hints to the deponent that her said husband had a design on his own life by means of knives, gallows, felling of trees and his gun. He had three fits in bed by which his whole body appeared agitated, and finally made the deponent fearful of her own life. On 28 or 29 November, your deponent left her husband, James' Houston's bed and house, and returned to the house of her mother "as much a Virgin as she was in a State of Celibacy." Her husband had expressed himself in these words: "That if he had to leave her (this deponent), he would leave her missing," by which she understood in plain terms that he designed taking her life. The deponent further saith on her oath "that if she was born a Maid, she still is so for any connexions she hath ever had with her said Husband." Nine other depositions are enclosed in this case regarding alleged impotency and homosexual inclinations on the part of said James Houston, including those of George Alexander (brother to said Cassandra), Augustus Alexander, Capt. Alexander Morrison, Marshall T. Alexander (grandson of Mrs. Jane Alexander), Atdam] Alexander (brother to said Cassandra), Francis B. Smart, John McCulloh, Jane Alexander (sister to Cassandra), Paris Alexander and Zeb Alexander. (GASR, Nov.-Dec. 1804, Box 2: folder "Petitions (Divorce, etc.)"). Committee of Divorce and Alimony to whom was referred the peti-

tion of Cassandra Alexander, alias Hou[torn] praying to be divorced from her husband James report that the accompanying documents are insufficient to authorize a belief that a separation would be just or reasonable. Both Senate and House concur in this decision. (GASR, Nov.-Dec. 1804, Box 2: folder "Senate Committee Reports").

123. **Johns(t)on, Sarah and John L. D.** Petition of Sarah Johns(t)on states she was married in the year 1794 to John L. D. Johns(t)on and lived with him until 11 Nov. 1803, when he left your petitioner. At the time of the marriage, your petitioner was possessed of considerable property, to wit: nine slaves, cash and other property. Prior to said John's departure, he had squandered the principal part of her property, leaving only three slaves. Your petitioner has sold two of the slaves and other personal property to pay her husband's debts. She has been informed that her said husband was in the Town of Fayetteville when she learned that he did not intend to return. In company with one of her brothers, your petitioner set out to find her said husband and went to Raleigh, Hillsborough and Fayetteville, but he had left the latter town some time previous to her arrival. She and her brother then proceeded to Guilford, Salem, Salisbury and then Charlotte. She then persuaded her brother to pursue the chase to Camden, SC, where he found that her husband was engaged in a school, but passed for a single man. Her said husband was detected in an attempt to debauch one of his scholars and was obliged to quit the town. From there, she learned that her husband went to Columbia, SC, then to Augusta, GA, and then to Charleston, SC, where he went by the name of Samuel Abbets. Shortly after, he found himself discovered, and he changed his lodgings and took a ship to Ireland, his native country. Your petitioner was told by her husband before he went away that he had another wife. Circumstances conspired to confirm the belief that this was true. The petitioner prays for a divorce. [No action noted.] (GASR, Nov.-Dec. 1805, Box 3: folder "Petitions (Divorce, name changes, etc.)").

124. **Knight, Nancy (Hill) and Murfree Knight.** Petition of Nancy Hill, alias Knight, states that about the month of October 1797, she married Murfree Knight of the town of Murfreesborough in Hertford Co., NC, and lived with him near two years. During this time, said Murfree engaged in a constant, uninterrupted pursuit of the vices of gaming and drunkenness and "dissipated the entire property belonging to your petitioner previous to her marriage with the said Murfree Knight..." Your petitioner was thus reduced to a state of extreme misery and want by being deserted by her said husband in pursuit of the aforesaid vices. She became sick and unable to provide for herself, and may have died had not relatives and friends interfered in her behalf and removed her to the house of her mother, where she has resided for upwards of six years. Since the separation, said Murfree has been engaged in an incessant career of vice, intemperance and debauchery. Your petitioner believes all of his friends have given up any hope of his being reclaimed, and there is not the remotest idea that reconciliation can ever take place between your petitioner and the said Murfree. In the year 1800, the Legislature secured such property as she might thereafter acquire, and now she once more "throws herself upon the compassion and Justice of her country" and prays for the dissolution of the bonds of matrimony and the restoration to her of her original name of Nancy Hill. The petitioner's prayer is rejected. (GASR, Nov.-Dec. 1805, Box 3: folder "Petitions (Divorce, name changes, etc.)"). Committee of Divorce and Alimony to whom was referred the petition of...Nancy Knight...reports that it is inexpedient to grant a divorce, and recommend rejection. (GASR, Nov.-Dec. 1804, Box 2: folder "Senate Committee Reports").

125. **Knight, Priscilla and Lewis.** Petition of Priscilla Knight of Hertford Co., NC, shows that her husband, Lewis Knight, deserted her and left her with several children without any means of support. Said Priscilla believes her husband has removed with another woman to the State of Georgia, and she

has no expectation that he will return. She prays for an act to secure to her such property as she may hereafter acquire by her own industry. (GASR, Nov.-Dec. 1805, Box 3: folder "Petitions (Divorce, name changes, etc.)"). Bill to secure to persons named such property as they may hereafter acquire, includes Priscilla Knight of Hertford Co., wife of Lewis Knight. (GASR, Nov.-Dec. 1805, Box 2: folder "Senate Bill 7 Dec."). Act made into law. (TV. C Laws, 1805, p. 42.)

126.   **Leck, Catharina.** Bill to secure to persons named such property as they may hereafter acquire, includes Catharina Leck of Lincoln Co., NC. (GASR, Nov.- Dec. 1805, Box 2: folder "Senate Bill 7 Dec."). N.C. Laws, 1805, p. 42, includes same wording as Senate Bill, but spells name as Luck. No husband is named for Catharina.

127.   **Lee, Elizabeth and Jesse.** Petition of Elizabeth Lee of Sampson Co., NC, notes that her husband, Jesse Lee, left her with several children in the year 1801. She prays for an act to secure to her the property she now has or may hereafter acquire. (GASR, Nov.-Dec. 1804, Box 2: folder "Senate Committee Reports"). Act passed into law. [N.C. Laws. 1804, p. 54.)

128.   **Limbaugh, Christian and Catharina (Hess) Limbaugh.** Petition of Christian Limbaugh, now Orderly Sergeant of Capt. McCaul's Company, 2nd United States Regiment, complains that it was his misfortune to marry Catharina Hess, daughter of John Hess of Rowan Co., NC, sometime in the year 1796. They lived together for a short time "in a state of the most poignant misery, owing to her rude, ungovernable temper, & particularly her incontinency, for I frequently had reason to believe that her immoral & indecent turn of mind led her to be connected with other men than myself." The petitioner left said Catharina on 24 April 1799, from which time they have never been together. Said Christian further states that his said wife removed to Lincoln Co., NC, where "she was looked upon as infamous by all with whom she was acquainted…, it being the general belief…that she was delivered of one or more mullato children…" At the March Term 1804 of Salisbury Superior Court, said Catharina "was convicted of having barbarously murdered her infant child which was generally believed…to have been a mulatto," but she was pardoned under the gallows by the Governor. The truth of the above can be learned from General Mumford Stokes, the Governor, and "all the members from the County of Rowan." Petitioner prays for a divorce. The signatures of fifteen subscribers are included on the bottom of the petition. The prayer of the petitioner is rejected by the North Carolina Assembly. (GASR, Nov.-Dec. 1805, Box 3: folder "Petitions (Divorce, name changes, etc.)").

129.   **Manning, Eli and Winnefred.** Petition of Eli Manning and his wife Winney (+) Manning of Edgecombe Co., NC, 10 Nov. 1805, states they were married about March 1805 and lived together until July 1806. At that time, petitioner "Winney" left her husband "under a belief (founded on repeated declarations both public and private) that said Eli intended to put her to death, abusing her with the most unjust & unfounded suspicions of incontinency." Said Winney further states "(and it is not deny'd by the sd. Eli…) that he the sd. Eli is absolutely impotent & by nature rendered a useless man as a husband; and disagreeable & unpleasant as that may appear to a young & healthy woman, yet, that is, compared with the consequences, but trifling; for haunted by the well founded belief of his own impotency, he suspects your Petr. Winney of illicit connection with every man, both white & black that may have seen her; and hurried off by this wild immagination, he the sd. Eli seeks to torment the sd. Winney yr. Petr. by the most refined & strident cruelty…" Said Winney prays for an act to divorce her from the sd. Eli Manning. Petitioner Eli Manning notes that due to the above circumstances, he too prays for a divorce. Petition is subscribed to by Jesse Cherry, J.P., and John Mhoon, "who married them and Pernounced them as man

& wife." (GASR, Nov.-Dec. 1805, Box 3: folder "Petitions (Divorce, name changes, etc.)"). Committee of Divorce and Alimony to whom was referred the above petition report that it is the opinion of the Committee that such prayers be rejected. Concurred in by Senate, 14 Dec. 1805, and by House, 19 Dec. 1805. (GASR, Nov.-Dec. 1805, Box 2: folder "Senate Committee Reports").[14]

130. **Moreign, Mary and Thomas.** Torn "petition of Mary Mareg_ [of Caswell] County who humbly sheweth that you[r Petitioner] was formerly the Widow of John Hughes De[cd. who died] some years ago & left her with a number of [infant? chiljdren…that she afterwards married Thoma[s Moreign/Morine and] lived with him Some time [?]. [H]e the said Thomas having the management of the property left by her deceasd. husband for the maintenance of his children. After some time it was made known to the Court of Caswell County, that the said Thomas was wasting the estate of the orphans, & did in no instance whatever treat them with Justice. [T]he aforesaid Court then appointed a new guardian who took the proper…[petition is torn and ends here]." (GASR, Nov.-Dec. 1805, Box 3: folder "Petitions (Divorce, name changes, etc.)"). Act is passed to convey to Mary Moreign, wife of Thomas, whatever property she has acquired and whatever she may acquire. (N.C. Laws, 1805, p. 42.)

131. **Norfleet, Peggy and Benjamin.** Petition of Peggy Norfleet of Gates Co., NC, wife of Benjamin Norfleet, states she intermarried with said Benjamin about 1789, and for causes unknown, their little property is entirely exhausted. Said Peggy is in indigent circumstances, and her said husband quit her bed in November 1803. He has never returned, and the cause of this injustice is unknown to the petitioner. She requests a law to secure to her such property, real and personal, that she may hereafter acquire, free and clear from any claim of her said husband. Dated 15 Oct. 1804 and signed by 43 subscribers. (GASR, Nov.-Dec. 1804, Box 1: folder "House Bill 26 Nov."). Committee of Divorce and Alimony to whom was referred the petition of…Peggy Norfleet…state that it is their opinion it would be inexpedient to grant a divorce and recommend rejection of the petitioner's prayer. (GASR, Nov.-Dec. 1804, Box 2: folder "Senate Committee Reports"). Bill is passed to secure to persons named such property as they may hereafter acquire, includes Peggy Norfleet of Chowan Co., wife of Benjamin Norfleet. (GASR, Nov.-Dec. 1805, Box 2: folder "Senate Bill 7 Dec."; N.C. Laws, 1805, p. 42.)

132. **Rains, Nancy.** Bill to secure to persons named such property as they may hereafter acquire, includes Nancy Rains of Randolph Co. [husband unnamed]. (GASR, Nov.-Dec. 1805, Box 2: folder "Senate Bill 7 Dec."; N.C. Laws, 1805, p. 42.)

133. **Rothhaus, Ann (Steiner) and Balser Rothhaus.** Petition of Ann Rothhaus, alias Steiner, states she married Balser Rothhaus several years ago, but "he deserted her, went to Baltimore, lived there with another woman as husband, & from thence he went to Europe & that for 5 years she heard nothing from him." She prays that her bond of matrimony be dissolved and that she be made secure on any property she now has or may hereafter acquire. (GASR, Nov.-Dec. 1805, Elox 3: folder "Petitions (Divorce, name changes, etc.)"). Bill to secure to persons named such property as they may hereafter acquire, includes Amy Rothhaas of Stokes Co., wife of Balser Rothhaas. Bill passed into law gives spelling of Roothoas and wife's name as Anny. (GASR, Nov.-Dec. 1805, Box 2: folder "Senate Bill 7 Dec."; N.C. Laws, 1805, p. 42.)

---

14   New petitions regarding this case will be shown in the next installment for 1806.

Divorces and Separations from Petitions to the North Carolina General Assembly from 1779

134. **Sawyer, Willis and Dinah.** Petition of Willis Sawyer of Camden Co., NC, states his wife, Dinah Sawyer, left his bed, board and house about six years ago. She removed into another county "and lives in an open & avowed State of Adultry and has had two or three children by Other men Since her elopement." At the time of, and previous to, the elopement, she "frequently threatened to burn up and distroy the House & property of your petitioner." Prays for a divorce from his said wife Dinah. Petitioner's prayer is rejected. (GASR, Nov.- Dec. 1805, Box 3: folder "Petitions (Divorce, name changes, etc.)").

135. **Seehon, Mary and Joseph.** Petition of Mary Seehon states she intermarried with Joseph Seehon on 19 March 1799. He treated her with "every cruelty and abuse that the Human System was able to bear, till the 5th day of October 1800." On that day, said Joseph "went away and left her confined to her bed with a small child under the age of four months and no person to assist her. He had disposed of all his property before leaving and without any reason known to your petitioner." Said Mary was "unable to seek friends or even the necessary s of life till at length a neighbor by accident found her in a Situation worse than can be described, and removed her to her friend's till she was able to provide for herself." Since that time, your petitioner has not seen the said Joseph or heard any account of him. Petitioner prays that the Legislature grant her a divorce from said Joseph. Prayer of petitioner is rejected. (GASR, Nov.-Dec. 1804, Box 2: folder "Petitions (Divorce, etc.)").

136. **Smith, Joseph and Elizabeth.** Petition of Joseph Smith of Randolph Co., NC, and Elizabeth Smith, formerly of said county, states that your petitioners were for some years married and lived with each other until 1802, at which time an irreconcilable difference took place between them ("the particulars of which it would be unnecessary & disagreeable to relate"), which caused a separation. Said Elizabeth removed herself to the State of South Carolina and has made her residence there ever since. There is no probability of a reconciliation, and your petitioners have made as equitable a division of property already acquired and have further agreed that each of them shall enjoy such estate as each now has or may hereafter acquire, free from the claim of the other, as if they had never been married. Petitioners pray for consideration to grant them relief. Dated 5 November 1804. (GASR, Nov.-Dec. 1804, Box 2: folder "Petitions (Divorce, etc.)"). Committee of Divorce and Alimony to whom was referred the petition of…Joseph and Elizabeth Smith…report that it is inexpedient to grant same and recommend rejection. Concurred in by Senate and House, 13-14 Dec. 1804. (GASR, Nov.-Dec, 1804, Box 2: folder "Senate Committee Reports").

137. **Stephens, Elizabeth.** Bill to secure to persons named such property as they may hereafter acquire, includes Elizabeth Stephens of Franklin Co. No husband is named. (GASR, Nov.-Dec. 1805, Box 2: folder "Senate Bill 7 Dec."). Bill is passed into law in N.C. Laws, 1805, p. 42, but spelling is Stevens.

138. **Taylor, John and Rachel (Gibbs) Taylor.** Petition of John Taylor of Beaufort Co., NC, 19 Oct. 1805, states he married Rachel Gibbs about seven years ago, "being desirous of ending his days in peace and quiet…" To his regret, marriage to him did not cheer and sweeten life. He did not find that sympathetic affection and reciprocity that helps to unite the characteristics of man and wife. He found that suspicion "began to draw her finger across the imagination of your Petitioner and point at her virtue." He was also embarrassed "by her domestic economy and involved in debt by her wild waste & thoughtless extravagance." Consequently, a voluntary separation and distribution of property ensued about four years ago, and your petitioner never after cohabited with the said Rachel, his wife. Prays for a divorce. Prayer of petitioner is rejected. (GASR, Nov.- Dec. 1805, Box 3: folder "Petitions (Divorce, name changes, etc.)").

139. **Vervell, Daniel and Mary.** Petition of Daniel (x) Vervell and Mary (x) Vervell, his wife, of Rowan Co., NC, 4 Nov. 1804, states they were married six years ago, but separated in four months, "not finding…the blessings and comforts usually attending the married life…" About a year ago, the father of your petitioner, Daniel Vervell, died, and said Daniel persuaded his wife, Mary, to return and live with him. Said Mary did return and remained three months. However, "the same unaccomodating spirit still prevailed in the breasts of both your petitioners," and they find they can never live together in peace. They pray the Legislature to grant them a divorce. (GASR, Nov.-Dec. 1804, Box 2: folder "Petitions (Divorce, etc.)"). Committee of Divorce and Alimony to whom was referred the petition of…Daniel and Mary Vervell…report that it is inexpedient to grant same and recommend rejection. Rejection concurred in by Senate and House on 13 and 14 Dec. 1804. (GASR, Nov.-Dec. 1804, Box 2: folder "Senate Committee Reports"). However, N.C. Laws, 1804, p. 54, secures to Daniel and Mary Vervell separately the property each now has and may hereafter acquire, free from any claim by the other.

140. **Walker, Elizabeth and Joseph.** Petition of Elizabeth Walker, 14 Nov. 1804, states she and her husband, Joseph Walker, have been separated at their own consent for several years, and there appears no probability of a reunion. She prays a law to secure to her such estate as she may lawfully acquire and to grant her all the privileges of a feme sole. (GASR, Nov.-Dec. 1804, Box 2: folder "Petitions (Divorce, etc.)"). Committee of Divorce and Alimony to whom was referred the petition of…Elizabeth Walker…report it is inexpedient to grant same and recommend rejection. Concurred in by Senate and House, 13 and 14 Dec. 1804. (GASR, Nov.-Dec. 1804, Box 2: folder "Senate Committee Reports").

141. **West, Rachel and William.** Petition of Rachel West of Wake Co., 6 Dec. 1805, shows that she married William West in said county in July 1805. She possessed at the time of her marriage, sufficient property for her support and maintenance. After this marriage, said William West showed "by his conduct that his only object was to obtain possession of your petitioner's property, thereby to gratify his disposition to Drunkenness and Extravagance. He sold and wasted nearly the whole of the property of your petitioner in dissipation and Riot, and when he could get no more to answer his vicious purposes, he beat and abused your petitioner in such a manner that her life was in danger. His barbarous and inhuman treatment compelled her to leave her home for the preservation of her life. Since that time, the said William West "has eloped and gone away she knows not where…" She prays an act to secure to her such property as she may hereafter acquire. Her prayer is approved, and an act is passed to secure her property. (GASR, Nov.-Dec. 1804, Box 2: folder "Petitions (Divorce, etc.)"; N.C. Laws, 1804, p. 42.)

142. **Witty, Ezekiel and Jean (Cumming) Witty.** Memorial of Ezekiel Witty of Rockingham Co., NC, states that he married Jean Cumming, daughter of John Cumming of said county on 30 June 1791. Said Ezekiel and Jean lived together in affection and love until after they had three children. Frequent appearances of discontent appeared in said Jean, and in January 1800, she withdrew herself from both her children and said Ezekiel, taking up abode with her father, who sanctioned her conduct. The said father demanded of your memorialist all of the property he had given his daughter at her marriage to said Ezekiel. After explaining to Jean's father that he, the said Ezekiel, had never misused her, and that she should stay with her children, he was rebuffed by said John Cumming. Eventually, Ezekiel gave up the property given to his wife by her father. Said Jean, who only lives three miles distant, has not since been on the property of your memorialist. The said Ezekiel is apprehensive of the situation and is aware that he is subject to pay all debts contracted by the said Jean, and yet is left to raise three small children under indigent circumstances. He prays for an absolute divorce. (GASR, Nov.-Dec. 1804, Box 2: folder "Petitions (Divorce, etc.)"). The Committee of Divorce and Alimony to whom was referred the peti-

tion of…Ezekiel Witty…report that it is inexpedient to grant a divorce to the petitioner and recommend rejection. Concurred in by Senate and House, 13-14 Dec. 1804. (GASR, Nov.- Dec. 1804, Box 2: folder "Senate Committee Reports").

143. **Woogard, Polly and William.** Petition of Polly Woogard, Wake Co., NC, dated 29 Nov. 1804, states she married William Woogard some years ago "in hopes to spend her live with him happily, but to her astonishment, in about six months after marriage he left her and went to South Carolina and is there married again." Since the departure of her said husband, she has acquired a little property and prays for assistance in securing said property to her. (GASR, Nov.-Dec. 1804, Box 2: folder "Petitions (Divorce, etc.)"). Committee of Divorce and Alimony to whom was referred petition of…Polly Woogard…report that it is inexpedient to grant prayer of petitioner and recommend rejection. Concurred in by Senate and House, 13-14 Dec. 1804. (GASR, Nov.-Dec. 1804, Box 2: folder "Senate Committee Reports").

144. **Woodyard, Polly and William.** Petition of Polly Woodyard of Wake Co., NC, wife of William Woodyard, shows that she intermarried with said William in March 1802, but for some unknown reason, "he eloped from her in about ten days after their marriage and has not returned - nor does she know where he is…[H]er father is a man in circumstances to justify her expectations of acquiring some property…" She prays for an act securing to her all such property as she may hereafter acquire. (GASR, Nov.-Dec. 1805, Box 2: folder "Senate Committee Reports"). Bill to secure to persons named such property as they may hereafter acquire, includes Polly Woodyard. Passed in Senate and House, 18-19 Dec. 1805. (GASR, Nov.-Dec. 1805, Box 2: folder "Senate Bill 7 Dec."; N.C. Laws, 1805, p. 42.)

1806

145. **Beedle, Nancy and husband, John.** Petition of Nancy Beedle of the City of Raleigh, 4 Dec. 1806, states she married John Beedle about twenty-two years ago and by whom she has four small children now living with her. About five years past, said John eloped and went off from your petitioner without any provocation on her part, leaving your petitioner with numerous debts. She has been compelled to support her children by her own labor, and had it not been for the assistance received from some of the inhabitants of Raleigh, she and her children would have felt more severely the stings of want. Her said husband John is reportedly living in Lexington, Kentucky, and has allegedly remarried. She prays for an act to secure to her such property as she now has or hereafter may acquire. (GASR, Nov.-Dec. 1806, Box 2: folder "Petitions (Divorce, etc.)"). Committee of Divorce and Alimony to whom was referred the petition of Nancy Beedle of the City of Raleigh, wife of John Beedle…praying to be secured in such property as [she] may hereafter acquire, recommend [her] prayers be approved. (GASR, Nov.-Dec. 1806, Box 2: folder "HCR"). Bill to secure…Nancy Beedle of City of Raleigh, wife of John Beedle…such property as [she] may now have or may hereafter acquire as if she had never been married. In House and Senate, 20 Dec. 1806, read third time and passed. (GASR, Nov.-Dec. 1806, Box 1: folder "HB 10 Dec."). Published in N.C. Laws, 1806, p. 52.

146. **Bond, Jemima and husband, Thomas.** Petition of Jemima Bond of Green[e] County states she married Thomas Bond about six years past. At that time, said Thomas possessed a considerable estate, both real and personal, all of which property has since been entirely exhausted through his intemperance and debauchery. For the past two years, your petitioner has been obliged to live separate from her said husband, and has supported herself and child through her own industry and some assistance from her mother. Prays for an act to secure to her such property as she may hereafter acquire. (GASR, Nov.-Dec. 1806, Box 2: folder "Petitions (Divorce, etc.)"). Committee of Divorce and Alimony recommends approval of prayer of Jemima Bond. (GASR, Nov.- Dec. 1806, Box 2: folder "HCR"). Bill to secure persons therein mentioned such property as they now have or may hereafter acquire:…Jemima Bond of Greene County, wife of Thomas Bond…(GASR, Nov.-Dec. 1806, Box 1: folder "HB 6 Dec."). Published in N.C. Laws, 1806, p. 52.

147. **Bracewell, Isaac and Nancy (Lee).** Petition of Isaac (x) Bracewell of Edgecombe County shows that he was married some years ago to Nancy Lee. At length, however, he came to believe "that her regard for him had abated and shortly after afforded unquestionable evidence of her total disregard to the vows which united them." The petitioner feared "that the reputation of his children would suffer from a knowledge of their Parents guilt to conceal her crime," but her conduct has become notoriously unchaste and an open violation of the marriage contract. Prays for legislative interference.

Divorces and Separations from Petitions to the North Carolina General Assembly from 1779

[Enclosed:] Committee of Divorce and Alimony to whom was referred the petition of Isaac Bracewell of Edgecombe County…praying to be divorced report they do not deem it expedient to grant the prayer [of said petitioner] and recommend rejection. Concurred in by House and Senate, 10 and 11 Dec. 1806. (GASR, Nov.-Dec. 1806, Box 2: folder "HCR").

148. **Caldwell, Thomas Given/Gavins and Elizabeth ("Betsey") (Black).** Deposition of James Caldwell before James Conner, Justice of Peace for Mecklenburg County, 1 Nov. 1805, notes that he was present on 2 May 1801 when James Conner, Esq., solemnized the marriage of Thomas Given Caldwell and Betsey Black, and that they lived together as husband and wife about five weeks and two or three days. Then said Thomas left his wife for no good cause and took up with a young woman named Polly Hanna. Shortly afterwards, said Thomas and Polly went away to the State of Tennessee. [Attached:] Deposition of Archibald Cathey and James Conner, same date and county, states essentially the same information as the preceding deposition. [Attached:] Committee of Divorce and Alimony to whom was referred a bill to divorce Elizabeth Caldwell from her husband, Thomas Gavins Caldwell, are of the opinion the said bill ought to pass into Law. In House, 6 Dec. 1806, read first time and passed. (GASR, Nov.-Dec. 1806, Box 1: folder "HB 27 Nov."). Bill enacted and published in N.C. Laws, 1805, p. 42.

149. **Chevers, Molly and husband, Andrew.** Petition of Molly Chevers of Rowan County states that her husband, Andrew Chevers, deserted his family, leaving many debts unpaid, and the whole of his property has been sold to satisfy his said debts. Prays for an act to secure to her what property she now has and what she may hereafter acquire. (GASR, Nov.-Dec. 1806, Box 2: folder "Petitions (Divorce, etc.)"). Committee of Divorce and Alimony recommend a bill to secure to persons therein mentioned such property as they now have or may hereafter acquire:…Molly Chevers of Rowan Co., wife of Andrew…(GASR, Nov.-Dec. 1806, Box 2: folder "HCR"). Bill to secure persons therein mentioned such property as they now have or may hereafter acquire:…Molly Chevers of Rowan County, wife of Andrew Chevers…In House and Senate, 19 Dec. 1806, read third time, passed, and ordered to be enrolled. (GASR, Nov.-Dec. 1806, Box]: folder "HB 6 Dec."). Published in N.C. Laws, 1806, p. 52.

150. **Collins, Elizabeth and husband, Isaac.** Petition of Elizabeth (C) Collins of Rutlnerford County states she married Isaac Collins of said county about twenty years past and lived with him about ten years "in which time he had several Bastard Children…and was guilty of other Crimes and misdemeanors untill he finally left…your memorialist with six small and helpless children to maintain…" By means of her own industry and the assistance of friends, she has lived in decency the past seven or eight years. Since said Isaac left, he married another woman and has had by her four or five children. He has now returned and is endeavouring to take from your petitioner and her small children the small property she has acquired. Prays an act securing to her such estate as she now has or may hereafter acquire. Endorsed by six subscribers. [Attached:] Paper fragment with writing- "Alston Rhodes wife of Arnold Rhodes of the County of Beaufort." (GASR, Nov.-Dec. 1806, Box 2: folder "Petitions (Divorce, etc.)"). Committee of Divorce and Alimony recommends a bill concurring in prayer of said Elizabeth Collins. (GASR, Nov.-Dec. 1806, Box 2: folder "HCR"). Bill to secure persons therein mentioned such property as they now have or may hereafter acquire:…Elizabeth Collins, wife of Isaac Collins of Rutherford County… (GASR, Nov.-Dec. 1806, Box 1: folder "HB 6 Dec."). Bill published in N.C. Laws, 1806, p. 52.

151. **Davis, Baxter and wife Lucretia.** Petition of Baxter Davis of Buncombe County, North Carolina, and Lucretia Davis, his wife, of Washington County, Tennessee, 8 Nov. 1806, states that the said petitioners had amicably agreed to part from each other of their own free will and accord, no longer

to be considered man and wife. Petitioners have not cohabited in anyway as man and wife for twelve years and pray an act to divorce them. (GASR, Nov.-Dec. 1806, Box 2: folder "Petitions (Divorce, etc.)"). Committee of Divorce and Alimony to whom was referred the petition of…Baxter Davis and Lucretia his wife of Buncombe County…to be divorced report they do not deem it expedient to grant the prayer…of said petitioners and recommend rejection. Concurred in by House and Senate, 10 and 11 Dec. 1806. (GASR, Nov.-Dec. 1806, Box 2: folder "HCR").

152. **Dennis, Francis and Nancy (Battel).** Petition of Francis Dennis of Carteret County, Nov. 1806, states he married Nancy Battel "about four years ago or upwards," and they lived together about three or four months. After that time, she left him "without any provocation or ill usage whatsoever on his part, and soon afterwards attached herself to one Morris Greenwood of Brunswick County…" She has resided with said Greenwood ever since, "has actually intermarried with him, has a child by him, and has renounced all intercourse and connection with your Petitioner." Said petitioner has a considerable estate, both real and personal, and at the time of his marriage with said Nancy, she had no property at all, nor has she acquired any since that time. The law states that in the case of his death, said Nancy and the child aforesaid, and any other children she may have by said Greenwood would be entitled to claim the petitioner's estate. Your petitioner is in the prime of his life, but conceives the hardships of being deprived of all matrimonial comforts, and desires that the General Assembly place him in a situation where he can lawfully consider some other woman "better disposed to regard his happiness and her unioned duties." Prays for a divorce from said Nancy and to secure his estate from her future claims and those of her children. [Attached:] Certificate of Nancy Greenwood, alias Dennis, from Smithsville, Brunswick County, NC, 1803, requests that her marriage with said Francis Dennis be dissolved and states she is satisfied to be barred of all future claims on the estate of said Francis in the event of his death. Witness: Benj. Smith, John Griffin, Fredk. Hargett. [Attached:] Committee of Divorce and Alimony to whom the petition of Francis Dennis of Carteret County was referred report that it has been proven that "said Nancy, wife of said Francis, has for some years past lived (and now is living) with another man as his wife, and does not acknowledge ever being married to the petitioner." Committee recommends the prayer of the petitioner be granted. In House of Commons, 3 Dec. 1806, read first time and rejected. (GASR, Nov.-Dec. 1806, Box 1: folder "HB 3 Dec.").

153. **Dodd, Lydia and husband, Robert.** Petition of Lydia (x) Dodd of the City of Raleigh states she has been married to Robert Dodd for a long time. She has always endeavoured to perform her duties as a wife and to raise and bring up children in the best manner. In her married life, she has met with the most unkind and ungenerous treatment from her husband, who has often beat and abused her. He has spent and dissipated what little property she has acquired. Your petitioner is not desirous of leaving her husband and children, but shall continue to bear with patience the injuries she receives. Prays an act to secure to her what property she may acquire so that same shall not be liable to the disposal and debts of her said husband. Subscribed to by twenty supporters. (GASR, Nov.-Dec. 1806, Box 2: folder "Petitions (Divorce, etc.)"). Committee of Divorce and Alimony to whom was referred petition of…Lydia Dodd of City of Raleigh, wife of Robert Dodd…recommend approval of said Lydia's prayer. (GASR, Nov.-Dec. 1806, Box 2: folder "HCR"). Bill to secure…Lydia Dodd, wife of Robert Dodd of City of Raleigh… what property she now has and may hereafter acquire. In House and Senate, 20 Dec. 1806, read third time, and approved. (GASR, Nov.-Dec. 1806, Box 1: folder "HB 15 Dec."). Published in N.C. Laws, 1806, p. 53.

Divorces and Separations from Petitions to the North Carolina General Assembly from 1779

154.	**Duty, Rebeccah and husband, Russell.** Petition of Rebeccah Duty, wife of Russell Duty of Chatham County, states that eight or nine years ago, said Russell left his said wife Rebeccah with two small children dependent on her labor for support. The petitioner believes her said husband has intermarried with another woman in Tennessee or Kentucky. Prays an act to secure such property as she may hereafter acquire. (GASR, Nov.-Dec. 1806, Box 2: folder "Petitions (Divorce, etc.)"). Committee of Divorce and Alimony recommends a bill concurring in the prayer of said petitioner. (GASR, Nov.-Dec. 1806, Box 2: folder "HCR"). Bill to secure persons therein mentioned such property as they now have or may hereafter acquire as if they had never been married:…Rebeccah Duty of Chatham County, wife of Russell Duty…(GASR, Nov.-Dec. 1806, Box 1: folder "HB6Dec.").

155.	**Eller, Mary and husband, Jacob.** Petition of Mary Eller, wife of Jacob Eller of Buncombe County, states that about five years ago, her said husband Jacob "absconded and left your petitioner in a distressed situation with a number of small children and no one to assist her to support them." Said Jacob has been back twice and taken what little she had acquired for her support, and she has heard that he is about to return a third time. Prays a law to secure her in what property she now has or may hereafter acquire. (GASR, Nov.-Dec. 1806, Box 1: folder "HB 20 Dec."). Bill confirming her prayer published in N.C. Laws, 1806, p. 53.

156.	**Fabre, Elizabeth (Tinker?) and husband, Peter, Jr.** Petition of Elizabeth Fabre, wife of Peter Fabre, Jr., 20 Nov. 1804, Newbern, reports that her said husband, Peter, departed from North Carolina several years ago and left your petitioner without any resources for her maintenance. He is now living an abandoned course of life in one of the West Indian Islands, declaring his determination never to return. Said Elizabeth requests a divorce from said Peter. Attested to by the signatures of 66 subscribers.

[Enclosure:] Deposition of Capt. Edward Tinker before John Sears, Justice of Peace for Craven County, NC, 27 Nov. 1804, states said Tinker was on the island of Antigua about two and one-half years ago and dined in the company of Pater Fabre, Jr. Tinker asked Fabre if he intended writing home to his wife, and Fabre answered that he never intended to write to his wife, nor return to Newbern. Fabre further said he would sell his wife to said Tinker for one hundred dollars.

[Enclosure:] Deposition of Capt. James Willson, 27 Nov. 1804, states substantially the same information as above Capt. Tinker.

[Enclosure:] Deposition of Capt. Thomas Hall, 27 Nov. 1804, states that he was in Antigua about two years ago and saw Peter Fabre, Jr., who was living with a mulatto woman.

[Enclosure:] Deposition of Samuel Simpson, 26 Nov. 1804, states that he was in the company of Peter Fabre, Jr., in Newbern in June 1801, and said Peter requested him to tell Mrs. Tinker, the mother of Mrs. Fabre, that if she would give him 100 dollars, he would give up his right to his said wife.

[Enclosure:] Committee of Divorce and Alimony to whom was referred the petition of Elizabeth Fabre of Newbern report that "the applicant is a young woman whom a tender and aged parent has placed at the feet of the Legislature of her country to solicit a relief…The lively interest which she has excited in the numerous and respectable inhabitants of the Town other residence evinces that her reputation is unblemished…But in an unlucky hour, sentiment beguiled reason, and she united herself to a man, equally devoid of sentiment and principal, who shortly afterwards abandoned her, and for the last six years has led a shameful and profligate life in one of the West [Indies] Islands…The merits of her petition have been fully proved by every cogent evidence, and your Committee, unable and unwilling to remain unconcerned of the unmerited suffering of a woman, recommend the passage of a bill granting the prayer of her petition." House and Senate concur. (GASR, Nov.-Dec. 1806, Box 1: folder "HB 29 Nov."). Bill published in N.C. Laws, 1806, p. 52.

1806 Session

157. **Freedle, Esther and husband, John.** Petition of Estar Freedle of Rowan Co., NC, Nov. 1806, states her husband, John Freedle, deserted his family without leaving any property of any kind. Prays for an act to secure to her such property as she now has or may hereafter acquire. (GASR, Nov.-Dec. 1806, Box 2: folder "Petitions (Divorces, etc.)"). Committee of Divorce and Alimony recommend a bill granting said Esther Freedle's prayer. (GASR, Nov.-Dec. 1806, Box 2: folder "HCR"). Bill to secure persons therein mentioned such property as they now have or may hereafter acquire includes Esther Freedle of Rowan Co., wife of John Freedle. In House and Senate, 19 Dec. 1806, read third time and passed. (GASR, Nov.-Dec. 1806, Box 1: folder "HB 6 Dec."). Bill published in N.C. Laws, 1806, p. 52.

158. **Grissum, Nancy and husband, Thomas.** Bill to secure persons therein mentioned such property as they now have or may hereafter acquire includes Nancy Grissum, wife of Thomas Grissum of Orange Co., NC. In House and Senate, read third time and passed, 20 Dec. 1806. (GASR, Nov.-Dec. 1806, Box 1: folder "HB 10 Dec."). Bill published in N.C. Laws, 1806, p. 52.

159. **Hofler, James and Deborah "Debory" (Outlaw).** Petition of James Hofler of Gates County states he married Debory Outlaw in the year 1802. A few months after the marriage, said Debory "deserted from your petitioner's Bed and bord, and lived with her father Jacob Outlaw…" Said Debory was solicited to return, "but to no Effect, and to the disgrace of herself, and Mortification of your petitioner, she…hath taken up with one John Lowance…" Petitioner requests a law be passed to secure to him all such estate he may hereafter acquire, free from the lawful claim of said Debory. Petition supported by signatures of over 160 subscribers. [Enclosure:] Committee of Divorce and Alimony report that the Committee is satisfied that Deborah Hofler, wife of said James, left his bed and board and took up with another man with whom she presently resides. Recommend passage of a bill to secure to James Hofler of Gates County such property as he may hereafter acquire. Concurred in by House of Commons and Senate, 6 Dec. 1806. Read second time in House, 17 Dec. 1806, and rejected. (GASR, Nov.-Dec. 1806, Box 1: folder "HB 6 Dec.").

160. **Horse, Simon and wife, Sarah.** Petition of Simon Horse and Sarah, his wife, 29 Oct. 1806.[15] Petition states they were married 21 July 1805 and hoped "to mutually experience the comforts of Domestic happiness." With deep regret, the petitioners realized at a very early period after their marriage that discontent and controversy presided over every consideration and produced a separation. They are compelled to declare that they have not in a single instance agreed on any proposition or occurrence of household concern except to obtain authority for a final and legal separation. There is no probability of an accommodation. Petitioners pray for relief by a law to dissolve the marriage contract.

[Enclosure:] Certificate signed by some eighteen subscribers who verify that said Simon Horse and his wife Sarah "hath lived and resided in this county [Lincoln County, NC] and neighborhood from their infancy untill the present time…They are Severally descended from respectable families and Parentage…"

[Enclosure:] The Committee of Divorce and Alimony to whom was referred the above petition "are of opinion that no evil could result from granting them a divorce, and to that end recommend the bill herewith submitted to be passed into law."

[Enclosure:] Bill to divorce Simon Horse of the County of Lincoln from his wife Sarah. In House on 3 Dec. 1806, read first time and rejected. (GASR, Nov.-Dec. 1806 Box 1- folder "HB22 Nov.").

---

15 In a separate petition, said wife Sarah signs "Sarey x Hass."

Divorces and Separations from Petitions to the North Carolina General Assembly from 1779

161. **Hughes, Lydia and husband, Francis.** Bill to secure Lydia Hughes in possession of certain property and such as she may hereafter acquire. Lydia Hughes and her husband, Francis Hughes, agreed by mutual consent some ten years ago to live separate and apart from each other forever. Whereas in consequence of said agreement, said Francis divided his property with his said wife Lydia, she giving security to pay certain debts of him, the said Francis, and did pay them. Whereas said Francis returned in a few years to his said wife Lydia and took from her the said property and continues to return occasionally and take other property from her, be it enacted that said Lydia Hughes have a full absolute title to all said property which has not been sold by her said husband, and shall be entitled to recover same as well as to be secure in any property hereafter acquired. In House and Senate, 10 Dec. 1806, read third time and passed. (GASR, Nov.-Dec. 1806, Box 1: folder "HB 3 Dec."). Bill published in N.C. Laws, 1806, p. 54.

162. **Lewis, Sophia and husband, Aaron.** Petition of Sophia Lewis, wife of Aaron Lewis of Guilford County, states her husband left her in the year 1801 with a large family of helpless children without any means of support, his property being sold to his creditors. Since that time, she has had no account of her said husband, but she has been able to acquire some property through her own industry. Prays for an act l;o secure such property as she now has or may hereafter acquire. Petition supported by signatures of 45 subscribers. (GASR, Nov.-Dec. 1806, Box 2: folder "Petitions (Divorce, etc.)"). Committee of Divorce and Alimony recommend a bill granting said petitioner's prayer. (GASR, Nov.-Dec. 1806, Box 2: folder "HCR"). Bill to secure persons therein mentioned such property as they now have or may hereafter acquire includes Sophia Lewis of Guilford County, wife of Aaron Lewis. In House and Senate, 19 Dec. 1806, read third time and passed. (GASR, Nov.- Dec. 1806, Box 1: folder "HB 6 Dec."). Bill published in N.C. Laws, 1806, p. 52.

163. **Manning, Winefred (Chappell) and husband, Eli Manning.** Petition of Winefred Manning of Martin County states she became acquainted with Eli Manning of Edgecombe County, NC, in 1805 and married him. To "her surprise and mortification, she found that she had been imposed on & entraped by a man that was really & absolutely impotent...," and said Eli executed every species of cruelty on your petitioner. She prays for relief by passing an act authorizing a divorce from said Eli. [Enclosures:] Two depositions from several inhabitants of Martin and Edgecombe counties support the petition of Winefred Manning and pray that the Legislature grant her request. [Enclosure:] Certificate of Eli Manning, November 1805, Martin Co., NC, accepts his incapacity and cheerfully gives his consent to his wife Winnefred's prayer for a divorce. [Enclosure:] Committee of Divorce and Alimony report that "the lamentable deficiency of the man [Eli], his inability to perform one of the essential undertakings on the part of the husband, the indispensable requisite to conjugal happiness, could not be guarded against or detected by the means in the power of a modest and virtuous woman. The Committee recommends granting the prayer of the petitioner. [Enclosure:] Act to divorce W nnefred Manning of Martin County from her husband, Eli. In House and Senate, 17 Dec. 1806, and passed. (GASR, Nov.-Dec. 1806, Box 1: folder "HB 29 Nov."). Published in N.C. Laws, 1806, p. 52.

164. **Martin, Sally and husband, Jesse.** Petition of Sally Martin of Rutherford County states she married Jesse Martin about seven years ago and lived with him four years. About three years ago, said Jessi: voided the obligations of his marriage contract with said Sally by carrying away "a certain Bett Brackett of 111 fame & went to the State of South Carolina where they live together as man and wife-" Prays an act to secure to her such property as she may hereafter acquire. (GASR, Nov.-Dec. 1806, Box 2: folder "Petitions (Divorce, etc.)"). Committee of Divorce and Alimony to whom was referred petition

of…Sally Martin of Rutherford County, wife of Jesse Martin, recommend granting prayer of petitioner. (GASR, Nov.-Dec. 1806, Box 2: folder "HCR"). Bill granting prayer of petitioner. Sally Martin of Rutherford County, read third time and passed in House and Senate, 20 Dec. 1806. (GASR, Nov.-Dec. 1806, Box 1: folder "HB 10 Dec."). Bill published in N. C Laws, 1806, p. 52.

165. **McKinley, Sarah and husband, James.** Petition of Sarah McKinley, wife of James McKinley of Guilford County, states she married James McKinley, and they lived together for three or four years. During this time, said James consumed the whole of his property by irregular conduct and then left the State, being absent now about seven years. The petitioner has heard that he married another woman in the State of Tennessee. Your petitioner has acquired some property through her own industry and has prospects of acquiring more. She prays that such property be secured to her by law. Dated 20 Sept. 1806. (GASR, Nov.-Dec. 1806, Box 2: folder "Petitions (Divorce, etc.)"). Committee of Divorce and Alimony recommend a bill to secure to persons therein mentioned such property as they now have or hereafter acquire:…Sarah McKinley of Guilford, wife of James…(GASR, Nov.-Dec. 1806, Box 2: folder "HCR"). Bill to secure to…Sarah McKinley of Guilford County…such property as [she] now has or may hereafter acquire…(GASR, Nov.-Dec. 1806, Box 1: folder "HB 6 Dec." and Box 2: folder "Miscellaneous Bills"). Bill published in N.C. Laws, 1806, p. 52.

166. **Millar, James and Gilly (Fullar).** Petition of James Millar of Randolph County states that in the Year 1792, he "accidentally happened to call at the House of Brittain Fullar of said County in the evening…" Said Fullar and his family engaged themselves in making "the petitioner so drunk that he was insensible of anything that passed, and while your petitioner was in that situation, the said Fullar…caused a magistrate, who was a brother to the said Brittain Fullar, to consummate the Marriage Ceremony between your Petitioner and a certain Gilly Fullar daughter to…said Brittain when your petitioner was so far intoxicated that he was…unable to stand without assistance…" The next morning, after your petitioner was informed of what had taken place, he "remonstrated with the said Fullar against the illegality of their proceedings…as he never had paid his addresses to the said Gilly Fullar or shown any signs of attachment to her." The said Fullar offered your petitioner a considerable quantity of property if the petitioner would acknowledge said Gilly as his wife and live with her as a husband. Your petitioner rejected this offer and advertised the facts stated in this petition in different parts of said county, forewarning all persons from giving said Gilly credit on his account. Your petitioner removed to the State of South Carolina and remained there until the said Gilly intermarried with Robert Arnold in said Randolph County, by whom she has had several children. Your petitioner, not considering himself bound by the fraudulent marriage to said Gilly, intermarried with Sarah Stanfield of South Carolina, who has borne him five children, viz., Alfred, James, John, Peter and Martin Millar. Upon being advised that the children may be considered illegitimate and deprived of their right of inheritance, your petitioner prays relief from his fraudulent marriage to said Gilly Fullar and a confirmation of his marriage to Sarah Stanfield, thus legitimizing the children. [Enclosures:] Depositions of Haman Miller, Esq., of Randolph County, 11 Dec. 1793, and of Rev. Richard Shackelford of Laurens County, South Carolina, 21 Aug. 1793, which support the details in James Millar's petition. (GASR, Nov.- Dec. 1806, Box 2: folder "Petitions (Divorce, etc.)"). Committee of Divorce and Alimony to whom was referred the petition of…James Millar of Randolph County's prayer for divorce recommend [his] petition be rejected. Concurred in by House and Senate, 13 Dec. 1806. (GASR, Nov.-Dec. 1806, Box 2: folder "HCR").

Divorces and Separations from Petitions to the North Carolina General Assembly from 1779

167. **Murray, Delilah and husband, Archibald.** Petition of Delilah Murry of Greene County states she married Archibald Murry. about eighteen years ago and lived for several years in the utmost harmony. About three [preceding word lined out] twelve years ago he left your petitioner without any means of subsistence and abandoned her to the raising and supporting of three small children. Through toil and extreme indigence she has supported herself and children and has accumulated a little property. She prays a law to secure what property she now has or may hereafter acquire. [Enclosure:] Committee of Divorce and Alimony to whom was referred petition of Delilah Murry of Green_ County, wife of Archibald Murray…praying to secure property recommend approval of petitioner's prayer. (GASR, Nov.-Dec. 1806, Box 2: folder "HCR"). Bill to secure property of Delilah Murray, wife of Archibald Murray of Greene County…read third time in House and Senate and passed, 20 Dec. 1806. (GASR, Nov.-Dec. 1806, Box 1: folder "HB 15 Dec."). Bill published in N.C. Laws, 1806, p. 53.

168. **Murray, Elizabeth and husband, Samuel, Jr.** Bill to secure Elizabeth Murray all such property as she may hereafter acquire and also to secure her husband, Samuel Murray, Jr., against all future demands of said Elizabeth. Said Elizabeth and Samuel Murray, Jr., have mutually agreed to live separate and apart from each other forever. In House and Senate, read three times, and passed. (GASR, Nov.-Dec. 1806, Box 1: folder "HB 28 Nov."). Bill published in N.C. Laws, 1806, p. 54.

169. **Pope, Elijah and Sarah (Parkes) Pope.** Petition of Elijah Pope of Northampton County states he married Sarah Parkes in 1796 and lived with her in conjugal affection for five years. Said Sarah then left her said husband's house and took up with Barnaba Bun of said county and has had three children since she left her said husband Elijah. She still continues to reside with said Bun. Prays for a divorce. (GASR, Nov.-Dec. 1806, Box 2: folder "Petitions (Divorce, etc.)"). Committee of Divorce and Alimony to whom was referred petition of…Elijah Pope of Northampton County…praying to be divorced…recommend rejection. Concurred in by House and Senate, 10 and 11 Dec. 1806. (GASR, Nov.-Dec. 1806, Box 2: folder "HCR").

170. **Redding, Jane and husband, Reham.** Petition of Jane Redding, 12 Nov. 1806, states she was married to Reham Redding upwards of twenty years before any material differences occurred in the family. However, for the past two years, her said husband has given himself up to a "profligate debauch'd and [lascivious] life and also much given to intoxication and has separated himself from your said petitioner and has married another woman…" Her said husband has appropriated any property your petitioner has acquired since the separation to support his other wife. Prays for an act to secure to her what property she now has or may hereafter acquire. (GASR, Nov.-Dec. 1806, Box 2: folder "Petitions (Divorce, etc.)"). Bill to secure to Jane Redding of Bladen County…such property as [she] may hereafter acquire as if [she] had never been married. Committee of Divorce and Alimony report that "it would not be more than common justice to grant the prayer of…[the petitioner] and recommend a law be passed to that effect. In House and Senate, 20 Dec. 1806, and passed. (GASR, Nov.-Dec. 1806, Box 1: folder "HB 3 Dec."). Published in N.C. Laws, 1806, p. 53.

171. **Sawyer, Willis and Dinah (Upton).** Petition of Willis Sawyer of Camden County states he married Dinah Upton, widow of Willis Upton, decd., and lived with her a few months. The said Dinah, without any just or reasonable cause, eloped and "has since led a life of abandoned profligacy [and] had several children by different persons." On 30 May 1801, the petitioner and his said wife Dinah entered into articles of separation whereby the petitioner secured the sum of $500 Spanish milled dollars to said Dinah as her dower share in lieu of any other claims on his Estate. The petitioner is satisfied there will

never be a reconciliation. Prays for a divorce. [Enclosure:] Committee of Divorce and Alimony to whom was referred petition of Willis Sawyer of Camden County…recommend said petition be rejected. Concurred in by House and Senate, 13 Dec. 1806. (GASR, Nov.-Dec. 1806, Box 2: folder "HCR").

172. **Seats, Mary and husband, Josiah.** Petition of Mary Seats of Iredell County states that her husband, Josiah Seats, left her in March 1804 with five small children and with no means to support them. Said Josiah "is a man of such bad habits that he makes use of every kind of support acquired by your petitioner for the use of her said family." She prays for act to secure to her such property as she shall hereafter acquire. (GASR, Nov.-Dec. 1806, Box 2: folder "Petitions (Divorce, etc.)"). Bill to secure to Mary Seats of lredell County such property as [she] may hereafter acquire as if [she] had never been married. Committee of Divorce and Alimony report that "it would not be more than common justice to grant the prayer of [said petitioner] and recommend a law be passed to that effect." In House and Senate, 20 Dec. 1806, and passed. (GASR, Nov.-Dec. 1806, Box 1: folder "HB 3 Dec."). Bill published in N.C. Laws, 1806, p. 53.

173. **Stewart, Thomas and Lovey (Robertson).** Petition of Thomas Stewart of Edgecombe County, Nov. 1806, states he married Lovey Robertson of said county on 15 February 1798. Unhappily, shortly after becoming his wife, said Lovey proved "that she had not been blessed with the gift of continency…"by openly and scandalously defiling her marriage bed. Your petitioner, "actuated by a desire to conceal her frailities…" continued to treat her with tenderness due as a wedded wife. In 1803, she absconded from his bed and board and has been living in adultery. Prays for a divorce. Subscribed to by sixty-two signatures. (GASR, Nov.-Dec. 1806, Box 2: folder "Petitions (Divorce, etc.)"). Committee of Divorce and Alimony to whom was referred the petition o f…Thomas Stewart of Edgecombe County…report they do not deem it expedient to grant the prayer of any of the said petitioners and recommend rejection. Concurred in by House and Senate, 10 or 11 Dec. 1806. (GASR, Nov.-Dec. 1806, Box 2: folder "HCR").

174. **Thomas, Charles Alien and Jane (Brewer).** Petition of Charles Alien Thomas of Wake County states he married Jane Brewer about twelve years ago, and for six years lived in "the utmost peace and harmony…" After this time, said Jane "attached her affections to a certain Henry Dillard by whom she had one child." Said Dillard moved with said wife, Jane, to the State of Tennessee. Prays for a divorce. (GASR, Nov.-Dec. 1806, Box 2: folder "Petitions (Divorce, etc.)"). Committee of Divorce and Alimony to whom was referred the petition of…Charles A. Thomas of Wake County…do not deem it expedient to grant the prayer of…[said petitioner]…and recommend rejection. Concurred in by House and Senate, 10 and 11 Dec. 1806. (GASR, Nov.-Dec. 1806, Box 2: folder "HCR").

1807

175. **Black, Elizabeth and husband, Frederick.** Bill to secure persons therein mentioned such property as they may hereafter acquire:…Elizabeth Black of Rockingham Co., wife of Frederic_…Read third time and passed. (GASR, Nov.-Dec. 1807, Box 2: folder "SB 10 Dec."). Published in N.C. Laws, 1807, p. 39.

176. **Boucher, Ann and husband, Thomas.** Petition of Ann Boucher [county not identified, but most supporters are from Warren Co., NC] states that about eight or ten years ago, she intermarried with Thomas Boucher. During the following years she endeavoured to discharge the various duties incumbent upon her, striving by industry and economy to obtain something for their material support and maintenance. About two years past, said Thomas left your memorialist and has removed himself to a distant State, leaving your petitioner with a young child in a situation little short of beggary and want. Said Thomas left her so considerably indebted that after exhausting the small pittance of property which he left behind, there will be a considerable surplus of debts remaining still unpaid. Petitioner prays for an act vesting the further productions of her labor and gifts from her friends to be secured to her. The following fifteen subscribers state that they are well acquainted with Mrs. Ann Boucher, believe the facts stated in the petition, and are of the opinion that said prayer should be granted: Jno. Hall, Oliver Kitts, Robt. H. Jones, Thos. B. Gloster, Peter A. Davis, Wake Falkener, M. Duke Johnson, Ro. R. Johnson, Wm. Falkener, Jacob Mordecai, J. G. Brehon, Stephen Davis, W. Ruffin, John Snow, Kemp Plummer. (GASR, Nov.-Dec. 1807, Box 3: folder "Divorces, etc."). Petition of Ann Boucher, praying that what property [she] may hereafter acquire be secured to [her]…that the bill before the House be amended by inserting [her] name. Concurred. (GASR, Nov.-Dec. 1807, Box 2: folder "SCR").

177. **Cain, Rebecca and husband, Elisha.** Petition of Rebecca (x) Cain, wife of Elisha Cain of Chatham County states that through the imprudence of my husband, the whole of his property is [wasted], and he himself has become an "invilead" and not able to support himself and yet being considerably in debt. Said Rebecca prays for an act for her "releaf, now being in years, yet thinking myself able to get my support, that whatever I may hereafter gain by my industry may be entirely for my own use…and clear from any encumbrance…of my husband, Elisha Cain…" Endorsed by fourteen subscribers. (GASR, Nov.-Dec. 1807, Box 3: folder "Divorces, etc."). Published in N.C. Laws, 1807, p. 39.

178. **Carpenter, Sally and husband, Joseph.** Petition of Sally Carpenter, wife of Joseph of Currituck County, states she was married about twelve years ago to said Joseph Carpenter, "whose dissipated conduct soon convinced your petitioner that what property they possessed would soon be consumed by his extravagance and waste - and, which ultimately proved to be the case." She further stated that sometime past, said Joseph left your petitioner in a state of indigence and want and dependent solely upon the clemency of her friends. She is yet desirous of accumulating by industry a portion of property sufficient for a comfortable support, but knowing what little she can acquire will be subject to his wasteful hands,

she prays a law to secure to her what property she may hereafter acquire. (GASR, Nov.-Dec. 1807, Box 3: folder "Divorces, etc."). The Committee of Divorce and Alimony, to whom was referred the petition of Sally Carpenter, are of opinion that the clemency of the Legislature ought to be extended to [her] relief and recommend a bill be passed. (GASR, Nov.-Dec. 1807, Box 2: folder "SCR"). Bill to secure persons therein mentioned such property as they may hereafter acquire:…Sally Carpenter of Currituck County, wife of Joseph…Read third time and passed. (GASR, Nov.-Dec. 1807, Box 2: folder "SB 10 Dec."). Published in N.C. Laws, 1807, p. 39.

179. **Dannell, David and wife, Susanna.** Petition of David Dannell of Rowan County, 23 Nov. 1807, states that in or about 1764, said petitioner, being then an inhabitant of Wake County, intermarried with a woman by the name of Susannah Ferrill of said county with whom he lived for the space of five years. He enjoyed all the comforts of conjugal felicity and had by his wife, two daughters. During this time your petitioner loved, honored and cherished his said wife, and she appeared to have an affectionate, loving and dutiful deportment. Your petitioner removed to the waters of Holsten with his wife and children and some others for the purpose of improving their situation in Life, but instead of answering those valuable ends, it proved a time of sorrow, disappointment and loss. His said wife (forgetful of those sacred ties of matrimony) absconded from his bed & board & to his astonishment without any just cause on his side, took up with & attached herself to a certain John Baker on said waters. Your petitioner was unable to reclaim his said wife to return to her duty as a wife and mother to two helpless females. After meeting with disappointment for about eight months, your petitioner removed to Wake County, where he continued to live with his children until the Year 1800, when he removed to Rowan County where he now lives. But as your petitioner understands, his said wife is still alive and continues to live with said Baker & by whom she has had several children. He further understands that his said wife and the children she has begotten since her elopement threaten that they will claim an equal part of whatever property your petitioner shall be seized with upon his decease. Prays consideration. (Enclosed:) Bill to secure David Dannell of Rowan County against all future claims of his wife Susanna. Read third time and passed. (GASR, Nov.-Dec. 1807, Box 2: folder "SB 14 Dec."). Committee of Divorce and Alimony, to whom the petition of David Dannell was directed, are of opinion that relief ought to be granted and recommend the passing of the bill. (GASR, Nov.-Dec. 1807, Box 2: folder "SCR"). Published in N.C. Laws, 1807, p. 39.

180. **Dennis, Sarah and husband, Francis.** Bill to secure persons therein mentioned such property as they may hereafter acquire:…Sarah Dennis, wife of Francis of Carteret County…Read third time and passed. (GASR, Nov.-Dec. 1807, Box 2: folder "SB 10 Dec."). Published in N.C. Laws, 1807, p. 39.

181. **Farr, Susanna and husband, Robert.** Petition of Susanna (+) Farr of Anson County sheweth that she intermarried with "a man who called himself Robert Farr" in 1788. Sometime in the Year 1790, said Robert made away with what little property he had and a horse belonging to her father, William Pratt, Sr., and "also a part other cloathes - went off & She has never since seen him…" She has reason to believe he is now living in the upper part of South Carolina with some other woman which he calls his wife & by whom he has several children. She prays for a divorce from said Farr or such other relief as the General Assembly may think proper. (Enclosed:) Deposition of William Pratt, Sr., before William Johnson, Justice of Peace for Anson County., 28 Oct. 1807, confirming statements made by the petitioner, Susanna (Pratt) Farr. (GASR, Nov.-Dec. 1807, Box 3: folder "Divorces, etc."). Committee of Divorce and Alimony, to whom the petition of Susanna Farr was referred, are of opinion that the clemency of the Legislature ought to be extended to [her] relief and recommend the bill be passed. (GASR, Nov.-Dec.

1807, Box 2: folder "SCR"). Bill to secure persons therein mentioned such property as they may hereafter acquire:…Susanna Farr of Anson County, wife of Robert…Read three times and passed. (GASR, Nov.-Dec. 1807, Box 2: folder "SB 10 Dec."). Published in N.C. Laws, 1807, p. 39.

182.   **Farrow, John and wife, Rebecca.** Petition of John Farrow of Currituck County sheweth that sixteen years ago "your unfortunate Petitioner Intermarried with a Rebekah Foulson, and for about 4 or 5 years livd. in the most Conjugall affection but finally to the utmost Injury & Total Destruction of the peace & Happiness of your Petitioner." She, the said Rebekah, "gave herself up first to Illicit amours with Other men and so increasd. in all manner of Indecent Behaviour till at Length She became an open public and debauchd. prostitute with any and all who woud partake in her wickedness; and Totally of Her own will Absconded & Eloped from the Bed and Board of your petitioner and took up with a Thomas Rolenson…After continuing with him perhaps 2 or 3 years, he went off and has never returnd.… then she took up with a William Oneel, who Remaind. with her 3 or 4 years & Lived as man and wife…by him She had Two Children, but he went off and Left her also:, and at this time She is living with a Jesse Brooks in the former manner without any prospects of amendment. She has from time to time notwithstanding her Brutall conduct Calld. on your petitioner for Support and Involvd. him in much Difficulties & Swears he Shall maintain her Bastards altho they Have Remained in a Separate Sittuation for more than 10 years." Your petitioner gave her much part of his Estate as she expressed herself Satisfyd. with as will appear by the Receipt and articles of agreement accompanying the Petition. He prays for a law to be passed to dissolve the marriage contract between the said John and Rebecca Farrow or to secure to each of the parties all such property as they now have or hereafter may acquire. In case of the death of either party, the surviving one shall not be entitled to any distribution right of Dower or otherwise to any Estate of the deceased and that no children begotten since the separation shall be considered as lawful heirs to the other property. [Enclosed:] Contract dated 24 May 1803 in Currituck County, NC, between John Farrow of Currituck County at Cape Hatteras and his wife, Rebekah Farrow, in which said parties mutually agree to separate and dissolve their marriage contract. Witnesses: Christopher Rolinson, Mayor Whidbee. (GASR, Nov.-Dec. 1807, Box 3: folder "Petitions-Divorces, etc."). Committee of Divorce and Alimony, to whom was referred the petition of John Farrow, is of opinion that it would be just and proper to grant the petitioner's prayer. (GASR, Nov.-Dec. 1807, Box 2: folder "SCR"). Bill to secure to Rebecca Farrow all property she may hereafter acquire and to secure to John Farrow, her husband, against all future demands of said Rebecca. Read third time and passed. Said John of Currituck County and his wife, Rebecca, have mutually agreed to live separately and apart from each other, and said John Farrow has made a fair and equitable division of his estate with said Rebecca. (GASR, Nov.-Dec. 1807, Box 2: folder "SB 14 Dec."). Published in N.C. Laws, 1807, p. 39.

183.   **Harris, Nancy and husband, William.** Petition of Nancy Harris of Richmond County sheweth that her husband, William Harris, has left her, and she declares she will never live with him again. Before he left her, he "beat and abused her in a most shamefully cruel manner…" Your petitioner, being quite a young woman and having lost all hopes of ever being reconciled to her husband, prays for an act to secure to her whatever property she may hereafter acquire free from claims of her said husband. In view of her youth, the petitioner would accept a divorce if "your honourable body will do that for her…" Endorsed by four subscribers. (GASR, Nov.-Dec. 1807, Box 3: folder "Petitions-Divorce, etc."). Committee of Divorce and Alimony, to whom was referred the Petition of Nailicy Harris, are of opinion that the clemency of the Legislature ought to be extended to [her] relief and recommend a bill be passed. (GASR, Nov.-Dec. 1807, Box 2: folder "SCR"). Bill to secure persons therein mentioned such property

1807 Session

as they may hereafter acquire:...Nancy Harris of Richmond County, wife of William...Read third time and passed. (GASR, Nov.-Dec. 1807, Box 2: folder "SB 10 Dec."). Published in N.C. Laws, 1807, p. 39.

184. **Hill, Nancy and husband, Seth.** Bill to secure persons therein mentioned such property as they may hereafter acquire:...Nancy Hill, wife of Seth of Randolph County...Read third time and passed. (GASR, Nov.-Dec. 1807, Box 2: folder "SB 10 Dec."). Published in N.C. Laws, 1807, p. 39.

185. **Toffler, James and wife, Deborah.** Petition of James Toffler of Gates County prays that what property he now has or may hereafter acquire be solely vested in him, and that his wife Deborah be precluded from any right of dower. Committee of Divorce and Alimony is of opinion that the petitioner's prayer be granted. [Attachment:] Petition of James Toffler of Gates County sheweth that in the Year 1802, he intermarried with Deborah Outlaw in hopes of enjoying the comforts of married life. After a few months, said Deborah left your petitioner and returned to her father, Jacob Outlaw, and refused to return to your petitioner. Said Deborah took up with a certain John Allowance by whom she had one child, and they continue to live in adultery. No hope of reconciliation has ever taken place between said Deborah and your petitioner. Said Deborah's father has taken into possession all the property she was possessed with and continues to hold the same. Petitioner prays for a law to invest him with power to dispose of his estate by will or otherwise so as to deprive said Deborah of right of dower and the child or children she may have by said John Allowance from any claim on your petitioner's estate, real or personal, that he now has or may hereafter acquire. Petition is endorsed by sixty-nine subscribers, including David Outlaw, James Outlaw, and George Outlaw. (GASR, Nov.-Dec. 1807, Box 2: folder "SCR"). Bill secures to James Toffler of Gates County all such property he now has or may hereafter acquire from any demand that his wife, Deborah Hoffler, may have in right of dower or otherwise. Read third time and passed. (GASR, Nov.-Dec. 1807, Box 2: folder "SB 10 Dec."). Published in N.C. Laws, 1807, p. 39.

186. **Lane, William and wife, Martha.** Petition of William Lane [of Wake County] states he was joined in wedlock in July 1793 with Martha Pastieur. In a few months, family feuds and misfortunes resulted in said Martha leaving his bed and board, and she still continues to absent herself with no hope of reconciliation. Petitioner prays for a divorce. (GASR, Nov.-Dec. 1807, Box 3: folder "Petitions-Divorce, etc."). Committee of Divorce and Alimony, to whom was referred the petition of William Lane, are of opinion that Legislative interference in such case is improper notwithstanding the disagreeable situation of the petitioner. Recommend petition aforesaid be rejected. Concurred with by Legislature. (GASR, Nov.-Dec. 1807, Box 2: folder "SCR").

187. **Manier, Ann B. and husband, Daniel J.** Petition of Anne B. Manier of Granville County sheweth that she intermarried with Daniel J. Manier in 1796 and lived with him until the Spring of 1802. At that time, her husband left her with three small children, the issue of their marriage, and removed himself and all his property to the State of Kentucky, where he presently resides. He disclaims all ideas of returning and has afforded no means of support for your petitioner or said children, who are dependent on the labour of your petitioner and the aid of an affectionate mother with whom your petitioner now resides. She does not wish to make any statement of the improper conduct of her husband but hopes to be able to show that their separation was not caused by any indiscretion of hers. She prays for a divorce from her husband. Dated 15 Nov. 1807, Granville County. (GASR, Nov.-Dec. 1807, Box 3: folder "Petitions-Divorce, etc."). Committee of Divorce and Alimony, to whom the petition of Ann B. Manier was directed, are of opinion that the clemency of the Legislature ought to be extended to [her] relief and recommend a bill be passed. (GASR, Nov.-Dec. 1807, Box 2: folder "SCR"). Bill to secure persons

therein mentioned such property as they may hereafter acquire:…Ann B. Manier of Granville County, wife of Daniel J…. Read third time and passed. (GASR, Nov.-Dec. 1807, Box 2: folder "SB 10 Dec."). Published in N.C. Laws, 1807, p. 39.

188. **Manlove, Hannah and husband, George.** Petition of Hannah Manlove of Guilford County states that her husband, George Manlove, deserted her six years ago, leaving her without support. He continues to create debts which creditors claim against her small earnings by hand labor. She prays for an act to secure property she may hereafter acquire. Endorsed by eight subscribers, including a Moses Craner, Jr., who has the same surname as said Hannah before her marriage.[16] (GASR, Nov.-Dec. 1807, Box 3: folder "Petitions- Divorce, etc."). Committee of Divorce and Alimony, to whom the petition of Hannah Manlove was referred, are of opinion that the clemency of the Legislature ought to be extended to [her] relief and recommend the bill be passed. (GASR, Nov.-Dec. 1807, Box 2: folder "SCR"). Bill to secure persons therein mentioned such property as they may hereafter acquire:…Hannah Manlove of Guilford County, wife of George…Passed. (GASR, Nov.-Dec. 1807, Box 2: folder "SB 10 Dec."). Published in N.C. Laws, 1807, p. 39.

189. **Massey, Olive and husband, Samuel.** Petition of Olive Massey, wife of Samuel Massey of Wake County, sheweth she intermarried with said Samuel about ten years past and lived with him for the space of six years. Unfortunately, said Samuel not only squandered and spent his own estate but also that of your petitioner due to attendant ill habits and neglect of that economy necessary for every man who has a family to provide for. About four years ago, said Samuel left your petitioner without any just cause and now resides in the State of Tennessee, during which time, your petitioner has not seen him. Since the departure of her husband, she has had to labor to support four children, which she had before said Samuel absconded. She prays for an act to secure to her such property as she may hereafter acquire. (GASR, Nov.-Dec. 1807, Box 3: folder "Petitions-Divorce, etc."). Committee of Divorce and Alimony, to whom the petition of Olive Massey was referred, are of opinion that the clemency of the Legislature ought to be extended to [her] relief and recommend the bill be passed. (GASR, Nov.-Dec. 1807, Box 2: folder "SCR"). Bill to secure persons therein mentioned such property as they may hereafter acquire:…Olive Massey of Wake County, wife of Samuel…Read third time and passed. (GASR, Nov.-Dec. 1807, Box 2: folder "SB 10 Dec."). Published in N.C. Laws, 1807, p. 39.

190. **Matthews, Mabel and husband, Reddick.** Petition of Mabel Matthews of Wake County sheweth that about three years past she intermarried with Reddick Matthews of said county, commonly known by the name of Reddick Jones, he being an illegitimate son of William Jones, deceased, of same county. At the time of her marriage with said Reddick, your petitioner had acquired a small portion of property through her own industry. Within a very short time after her said marriage, said Reddick had squandered all the property she had "and even broke open her chest to procure what money she had concealed therein to prevent him entirely reducing her to beggary - all of which he spent in Drinking & Rioting, in which dissipated course he continued until having contracted debts, he finally absconded and is now living in Tennessee or some other part of the western country. Your petitioner further states that whatever she can now acquire is continually taken from her to pay the debts other said husband, contracted before his departure." She prays an act to secure her in such property as she may hereafter acquire. (GASR, Nov.-Dec. 1807, Box 3: folder "Petitions-Divorce, etc."). Committee of Divorce and

---

16 Marriage Bond, dated 17 January 1799, Guilford County, North Carolina, between George Manlove and Hannah Craner, is on the North Carolina Statewide Marriage Bond Index, compiled on microfiche by the North Carolina State Archives.

Alimony, to whom the petition of Mabel Matthews was referred, are of opinion that the clemency of the Legislature ought to be extended to [her] relief and recommend the bill be passed. (GASR, Nov.-Dec. 1807, Box 2: folder "SCR"). Bill to secure persons therein mentioned such property as they may hereafter acquire:…Mabel Matthews of Wake County, wife of Reddick…Read third time and passed. (GASR, Nov.-Dec. 1807, Box 2: folder "SB 10 Dec."). Published in N.C. Laws, 1807, p. 39.

191. **Morgan, Mary and husband, Benjamin.** Committee of Divorce and Alimony, to whom the petition of Mary Morgan was referred, are of opinion that the clemency of the Legislature ought to be extended to [her] relief and recommend the bill be passed. (GASR, Nov.-Dec. 1807, Box 2: folder "SCR"). Bill to secure persons therein mentioned such property as they may hereafter acquire:…Mary Morgan, wife of Benjamin…[no county given] Read third time and passed. (GASR, Nov.-Dec. 1807, Box 2: folder "SB 10 Dec."). Published in N.C. Laws, 1807, p. 39.

192. **Morrison, Elizabeth and husband, Archibald.** Petition of Elizabeth Morrison of Bladen County states she was married to Archibald Morrison, and they lived together for a considerable time in peace and harmony. At length, in consequence of his dissipated conduct, she discovered that the hard earnings of her labor were destroyed by his extravagance and waste. They soon became prey to misery and want, and the said Archibald abandoned your petitioner, removing to parts unknown. Nevertheless, your petitioner made every exertion to acquire by industry a sufficient support and prays for an act to secure what property she may hereafter acquire from the claims of said Archibald. (GASR, Nov.-Dec. 1807, Box 3: folder "Petitions-Divorce, etc."). Committee of Divorce and Alimony, to whom the petition of Elizabeth Morrison was referred, are of opinion that the clemency of the Legislature ought to be extended to [her] relief and recommend the bill be passed. (GASR, Nov.-Dec. 1807, Box 2: folder "SCR"). Bill to secure persons therein mentioned such property as they hereafter acquire:…Elizabeth Morrison of Bladen County, wife of Archibald…Read third time and passed. (GASR, Nov.-Dec. 1807, Box 2: folder "SB 10 Dec."). Published in N.C. Laws, 1807, p. 39.

193. **Murray, Samuel, Jr.** Committee of Divorce and Alimony, to whom was referred [the petition of Samuel Murray, Jr.] for a divorce, are of opinion that Legislative interference in such cases are improper, notwithstanding the disagreeable situation of the petitioner. Recommend [petition] aforesaid be rejected. (GASR, Nov.-Dec. 1807, Box 2: folder "SCR").

194. **Norfleet, Peggy and husband, Benjamin.** Bill to secure Peggy Norfleet, wife of Benjamin Norfleet of the Town of Edenton, such property a$ she may hereafter acquire against all claims of said Benjamin Norfleet, her husband, as if she and said husband had never been married. (GASR, Nov.-Dec. 1807, Box 1: folder "HB 21 Nov.").

195. **Ogle, Sally and husband, Hiram.** Petition of Sally (-) Ogle [of Burke County] states she intermarried with Hiram Ogle in 1801 and happily lived together in the first week of November 1802. At that time, said Hiram left his said wife and child to go visit friends and relatives on New River in Virginia. Prior to his leaving, a "report prevailed that he had a wife in that part of the country, but it was not then believed by your petitioner…" Since that time, your petitioner believes that it was true that her said husband had a wife and three children, but that he would return to her as her husband. However, she has not heard from him since he left, nor does she know what has become of him. She notes that the small amount of property he left has been taken by creditors. She is now destitute of any means of subsistence for her and her child except from the bounty of her father, who is now an aged and infirm man. She is

Divorces and Separations from Petitions to the North Carolina General Assembly from 1779

desirous of a situation to have a home and a protector, and therefore prays for a divorce and to be at liberty to marry again. In the meantime, she would like to be entitled to hold any property she might acquire by her own industry. Sworn to before William W. Erwin, Justice of Peace of Burke County, 6 Nov. 1807. Deposition of William W. Erwin before Waightstill Avery, Justice of Peace of Burke County, 7 Nov. 1807, who deposes that Sally Ogle, formerly Sally Moore, was married to Hiram Ogle about or in the Year 1801. He lived with her until they had one child and until about 1 Nov. 1802, when he left her to visit friends on New River in Wythe County, Virginia. He has never returned. A report prevailed shortly before he went away that he was married to another woman before he came into this country, which report this deponent verily believes was true. Deponent further states that before and since the marriage of the said Sally to the said Hiram that he had been acquainted with the said Sally and lived near her. She had always conducted herself with propriety and sustained an unblemished reputation. She married at about seventeen years of age and is now about twenty-three or four years of age. He is informed that Hiram Ogle is again married to a woman in the Cumberland country "low down in the State of Tennessee." Depositions of Albert Corpening, James Kincaid, Henry Hiland, and Landry Persons all attest to the good character of said Sally (Moore) Ogle. Endorsed by twelve other subscribers. (GASR, Nov.-Dec. 1807, Box 3: folder "Petitions-Divorce, etc."). Committee of Divorce and Alimony, to whom the petition of Sally Ogle was referred, are of opinion that the clemency of the Legislature ought to be extended to [her!] relief and recommend the bill be passed. (GASR, Nov.-Dec. 1807, Box 2: folder "SCR"). Bill to secure persons therein mentioned such property as they may hereafter acquire:...Sally Ogle, wife of Hiram...Read three times and passed. (GASR, Nov.-Dec. 1807, Box 2: folder "SB 10 Dec."). Published in N.C. Laws, 1807, p. 39.

196. **Pope, Elijah and wife, Sarah.** Committee of Divorce and Alimony, to whom the petition of Elijah Pope; of Northampton County was referred, praying to be divorced from his wife, Sarah, are of opinion that it is inexpedient to grant the relief prayed for and recommend the prayer be rejected. Concurred in by the Legislature. (GASR, Nov.-Dec. 1807, Box 2: folder "SCR").

197. **Sadler, Averelles/Averiller and husband, William.** Petition of Averiller Sadler states she intermarried with William Sadler in 1798 and lived with him until July 1803, when he left her with a two year old child, the issue of their marriage. He removed himself with all his property to Salem in Stokes County and from there to the State of Tennessee or Kentucky, endeavouring, as your petitioner understands from respectable authority, to impose on others by [illegible] disclaiming all ideas of a return. Since his removal, he has afforded no means of support for herself or child, and who are maintained entirely by her own labor and the aid of an affectionate grandfather. Said petitioner does not want to make any statement on the improper conduct of her husband, but hopes to be able to show that their separation was not caused by any indiscretion of hers. She further says she was raised as an orphan by her grandfather, who wants her secure in her property after his death. She prays for a divorce and to be secure in her property separate from her husband. [The original petition is very faded.] (GASR, Nov.-Dec. 1807, Box 3: folder "Petitions-Divorce, etc."). Committee of Divorce and Alimony, to whom the petition of Averiller Sadler was referred, are of opinion that the clemency of the Legislature ought to be extended to [her] relief and recommend the bill be passed. (GASR, Nov.-Dec. 1807, Box 2: folder "SCR"). Bill to secure persons therein mentioned such property as they may hereafter acquire:...Averelles Sadler of Granville County, wife of William...Read third time and passed. (GASR, Nov.-Dec. 1807, Box 2: folder "SB 10 Dec."). Published in N.C. Laws, 1807, p. 39.

1807 Session

198. **Salisbury, Polly and husband, Willis.** Petition of Polly Salisbury of Pitt County states that her husband, Willis Salisbury, left her eight or ten years ago in the utmost indigence and want and has never returned to render her the least assistance in acquiring the common necessaries of life. She has made exertions to acquire by labour a common support, but believes what she has acquired will be subject to seizure or waste and prays for an act to secure what property she now has or may acquire against any claim by her said husband. (GASR, Nov.-Dec. 1807, Box 3: folder "Petitions-Divorce, etc."). Committee of Divorce and Alimony, to whom was referred the petition of Polly Salisbury, are of opinion that the clemency of the Legislature ought to be extended to [her] relief and recommend the bill be passed. (GASR, Nov.-Dec. 1807, Box 2: folder "SCR"). Bill to secure persons therein mentioned such property as they may hereafter acquire:...Polly Salisbury of Pitt County, wife of Willis...Read third time and passed. (GASR, Nov.-Dec. 1807, Box 2: folder "SB 10 Dec."). Published in N.C. Laws, 1807, p. 39.

199. **Sessums, Susannah and husband, James.** Committee of Divorce and Alimony, to whom was referred the petition of Susannah Sessums of Hertford County, who prays for a divorce from her husband, James Sessums, report that they are of the opinion that it is inexpedient to grant the relief prayed for and recommend the prayers be rejected. (GASR, Nov.-Dec. 1807, Box 2: folder "SCR"). Concurred in by the Legislature.

200. **Skidmore, Ann.** Committee of Divorce and Alimony, to whom was referred the petition of Ann Skidmore of Randolph County...praying that what property [she] may hereafter acquire be secured to [her]...recommend that the bill before the House be amended by inserting [her] name. (GASR, Nov.-Dec. 1807, Box 2: folder "SCR").

201. **Stokes, Nancy and husband, David.** Petition of Nancy Stokes [no county listed] states she married David Stokes in December 1805 and lived with him for three months. For some unknown reason, said David quit her bed and board and "went to some other part of the world of which your petitioner has no knowledge, declaring at the same time his determination never to return to your petitioner again, leaving her pregnant of which child she was delivered in seven months after his departure, which infant is now living in the care of your petitioner." All hope of a reconciliation is lost. She prays for an act to secure to her all such estate as she may hereafter acquire. (GASR, Nov.-Dec. 1807, Box 3: folder "Petitions-Divorce, etc."). Committee of Divorce and Alimony, to whom the petition of Nancy Stokes was referred, are of opinion that the clemency of the Legislature ought to be extended to [her] relief and recommend the bill be passed. (GASR, Nov.-Dec. 1807, Box 2: folder "SCR"). Bill to secure persons therein mentioned such property as they may hereafter acquire:...Nancy Stokes, wife of David...Read third time and passed. (GASR, Nov.-Dec. 1807, Box 2: folder "SB 10 Dec."). Published in N.C. Laws, 1807, p. 39.

202. **Thomas, Lewis and wife, Levinah.** Petition of Lewis (x) and Levinah (x) Thomas of Robeson County, who married "a number of years ago" note that "since that time a seperration has taken place and not the least prosspect of a Reconciliation." Petitioners pray for a divorce. Referred to Committee of Divorce and Alimony and rejected. (GASR, Nov.-Dec. 1807, Box 3: folder "Petitions-Divorce, etc.").

203. **Utley, Young and wife, Polly.** Petition of Young Utley of Wake County states he was married to a young woman named Polly Woodward about twelve months past. By her deceitful speeches, actions and behavior, she caused your petitioner to believe she was an honest and virtuous young woman. But in the course of a few months after your petitioner was married to the said Polly, she was delivered of a

Divorces and Separations from Petitions to the North Carolina General Assembly from 1779

"Female Child which appears to a demonstration from its features and complection to have been begotten by a Negro or a very dark mulatto - which is the general opinion of all persons that has ever seen the said child which renders your petitioner Exceedingly unhappy." He prays relief by passing an act to divorce him from the bonds of matrimony. Dated 4 Dec. 1807. Subscribed to by fifteen witnesses. Deposition of Peyton Norris before William Peace, Justice of Peace of Wake County, agrees with the remarks of the petitioner. Prayer of petitioner is rejected. Bill withdrawn by Mr. Alien Rogers, 17 Dec. 1807. (GASR, Nov.-Dec. 1807, Box 3: folder "Petitions-Divorce, etc.").

204.   **Wilfong, Elizabeth and husband, Jacob.** Bill to secure persons therein mentioned such property as they may hereafter acquire:…Elizabeth Wilfong of Orange County, wife of Jacob…Read third time and passed. (GASR, Nov.-Dec. 1807, Box 2: folder "SB 10 Dec."). Published in N.C. Laws, 1807, p. 39.

205.   **Williams, Milley and husband, John.** Bill to secure persons therein mentioned such property as they may hereafter acquire:…Milley Williams, wife of John of Granville County…Read third time and passed. (GASR, Nov.-Dec. 1807, Box 2: folder "SB 10 Dec."). Published in N.C. Laws, 1807, p. 39.

1808

206. **Blalock/Blelock, David and wife, Nancy (Mathews).** Petition of David Blelock of Lincoln County sheweth that he married Nancy Mathews in 1802, and they lived together for about three years, at the end of which time said Nancy eloped from your petitioner without any known cause and "went with a certain Francis Dunn (a painter of Houses) to some of the northern counties in this State or to the State of Virginia" and has never returned. Said petitioner has had no word of his said wife's place of residence although it has been three years since her elopement. Prays for a divorce from his said wife, Nancy. Petition referred to Committee on Divorce and Alimony. (GASR, Nov.-Dec. 1808, Box 3: folder "Petitions - Divorce, Name Change, etc.")

    Committee on Divorce and Alimony to whom was referred the petition of David Blelock of Lincoln County praying to be divorced from [his wife, Nancy Blelock] are of opinion it would be improper to grant the prayer of the [petitioner] and recommend [it] be rejected. Read and concurred with by the House of Commons, 12 Dec. 1808, and the Senate, 13 Dec. 1808. (GASR, Nov.-Dec. 1808, Box 2: folder "JCR - Divorce and Alimony.")

207. **Bracewell [Braswell?], Isaac and wife, Nancy (Low).** Petition of Isaac Bracewell of Edgecombe County notes that he "married in the year 1798 to his present wife, whose maiden name was Nancy Low…[and] for several years they enjoyed uninterrupted happiness, and he had no reason to suspect either the affection or chastity of his wife. Circumstances however soon after occurred to prove incontestibly the fallacy of his hopes, and that regardless of her duty, she had openly and shamefully violated her marriage vow - although your petitioner with a vow to protect from injury the reputation of his children who must of necessity partake of the mother's guilt, would have been willing to conceal from the world the acts of their parents, yet her conduct for the last four years has been so openly at variance with either modesty or chastity that no hope of this kind remains…" Prays for a divorce from his wife aforesaid. Dated 15 Nov. 1808. /s/ Isaac Bracewell, Nancy (x) Bracewell. Bill to divorce Isaac Bracewell from his wife Nancy…that Isaac Bracewell be hereby divorced from his wife Nancy and that the said marriage be annulled and dissolved. In Senate, 19 Dec. 1808, read first time and passed; in House of Commons, 19 Dec. 1808, read first time and rejected. (GASR, Nov.-Dec. 1808, Box 1: folder "Senate Bills - 19 Dec.")

208. **Byars/Byers, Drusilla and husband, Nathan.** Petition of Drusilla Byars of Rutherford County, wife of Nathan Byars of the same county, sheweth that when they were married, your petitioner was worth a considerable estate and that her husband had little or no property. They lived together in harmony for "a great many years in which time she had Ten children." She states that she used unremitted exertions to render her husband happy. About seven years ago, her husband withdrew his affections from her, refused to give her any protection or support, and compelled her to leave his house. She "repeatedly returned & was as often obliged to abandon his house & resort to the cold charity of the world for sustenance." Prays for an act to authorize her to hold property in her own name. /s/ Drusilla (x) Byars,

Divorces and Separations from Petitions to the North Carolina General Assembly from 1779

11 Oct. 1808. Referred to Committee on Divorce and Alimony. (GASR, Nov.-Dec. 1808, Box 3: folder "Petitions - Divorce, Name Change, etc.")

    The Committee on Divorce and Alimony to whom was referred the [petition] of Drusilla Byers of Rutherford County…are of opinion the prayer of the [petition] ought to be granted and recommend the Bill herewith presented be passed into law: "A Bill to secure to the persons therein mentioned such property as they may hereafter acquire." Read and concurred with by the House of Commons, 17 Dec. 1808, and by the Senate, 19 Dec. 1808. (GASR, Nov.-Dec. 1803, Box 2: folder "JCR - Divorce and Alimony") Published in North Carolina Laws, 1808, p. 39.

209.   **Cain, Rebecca.** Committee of Divorce and Alimony to whom was referred the following [petition]…Rebecca Cain of Chatham County…praying to be divorced are of opinion that Legislative interference in such cases are…improper and therefore recommend that the aforesaid [petition] be rejected. In Senate, 10 Dec. 1807 [sic], read and concurred with. In House of Commons, 15 Dec. 1807 [sic], read and concurred with. (GASR, Nov.-Dec. 1808, Box 2: folder "JCR - Divorce and Alimony")[17] Published in North Carolina Laws, 1807, p. 39.

210.   **Chappell, Ruth and husband, Solomon.** Petition of Ruth Chappell of Randolph County sheweth that she intermarried with Solomon Chappell of Guilford County in 1787, and they lived together for about nine years, in the course of which your petitioner had two children by her said husband. However, said husband became entirely dissipated, and after exhausting nearly all the property he possessed, he left your petitioner and children and removed to the State of Kentucky. Since that time, all the property he left with your petitioner has been sold to pay the debts contracted by said husband, "and had it not been for the Generosity of Neighbours, your Petitioner & her children must have been in the Most Deplorable Situation for the want of Something to subsist on." Prays for a law to secure to her such property as she may hereafter acquire. Subscribed to by four signatures. The Committee on Divorce and Alimony to whom was referred the [petition] of Ruth Chappell of Randolph County…are of opinion that the prayer of [the petitioner] ought to be granted and recommend the Bill herewith presented be passed into law: "A Bill to secure to the persons therein mentioned such property as they may hereafter acquire." Read and concurred with by the House of Commons, 17 Dec. 1808, and by the Senate, 19 Dec. 1808. (GASR, Nov.-Dec. 1808, Box 2: folder "JCR - Divorce and Alimony"). Published in North Carolina Laws, 1808, p. 39.

211.   **Crockett, Luc(e)y and husband, William.** Petition of Lucy Crockett [of Person County], wife of William Crockett, sheweth that "about three years ago your Petitioner being of reputable family and connection was falsely influenced to intermarry with the said William Crockett, who after a short time left her disconsolate and poor to wander about and depend altogether on the generosity of her friends for a support. At the time of her [said] intermarriage…she was possessed of several valuable slaves and other property which he in a few months squandered and sold, and soon afterwards left your Petitioner quite in a dependent situation, she being at the time without a home and pregnant of a son of which she has since delivered…Since the said Crockett has left your Petitioner, he has Traversed several of the States engaged in practices highly dishonorable to himself and your Petitioner - and for the commission of some of his evil practices he has been apprehended and convicted in the Federal Court of this State for the passing of counterfeit Bank Notes and sentenced to Two Years imprisonment in the [Jail] of Hillsboro." Prays for a law to secure to her all property which she may hereafter acquire free from the control of her said husband or the molestation of his creditors. Subscribed to by the names of seven resi-

---

17   This document is out-of-place and may be removed to the GASR, 1807 records.

dents of Person County. Referred to Committee on Divorce and Alimony. (GASR, Nov.-Dec. 1808, Box 3: folder "Petitions - Divorce, Name Change, etc.") The Committee on Divorce and Alimony to whom was referred the...[petition] of Lucey Crockett of Person County...are of opinion the prayer...ought to be granted and recommend the Bill herewith presented be passed into law: "A Bill to secure the persons therein mentioned such property as they may hereafter acquire." Read and concurred with by House of Commons, 17 Dec. 1808, and by the Senate, 19 Dec. 1808. (GASR, Nov.-Dec. 1808, Box 2: folder "JCR - Divorce and Alimony") Published in North Carolina Laws, 1808, p. 39.

212. **Davis, Elizabeth and husband, Edward Patrick.** Petition of Elizabeth Davis of Warren County sheweth that her husband, Edward Patrick Davis, left her and an infant daughter destitute of property about three years ago without any just cause. He is now wandering in the western country without a home, but took with him property to the amount of $2,000, which she is informed he has entirely exhausted. Since he departed, he has married a Mrs. Ragland of the Town of Petersburg in the State of Georgia "whom he remained but a few days." There is no prospect of his return. Prays for a law to secure to her the property she has acquired through her own industry. Dated 24 Nov. 1808. Enclosed: Statement of three subscribers conferring their support for said Elizabeth P. [sic] Davis. Referred to Committee on Divorce and Alimony. (GASR, Nov.-Dec. 1808, Box 3: folder "Petitions - Divorce, Name Change, etc.")

The Committee on Divorce and Alimony to whom was referred the [petition] of...Elizabeth Davis of Warren County...are of opinion the prayer...ought to be granted and recommend the Bill herewith presented be passed into law: "A Bill to secure to the persons therein mentioned such property as they may hereafter acquire." Read and concurred with by House of Commons, 17 Dec. 1808, and by the Senate, 19 Dec. 1808. (GASR, Nov.-Dec. 1808, Box 2: folder "JCR -Divorce and Alimony") Published in North Carolina Laws, 1808, p. 39.

213. **Dollar, Patience and husband, William.** Petition of Patience Dollar sheweth she intermarried with one William Dollar, but he exhausted the whole of the property acquired by such marriage, maltreated your Petitioner and finally deserted her. Prays for an act to secure such property as she may hereafter acquire. Referred to Committee on Divorce and Alimony. (GASR, Nov.-Dec. 1808, Box 3: folder "Petitions - Divorce, Name Change, etc.")

The Committee on Divorce and Alimony to whom [was] referred the [petition] of Patience Dollar of Sampson County...are of opinion the prayer...ought to be granted and recommend the Bill herewith presented be passed into law: "A Bill to secure to the persons therein mentioned such property as they may hereafter acquire." Read and concurred with by the House of Commons, 17 Dec. 1808, and by the Senate, 19 Dec. 1808. (GASR, Nov.-Dec. 1808, Box 2: folder "Divorce and Alimony") Published in North Carolina Laws, 1808, p. 39.

214. **Fannigan, Trecy/Tricey and husband, John.** Petition of Trecy Fannigan of Duplin County sheweth that "she intermarried with John Fannigan about ten years past[18] and that they lived together nearly nine years, during which time, the said Fannigan treated her extremely ill by giving her every abusive language and threats until] the year [1807], when the said John entirely left her without any visible support with Five small children, after which she went to him, he then abused her, and cruelly beat her, so that she could not stay with him, without endangering her life, which he frequently threatened to take. She then concluded to live and support part of her children by her industry in the Houses of her

---

18   Marriage Bond, Duplin County, North Carolina, dated 1 August 1798, for John Flanakin and Teresy Taylor.

Divorces and Separations from Petitions to the North Carolina General Assembly from 1779

friends. That design he frustrated by for warning all persons from harboring her in their houses or letting her stay therein." Prays for serious consideration to secure to her such property as she may hereafter acquire free from the claims or control of her said husband. Referred to Committee on Divorce and Alimony. The Committee on Divorce and Alimony to whom [was] referred the [petition] of…Tricey Fannigan of Duplin County…are of opinion the prayer…ought to be granted and recommend the Bill herewith presented be passed into law: "A Bill to secure to the persons therein mentioned such property as they may hereafter acquire." Read and concurred with by the House of Commons, 17 Dec. 1808, and by the Senate, 19 Dec. 1808. (GASR, Nov.-Dec. 1808, Box 2: folder "JCR - Divorce and Alimony")

215. **Farrar, Milly and husband, John.** Petition of Milly Farrar of Chatham County sheweth that she intermarried with a certain John Farrar of said county in 1804 and lived with him "upwards of two years, in which time they had one child, and in that Station She well hoped to have spent a happy life…But so it was the said John, laying aside all paternal affections and the more engaging ties of a husband, went off to the Western country and carried with him four Negroes, which were given her by her Father - and left your Petitioner and her Infant child destitute of any means of Support…" Prays for an act to secure to her such property as she may hereafter acquire, /s/ Milly Farrar. Dated 3 Dec. 1808. Subscribed to by the following signatures: Thos. Sniper, M. Bynum, Oliver Prince, William Horton, Zach. Harman, Stephen Ellington, Herbert Haynes, Luke Bynum, Tapley Bynum, Ashkenaz Williams, Joseph Williams, Isaiah Riceson, Wm. Bynum, James Bynum. Referred to Committee on Divorce and Alimony. (GASR, Nov.-Dec. 1808, Box 2: folder "JCR Divorce and Alimony") Act to secure to Milly Farrar of Chatham County such property as she may hereafter acquire published in North Carolina Laws, 1808, p. 39.

216. **Foster, Sall(e)y and husband, Asa.** Petition of Salley Foster of Person County sheweth that about nine years ago she married Asa Foster,[19] who lived with your petitioner about four years, after which time he left your petitioner with one small child and no visible property for the maintenance and support of herself and child. For about the past five years your petitioner has lived with her parents and has endeavoured to support herself and her child in an honest way by her own industry. She has not seen her husband for five years, and she heard that he was about to go to Louisiana. Prays an act to secure to her such property as she has acquired through her own industry or may hereafter acquire. Subscribed to by seven residents of Person County. Referred to Committee on Divorce and Alimony. (GASR, Nov.-Dec. 1808, Box 3: folder "Petitions- Divorce, Name Change, etc.")

The Committee on Divorce and Alimony to whom was referred the [petition] of…Sally Foster of Person County…are of opinion the prayer…ought to be granted and recommend the Bill herewith presented be passed into law: "A Bill to secure to the persons therein mentioned such property as they may hereafter acquire." Read and concurred with by the House of Commons, 17 Dec. 1808, and by the Senate, 19 Dec. 1808. (GASR, Nov.-Dec. 1808, Box 2: folder "JCR - Divorce and Alimony") Published in North Carolina Laws, 1808, p. 39.

217. **Gregory, Mary and husband, Edmund.** Petition of Mary Gregory of the Town of Tarborough represents that "the conduct of her husband Edmund Gregory, to whom in an unlucky moment she united herself, has evidenced such a total want of regard for her, and so little desire to acquire a Support, or even to preserve that of which by her industry she was previous to marriage, and is in part, now possessed, that she feels it her duty, one which she owes not only to herself, but in a far greater degree to a child in whom are now centered all her hopes and desires, to apply to your honourable body for releif…

---

19 Marriage Bond, Orange County, North Carolina, dated 3 October 1800, for Asa Foster and Sally Haley.

She was told that he [her said husband] possessed an amiable temper, but the most abusive language and treatment are the only proofs he has ever offered." Prays for an act to secure to her such property as she may hereafter acquire. Subscribed to by the signatures of thirteen persons. Referred to Committee on Divorce and Alimony. (GASR, Nov.-Dec. 1808, Box 3: folder "Petitions- Divorce, Name Change, etc.")

      The Committee on Divorce and Alimony to whom was referred the [petition] of…Mary Gregory of Edgecombe County…are of opinion the prayer…ought to be granted and recommend the Bill herewith presented be passed into law: "A Bill to secure to the persons therein mentioned such property as they may hereafter acquire." Read and concurred with by the House of Commons, 17 Dec. 1808, and by the Senate, 19 Dec. 1808. (GASR, Nov.-Dec. 1808, Box 2: folder "JCR - Divorce and Alimony")

218.   **Gunter, Anne/Hanna and husband, Jesse.** Petition of Anne Gunter [signature: Hanna (+) Gunter] sheweth that she married Jesse Gunter of Wilkes County,[20] "who for ten tears past has lived in a riotous & idle manner and has wasted her estate and for some time has absolutely left your petitioner and taken up and lives & beds with another woman." Your petitioner has always conducted herself as a prudent and dutiful wife. Prays for an act to divorce her from her said husband or to secure all such property as she may hereafter acquire. She states she has a considerable family to maintain. Dated 2 Nov. 1808. Subscribed to by the signatures of five persons. Referred to Committee on Divorce and Alimony. (GASR, Nov.-Dec. 1808, Box 3: folder "Petitions- Divorce, Name Change, etc.") The Committee on Divorce and Alimony to whom [was] referred the [petition] of…Anne Gunter of Wilkes County…are of opinion the prayer…ought to be granted and recommend the Bill herewith presented be passed into law: "A Bill to secure to the persons therein mentioned such property as they may hereafter acquire." Read and concurred with by the House of Commons, 17 Dec. 1808, and by the Senate, 19 Dec. 1808. (GASR, Nov.-Dec. 1808, Box 2: folder "JCR - Divorce and Alimony") Published in North Carolina Laws, 1808, p. 39.

219.   **Kerr, William and wife, Sarah.** Petition of William Kerr of Stokes County states he is "one of the most unfortunate of mankind." Early in life, his father died, leaving said William with little knowledge on how to conduct his life. "At about fifteen or sixteen years of age through the folly of my mind [I] was Indued. to marry Sarah Guymon of Stokes County who after living a few months with your Petitioner went to her Father and there has livd. ever since…about four years we have been apart and passd. all hope of ever living together any more." Prays for a divorce. Deposition of Edward (E) Edwards that he was well acquainted with the circumstances between William Ker[r] and his wife and has no reason to believe that said William was at fault "but that he would have livd. with her and would have done by her and for her the best he Could and that he thinks she left him two or three times…that he was but a youth when he mar[r]ied." Sworn to before J. Venables, J.P. of Stokes County, North Carolina, 5 Nov. 1808. Deposition of William Steele states that William Ker[r] requested him to go to his wife, Sarah Kerr, and try to persuade her to live with her said husband again. Your deponent went to the said Sarah "and askd. her the reason why She could not live with her husband William Ker and her answer was that she hated him so bad that she could not live with him nor never would again…at the same time she acknowledged that her husband never had abused her nor treated Ill in the least respect…" Sworn to before J. Venables, J.P. of Stokes County, North Carolina, 5 Nov. 1808. Petition and depositions referred to Committee on Divorce and Alimony. (GASR, Nov.-Dec. 1808, Box 3: folder "Petitions- Divorce, Name Change, etc.") Committee on Divorce and Alimony to whom was referred the petition of William Kerr of Stokes County, praying to be divorced from his wife, Sarah, are of opinion that the same should not

---

20   Marriage Bond, Wilkes County, North Carolina, dated 18 February 1792, for Jesse Gunter and Ann Manton.

Divorces and Separations from Petitions to the North Carolina General Assembly from 1779

be granted. Read and concurred with by House of Commons, 30 Nov. 1808, and by the Senate, 1 Dec. 1808. (GASR, Nov.-Dec. 1808, Box 2: folder "JCR - Divorce and Alimony")

220.   **Miers, Jacob and wife. Sally.** Petition of Jacob Miers of Rowan County states that his wife. Sally Miers, deserted his bed and board "Some ten or twelve years ago" and has ever since, as your petitioner believes, cohabited with a certain Fowler Jones. Your petitioner, who is now an old man, has with care and industry gathered together a little property, "which it is his wish to leave at his death to his children." Prays an act to secure to him "the right of so doing & to exclude his said wife Sally from her right of dower on any distributive share of his estate." /s/ Jacob (x) Miers. Committee on Divorce and Alimony to whom was referred the petition of Jacob Miers of Rowan County report that your Committee are of opinion that the prayer of the petitioner ought to be granted and recommend the accompanying Bill be passed: "A Bill to secure Jacob Miers of the County of Rowan against all future demands of his wife Sally." In House of Commons, read first and second time and passed. In Senate, read first time and passed; read second time and rejected. (GASR, Nov.-Dec. 1808, Box 2: folder "JCR - Divorce and Alimony")

221.   **Murry, Samuel, Jr., and wife, Elizabeth.** Petition of Andrew Erwin and thirteen others sheweth that they have been intimately acquainted with Samuel Murry, Jr., his family and relations for a number of years. They regret to say that about eighteen months past, the said Samuel and his wife, Elizabeth, decided they could not live happily together and separated, the said Elizabeth receiving a division of their property. In the last session of the Assembly, a law was passed that secured to each of these persons the property they had independent of any marriage claim on each other. [See North Carolina Laws, 1806, p. 54.]

Said Elizabeth is about to remove to the State of Tennessee, and the said Samuel Murry, who possesses a fair moral character, is desirous of obtaining a complete divorce from his former wife. Said petitioners pray that the said Samuel be given a final divorce from his said wife and also to allow "the unfortunate woman, viz., Elizabeth, his former wife…to try to Live a Better life with some other man as they are both in the prime of Life." Referred to Committee on Divorce and Alimony. The Committee's report has not survived, but the prayer of the petitioners for a divorce was rejected. (GASR, Nov.-Dec. 1808, Box 3: folder "Petitions- Divorce, Name Change, etc.")

222.   **Mus(t)grave, Micajah and wife, Zilpha.** Petition of Micajah Musgrave of Wayne County states he intermarried with Zilpha Harrel of the same county about twelve years ago. He lived peacefully with said wife until about two or three years last past, when she voided the bond of matrimony by cohabiting with other men. In the past year "she has taken up and lives with one Isaac Bizzel and has left with your petitioner five small children which he is oblige, to support and take care of…" Prays for a law to divorce him from the said Zilpha. Dated 9 Nov. 1808. Subscribed to by the signatures of eight persons. Referred to Committee on Divorce and Alimony. (GASR, Nov.-Dec. 1808, Box 3: folder "Petitions Divorce, Name Change, etc.") Committee on Divorce and Alimony to whom was referred the petition of Micajah Mustgrave of Wayne County…praying to be divorced from [his wife]…are of opinion that it would be improper to grant the prayer of the [petitioner] and recommend [it] be rejected. Read and concurred with by the House of Commons, 12 Dec. 1808, and by the Senate, 13 Dec. 1808. (GASR, Nov.-Dec. 1808, Box 2: folder "JCR - Divorce and Alimony")

223. **Norcom, Dr. James (physician) and wife, Mary.** In September 1807, Mrs. Mary Norcom by her next friend, Frederick B. Sawyer, and John Hamilton, Esq., her attorney, submitted a Bill of Complaint and petition against her husband, James Norcom, for maintenance to the Superior Court of Equity for Pasquotank County, North Carolina. This petition noted she was married about "two years past" to Dr. James Norcom of Edenton[21] by whom she had one child. About "two years past" said James deserted his house and family without any cause, wandered through the eastern states, took a voyage to the East Indies, and returned to "his former connection." He arrived by way of Edenton in July 1807 but again "bids her adieu & vows…to abandon and desert her." In the meantime, said husband "left her no means of support for the maintenance of herself and child," and had it not been for the kindness of her father-in-law, Hamilton, residing in Elizabeth City, she would have "been an outcast and her child a pauper." Said James possessed a considerable estate from his father, Jno. Norcom, practiced as a physician in Edenton for a considerable time and also inherited a fourth of the estate of his brother, Abner Norcom. Your petitioner has always conducted herself "as became a virtuous & prudent wife, jealous of her honor, and gave no just cause to the said James to desert his family. Prays for action to provide her with maintenance and support from the said James. The Court decreed that the defendant, James Norcom, would have four months to file an answer. John Hamilton was appointed guardian to John Hamilton Norcom, an infant. Letter from James Norcom in Edenton to Mrs. Mary Norcom, 24 October 1808, notifies his wife of his appeal to the North Carolina General Assembly for a divorce at the next session and of the testimony he has submitted. He notes that his actions are "not intended to affect the suit you have instituted for maintenance." In his appeal to the North Carolina General Assembly, James Norcom submits the following petition and accompanying depositions:

(a). Petition of James Norcom, Physician of Town of Edenton, North Carolina, states that in August 1801, said Norcom married Mary Custis and lived happily with her until the commencement of the year 1804, when he discovered in her an imprudent attachment to opium and intoxicating liquors. Believing that she was not conscious of her weakness, said Norcom remonstrated with her on the extreme indelicacy and impropriety of her conduct in terms of the tenderest affection. However, he found that gentleness and persuasion were ineffectual and so took recourse to threats and rebuke and told her "that if she did not forsake the practice to which she was addicted, she would ere long have cause to lament her folly & might be compelled to weep over her errors when tears would be of no avail." Finally, your petitioner deemed it impossible to live with his said wife, as all of his entreaties to change were ignored. In July 1805, said Norcom left his home, his wife and a child, and an extensive practice in which he had been engaged for more than five years, and wandered through the Eastern States for several months under the most poignant and agonizing distress. In April 1806, he embarked on a voyage to the East Indies and recovered both his physical and mental health and gained an ardent desire to return to his family. In July 1807, he did intend to go to the place of his former residence, but then considered it inconsistent with his reputation, his peace of mind and the conduct of his wife in his absence and decided to renounce her and never see her again. When he left his home in 1805, he did not leave Mrs. Norcom destitute but left her in the house under the protection of her father-in-law and furnished her a servant and every necessary and convenience. Petitioner prays for a divorce.

(b). Deposition of Stephen R. Hooker states he lived in the house of said James Norcom from 6 January 1802 to mid-July 1805 and recollected that during the first year of marriage, Mrs. Mary Norcom conducted herself in a tolerable prudent manner towards her husband but by the second year was throwing off her veil of respectability. The deponent supported said James' reports of his wife's growing intoxication and that she became more licentious. On one occasion, she came into a room where several

---

21   Marriage Bond, Chowan County, North Carolina, dated 8 August 1801, for James Norcom and Mary Custus.

Divorces and Separations from Petitions to the North Carolina General Assembly from 1779

young men were in bed, and she had nothing on but her shift. She made use of language and appropriate actions "as to clearly evince to the deponent that either intoxication or violent carnal desires had made her forget all appearance of modesty, virtue and propriety." Eventually her said husband James left his family and sailed for New York in July 1805. This deponent received letters from New York, Boston and Philadelphia and from Calcutta in the East Indies. The said James did not return to America until April 1807 at Philadelphia and not to Edenton until mid-July in the same year, but there were reports that Mary Norcom was pregnant and delivered of a child in September following.

    (c).   Deposition of Joseph S. Creecy, who lived in the house of James Norcom about one year from 4 July 1804. He confirmed the deposition of Stephen R. Hooker regarding Mrs. Mary Norcom and added that she sometimes would pull off the bedclothes to expose the nakedness of himself and others and "evince a desire to have that sensual appetite gratified…" He had "heard her when her husband had been called to visit country patients wish that the horse might brake his neck & he be in hell before morning…"

    (d).   Deposition of Mary Caskeden at house of George Caskaden in Elizabeth City…notes that she became acquainted with said Mary at Elizabeth City and knew her for about two years. She deposed that the said Mary was delivered of a child in the house of Col. John Hamilton at Elizabeth City about 1 October 1807 in the presence of three women, but the child was born dead and was buried.

    (e).   Certificate signed by forty-three persons, all inhabitants of Edenton and vicinity, who have been acquainted for several years with James Norcum, Practitioner of Medicine in said town, certify "that in every status in which we have known him he has conducted himself virtuously and respectable" and "heartily concur with him in his petition to be divorced from his wife, Mary Norcum, who we have reason to believe…has dishonored the obligation subsisting between them [and has] forfeited her right to her protection and rendered herself unworthy of his affection and esteem-."
House Bill: That James Norcum of Edenton is hereby divorced from his wife Mary and that the marriage tie between said James and Mary be annulled and dissolved…as if they had never been married. Read third time and passed by the North Carolina Assembly. (All of the above in GASR, Nov.-Dec. 1808, Box 1: folder "House Bill (Dec. 2) to Divorce James Norcum of Edenton from His Wife Mary")

224.   **OBriant/OBryant, Jane and husband, William.** Petition of Jane (+) OBriant of Mecklenburg County, 24 October 1808, sheweth that she married William OBriant sometime in the Year 1804, and they lived together for about five months, in which time he wasted what property of which she was possessed when they married and contracted debts to a much larger amount. He abandoned your petitioner and has been absent ever since. Prays for an act to secure to her such property as she may hereafter acquire. Subscribed to by the signatures of seven persons. Referred to Committee on Divorce and Alimony. (GASR, Nov.-Dec.1808, Box 3: folder "Petitions - Divorce, Name Change, etc.") The Committee on Divorce and Alimony to whom [was] referred the [petition] of…Jane O'Briant of Mecklenburg County…are of opinion the prayer…ought to be granted and recommend the Bill herewith presented be passed into law: "A Bill to secure to the persons therein mentioned such property as they may hereafter acquire." Read and concurred with by the House of Commons, 17 Dec. 1808, and the Senate, 19 Dec. 1808. (GASR, Nov.-Dec. 1808, Box 2: folder "JCR Divorce and Alimony")

225.   **Pit(t)man, Mary and husband, Robert.** Petition of Mary (Summerlin) Pitman of Edgecombe County sheweth that she intermarried with a certain Robert Pitman in 1798. After two years of marriage, the said Robert began to show uncommon indifference and want of attention towards your petitioner, followed by personal abuse and an intention to disregard his marriage vow. He formed a close connection with a certain Nancy Walters and spent the greater part of one year cohabiting with her and

"lavished almost everything we possessed" on her. In the year 1801, the said Robert "formed a base & wicked connection with a certain Jemima Melton, whom he took into his house" and with whom lie cohabited. He "used every effort in his power to compel your petitioner to desert his house & home, all of which attempts he found in vain…" He continued in this manner for about six months, "at the expiration of which time he formed a connection equally base & wicked with another woman by the name of Catharin Griffis" and took up lodging at the house of Mrs. Griffis, said Catharin's mother. Your petitioner continued to hope that the said Robert would see the errors of his ways and return to your petitioner, but in the year 1804, these hopes vanished. He "moved with his Harlot & her friends to the State of Tennessee, where I am informed he yen remains, leaving your petitioner & two Infants without the smallest means of support." Prays for a law to secure to her all such property as she may hereafter acquire free from the molestation of the aforesaid Robert Pitman. Subscribed to by the signatures of five supporters. Referred to the Committee on Divorce and Alimony. (GASR, Nov.-Dec. 1808, Box 3: folder "Petitions-Divorce, Name Change, etc.")

  The Committee on Divorce and Alimony to whom [was] referred the [petition] of…Mary Pitman of Edgecombe County…are of opinion the prayer…ought to be granted and recommend the Bill herewith presented be passed into law: "A Bill to secure to the persons therein mentioned such property as they may hereafter acquire." Read and concurred with by the House of Commons, 17 Dec. 1808, and by the Senate, 19 Dec. 1808. (GASR, Nov.-Dec. 1808, Box 2: folder "JCR - Divorce and Alimony") Published in North Carolina Laws, 1808, p. 39.

226. **Pope, Elijah and wife, Sarah.** Petition of Elijah Pope of Northampton County states he married a certain Sarah Parks of said county in the year 1796. They lived together until 1802, when the said Sarah "for some cause unknown" left his "bed and lodging and took up with a Certain Barnaba Bunn of said County and has lived with him ever since and had two children as if she was his Lawfull wife." Prays for a divorce. Signed by Sarah (x) Pope and fifty other subscribers. Referred to Committee on Divorce and Alimony. (GASR, Nov.-Dec. 1808, Box 3: folder "Petitions - Divorce, Name Change, etc.")

  Petition of Elijah Pope of Northampton County sheweth that he intermarried with Sarah Parks of said county sometime in March 1797. After three or four years, said Sarah "made her elopement from him & took up with a certain Barnaba Bunn, who has kept her as a wife ever since, having Begotten Several children by her to the best knowledge and belief of all who know them." Prays "to be divorced from So Vile & polluted a creture as She has proven herself to the World to be, who as will appear from her signiture Anext to his in This Petition is Eaqually As himself Anxious for the Seperation That has Taken place between them…" /s/ Elijah Pope, Saley (x) Pope. Subscribed to by the signatures of twenty-eight persons. The Committee on Divorce and Alimony to whom was referred the petition of Elijah Pope of Northampton County deem it improper to grant the prayer of the Petitioner and recommend it be rejected. In House of Commons, 14 Dec. 1808, and in Senate, 15 Dec. 1808, read and concurred with. (GASR, Nov.-Dec. 1808, Box 2: folder "JCR - Divorce and Alimony")

227. **Rogers, Sarah and husband, Benajah.** Petition of Sarah Rogers of Wake County states she intermarried with a certain Benajah Rogers some years ago, but he abandoned her in 1806 without any cause whatsoever. The petitioner is fearful that her said husband may return and take from her the earnings of her industry and care. She therefore prays that such property as she may hereafter acquire be secured to her. Referred to Committee on Divorce and Alimony. (GASR, Nov.-Dec. 1808, Box 3: folder "Petitions- Divorce, Name Change, etc.") The Committee on Divorce and Alimony to whom [was] referred the [petition] of…Sarah Rogers of Wake County are of opinion the prayer…ought to be granted and recommend the Bill herewith presented be passed into law: "A Bill to secure to the persons therein

Divorces and Separations from Petitions to the North Carolina General Assembly from 1779

mentioned such property as they may hereafter acquire." Read and concurred with by the House of Commons, 17 Dec. 1808, and by the Senate, 19 Dec. 1808. (GASR, Nov.-Dec. 1808, Box 2: folder "JCR - Divorce and Alimony") Published in North Carolina Laws, 1808, p. 39.

228.   **Self, Lucey.** The Committee on Divorce and Alimony to whom [was] referred the petition of Lucey Self of Anson County…are of opinion the prayer…ought to be granted and recommend the Bill herewith presented be passed into law: "A Bill to secure to the persons therein mentioned such property as they may hereafter acquire." Read and concurred with by the House of Commons, 17 Dec. 1808, and by the Senate, 19 Dec. 1808. (GASR, Nov.-Dec. 1808, Box 2: folder "JCR - Divorce and Alimony") Published in North Carolina Laws, 1808, p. 39.

229.   **Smith, Alexander.** The Committee on Divorce and Alimony to whom was referred the following [petition], vizt.,…Alexr. Smith of Ashe County…praying to be divorced are of opinion that Legislative interference in such cases are largely improper and therefore recommend that the…[petition] be rejected. Read and concurred with by House of Commons, 15 Dec. 1807, and by Senate, 10 Dec. 1807.

230.   **Snipes, Delia/Dilly and husband, John.** Petition of Dilly Snipes [of Wake County] sheweth that some years past she intermarried with John Snipes, who has from time to time caused her property to be sold and left herself and family destitute of support. In the year 1808, the said "John left his unfortunate wife to maintain herself & three children…Fearful the said Snipes may return and take from her the little property she may gather together…," she implores an act to secure such property as she may hereafter acquire. Referred to Committee on Divorce and Alimony. (GASR, Nov.-Dec. 1808, Box 2: folder "JCR - Divorce and Alimony") Prayer of petitioner approved and published in North Carolina Laws, 1808, p. 39.

231.   **Staley, Eve.** Committee on Divorce and Alimony to whom was referred the following petitions, vizt.,…Eve Staley of Wilkes County…praying to be divorced are of opinion that Legislative interference in such cases are largely improper and therefore recommend that the aforesaid petitions be rejected. Read and concurred with by House of Commons, 15 Dec. 1807, and by Senate, 10 Dec. 1807. (GASR, Nov.-Dec. 1808, Box 2: folder "JCR - Divorce and Alimony") Bill to secure the property of Eve Staley of Wilkes County that she may thereafter acquire from her husband, Jacob Staley, was approved and published in North Carolina Laws, 1803, p. 56.

232.   **Stephens/Stevens, Elizabeth and husband, Ebenezer.** Petition of Elizabeth Stevens of Robeson County states she intermarried with Ebenezer Stevens several years ago, but soon discovered he "exercised the utmost cruelty towards her and soon reduced her by his extravagance and waste into a state of indigence and want and at all times failing to pursue any occupation which would in the least degree contribute towards the support of your petitioner & children…Being thus treated, and ultimately abandoned by her husband, no alternative was left her except a dependence upon the clemency and Goodness of her Friends…" Prays for a law to secure what property she may hereafter acquire from the claims of said Ebenezer Stevens. Read and referred to Committee on Divorce and Alimony. Deposition of Moses Hill, father of above Elizabeth Stevens, before Alexander Rowland, J.P of Robeson County, North Carolina, supports the statements of said Elizabeth as claimed in her petition. In addition, said Moses Hill notes that said Ebenezer was absent six months, and when he returned, he was still without any preparation for the support of his family and appeared more dissipated than when he left. Said Ebenezer stayed a few days, went away again, and has not returned. Dated 16 Nov. 1808. (GASR, Nov.-Dec. 1808, Box

3: folder "Petitions- Divorce, Name Change, etc.") The Committee on Divorce and Alimony to whom [was] referred the [petition] of…Elizabeth Stephens of Robeson County…are of opinion the prayer… ought to be granted and recommend the Bill herewith presented be passed into law: "A Bill to secure to the persons therein mentioned such property as they may hereafter acquire." Read and concurred with by the House of Commons, 17 Dec. 1808, and by the Senate, 19 Dec. 1808. (GASR, Nov.-Dec. 1808, Box 2: folder "JCR - Divorce and Alimony") Bill published in North Carolina Laws, 1808, p. 39.

233. **Starling/Sterling, Stephen and wife, Bersheba.** Petition of Stephen Starling of Robeson County states he has been a resident of the State since infancy and that "some years past he unfortunately married a woman by the name of Bersheba Dawson, who in a short space thereafter, proved to be a most notorious prostitute & violation of the sanctity of the Conubial vow." The said Bersheba "did at length wholly associate, live & cohabit with a certain John Bond, a resident of South Carolina, with whom your Petitioner has caught his said wife in the act of Adultery, & with whom she has for the space of fifteen months lived & cohabited, & by whom she had a child twelve months after absenting herself from your Petitioner." Prays for an act to secure to him such property as he now has or may hereafter acquire from the claims of said Bersheba. Referred to Committee on Divorce and Alimony. (GASR, Nov.-Dec. 1808, Box 3: folder "Petitions - Divorce, Name Change, etc.") The Committee on Divorce and Alimony to whom was referred the [petition] of…Stephen Sterling of Robeson County…are of opinion the prayer… ought to be granted and recommend the Bill herewith presented be passed into law: "A Bill to secure to the persons therein mentioned such property as they may hereafter acquire." Read and concurred with by the House of Commons, 17 Dec. 1808, and by the Senate, 19 Dec. 1808. (GASR, Nov.-Dec. 1808, Box 2: folder "JCR - Divorce and Alimony") Bill published in North Carolina Laws, 1808, p. 39.

234. **Sumerset, Simon and wife, Hannah.** Petition of Hannah Sumerset notes that she married Simon Sumerset on 6 August 1807, both of Bladen County. From that time, she lived a discontented life, and a few months ago, she left the said Simon "and fled to the State of Georgia and tuck up with another man to which place I was persued by his friends and Brought Back But finding it is imposible for me Ever to live with him the said Simon Sumerst any moore must Beg Legislature interfearance and pray that your Honorable Boddy would…divorce me from him the said Simon Sumerst." /s/ Hannah Sumarset. Petition of Simon Sumerset states he married Hannah Flinn on 6 August 1807, both of them of the County of Bladen. From that time he lived a discontented life, and a few months ago, the said Hannah left him and fled to the State of Georgia where she was married to another man. She was pursued by some of my friends and brought back, but then "she took up with another man and are living together at this time and have Brought a Child by the said man…" Prays for a divorce from the said Hannah Sumerset. Dated 24 Nov. 1808. /s/ Simon Sumerset. The Committee on Divorce and Alimony to whom was referred the petition of Simon Sumerset of Bladen County report that they have taken said petition under consideration and are of the opinion it would be inexpedient to grant the prayer of the petitioner and recommend that it be rejected. Concurred in by the House of Commons, 17 Dec. 1808, and by the Senate, 19 Dec. 1808. (GASR, Nov.-Dec. 1808, Box 2: folder "JCR - Divorce and Alimony")

235. **Thomas, Lewis and wife, Levina.** Committee of Divorce and Alimony to whom was referred the following petitions, vizt.,…Joint petition of Lewis and Levina Thomas of Robeson County, praying to be divorced are; of opinion that Legislative interference in such cases are largely improper and therefore recommend that the aforesaid petitions be rejected. Read and concurred with by House of Commons, 15 Dec. 1807, and by the Senate, 10 Dec. 1807. (GASR, Nov.-Dec. 1808, Box 2: folder "JCR - Divorce and Alimony")

Divorces and Separations from Petitions to the North Carolina General Assembly from 1779

236. **Vervell, Daniel and wife, Mary.** Petition of Daniel and Mary Vervell of Rowan County states they were married about ten years ago, "but from causes which it is not necessary to explain at this time, your petitioners mutually agreed to separate and did not live together three months in the ten years." About five years ago, they jointly petitioned the General Assembly, and a Law was passed securing to each the property they might thereafter acquire. [North Carolina Laws, 1804, p. 54.] Your petitioner, Daniel Vervell gave to the said Mary a portion of his property with which both parties were content. However, your petitioners are now desirous of a law to divorce them from the bonds of matrimony, /s/ Daniel Vervell [written in German script], Mary (x) Vervell. They have lived apart for ten years and have been legally separate for near five years. Subscribed to by the signatures of twenty-two persons. Referred to Committee on Divorce and Alimony. (GASR, Nov.-Dec. 1808, Box 3: folder "Petitions- Divorce, Name Change, etc.")

    Committee on Divorce and Alimony to whom was referred the petition of Daniel Varnell and wife [unnamed] of Rowan County, praying to be divorced, are of opinion that it ought not be granted. Read and concurred with by House of Commons, 30 Nov. 1808, and by the Senate, 1 Dec. 1808. (GASR, Nov.-Dec. 1808, Box 2: folder "JCR - Divorce and Alimony")

237. **Warmoth/Wormoth, Betsy and husband, James.** Petition of Betsy Warmoth, wife of James Warmoth, sheweth that your petitioner has been "under the necessity of throwing herself under the protection of her aged parents, who are very far from being welthy" because she is afraid of her personal safety when her said husband is in a state of inebrity, "which is ever the case…" Prays for a law to secure such property as she may hereafter acquire as if she had never been married. Referred to Committee on Divorce and Alimony. (GASR, Nov.-Dec. 1808, Box 3: folder "Petitions- Divorce, Name Change, etc.")

    The Committee on Divorce and Alimony to whom was referred the [petition] of…Betsy Warmoth of Franklin County…are of opinion the prayer…ought to be granted and recommend the Bill herewith presented be passed into law: "A Bill to secure to the persons therein mentioned such property as they may hereafter acquire." Read and Concurred with by the House of Commons, 17 Dec. 1808, and by the Senate, 19 Dec. 1808. (GASR, Nov.-Dec. 1808, Box 2: folder "JCR - Divorce and Alimony")

1809

238. **Alexander, Mary (Scott) and husband, John.** Petition of Mary Scott of Buncombe Co., NC, requests the North Carolina General Assembly to take under serious consideration her unhappy situation. She was married in 1803 to John Alexander, who absconded with a considerable part of her property. It is also evident that the said Alexander was previously married to another woman who is still living. Prays for a final and total divorce. N.B. by Justice of Peace, Thos. Rogers, "that in March last 1809, the same John Alexander did marry another woman in Abivil [Abbevillle] South Carlinah wich has been Searty Fyed beafore me." (GASR, Nov.-Dec. 1809, Box 3: folder "Petitions (Divorce, etc.)").

The Committee to whom was referred [the petition of Mary Scott] praying for a divorce from bonds of matrimony are of opinion that it is inexpedient to grant the relief prayed for and recommend that the same be rejected. Read and concurred with by Senate and House, 19 Dec. 1809. (GASR, Nov.-Dec. 1809, Box 2: folder "JCR (Divorce & Alimony - Emancipation)").

239. **Alley, Elisabeth and husband, John.** Petition of Elisabeth Alley of Montgomery County states that she intermarried with one John Alley some time in the Year 1802 "under the fondest hopes of enjoying the unsullied sweets of the Conjugal State but unfortunately for your Petitioner in about six months after the marriage he the said John Alley absconded from your petitioner leaving her in a state of the utmost distress for about five months, when he returned and promised your petitioner that he would then live with her and take care of her during life." Instead, your petitioner "had the mortification of experiencing his final desertion in which forlorn and helpless state your petitioner has ever since lived." Prays for a law divorcing her from the said John Alley, 20 Nov. 1809.

Affidavit of Benjamin (x) Merit, 28 Oct. 1809, Montgomery Co., NC, before Justice of Peace Mark Bennett, that "he saw John Alley husband to Elisebeth Alley after he had left her & he the sd. Alley told him the sd. Merit that he never would live with her any more as long as he lived."

Affidavit of John (0) Merit, 28 Oct. 1809, Montgomery Co., NC, before Justice of Peace Mark Bennett, deposeth "that the sd. Alley & his wife has not lived together for near about five year & she had to live as she could..." (GASR, Nov.-Dec. 1809, Box 3: folder "Petitions (Divorce, etc.)").

The Committee to whom was referred the [petition of Elizabeth Ally] praying for a divorce from bonds of matrimony are of opinion that it is inexpedient to grant the relief prayed for & recommend that the same be rejected. Read & concurred with by Senate & House, 19 Dec. 1809. (GASR, Nov.-Dec. 1809, Box 2: folder "JCR Divorce & Alimony - Emancipation")

240. **Armstrong, Elizabeth and husband, Martin.** Memorial of Elizabeth Armstrong of Surry County sheweth that she has been abandoned for some time by her husband, Martin Armstrong, and left to support a helpless family of children by her own industry and the charitable assistance of her parents. Prays to the General Assembly to secure to her by Law the property she may hereafter acquire. (GASR, Nov.-Dec. 1809, Box 3: folder "Petitions (Divorce, etc.)").

Divorces and Separations from Petitions to the North Carolina General Assembly from 1779

The Committee to whom was referred the Petition of [Armstrong, Elizabeth of Surry Co.] are of opinion that the clemency of the Legislature ought to be extended to [her] relief and recommend the accompanying Bill be passed into law. Concurred with by Senate (15 Dec.) and House (16 Dec.). (GASR, Nov.-Dec. 1809, Box 2: folder "JCR - Divorce & Alimony - Emancipation")

To secure to persons therein mentioned such property as they may hereafter acquire: "Armstrong, Elizabeth of Surry Co., wife of Martin Armstrong." 21 Dec. 1809 - read 3d time by House and Senate and ordered to be engrossed. (GASR, Nov.-Dec. 1809, Box 2: folder "SB, 15 Dec.")

241. **Armstrong, Martin.** The Committee [JCR] was referred the petition of David Bray, John Critchfield, Aaron Owen and Robert Harris of Surry Co., praying to be released from their recognizances as thereon mentioned. It appears from evidence adduced to your Committee that the said petitioners entered into recognizances for the appearance of a certain Martin Armstrong and Patsey Mask at the Superior Court for the County of Surry on a charge of their having illicit intercourse with each Other & that they failed to appear and answer to the August 1995 255 charge - that every reasonable effort has been made use of to compel their appearance, but all in vain…therefore are of opinion that legislative interference ought to be extended to their relief. House concurred on 7 Dec. 1809, but Senate did not concur. (GASR, Nov.-Dec. 1809, Box 2: folder "JCR, Prop. & Griev.")

242. **Bell, Miles and wife, Penelope (Adams).** Petition of Miles Bell of Carteret Co. states that he was married to Penelope Adams of said county in the year 1801, and that they lived in peace and harmony together for about two years. At the end of that time, said Penelope eloped from your petitioner's bed and board and went to the State of Tennessee without any just cause and for reasons unknown. Said Penelope intermarried with a certain Philip Sanders of Tennessee and has remained his wife for about six years. Your petitioner is young (about 28 years of age) and in the prime of life and considers his case an extreme hard one. Prays for a Bill of Divorce from his wife Penelope. Dated 14 Nov. 1809.

Affidavit of John Adams, father of Penelope Bell, wife of Miles Bell, before Richard Canaday and Jno. Roberts, Justices of Peace of Carteret Co., 20 Oct. 1809, that he, said Adams, was in the State of Tennessee in 1804 and saw the said Penelope Bell, wife of Miles Bell, married to a certain Philip Sanders of that State and living together as man and wife.

Committee of Divorce and Alimony to whom was referred the Petition of [Miles Bell] of Carteret Co. praying to be divorced from wife Penelope report that your Committee have maturely considered the Petitioner's prayer and examined the evidence adduced in support thereof: They are of opinion that [Penelope] the wife of said Miles Bell has committed an Act inconsistent with the matrimonial vow and contrary to the purpose for which it was instituted: therefore recommend that the Bill accompanying this report - entitled "A Bill to Divorce Miles Bell, of the County of Carteret from his wife Penelope" be passed into a law. In Senate, 4 Dec. 1809, read and resolved non-concurrence with said report. (GASR, Nov.-Dec. 1809, Box 1: folder "Senate Bills, Dec. 4")

243. **Bracewell [Braswell?], Isaac and wife. Nancy (Low).** Letter to Mr. Isaac Bracewell, Edgecombe Co., from Nancy Bracewell, Beaufort Co., 12 Aug. 1808: "Sir, this is to inform you that I am predetermined never to attempt to live with you again & also to inform you that If you will come or send that I will assign any Instruments of writing that you think May tend to Induce the General Assembly to Grant us a Divorce. Please to signify your Intentions as soon as possible, for I Do not care How Soon we get clear of each other. Remember My love to My Children & take this as a positive Declaration from

me of My Determination Never to risk My Self In your Power again. I am &: c." /s/ Nancy Bracewell.[22] (GASR, Nov.-Dec. 1809, Box 3: folder "Miscellaneous Correspondence")

  The Committee to whom was referred the following petitions: "…Bracewell, Isaac…" respectively praying for a divorce from bonds of matrimony are of opinion that it is inexpedient to grant the relief prayed for and recommend that the same be rejected. Read and concurred with by Senate and House, 19 Dec. 1809. (GASR, Nov.-Dec. 1809, Box 2: folder "JCR - Divorce & Alimony -Emancipation")

244. **Braswell, Sarah and husband, John.** To secure to persons therein mentioned such property as they may hereafter acquire: "…Braswell, Sarah of Nash Co., wife of John Braswell…" Read 3d time by House and Senate and ordered to be engrossed. (GASR, Nov.-Dec. 1809, Box 2: folder "SB, 15 Dec.")

245. **Bright/Brite, Richard and wife, Jane.** Petition of Richard Brite of Pasquotank Co. sheweth that his wife, Jane Brite, has forsaken his bed and board for upwards of two years without provocation and has taken up with a "person as base as herself and living in the same neighbourhood in an audacious & daring State of adultry…" Prays for an act to divorce him from the ties of matrimony with said Jane Brite.[23] (GASR, Nov.-Dec. 1809, Box 3: folder "Petitions- Divorce, etc.")

  The Committee to whom was referred the following petition "…Bright, Richard…" respectively praying for a divorce from bonds of matrimony are of opinion that it is inexpedient to grant the relief prayed for and recommend that the same be rejected. Read and concurred with by Senate and House, 19 Dec. 1809. (GASR, Nov.-Dec. 1809, Box 2: folder "JCR - Divorce & Alimony - Emancipation")

246. **Brown, Bond V. and wife, Susanna (Kearns).** Petition of Bond V. Brown of Caswell Co., NC, that he intermarried with Susanna Kearns in the year 1791 and lived with her nine years, enjoying the comforts commonly derived from a married state. At the expiration of that time, the said Susanna eloped "with a young man of dissipated character to the State of Tennessee. She has had four children by him and continues to live in open adultry, having taken with her a valuable horse and forty dollars in cash, the property of your petitioner, and leaving him with four small children. Your petitioner has been informed that the said Susanna has frequently boasted of her right of dower from your petitioner's estate…" He therefore prays for a law to "invest him…with power to dispose of his property by will, or otherwise, so as to deprive the said Susanna of her right of dower and the children she may have had since her elopement…" (GASR, Nov.-Dec. 1809, Box 3: folder "Petitions- Divorce, etc.")

  The Committee to whom was referred the [petition of V. Brown] praying for a divorce from bonds of matrimony are of opinion that it is inexpedient to grant the relief prayed for and recommend that the same be rejected. Read and concurred with by Senate and House, 19 Dec. 1809. (GASR, Nov.-Dec. 1809, Box 2: folder "JCR Divorce & Alimony -Emancipation")

247. **Clark, Rebeccah and husband, William.** Petition of Rebeccah Clark of Lincoln Co., NC. She was married to William Clark on or about 4 March 1785. They lived together for about three years, when the said William Clark left your petitioner with two small children without any provocation or support. Your petitioner has supported them in a decent and Christian manner through her own industry. She prays that an Act be passed securing to her such property as she now has or may hereafter acquire. Subscribed to by ten supporters of her petition, 2 Nov. 1809. (GASR, Nov.-Dec. 1809, Box 3: folder "Petitions- Divorce, etc.")

---

22 There is also a similar letter dated 21 Sept. 1808.
23 This petition is subscribed to by the names of fifty-nine supporters.

Divorces and Separations from Petitions to the North Carolina General Assembly from 1779

    The Committee to whom was referred the petition of…Rebecca Clark of Lincoln Co.…are of opinion that the clemency of the Legislature ought to be extended to [her] relief and recommend the accompanying Bill be passed into law. Concurred with by Senate (15 Dec.) and House (16 Dec.). (GASR, Nov.-Dec. 1809, Box 2: folder "JCR - Divorce & Alimony - Emancipation")

    To secure to persons therein mentioned such property as they may hereafter acquire: "…Clark, Rebecca of Lincoln Co., wife of William Clark…" Read 3d time by House and Senate and ordered to be engrossed, 21 Dec. 1809. (GASR, Nov.-Dec. 1809, Box 2: folder "SB 15 Dec.")

248. **Coffin, Hannah and husband, William.** Petition of Hannah Coffin of Guilford Co., NC. Your petitioner, wife of William Coffin, sheweth that her husband absented himself from her for more than seven years, leaving with her, two small children. Requests the General Assembly to secure to her such property as she may hereafter acquire clear of her husband's claims or debts. 15 Nov. 1809. (GASR, Nov.-Dec. 1809, Box 3: folder "Petitions- Divorce, etc.")

    The Committee to whom was referred the petition of…Coffin, Hannah of Guilford Co.… are of opinion that the clemency of the Legislature ought to be extended to [her] relief and recommend the accompanying Bill be; passed into law. Concurred with by Senate (15 Dec.) and House (16 Dec.). (GASR, Nov.-Dec. 1809, Box 2: folder "JCR - Divorce & Alimony - Emancipation")

    To secure to persons therein mentioned such property as they may hereafter acquire:…Coffin, Hannah, wife of Wm. Coffin of Guilford Co.…Read 3d time by House and Senate and ordered to be engrossed. (GASR, Nov.-Dec. 1809, Box 2: folder "SB 15 Dec.")

249. **Craig, James and wife. Nancy.** Petition of James Craig of Burke County sheweth that Nancy, his wife, deserted his abode about three years ago without any provocation or cause whatsoever and removed herself to Kentucky where she has remained ever since. Prays for an Act to divorce him from his said wife. (GASR, Nov.-Dec. 1809, Box 3: folder "Petitions- Divorce, etc.")

    The Committee to whom was referred the [petition of]…Craig, James…respectively praying for a divorce from bonds of matrimony are of opinion that it is inexpedient to grant the relief prayed for and recommend that the same be rejected. Read and concurred with by Senate and House, 19 Dec. 1809. (GASR, Nov.-Dec. 1809, Box 2: folder "JCR - Divorce & Alimony - Emancipation")

250. **Crutchfield, Lidea and husband, Eusebius.** Petition of Lidea Crutchfield of Jones Co., NC, states that "about thirty years ago, your petitioner was married to Eusebius Crutchfield of said county, that she had by him eleven children…that about two years ago, he absented himself from her and went, as she believes, into the State of South Carolina…that he left with your petitioner's three small children…that he left her with no means whereby either these children or herself was to be supported…that he has since, as she is credibly informed, and verily believes, been married to a certain Elizabeth Bradford of the said State of South Carolina, where he now lives with the said Elizabeth as if she were his proper lawful and only wife. Prays a law to be passed securing to her whatever property she may have acquired since the absence of her husband." (GASR, Nov.-Dec. 1809, Box 3: folder "Petitions- Divorce, etc.")

    The Committee to whom was referred the petition of…Crutchfield, Lydia of Jones Co.… are of opinion that the clemency of the Legislature ought to be extended to [her] relief and recommend the accompanying Bill be passed into law. Concurred with by Senate (15 Dec.) and House (16 Dec.). (GASR, Nov.-Dec. 1809, Box 2: folder "JCR - Divorce & Alimony - Emancipation")

To secure to persons therein mentioned such property as they may hereafter acquire…Crutchfield, Lydia of Jones Co., wife of Eusebius Crutchfield. Read 3d time by House and Senate and ordered to be engrossed, 21 Dec. 1809. (GASR, Nov.-Dec. 1809, Box 2: folder "SB 15 Dec.")

251. **De Loach, John and wife. Nancy.** Petition of John (x) De Loach and Nancy (x), his wife, sheweth that they intermarried with each other about 1807, and after living together in "Conjucal Affection about one year," harmony and union between them broke down, and they've been separated about 18 months with no likelihood of their living together again as man and wife. They pray for a law to secure to each of them what property they may hereafter acquire. Dated 18 Nov. 1809 [probably of Northampton Co., NC]. (GASR, Nov.-Dec. 1809, Box 3: folder "Petitions - Divorce, etc.")

The Committee to whom was referred the [petition of De Loach, John] praying for a divorce from bonds of matrimony are of opinion that it is inexpedient to grant the relief prayed for and recommend that the same be rejected. Read and concurred with by Senate and House, 19 Dec. 1809. (GASR, Nov.-Dec. 1809, Box 2: folder "JCR - Divorce & Alimony - Emancipation")

252. **Dough, Ambrose N. and wife, Barbara (Midgett).** Memorial of Ambrose N. Dough of Currituck Co., NC, mariner, sheweth that he intermarried Barbara Midgett of Roanoke Island in the county aforesaid in the year 1802. At that time, your memorialist was at the age of eighteen years, and the said Barbara was in her fifteenth year. They cohabited with each other about two years and four months, when during your memorialist's absence in his seafaring occupation, he discovered that his said wife had proved faithless and cohabited with a certain John Westcott. She has since openly lived and cohabited with this man and has two children by the said Westcott, but some by your memorialist. At the time of their marriage, said Barbara was seized and possessed of 76 acres of land which your memorialist improved as far as he could. He desires an amicable separation from his wife and prays for a suitable relief. (GASR, Nov.-Dec. 1809, Box 3: folder "Petitions - Divorce, etc.")

The Committee to whom was referred the following [petition from Dough, Ambrose N.] praying for a divorce from bonds of matrimony and of opinion that it is inexpedient to grant the relief prayed for and recommend that the same be rejected. Read and concurred with by Senate and House, 19 Dec. 1809. (GASR, Nov.-Dec. 1809, Box 2: folder "JCR - Divorce & Alimony - Emancipation")

253. **Hall, Sally and husband, Willoby.** Petition of Sally (x) Hall of Wake Co., NC. Your petitioner intermarried with a certain Willoby Hall sometime in the year 1807 and lived in perfect love and peace with her said husband about five weeks, after which time he left her to the mercy of a charitable world and her own industry. Prays that consideration be given to secure to her such property as she may hereafter acquire. Subscribed to by fifty-two supporters, 18 Nov. 1809. (GASR, Nov.-Dec. 1809, Box 3: folder "Petitions- Divorce, etc.")

The Committee to whom was referred the petition of…Hall, Sally of Wake Co.…are of opinion that the clemency of the Legislature ought to be extended to [her] relief and recommend the accompanying Bill be passed into law. Concurred with by Senate (15 Dec.) and House (16 Dec.) (GASR, Nov.-Dec. 1809, Box 2: folder "JCR - Divorce & Alimony - Emancipation")

To secure to persons therein mentioned such property as they may hereafter acquire:…Hall, Sally of Wake Co., wife of Willoughby Hall…Read 3d time by House and Senate and ordered to be engrossed, 21 Dec. 1809. (GASR, Nov.-Dec. 1809, Box 2: folder "SB 15 Dec.")

254. **Heuster/Huster, Rebecca and husband, John.** Petition of Rebecca Heuster of Wilkes Co., NC. She intermarried with one John Heuster of Wilkes Co., who lived with your petitioner until she had

five children, and then, without any provocation, he abandoned her, leaving her without the common necessary s of life. Your petitioner's father did assist her to raise; her infant children and also gave her some property. As soon as the said John Heustis heard of your petitioner's father giving her support, he returned and has taken everything your petitioner possessed. Her father wishes to give her considerable property but will not do so. Prays a law to secure to her such property as she may hereafter acquire by will, gift, devise or otherwise. (GASR, Nov.-Dec. 1809, Box 3: folder "Petitions Divorce, etc.")

The Committee to whom were referred the petition of...Huster, Rebecca of Wilkes Co....are of opinion that the clemency of the Legislature ought to be extended to [her] relief and recommend the accompanying Bill be passed into law. (GASR, Nov.-Dec. 1809, Box 2: folder "JCR - Divorce & Alimony - Emancipation")

To secure to persons therein mentioned such property as they may hereafter acquire...Huster, Rebecca of Wilkes Co., wife of John Huster. Read 3d time by House and Senate and ordered to be engrossed, 21 Dec. 1809. (GASR, Nov.-Dec. 1809, Box 2: folder "SB 15 Dec.")

255. **Johnson, Nancy and husband, Thomas.** Petition of Nancy Johnson of Wake Co., NC, sheweth that she intermarried with a certain Thomas Johnson of said county on 3 Mar. 1805 and lived with him nearly four years, "during which time the said Thomas her husband was a constant attendant on all dissipated and vicious company he could find, taking no care to provide for the maintenance of a family, but dissipating and squandering his daily earnings among his vagabond Bachanalian companions, and finally, after having disposed of every species of property, which himself or your petitioner had; which with any colour he could sell or dispose of and wasting the money, he enlisted himself a Soldier, in the United States troops which were soon after removed from Raleigh to Washington in this State, & from thence, as your petitioner has been inform'd to or near the City of New Orleans -from whence your petitioner has no expectation of his returning; his conduct in many respects, having been such before he left this place as to induce a well grounded belief that if he was now discharged he would go elsewhere rather than return to Raleigh or any where near it.... Your petitioner further states to your Honours that her said Husband had so involved himself in debt before his enlistment and departure from Raleigh, that what little property she had left was immediately seized on by his creditors and has been sold for the payment of his debts - which tho' your petitioner is well assured & does believe were not half discharged by the proceeds of such sale...In which case any property which your petitioner may hereafter acquire by her industry...would be subject to the grasp of her said Husband's creditors..." Prays for Act securing to her such property as she may hereafter acquire. Dated December 1809, Raleigh. (GASR, Nov.-Dec. 1809, Box 3: folder "Petitions Divorce, etc.")

The Committee to whom was referred the following petitions:...Johnston, Nancy...praying for a divorce from bonds of matrimony are of opinion that it is inexpedient to grant the relief prayed for and recommend that the same be rejected. Read and concurred with by Senate and House, 19 Dec. 1809. (GASR, Nov.-Dec. 1809, Box 2: folder "JCR - Divorce & Alimony - Emancipation")

256. **Lane, William and wife, Martha (Pasteur).** Petition of William Lane states that he was joined in matrimony in the year 1791 with Martha Pasteur, but in the same year the said Martha absconded from his bed and board and refused to dwell with him. She still continues to absent herself from him. Your petitioner has not the least hope of a conciliation and prays for an Act to divorce him from his said wife. Dated 4 Dec. 1809. (GASR, Nov.-Dec. 1809, Box 3: folder "Petitions Divorce, etc.")

The Committee to whom was referred the following petitions:…Lane, William…praying for a divorce from bonds of matrimony are of opinion that it is inexpedient to grant the relief prayed for and recommend that the same be rejected. Read and concurred with by Senate and House, 19 Dec. 1809. (GASR, Nov.-Dec. 1809, Box 2: folder "JCR - Divorce & Alimony - Emancipation")

257.　**Lunceford/Lunsford, Abraham and wife, Eleanor (Humphr(e)y(s)).** Petition of Abram Lunsford of Burke Co., NC, sheweth "that he was married to a woman of the name of Elenor Humphrys, and she the sd. Elenor hath absconded My bed without any cause and hath been absent near two years and hath had a child by another man which is about seven months old…" Prays to be separated and divorced from his said wife Elenor. Affidavits in support of above petition by John Hendrexson, Samuel Hendrexson, Josiah Hendrexson, General Wilson and William Lunsford before a Justice of Peace in Burke Co., NC, 19 Oct. 1809, are attached. (GASR, Nov.-Dec. 1809, Box 3: folder "Petitions- Divorce, etc.")

Petition of Abraham Lunceford of Burke Co., NC, "sheweth that a little more than two years ago, he was married to Eleanor Humphrey, who remained with him only three weeks, after which she without cause or pretence whatsoever deserted his abode & obstinately refused to live any longer with your memorialist. Long since she has so deserted, she has had a child which is about seven months old, altho he had never bedded nor cohabited with his said wife during the term of her desertion…which [is] about two years." Prays for a divorce from the bond of matrimony. Dated 24 Oct. 1809 (GASR, Nov.-Dec. 1809, Box 3: folder "Petitions -Divorce, etc.")

The Committee to whom was referred the following petitions:…Lunceford, Abraham…praying for a divorce from bonds of matrimony are of opinion that it is inexpedient to grant the relief prayed for and recommend that the same be rejected. Read and concurred with by Senate and House, 19 Dec. 1809. (GASR, Nov.-Dec. 1809, Box 2: folder "JCR - Divorce & Alimony - Emancipation")

258.　**Murden/Murdin, Frances and husband, David.** Petition of Frances Murden/Murdin states she married David Murdin about December 1798. They lived together about nine years, and she became the mother of several children. Said David obtained by his marriage with your petitioner some handsome property. "By a constant round of dissipation and extravagance he was embarrassed by debts he had considerably lessened his property. He was cruel in the extreme to your petitioner by unmanly usage and savage barbarity." He ultimately fled and left me in the most dependent and wretched situation with three children. Your petitioner has just cause that this unfeeling monster will return from Georgia (to which State he fled in 1807 and took with him about eight negroes). By her manual labor, she has collected scanty necessaries of life. She would not trouble your Honorable Body, but she has lost her brother, friend and protector, the late unfortunate Col. Thomas Alston, during whose life she had no fears about her unfeeling husband returning. Prays for a law to secure to her what she presently possesses or may hereafter acquire, free from the debts or power of her said husband. (GASR, Nov.-Dec. 1809, Box 3: folder "Petitions- Divorce, etc.")

The Committee to whom was referred the petition of…Murden, Frances of Franklin Co.…are of opinion that the clemency of the Legislature ought to be extended to [her] and recommend the accompanying Bill be passed into law. Concurred with by Senate (15 Dec.) and House (16 Dec.) (GASR, Nov.-Dec. 1809, Box 2: folder "JCR - Divorce & Alimony - Emancipation")

To secure to persons therein mentioned such property as they may hereafter acquire:…Murdin, Frances of Franklin Co., wife of David Murdin…Read 3d time by House and Senate and ordered to be engrossed. (GASR, Nov.-Dec. 1809, Box 2: folder "SB 15 Dec.")

Divorces and Separations from Petitions to the North Carolina General Assembly from 1779

259. **Murray, Samuel, Jr., and wife, Elizabeth (Morrow).** Petition of Samuel Murray, Jr., of Buncombe Co., NC, sheweth that in the year 1798 he was joined in matrimony with Elizabeth Morrow of said county and state. The said Elizabeth left the bed and board of your petitioner, and every effort to bring about a reconciliation proved impractical. In 1806, your petitioner applied for and obtained a bill of alimony from the Honorable Legislature. In the year 1807, with the consent of said Elizabeth, a petition was forwarded to the General Assembly of North Carolina praying for a divorce to be granted to both parties, however the petition was lost or mislaid. In the meantime, she has left the State and has gone with her family connections to the State of Kentucky and never intends to return to North Carolina. Prays for a bill of divorce from his said wife. Subscribed to by forty-eight citizens of Buncombe Co., NC. (GASR, Nov.-Dec. 1809, Box 3: folder "Petitions-Divorce, etc.")

    The Committee to whom was referred the following petition...Murray, Samuel...praying for a divorce from bonds of matrimony are of opinion that it is inexpedient to grant the relief prayed for and recommend that the same be rejected. Read and concurred with by Senate and House, 19 Dec. 1809. (GASR, Nov.-Dec. 1809, Box 2: folder "JCR - Divorce & Alimony -Emancipation")

260. **Oel, Catherine and husband, Peter F.** Petition of Catherine Oel that she intermarried about five years ago with Peter F. Oel. They lived together a short time, but said Peter absconded from your petitioner for reasons unknown after stripping the house of the best of the property. At the time said husband left her, he was considerably in debt, and the property he lifted was to pay his debts. Since then, your petitioner has acquired some property and flattered herself - And she would be able to procure a comfortable subsistence, but her husband's creditors have come to sweep away what little has been accumulated. Prays that a law be passed to secure to her such property as she may hereafter acquire. Subscribed to by twelve residents of Lincoln Co., NC. (GASR, Nov.-Dec. 1809, Box 3: folder "Petitions- Divorce, etc.")

    The Committee to whom was referred the petition of...Oel, Catharine...are of opinion that the clemency of the Legislature ought to be extended to [her] relief and recommend the accompanying bill be passed into law. Concurred with by Senate (15 Dec.) and House (16 Dec.). (GASR, Nov.-Dec. 1809, Box 2: folder "JCR Divorce & Alimony - Emancipation")

    To secure to persons therein mentioned such property as they may hereafter acquire...Oel, Catharine, wife of Peter F. Oel of Lincoln Co.... Read 3d time by House and Senate and ordered to be engrossed, 21 Dec. 1809. (GASR, Nov.-Dec. 1809, Box 2: folder "SB 15 Dec.")

261. **Simpson, Sally and husband, Solomon.** Petition of Salley (x) Simpson sheweth that she married Solomon Simpson in May 1806, but sometime in February 1808. the said Solomon left your petitioner and has not returned. Prays for a law to secure to her what property she may hereafter acquire, free from any claim or demand of said Solomon Simpson as if they had never been married. (GASR, Nov.-Dec. 1809, Box 3: folder "Petitions- Divorce, etc.")

    The Committee to whom was referred the following petitions...Simpson, [blank]...praying for a divorce from bond of matrimony are of opinion that it is inexpedient to grant the relief prayed for and recommend that the same be rejected. Read and concurred with by Senate and House, 19 Dec. 1809. (GASR, Nov.-Dec. 1809. Box 2: folder "JCR - Divorce & Alimony - Emancipation")

262. **Smith, Alex and wife, Sarah (Dickson).** Petition of Alex Smith, Esq., of Ashe Co., NC, states that he married Miss Sarah Dickson in 1784 and lived with her for many years in domestic peace and pleasure. During this time, she had five children - all girls and "he never had the most distant thought they were not his own. He made use of Every means...to make them happy in Life, but in the year 1800, the said Sarah became base in her conduct...on the 14th day of April 1801. She eloped from your

petitioner's Bed and Board, not regarding the safety of her children, which your petitioner has carefully provided for ever since." When she eloped, she went off with a "Mallatoe" man…and has lived out of state ever since. Requests that his property be secured so that he may dispose of it at his own pleasure for the good of his children and requests a divorce from his wife Sarah. He wants a law to prevent her from claiming any right, title or interest to any part of his estate or property, real or personal. Dated 23 Nov. 1809. (GASR, Nov.-Dec. 1809, Box 3: folder "Petitions- Divorce, etc.")

The Committee to whom was referred the following petitions…Smith, Alexander…praying for a divorce from bonds of matrimony are of opinion that it is inexpedient to grant the relief prayed for and recommend that the same be rejected. Read and concurred with by Senate and House, 19 Dec. 1809.

263. **Smithwick, Edmund.** The Committee to whom was referred the following petition…Smithwick, Edmund…praying for a divorce from bonds of matrimony are of opinion that it is inexpedient to grant the relief prayed for and recommend that the same be rejected. Read and concurred with by Senate and House, 19 Dec. 1809. (GASR, Nov.-Dec. 1809, Box 2: folder "JCR - Divorce & Alimony - Emancipation")

264. **Stephens, Elizabeth and husband, Ebenezer.** Petition of Elizabeth Stephens [of Robeson Co.] states that sometime in the year 1803, "your petitioner Entermarried with a certain Ebenezer Stephens with whome she thought to spend her life in Joy and Felicity, but soon after to her sad disappointment and Grief, all her prospects was changed into Misery and he became the Subject of almost all the Vices and Dissipations of the world…however through many Dificulties she lived with the said Ebenezer about three years and by whom she had two children During which time he treated her with the utmost cruelty & contempt…he then left her with her two little Infants, Destitute of any means of support only the labour of herself and the Charity of her friends. Seeing that all hopes of a reconciliation is lost…and being young and in the bloom of life, she thinks her case to be a hard one, and therefore prays…your Honorable body…[to] grant her a divorce from…the said Ebenezer Stephens…" (GASR, Nov.-Dec. 1809, Box 3: folder "Petitions Divorce, etc.")

The Committee to whom was referred the following petitions…Stephens, Elizabeth…praying for a divorce from bonds of matrimony are of opinion that it is inexpedient to grant the relief prayed for and recommend that the same be rejected. Read and concurred with by Senate and House on 19 Dec. 1809. (GASR, Nov.-Dec. 1809, Box 2: folder "JCR - Divorce & Alimony - Emancipation")

265. **Stephney, William and wife, Elizabeth (Phillips).** Petition of William Stepney and Eli[za]beth (x) Phillips sheweth that they intermarried in 1807 "& that your female petitioner was at the time of her marrege & and [sic] is now Subject to a Certain Complaint which Was unknown to your male petitioner at the time of His intermarriage with her - this being the case it Renders your petitioners altogether unhappy to be confined to each other…" Pray an act to "Brake the bond of marrage…" [Perquimans Co., NC?] (GASR, Nov.-Dec. 1809, Box 3: folder "Petitions - Divorce, etc.")

The Committee to whom was referred the following petitions…Stepney, Wm…. praying for a divorce from the bonds of matrimony are of opinion that it is inexpedient to grant the relief prayed for and recommend that the same be rejected. Read and concurred with by Senate and House, 19 Dec. 1809. (GASR, Nov.-Dec. 1809, Box 2: folder "JCR - Divorce & Alimony - Emancipation")

266. **Utley, Young and wife, Polly.** Committee of Divorce and Alimony to whom was referred the Petition of Young Utley of the County of Wake praying to be divorced from his wife Pol[l]y report that your committee have maturely considered the Petitioner's prayer and examined the evidence adduced

Divorces and Separations from Petitions to the North Carolina General Assembly from 1779

in support thereof. They are of opinion that Polly, the wife of said Young Utley, has committed an act inconsistent with the matrimonial vow and contrary to the purposes for which it was instituted: therefore recommend that the Act accompanying this report, entitled "A Bill to divorce Young Utley of the County of Wake from his wife Polly" be passed into a law. In Senate, 4 Dec. 1809, read and resolved nonconcurrence with said report. (GASR, Nov.-Dec. 1809, Box 1: folder "Senate Bills, Dec. 4")

267.   **Warren, Mary and husband, William.** Petition of Mary Warren of Caswell Co. sheweth that sometime in 1805 she intermarried with William Warren in hopes of enjoying the comforts of a married life. To her great mortification, she soon found a man very much in debt, and the property she possessed prior to her marriage was actually sold by him. He finally left her with one child in a distressed situation. She prays for a law to secure to her such property as she may hereafter acquire. (GASR, Nov.-Dec. 1809, Box 3: folder "Petitions- Divorce, etc.")

The Committee to whom was referred the petition of…Warren, Mary of Caswell Co…. are of opinion that the clemency of the Legislature ought to be extended to [her] relief and recommend the accompanying Bill be passed into law. (GASR, Nov.-Dec. 1809, Box 2: folder "JCR - Divorce & Alimony - Emancipation")

To secure to persons therein mentioned such property as they may hereafter acquire…Warren, Mary of Caswell Co., wife of William Warren…Read 3d time by House and Senate and authorized to be engrossed, 21 Dec. 1809. (GASR, Nov.-Dec. 1809, Box 2: folder "SB 15 Dec.")

268.   **Wood, William, Sr.** Petition of William Wood, Sr., of Sampson Co., NC, presented by James Mathis, states that "your petitioner in his youthful days married the wife of his choice by whom he had a numerous progeny of children whose tender endearments greatly increased his domestic comforts; that your petitioner and his said wife lived together in perfect harmony, each contributing their utmost efforts to rear up their children so as to render them useful and worthy members of society, and then discharge that duty enjoined on them by the laws of nature. But the time at length arived when your petitioner's head was silvered o'er with age, that it please the devine deposer [?] of events to summon to the ma[n]sions of eternal rest the wife of his earliest and latest affections - Your petitioner thus left alone, for his children had arived at that age when it became necessary they should pursue their own separate interests; became desirous to procure a companion who could contribute to the comforts of his declining years and measurably smooth his passage to the grave; prudence he conceived directed this selection, as he chose one old like himself in whom the passion of youth must have long since subsided: neither was your petitioner guided in his choice by avaricious motives, the lady being perfectly destitute of fortune. It is with regret therefore your petitioner finds himself imperiously called upon by that duty he owes to himself and his children to state to your honorable Body that his wife Elisabeth in a verry short time after her intermarriage with your petitioner did without any justifiable cause whatever elope from his bed and board, and cannot by any persuasions be again induced to return." Prays that his melancholy situation be seriously considered and pass a law securing to your petitioner free from all claim of his said wife Elizabeth the property which he now posseses or which he may hereafter acquire in order that his estate ultimately descend to the children of his first wife. (GASR, Nov.-Dec. 1809, Box 3: folder "Petitions - Divorce, etc.")

The Committee to whom was referred the following petition…Wood, William…praying for a divorce from bonds of matrimony are of opinion that it is inexpedient to grant the relief prayed for and recommend that the same be rejected. Read and concurred with by Senate and House, 19 Dec. 1809. (GASR, Nov.-Dec. 1809, Box 2: folder "JCR - Divorce & Alimony - Emancipation")

269. **Younger, Rebecca and husband, John.** Petition of Rebecca Younger. Her husband, John Younger, left her in 1804 in a helpless and defenseless situation with five children to support and maintain. Prays for an act to entitle her to property as she may hereafter accumulate and acquire and to what she has already acquired. Subscribed to by seventeen supporters circa November 1809. (GASR, Nov.-Dec. 1809, Box 3: folder "Petitions- Divorce, etc.")
The Committee to whom was referred the petition of…Younger, Rebecca…are of opinion that the clemency of the Legislature ought to be extended to [her] relief and recommend the accompanying bill to be passed into law. (GASR, Nov.-Dec. 1809, Box 2: folder "JCR - Divorce & Alimony -Emancipation")

To secure to persons therein mentioned such property as they may hereafter acquire…Younger, Rebecca, wife of John Younger of Chatham Co.…Read 3d time by House and Senate and ordered to be engrossed, 21 Dec. 1809. (GASR, Nov.-Dec. 1809, Box 2: folder "SB 15 Dec.")

1810

270. **Bizzell (Bezzell), Elizabeth and husband, Isaac.** Petition of Elizabeth Bezzell of Sampson County states that she intermarried with Isaac Bezzell in 1804 with whom she removed to the State of Tennessee. She lived with him until a short time before the birth of her child, which was born about twelve months after her marriage. During this time your petitioner discharged with fidelity and affection the duties of a wife "and entertained a hope that she would be able to spend her days in peace and quietness and rear up her offspring to usefulness, but the hopes of Your petitioner were all blasted by the gloominess and discontent of which her husband was pervaded...the cause of which when interrogated he assigned to his connection with her - stating that he had not received as large a fortune as he himself had calculated on." Your petitioner hoped that by her affectionate conduct and unwearied attention, she would affect a change in her husband as well as endure with patience "the intolerable sufferings imposed by her husband, until he made a deliberate attempt to poison your petitioner - the wife of his Bosom and the mother of his Babe..." She fled from his house and "returned to her fathers who resided in the County of Sampson in this State..." She has employed her time since the separation in raising her infant son, the only issue of this unfortunate marriage. Her husband has taken the wife of Micajah Musgrove of Wayne County with whom he lives and [they] have had one more child. No prospect remains that your petitioner can ever again be united with her said husband - "a man whose baseness and turpitude know no bounds." Prays for a law to divorce her from her said husband, Isaac Bezzell. (GASR, Nov.-Dec. 1810, Box 2: folder "JCR (Divorce and Alimony - Finance)").

271. **Bracewell, Isaac and wife. Nancy (Low).** Petition of Isaac (x) Bracewell of Edgecombe County, North Carolina, represents that he married Nancy Low some years ago and enjoyed happiness and content for a considerable length of time. About seven years ago, without just cause or provocation, the said Nancy left his house "and has ever since lived in open and notorious adultery extending her favors (if since then they can be called) to all, without distinction of color." Prays an act of separation from said Nancy. (GASR, Nov.-Dec. 1810, Box 2: folder "JCR (Divorce and Alimony - Finance)").

272. **Bryan, Nathaniel and wife, Eleanor/Nelly (Singletary).** Memorial of Nathaniel Bryan of Bladen County, North Carolina, sheweth that on 5 January 1809, "he was, as he supposed, lawfully married unto Eleanor Singletary of the state and county aforesaid, daughter of Ithamon Singletary. He lived with the said Eleanor until 9 April 1810, notwithstanding he was fully concerned in a short time after marriage that she, the said Eleanor, laboured under an imbecility of the body which totally disqualified her...to the marriage state, and which naturally result from the force of Conjugal affections." A confirmation of your memorialist's concern is shown by the accompanying depositions of Mary Chesher and Elizabeth Newberry. A separation did arise from mutual consent of the said Eleanor and your memorialist. Prays for a divorce from said Eleanor.

[Attachment:] Deposition of Elizabeth Newberry and Mary Chesher, midwives, of Bladen County, North Carolina, state that they examined Eleanor Bryan (formerly Eleanor Singletary), wife of

Nathaniel Bryan, on 1 April 1810 and found her to have a natural defect which disqualified her in the exercise of those duties related to the marriage state. Sworn before Amos Richardson and Isaac Wright, Justices of Peace for Bladen County, North Carolina, 3 November 1810.

[Attachment:] Certificate of Dr. Alexander McDowell that he has examined Nelly Bryan, otherwise Nelly Singletary, and found her an incapable person to perform the duties of a wife. Signed at "Elizabeth 16th 1810." (GASR, Nov.-Dec. 1810, Box 3: folder "Petitions- Divorce").

273. **Capehart, Rosan(n)a and husband, John.** Petition of Rosana Capehart of Burke County, North Carolina, represents that her husband, John Capehart, without any disagreement or cause of dissatisfaction known to her, has deserted her and removed to New Orleans or some of the adjacent settlements, "having taken off everything which was not afterwards taken by execution." His pretence when about to remove was that of viewing a place to settle, and he is now about nine years absent. Sometime after his desertion, your memorialist had furnished herself with many necessaries of life by her own industry, but a fire destroyed all of these. She is nearly sixty years of age, [and] her children have left her. She prays for a law allowing her the exclusive right to such property as she may acquire. Dated 26 October 1810. Subscribed to by five citizens; of Burke County, North Carolina. (GASR, Nov.-Dec. 1810, Box 3: folder "Petitions-Divorce").

274. **Crowder, Mary and husband, Elijah.** Memorial of Mary Crowder of Buncombe County, North Carolina, states that her husband, Elijah Crowder, deserted her about three years ago and removed himself to Kentucky. Your memorialist is left desolate and unable to protect herself or any property she may acquire by her own industry. Prays for a law to secure to her such property as she may hereafter acquire. Dated 5 October 1810. (GASR, Nov.-Dec. 1810, Box 2: folder "JCR (Divorce and Alimony -Finance)").

275. **Davis, Eady and husband, Lewis.** Petition of Eady Davis of Pitt County, North Carolina, represents that "about twenty years ago, she intermarried with a certain Lewis Davis with whom she lived many years, and by whom she had three children and calculated upon enjoying that felicity which is the desire of all who enter into that State - but in this pleasing expectation she was entirely disappointed..." Her husband, Lewis Davis, left her in a state of indigence and want, and she had to raise her children by her own industry. Her said husband has taken another woman and No hope remains of his ever contributing to the least degree to the support of herself or her children. Prays for a law to secure to tier such property as she may hereafter acquire. (GASR, Nov.-Dec. 1810, Box 2: folder "JCR (Divorce and Alimony -Finance)").

276. **Davis, Mildred and husband, William.** Memorial of Mildred Davis of Buncombe County, North Carolina, represents that her husband, William Davis, "took the chief of our property and removed himself to the State of Kentucky and there married About two years and then Returned to the same Segment and sold and wasted the ballance of the property & tooke Annother woman and I am informed is living in Kentucky about twelve months since...now your memorialist is left disolate and unable to protect herself or any property she may by hir industry Afluire." Dated 5 October 1810. (GASR, Nov.-Dec. 1810, Box 2: folder "JCR (Divorce and Alimony -Finance)").

277. **Herring, Susanna(h) and husband, Frederick.** Petition of Susannah Herring [of probably Sampson County, North Carolina] sheweth that she was intermarried with Frederick Herring and lived with him for twelve years, during which time they had six children. "Your petitioner has now to lament that the beneficial practice of indulging to an excess in the use of ardent spirits which her husband

Divorces and Separations from Petitions to the North Carolina General Assembly from 1779

unfortunately contracted produced the ruin of himself, your petitioner and their infant children. [A] very considerable fortune of which they were possessed first fell a sacrifice to his intemperance, and your petitioner found herself & her six little children thrown from a state of affluence to the most abject poverty. Your petitioner found herself with her little children driven from their home to seek protection from the humanity of his relations. Two years have now expired and no prospect remains of her ever being able again to live with her husband. Your petitioner has an aged mother with whom she and her children now live. Prays for a law to secure to her what property she may hereafter acquire." (GASR, Nov.-Dec. 1810, Box 2: folder "JCR (Divorce and Alimony - Finance)").

278. **Holtzclaw, Susannah and husband, Nathan.** Petition of Susannah Holtzclaw of Robeson County, North Carolina, represents that about six years ago she intermarried with Nathan Holtzclaw and by whom she had two children. Her said husband was committed to Hillsborough Jail for passing counterfeit money and was sentenced to two years imprisonment. After his release, he left your petitioner for parts unknown. When he was committed to jail, he was considerably in debt, and the property he left has been sold to satisfy the same. She has made case of every execution to procure by her industry a competency to raise and support her children, but all she acquires is subject to the payment of his debts. Prays for a Law to secure what property she may hereafter acquire free from the claims of her husband or any other person. (GASR, Nov.-Dec. 1810, Box 2: folder "JCR (Divorce and Alimony - Finance)").

279. **Hudson, Eleanor/Ellen and husband, Jacob.** Petition of Ellen Hudson states that for nine years she was joined in the bonds of wedlock with Mr. Jacob Hudson, who has from the space of two years absented himself "from me and his children…and finally Has Deprived us of Every necessary Comfort of Life and had Commited other wrongs Highly derogatory to me in a Parental Station…and is also well known to the gentlemen who represents the County of Cabarrus at the present Session [and] who have been acquainted with my ancestors and myself from an Early period of my life…" Said Mr. Hudson took his final farewell on 13 October saying he would not return for some years. Prays for a bill of Divorce from said Mr. Hudson. Oath of James Daugherty before P. Barringer, Justice of Peace for Cabarrus County, North Carolina, 29 October 1810, that Jacob Hudson told the deponent last month that he, the said Hudson, would be damned to everlasting perdition if he would ever cohabit with his wife, Eleanor Hudson, to the day of his Death and likewise that the said Hudson had kept a woman in the State of Tennessee the time he absconded himself from his wife Eleanor and that she was pregnant to him and that he intended to return to the said woman. Oath of Jno. B. Misters before P. Barringer, Justice of Peace of Cabarrus County, North Carolina, 2 November 1810: Jacob Hudson repeatedly told him that while said Hudson was absent from his wife Ellen in the western country, "he had kept three women at times and that one of them was pregnant by him, i.e., a certain Miss Peggy Hinsley or Hinslars, and that the said Peggy and her friends had him arrested by an officer, and that he had no alternative but to marry her the said Peggy or go to gaol…he then told her that if she would take up the papers from the officer that he would take her away into some other county and marry her, and he the said Hudson also told this deponent that he did carry away the said Peggy a considerable distance from her parents under these impressions, and finally awaited his opportunity to leave her which he performed by going to water their horse one morning, and by that strategem came off and left her in the situation which he mentioned to me that I have aluded to and the said Hudson has frequently boasted in my hearing of his success in similar occasions…and told me that the child the said Miss Peggy charged him with was his and that he had told her what name to give it agreeable to its sex, and he the said Hudson has also told me since his return from the western country that he had learned by letter that the said Peggy was delivered of a son which he did not scruple to be his, and this deponent further sayeth that said Hudson told him that since

his return from the western country which was on the 26th of deer. 1809 at night, he had not had with Ellen his wife as a Husband, and this deponent says that he friendly recommended him at different times to foresake his disapated way of living and go to house keeping, to which the said Hudson replyed that would be d...d if he would live with his wife Ellen again as long as he lived.... this deponent says this conversation took place after Hudson's return from the western country after he had been absent from his family fifteen months...under pretence of going to Salisbury or at furthest to Salem...which would have been performed in three or four days...the said Hudson has frequently in the hearing of this deponent said that he intended to travel again or sail to the West Indies and there marry a fortune, and on the evening of the 13th October 1810 in presence of Messrs. Russel, Parks, Edington & this deponent the said Hudson told this deponent that he was determined to go off...and would not see him for some years, and perhaps never and bade this deponent a final farewell...This deponent further sayeth that he was informed by a Mr. Richd. Brandon on the 15th of October 1810 that he had seen said Hudson and spoke with him on the main Road leading from Concord to Salisbury and that he said he was gone..." (All above from GASR, Nov.-Dec. 1810, Box 2: folder "JCR (Divorce and Alimony Finance)").

280. **James, Nancy and husband, George.** Petition of Nancy James of Surry County, North Carolina, that "George James, a man descended from a good family married a wife descended from a respectable family & once possessed of a good living...by his Intemperance, has spent all his property, & his wife by her industry has acquired a little property to support their children...he has at length become so Illnatured as to threaten the life of his wife & has drove her of_ to Seek her own living. We the citizens of Surry County & neighbors of sd. James do pray your Honorable Body to take into consideration the pitiable case of Nancy James, wife of sd. George James & grant her relief by passing an act to Enable her to...possess such property as she may hereafter acquire." Signed by thirty citizens of Surry County, North Carolina. (GASR, Nov.-Dec. 1810, Box 2: folder "JCR (Divorce and Alimony - Finance)").

281. **Lowe, Eve and husband, Thomas.** Petition of Eve Lowe states that husband Thomas Lowe of Rowan County, North Carolina, has absconded after "Taking away with Him all the property he was possessed with Leaving me with Six children...three of which is not able as yet to work for their Support also leaving many Creditors that will take away from me what I may in future Earn by my labor." Prays for an act securing to her what property she may hereafter acquire. Dated 1 August 1810. Subscribed to by one hundred nineteen residents of Rowan County, North Carolina. (GASR, Nov.-Dec. 1810, Box 2: folder "JCR (Divorce and Alimony - Finance)").

282. **Murray, Samuel, Jr. and wife, Elizabeth (Morrow).** Petition of Samuel Murray, Jr., of Buncombe County, North Carolina, sheweth that in the year 1798, he married Elizabeth Morrow of the same state and county and lived with her until 1805. In that year, the said Elizabeth left his bed and board "without any known cause or provocation given on the part of your Petitioner...", and every effort to bring about a reconciliation proved impracticable. In 1806, your petitioner obtained a Bill of Alimony (Laws of North Carolina, 1806, Chapter 114, pages 53, 54). In 1807, your petitioner and the said Elizabeth forwarded a petition to Your Honorable Body praying for a Bill of Divorcement to take place, but by some means it was lost or mislaid. Since that time, the said Elizabeth has left the State of North Carolina and gone with her family connections to the State of Kentucky and intends never to return. Prays for a divorce. Subscribed to by the signatures of twenty-nine residents of Buncombe County, North Carolina. (GASR, Nov.-Dec. 1810, Box 2: folder "JCR (Divorce and Alimony - Finance)").

Divorces and Separations from Petitions to the North Carolina General Assembly from 1779

283. **Pannel (Pannal), Martha and husband, William.** Petition of Martha Pannel of Granville County, North Carolina, represents that she was intermarried with William Pannel about eighteen years ago, who at that time possessed considerable property, and she lived with him for nine or ten years in terms of the greatest friendship. However, said husband gave into incessant intoxication, spent all his property and still continues in his ruinous course. "Even the little earnings of the daily labour of your petitioner are seized upon to pay the expenses of his midnight riots." Prays for a law to secure to her what property she may hereafter acquire. (GASR, Nov.-Dec. 1810, Box 2: folder "JCR (Divorce and Alimony - Finance)").

284. **Potter, Archibald and wife, Lemender (Harris).** Petition of Archibald Potter of Franklin, Williamson County, Tennessee, sheweth that in or about the year 1796, he was married to a certain Lemender Harris of Granville County, North Carolina[24] with whom he peaceably and quietly lived until about 1801, "at which time for causes not in his power to control, and which were entirely irreconcilable to his feelings, he absented himself from her & has since resided in the State of Tennessee." He begs to suggest "that his departure did not result from any dissatisfaction incident to the connection but from a full & entire conviction on his part, derived as well from the confessions of his wife freely and without force or coercion used, as from the General opinions & belief of the neighbourhood, that the said Lemender was a lewd, licentious & adulterous woman-" Since the period of his departure he has principally resided at Franklin, Tennessee, and he has had no communication with the said Lemender. She "has still continued in her incestuous and adulterous practices, and that as he has been credibly informed, she had three children born of her body since his said departure…which is a fact he believes known to some of the members of your honorable body, particularly those from the County of Granville." He entreats the Honorable Body not to "view his voluntary seperation as affording a plausible pretext for the rejection of his petition; his unducement alone was that he might be relieved from a connection clouded & made wretched by unpardonable prostitution which destroyed his peace of mind and marred every effort of his life." He rests full confidence that "your honorable body will extend that relief which the equity & justice of his entreaty may seem to require and give claim to…He solicits your Honorable body thoroughly to investigate it…" (GASR, Nov.-Dec. 1810, Box 2: folder "JCR (Divorce and Alimony -Finance)").

285. **Smithwick, Edmund and wife, Mary (Walker).**
 (a).   Letter from Edmund Smithwick, Sr., to Mrs. Mary Smithwick, Martin County, North Carolina, dated 23 September 1809: "Madam - Intending to present to the Legislature of this State a petition for the purpose of obtaining a Divorce from the bonds of matrimony contracted with you. I hereby notify you that the Depositions of Witnesses in support of the facts stated in the said petition will be taken before Ebenezer Smithwick, Esquire, one of the justices of the peace in and for this County or some other justice at the following times and places, viz., on the first Saturday in next month at two o'clock in the afternoon at the House of Jesse Peal near where Ebenezer Smithwick resides and on the second Saturday in next month at the same time of the day at the house of Solomon Jones in Jamestown at which several times and places you may attend if you think proper, from your friend…" [Note at bottom in different handwriting:] "the persons that is to be sworn on this acation is Soloman Jones and his wife and othirs" [On reverse:] "Personally Appeared before me Baldy Smithwick & after being sworn Saith that he delivered a copy of this notice to Mrs. Mary Smithwick on the fourth day of the present Month October 14th 1809…at the same time She Said She Should not attend…" /s/ Thos. Hyman, J.P. (GASR, Nov.-Dec. 1810, Box 3: folder "Petitions-Divorces").

---

24   Marriage Bond of Granville Co., NC, for this marriage is dated 5 June 1795

1810 Session

(b).   Petition of Edmund Smithwick Snr. sheweth that between twelve and thirteen years ago, he was lawfully married to Mary Walker with whom he lived upwards of seven years. During this time he faithfully and justly discharged all the duties incumbent upon him by the marriage vow. Despite the tenderness and affection uniformly manifested to her by your petitioner, the said Mary, "after repeated wanton and unprovoked exertions of a restless, discontented and ungovernable temper towards him, in the month of February in the year of our Lord one thousand eight hundred and four, in violation of her plighted faith, without any reasonable cause, and without even the knowledge of your petitioner, during his absence from home on his lawful and necessary business, withdrew herself from his bed and board taking with her, not only all the effects which originally belonged to her, but also a considerable part of your petitioner's own property…" Since her elopement, she has lived separate from your petitioner, and although asked to return, she has refused to do so without assigning any reason for not living with him. Your petitioner, thus injured, is compelled by duty he owes himself and his children by a former marriage to appeal to you to grant him a divorce from his said wife Mary. Subscribed to by the signatures of one hundred fifty-one citizens of Martin County, North Carolina. (GASR, Nov.-Dec. 1810, Box 3: folder "Petitions-Divorces").

(c).   Deposition of Martin (x) Griffin that he hath been acquainted with Edmd. Smithwick Senr. for many years (say twenty)- that he was Raised within three miles of his house, and frequently worked for him- that he never knew or heard of his abusing or ill treating his former or present wife- that he understood that She…Mary Smithwick, after L[e]aving him contracted debts to a considerable amount which the said Smithwick had to pay…" Sworn to before Thomas Hyman, J.P. for Martin County at Jamestown, 14 October 1809, at the house of Solomon Jones. (GASR, Nov.-Dec. 1810, Box 3: folder "Petitions-Divorces").

(d).   Deposition of David Jones states that he was well acquainted with Edmund Smithwick, Senr., for a number of years and lived with him as a hireling five years. He never knew or heard of said Edmund misusing or ill treating his former or present wife. Sometime before Mary Smithwick left her husband, said Edmund, she told your petitioner that she intended to leave said husband. Your petitioner asked her for what cause, for he was a kind husband. She replied that she had no fault to find with him, for he was a kind man to her but "would not join him against his children and for that reason She wanted to go away…" Shortly after, she did go away and asked this deponent to let her have a horse to carry a load. He told her he had no cart and asked her if she could hold the property if she got it away. She said if she could get it in the hands of James Bennet or Mr. Walker, she believed she could. This was in the Fall season between four and six years ago. She offered for sale for cash in hand- corn, meat, fat, flax or cotton. This deponent asked her her reason for it, and she replied she was going away, and he believes she used every means in her power to sacrifice the interest of the said Smithwick. Sworn to before Thomas Hyman, J.P. for Martin County, North Carolina, at house of Solomon Jones, Jameston, 14 October 1809. (GASR, Nov.-Dec. 1810, Box 3: folder "Petitions-Divorces").

(e).   Deposition of Solomon Jones states that he has been acquainted with Edmd. Smithwick Sr. for thirty-five or forty years and [said Smithwick] has been a peacable, orderly and good citizen during this time. Eleven or twelve years ago, he [the said Edmund] "entermaryed with Mary Walker whom he cohabited with for [nearly] Seven Year all of which time he believes the Said Edmond Treated the Said Mary in a friendly maner and that he hath heard the Said Mary Say that it was on the acount of the Said Edmonds Children that She was disatisfyed…That about five years ago the Said Mary Smithwick in the night time applyed to one of his Sons to help her move property at which he Solomon was much disatisfyed and that the Said Edmd. Got a Search Warrint and applyed to him as an officer to obtain the Property if to be found - and after the most diligent Search the Said Mary had So Conected the property that the said Solomon could not find it (or but a Small part) and she said that if the Matur Could be droped at that, the property Should come back, and that the proceedings of the warrant was droped, but never knew of any property being Returned - and this deponent further Saith that the said Mary hath Continued...to Seperate herself from the said Edmd." Sworn to before James Carmer, J.P. for Martin County, North Carolina, 28 October 1809. (GASR, Nov.-Dec. 1810, Box 3: folder "Petitions-Divorces").

(f). Deposition of Esther (x) Jones, wife of Solomon Jones and of lawful age, states that "she has been well acquainted with Edmund Smithwick Sr. and Mary his wife for a number of years...that for a considerable time before and at the time of the elopement of the said Mary was not owing to any mistreatment of the said Edmund...on the contrary after the said Mary left him she has heard her say that the only reason of it was that he would not put away his children by a former wife, that the said Edmund was not at home when the said Mary eloped, and this deponent at the time heard the said Mary say she wished to get away before her husband the said Edmund returned home...the said Mary called at this deponents house about midnight and hired one of Deponents sons to assist her in getting away the property of the said Edmund which she took with her saying that she was afraid the creature she had with her in a cart would give out before she got to where she was going. This according to the best of Deponents knowledge and belief happened about five years ago since which the said Mary has never lived with the said Edmund. That since the said Mary's elopement Deponent has seen her and asked her if she intended ever to return and live with the said Edmund again and the said Mary replied that she would never do so..." Sworn to before James Carmer, J.P. for Martin County, at house of Solomon Jones, Jameston, 28 October 1809. (GASR, Nov.-Dec. 1810, Box 3: folder "Petitions-Divorces".

(g). Deposition of Elizabeth (x) Hatfield of lawful age states that she was present where a notice was handed to Mrs. Mary Smithwick...that she was asked whether she intended to attend...her answer was- I shall not give myself any trouble about it for if it is his desire to be divorced I have no objection. I am perfectly willing & I would thank you if you see Mr. Smithwick to tell him the same and that I shall not attend. Sworn to before James Burroughs, J.P. for Martin County, North Carolina, 1 November 1809. (GASR, Nov.-Dec. 1810, Box 3: folder "Petitions-Divorces").

(h). Memorial of Mary Smithwick, late wife of Edmond Smithwick of Martin County, North Carolina. Your memorialist, Mary Smithwick, and her said husband, Edmund Smithwick, have been separated from each other for several years, and both are equally desirous and willing to be divorced from each other. Prays that this case be taken under consideration. Dated 6 November 1810, witnessed by Elizabeth Sutton, and sworn to before Benja. Fessenden, J.P. (GASR, Nov.-Dec. 1810, Box 3: folder "Petitions-Divorces").

286. **Townsend, Thomas and wife, Sally (Stewart).** Memorial of Isaac Alexander, John Harris and other subscribers in behalf of Thomas Townsend, an orphan whose father and mother died in Mecklenburg County, North Carolina. When said Thomas was a minor, a single woman by the name of Sally Stewart (supporting the role of a courtesan) claimed that the said Thomas had made her pregnant. We, your subscribers, say that the said Thomas Townsend "is of unimpeachable character, a youth remarkable for his innocent simplicity of manners and goodness of disposition." We are alarmed of this charge of the said Sally Stewart, which charge he denies. The said Thomas thought it advisable from the council of his friends to remove from the county and state. Accordingly, "on his way to Georgia was overtaken (in the District of York and State of South Carolina) by this Sally Stewart aided and accompanied by a certain John Clark." They threatened and alarmed the said Thomas so as to compel him to go with them to the Magistrate of the said district and against his will, then expressed before the Magistrate to marry the said Sally Stewart. The said Thomas declared that he never could nor never would live with her, but they were married, and he was not twenty-one years of age. They came back to Mecklenburg County, but three days after the marriage ceremony, the said Thomas Townsend left the neighborhood of this

woman, Sally Stewart, and declared that he would never live with her and was still under twenty-one years of age. We pray that a divorce be granted said Thomas. (GASR, Nov.-Dec. 1810, Box 2: folder "JCR (Divorce and Alimony Finance)").

287. **Utley, Young and wife, Mary (Woodard).** Young Utley of Wake County, North Carolina, represents that about three years ago, he was united in wedlock to Mary Woodard of the same county. Sometime after the marriage, the said Mary was delivered of a black child and soon after removed herself to Tennessee, where your petitioner has been informed that she cohabits with a man of colour. Your petitioner represents that he is a young man about twenty-five years of age, and though of obscure birth and condition, has sustained an upright character and endeavoured to discharge his duty as became a quiet citizen. Prays for a divorce from his said wife. (GASR, Nov.-Dec. 1810, Box 3: folder "Petkions-Divorce").

288. **Walker, Elizabeth and husband, Joseph.** Petition of Elizabeth "Betsy" Walker [probably of Surry County, North Carolina], wife of Joseph Walker, states that said husband "hath for the space of eleven years ceased, to abide with me as head & guide..." She had hoped that he would have left her with some part of the small estate they had gathered but instead let her shift for herself. Prays an act to secure to her what property she may hereafter acquire. Subscribed to by seven citizens [apparently all of Surry County, North Carolina]. (GASR, Nov.-Dec. 1810, Box 2: folder "JCR (Divorce and Alimony - Finance)").

289. **Wilkinson, Barbara (x) and husband, John.** Memorial of Barbara (x) Wilkinson [of Duplin County, North Carolina] sheweth that after the death of her former husband, Robert Dickson, his will left her in comfortable and opulent circumstances in life. He had left her his manor plantation with the buildings, orchards etc. during her life. He had left her certain slaves, stock of every kind, household and kitchen furniture of every necessary kind with provisions etc., independent at her own disposal. During the term of her widowhood (which continued for several years), she had improved and increased her stock and lived in affluence and independence, "until by the Insinuating address of Doctor John Wilkinson, a young man, then in good credit, and much Esteemed by those who were acquainted with him, and by the advice of her friends, she was prevailed upon to Intermarry with him. Her felicity was of short duration. She found herself in many respects treated more like his Servant than his wife. The Property she possessed Previous to her manage with him was sold or changed to his own use and her Exclusion. And in February 1809, he finally left her destitute of almost every means of support- without Provisions, scarcely a Bed to lie on, or cloaths to wear. He carried off all that was worth taking out of the House. Your Memorialist is now Reduced to Indigent Circumstances in life, having little more than her House and Plantation left her by her former husband..." Prays for a consideration to secure her in the future from being again stripped of her all by the said John Wilkinson. Dated 20 November 1810, Duplin County, North Carolina. Subscribed to by the signatures of six residents of Duplin County, North Carolina, who further state that "it is almost two years since [Dr. Wilkinson] left her and went towards the Western Country, Richly loaded and Seven or Eight Slaves, leaving his said wife indigent and base of almost every Necessary of life." (GASR, Nov.-Dec. 1810, Box 2: folder "JCR (Divorce and Alimony -Finance)").

290. **Wren, Sarah and husband, Howell.** Petition of Sarah Wren of Nash County, North Carolina, sheweth that she was married about the year 1795 to Howell Wren and was then possessed of a good and substantial property in land and negroes etc., all of which her said husband has wasted and destroyed by

extravagance and dissipation, "after which, in 1805, he deserted & left me to struggle with the world and went to the State of Tennessee as your petitioner has reason to believe -not having seen him since his departure." Prays a consideration so as to secure what property she now has, or may acquire hereafter not subject to the debts of the said Howell Wren. Dated 21 November 1810. (GASR, Nov.-Dec. 1810, Box 2: folder "JCR (Divorce and Alimony - Finance)").

291.   **Reference A.**
A Bill to Divorce Young Utley of Wake County from his wife Mary. In House, 18 December, passed. In Senate, 18 December, rejected. (GASR, Nov.-Dec. 1810, Box 2: folder "SB, Dec. 13").

292.   **Reference B.**
A Bill to secure to persons therein mentioned such property as they may hereafter acquire: Mary Crowder of Buncombe County, wife of Elijah; Susanna Herring, wife of Frederick Herring; Nancy James of Surry County, wife of George; Sarah Wren of Nash County, wife of Howell; Barbara Wilkinson of Duplin County, wife of John; Betsey Walker, wife of Joseph; Susannah Holtzclaw of Robeson County, wife of Nathan; Eady Davis of Pitt County, wife of Lewis; Eve Low of Rowan County, wife of Thomas; Mildred Davis of Buncombe County, wife of William; Elizabeth Bizzell, wife of Isaac Bizzell of Sampson County; Rachel McGonnigold, wife of Eli of Guilford County. In Senate, 13 December, and passed; in House, 15 December, amended and passed. 21 December 1810 - read third time, passed and ordered to be engrossed. (GASR, Nov.-Dec. 1810, Box 2: folder "SB, Dec. 13").

293.   **Reference C.**
The Committee of Divorce and Alimony to whom was referred the following petitions for Divorce, to wit: Samuel Murray Jr. of Buncombe County, Thomas Townsend of Mecklenburg County, Eleanor Hudson, Elizabeth Bezzell, Isaac Bracewell, Betsy Fulwood, Archibald Potter, Edmund Smithwick and Michael Shoftner...are of opinion that it is inexpedient and highly improper to grant the relief prayed for and recommend said petitions be rejected. In Senate [and House], 13 December - read and [concurred in]. (GASR, Nov.-Dec. 1810, Box 2: folder "JCR (Divorce and Alimony - Finance)").

294.   **Reference D.**
The Committee of Divorce and Alimony to whom was referred the following petitions, to wit: Mary Crowder, Susanna Herring, Nancy James, Sarah Wren, Barbara Wilkinson, Betsey Walker, Susanna Holtzclaw, Eady Davis, Eve Lowe, Mildred Davis and Martha Pannal - praying a law to be passed securing what property they may hereafter acquire report that your Committee are of opinion that they are justly entitled to the clemency of the Legislature and to the relief respectively prayed for and recommend that the Bill accompanying this report entitled "A Bill to Secure to the Persons therein mentioned such property as they may hereafter acquire" be passed into law. In Senate, 13 December, and House, 15 December, read and concurred with. (GASR, Nov.-Dec. 1810, Box 2: folder "JCR (Divorce and Alimony -Finance)").

295.   **Reference E.**
A Bill to secure to Barbara Wilkinson of Duplin County such property as she may hereafter acquire...(GASR, Nov.-Dec. 1810, Box 2: folder "JCR (Divorce and Alimony - Finance)").

1810 Session

296. **Reference F.**
A Bill to Divorce Nathaniel Bryan of the County of Bladen from his wife Eleanor: Be it enacted...that from the passing of this Act, Nathaniel Bryan of the County of Bladen, be, and he is hereby divorced from his wife Eleanor...Read the first time and passed - In Senate, 1 December 1810, and House, 4 December 1810. (GASR, Nov.-Dec. 1810, Box 3: folder "Petitions-Divorce").

297. **Reference G.**
Laws of North Carolina, November-December 1810 Session. The persons first listed on each line below, except those preceded by the letter "D", were entitled to hold, possess and enjoy, in their sole right, all such estate, real or personal, as they may hereafter acquire by industry, purchase, gift or otherwise, in as full and ample manner as if they had never been married. The persons whose names are preceded by a "D" were granted full divorces from each other.

Bezzell, Elizabeth of Sampson County; husband - Isaac, page 48.
Bloom, Patsy of Stokes County; husband - Lewis, page 48.
Capehart, Rosanna of Burke County; husban - John, page 48.
Carven, Sarah of Currituck County; husband - Thomas, page 48.
Crowder, Mary of Buncombe County; husband - Elijah, page 48.
Davis, Eady of Pitt County; husband - Lewis, page 48.
Davis, Mildred of Buncombe County; husband - William, page 48.
Edwards, Lucy; husband - Michael of Warren County, page 48.
Herring, Susannah; husband - Frederick [county unnamed], page 48.
Holtzclaw, Susannah of Robeson County; husband - Nathan, page 48.
Hudson, Eleanor; husband - Jacob of Cabarrus County, page 48.
James, Nancy of Surry County; husband - George, page 48.
Low, Eve of Rowan County; husband - THomas, page 48.
M'Gonnigold, Rachel; husband - Eli of Guilford County, page 48.
M'Naughton, Barbara of Cumberland County; husband - Neill, page 48.
Pannal, Martha of Granville County; husband - William, page 48.
Walker, Betsy; husband - Joseph [county unnamed], page 48.
Wilkinson, Barbara of Duplin CO.,; husband - Jehu, page 48.
Wren, Sarah of Nash County; husband - Howel, page 48.

1811

298. **Adams, Sally and husband, Robert.** Petition of Sally Adams of Franklin County, North Carolina, represents "that many years ago she intermarried with Robert Adams of said county - that since then he has exhausted the estate of which they were possessed at the time of their marriage - In consequence of which she is now in a great degree dependent on the charity of her relations not only for her support but for the support of a numerous family of children - and that the proceeds of her industry are liable to the payment of his debts…" Prays for a law securing to her such property as she may hereafter acquire. Nine subscribers sign their signatures in support of this petition. (GASR, Nov.-Dec. 1811, Box 3: folder "Petitions - Divorces").

299. **Bezzell/Bizzell, Elizabeth and husband, Isaac.** Petition of Elizabeth Bezzell of Sampson County, North Carolina, sheweth that on 29 February 1805, she intermarried with a certain Isaac Bezzell of Wayne County, North Carolina, and was immediately after carried by him to the State of Tennessee, where said Elizabeth continued to live until July following, at which time she had the necessity to absent herself from his house, as she had every just reason to believe that her life was in continued danger as the said [Isaac] Bezzell had made an attempt to poison her by giving her a mixture of wine and arsenic - Your petitioner suspected her husband because of repeated threats he uttered and refused to drink the same, notwithstanding his assurances of its palatable and inoffensive nature. In order to induce your petitioner to drink the same, he drank some himself, and this would have taken his life had he not called a physician to his assistance.

Your petitioner further states that after leaving said Bezzell, she went to some of her relatives a few miles away and continued with them until the May following and then returned to her father in Sampson County, North Carolina, where she now resides. She has never seen her husband since her return, but that he has returned to Wayne County, North Carolina, "and purchased the wife of Micajah Musgrave and carried her to the State of Tennessee, with whom he has lived (as your petitioner is informed) ever since, and Cohabits together as man & wife and who has had by him one or two Children."

(a). Certificate of Isaac Bizzel, Williamson County, Tennessee, dated 10 February 1806: I have undertaken to establish the reputation of Elizabeth Bizzell as "she is intended to remove Hur Self To the State of North Carolina, Sampson County To Hur fathers To Live there Being a Separation Between my Self and Hur…it mite Stroke the minds of Sum of Hur aquaintance that She was Blamable in our Separation…I Hire By acnoledge and Do Acant that the Blame Dose Not Lay in Hur…I hire By Certyfy to all persons whome may inquire that She was industris prudent woman with grate Conduct and I Never Had no fault to find of Hur in no Shape what Ever and I Do Hire By Certify that I Never Chaged Hur with any thing Disrespectful in any manner to No person what ever But must Here By accnoledge and Take the Hole Blame of our Separation on my Self…" Test: Bennet Blackman
[On reverse:] Certificate of eleven subscribers on the conduct of Elizabeth Bizzel while a near neighbor as she prepared to separate from her husband and return to North Carolina, dated 10 February 1806, Williamson County, Tennessee: "She conducted Hurself in a most genteal manner…and apeared To Be

a industrss curfel person...very kind to Hur Husband and Treated Him very well...We never Herd Mr. Bizzell Say anything other of Hur But Charges Himself with His and Hur Sepraration..." /s/ Dorety Deens & Dempsey Deens, Henry Sharp and Hzziah Sharp, Henry Davis & Elizabeth Davis, Mark Pipkin & Sareigh Pipkin, Mary Edwards & Thomas Edwards, Isaac Crow.

(b). Deposition of Ethelred (+) Boyet and James Boyet of Williamson County, Tennessee, before Ezekiel Slocumb and Bama McKinne, Justices of Peace for Wayne County, North Carolina, 2 October 1810: The said Ethelred Boyet lives within a mile of Isaac Bizzell & says that they (Isaac & female companion) appear at home and in company as though they were lawfully married. Said Ethelred also said that he heard Isaac Bizzell say "that he has a fine daughter by the woman he lives with -Zilpah Musgrave." James Boyet says he has heard said Isaac Bizzell say "that he has bedded with Zilpah Musgrave & that he had a right to do so and that he would do it as long as he lived for that he had Bought her & paid for her..."

(c). Deposition of Col. Jethro Oates and William Blackman before Peter Frederick, Justice of Peace for Sampson County, North Carolina, 16 November 1811: "They have been acquainted with Elizabeth King, now Elizabeth Buzzell, from her infancy until her marriage with Isaac Bizzell (when she removed to the State of Tenisee) and since her return...until the present time...The said Elizabeth ever has supported the character of a Virtuous, Industrious, prudent and discreet woman..."

(d). Committee of Divorce and Alimony to whom was referred the petition of Elizabeth Bizzell of Sampson County, North Carolina, report that they are of opinion that the relief prayed for by the petition ought to be granted and recommend the bill of divorce accompanying this report. In Senate (14 December) and House of Commons (18 December) - read and concurred with.

(e). A Bill to Divorce Elizabeth Bezzel of the County of Sampson from her Husband Isaac Bezzell. In House of Commons (20 December), read second time and passed; in Senate (21 December), read third time and passed.

(All of the papers above in GASR, Nov.-Dec. 1811, Box 1: folder "SB 14 Dec.").

300. **Blackwell, Jemima (+) and husband, Robert.** Petition of Jemima Blackwell of Stokes County, North Carolina, sheweth that her husband, Robert Blackwell, "absconded from her bed and board between four and five years ago & hath remained from her ever since, having from credible information intermarried with another woman since, in me State of Georgia, he having thus absconded from the presence of your petitioner without the least cause known...leaving his just creditors unpaid, whereby all his property was taken to satisfy his debts, leaving your Petitioner to Shift for a living, stripted of every thing She had, nothing to depend on for Subsistence but her own labour & the mercy of her friends - and as your Petitioners Father is willing to give some aid to your Petitioner were it not for fear of the same being liable to Be arrested out of the Possession of your Memorialist to satisfy demands coming against her husband & c." Prays for an act to secure her all such property, either real or personal, as she may hereafter acquire by her own industry. Dated 18 October 1811 and affirmed before Charles Banner, Justice of Peace of Stokes County, North Carolina. [At bottom:] "Granted." (GASR, Nov.-Dec. 1811, Box 3: folder "Petitions -Divorces").

301. **Brown, Bond V. and wife, Susannah.** Bond V. Brown of Caswell County, North Carolina, "sheweth that he intermarried with a certain Susannah Kerns in the month of August one thousand seven hundred & ninety one. [W]e lived in Peace & harmony untill the year [1800] when without any provocation whatever that I had any knowledge of...the said Susannah left my bed and board leaving with me four children - one of which was at the breast, and went of[f] with a man by the name of Joshua Pyron to the State of Tennessee with whom she has lived in a state of adultery & abandonment ever since." Your

Divorces and Separations from Petitions to the North Carolina General Assembly from 1779

petitioner has been credibly informed the said Susannah is still living with said Pyron and has had five children by him. "Your petitioner has some property which may be serviceable to his said children at his death & having a wish that the said Susannah nor her children should enjoy any lawfull title or claim to the same...," he prays a law securing to him what property he now has or hereafter may acquire. [On reverse:] "Rejected." (GASR, Nov.-Dec. 1811, Box 3: folder "Petitions - Divorces").

302. **Daniel, Orpah and husband, Drury.** Petition of Orpah Daniel of Rowan County, North Carolina, states that she married Drury Daniel of the same county in the year 1808. After living together for "some time," she found her said husband "to be fals (or as the Law states that before the age of puberty...generation is imposible) (Rolls Abr. 358 & 359)...[F]inding him precisely in that situation and willing to live with him, but without any cause or provication by her...that hoi-id monster Jelosy arose in his breast as he pretended it did and led me such a life that it is impossible for me to live with or do the dutys of a wife towards him...he still threatinning my life and he also has forced me to leave his home and protection by Violence & I having done all in my power to promote his welfare and my own peace...I also have many other Greavances which I could state...but relief for myself and not Injury to him being my aim I forebear to mention them..." The "said Drury Daniel is man worth about Seven Hundred Dollars in good property which [I] shall not aske or demand any part though having taken a considerable part of it to him...but to be free from him is my wish and the law I think would clear me of him from his Situation which there are no doubts of for he first told it himself." Prays for a divorce from said husband, Drury Daniel. Dated 11 November 1811. [At bottom:] "Rejected." (GASR, Nov.-Dec. 1811, Box 3: folder "Petitions Divorces").

303. **Davis, Downing D. and wife, Penelope.** Petition of Downing D. Davis of Washington County, North Carolina, states that he was lawfully married to Penelope Collins of the same county in March 1804 by the Reverend Amariah Biggs, a Baptist Minister of the Gospel. During the time of his cohabitation with her, your petitioner performed to the utmost of his abilities the duties of his marriage vow, including that affection, tenderness and fidelity becoming a husband. In the month of December following their marriage, your petitioner, in the exercise of his only means of supporting his family, departed from home on a voyage to Charleston, South Carolina, as mate of the schooner Betsey of Plymouth in the county aforesaid. He left his said wife in a comfortable house with suitable furniture and amply provided her with every necessary convenience. The said Penelope, unmindful of the several obligations she owed your petitioner, and disregarding the delicacy of her sex, and in violation of her plighted faith, eloped from your petitioner's bed and board without any reasonable cause whatever. She "sold every article of his property on which she could lay hands, involved him in debts of her contracting to the amount of seventy-five dollars and upwards, and took up her residence in the house of a certain William Davenport, a single man, residing in said County, with whom she was living when your petitioner arrived." No explanation of her conduct was received, and finding "no prospect of her reformation, your petitioner shortly afterwards embarked on a voyage to the West Indies." Before his return, the said Penelope removed to Georgia, where she now resides. She is living there "in open adultery with a certain John Hill, by whom she had a child, the fruit of the illicit and scandalous connection." Prays for an act to divorce him from the bonds of matrimony contracted with the said Penelope. Sworn before Ezekiel Hardison, Justice of the Peace of Washington County, North Carolina, 12 October 1811. Subscribed to by seventeen residents of Washington County, North Carolina, in support of the petitioner. [On reverse:] "Rejected". (GASR, Nov.-Dec. 1811, Box 3: folder "Petitions -Divorces").

1811 Session

304. **Dudley, Lean and her husband, Christopher, Jr.** Petition of Leah Dudley, wife of Christopher Dudley of the Town of Wilmington, North Carolina, represents that she intermarried with one Christopher Dudley, and at that time she possessed property inherited from her father and which was settled on her by the said Christopher before marriage. Previous to said marriage, the said Christopher was security for several persons in very large sums, and upon such undertakings, judgment was rendered against him. As these undertakings were previous to his intermarriage with your petitioner, it is reasonable that she should be permitted to make the most of the property left her by her father to the benefit of herself and children. Prays that she be allowed to possess and enjoy in her own separate right such property as by her industry she may hereafter acquire.

    (a). Committee of Divorce and Alimony to whom above petition was referred report that the petitioner is entitled to the relief prayed for. Concurred with by the Senate (18 December) and House of Commons (19 December).

    (b). Bill to secure to Leah Dudley, wife of Christopher Dudley, Jr., of the Town of Wilmington, such property as she may hereafter acquire. Read second time in both Senate (18 December) and House (19 December) and passed. (GASR, Nov.-Dec. 1811, Box 1: folder: "HB 9 Dec.").

305. **Duke, Mary and husband, Hardaman/Hardiman.** Mary Duke of Orange County, North Carolina, sheweth that she intermarried with Hardaman Duke of the same county in 1789. For causes unknown to your petitioner, said husband left her and "never lived one day with her." He "soon after associated himself with another woman and has had children by three or four other women. Since that time…your petitioner thus finding herself thrown Friendless upon the world without fortune or Friends save an old and infirm mother - was taken under the care and protection of one Claborn Parrish with who she has lived ever since…that your petitioner has ever lived with the said Claborn upon terms of the greatest Harmony and happiness…that they have even felt that mutual esteem and Friendship for Each other which subsists in the more near and Dear relation of husband and wife…that they have raised a large famely of Children…Some of whom are married and settled in the world. That since the year 1789 your Petitioner and the said Duke have lived in the same neighbourhood compleatly Destitute of all those feelings subsisting between man and wife - in fact as utter strangers to each other. Your petitioner further states that She has lately been presented by the Grand Jury of Orange County for living with the said Parrish contrary to an act of assembly passed in 1805 to the unspeakable mortification of your Petitioner and her Children…some of whom as before stated are married into Respectable famalys. Your petitioner prays that the affidavits herewith sent may be received by the General assembly as proof of the allegations sent forth in the petition and that your honourable Body will take into Consideration the… hardship of the situation of your petitioner and that you will grant to her prayer an act Divorcing her from her husband the said Hardaman Duke that she may be Enabled to Intermarry with the said Claborn Parrish whom she has Ever treated and loved as a Husband…and your petitioner with Claborn Parrish prays that their Children may be called Parrish and in every Respect Legitimated." Dated 29 November 1811.

    (a). A Deposition by James Walker and William Robards and a Deposition by Benjamin Bullock - both depositions signed in Granville County, North Carolina support the petition of Mary Duke.

    (b). A Certificate by Micajah Bullock, dated 2 December 1811, states "that about the Time set forth in the Petition [above] I married Hardiman Duke to Mary Wallis at Granville Court House & in about Ten days I believe I heard the said Duke had parted from his wife & I never heard that they lived together since." [On reverse:] "Rejected". (GASR, Nov.-Dec. 1811, Box 3: folder: "Petitions - Divorces").

Divorces and Separations from Petitions to the North Carolina General Assembly from 1779

306. **Fesler, Judith and husband, Adam.** Judith Fesler of Stokes County, North Carolina, "sheweth that her husband Adam Fesler hath absconded from her bed and bord & hath remained so for almost three years…he having inlisted himself as a Soldier in Capt. Benjn. Forsyth's Company." Your petitioner has no hope of said Adam ever living with her in peace and prays an act to secure to her such property as she may hereafter acquire by her own industry or otherwise. Dated 15 November 1811. [On reverse:] "Rejected". (GASR, Nov.-Dec. 1811, Box 3: folder: "Petitions -Divorces").

307. **Finder/Fender, Elizabeth and husband, John.** Petition of Elizabeth Finder of Suny County, North Carolina, sheweth "that about five year ago she intermarried with a certain John Finder & lived with him for sometime in love & Harmony…at length, however, it so turned out that I was deprived of all domesteck Happiness that belongs to a Married life…a separation was the result. I could no longer have his protection. No Intreaties or pursuasive arguments would avail, but I must shift for myself, yet no charge of fedelity or Industry was ever brought against me." Prays for a law to secure to her such property as she may hereafter acquire by her own industry. Signatures of twenty-five subscribers support her petition. [On reverse:] "Granted alimony". (GASR, Nov.-Dec. 1811, Box 3: folder: "Petitions - Divorces").

308. **Fitzgerald, Nancy and husband, Thomas.** Petition of Nancy Fitzgerald of Caswell County, North Carolina, represents that she intermarried with a certain Thomas Fitzgerald with whom she lived about six years and by whom she had three children. Her said husband eventually gave in to intoxication and other kinds of dissipation and extravagance, and "after spending the whole of his property, left your petitioner & children in a lamentable situation dependent wholy upon the benevolence of her father, and fled to the State of Kentucky, where he has or is about to marry another woman, as appears from a letter accompanying this petition." Prays for a law securing to her such property as she may hereafter acquire by industry or otherwise.[25] [On reverse:] "Granted".. (GASR, Nov.-Dec. 1811, Box 3: folder: "Petitions - Divorces").

309. **Forsett/Forseth, John and wife, America.** Petition of John Forsett/Forseth of Halifax County, North Carolina, sheweth that he intermarried with America Jackson and led a virtuous and peaceful life with her until "about three years past, when your Memorialists said wife America, being moved & Seduced by the Devil & a certain Benjamin Lewis, eloped from your Memorialists house & has gawn with the said Benj. Lewis to parts unknown…" Prays for a divorce. [On reverse:] "Rejected". (GASR, Nov.-Dec. 1811, Box 3: folder: "Petitions - Divorces").

310. **Forster/Foster/Forester, Samuel and wife Dinah.** Petition of Samuel Foster [signed Samuel Forester] of the First Bitalion Rowan County, North Carolina, sheweth that he married Dinah Short in the year of 1798.[26] "After about ten years (all of which time she neglected the duties of a wife and mother) she left his house and protection…[P]revious to the seperation she had two children, and since her departure and before she has violated both the laws of God and man…" He has tried in vain to reclaim his wife. He desires to be respectable and bring up his two children under such circumstances as exclusively entitles them to the benefit of your petitioner's exertions and property. He is a man brought up to hard labour and owns a small tract of land with a few cattle, horses and hogs. He could state many

---

25 Said letter is not with the petition.
26 Marriage Bond of Rowan County, North Carolina, lists Samuel Forster and Dinah Short, dated 28 August 1795.

instances of neglect of family duty, but he desires relief for himself and not injury to his said wife. Prays for a divorce. Dated 12 November 1811. Signed by fifteen subscribers in support of his petition. [On reverse:] "Rejected". (GASR, Nov.- Dec. 1811, Box 3: folder: "Petitions Divorces").

311. **Garrett, John and wife, Easter.** "Whereas John Garrett of the County of Rowan & State of North Carolina has solicited us the subscribers - all Cytizens of said County to petition your Honnarable Body, the said John Garret's wife Easter[27] has left his bed & Board with out any Just cause and hath continued absent near Six years to the Great Injury of him the Said Jno. Garret…" Pray for a divorce. Signed by eighty-nine subscribers in support of John Garrett. [On reverse:] "Rejected". (GASR, Nov.- Dec. 1811, Box 3: folder: "Petitions - Divorces").

312. **Hammonds, Mary and husband, James.** Petition of Mary Hammonds of Iredell County, North Carolina, shows that she was married to James Hammonds "usually appellated Doctor Hammonds" on 21 May 1809. The said James obtained possession of all her property, disposed of it, and on 6 December 1810, he left her and their nine months old infant with no cause or provocation. She believes he left Iredell County and does not know if he is dead or alive, by which she and her child are deprived of their property and maintenance. Prays that she be granted such relief as shall appear proper, either by divorce or by granting her such estate as she may hereafter acquire. Signed by twenty-two subscribers who believe her case presents a proper object for legislative interference. [On reverse:] "Granted". (GASR, Nov.-Dec. 1811, Box 3: folder: "Petitions - Divorces").

313. **Hatcher, Margaret and husband, Thomas.** Margaret Hatcher of Buncombe County, North Carolina, sheweth "that some years ago she unfortunately intermarried with one Thomas Hatcher and continued but a short time to live with him when he abandoned her. He has now been absent from her for five years, during four of which she has not received the least intelligence concerning him. Throughout this period she has supported herself by her own economy and labour but is apprehensive that at some future time he will return, and after again despoiling her of the little she has been able to acquire, leave her to repeat her exertions until she shall again obtain something to awaken his cupidity." Prays for an act securing to her such property as she may hereafter acquire. Dated 23 November 1811. (GASR, Nov.-Dec. 1811, Box 3: folder: "Petitions Divorces").

314. **Houston, James and wife, Cassandra.** Petition of James Houston [of Mecklenburg County, North Carolina] that "having been heretofore been connected in the Marriage Relationship with Cassandra Houston[28] with whom he lived in this sacred union a time not exceeding Twelve Months, when she voluntarily absented his Bed & Board and made application to your Honorable body to release her from the obligations and other Legal restrictions under which she was placed…[Y]our Honorable Body thought proper not to grant her that relief which she pray'd for…" Your petitioner shews that they have lived separately nearly seven years, therefore destroying the design of that secret relationship. Prays that he be released from the obligation and legal restrictions peculiar to their present relationship. Dated 8 November 1311, Mecklenburg County, North Carolina. [On reverse:] "Rejected". (GASR, Nov.-Dec. 1811, Box 3: folder: "Petitions -Divorces").

---

27 Marriage Bond of Rowan County, North Carolina, lists John Garrett and Easter Hadly, dated 27 January 1803.

28 Marriage Bond of Mecklenburg County, North Carolina, lists James Houston and Casandra Alexander, dated 1 January 1803; bondsman - A(aron) Alexander.

Divorces and Separations from Petitions to the North Carolina General Assembly from 1779

315. **Ingram, Jennet(t) and husband, Matthew.** Petition of Jennett Ingram of Montgomery County, North Carolina, sheweth that about two years ago she married Matthew Ingram of the same county "with whom she lived until the indolence and extravagance of said Matthew had exhausted the earnings of several years labour and frugality of your petitioner and a separation having taken place and the said Matthew being much in debt and making no provision for the payment of such debts and your petitioner having herself and one child to support by her labour alone…" Prays for a law to secure to her such property as she may hereafter acquire. [On reverse:] "Granted". (GASR, Nov.-Dec. 1811, Box 3: folder: "Petitions - Divorces").

316. **McKinne(y), Nancy and husband, George.** Nancy McKinney of Guilford County, North Carolina, wife of George McKinney sheweth "that she intermarried with the said George in the year 1794 when he was an itinerant preacher in the Methodist Church, who continued a Local preacher in the same for a number of years after being married. During cohabitance he conducted himself as an affectionate husband, taking all necessary care for the Support of his family [and at] the same time was respected as a useful preacher in said Church." About four or five years ago, he abandoned his former habits of taking care of his family and attending to his duties of Religion. To the distress of your petitioner and family, he has ever since paid little care towards their support. He has taken to gambling and intoxication and has destroyed almost all they had for subsistence and has often absconded from the bed and board of your petitioner. Were it not for the help of friends and relations of your petitioner who bestowed their charity upon her and her children, the latter would have come to suffering circumstances. With no hope of a reformation, your petitioner prays an act securing to her all such estate as she may hereafter acquire by her own industry, or by gift from the claims of her husband and his creditors." Subscribed to by eight supporters of her petition. (GASR, Nov.-Dec. 1811, Box 3: folder: "Petitions - Divorces").

317. **Miles, Eleanor and husband, Thomas.** Eleanor Miles of Person County, North Carolina, represents she married Thomas Miles in 1799[29] and lived in the utmost harmony for several years and "cherished the most sanguine hopes that in all the vicissitudes of life she would find in him a husband, a friend and Protector - but to the great mortification of your Petitioner, and from causes to her unknown, the said Thomas Miles has deserted his family and gone to some parts of the Western Countries from whom she has heard nothing for nearly three years." She further states that said Thomas left her in a state of indigence and want with five small children to maintain. Prays for a law securing to her what property she may hereafter acquire. [On reverse:] "Rejected". (GASR, Nov.-Dec. 1811, Box 3: folder: "Petitions - Divorces").

318. **Randell/Randol, Jean and husband, Thornton.** Petition of Jean Randell of Rutherford County, North Carolina, sheweth that she was married to one Thomton Randell "a number of years ago[30] and the said Randell has left your memorialist for the space of three or four years…" She supports herself through her own labor, but if he came and took away what she has saved, "she might come to want in old age when she was unable to work." Prays for an act securing to her what she may hereafter make. The signatures of seventeen subscribers support this petition. [On reverse:] "Granted". (GASR, Nov.-Dec. 1811, Box 3: folder: "Petitions - Divorces").

---

29   Marriage Bond of Person County, North Carolina, lists Thomas Miles and Eleanor Rainey, dated 25 December 1798; bondsman - Thos. Neeley.

30   Marriage Bond of Rutherford County, North Carolina, lists Thornton Randol and Jane Owins, dated 18 October 1804; bondsman - George Randol.

319. **Shofner, Michael and wife, Sarah.** Petition of Michael Shofner of Orange County, North Carolina, sheweth "that he was intermarried to Sarah Smith in said county on or about the 25th day of December 1803[31]...that the said Sarah possessed beauty and art sufficient to snare most men, and particularly an inocent and unsuspecting youth as was your petitioner at that time. hi the State of matrimony your petitioner calculated alone on peace and happiness, but unfortunately for him and to his great disappointment and surprize he soon found what he looked upon as a blessing to prove a curse - a demon...[D]isreguarding the sacred obligations of her marriage vow unmindftill of her duties as a wife, and being insensible to shame...to virtue or the benefits of a clear conscience, she gave a look to the barest Sensuality and Guilty passions, throughing off all appearance of modesty, she sought Criminal intercourse with every man who was wicked enough to perpratrate the crime of adultry with her..." The petitioner tried in vain "to reclaim her from the paths of vice and debauchery..." and offered forgiveness for a promise of future good conduct. However, she returned to her "former ways of folly and wickedness and...abandoned his bed and board...for many months..." Finally, she returned "to his house and protection and there for a short time remained until instigated by her ungovernable lusts and wicked desires She again abandoned her home and carried with her much of the property of your petitioner... which she sold..." Since then "the said Sarrah Shofner lead the most abominable course of life and Sensual pleasures and obstinately refused to return to her home..." Prays for a divorce. Dated 25 November 1811, Orange County, North Carolina. [On reverse:] "Rejected". (GASR, Nov.-Dec. 1811, Box 3: folder: "Petitiions - Divorces").

320. **Stephens, Elizabeth and husband, Ebenezer.** Elizabeth Stephens of Robeson County, North Carolina, represents she intermarried with Ebenezer Stephens sometime in January 1803 "...with whom she flattered herself to spend her life in the Utmost Felicity and delight. But soon after to the astonishment and grief of your Petitioner - all her Pleasure was changed to Mesiry and Woe when the said Ebenezer Ingaged himself in allmost every Vice and imprudent habit that human nature could Invent. In his dissipation he spent all his Estate...which subjected her to depend alone on her parents for the support of herself and two little Infants. [H]e further abused and ill treated her and Verily believes would have seeked her life had it not been for fear of her friends." About four years ago, said Ebenezer abandoned the bed and board of your petitioner and went to some unknown parts where she has not learned of him since. "Being young and in the bloom of life [and] also anxious to answer the purpose of her creation in an Honorable & decent manner...," she prays for a divorce from said Ebenezer or otherwise as your wisdom may deem proper. The signatures of seven subscribers support this petition. [On reverse:] "Rejected". (GASR, Nov.-Dec. 1811, Box 3: folder: "Petitions - Divorces").

321. **Sutton, Hannah and husband, John.** Petition of Hannah (H) Sutton of Rowan County, North Carolina, sheweth "that Francis Winkler her first husband died sometime in the year 1803 leaving your petitioner with four small children and a considerable property to maintain them..." In "the year 1806 your petitioner intermarried with a certain John Sutton, who, after having wasted all the property of your petitioner...early in the year 1810 left your petitioner to shift for herself and support her children as she could without a house to shelter them." She supported herself and children for nearly two years by her own industry without any assistance from the said John Sutton. Prays for an act to secure to her such property as she may acquire for the maintenance of herself and family. Certificate signed by twenty-seven subscribers supports this petition. [On reverse:] "Granted alimony". (GASR, Nov.-Dec. 1811, Box 3: folder: "Petitions - Divorces").

---

31   Marriage Bond of Orange County, North Carolina, lists Michael Shofner (German script) and Sarah Smith, dated 26 December 1803; bondsman - Henry Fogleman.

Divorces and Separations from Petitions to the North Carolina General Assembly from 1779

322. **Tucker, Aaron and wife, Nancy.** Petition of Aaron Tucker of Rowan County, North Carolina, "sheweth that he was married in the year 1800 to Nancy Hagins. We lived together four years, had two children born while we lived together and one shortly after she left me, what she did in company with one Michael Hinkle and hath gone to the new countries." He prays for relief "by divorcing me from my said wife. Nancy. Permit me to call to your recollection a Law which you have passed against fornication and adultry and a Law against marrying a second time. Those Laws compleatly puts it out of my power to have a female on my plantation and reduces me to the necessity of cooking & washing for myself or getting it done to great disadvantage and inconvenience. I need only hint to you that I cannot suppress those propensities which are so natural to all men and that between my wish to be an orderly citizen and to gratifie these desires I have a trial which I find more than I am capable of regulating to my own & your wishes. Should you grant me a Divorce, I shall humbly thank you. If not, I shall conclude that you intend I shall do that abroad which I had beter do at home. You will herewith receive a statement of facts signed by my neighbours which X hope will have its own weight -"

Statement signed by sixty-six subscribers to the petition above: "We the subscribers citizens of Rowan - are well acquainted with Aaron Tucker, He is an orderly and well disposed man. His wife left him about seven years ago as we verily believe, without provocation and much against the wish & will of said Aaron. She is now living in Kentucky and has several children as we have heard and believe. We' join said Aaron in the wish that you will grant him a divorce and will venture an opinion that unless relief is granted in such like cases, our country will be overrun with Bastards which is an evil that is every day increasing and must continue unless your laws are altered or amended." [At bottom of page:] "Rejected".

(GASR, Nov.-Dec. 1811, Box 3: folder: "Petitions - Divorces").

323. **Utley, Young and wife, Polly.** Memorial of Young Utley of Wake County, North Carolina, represents that he was lawfully married to Polly Woodward of the same county in 1804.[32] At that time, said Polly was in an advanced stage of pregnancy "which was unknown to your orator, but from circumstances which had previously taken place between them, he had reason to believe that he himself was the cause of her situation…[H]e resolved without delay not only to convince her that the professions of love which he had made were sincere, but publickly to evince to the world the sincerity of that attachment…How painful was his situation when within two months and eight days after marriage, the wife he so tenderly loved was delivered of a mulatto child…" Prays for a divorce from his said wife Polly.

(a). Deposition of Robert T. Daniel, Silas Greene and Henry Brown before William Boylan, J.P. of Wake County, North Carolina, 11 December 1810: Young Utley of Wake County intermarried with Mary Woodard about three or four years ago and within three or four months after the marriage, said Mary was delivered of a female child which we believe to be a negro or mulatto. Sometime after the birth of said child, the said Polly [Mary] went to the State of Tennessee and lives with another person.

(b). Deposition of Michael Duskin, Jr., J.P. of Wake County, North Carolina, 30 November 1809: On 20 October last, he was at the house of Richard Woodward who lives near the line of Tennessee and Kentucky, where Polly Utley, the reputed wife of Young Utley of this State and County resided at that time. He further deposeth that he observed a child that said Polly was reputed to have had born before she left this State. From his own observation, the said child was of mixed blood and either a negro or very dark mulatto.

---

32 Marriage Bonds of Rowan County, North Carolina, list Young Utley and Mary Woodward, dated 20 October 1806, with bondsman - Richd. Woodward; also Young Utley and Lotty Norris, dated 3 February 1812, with bondsman - Wm. Utley.

(c).   A Bill to Divorce Young Utley of the County of Wake from his wife Polly. In Senate (19 December) and in House (20 December) - read third time and passed.
(GASR, Nov.-Dec. 1811, Box 1: folder: "SB 14 Dec.").

324.   **Weston, Elizabeth and husband, Benjamin.** Petition of Elizabeth Weston of Hertford County, North Carolina, sheweth that she intermarried with Benjamin Weston about thirteen years ago and lived with him until they had two children. The said Benjamin "then gave himself up to the dreadful crime of habitual intoxication…until he had totally disapated the little estate she was possessed of and sold the land on which she lived at the time of the intermarriage. Her husband then left her and was absent about twelve months, during which time your Petitioner made a tolerable crop of corn &c., which would have supported her and children the ensuing year…but…he returned and sold the said crop of corn &c. leaving your Petitioner and children in a very distressed situation…" She has been treated by the said Benjamin in the most inhuman manner and that a reconciliation is utterly impracticable. Prays that she be secured to any property she may hereafter acquire. [On reverse:] "Granted". (GASR, Nov.-Dec. 1811, Box 3: folder: "Petitions - Divorces").

325.   **Williams, Ann L. and husband, James.** Petition of Ann L. Williams of Hertford County, North Carolina, sheweth that sometime in the month of December 1807, she intermarried with a certain James Williams. Shortly after the marriage, the said James "gave himself over to the heinous crime of intoxication and has almost without intermission continued to do so, until he has destroyed all the estate your Petitioner was possessed of at the time of the intermarriage, and in fact has sold the Lands on which your Petitioner lived and was comfortably situated…" She has made every exertion to bring about a reconciliation, but all her efforts proved ineffectual. Prays for relief by securing to her such property as she may hereafter acquire. She further represents that "she has a number of friends, some of whom are tolerably wealthy, amongst whom is her mother who would willingly render her any assistance necessary to subsist on provided it could be secured to your petitioner…" [On reverse:] "Granted alimony". (GASR, Nov.-Dec. 1811, Box 3: folder: "Petitions - Divorces").

326.   **Yarborough, Philis and husband, William.** Philis Yarborough of Franklin County, North Carolina, sheweth "that a few years past she intermarried with one William Yarborough, and for some time continued to live with him, but about three years ago, after having suffered from him much ill treatment, and in vain endeavoured by all means in her power to continue their union, finding from his content and disposition, that her efforts to do so were unavailing, they by mutual consent separated, and have since continued to live apart…" Her said husband "has been willing to avail himself of the rights which the laws of the county gave him over her person and property without complying with those duties which those laws impose [and] frequently deprives her of the hard earnings of her labour…" Prays such relief us the nature of her case requires. Dated 20 November 1811. [On reverse:] "Rejected". (GASR, Nov.-Dec. 1811, Box 3: folder: "Petitions - Divorces").

Divorces and Separations from Petitions to the North Carolina General Assembly from 1779

327. **Reference A.**
Committee of Divorce & Alimony to whom following petitions were referred:

>Jennet Ingram of Montgomery County;
Elizabeth Weston of Hertford County;
Hannah Sutton of Rowan County;
Ann L. Williams of Hertford County;
Nancy McKinne of Guilford County;
Elizabeth Fender of Surry County;
Margaret Hatcher of Buncombe County;
Eleanor Miles of Person County;
Orpah Daniel, of Rowan County;
Mary Hammon[d]s of Iredell County;
Sarah Taylor - wife of Alfred Taylor;
Elizabeth Arnold - wife of William Arnold; and
Nancy Laxton - wife of Meador Laxton of Randolph County

...report that the petitions are respectively entitled to relief and recommend a bill accompanying this Report be passed into Law. In Senate (13 December) and House of Commons (17 December), read and concurred with.

Bill to secure to persons therein mentioned such property as they may hereafter acquire, includes all of the above persons plus - Sally Adams of Franklin County, Jemima Blackwell of Stokes County, Jean Randall of Rutherford, Nancy Fitzgerald of Caswell County, Philliss Yarborough -wife of William Yarborough of Franklin County, Mary Yarrell - wife of Matthew Yarrell of Martin County. In House of Commons (19 December), read second time and passed. In Senate (20 December), read third time and passed. (GASR, Nov.-Dec. 1811, Box 1: folder: "SB 13 Dec.").

328. **Reference B.**
Laws of North Carolina, November-December 1811 Session. The persons first listed on each line below, except those preceded by the letter "D", were entitled to hold, possess and enjoy, in their sole right, all such estate, either real or personal, as they may hereafter acquire by industry, purchase, gift or otherwise, in as full and ample manner as if they had never been married. The persons whose names are preceded by a "D" were granted full divorces from each other.

>   Adams, Sally of Franklin County; husband unnamed, page 38
    Arnold, Elizabeth; husband - William of Randolph, page 38
D Bezzell, Elizabeth of Sampson County; husband - Isaac, page 38
    Blackwell, Jemima of Stokes County; husband unnamed, page 38
    Daniel, Orpah of Rowan County; husband unnamed, page 38
    Dudley, Leah; husband - Christopher, Jr., of Wilmington, page 38
D Dumas, Amos of Richmond County; wife - Drusilla, page 38
    Fitzgerald, Nancy of Caswell County; husband unnamed, page 38

1811 Session

Hammonds, Mary of Iredell County; husband unnamed, page 38
Hatcher, Mary of Buncombe County; husband unnamed, page 38
Ingram, Jennet of Montgomery County; husband unnamed, page 38
Miles, Eleanor of Person County; husband unnamed, page 38
Randall, Jane of Rutherford County; husband unnamed, page 38
Sexton, Nancy; husband - Thomas of Randolph County, page 38
Sutton, Hannah of Rowan County; husband unnamed, page 38
Taylor, Sarah; husband - Alfred of Randolph County, page 38
Tender [should be Fender], Elizabeth of Surry County; husband unnamed, page 38
D   Utley, Young of Wake County; wife - Polly, page 38
Weston, Elizabeth of Hertford County; husband unnamed, page 38
Williams, Ann L. of Hertford County; husband unnamed, page 38
Yarborough, Philis; husband - William of Franklin County, page 38
Yarrell, Mary; husband - Matthew of Martin County, page 38

1812

329. **Bass, Benjamin and wife, Susanna.** Petition of Benjamin Bass of Randolph County, North Carolina, represents that some time ago he intermarried with a certain Susanna Wray under the impression that peace and harmony would result from the union and that he should spend the rest of his life with her...daily experiencing the utmost connubial joys and domestic felicity. In less than six months he was entirely disappointed, for she removed from his habitation and left your petitioner a complete victim to misery and distress without the least provocation on his part. He attempted with the utmost solicitation to recall her to a sense of her duty - all in vain. Prays for a divorce. (GASR, Nov.-Dec. 1812, Box 3: folder "Petitions - Divorces").

(a). The Committee of Divorce and Alimony to whom was referred the...[petition of]...Benjamin Bass, praying for [divorce]...report that [this petition]...is [not] entitled to relief. Recommend [this petition]...be rejected. In Senate (16 December 1812) and House (17 December 1812), read and concurred with. (GASR, Nov.-Dec. 1812, Box 2: folder "Joint Committee Reports").

330. **Davis, Downing D. and wife, Penelope.** Petition of Downing D. Davis states that he married Penelope Collins in 1803. In the Spring of 1804, he was on a voyage to the West Indies in pursuit of his regular occupation, and during his absence, the said Penelope without any reasonable cause, eloped from his bed and board of your petitioner and fled to the State of Georgia where she cohabited with a certain Nathaniel Hill by whom she had a female child. She has refused to return. Prays for a divorce from the bonds of matrimony.

(a). Deposition of James A. Davis before Ezekiel Hardison, J.P. of Washington County, North Carolina, dated 7 November 1812: Said Davis was born and raised in Washington County, North Carolina, and was well acquainted with Downing D. Davis and Penelope Collins who were intermarried in the Spring of 1804. This deponent went to sea on a voyage to the West Indies, and on his return, understood by the general report of the neighborhood that the said Penelope had eloped from the bed and board of the said Downing and had gone to Georgia. In 1809, this deponent saw the said Penelope in the house of a certain Mathew Shaw in Washington County, Georgia, where she showed a female child of about two years. She acknowledged herself to be the mother and that the child had been begotten and born after she left the said Downing. She also said the father was Nathaniel Hill who she had expected would have married her. Upon inquiring whether she meant to return home to North Carolina, she replied that she was well satisfied where she was and had no wish or intention to return and never wanted to see the said Downing any more. (GASR, Nov.-Dec. 1812, Box 3: folder "Petitions - Divorce").

(b). The Committee of Divorce and Alimony to whom was referred the...[petition] of Downing D. Davis...praying for a divorce report that...[this petition is not] entitled to relief. Recommend... [it] be rejected. In Senate (16 December 1812) and Commons (17 December 1812), read and concurred with. (GASR, Nov.-Dec. 1812, Box 2: folder "Joint Committee Reports").

1812 Session

331. **Ful(l)wood, Betsey and husband, Andrew.** Petition of Betsey Fulwood of Onslow County, North Carolina, states that "about six years ago, being then only of the age of fifteen years, was persuaded on without the knowledge or consent of her parents and friends to intermarry with a certain Andrew Fullwood." From that "date of her ill Judged and most unfortunate connection with her said husband untill he finally abandoned and deserted her, she had experienced at his hands every specie of neglect, cruelty and personal outrage that the most wanton humanity could inflict, and upwards of four years ago, the said Andrew Fullwood entirely left your pitioner and this state with an intention as petioner has good reason to believe never to return to the same." Your petitioner is ignorant of his place of abode and whether he is alive or dead. She has had no communication or assistance with her said husband since he left, but has been dependent upon the kindness and generosity of an indulgent and forgiving father for the support and comfort of herself and child "(the fruit of her imprudent marriage)." Your petitioner, being of very tender years, sheweth that her affection was reduced and her judgment blinded by her said husband, "who by a constant series of unprovoked cruelties towards her soon proved himself unworthy other esteem. Your petitioner will not offend your honorable body with the disgusting particulars of his ill treatment…" Her life was in constant jeopardy by night and day, and her said husband "had a knife at her throat to destroy her." Further, your petitioner sheweth that she always behaved as a loving, affectionate and dutiful wife and used every means in her power to bring about a state of tolerable comfort and harmony. Prays that she be extended relief by a law "directing her from the claim of matrimony with her said husband."

(a). Statement of James Thompson, 8 November 1812: The said Andrew and his wife Betsey lived in a few miles of my home, and I was well acquainted with them as well as the family of said Betsey. Andrew was a man of ill-fame and bad reputation in Onslow County and left his wife five years ago in a distressful situation, including much debt. The said Betsey is a very decent, well-behaved woman and was extremely kind and obliging to her said husband. The family of said Betsey is highly respected in Onslow County, and these distressing circumstances appear to cause an uneasiness in said Betsey and her parents.

(b). Statement of R. Ward, J.P. of Onslow County, North Carolina, 15 November 1812: was well acquainted with Andrew Fullwood when he lived with his wife, the said Betsey, and am some acquainted with the usage he gave her. He treated her in the most unhumane manner that a man could treat his own bosom friend. Instead of love and harmony, it was cussing and threatening to take her life, and many times my family was sent for to her relief. It is out of my power to state the misconduct of Mr. Fulwood, or the abuse was cruelty he gave his wife.

(c). Statement of Willm. French, Onslow County, North Carolina, 13 November 1812: Andrew Fulwood, after having married his wife Betsey, a young lady of very respectable family, did so conduct himself that in some short time, he: was compelled by his misconduct to leave the county and perhaps the State as a refugee from offended Justice…[H]is long absence [and] the nature of his crimes…would probably render his return dangerous to some of his members…He will probably never return. Prays that Mrs. Fulwood's case for divorce be granted.

(d). Statement of Leml. Doty, Onslow County, North Carolina, 8 November 1812: I was personally acquainted with Andrew and Mrs. Fullwood, they having lived on my land and within a half mile of me sometime before he left her. [I] do believe he treated his wife in a very inhuman manner and without the least provocation, as she always appeared to me to act in an affectionate and discrete manner towards him, when to my knowledge he would be frequently ridiculing both her and connections- And (as I have understood) after frequently abusing her in the most brutal manner, he finally abandoned her, and her parents took her home. She is of respectable parents and connection, [and] her Father is Pos-

Divorces and Separations from Petitions to the North Carolina General Assembly from 1779

sessed of a handsome fortune. She is a handsome gentle little woman and in the bloom of youth- and therefore worthy of your consideration.

(e). The Committee of Divorce and Alimony to whom was referred the above petition report "That the Petitioner...a young lady of respectable parentage, when of tender years, became the wife of Andrew Fullwood, who soon dissipated his Estate & the fortune he obtained with her, contracted criminal connexions with other women, used his wife in a most brutal manner, was guilty of the crimes of Forgery and Larceny, and fled his country to escape the punishment which awaited him. That he has now been absent several years & it is doubtful whether he be dead or alive. The Petitioner, since his departure and for some time before (he having exhausted all means of supporting her), has found an asylum in the house of her father, a man of great respectability. As this connexion was found when the Petitioner was very young & when her husband was not suspected to be of that base character he has since exhibited; as it is doubtful if he be not dead; and as if he be living, his crimes must prevent his ever visiting the State with safety, wherefore it is most probable that he will never return. Your Committee recommend that the Petitioner be relieved by an Act divorcing her from him & that the Bill to that effect accompanying this report be passed into law." Concurred in by Senate (1 December 1812) and by House of Commons (3 December 1812).

(f). A Bill to divorce Eliza Fullwood of Onslow County from her husband Andrew Fullwood. In Senate (21 December 1812) and House of Commons (22 December 1812), read third time, passed and ordered engrossed.

(All of the above from GASR, Nov.-Dec. 1812, Box 1: folder "SB 1 Dec.").

332. **Massey, Levina and husband, Adkins.** Petition of Levina Massey of Tyrrell County, North Carolina, "sheweth that she was married to Adkins Massey on [blank] day of August 1809, that shortly after which she was much abused by her husband, that she struggled under it from time to time with hopes of reformation, but unfortunately for her the abuse increased, until to complete his malignant designs she was so violently beaten, scourged, mangled, & unconsciously abused, that it appeared only to be the Will of God that she did not meet what she almost suffered the Pangs of Death. The Law then seized him for trial, in order to do her all the justice it could, but he knowing his guilts broke gaol & absconded. Your Petitioner then is left in this awkward situation – abused nearly 'unto death,' her property injured, and a young child to take care of, and now her absconded husband in what part of the world she knows not. Prays for a divorce from her husband, Adkins Massey. Dated 24 October 1812. [Below:] Signatures of thirty supporters of her petition and requesting the North Carolina Legislature to grant relief.

(a). Deposition of Levina (X) Massey before Joseph Ansley, Justice of Peace of Tyrrell County, North Carolina, 10 November 1812: Her husband, Adkins Massey, came home from a journey and appeared to be in a vehement passion. He came into the room where she was sitting on a bed and hit her with a pistol "and in a few Moments I was of a full gone from my head...and then the said Adkins tuck Me by the arm and Did Drag Me out of the house and as I was in the yard near the Dore he gave me a Most fatal blow that had Ended My time in this life and then the said Massey Did order Me to go up Stares and Call to a negro woman that was about house and told her to bring unto him Sum hot water as we war both up Chamber together and there he stamped Me with his feet and having his Boots on he gave Me the Most Terrible wounds in My Body and having the water brought he made use of Read pepper and water in a most indeasent Manner as a Deavil or man Cud invest and further more...the said Massey Did Stamp and abuse her body and Slaps her mouth So that the Crys of her Moan Cud not be heard by people and after...he demanded of Me to Clean up the floor but my infermitys...was so grate and weakness had over came Me by the loss of Blood So that I was not able..."

1812 Session

    (b).   Depositions by Esther (X) Alexander, Deborah (X) Philips and Nancy (X) Davenport support the statements in the deposition of Levina Massey above.

    (c).   Certificates of six Justices of the Peace for Tyrrell County, North Carolina, November 1812: State that in the case of the State vs. Adkins Massey for abusing his wife, Levina Massey, that the testimony was such that the said Adkins was initially committed for trial at the next Superior Court…but shortly after, said Massey broke gaol and absconded.

    (All of the above from GASR, Nov.-Dec. 1812, Box 3: folder "Petitions - Divorce").

333.   **Murray, Samuel, Jr., and wife, Elizabeth.** Memorial of Samuel Murray, Jr., of Buncombe County, North Carolina, represents that about the year 1798, he intermarried with Elizabeth Morrow with whom he lived until the year 1805, when she left his bed and board. Every effort to bring about a reconciliation proved impracticable. In 1807, he forwarded a petition for a Bill of Alimony with the consent of said Elizabeth, but by some means, it was mislaid and never presented. She has since left the State and has gone with her connections to Kentucky and never intends to return. Prays for a divorce from the said Elizabeth.

    (a).   Deposition of Susannah (X) Stone before Samuel Chunn, Justice of Peace for Buncombe County, North Carolina, 2 January 1806: "…sometime last Fall, being frequently in company with Mrs. Elizabeth Murray, wife of Samuel Murray, Jr., she, the said deponent heard the said Mrs. Murray say she liked Simpson Lee better than she did her own husband, and if it was not for committing adultery and leaving her children, she would go along with the said Lee when he returned at the risque of her life and further observed that the said Lee told [her] that if she would say the word when he returned he would pick a quarrel with the said Murray and whip him…"

    (b).   Deposition of Ann (X) Stone before the same JP as above on the same date generally supports the deposition of Susannah Stone above.

    (c).   Deposition of John Thomas, Sr., before Robert Hamilton, Justice of Peace of Buncombe County, North Carolina, 7 May 1810: The deponent undertook to finish a dwelling house for Samuel Murray, Jr., of said county and State about six years ago. During a two year period he was well acquainted with the family proceedings and conduct until the said Samuel and his wife, Elizabeth, made a final separation. At that time the deponent and the said Elizabeth were members of the Methodist Church, and he never was "acquainted with a man that took more pains to gain the affection of his wife & appeared to use his utmost exertion to please her & recall her tenderness than Mr. Murray, but alas! to no purpose. On the contrary Elizabeth Murray seemed to make it her daily Study to cross and contradict her husband in all his laudable undertakings from the Turbulency & insupportable overbearing obstinacy of her temper." The deponent at the time was "sixty years of age and generally esteemed by his neighbors as a quiet, easy, peaceable man," his frequent witnessing "her exertions of temper towards her patient, suffering husband & applying the case to himself, after mature consideration concluded…that it was next to impossible (if not quite) to dwell in peace with her…" He "took the liberty two or three times to admonish her to alter her conduct towards her husband (thinking perhaps she would pay some attention to him, being a member of the same Church), but she abruptly ordered him to hold his tongue…"

    (d).   Deposition of Rheuben (X) Stone before Philip Read, J.P. for Greene County, Kentucky, 2 October 1812: About eight years ago, this deponent took to make a crop with Samuel Murray, Jr., of Buncombe County, North Carolina, and lived with said Murray until Murray's wife Elizabeth absconded from him. The deponent was acquainted with Simpson Lee and was aware of the conduct of Elizabeth Murray as sworn to by Ann and Susannah Stone. Afterwards, this deponent moved to Greene County, Kentucky, and in his travels in that county saw Elizabeth Murray, the wife of Samuel Murray, Jr., nursing a child "what got a child years what maried now of living with Simson Lee whome of allways told you that of Loved him beter than my husband…"

(e). The Committee of Divorce and Alimony to whom was referred the Petition of Samuel Murray, Jr., of Buncombe County report that in the year 1798 the Petitioner, Samuel Murray, intermarried with one Elizabeth Morrow who lived with him for seven years, during which span of time he was condemned to suffer every mortification, which a woman of unfeeling and perverse temper, could inflict on one who looked for happiness in domestic life. He endeavoured by every means in his power to conciliate her affections, and by a mild and gentle demeanor to win her over to her duty. But at the end of seven years, her conduct became still more unsupportable. She left his house, declaring that she had more affections for another man, with whom there was strong to believe that she indulged in criminal intercourse. The Petitioner notwithstanding the stab thus given his honor, endeavoured to prevail upon her to return to him and to abandon the course she was pursuing. She refused, and after a short time, went with her adulterer to the State of Tennessee where they have lived for the last seven years and have had some children. The Committee recommends the passage of the bill herewith submitted, entitled "A Bill to divorce Samuel Murray Junr. of the County of Buncombe from his wife Elizabeth." In Senate (14 December 1812) and House (17 December 1812), read and concurred with. (All of the above from GASR, Nov.-Dec. 1812, Box 2: folder "Joint Committee Reports").

(f). Bill to Divorce Samuel Murray Jr. of County of Buncombe from his wife Elizabeth. In Senate (21 December 1812) and House (22 December 1812), read third time, passed and ordered engrossed. (GASR, Nov.-Dec. 1812, Box 1: folder "HB 8 Dec.").

334. **Philips, Willis and wife, Susanna.** Petition of Willis Philips of Randolph County, North Carolina: He intermarried with Susanna Cruthis with whom he entertained the most sanguine hopes of enjoying the utmost harmony and conjugal felicity. For sometime after the marriage, he experienced the joys which flow from a matrimonial union cemented by love and sincere affection, "But alas! How delusive were his hopes - he soon had the most incontrovertible evidence that her affection was fixed upon another person by whom she has had several children and left your petitioner abandoned to grief and despair." Your petitioner endeavoured to recall her from the paths of vice and debauchery, but all in vain. She eventually entered into connection and is now living with a free negro man by whom she has a mulatto child. No hope remains of a reconciliation. Prays for an act divorcing him from the bonds of matrimony with said Susanna.

(a). Certificate of seventy-one subscribers who state they are well acquainted with the circumstances of the above named petitioner and certify that the statements made in the above petition are correct and join him in his prayer.

(b). Deposition of Alexander Gray of Wake County, North Carolina, 21 December 1812: "[A] certain Susannah Phillips, said to be the wife of Willis Phillips of Randolph Co., NC, took up and lived for a number of years in the neighborhood of this deponent with a certain John Swearingam in a State of Adultery and during the time of their living together she the said Susannah had several children which the said Swearingam openly acknowledged to be his…that the said Swearingam & Susannah Phillips afterwards Removed to Montgomery County and there the said Swearingam died - that the said Susannah has since as this deponent is informed & believes removed into Randolph County and has for some time been living with a free negro by whom she has a mulatto child…and further this deponent saith he believes that the said Susannah does not at this time exceed forty years of Age…"

(c). Committee of Divorce and Alimony to whom was referred the Petition of Willis Philips and others of the County of Randolph report that Susannah, the wife of the Petitioner, several years ago, without any fault on his part, separated herself from him and attached herself to a man by whom she had several children. The said Willis endeavoured to prevail upon her to return and that he would forget the past and look to her future conduct for that happiness which he had promised himself in a union with her. But, as deaf to his invitation as to the voice of duty, honour and female virtue, she has not only refused her compliances but has lately left her former paramour and has formed a connexion with a free negro by whom she had a child. Your Committee views the petitioner as the victim of an unfortunate connexion from which he ought to be released. They recommend the bill accompanying this report, entitled "A Bill to divorce Willis Philips of the County of Randolph from his wife Susannah." In Senate (19 December) and House (22 December), read third and last time, passed, and ordered to be engrossed. (GASR, Nov.-Dec. 1812, Box 1: folder "SB 1 Dec.");

335. **Shof(f)ner, Sarah and husband, Michael.**

(a). Orange County, North Carolina- In Equity: Bill of Complaint of Sarah Shofner against Michael Shofner of said county, 3 September 1808: Your oratrix, Sarah Shofner, formerly Sarah Smith, by her father and next friend Thomas Smith, states that in the Year 1803, the foresaid Michael Shofner "paid his addresses to her the said Sarah for the purposes of inducing her to marry him." On 25 December 1803, she consented to and did unite with him in marriage. They lived together for a short time "as man & wife ought ever to do in peace and quietness. Your oratrix was happy for she was treated with kindness and affection. However, not long afterwards the affections of Michael Shofner wandered from her to another. From that period your Oratrix has not been merely a stranger to domestic happiness but the sufferer of every species of violence & injury. Michael Shofner, in ceasing to regard your Oratrix as a wife ceased to regard her as a woman & as a human being…[A]t various times he has beaten her with whips, with sticks & with fists, until she has sunk upon the floor, almost deprived of life, and while in that situation, he has proceeded to kick & spurn her until rescued from his merciless hands at times by his neighbours and at others by her parents. Notwithstanding her husband's cruel procedure, she continued to discharge her duties as a wife until 10 August 1806, when the said Michael turned her from his door after violently beating her. Your oratrix resided with her parents until November 1807, when the said Michael persuaded her to return and live with him, promising to use her differently and treat her kindly. She returned to his house, [but] scarcely was she within his doors when she began to feel the effects of his malignant passions; what she had suffered previously…was mercy to what she was now forced to endure…[O]n the 2d of July 1808 tho far advanced in pregnancy she was most cruelly beaten by him…and that night she suffered a miscarriage. [F]ourteen days afterwards, namely on the 16th day of the month, she was drag[g]ed from her bed and turned out of doors…" He has refused to give your oratrix any kind of support or contribute in any way to her maintenance. Request that the said Michael be decreed to convey to your oratrix such portion of his property for her support (schedule of such property is annexed hereto) and that he be required to appear before the Court to answer the premises. Schedule of Michael Shofner's property: 200 acres of land, four head of horses, 38 head of hogs, 3 head of cattle, a set of blacksmith tools (sold since 10 July).

(b). Answer of Michael Shofner to Bill of Complaint of Sarah Shofner at a Court of Equity, Orange County, North Carolina: He was intermarried with complainant about the time as set forth in the Bill, and they lived together in peace and quietness, and he treated the complainant with kindness, and she returned it with much apparent affection. He denies that this peace and quietness was but of short duration owing to any cruel or barbarous conduct on his part or to any wandering of affection. He denies that he laid violent hands upon the complainant or whipped her or beat her until she was rescued by her neighbors or parents. He denies that on 10 August 1806 or at any other time that he beat her and turned her from his door. He believes his said wife never entertained any affection for him though she made great pretenses before their intermarriage and for a short time afterwards. Her moral principles were so

Divorces and Separations from Petitions to the North Carolina General Assembly from 1779

much depraved, arid a common sense of propriety did not uphold those pretenses but a little time. She gave them up and abandoned herself to loose and criminal pleasures and to angry and malignant passions. This defendant in vain exerted himself to correct her wanderings and improprieties. He treated her kindly and affectionately, and she repaid him with ill-humor and violent passion. She would often absent herself from his bed and board without any apparent cause. This defendant chided her for such improprieties, but he did it with gentleness. The complainant was above reproof, disdained his admonitions and more than once attempted to take away the life of this defendant. In one other passions, she attempted to throw boiling water upon him but scalded her infant instead causing one-half of the hair on its head to come off. Her elopement on 10 August 1806 was without any provocation or threats on his part. She continued away from his bed and board for nearly fourteen months wandering through the country in sensual gratification of the most criminal kind. His house was always open for her return willing to receive and forgive her. He denies beating her on 2 July 1808 when she was far advanced in pregnancy. On the contrary, the complainant and he had been at her father's, Tobias Smith. On 30 June, many people were assembled to assist in gathering the harvest. The complainant, although far advanced in pregnancy, became much intoxicated with ardent spirits, and as she and this defendant were returning home that evening, she fell from her horse and received an injury that produced the miscarriage. She herself has said that this injury caused the miscarriage. The next morning they both went to her father's house about a mile and a half distant and remained there day and night. It was that night that the miscarriage occurred. During her illness, this defendant was assiduous in his attentions to her. He denies that he dragged her from bed and turned her out of doors, that he used any violence against her person. He is informed and believes that she has again abandoned herself to her criminal propensities, wandering through the country in quest of vicious pleasures. In short, she has lived and continues to live in adultery. The infant which is the offspring of this unhappy marriage is with this defendant, and it will be his care to raise it decently and virtuously.

(c).   Depositions in support of the answer of defendant Michael Shoffner, including cross-examinations, are enclosed for this case from: Martin Mease, Nathaniel Robinson, Polley Smith, Jacob Shaddy, John Coble, Betty Nease, Barbara Courtner, William Neese, James Robertson, Eve Robertson, John Nease, Michael Shofner Sr. and Elizabeth Warren. Depositions of John Teague, Joseph Teague, Jacob Fox and Absalom Cenlee identify Isaac Teague of Burke County, North Carolina, as the man whom Sarah (Smith) Shoffner lived with as man and wife.

(d).   Committee of Divorce and Alimony to whom was referred the Petition of Michael Shoffner of Orange County praying that he may be divorced from his wife Sarah, report that from evidence of the most satisfactory nature when an opportunity was afforded to the parties to cross-examine in a Court of Equity of Orange County, the petitioner is a man of honest and industrious habits, and one who stands high in the estimation of those who know him. Sometime in the year 1803, being very young, he intermarried with Sarah Smith, the woman from whom he now prays to be divorced. That her character and disposition which before her marriage had exhibited nothing reprehensible, soon afterwards displayed traits very different from those which her husband had a right to expect. After having borne one child, which she openly and shamelessly declared not to be the child of her husband, she without any provocation, left him and her infant and wandered about the country indulging herself in every act of profligacy and debauchery. That her husband uniformly during her continuance with him, treated her with a tenderness not only much above her merits but sufficiently to have rivetted the affection of a virtuous wife: After her departure, he solicited her return which she refused but filed a Bill in the Court of Equity for the County of Orange, saying that alimony be allowed her, but from the evidence produced in that Cause appeared in so odious a light, her bill was dismissed. She afterward returned to her husband who…treated her with kindness and endeavoured to wean her inclinations from the course of life she had adopted. She soon after left him after having attempted and repeatedly threatened to take away his life. Since her last elopement her husband has used his endeavours to reclaim her, but she has taken up with one Teague of a character as infamous as her own [and] has had a child by him and passes for his wife…Recommend the Petitioner as a subject worthy of relief and that the Bill herewith submitted be passed into a law. In Senate (1 December 1812) and House (3 December 1812), read and concurred with.

(e). A Bill to Divorce Michael Shoffner of the County of Orange from his wife Sarah. In Senate (19 December 1812) and House (20 December 1812), read third and last time, passed and ordered to be engrossed.

(All of the above in GASR, Nov.-Dec. 1812, Box 1: folder: "SB 1 Dec.").

336. **Reference A.**
Bill to secure to certain persons therein mentioned such property as they may hereafter acquire:
Nancy Waldron of Onslow County, wife of John Waldron;
Nancy Christopher of Guilford County, wife of Simon Christopher;
Jenny Dillon of Guilford County, wife of Leven Dillon;
Christian Hosea of Perquimans County, wife of Hugh Hosea;
Mary Coval of Rutherford County, wife of Jacob Coval;
Anna Hyatt of Burke County, wife of Seth Hyatt;
Martha Russel of Guilford County, wife of William Russell;
Polly Mira Poor of Burke County, wife of Caleb Poor;
Nancy McKinnie of Guilford County, wife of George McKinney;
Nancy Philmon of Robeson County, wife of James Philemon;
Rebecca Abbot of Burke County, wife of William Abbot;
Rachel Landreth of Guilford County, wife of Thomas Landreth;
Martha Sanders of Chatham County, wife of Tilman Sanders;
Mary Dickey, wife of Zachariah Dickey of Orange County.
(GASR, Nov.-Dec. 1812, Box 2: folder "SB 16 Dec.").

337. **Reference B.**
Laws of North Carolina, November-December 1812 Session.

The persons listed on each line below, except those preceded by the letter "D" were entitled to hold, possess and enjoy, in their sole right, all such estate, either personal or real, as they may hereafter acquire by their own industry, purchase, gift or otherwise, in as full and ample manner as if they had never been married. The persons whose names are preceded by a "D" were granted full divorces from each other.

Abbot, Rebecca of Burke County; husband- William, p. 20
Christopher, Nancy of Guilford County; husband- Simon, p. 20
Coval, Mary of Rutherford County; husband- Jacob, p. 20
Dickey, Mary; husband- Zachariah of Orange County, p. 20
Dillon, Jenny; husband- Levin (county unnamed), p. 20
D   Fullwood, Eliza of Onslow County; husband- Andrew, p. 20
Hosea, Christian of Perquimans County; husband- Hugh, p. 20
Hyatt, Anna of Burke County; husband- Seth, p. 20
Landreth, Rachel of Guilford County; husband- Thomas, p. 20
D   Massey, Levina of Tyrrell County; husband- Adkins, p. 21
McKinnie, Nancy of Guilford County; husband- George, p. 20

Divorces and Separations from Petitions to the North Carolina General Assembly from 1779

    Murray, Samuel Jr. of Buncombe County; wife- Elizabeth, p. 21
    Philemon, Nancy of Robeson County; husband- James, p. 20
    Philips, Willis of Randolph County; wife- Susannah, p. 21
    Poor, Polly Mira of Burke County; husband- Caleb, p. 20
    Russell, Martha of Guilford County; husband- William, p. 20
    Sanders, Martha of Chatham County; husband- Tilmand, p. 20
D   Shoffner, Michael Jr. of Orange County; wife- Sarah, p. 21
    Waldron, Nancy ofOnslow County; husband- John, p. 20

1813

338. **Alexander, Catharine and husband, William.** Memorial of Catharine Alexander of Rockingham County states she married one William Alexander, but after bearing a child and living with him a few years, her said husband sold all his property and left your petitioner without any means to support herself and her helpless offspring. Her husband has been absent about four years, but she has made use of her own industry to support herself and child. Prays for a divorce from her said husband. Subscribed to by the signatures of three persons. [On reverse:] Rejected. (GASR, Nov.- Dec. 1813, Box 2: folder "Petitions - Divorces").

339. **Bal[l]ance, Nancy and husband Charles.** Petition of Nancy Balance of Currituck County shews that in March 1802 at about the age of 22 years, she married one Charles Ballance of said county, and they lived together peaceably for about nine months. At the end of that time, the said Charles "became utterly crazy and deranged in mind and continued so for about nine months more." He then somewhat came to his senses and conducted a business in a poor manner for three months, wasted all his property and became again more deranged than before. This spell lasted for three years and included violence towards your petitioner. His reason was restored in some measure, and the said Charles and your petitioner undertook to live together for five years more, but he often became delirious in the extreme and violently abused your petitioner until in March 1812, the said Charles became deranged again. His violent conduct resumed, and your petitioner was under the necessity of separating from him entirely. The Wardens of the Poor took possession of his property and sold it for his support, not leaving your petitioner a part of it. The said Charles "is now running up and down the county like a madman…and is not rational enough to do any kind of labor. He has threatened to take her life, and she has gone to her brother's house. The said Charles has now advanced to the age of forty-eight or fifty years and shows no prospect of getting better." Prays for a divorce from her said husband. [Below:] Subscribed to by the signatures of nineteen supporters. [On reverse:] "REJECTED." (GASR, Nov.-Dec. 1813, Box 2: folder "Petitions - Divorces").

340. **Banks, Alsey and husband, William.** Petition of Alsey Banks of Burke County represents that her husband, William Banks, left her about five years ago with seven helpless children, the eldest of whom had lost one hand. Her said husband has been of no advantage to her in raising the children and left no property. Prays for a law to secure to her such property as she may hereafter acquire. [Below:] Subscribed to by signatures of nineteen supporters. [On reverse:] "Alimony granted". (GASR, Nov.-Dec. 1813, Box 2: folder "Petitions - Divorces").

341. **Bass, Benjamin and wife, Susannah.** Petition of Benjamin Bass of Randolph County states he married on 24 March 1810 to Susannah Wray with whom he expected to live in peace and happiness and to enjoy the mutual satisfaction incident to married life, but "Alas! a circumstance shocking to relate happened, which at once Rendered your petitioner not only unhappy, But miserable in Life…on the 17th of September, while your petitioner was Employed in his Agricultural affairs and absent from his house.

Divorces and Separations from Petitions to the North Carolina General Assembly from 1779

She the said Susanna- without the Knowledge of your petitioner and without any cause or provocation on his part- Eloped from his bed and Board and left him in a Lonesome Wretched and Miserable Condition Bereft of all future hopes of happiness." He has prevailed upon his wife Susanna to return to live with him again and to perform the duties of a wife and mother, but she turned a deaf ear to his entreaties and "shews a Disposition to Seal the Measure of his misfortunes by other Improper Conduct perhaps not necessary to mention…" She is also petitioning your Honorable Body in her behalf. Prays for a divorce from his said wife, Susanna. [Below:] Subscribed to by five supporters. [On reverse:] "Rejected." (GASR, Nov.-Dec. 1813, Box 2: folder "Petitions - Divorces").

(b). Petition of Susannah Bass of Randolph County sheweth that she intermarried with a certain Benjamin Bass of said county in 1810 and "lived with him until she discovered that her said husband was guilty of practices which delicacy forbids her to name, which eventually tended to destroy all that peace, happiness and confidence which she had formerly placed in him and rendered her life miserable." Although your petitioner has frequently pointed out to her said husband of his indecent and improper conduct, he still persists "in committing acts in violation of his duty to her…in violation of his marriage covenant." It has been impossible for your petitioner to remain with her said husband and [she] has separated from him and returned to her father's house. Prays for a law to secure to her such property as she may hereafter acquire. [On reverse:] "Granted alimony." (GASR, Nov.-Dec. 1813, Box 2: folder "Petitions - Divorces").

342.   **Beckham, Martha "Patty" and husband, Zachariah.** Petition of Martha Beckham states she has been married to Zachariah Beckham of Warren County for upwards of nine years and has conducted herself with prudence and economy, however her said husband has not contributed to their mutual support, and she has submitted to "multiplied inconvenience almost without murmuring." However she seeks protection from the General Assembly and prays for an Act to secure to her any "Acquirements she may hereafter obtain." [Below:] Subscribed to by fifteen supporters. (GASR, Nov.-Dec. 1813, Box 2: folder "Petitions - Divorces").

343.   **Bell, Sarah and husband, Samuel.** Petition of Sarah Bell of Camden County sheweth that she was the widow of William Granby and possessed a handsome property in lands, negroes and stock. She married one Samuel Bell of the same county who was in far inferior circumstances, but [she] lived with him until 1808, having by him two sons and one daughter. During this time she lived a very disagreeable life compared to the one with her first husband. Samuel Bell not only wasted her personal property by selling her negroes and stock, but treated her person in a very harsh and cruel manner, including "Blows with Cruel and Barbarous Weapons on the Body of your Orator, then far advanced in years and Mother of Ten children." Because of this bad treatment, your Orator proposed a separation from the said Samuel Bell and a day set apart for the purpose of dividing the personal property between them. Before the day arrived, the said Samuel promised to mend his ways and treat your Orator as a wife should be treated. At this time your Orator joined the church with the Baptist Society and hoped to live and die as became a Christian with love and harmony absolutely necessary in the home. However, the said Samuel resumed his beatings upon your Orator, and she fled his bed and board with her young daughter and took refuge with a married daughter. She then proposed a final separation and the division of the property in an agreement between your Orator, her son-in-law Charles Grice, and the said Samuel Bell, in which the said Bell would give up the plantation to said Grice, and the said Grice would support your Orator and daughter Sarah. All of these arrangements were made, but your Orator wants a more comfortable

situation, and prays for a complete divorce from her said husband, Samuel Bell. [Below:] Subscribed to by the signatures of six supporters. [On reverse:] "Rejected." (GASR, Nov.-Dec. 1813, Box 2: folder "Petitions - Divorces").

344. **Benton, Thomas and wife, Polley.** Petition of Thomas Benton of Rockingham County states that when he was about eight years of age, his parents departed this life, leaving your petitioner and three sisters in a helpless and forlorn situation. Eventually, your petitioner was put to live with a certain Willis Prutt in Stokes County, whose severe treatment while young caused your petitioner to feel constrained and repugnant to comply to the mandates of said Willis. When your petitioner became seventeen years of age, the said Willis through insinuations and threats compelled your petitioner to intermarry with a certain Polley Wright, a step-daughter of the said Willis, "who then lived in this family and who was only about fourteen years of age- Your petitioner at the time of his intermarriage…was entirely ignorant of the views and nefarious schemes of the said Willis Pruit…Your honorable Body will better conceive than I can express the surprise and indignation I felt when I came to learn that the whole trick had been plan'd and played off…your said petitioner for the sole purpose of gitting the Estate of the said Polley (which was considerable) into the hands of the said Willis, which at length he has done." The said Polley from the first night of their marriage absolutely refused to bed and cohabit with your said petitioner, nor have they lived together, nor is there any prospect that they ever will. It has been upwards of four years since the said marriage took place "in which said time the said Polley has been delivered of a child which your said petitioner entirely disowns." The said Polley "hath entirely devoted herself to every evil and shameful practice of a common prostitute. Your petitioner deems it unnecessary to go any further into a detail of a subject as disagreeable to himself as it must be unpleasant for you." Prays for a law to divorce him from the said Polley. [Below:] Citizens of the Counties of Rockingham and Stokes Certify that the facts set forth in the foregoing petition are believed to be true and that the said Thomas Benton has always supported a good character and that he is justly entitled to the clemency of the Legislature. The signatures of some ninety-four subscribers follow. [On reverse:] "Rejected." (GASR, Nov.-Dec. 1813, Box 2: folder "Petitions - Divorces").

345. **Bond, Rebecca and husband, Samuel.** Petition of Rebecca Bond of Wilmington, North Carolina, sheweth that she intermarried in August 1808 with one Samuel Bond, officer on one of the gunboats stationed in Wilmington. After four weeks, said Samuel set out for the State of Maryland, saying that he had to settle some property affairs but would return in six weeks. However, said Samuel has never returned, nor has she received any communication from him. Your petitioner further states that letters from friends and relations of her said husband noted that he has contracted habits of dissipation and has refused to return to his wife despite the solicitations of his acquaintances that he should at least make some provision for his wife and child. The said Samuel has left the State of Maryland and taken up residence in the State of Kentucky, where your petitioner has learned that he has contracted another marriage. Your petitioner states that he left her without any cause of dissatisfaction, and that when he left, she had every reason to believe that he still viewed her with the eyes of affection. However, because of his refusal to return to her, she can never look upon him again with respect, much less with affection, even if he were to return. Prays for a divorce from said husband. [Below:] Subscribed to by the signatures of thirteen supporters. [On reverse:] "Rejected…laid over." (GASR, Nov.-Dec. 1813, Box 2: folder "Petitions - Divorces").

Divorces and Separations from Petitions to the North Carolina General Assembly from 1779

346. **Braddy, Polly and husband, Richard.** Petition of Polly Bailey Braddy of Johnston County represents she married a certain Richard Brade'y some few years ago, but he has treated her "with great cruelty and contempt and finally abandoned her by enlisting in the service of the United States." Your petitioner entertains no hope of a reconciliation. Prays for a law to secure to her such property as she may hereafter acquire. [On reverse:] "Granted." (GASR, Nov.-Dec. 1813, Box 2: folder "Petitions - Divorces").

347. **Brightman, Margaret and husband, Joseph.** Petition of Margaret Brightman of New Hanover County represents "that she was possessed of a considerable estate the most of which she acquired by her own industry. That a few years ago she intermarried with one Joseph Brightman who was not worth a shilling. In a very short time her said husband began to contract debts and dispose of her property, and about a year ago sold everything she had in this world and let; her with a determination never to return…" Your petitioner is afraid that her said husband may return again when she has acquired sufficient property to make it an inducement. "She is now old and can only expect to make enough to support herself for the remainder of her life." Prays for "a law to authorize to hold in her own right such property as she may hereafter acquire." [On reverse:] "Granted".. (GASR, Nov.-Dec. 1813, Box 2: folder "Petitions - Divorces").

348. **Brown, Ann and husband, William.** Petition of Ann Brown of Rowan County sheweth that her husband, William Brown, has abandoned from his wife and family for four years or more and left them in indigent circumstances. Prays for a law securing to her such property as she may hereafter acquire. Dated November 1813. [Below:] Signatures of thirty-one supporters of this petition. [On reverse:] "Granted alimony." (GASR, Nov.-Dec. 1813, Box 2: folder "Petitions - Divorces").

349. **Butler, Ann and husband, Reuben.** Memorial of Ann Butler of Granville County states "she was married to Reuben Butler her present husband many years past, by whom she has had a number of children." At the time of her marriage, she was possessed of a handsome property, but her husband wasted it all through a long course of idleness, extravagance and dissipation. He has abandoned her and her little children without a cent to purchase the necessaries of life. "The indulgence of her parents, who were wealthy and affluent, had raised her in a genteel and fashionable manner, but that the wants of herself and a large family of small children have subjected her to most of the common drudgeries of life. She has been able to collect some of the necessaries of life and a small stock of horses, cattle and hogs, but she is continually subjected to the demands of her husband's creditors." Prays for a law to secure to her such property as she may hereafter acquire. [On reverse:] "Alimony granted." (GASR, Nov.-Dec. 1813, Box 2: folder "Petitions - Divorces").

350. **Crossland, Alexander and wife Catherine.** Petition of Alexander Crossland of Warren County sheweth that he intermarried with one Catherine Durrell, a widow of a respectable family, in 1804. He lived with her for three years and treated her with all the regards and tenderness "which a wife has a right to expect and which it is the duty of a husband to bestow." However, "neither a virtuous education, honest parentage, or a demeanor…so modest as would awe a libertine into respect, afford a sufficient guarantee for female honour; and that when the heart and dispositions of a woman are once tainted, human art cannot form a corrective." After some time, she left your petitioner's house and openly and publicly hired lodgings in the Town of Petersburg and received such male visitors as thought proper to solicit her favours. Although stabbed in his heart, your petitioner went to her and told her that she was not only destroying his peace but preparing for herself a fund of wretchedness, disgrace and infamy. He

proposed to her to leave the course of life she had adopted, return to her duties as a wife, and that the past would be forgiven. She consented to this plea and returned to your petitioner, but a virtuous life was not suited to her disposition. She soon returned to the iniquity of her ways, and for seven years past has given up to open and shameless prostitution. Her conduct does not rest upon whispers or suspicion, but prostitution is her averred trade and occupation. Prays for a divorce.

(a). Accompanying this petition are depositions from William B. Robinson, John Banks, John Loughbridge, Alexander Gordon, William Thweatt, Benjamin Curtis, Martin Eaves and Eaton Lamb - all of the town of Petersburg, Virginia, who confirm the statements made by Alexander Crossroads above and add a few of their own.

(b). Committee of Divorce and Alimony to whom was referred the Petition of Alexander Crossland of Warren County, praying for a divorce from his wife Catherine, state that every allegation contained in the petition has been substantiated and recommend the bill accompanying the report be passed into law and honor the prayer of the petitioner. Concurred in by House (7 December 1813) and North Carolina Senate (8 December 1813).

(c). Bill of Divorce for Alexander Crossland of Warren County from his wife Catherine. In House (17 December 1813), read third time and passed; in Senate (17 December 1813), read third time, passed, and ordered engrossed.

(All of the above from: GASR, Nov.-Dec. 1813, Box 1: folder "HB 7 Dec.").

351. **Deeton, Nancy and husband, Thomas.** Petition of Nancy Deeton of Chatham County "sheweth that in the year 1797 her husband Thomas Deeton ran away takeing with him another Woman, and being much in debt leaving your petitioner with a very small quantity of property all of which has been liable to his debts…also with two small children whom your petitioner with her own labour have since raised and maintained." Prays a law to secure to her such property as she may hereafter acquire. [On reverse:] "Granted." (GASR, Nov.-Dec. 1813, Box 2: folder "Petitions - Divorces").

352. **Dever, John and wife, Elizabeth.** Committee of Divorce and Alimony to whom was referred the petition of John Dever of Duplin County praying to be divorced from his wife Elizabeth report the following facts: "the said John Dever some time in the year 1804 became connected in wedlock with Elizabeth Gray; that the said Elizabeth within two or three years after the Bonds of matrimony were solemnized left the house and protection of the said John; that since the period of her elopement, she has more than once become a mother, and shameful as it is to relate, it appears that these adulterous connections have not been confined to persons of her own colour; that the said Elizabeth for the last two years has resided under the roof of a Slave, and that she actually claims as her child and has suckled at her breast an infant bearing the most certain marks of a coloured Father-" Recommend the Bill accompanying this report entitled A Bill to Divorce John Dever of Duplin County from his wife Elizabeth be passed into a Law. Concurred with by House (30 November 1813) and Senate (1 December 1813).

(a). Bill to Divorce John Dever of Duplin County from his wife Elizabeth. In Senate (1 December 1813), read first time and passed. In House (30 November 1813), read first time and passed; in House (20 December 1813), read second time and rejected.

(All of the above from: GASR, Nov.-Dec. 1813, Box 1: folder "HB 30 Nov.").

353. **Emery, Jinny and husband, Stephen.** Petition of Jinny Emery of Randolph County sheweth that her husband, Stephen Emery, being charged with committing rape of "a poor old decripted woman" in 1811, fled his country and has not been heard of since. He left your petitioner with two small children in a deplorable condition, the whole of his property being immediately attached to satisfy his creditors.

Your petitioner and family would have starved had it not been for the humanity of her neighbors. There is no probability other husband ever returning. Prays for a divorce from her said husband or securing to her such property as she may hereafter acquire. [On reverse:] "Alimony granted." (GASR, Nov.-Dec. 1813, Box 3: folder "Petitions - Miscellaneous").

354. **Gilmour, Stephen and wife. Charity.** A Bill to divorce Stephen Gilmour and his wife, Charity. In Senate (21 December 1813) and in House (22 December 1813), read third time, passed and ordered to be engrossed. (GASR, Nov.-Dec. 1813, Box 1: folder "SB 9 Dec.").

355. **Grantham, William and wife, Rachel.** Petition of sundry inhabitants of Buncombe County sheweth that William Grantham of said county married Rachel Cox in February 1807 when he was only 16 years of age. The said William soon found that said Rachel was better calculated to destroy than to ensure conjugal happiness, but he did everything in his power to reclaim her manners and to render her life comfortable for the space of two years. She finally eloped from his bed and board without any cause, and "from that time…has conducted herself in the most unworthy manner…She is now bound over to stand her trial at the next Superior Court for the County of Lincoln in this State charged with the murder of one of her spurious children." Pray that "such relief as is in your wisdom may deem proper" be applied in this case. [Below:] Signatures of thirty-four petitioners. [On reverse:] "Rejected." (GASR, Nov.-Dec. 1813, Box 2: folder "Petitions - Divorces").

356. **Hancock, Joseph and wife, Tabitha.** Petition of Joseph Hancock represents that he married a certain Tabitha Askew of Hertford County a few years ago. His said wife "evinced a disposition to destroy the peace and harmony" of their marriage until about five years ago, when a separation took place between them. Your petitioner claims that his said wife "has perpetrated crimes repugnant to the intentions of the marriage institution [which are] derogatory to the dignity of her sex, abandoned herself to the most vile prostitution and debauchery, has had children of various colours and complexions, and nearly effected the ruin of your petitioner!" Prays that his marriage with the said Tabitha may be entirely abrogated.
    (a). Deposition of Thomas Hancock before Southey Bond, Justice of Peace of Wake County, supports the remarks made in the above petition of Joseph Hancock. [On reverse:] "Rejected." (GASR, Nov.-Dec. 1813, Box 2: folder "Petitions - Divorces").

357. **Hatch, Polly and husband, Henry.** Petition of Polly Hatch of Lenoir County represents that in the year 1807 she intermarried with Henry Hatch, who "reduced himself and family to a wretched state of poverty and then left your petitioner with two small children to shift for herself and them and has been absent from her about two years and gone to the State of Georgia…" Prays for relief to secure her such property as she may hereafter acquire. [Below:] Endorsed by signatures of four supporters. [On reverse:] "Granted".. (GASR, Nov.-Dec. 1813, Box 2: folder "Petitions - Divorces").

358. **Higbie, Thisbe J. and husband, David.** Petition of Thisbe J. Higbie shews "that about eight years ago she intermarried with David Higbie with whom she lived in the State of New York about five years during which time a competency for the comfortable and decent maintenance of a family was wasted by him by his imprudence and dissipations…" The said David then left your petitioner and his infant child without means of support and "has gone into distant parts…" Your petitioner and child [daughter] removed to the State of North Carolina where they are now dependent on the bounty of her

brothers and relations. She has expectation of acquiring some property in North Carolina and is desirous of securing such property for herself and infant against the claims of her said husband.

(a). Deposition of Calvin Jones of the city of Raleigh, brother of said Thisbe J. Higbie, and of Sylvester K. Fuller of the city of Raleigh support the statements made in the above petition of Thisbe J. Higbie. Both depositions are dated 2 December 1813. (GASR, Nov.-Dec. 1813, Box 2: folder "Petitions - Divorces").

359. **Hinkle, Hanah and husband, Jacob.** Petition of Hanah Hinkle of Lincoln County sheweth she intermarried with a certain Jacob Hinkle about fifteen years ago, and they lived together until they had three children…"that your pitioner entertained flattering hopes for a short time after their marriage that they would live a comfortable life." However, her said husband Jacob gave himself up to "almost every kind of dispatations but finally run in debt to a greater amount thin our little property was worth - and finally left your Petioner with his helpless children without any subsistence…" Her said husband has been gone for eight years, and she does not want to be held responsible for his debts. Prays for a law securing to her such property as she may hereafter acquire by her own industry. [Below:] Signatures of thirteen supporters subscribe to statements made in her petition. (GASR, Nov.-Dec. 1813, Box 2: folder "Petitions - Divorces").

360. **Hoffler, James and wife, Deborah.** Petition of James Hoffler of Gates County represents that he married Deborah Hoffler of said county in September 1802.[33] Three months later, said Deborah deserted his bed and board without cause and returned to her father, Jacob Outlaw, and in the course of six or eight months had a child. Not long afterwards, the said Deborah took up with a man by the name of John Lowance, "a person of Collow," by whom she the said Deborah had a child. A few years later the said Lowance left her, but she soon took up with a man named Thomas Ball and went to Charleston, South Carolina. For three years, your petitioner has had no word about the said Deborah. A few years past, the Legislature favored your petitioner by passing a law divesting the said Deborah of all right of dower in my property. Prays that the Legislature take his situation into consideration and pass a law to divorce him from said Deborah. [Below:] Signatures of 116 supporters, including Deborah's brother, John Outlaw, and the following Hofflers: James, Garrett, and William. [On reverse:] "rejected". (GASR, Nov.-Dec. 1813, Box 2: folder "Petitions - Divorces").

361. **Holland, Milley and husband, James.** Petition of Milley Holland, wife of James Holland of Greene County sheweth that she has four small children unable to work for their support, "and her Husband the said James Holland does not use the necessary industry for the support of his family, but on the other hand, employs his time in drinking, gambling and other dissipated practices, and through those means spends and wastes the earnings of your petitioner, having no property to support on except such as your petitioner Earns through her Endustry." Prays a law securing to her such property as she may hereafter acquire. Dated 8 November 1813. (GASR, Nov.-Dec. 1813, Box 2: folder "Petitions - Divorces").

362. **Horney, Lydia and husband, Manlove.** Petition of Lydia Horney of Guilford County sheweth that "Manlove Horney the husband of your petitioner hath inlisted in the Army of the United States and left your petitioner with six small children in a helpless and disconsolate situation." Prays for a law to secure to her such property as she may hereafter acquire. [On reverse:] "Alimony granted".

---

33   Marriage Bond of Gates County, North Carolina, lists James Hofler and Deborah Outlaw, dated 22 September 1802.

Divorces and Separations from Petitions to the North Carolina General Assembly from 1779

363. **Hyatt, Anna and husband, Seth.** Petition of Anna Hyatt sheweth that she was married on 14 March 1806 to Seth Hyatt. Her father, Joseph Dobson, gave them a plantation on the north side of the Catawba River "with a tolerable good house thereon and a good orchard and made a full conveyance thereof by Deed - the same estimated to be worth nearly One Thousand Dollars. Her said father also gave them some household furniture, cattle and hogs. There was always the appearance of plenty. She endeavoured to carry out her duties of a good wife and bore him two sons and also became pregnant a third time. Her husband, however, formed a connection with one Nancy Smith, and on 8 Jan. 1810, these two went off to the Duck River in West Tennessee, and from thence it is said they went to Louisiana where they cohabit together as man and wife. Your petitioner further sheweth that for one whole year before going away, the said Seth neglected his plantation, and during the summer of 1809, your petitioner took upon herself to tend a crop of corn for bread. A man was engaged to work in the crop for a share in it, and another man was engaged to plow the corn for which your petitioner promised to make a shirt for him. She also worked with her own hands, putting her child in the field while she hoed. She hired some girls to assist, and with this help, they made a crop of corn and had aplenty. The said Seth did not do one day's work in support. There were at least 100 bushels of corn standing in the crib on 8 Jan. 1810 when Seth went off, and your Petitioner knew not of his intention until after his departure. To add to your Petitioner's distress and anguish, she learned that her said husband had sold the plantation and made a deed for the same and had also sold the cattle, hogs, household furniture, and the crib of corn which your petitioner with many hard days of labor with her own hands had assisted to make. In a few days after he was gone, the creditors of her husband were contending one against another who should first seize the property and be the first to carry it off…which they proceeded to do and left the house empty."

"Soon after this scuffle of creditors and purchasers, William Murphy, who had purchased the plantation, sent a tenant, who with his family came into the house, took possession thereof and of the said plantation, and your petitioner had to go away. This was within one month of the time of delivery of her third and last child."

"Previous to your Petitioner's misfortunes, her father, the said Joseph Dobson, had failed, became unable to pay her debts, was confined in Gaol, gave up his property for the benefit of his creditors, and took the benefit of the Insolvent Act. Her said husband, Seth Hyatt, has now left your petitioner almost four years & deserted her as she believes, forever." Prays for a divorce.

(a). Deposition of William (X) Stallcup before Waightstill Avery, J.P. of Burke County, North Carolina, 27 September 1813: "The deponent states he was living with his father in Burke County in 1806 and heard of the marriage of Seth Hyatt, son of Hezekiah Hyatt, with Anna Dobson, daughter of Joseph Dobson, Esqr., of the same County of Burke, and some time after the marriage, this deponent became acquainted with said Hyatt and his wife Anna. On 27 Oct. 1808, this deponent courted and married the sister of Seth Hyatt, and in the year 1810, they were living in Jackson Co., TN, on the waters of the Cumberland River. In the month of June, he heard a report that Seth Hyatt, his said brother-in-law, had left his said wife Anna and had taken up with one Nancy Smith, a young single woman who lived in a family near the said Seth. This couple, Seth and Nancy, went off to the Duck River in West Tennessee and cohabited as man and wife. This report was grievous to this deponent and his wife, and after consultation, left together in early July to travel to the Duck River to see the said Seth to persuade him to return to his wife in Burke County. Unfortunately, their best endeavours did not prevail upon the said Seth to leave the said Nancy and return to his wife, Anna. This deponent and his wife lived in the same cabin with said Seth and Nancy Smith from July to October 1810, but suffered much grief and sorrow to see and know that Seth and Nancy did cohabit and bed together in the same bed a.s this deponent and his wife did bed together in one bed." In October, the said "Seth Hyatt declared his intention to go over the Ohio and the Mississippi, and up the Arkansaw River- as far as any white people were living. This deponent offered to give the said Seth a valuable mare as a free gift on condition that he would go home to Burke County & live with his wife Anna. The said Nancy Smith overheard this offer and replied- 'You need not try to persuade Seth for he may go where he pleases and I will go there [with him].' Seth said that he supposed he must go away anyhow and refused to accept this deponent's offer. In October 1810, the said Seth and Nancy were in Nashville and set off to go to the Arkansaw River as they had declared. This deponent and his wife at the same time set off for Burke County, NC. While they all were within speaking distance, the said Seth called back: 'Tell my people in Burke that my Bond and their Bond will be buried a long ways apart.'"

(b). Deposition of Berry Burnett before Waightstill Avery, Justice of Peace of Burke County, North Carolina, 14 August 1813, attests to similar circumstances regarding Seth Hyatt, his wife Anna (Dobson), and Nancy Smith.

(c). Deposition of Killian Jarratt before Waightstill Avery. Justice of Peace of Burke County, North Carolina, 15 August 1813: Deponent attests to his knowledge of the marriage of Seth Hyatt and Anna Dobson and the subsequent flight of said Seth and said Nancy to Tennessee. The deponent said that Seth Hyatt sold the plantation conveyed to him by Joseph Dobson to William Murphy. The plantation where said Hyatt lived was taken possession of by James Henderson and by Mr. Murphy a few months after Hyatt went away. The deponent further said that he well knows the handwriting of Seth Hyatt and saw a letter written by Hyatt to the deponent's wife, the mother of said Nancy Smith, and a second letter from the said Hyatt, dated September 1811, remarked about his wife. Nancy, and called this deponent's wife "his mother." The said Hyatt at that time said he was living at or near the Lead Mines in Louisiana. A third letter dated in December 1812 to this deponent's wife from her said daughter Nancy stated that Nancy and Seth Hyatt were living within 15 miles of the lead mines in Louisiana, and that said Seth intended to live there a long time if "he should have days to live."

(d). The Committee of Divorce and Alimony to whom was referred the petition of Anna Hiatt of Burke County to be divorced from her husband, Seth Hiatt, report that it appears that on 14 March 1806, said Anna was married to said Seth and lived with him until 8 June 1810 when he left her without any cause and formed a connection with one Nancy Smith with whom he removed to Duck River in West Tennessee and from thence the said Seth and Nancy have gone to Louisiana and continue to live together as man and wife. Your Committee recommends the Bill accompanying this report entitled- a Bill to divorce Anna Hiatt of Burke County from her husband, Seth Hiatt, be passed into law. Concurred in House (3 December 1813) and in Senate (4 December 1813).

(e). A Bill to Divorce Anna Hiatt of Burke County from her husband Seth Hiatt. In House (22 December 1813), read third time and passed. In Senate (23 December 1813), read third time and passed. (The above documents found in: GASR, Nov.-Dec. 1813, Box 1: folder "HB 3 Dec.").

364. **Jones, Mary H. and husband, [Alexander],** Memorial of Mary H. Jones of Lincoln County sheweth that she and her husband [unnamed] have been separated for "upwards of three years," and that he is living in the western country at least 500 miles distant. There is no probability of a reconciliation. Prays for a law to secure to her such property as she may hereafter acquire. [Below:] Signatures of eight supporters of the facts in her petition. (GASR, Nov.-Dec. 1813, Box 2: folder "Petitions - Divorces").

365. **Mask, John D. and wife, Peggy.** Memorial of John D. Mask of Richmond County represents that he married one Peggy Vining about twenty-three years ago and "calculated to live in the utmost harmony and content…" After some time had elapsed, his said wife disregarded the obligations of the matrimonial vow and treated your petitioner with the utmost contempt and derision, and finally abandoned her house and moved to an adjacent county. She contracted debts to a considerable amount which

your petitioner has paid by the utmost exertion while supporting five small and helpless children - the fruits of this unhappy union. Your petitioner has entreated her in the most affectionate manner to return to his house and render to her helpless offspring that material aid so desirable. She yielded and returned, but in February 1803, she eloped from his company and fled to the State of Georgia, and he has not seen her since. Prays for a law to divorce him from the said Peggy. [Below:] Subscribed to by four supporters. [On reverse:] "Rejected". (GASR, Nov.-Dec. 1813, Box 2: folder "Petitions - Divorces").

366. **McKinsey, Elizabeth and husband, James.** Petition of Elizabeth McKinsey of Iredell County sheweth that she was in her youth married to William Bowman with whom she lived very comfortably for a number of years, but he died, and she was left with a small and helpless family. In time, she married one James McKinsie and hoped to find in him a loving husband. Alas, she was disappointed, for said James has spent the whole of the estate acquired by her own and her former husband's industry except her dower rights to the land. She is now advanced in age and prays for a law to secure to her such property as she may hereafter acquire. [Below:] Petition of seven supporters of said Elizabeth requesting that her prayer be answered. (GASR, Nov.-Dec. 1813, Box 2: folder "Petitions - Divorces"). [34]

367. **Neilly, Elsey and husband, William.** Memorial of Elsey Neilly of Buncombe County "sheweth that some more than seven years past your memorialist got Personly acquainted with a Person by the name of William Neilly, who was at that time a hireling to your Memorialist's father in which time your memorialist thought she had got Sufficiently acquainted with him and Blundered into wedlock." She lived in peace and harmony with him for nearly two years, when the said William left for a number of weeks, returned and behaved himself tolerable well, but then broke out with "execrable invectives…he Developed from your Memorialist in a Rage and has been near four years absent…" She then returned to her parents. Prays for an act to secure to her such property as she may hereafter acquire by her own industry. [Below:] Signatures of eight supporters of said Elsey. (GASR, Nov.-Dec. 1813, Box 2: folder "Petitions - Divorces").

368. **O'Quin, John and wife, Mary.** Petition of John O'Quin of Wayne County states that about eight or ten years ago in the town of Wilmington, North Carolina, he and sundry others, "who were disposed to spend the evening in a convivial manner (after having recourse to the inebriating liquors, as an impetus to their actions) repaired to a House in the Town where the Occupants were of the Female sex and notorious for their Prostitution. Your Petitioner being then in the prime of life, and a. disposition rather volatile, he did not hesitate to become one of the company, and expatiated freely on the subject of matrimony. He did not believe that any scandal would result from such conduct, as a Justice of the Peace was in company with him, and as his sole object was the acquisition of knowledge to enable him the better to discriminate between women of virtuous and vicious habits. He further states that but a short time had elapsed before the inebriating liquors proved absolutely predominant, and your petitioner became utterly insensible of the Transactions of the Night…[I]n the morning when he awoke, to his inexpressible Mortification, there lay by his side a Huge Mass of Creation, purporting to be of the Female sex, who called herself Mary Jackson- whose uncouth appearance indicated that she was formed by nature in a rude and ranting frolic- and whose touch alone was amply sufficient to recoil the feelings of the most profligate wretch in society—…[H]e hastily arose from his bed and enquired into the cause of her intrusion upon his repose…[H]e was informed that a Justice of the Peace who was in company in a fit of intoxication had joined them together as man and wife, and at a time when your Petitioner was utterly insensible of

---

34 Marriage Bond of Rowan County, North Carolina, lists William Bowman and Elizabeth McPherson, dated 14 May 1785.

the whole transaction…Upon this information he precipitately retired with pungent feelings of grief; and Alas! when too late protested against the proceedings of that fatal night. This fortuitous occurrence has proved as destructive to the repose of your Petitioner and has excited as much consternation among his friends, as was experienced by the Trojans upon the introduction of the Grecian Horse into Troy. "Your Petitioner further states that he is firmly impressed with the Belief that if none of the fair sex were ornamented with features and forms more enchanting than this Mary Jackson, procreation would certainly cease and be forgotten…[T]he said Mary Jackson has gone off as a Prostitute to Canada with the Troops of the United States, and it is as reasonable an expectation that a Camel can go through the eye of a needle or the Leopard change his skin, as to believe that the said Mary and your Petitioner will ever dwell together…as our Moral and Civil institutions require that all contracts (if obligatory) should be entered into with the free and full consent of both parties." Prays that the marriage aforesaid be abrogated by an Act of your Honorable Body. (GASR, Nov.-Dec. 1813, Box 2: folder "Petitions - Divorces"). [On reverse:] "In House of Commons, 25 November 1813, Read and rejected."

    (a).   Deposition of Uriah Bass before Jacob Kennedy and William Bizzell, Justices of the County Court of Wayne County, North Carolina, 11 November 1816, at the house of Jacob Kornegay "saith in May last he went to Wilmington…that John O'Quin gave him a Letter to carry to John Darden for the purpose of Inquiring for a woman by the name of Mary Jackson…that he could not find Darden in town…that he gave the letter to William B. Miller, and the sd. Miller Read the letter and said there had been such a Woman in Town but [she] was then gone of[f] with the Soldiers, and if O'Quin wanted to marry, he might do so- that she never would come back to interrupt him." (GASR, Nov.-Dec. 1813, Box 3: folder "Petitions - Miscellaneous").

369.   **Perry, Elizabeth and husband, Reuben.** Petition of Elizabeth (X) Perry states she intermarried with Reuben Perry of Johnston County sometime in the year 1790. She believed that a wife was entitled to receive protection from her husband and continued in this mode for fourteen years, at which time he began to drink heavily and shamefully abused and threatened your petitioner. She further states that the said Reuben has "taken other women into his house and suffered them to domineer and shamefully abuse your petitioner." Her said husband has had three base born children by these women and has made a will in which he has given away nearly all his property to said children. It is true that she and her husband have no children of their own, but she has offered to take care and raise the base born children as a mother would. Your petitioner has lived in this disgraceful manner for six or seven years and prays for a law to divorce her from the said Reuben Perry. Dated 2 December 1813. Reuben (X) Perry gives his assent to the prayers of the Petitioner. [Below:] "Rejected." (GASR, Nov.-Dec. 1813, Box 2: folder "Petitions - Divorces").

370.   **Perry, Jacob and wife, Sarah.** Petition of Jacob Perry of Pasquotank County sheweth "that some time in the year 1808 while in a state of intoxication, He fell in with a woman who was a stranger to him and from persuasion was induced while in that situation to have the Right of matrimony solemnized." He lived with her for a very disagreeable period of eighteen months, during which time she bore a child and then abandoned his bed and board. She "was strolling from House to House in the State of Virginia for about Eighteen months" and then I learned that she was in Camden County, North Carolina, where I went to her to persuade her to return. She came back with me and stayed ten days, but then absconded with our son Willis Perry in August 1811. I have made inquiries of her presence since that time, but to no avail. I do not expect to see her again. Prays for a divorce from his wife Sarah Perry, formerly Sarah Dozier. Dated 28 October 1813. [Below:] Signatures of twenty-nine subscribers support the peti-

tion of the above Jacob Perry for a divorce. [On reverse:] "Rejected." (GASR, Nov.-Dec. 1813, Box 2: folder "Petitions - Divorces").

371.   **Perry, Nancy and husband, David.** Bill to enable Nancy Perry of Carteret County to hold and enjoy…such property as she may hereafter acquire…from any controls of her husband David Perry. In House (20 December 1813) and Senate (21 December 1813), read second time and passed. (GASR, Nov.-Dec. 1813, Box 1: folder "HB 7 Dec.").

372.   **Poor, Polly Mira and husband, Caleb.** Petition of Polly Mira Poor, wife of Caleb Poor, notes that at the last North Carolina Assembly, she was entitled to have secured to her such property as she might thereafter acquire and hoped to peaceably possess such property as her good father would give to her, especially some slaves and a plantation called Horse Shoe Neck of the French Broad River, some eighty miles from her father's place of residence. Your petitioner states she is apprehensive that if she had said property in her possession, she could not peaceably possess it: Caleb Poor has exhibited many acts of violence and outrage, and "he might take the Property from her by force and carry it off…[T]he said Caleb Poor may have addicted some chimney corner law opinion [and] that your Humble Petitioner being the Wife of said Caleb Poor could not give Evidence against him for rob[b]ery…" Further, if said Caleb forcibly took the negroes away to the State of Tennessee or Kentucky, the judicial and civil officers would not be so ready to extend their legal assistance to your petitioner and against the said Caleb "as long as he might call your Petitioner his wife, make light of it, and say it was a small Dispute Between Husband and wife. Your Petitioner would be more Diffident, more intimidated and fearful of following the said Caleb Poor to recover the said property." A few of the actions of said Caleb are mentioned:

(1).   In a deposition of your Petitioner's father to the Assembly last session, it appeared that in September or October 1812, said father felt his life threatened by the conduct of said Caleb. On 8 January 1813, the said Caleb came to my father's house and without any known cause, "fell upon and Beat her eldest Son, then fifteen years old, with a Hickory as Big as a large Mans thumb with great Severity." The blows landed on both shoulders and arms, and the subsequent bruises and discolorations remained visible for more than three weeks. As said Caleb was beating his son, your petitioner stepped up to him, took hold of the stick and entreated him to desist in this violence. The said Caleb responded- "I would as soon give you a little or as much as not, and I would as soon kill the whole family as not." Your petitioner believes that said Caleb meant the family of your Petitioner's good father, Col. W. Avery, including which your Petitioner and her children are a part. Said Caleb then rode off in great haste about a mile to Mr. Charles Persons and soon returned with a gun. He was in a rage and used words of violence and rushed at your Petitioner's aged father saying that "he would be justifiable to massacre him that moment." Your petitioner and her aged mother were truly alarmed and were glad to see James Murphy, Esq., a Justice of the Peace, come up and seize the gun, restraining said Caleb from shooting your petitioner's father who is a cripple.

(2).   "On 6 September 1813, the said Caleb threatened the life of your petitioner's aged father again with tremendous oaths and curses…. [T]he said Caleb said that he was not too good to kill your Petitioner's father, and that he ought to kill him, or would kill him before he died. Although your Petitioner knew Caleb Poor's bad conduct, she was not in the habit of scolding at him. He is the father of all her children who are dear to her. She long suffered his rage in silence while she remained at the house where her father permitted the said Caleb to live on his land. During part of the time, it was known to your Petitioner that the said Caleb Poor kept two other women with whom he prostituted himself…[B]y the Laws of God and man [, your petitioner] hath sufficient Cause of Divorce from Caleb Poor. [She] cannot Live with him [and] it would be positively improper to put herself into his Power, as to put herself into a Lyons Mouth or the Jaws of a Bear...If a Man of Common Fortitude when a Robber Presented a Pistol to his Breast & threatens him with instant Death unless he will give up his money...does in such case Deliver his money to save his life...is he to blame for so doing? And could a weak woman be blamed for giving up her property to save her life?...Your petitioner hath much to fear from Caleb Poor." Prays an act of Assembly to grant her a divorce from her said husband. For further evidence in this case, see annexed Exhibits no. 1 and no. 2 and a certificate from the Elders of the Presbyterian Church at Quaker Meadows, Burke County, North Carolina.

(a). Exhibit no. 1. Memorial of Polly Mira Poor, wife of Caleb Poor to the North Carolina Gen'l Assembly, 1812: In July 1796, your petitioner "then being under the Age of 17 years was clandestinely married to Caleb Poor without the consent of her parents who had forbidden...[her] keeping company with the said Caleb and forbidden him the House." Your petitioner's father permitted said Caleb to live on one of his plantations and set up a tanyard to give him a chance to make a living. She lived with said Caleb and had six children- three sons and three daughters, all the time receiving considerable support of the necessaries and comforts of life from her kind parents. However, the distress, afflictions and griefs she received from her said husband made a black cloud. She did not complain to her neighbors but bore her wrongs in silence. Caleb Poor had treated her with great cruelty about the time of the birth of the sixth child in February 1808 and expressed threats of personal violence to turn her out of the house. They took up separate beds, and your petitioner complained to her father, asking permission to come home, but she was advised to stay longer, take care of her children, and try to keep this marriage together. She thereupon stayed for one more year with said Caleb, but she was unable to bring about a reconciliation, and asked her father once more if she could come home. He consented, and ever since she has lived in her chamber secluded from the world, but spends her time bringing up her children in habits of morality and industry. Your petitioner's father is an old man in the decline of life and very infirm. If your petitioner should survive him, she would lose his protecting arm for her support and could not possess property in her own right as a married woman without permission of an Act of the Assembly. The property in land and slaves intended for your Petitioner is supposed to be of the value of £10,000. Such property would enable her to support herself and her children and give them a chance of learning at an English school. Prays an Act of Assembly to secure to her such property as she may hereafter acquire.

(b). Exhibit no. 2. Deposition of Waightstill Avery before J.P. James Murphy. dated 8 September 1813, Burke County, North Carolina: Deponent slated he was at Caleb Odel's house on 6 September, and Caleb Poor came up and asked if this deponent would give up to him the Indentures for the children of said Caleb, saying- "By the Holy Jesus & by the Heavenly God, if you don't give them up I will take your Life, and I will be damned if I don't kill you." This deponent said it would not suit him to give them up, and the said Caleb then repeated the identical words four or five times. Your deponent said that "he was an old man and had not long to live...that he was a cripple unable to make any Defense, that...if [said Caleb] did kill the Deponent, it would not rob him of any great Part of Life as he had lived already nearly to the End of it-". Said Caleb Poor then said that if the deponent would not give up the Indentures in four days, he would be a dead man...and again swore by the Holy Jesus and by the Heavenly God... and followed up with "...damn your Law, I regard nothing you can do, send your Sheriff & be damned."

(c). Certificate of the Ruling Elders of the Presbyterian Church at the Quaker Meadows in Burke County, North Carolina, 12 November 1813: "We have been acquainted with Col. Waightstill Avery and his family for nearly Thirty years last past; that we have known his Daughter the said Polly Mira Poor from her childhood; that we have thought her blameable for making a runaway match with Caleb Poor; but never knew or heard of her being blamed before or since her marriage with any levity or imprudence with any other man…but believe her conduct hath been prudent and exemplary…We further certify and do believe that there is probably sufficient cause for a divorce."

(d). The Committee of Divorce and Alimony to whom was referred the Petition of Polly Mira Poor of Burke County praying for a divorce, report: The petitioner at an early age in disobedience to the wishes of her parents intermarried with the person for whom she seeks to be divorced. After living with him for twelve years and having six children by him, she was by her own solicitation received with her children into the House of her father where they have continued to receive his support. Except for the first act of disobedience, she has performed every duty of a wife and a mother, but after having suffered a series of wrongs and abuses and after seeing her marriage bed polluted by him, and herself not only neglected but personally and violently abused, and her substance divested by his debauchery and herself and children deprived of a home by his extravagance- then, and not until then, did she seek asylum in the house of her father…. The Justices of Burke County have [declared] the said Caleb Poor as unfit to have the government of his own children and have bound them by indenture to another. Several instances of the violence and depravity of said Caleb have been laid before your Committee, and we are unanimously of the opinion that her prayer should be granted and recommend the accompanying Bill. Concurred in by House (1 December 1813) and Senate (2 December 1813).

(e). Bill to Divorce Polly Mira Poor of Burke County from her husband Caleb Poor. In House (18 December 1813) and in Senate (18 December 1813), read third time, passed, and ordered to be engrossed.

(All of the above from: GASR, Nov.-Dec. 1813, Box 1: folder "HB 1 Dec.").

373. **Porter, Daniel and wife, Rhody.** Petition of Daniel Porter of Anson County represents that he married Rhody Ingrim in 1800, but a short time after said marriage, said wife lived in adultery with another man for several years and had a bastard child. Your petitioner has requested her to return and live with him, but she has utterly refused to do so. She now lives apart and has not cohabited with him for upwards of four years past. Prays for a divorce from said wife, Rhody. [Below:] Signatures of five supporters. (GASR, Nov.-Dec. 1813, Box 2: folder "Petitions - Divorces").

374. **Richardson, Sarah and husband, John.** Petition of Sarah Richardson of Randolph County states she married one John Richardson in 1799 and lived with him about two years. He "left your petitioner with a small infant in her arms and took with him what property they possessed at that time. It is reported that he resides in Tennessee and is married to another woman." Prays for a law to secure to her such property as she may hereafter acquire. (GASR, Nov.-Dec. 1813, Box 2: folder "Petitions - Divorces").

375. **Riley, Peter and wife. Patsy.** Petition of Peter Riley of Rowan County sheweth that in the year 1796, he intermarried with one Patsy Wade "whose character he had never heard questioned, and whom he believed to be amiable and virtuous. A very short time proved to him that he had been fatally mistaken in his opinion, and at the time he married her, she was actually pregnant by another man. Your petitioner could not but be sensibly affected by a discovery which at once blasted all his prospects." After repeated efforts to reclaim her proved unavailing, your petitioner was forced to separate himself from her injustice to his own reputation. The separation took place by mutual consent, and she now "has had two children by different fathers." Prays for a divorce from his said wife. (GASR, Nov.-Dec. 1813, Box 2: folder "Petitions - Divorces").

376. **Roberts, Thomas and wife, Phoebe.** Petition of Thomas Roberts and Phebe (+) Roberts, his wife, of Camden County sheweth that they "were joined together in holy wedlock in the year 1805…[and] led a very disagreeable life together until the year 1810, when your petitioner Phebe separated from your Petitioner Thomas…Your petitioners think it not necessary to detail the disagreeable circumstances that caused the separation, but they are as such as will forever prevent a reunion." Your petitioner Phebe has become attached to another man with whom she now lives and by whom she has a son. Pray for a law to divorce them from each other. (GASR, Nov.-Dec. 1813, Box 2: folder "Petitions - Divorces").

377. **Thomas, Elizabeth and husband, William.** Petition of Elizabeth Thomas of Sampson County states she intermarried with William Thomas some few years ago, but he "pursued a course of dissipation and extravagance until the property was exhausted, and she was reduced to a state of indigence and want. After six years of marriage, said William abandoned your petitioner and has gone to parts unknown to her. She is fearful that her said husband will return and waste what little property she may acquire." Prays for a law securing to her such property as she may hereafter acquire. [On reverse:] Alimony granted. (GASR, Nov.-Dec. 1813, Box 2: folder "Petitions - Divorces").

378. **Tores, Elizabeth and husband, Benjamin.** Petition of Elizabeth Tores states that "some years ago [she] unfortunately intermarried with Benjamin Tores of Salisbury, by whom she had two infant children. Your petitioner is unwilling to shew any kind of resentment towards her said husband by laying before the public the manner in which he has abandoned her and her children…[W]ere it not for the bounty of an affectionate mother, your petitioner & her two infant children would long ago have suffered for comfortable subsistence." Prays for a law to divorce her from said husband or a law to secure to her such property as she may acquire.

    (a). Petition of "Margaret Beard [signed Margaret the mother of Elizabeth Tores Humbly prays the Legislature to grant a divorce to her beloved daughter inasmuch as she is advancing in years, and having to support her said daughter and her two infant children, she wishes to provide for their welfare in a manner that shall not be subject to Debts or claims of any other person as she has honestly earned what it is now her wish to bestow upon her children…" [Below:] Signatures often persons, including one Jno. Beard, who support the above petitions. [On reverse:] "Alimony granted." (GASR, Nov.-Dec. 1813, Box 2: folder "Petitions - Divorces").

379. **Ward, Frederick and wife, Catharine.** Petition of Frederick Ward of Lincoln County sheweth that he was lawfully married about fifteen or sixteen years ago to Catharine Snider with whom he lived one year, "during which time he conducted himself as a good & affectionate husband, notwithstanding the said Catharine left your petitioner and took up with another man…[B]efore said Catharine left him, she conducted herself in a lewd way and has now moved to New Spain and…married another man." Prays aid in dissolving the bonds of matrimony by granting a divorce. [Below:] Signatures of fifty supporters of petition above.

    (a). Deposition of Barnet Snider before Jesse Perkins, JP of Lincoln County, 9 November 1813, that he is "the Brother of the Reputed wife of sd. Ward and made oath that Since the Departure of his Sister to the Louisanna he has Received a Letter Directed from his father which informd him that She was mared to a man by the name of Daniel Hubble…" [Below:] Certificate of Jesse Perkins "that in the year 1810 I was at the house of John Snider the Reputed father of Mrs. Ward which I was well acquainted with and her father and mother told me She was mared to Mr. Daniel Hubble who was then living close by them…."

Divorces and Separations from Petitions to the North Carolina General Assembly from 1779

    (b).   Committee of Divorce and Alimony to whom was referred the petition of Frederick Ward of Lincoln County…report that they have taken the prayer of the petitioner into consideration and recommend the Bill accompanying this report intitled "a Bill to Divorce Frederick Ward of Lincoln County from his wife Catharine" be passed into law. [Below:] Concurred in by House (30 November 1813) and Senate (1 December 1813).

    (c).   Bill to Divorce Frederick Ward of Lincoln County from his wife Catharine. In Senate, 1 December 1813, read first time and passed. In House, 20 December 1813, read first time and passed; read second time and rejected. (All of the above from: GASR, Nov.-Dec. 1813, Box 1: folder "HB 20 Nov.").

380.   **Wells, Fanny and husband, John.** Memorial of Fanny Wells of Caswell County states she was married some years ago to John Wells with whom she lived in tolerable harmony for many years, long enough to bear to him six children. For causes unknown, her said husband left her and the children without any means of support except for her own industry. In addition, said husband "took with him your memorialist's sister with whom he has lived in the habits of husband and wife for more than two years." Prays for either an act to grant her an absolute divorce from the bonds of matrimony from her said husband or a law to secure to her such property as she may hereafter acquire. [Below:] Deposition of Alexander Murphey of Caswell County supports statements made in the above memorial, dated 9 December 1813. (GASR, Nov.-Dec. 1813, Box 2: folder "Petitions - Divorces").

381.   **Reference A.**

    (a).   Committee of Divorce and Alimony…petition of sundry persons [unnamed] desiring to be secured in property as they may hereafter acquire- recommend approval.

    (b).   Committee of Divorce and Alimony…petition of Rebecca Bond of Wilmington praying for a divorce from her husband Samuel Bond;…Nancy Balance of Currituck County praying for a divorce from husband Charles Balance;…Catherine Alexander of Rockingham County praying for a divorce from husband William Alexander; petition of sundry inhabitants of Buncombe County praying that William Grantham of said county may be divorced from his wife Rachel:,…Jacob Perry of Pasquotank County praying to be divorced from his wife Sarah;…John D. Mask of Richmond County praying to be divorced from wife Peggy;…Thomas Benton of Rockingham County praying to be divorced from his wife Polly;…Sarah Bell of Camden County praying to be divorced from her husband Samuel Bell; Thomas Roberts and wife Phoebe of Camden County. In opinion of your Committee, neither of the petitioners is entitled to relief and recommend their petitions be rejected. In House (7 December 1813) and in Senate (8 December 1813), and concurred in. (GASR, Nov.- Dec. 1813, Box 2: folder "House Committee Reports").

    Committee of Divorce and Alimony to whom was referred the petition of Elizabeth Perry of Johnston County, praying for a divorce from her husband Reuben Perry; the petition of Joseph Hancock of Hertford County praying a divorce from his wife Tabitha; the petition of James Hoffler of Gates County praying a divorce from his wife Deborah; the petition of Nancy Perry of Carteret County playing for a divorce from her husband David Perry; and the petition of Benjamin Bass of Randolph County praying for a divorce from his wife Susannah- report that neither of the petitions merits relief and recommend they be rejected. Concurred in by House (18 December 1813) and Senate (20 December 1813). (GASR, Nov.-Dec. 1813, Box 2: folder "House Committee Reports").

    Bill to secure to Patty Beckham, wife of Zachariah Beckham of Warren County; Susanna McQuistion, wife of William McQuistion of Orange County; Elizabeth Tores, wife of Benjamin of Rowan County…any property that they may hereafter acquire. In Senate (21 December 1813) and House (22

December 1813)- read third time, passed, and ordered to be engrossed. (GASR, Nov.-Dec. 1813, Box 2: folder "SB 17 Dec.").

382. **Reference D.**
Laws of North Carolina, Nov.-Dec. 1813 Session. The persons listed on each line below, except those preceded by the letter "D", were entitled to hold, possess and enjoy, in their sole right, all such estate, either personal or real, as they may hereafter acquire by their own industry, purchase, gift or otherwise, in as full and ample manner as if they had never been married. The persons whose names are preceded by a "D" were granted full divorces from each other.

    Banks, Alsey of Burke Co.; husband - William, p. 34
    Bass, Susannah of Randolph Co.; husband - Benjamin, p. 34
    Beckham, Patty; husband - Zachariah of Warren Co., p. 24
    Braddy, Polly Bailey of Johnston Co.; husband - Richard, p. 34
    Brightman, Margaret of New Hanover Co.; husband - Joseph, p. 34
    Brown, Ann of Rowan Co.; husband - William, p. 34
    Butler, Ann L. of Granville Co.; husband - Reuben, p. 34
D   Crossland, Alexander of Warren Co.; wife - Catharine, p. 37
    Deeton, Nancy of Chatham Co.; husband - Thomas, p. 34
    Emmery, Jinny of Randolph Co.; husband - Stephen, p. 34
D   Gilmour, Stephen of Cumberland Co.; wife - Charity, p. 37
    Hatch, Polly of Lenoir Co.; husband - Henry, p. 34
    Higbie, Thisbe J.; husband - David [county unnamed], p. 34
    Hinkle, Hannah of Lincoln Co.; husband - Jacob, p. 34
    Holland, Milly of Greene Co.; husband - James, p. 34
D   Hyatt, Anna of Burke Co.; husband - Seth, p. 25
    Jones, Mary H. of Lincoln Co.; husband - Alexander, p. 34
    McKinsie, Elizabeth of Iredell Co.; husband - James, p. 34
    McQuestion, Susanna; husband - William of Orange Co., p. 34
    Neilly, Elsey of Buncombe Co.; husband - William, p. 34
    Perry, Nancy of Carteret Co.; husband - Daniel, p. 34
D   Poor, Polly Mira of Burke Co.; husband - Caleb, p. 37
    Thomas, Elizabeth of Surry Co.; husband - William, p. 34
    Tores, Elizabeth; husband - Benjamin of Rowan Co., p. 24
    Wells, Fanny of Caswell Co.; husband - John, p. 34

1814

383. **Bass, Susannah and husband, Benjamin.** Petition of Susannah Bass of Randolph County sheweth she intermarried with a certain Benjamin Bass of the same county in 1810 and lived with him but a short time. She "discovered that in violation of the marriage vows and…of the duty he owed your petitioner, he pursued measures for his own gratification which decency forbids her to name, and which placed him upon an equality with the lowest Class of Human beings we have in this Country." She advised him to refrain from such practices, for it "might eventually destroy that affection, confidence and harmony which ought to exist between man & wife…" Unfortunately, her husband, regardless of his promise to change, continued his wicked, immoral and shameful conduct, and a separation took place. Your petitioner "repaired to her father's house for shelter and protection, at which place she has ever since resided." Her said husband at length removed himself westward with full determination never to see your petitioner again. It is improbable that a reconciliation will take place, and she prays for a law to divorce her from the said Benjamin Bass. [Below:] Signatures of five persons who affirm that said petitioner is a girl under a good carractor [sic] & well respected by all her neighbours. (GASR, Nov.-Dec. 1814, Box 2: folder "Petitions - Divorce and Alimony"). See number 549 (Bass, Benjamin and wife, Susannah) in this magazine, August 1997, pages 277, 278.

384. **Boyce, Isaac and wife, Nancy (White)**[35]. Petition of Isaac (X) Boyce sheweth that in January 1805, his wife. Nancy, "…absconded from his bed and board without any just cause and has ever since taken up with another man and is now living in open acts of adultery…" Your petitioner has endeavoured to induce said Nancy to return and live with him but has never succeeded. Prays for a divorce from said Nancy Boyce. [Below:] Signatures of forty-four persons support the above petition.
Petition of Nancy (X) Boyce of Chowan County humbly sheweth that she was married to Isaac Boyce some years ago, and for the past eight years, she has not been able to live with him. Prays for a divorce from said Isaac Boyce. (Petitions above from GASR, Nov.-Dec. 1814, Box 2: folder "Petitions - Divorce and Alimony").

385. **Brady, Love (Sears) and husband, Mills.** Memorial of Love (+) Brady, formerly Sears, represents she intermarried with one Mills Brady upwards of two years last past, and your memorialist was possessed of considerable property at the time, including negroes. The said Mills "…did beat and iltreat your memorialist without cause on her part and spent and wasted the whole of the property and finally left your memorialist without anything to subsist on other than the Charity of Friends…" The said Mills "took up with a certain Selah Eure with whom he lives, and there is no probability of a reconciliation between us…" Prays that a law be passed to secure to her any property she may hereafter acquire and barring said Brady from any claim on such property. [Below:] Signatures of fifteen persons who subscribe to the above petition.

---

35 Marriage Bond of Chowan County, dated 17 October 1798, lists the parties as Isaac Boyce and Nancy White.

Deposition of Jesse Savage, former guardian to Love Brady, the petitioner named above, before Charles W. Harvey and Hillery Willey, Justices of Peace of Gates County, 22 November 1814, states the said Love Brady lived with this deponent until within a few days of her intermarriage with said Mills Brady, and "that she was nearly fourteen years of age, had property of four negroes and some cash, that from general report and bruses and wound he had seen on her the said Love…," he has reason to believe that said Brady did often beat and illtreat the said Love.

Deposition of William Sears before Charles W. Harvey and Hillery Willey, Justices of the Peace of Gates County, 22 November 1814, states the said Love had at different times come to the deponent's house, beaten and bruised, saying that her husband, Mills Brady, had beat her. This deponent had seen said Mills Brady leaving with Selah Eure, and the property was all spent.

Deposition of Capt. Mills Lewis before Charles W. Harvey and Hillery Willey, Justices of Peace of Gates County, 22 November 1814, states Love Brady came to his house "considerably beaten and bruised saying her husband had done it…" A short time later. Mills Brady came to this deponent's house enquiring after the said Love, saying "if she would Emediately return home…Well, if not, he would beat her worse than he had done…[and] this deponent heard Mills Brady say he intended to try to get divorced from the said Love…"

(Papers above from GASR, Nov.-Dec. 1814, Box 2: folder "Petitions - Divorce and Alimony").

386. **Clark, Lucy and husband, William Henry.** Petition of Lucy Clark of Chatham County represents that "at an early period of life and before her Judgment had been tempered by experience and discretion, she intermarried with a certain William Henry Clark of said county and…her prospects of hapiness were as bright, and her hopes of conjugal felicity as sanguine as any other person of her sex…, and she made use of every exertion and precaution on her part to prevent a dimunition of those connubial enjoyments, which usually afford a rich relish to the cup of matrimony." However, after a few months had elapsed, the conduct of said William Henry Clark towards your petitioner proved that her confidence had been misplaced, and her "prospects therefore became blasted, and all her hopes of hapiness inveloped in Misery and delusion. To recite the tyranical conduct of the said William…towards your Petioner would only tend to Mortify her feelings already wounded…" Instead, your Petitioner "will only add that by the extravagance & waste of her husband…their little property was soon consumed and your Petitioner abandoned." Prays for an act to secure to her what property she may hereafter acquire. Dated 13 October 1814. (GASR, Nov.-Dec. 1814, Box 2: folder "Petitions - Divorce and Alimony").

387. **Collins, Benjamin and wife, Avis.** Petition of Benjamin Collins sheweth he intermarried with one Avis Bowen and had the fondest anticipation of finding mutual satisfaction among his family, but such hopes were "most suddenly blasted. Urged on by lust and a most criminal attachment to another man, Avis within little more than twelve months deserted the house and refused all intercourse with her husband." Your petitioner tried all suitable means to reclaim her and was conscious of having at all times acted towards her as a kind and obliging husband. "It is now about eight years since Avis went away…," and he has had no communication with her. "She, however, has become one of the most abandoned prostitutes- is now the mother of three bastard children and at present pregnant with another- and has gone to the State of Virginia where her prostitution is notorious." Prays for a divorce. Supported by the signatures of twenty-eight subscribers. A Bill to Divorce Benjamin Collins from his wife Avis Collins. In Senate 28 November, read first time and passed. In House of Commons, 27 December 1814, read first time and postponed indefinitely. (GASR, Nov.-Dec. 1814, Box 1: folder "SB 28 Nov.")

Divorces and Separations from Petitions to the North Carolina General Assembly from 1779

388. **Colyear, Polly (Phillips) and husband, John.** Petition of Polly Colyear of Buncombe County sheweth that she intermarried with a certain John Colyear in 1804 and hoped to enjoy peace and harmony. To the contrary, in about three months, he misused and ill-treated her in such a way that no satisfaction of life could be had, and in about eight months from the time of marriage, a final separation took place. He removed himself to the "State of Caintucky Leaving your petitioner in a state of pregnancy & there has married another woman & has several children by her & from his many threats your Memorialist knows not when he may return & strip your petitioner of what Little she has acquired by her hard Industry, haveing no other way to support herself & one child…" Prays for relief by granting alimony to her and securing to her such property as she may hereafter acquire. [Below:] Signatures of five persons who are neighbors and "have had a long acquaintance with her."

    Deposition of William Colyear before William P. Chester, Justice of Peace of Washington County, Tennessee, 14 November 1814, states that John Colyear, formerly a citizen of Tennessee, married Polly Phillips of Buncombe County, North Carolina, in the year of 1804, but has since removed himself to the State of Kentucky and married there a second wife with whom he has lived for seven years. The deponent has been in said john's neighborhood, and it was the general understanding that said john was married, and this deponent has also been told the same story by john's parents and brothers. (GASR, nov.-Dec. 1814, Box 2: folder "petitions - divorce and alimony").

389. **Davis, Jane and husband, Wiley J.** Petition of Jane Davis of Richmond County states she intermarried with Wiley J. Davis on 19 April 1809, "who at that time was a practitionary of Psychic…" On entering into the State of Matrimony, she was determined to add to the common stock of domestic felicity. However, her said husband abandoned your Petitioner to the utmost distress - including the withholding of all means of subsistence and she was compelled "to bid farewell to every spark of domestic tranquillity." The said Wiley J. Davis, in a fit of intoxication, enlisted for the term of five years in the service of the United States, and in which service he still remains. Prays for a law annulling the ties of matrimony between them. [Below:] Signatures of seven persons subscribe to this petition. [On reverse:] Ordered to lie on table. (GASR, Nov.-Dec. 1814, Box 2: folder "Petitions - Divorce and Alimony").

390. **Dowday, Eliza and husband, John.** Petition of Eliza (X) Dowday of Currituck County sheweth that about seven years ago she intermarried with John Dowday, hoping to enjoy the blessing of married life. However, in a short time, said husband began to treat your petitioner in a most horrid manner and continued to do so until about "five or six years ago, he turned me out of his house without the least means of support. Despite frequent solicitations by your petitioner to return to live with him as a loving wife, his answer is accompanied by threats of violence. He has taken up with another woman and by her has had three children and he still lives with her as his wife. His conduct has reduced his circumstances to insolvency and he is unable to properly support his Miss and children. Your petitioner is likely to inherit a small sum by the death of her father, and prays an act securing to her any property she may hereafter acquire." (GASR, Nov.-Dec. 1814, Box 2: folder "Petitions - Divorce and Alimony").

391. **Dunagan, Nancy and husband, James.** Petition of Nancy Dunagan states that "in the year 1810 it was her misfortune to become acquainted with a man by the name of James Dunagan who paid his addresses to her in the way of Honorable courtship - that after some time she consented to marry him…" in the same year. A "year had scarcely elapsed before the said James Dunagan left her & has never returned. She has been informed & does believe that he was, at the time he married her, the husband of another woman - that since he has left her he has again married & has announced to your Petitioner

his intention of not returning to this State." Prays for an act to divorce her from said James Dunagan. (GASR, Nov.-Dec. 1814, Box 2: folder "Petitions - Divorce and Alimony").

392. **Ferguson/Farguson/Fargerson, Mary G. and husband, Joel.** Petition of Mary G. Farguson of Granville County sheweth that her husband, Joel Ferguson, abandoned her a few years ago without leaving any means of subsistence and entirely dependent upon her own exertion and the hospitality of friends for the daily support of herself and child. Prays that she be secured in what property she may hereafter acquire, free from the claims of her said husband. (GASR, Nov.-Dec. 1814, Box 2: folder "Petitions - Divorce and Alimony").

Committee to whom was referred the Petition of Mary G. Fergusson and a Bill to secure to her such property as she may hereafter acquire report they are satisfied of the truth of the facts and recommend the passage of the Bill. (GASR, Nov.-Dec. 1814, Box 2: folder "HCR").

Bill to secure to Mary C. Fargerson of Granville County, wife of Joel Fargerson, Jr., such estate, real or personal, as she may hereafter acquire. In House, read third time and passed (10 December). (GASR, Nov.-Dec. 1814, Box 1: folder "HB 2 Dec.")

393. **Field, Peggy and husband, Jeremiah.** Petition of Peggy Field of Guilford County sheweth that her husband, Jeremiah Field, enlisted in the Army of the United States and left your petitioner with a number of small children in low and indigent circumstances without a means of support and faced to pay debts contracted by her said husband. Prays for a law to secure to her such estate as she may acquire either by gift or her own industry during the absence of her said husband. [On reverse:] "Granted." (GASR, Nov.-Dec. 1814, Box 2: folder "Petitions - Divorce and Alimony").

394. **Gregory, Edmond and wife, Mary (Loyd).** Petition of Edmond Gregory states he was lawfully married to Mary Loyd in the Town of Tarborough in 1807, and a short time later, urgent business compelled him to leave home and go to the State of Tennessee for a period not exceeding three months. While he was away, his said wife, assisted by some male inhabitants of Tarborough, managed to run into considerable debt, and your petitioner's property was attached to them without advertising this event as directed by law. In consequence, property in the amount of nearly two thousand dollars was seized and sold in a clandestine manner. Although the amount of the attachment did not exceed $120, the said Mary Gregory laid a petition before the Honorable General Assembly praying that all property hereafter acquired might be secured to her. A bill was passed which honored the petition. [See number 330 (Gregory, Mary and husband Edmond) in this magazine, February 1995, page 54.] Your petitioner requests an investigation of facts in this memorial which has resulted in injuries to your petitioner brought about by a depraved conspiracy of a deluded woman and designing men.

Memorial of sixty-four persons in support of the above petition of Edmond Gregory state that said Gregory is of a respectable family in this State. In the early period of his life, he married an amiable woman, and they lived in a happy state until his said wife died within a few years. After his wife's death, said Gregory was in Tarborough, met his present wife, and they married and lived happily for some time. The said Gregory was compelled to settle some business in Tennessee, and during his absence, "vipers under the mask of friendship stole into his family, deluded his wife, and ruined his peace forever. Yes, Gentlemen, deceived by their Sophistry, an act you were innocently led to commit - an act of oppression which would have disgraced the arbitrary sway of an Eastern Prince and more like a Turkish Bashaw [now written Pasha] than the cool decision of an enlightened Senate; for by the passing of that bill, the repeal of which I now claim, an injured citizen already wounded in the nicest point - his feelings trampled to dust...is drove from his home, his wife torn from his arms, and his property delivered as a reward to [villainy] and vice & by that Assembly which should have guarded his liberty and his wrights…he has a little Daughter the only pledge of his affection…" He therefore places confidence in this Honorable Body for relief by repealing the bill now in question. (GASR, Nov.-Dec. 1814, Box 2: folder "Petitions - Divorce and Alimony").

    Committee of Alimony to whom was referred the petition of Edmond Gregory praying for alimony had the same under consideration and recommend the same be rejected. In House and Senate (23 December) and concurred with. (GASR, Nov.-Dec. 1814, Box 2: folder "HCR").

395. **Griswould, Mary and husband, James.** Memorial of Mary Griswould represents she intermarried with one James Griswould about five years ago and lived in harmony and mutual satisfaction until September 1812, when he "left on a journey, as he said, to the State of New York to sell some property he had there, and has never since returned." During his absence, all the property belonging to your memorialist has been sold to satisfy debts contracted by the said husband. Information has been received from that part of New York where the said Griswould claimed he owned property that no such person was ever known there. From information available, it is generally believed that the said Griswould never intended to return, "and if living is probably now in the embraces of another wife." Prays for a law securing to her such property as she may hereafter acquire. (GASR, Nov.-Dec. 1814, Box 2: folder "Petitions - Divorce and Alimony").

396. **Hackett, Alley and husband, Thomas.** Letter from H. Branson, Fayetteville, North Carolina, 20 December 1814, states that Thomas Hackett has not been able to attend to his own business, and the County Court appointed a guardian for him. His real and personal property was sold some time past to pay his debts, and his wife (Alley Hackett) is left without house or home. On the last day of the County Court, said Thomas was represented as being able to transact his own business, and the Court released him from guardianship. However, there is no hope of his ever doing anything for his family. Request that an amendment be made to the Bill to secure to his wife such property as she may hereafter acquire. [Below:] An endorsement by seven persons support the request. (GASR, Nov.-Dec. 1814, Box 2: folder "Petitions - Divorce and Alimony").

397. **Hannah, Nancy and husband, Robert, Jr.** Petition of fifteen inhabitants of Guilford County state that Nancy Hannah, consort of Robert Hannah, Jr., of said county, has been left by her said husband in a destitute and helpless simation with a large family and little or nothing upon which to subsist except what she acquired by her own labor. The said Robert has absconded, having previously become debt-ridden and all his property sold. Pray for an act securing to the said Nancy what property she has or may acquire by her own labor. (GASR, Nov.-Dec. 1814, Box 2: folder "Petitions - Divorce and Alimony").

398. **Heath, John and wife, Rachel.** Petition of John Heath of Craven County sheweth "That he has the misfortune to have for wife a woman who utterly unmindful of the duties of the connection, has for many years treated your petitioner with unkindness and disrespect, and at length in contempt of decency, morality and religion, has for nearly two years deserted your petitioners house, and associated herself with a negro fellow, a slave, with whom there is but too much reason to believe she keeps up an adulterous intercourse." For proof of this conduct, refer to accompanying petitions. Prays for a divorce from his said wife. Dated 10 November 1814. (GASR, Nov.-Dec. 1814, Box 2: folder "Petitions - Divorce and Alimony").

Deposition of Polly Carmack before Daniel Simmons, Justice of Peace of Jones County, states she was at Mr. [John] Heath's…"when there was a Neagre fellow by the Name of Dublin belonging to Mr. James Bright came there and he said Good Nighty and Mrs. Heath the wife of sd. John Heath said-Lord…Dublin…is that you. Yes Madam he replide. She said aint you a cold…if you are come in and warm and if you are - fetch in some wood and put on the fire and he so did and She the Sd. Mrs. Heath got up out of her Seet and went to Mr. Heath and laide hir Child in his Lap. She then told Doublin to take hir chear and Set near the fire and warm and he So Did…She then ast him how is Mr. Bright people…he said they were well madam…She then Said how is my Mothers people…he replide they was well…She then ast him if he was a hongry. no madam…I have vittels in my cart…She then went and got him warm Vittuels and Sat it on the table and ast him to Set nigh and Eate his Supper which he the Sd. Doublin Did…. Mr. Heath then ast his wife if she had Supper for us. 0 yes say she…She then stept away to the shelf and took Down a Bason with some Colde Soope in it and porde Some in the Skillet and Set to Mr. Heath in the corner. Mr. Heath reacht Down & took hold of it and Set it Still further in the corner and did not Eate any of it…further the Deponant Sayeth not.

"Mrs. Davice personally appeared at the sd. time and Deposeth and Sayeth that the Day after [Mrs. Heath]…left Mr. Heath She came to hir house and Mrs. Davice ast hir the said Mrs. Heath if She Did tell Mr. Heath that she had rather be Doublin's wife than his…hir reply was She Did. Sd. Mrs. Davice ast hir what Did She Do it for…She said She did it for aggravation and further the Deponent Sayeth Not.

"Also at the same time Mr. William Watson and his wife Sinthy and Nancey Watson Did all three appear & Deposeth and Sayeth they were all at Mr. Heath's one Night…that Rachel Heath Said that her husband had had a Child by hir - know thanks to him after the Neagre." 3 September 1813. (GASR, Nov.-Dec. 1814, Box 3: folder "Miscellaneous").[36]

399. **Hobbs, Sarah and husband, Nehemiah.** Petition of Sarah Hobbs of Guilford County states she was married to Nehemiah Hobbs in 1796, and they lived together about eleven years. During this time, he did little to make a living and finally left for Ohio, leaving her with five small children and little or no support as well as large, unpaid debts. Prays for a law to secure to her what little property she now has or may hereafter acquire. [Below:] Subscribed to by the signatures of twelve supporters. Dated 17 November 1814. [On reverse:] "Granted." (GASR, Nov.-Dec. 1814, Box 2: folder "Petitions - Divorce and Alimony").

400. **Hunt, Martha and husband, William.** Petition of Martha Hunt of Granville County represents that about the year 1801, she married her present husband, William Hunt, at which time she was possessed of "a handsome little property, all of which by bad management & Imprudance of said William has been since consumed and distributed towards the payment of his debts And now the said William without making any provision for Her future support has absented himself from her & As she supposes gone to some distant part of the Union." Prays for a law to secure to her the possession of such property as she may hereafter acquire. Dated 15 December 1814. [Below:] Signatures of six neighbors and acquaintances support her request. [On reverse:] "Report in favor." (GASR, Nov.-Dec. 1814, Box 2: folder "Petitions - Divorce and Alimony").

---

36 One other deposition by John Heath is filed in the same location as the one above. It is lengthy (four pages), very colloquial in speech and spelling, includes several long oaths uttered by Mrs. Rachel Heath to her husband, and includes the same incidents as related in the deposition of Polly Carmack but from a different point of view. This deposition is not abstracted here.

Divorces and Separations from Petitions to the North Carolina General Assembly from 1779

401. **Johnson, Polly (Record) and husband, Moses.** Petition of Polly Johnson in Chatham County sheweth she was married to Moses Johnson in 1810 in Randolph County [37] and had confidence of enjoying connubial happiness to a superlative degree. Alas, he neglected to provide for his family, and what little they has was used to discharge his tavern and other debts occasioned by his disorderly conduct. He frequently abused and beat his wife in a manner that decency forbids her to mention. Your petitioner has been turned adrift in a state of pregnancy…[and with] two small children. Prays that her case be taken into consideration and that she be granted alimony. [Below:] Signatures of ten persons support her petition. [On reverse:] "Granted."

    Depositions of Peter Foust, Samuel Russell, and J. Marly affirm that Moses Johnson of Randolph County abused and beat his wife without any provocation. (GASR, Nov.-Dec. 1814, Box 2: folder "Petitions - Divorce and Alimony").

402. **Jordan, Sarah and husband, George.** Petition of Sarah Jordan (wife of George Jordin) of Stokes County shows that her said husband has involved your petitioner and himself in debt…[and] they are in indigent circumstances…and…the creditors have executions levied on the corn, meat, yam and cloth in the loom, which your petitioner and her children "honestly labour for-". Almost all the property of said George has been sold at public sale by the Sheriff. Her husband has been in close confmement in Stokes County jail but came out by the act of insolvency. She has a father and brothers who would be willing to contribute something towards the support of your petitioner and her children, provided it was secure from the said George and his creditors. Prays for a law to secure to her such property as she may hereafter acquire by her own industry, gift, will or otherwise. [Below:] Subscribed to by the signatures of ten supporters. [On reverse:] "Rejected." (GASR, Nov.-Dec. 1814, Box 2: folder "Petitions Divorce and Alimony").

403. **Leigh, Sarah and husband, Benjamin.** Petition of Sarah (X) Leigh of Perquimans County sheweth she married Benjamin Leigh of said county in 1806, and at that time, she was in possession of a considerable amount of property. About twelve months ago, said Benjamin "left her & removed to the State of Tennessee, taking with him another woman (who she is informed he has since married) as also the greatest part of the property which he had by her at the time of their intermarriage." Prays for an act to secure to her such property as she now has and what she may thereafter acquire. Dated 28 September 1814. [Below] Signatures of fifteen supporters of her petition. (GASR, Nov.-Dec. 1814, Box 2: folder "Petitions - Divorce and Alimony").

404. **Lewis, Patsey (Cox) and husband, Stephen.** Petition of Patsey Lewis of Randolph County states she intermarried with Stephen Lewis of said county in September 1811.[38] They lived together for about three months, but for some unknown cause, the said Stephen removed himself to the western country leaving your petitioner to depend entirely upon her own industry and the assistance other friends for subsistence. In the latter part of 1812, her said husband returned to Randolph County but showed no disposition to return to his duty as a husband and live with your petitioner. In January 1813, he removed himself to some of the settlements on the Mississippi River, as she has been informed and believes. Prays for an act to secure to her such property as she may hereafter acquire. [Below:] Signatures of

---

37   Marriage Bond of Randolph County, dated 28 November 1810, lists the parties as Moses Johnson and Mary Record.

38   Marriage Bond of Randolph County, dated 19 September 1811, lists the parties as Stephen Lewis and Marther Cox.

supporters. [On reverse:] "Granted." (GASR, Nov.-Dec. 1814, Box 2: folder "Petitions - Divorce and Alimony").

405. **Machen, Thomas W. and wife, Mary (Rowe?).** Petition of Thomas W. Machen of Craven County "sheweth that his wife Mary has for some time past abandoned herself to shameless prostitution and forfeited every claim to the affection of a husband or to the respect of Society."[39] (GASR, Nov.-Dec. 1814, Box 2: folder "Petitions - Divorce and Alimony").

Bill to divorce Thomas W. Machen of Craven County from his wife Mary. In Senate (17 December), read first time and passed. In House of Commons (19 December), read first time and ordered to be indefinitely postponed. (GASR, Nov.-Dec. 1814, Box 1: folder "SB 13 Dec.")

406. **Mason, Richard and wife, Margaret (Walker).** Petition of Richard Mason shews he intermarried in 1811 with Margaret Walker, a woman of good character and of a respectable family. However, instead of enjoying a degree of happiness in this Union, said Margaret eloped from his house without any reason whatever, and for some time has been living in open adultery with David Cowen, a man whose character has been corrupt and perfidious. In order to effect such a connection it was necessary for said David and Margaret to expel from David's house a defenseless, unoffending wife and three small children. Your petitioner is now compelled to remain in this situation…equal to a sentence of misery and distress the balance of his life. Prays for a divorce from his wife, Margaret.

Deposition of James Porter, Francis Irwin, and Robert McComb before Robert Robinson and William Davidson, Justices of the Peace of Mecklenburg County, 16 November 1814: James Porter stated he resided in the house of Richard Mason some six to twelve months before the separation of Mr. Mason and his wife and had opportunity of observing their conduct. Mr. Mason always supplied his wife and family with all the necessarys of life, but the conduct of Mrs. Mason towards her husband was not that becoming of a wife. Last Fall, when Mr. Mason was on a trip to Virginia, "it was evident that Mrs. Mason held improper intercourse with David F. Cowan. On Mr. Mason's return, he received information of his wife's behaviour. He asked your deponent to be with him to see if the report was correct, and they concealed themselves for this purpose. The said David F. Cowan came to said Mason's house in the night, and they heard Mrs. Mason agree to go and be with said Cowan. Mr. Mason then went in and drove her off, but on her promise to behave better, he took her back. They lived together again but a short time, and the said Mrs. Mason and said Cowan have been living together for a considerable time."

Deposition of Francis Irwin and Robert McComb state that Mr. Richard Mason treated his wife well, but that Mrs. Mason has been living with David F. Cowan for a considerable length of time and that Cowan left his own wife.

All of the above from: (GASR, Nov.-Dec. 1814, Box 1: folder "HB 2 Dec.")

Signatures of six persons in Charlotte, North Carolina, November 1814, support the petition of Richard Mason for a divorce and solicit the Legislature to grant him the relief for which he prays. (GASR, Nov.-Dec. 1814, Box 2: folder "Petitions - Divorce and Alimony").

Bill to divorce Richard Mason of Mecklenburg County from his wife, Margaret. Read and ordered to be on the table until called up. (GASR, Nov.-Dec. 1814, Box 1: folder "HB 2 Dec.")

407. **Mitchell, James G. and wife, Faith(ey)(Davis).** Memorial of James G. Mitchell of Raleigh, Wake County, represents that he married Faith Davis in December 1811 by license from the Clerk of

---

39 Marriage Bond of Craven County, dated 10 May 1808, lists the parties as Thomas W. Machen and Mar/ Rowe.

Divorces and Separations from Petitions to the North Carolina General Assembly from 1779

Wake County. [40] A short time after the marriage, as your memorialist endeavoured to be an affectionate husband and fulfill his duties under the civil and religious institutions of this country, his said wife, Faith, left his bed and board. Neither partners now desire to continue the marriage. Prays for a divorce from his said wife, Faith. (GASR, Nov.-Dec. 1814, Box 2: folder "Petitions - Divorce and Alimony"). Bill to divorce James G. Mitchell of Wake County from his wife Faithy. Read and ordered to lie on the table. (GASR, Nov.-Dec. 1814, Box 1: folder "Miscellaneous Bills").

408. **Patton, Joseph and wife, Patsey (Person).** Petition of Joseph Patton "Shews that he was married about seven years past to a woman of the name of Patsey Person as I thought amiable for Beauty and Virtue but her charms was only an outward show, for we had not lived together more than a few months before…to my great sorrow…all her amiable quallities and her affections to me were transfered to another man and so lost to Virtue and Shame was Shee that I have Caut her often in the act of adultery. Yet unwilling to leve her or make a Publick Example of her I took her and removed to another State hopeing…to reclaim her back to the path of Vertue and Honor…but all in vain. She proved if anything reather worse…She left my bed and board and went home to her fathers house whare she Remaind…not long before the Birth of an unlawful begotten Child and now to Crown the whole She has married another man and gone whare I know not." Prays for a divorce. Dated 10 November 1814. [On reverse:] "Ordered to be on the table indefinitely." (GASR, Nov.-Dec. 1814, Box 2: folder "Petitions - Divorce and Alimony").

409. **Perry, Nancy and husband, David.** Bill to divorce Nancy Perry of Carteret County from her husband, David Perry. Petition and vouchers withdrawn by Col. Roberts. (GASR, Nov.-Dec. 1814, Box 1: folder "Miscellaneous Bills").

410. **Powell, Elizabeth and husband, John.** Petition of Elizabeth Powell of Richmond County states she intermarried with John Powell of said county in 1808 and hoped "that her days would be spent in the utmost conjugal felicity". However, in a few days, she found "that her exertions were in vain…her hopes were delusive." The said John Powell became a victim to vicious habits, and he "would return to his fireside where love and harmony should hold their easy sway, but…he would often commit the most horrid acts of brutality." Further, he totally neglected to furnish her with the means of subsistence and then "abandoned her to the protection of the world and the aid and clemency of indigent friends." A few weeks ago, the said John "…[b]argained, sold…and conveyed your Petitioner to a certain Josiah Sheppard for a trivial consideration, and she…has thus become a species of personal property…" Prays for an absolute divorce and that she may be allowed to enjoy what property she may hereafter acquire. [Below:] Subscribed to by the signatures of nine persons. (GASR, Nov.-Dec. 1814, Box 2: folder "Petitions - Divorce and Alimony").

411. **Powers, Lucy and husband, Rodham.** Petition of Lucy Powers of Wake County states she is a poor woman with four small children. Her husband, Rodham Powers, from his intemperance and misfortunes, became involved in debts to the amount of all his little property. He is now serving his country as a drafted militiaman from Wake County at Norfolk [Virginia]. Since his departure, his creditors have pressed for what is owed them, and the whole of the little property he left to support his family will in a few days be sold. Prays for a law granting to her the privilege of holding such property as she may hereafter acquire. [On reverse:] "Rejected."

---

40   Marriage Bond of Wake County, dated 27 December 1811, lists the parties as James G. Mitchell and Faithey Davis.

412. **Pugh, Rebecca and husband, James.** Petition of Rebecca Pugh of Sampson County represents she intermarried with James Pugh some years ago, and at that time, she "was in tolerable circumstances." However, her said husband was negligent and extravagant, and she has been reduced to "almost perfect want." In this situation with three small children to support, he left her in considerable debt and enlisted in the United States Army. Prays for an act to secure to her whatever property she may hereafter acquire. [On reverse:] "Allowed." (GASR, Nov.-Dec. 1814, Box 2: folder "Petitions Divorce and Alimony").

413. **Rankin, Samuel and wife, Jean (Meek).** Petition of Samuel Rankin of Mecklenburg County sheweth he intermarried with Jean Meek in September 1806 with the expectation that "their days in this life would be crowned with felicity and happiness...during the time they lived together, which was about six years, the said Jean became the mother of two children-". But alas, it was plainly demonstrated that others were more the objects of her affections. When her infidelity to him became publicly known, a separation took place, and a division of his property was made by six persons, who allotted to said Jean her part. Prays for a divorce. [On reverse:] In House of Commons (2 December) and ordered to lie on the table until called up. (GASR, Nov.-Dec. 1814, Box 1: folder "Miscellaneous Bills").

414. **Riddle, Susannah and husband, Harmon.** Petition of Susannah Riddle shows she married Harmon Riddle of Buncombe County at the age of fifteen years. After four weeks of marriage, said Harmon left her without any cause, and your petitioner returned to her father. She has since learned that her said husband has married another woman, has three children, and lives in the Mississippi Territory. Your petitioner's father is an old man possessed of a large property. Prays an act to secure to her such property as she may hereafter acquire by her own industry as well as by her father's donation. [On reverse:] "Granted." (GASR, Nov.-Dec. 1814, Box 2: folder "Petitions - Divorce and Alimony").

415. **Riley, Peter and wife, Patsy (Wade).** Petition of Peter Riley of Rowan County "sheweth that about twenty years ago he intermarried with a certain Patsey Wade who was Pregnant at the time of their marriage...[and] shortly after, she was delivered of a Son which your petitioner is conscious is none of his, but which he was unwilling to Disclaim - hoping to Enjoy in the then happy union with the woman the fascinating pleasures of Connubial happiness..." Your petitioner further states that he had business which required him to go to South Carolina less than two years after said marriage, and he was absent about eight months. On his return, "said wife had Voluptuously destroyed his property and abandoned her duties as a wife and mother...the wife of your petitioner has ever since lived in adultry and has supported the Character of a Base Lewd Woman and has frequently Carried in her arms the fruits of her abominable licentious and lewd habits..." Prays for a divorce from said wife, Patsey. [Below:] The signatures of fourteen persons support the above petition.

[Below:] Certificate of Patsey (X) Riley, wife of Peter Riley: "...Being conscious of the truth of the facts alledged in the [above] petition...Do believe that there is not a probability (nor even a possibility) of a Reconciliation taking place Between myself and husband." Prays that he be granted relief prayed for in his petition. [On reverse:] In House of Commons, 30 November 1814, read and ordered to lie on table, subject to be taken up at a future day.

[Attachment:] Deposition of Manring (X) Brookshire and Joseph Robbins before Colen Steel, Justice of Peace of Randolph County, 17 November 1814, who depose that they are well acquainted with Patsy Ryley, wife of Peter Ryley, "who ever since She Eloped from her husband has been under the Character of a lewd Base woman and that we are both nearly connected Unto her by mariage and have generally lived a Near Neighbour unto her and have had an Opportunity of Observing her general conduct…"

[Attachment:] Deposition of James Miller before Josiah Lyndon, Justice of Peace of Randolph County, sayeth that he is personally acquainted with Peter Riley of Rowan County both before and after his intermarriage with Patsey Wade and supports the facts in the petition of said Peter. The deponent has been "well acquainted with the aforesaid Patsey…and her conduct has been so base that he, this deponent, never Blamed the said Riley, your petitioner." Dated 17 November 1813.

Depositions of Herman Miller and Rhodus Riley are similar in content as the depositions above. (GASR, Nov.-Dec. 1814, Box 2: folder "Petitions - Divorce and Alimony").

416. **Roane, Margaret and husband, Jesse.** Memorial of Margaret Roane states she married Jesse Roane in October 1812 and hoped they would live together in peace and harmony. However, in a few weeks, her husband abused and ill-treated her without any just cause of provocation. He compelled her often "to take refuge in the woods and to lie out. This cruel treatment continued until the Winter of 1813, when her husband absconded and left her destitute of the Common Necessaries of Life and has continued absent ever since in parts unknown to your Memorialist." Her husband was often rebuked by his neighbors for his shameful conduct, and many efforts were made to induce him to reform, but all to no purpose. Prays that her case be taken into consideration and that she be granted such relief as "you shall think her entitled to…" Dated 26 October 1814. Signatures of sixteen persons subscribe to the plight of the memorialist.

[Below:] Certificate of Benjamin Suddath states "that Margrit Roan was obliged to lay qu[ie]te in the woods for some days in consequence of this in treatmente of her Husband & further say that I heard the said Rone when braught by the offisser that he treated her with Evry onbecoming Languig that a heathing will note make use of & further say that he is one of the ilist Disposed men that I ever was acquainted with…"

(GASR, Nov.-Dec. 1814, Box 2: folder "Petitions - Divorce and Alimony").

417. **Shaw, Polly and husband, Ha(i)ley.** Petition of Polly Shaw of Randolph County represents that she intermarried with Haley Shaw on 17 September 1807. They lived together for some considerable time in an agreeable manner and enjoyed the sweets and pleasures of conjugal happiness but without issue. At length, her said husband "betook himself to base, lewd, vile practices running about and keeping company with other women as base and as lewd and as vile as himself and cohabiting with them…" Your petitioner would have been willing to live with him provided he gave up these abominable practices. Alas, he continued "to fill up the Cup of his Iniquity" and "has formed an acquaintance with a woman of Colour and She now carries in her Arms the fruits of their Illicit Amours." Furthermore, previous to 4 February last, her said husband abused her in such a manner that she considered her life in danger and fled to the house of one of the neighbors. On 4 February, your petitioner and her said husband agreed to separate and live apart. Prays for an act to divorce her from her said husband. [Below:] Signatures of five persons subscribe to the petition above.

Bill to divorce Polly Shaw of Randolph County from her husband, Hailey Shaw. Read and ordered to lie on the table. (GASR, Nov.-Dec. 1814, Box 1: folder "Miscellaneous Bills").

418. **Spears, Sally and husband, Absalom.** Petition of Sally Spears of Edgecombe County states she possessed some property when she intermarried with one Absalom Spears a few years ago, but said Absalom wasted "the whole of his subsistence, became a common drunkard, and about two years ago left your petitioner with one child to shift for themselves…" Prays for an act to secure to her such property

as she may hereafter acquire. [Below:] Signatures of eight persons of Edgecombe County subscribe to petition above. (GASR, Nov.-Dec. 1814, Box 2: folder "Petitions - Divorce and Alimony").

419. **Tapley, Tempy and husband, Robert.** Petition of Tempy Tapley of Montgomery County sheweth she intermarried with Robert Tapley about eight years ago. They lived together for about two years, and "she neglected no means on her part to render the situation of her husband as agreeable and happy as circumstances could admit but the said Robert in removing with your petitioner on the road to Tennessee abandoned her…finally leaving her in a State of pregnancy without any means of support or return to her friends, since which time she has to rely solely for the support of herself and child on her own industry…" Further, her husband has been absent for six years "during which time he has several times inlisted into the service of the United States and as many times deserted and been advertised as such, and has once been advertised in the publick papers as having broke jail where he was confined for stealing money…" Prays for an act to divorce her from said husband, Robert Tapley. [Below:] Signatures of nine persons subscribe to above petition. (GASR, Nov.-Dec. 1814, Box 2: folder "Petitions - Divorce and Alimony").

420. **Thomas, Anna and husband, James.** Petition of Anna Thomas of Guilford County represents that she intermarried in 1808 with James Thomas and hoped to spend her days in peace and happiness, but the said James "sometime since left her bed and board without any just cause, and his sole aim appears to be to squander what little property she may acquire from time to time for the support other family…" Prays for a law to secure to her such property as she may hereafter acquire. (GASR, Nov.-Dec. 1814, Box 2: folder "Petitions - Divorce and Alimony").

421. **Tores, Benjamin and wife, Elizabeth.** Petition of Benjamin Tores of the Town of Salisbury, Rowan County, represents that he and his wife, Elizabeth, have lived separate and apart from each other for several years, and there is no prospect of a reunion. The General Assembly at the last session passed a law securing to his wife such property as she may thereafter acquire. Your petitioner prays that he may be secured from the claims of his said wife upon any part of his property. [On reverse:] "Allowed." (GASR, Nov.-Dec. 1814, Box 2: folder "Petitions - Divorce and Alimony").

Act that bars Elizabeth Tores, wife of Benjamin Tores, from all right to dower or claim of any kind on estate of which her husband, Benjamin Tores, may be seized. "Referred to Committee on Alimony." (GASR, Nov.-Dec. 1814, Box 1: folder "HB 13 Dec.")

422. **Vannoy, Sary/Sarahj and husband, Nathaniel.** Petition of Sary Vannoy states she intermarried with one Nathaniel Vannoy of Wilkes County, but a short time after the marriage, her said husband began to abuse her and whipped her severely. With all her industry and kindness, she prevailed upon her husband to desist, but the more she humbled herself, the more he abused her, and at length, he ordered her to leave his house and abandon her children, and also said he would kill your petitioner. She then left her husband and went to live with her father. It has been upwards of one year, and she has acquired sufficient maintenance for herself and one child through her own industry. Prays for a law to secure to her such property as she may hereafter acquire by her own industry. [Below:] Subscribed to by the signatures of twenty-seven persons. [On reverse:] "Granted." (GASR, Nov.-Dec. 1814, Box 2: folder "Petitions - Divorce and Alimony").

Divorces and Separations from Petitions to the North Carolina General Assembly from 1779

423. **Ward, Silvia and husband, Joshua.** Petition of Silvia Ward of Bertie County sheweth she intermarried with Joshua Ward some years ago, but from his profligacy and imprudence, she has been reduced to extreme poverty with a large family of children to support. Her small earnings are often seized by his merciless creditors. Prays for a law to secure to her such property as she may hereafter acquire. Dated 1 November 1814. [On reverse:] "Allowed." [41]

424. **Whitsenhunt, Holland and husband. Henry.** Petition of Holland Whitsunhltnt sheweth she intermarried eighteen or twenty years ago with Henry Whitsunhunt, late of Randolph County, and they lived together in mutual love until 1 August 1813, when said husband (as she has been induced to believe) enlisted himself as a soldier in the Service of the United States. Previous to his enlistment, her said husband had been reduced almost to indigent circumstances and had contracted debts which your petitioner feels under obligation to discharge. Prays for a law to secure to her such property as she may hereafter acquire. (GASR, Nov.-Dec. 1814: folder "Petitions Divorce and Alimony").

425. **Wortham, Elizabeth P. and husband, Charles.** Petition of Elizabeth P. Wortham represents she intermarried with her present husband, Charles Wortham of Warren County, in the year 1804. She lived with him two years, and she had two children by him. However, in 1806 she abandoned his house because of the cruel and inhuman treatment he had exercised towards her. She went to her father's house for support, as her said husband had squandered the property of which he was possessed. Prays for an act to secure to her such property as may hereafter acquire. [Below:] Signatures of sixteen persons subscribe to the above petition. (GASR, Nov.-Dec. 1814, Box 2: folder "Petitions - Divorce and Alimony").

426. **Reference A.**
The following persons are made capable of exclusive right to such estate, real or personal, as they may hereafter acquire by descent, purchase or otherwise as if they had never been married to their respective husbands, and they are made capable to prosecute and defend suits either in Law or Equity in their own names:

> Susannah Riddle, wife of Harmon Riddle of Buncombe County;
> Sarah Vannoy, wife of Nathaniel Vannoy, Jr., of Wilkes Co.;
> Patsey Lewis of Randolph Co., wife of Stephen Lewis;
> Polly Johnson of Chatham Co., wife of Moses Johnson;
> Polly Colyear of Buncombe Co., wife of John Colyear;
> Mary Griswould, wife of James Griswould of Edgecombe Co.;
> Anna Thomas of Guilford Co., wife of James Thomas;
> Margaret Roane, wife of Jesse Roane of Guilford Co.;
> Nancy Hannah of Guilford Co., wife of Robert Hannah, Jr.;
> Sarah Hobbs of Guilford Co., wife of Nehemiah Hobbs;
> Elizabeth P. Wortham of Franklin Co., wife of Charles Wortham;
> Peggy Field of Guilford Co., wife of Jeremiah Field;
> Sally Spears of Edgecombe Co., wife of Absalom Spears;
> Eliza Dowday of Currituck Co., wife of John Dowday;
> Lucy Clark of Chatham Co., wife of William Hen[r]y Clark;
> Rebecca Fugh of Sampson Co., wife of James Pugh;
> Sylvia Ward of Bertie Co., wife of Joshua Ward;

---

41   Marriage Bond of Bertie County, North Carolina, dated 19 May 1797, lists parties as Joshua Ward and Silvey Ward.

1814 Session

      Mary G. Furgeson of Granville Co., wife of Joel Furgeson;
      Sarah Jordan, wife of George Jordan of Stokes Co.;
      Alley Hackett, wife of Thomas Hackett of Fayetteville;
      Martha Hunt, wife of William Hunt of Granville Co.;
      Holland Whitsenhunt of Randolph Co., wife of Henry Whitsenhunt;
      Elizabeth Powell of Richmond Co., wife of John Powell;
      Love Brady, wife of Mills Brady of Gates Co.
  Further, they are hereby barred from all right of dower or claim of any kind on the real or personal estate of which their respective may be seized:
      Susannah Riddle,
      Sarah Vannoy,
      Patsy Lewis,
      Polly Johnson,
      Polly Colyear,
      Mary Griswould,
      Anna Thomas,
      Margaret Roane,
      Nancy Hannah,
      Sarah Hobbs,
      Elizabeth P. Wortham,
      Peggy Field,
      Sally Spears,
      Eliza Dowday,
      Lucy Clark,
      Rebecca Pugh,
      Sylvia Ward,
      Mary G. Furgeson,
      Sarah Jordin,
      Alley Hackett,
      Martha Hunt,
      Holland Whitsenhunt,
      Elizabeth Powell,
      Love Brady,
      Lucy Powers,
      Sarah Leigh;
      Tempy Tapley, wife of Robert;
      Elizabeth Tores, wife of Benjamin Tores; and
      Mary Gregory, wife of Edmond Gregory.
  (GASR, Nov.-Dec. 1814, Box 1: folder "HB 23 Dec.")

Divorces and Separations from Petitions to the North Carolina General Assembly from 1779

427. **Reference B.**
Laws of North Carolina, November-December 1814 Session.
The persons listed on each line below were entitled to hold, possess and enjoy in their sole right, all such estate, real or personal, as they may hereafter acquire by industry, purchase; gift or otherwise, in as full and ample manner as if they had not been married.

Brady, Love; husband Mills of Gates Co., p. 26
Clark, Lucy of Chatham Co.; husband, William Henry, p. 26
Colyear, Polly of Buncombe Co.; husband, John, p. 26
Dowdy, Eliza of Currituck Co.; husband, John, p. 26
Ferguson, Mary G. of Granville Co.; husband, Joel, p. 26
Field, Peggy of Guilford Co.; husband, Jeremiah, p. 26.
Gregory, Mary; husband, Edmund [County unnamed], p. 27
Griswold, Mary; husband, James of Edgecombe Co., p. 26
Hackett, Alley; husband, Thomas of Fayetteville, p. 26
Hannah, Nancy of Guilford Co.; husband, Robert Jr., p. 26
Hobbs, Sarah of Guilford Co.; husband, Nehemiah, p. 26
Hunt, Martha; husband, William of Granville Co., p. 26
Johnson, Polly of Chatham Co.; husband, Moses, p. 26
Jordan, Sarah; husband, George of Stokes Co., p. 26
Leigh, Sarah of Perquimans Co.; husband, Benjamin, p. 26
Lewis, Patsey of Randolph Co.; husband, Stephen, p. 26
Powell, Elizabeth of Richmond Co.; husband, John, p. 26
Powers, Lucy of Wake Co.; husband, Rodham, p. 26
Pugh, Rebecca of Sampson Co.; husband James, p. 26
Riddle, Susanna; husband, Harmon of Buncombe Co., p. 26
Roane, Margaret; husband, Jesse of Guilford Co., p. 26
Spears, Sally of Edgecombe Co.; husband, Absalom, p. 26
Tapley, Tempy; husband, Robert of Montgomery Co., p. 26
Thomas, Anna of Guilford Co.; husband, James, p. 26
Toris [Tores], Elizabeth; husband, Benjamin of Rowan Co., p.27
Vannoy, Sarah; husband, Nathaniel Jr. of Wilkes Co., p. 26
Ward, Sylvia of Bertie Co.; husband, Joshua, p. 26
Whit(e)senhunt, Holland of Randolph Co.; husband, Henry, p. 26
Wortham, Elizabeth P. of Franklin Co.; husband, Charles, p. 26

1816

428. **Alford, Eunice and husband, Roy.** Petition of Eunice Alford of Guilford County shews that she intermarried with Roy Alford in March 1812, and they had a child. In September 1813, her husband, having squandered his property, left his family and went into parts unknown to your petitioner. By her own industry, she has acquired a sufficiency for the support of herself and child. She refers to the affidavits of reputable men heretofore annexed who have known her since childhood. She despairs of ever seeing her husband again. Prays for a divorce or a law to secure to her such property as she may hereafter acquire. Dated 19 November 1816. [Below:] We certify that we have known Eunice Alford since her infancy. She has acquired the respect and affection of her neighbors and deserves a much better fate than has befallen her. (Signed by twenty-one persons). [On reverse:] In House of Commons (28 November 1815) and Senate (30 November 1815), read, and ordered that so much as relates to a divorce be indefinitely postponed, but so much as relates to the security of property be referred to Committee of Propositions and Grievances. (GASR, Nov.-Dec. 1816, Box 3: folder "Petitions - Divorce and Alimony").

429. **Bal(l)ance, Nancy and husband, Charles.** Petition of Nancy (X) Ballance of Currituck County sheweth she intermarried with Charles Balance in 1802, "…and in seven months after their marriage, he unfortunately became deranged and remained so nine months, when he suddenly came to his understanding and continued for two and a half months, when he again became deranged…began to buy and sell and make bargains, used all kinds of violence towards your Petitioner, making many and repeated attempts to take away her life…destroyed every vistage of his property and continued distracted for about twelve months when he became helpless…and after continuing in this state for the space of three years, he again came to his understanding, was prudent and Economical, and we lived together for the space of five years and accumulated property sufficient to live on with care and industry. When your Petitioners husband again became deranged…was raving…distracted…spent and wasted the whole of his property…set fire to his House and repeatedly endeavoured to kill your petitioner. Your Petitioner then left him and went home to her Fathers where she continued four years when her Father died, and some property hath fell to her by her said Fathers death: Your petitioners unfortunate husband has remained insane and entirely helpless…he may be said to be in a state of Idiotism. Your Petitioner has kept her unfortunate husband from being at any expence since she has property of her own to support him with and is willing to do so…so long as he is peaceable and can be managed." If "her unfortunate husband Charles Ballance should again become a lunatic of which there is a strong probability, he will destroy the property of your Petitioner and reduce her and himself to want and misery. Prays for a law to secure to her such property she has or may fall to her by descent or that which she may acquire…" [On reverse:] "granted as to property yet to be acquired." (GASR, Nov.-Dec. 1816, Box 3: folder "Petitions - Divorce and Alimony").

Divorces and Separations from Petitions to the North Carolina General Assembly from 1779

430. **Barker, Mary and husband, Charles.** Petition of Mary (1^) Barker states she married Charles Barker in 1815 and lived with him a short time, but that he has now been living with another woman for more than a year. Prays for a law to secure to her what property she may hereafter acquire. Dated 20 November 1816. [On reverse:] "Petition Indefinitely Postponed." (GASR, Nov.-Dec. 1816, Box 3:folder "Petitions Divorce and Alimony").

431. **Bray, Hannah and husband, Solomon.** Petition of Hannah (X) Bray of Randolph County before Superior Court of Law of the same county at March Term 1815: "She has resided within the state ever since her birth and for several years in said county. She intermarried with Solomon Bray in 1800 and lived in much harmony for a considerable time. She had two children by him, one of which is still living. In the year of 1806 or 1807, the said Solomon separated himself from her without any just cause and went to Tennessee. Your petitioner is informed that he made an adulterous connection with another woman and took her into his house, lived with her in open adultery and has had several children by her. Your petitioner has lost all hope of his reformation." Prays for a divorce.

    Suit of Hannah Bray vs. Solomon Bray. Jury fmds that a marriage was duly celebrated between the plaintiff and defendant, that the defendant separated himself from the plaintiff and was living in adultery at the time of the filing of the petition. Ordered that the petitioner, Hannah Ray, be divorced from the bonds of matrimony.

    (Above from GASR, Nov.-Dec. 1816, Box 3: folder "Petitions - Divorce and Alimony").

    Bill to establish and confirm the judgment of the Superior Court of Law of Randolph County divorcing Hannah Bray and her husband, Solomon Bray from the Bonds of Matrimony. In Senate and House of Commons on 19 December, read third time, passed, and ordered to be engrossed. (GASR, Nov.-Dec. 1816, Box 1: folder "SB 6 Dec.").

432. **Chiles, Sarah and husband, Thomas.** Petition of Sarah Chiles of Anson County states she "…intermarried with General Thomas Chiles of the same county about thirty years past, who at the time of said marriage was in affluent circumstances, and that he received in marriage with your Petitioner a considerable personal estate…" Shortly after said marriage, her husband "…fell into fits of intemperance and dissipation and has long since entirely Squandered and dissipated away all his estate…" About ten years ago, "…he abandoned your petitioner and refused to keep house but removed himself and resided with a neighbor where he supports on a small pension which he received from the United States." The said Thomas "…has ever since refused to support or assist your Petitioner in any manner." Since that time, "…she has lived in the Houses of her relatives and friends, and has no other means of support other than her own industry and this county." She is now old, infirm and unable to support herself. Further, she has many relatives and friends who are in affluent circumstances who are willing to aid her. Prays for a law to secure to her such estate as she may hereafter acquire. Said Thomas has given his consent thereto. Dated 14 November 1816. [Below:] Signatures of five persons support this petition. (GASR, Nov.-Dec. 1816, Box 3: folder "Petitions - Divorce and Alimony"). Committee of Propositions and Grievances to which was referred tile petition of Sarah Chiles report they examined the facts in said petition and recommend adoption of the attached bill: Bill to secure to Sarah Chiles, wife of Thomas Chiles, such estate as she may hereafter acquire. In Senate (14 December) and House of Commons (17 December), read third time, passed, and ordered engrossed. (GASR, Nov.-Dec. 1816, Box 1: folder "SB 4 Dec.").

433. **Cole, Matthew and wife, Elizabeth (Strickland).** Petition of Matthew Cole of Richmond County states he married Elizabeth Strickland in the year 1810. In order to promote harmony and domestic felicity, he exerted his power to render the situation agreeable. In October 1814, he became aware that "…the said Elizabeth was unfaithful to his bed, and that she had committed acts of lewdness and adultery…[and] he thereupon declined living with her." At the Superior Court for Richmond County, September 1815 Term, he filed his petition against said Elizabeth, praying for a divorce. At the September 1816 Term of said court, the allegations against said Elizabeth were found true by a lawful jury. Your petitioner prays that the said sentence and decree be confirmed by an Act of the Assembly.

Depositions of Aggy (X) Cole, Drusilla (X) Yates, Elizabeth Cain, and Samuel Watkins provide eye-witness detail to the illicit behavior of Elizabeth Cole, wife of the petitioner, Matthew Cole, with a neighborhood man on several occasions in the house of said Matthew Cole.

(All of the above in GASR, Nov.-Dec. 1816, Box 3: folder "Petitions - Divorce and Alimony").

A Bill to divorce Matthew Cole of Richmond County from his wife, Elizabeth. It appears from a transcript legally authenticated that Matthew Cole of Richmond County filed his petition in the Clerk's Office of the Superior Court at Law for said county containing allegations against his wife, Elizabeth, for committing the crime of adultery and praying a divorce. At the last September term of said Court, the Petition was heard, and the allegations were substantiated and found true by a lawful jury. Whereupon it was ordered by said Court that said Matthew Cole and his wife, Elizabeth, be divorced from the bonds of matrimony. Be it enacted by the General Assembly that Matthew Cole of Richmond County is hereby divorced from his wife, Elizabeth. In House of Commons (26 November) and Senate (27 November), read third time, passed, and ordered engrossed. (GASR, Nov.-Dec. 1816, Box 1: folder "HB 21 Nov.").

434. **Denson, Sarah and husband, Benjamin.** Petition of Sarah Denson of Moore County shews that she intermarried with one Benjamin Denson several years ago with whom she lived until about two years ago. At that time, without any provocation on her part, he left her to maintain herself and his infant child. Prays for an act to secure to her separate use any property which she may hereafter acquire. [On reverse:] "Granted." (GASR, Nov.-Dec. 1816, Box 3: folder "Petitions - Divorce and Alimony").

435. **Dorsey, Mary Ann and husband, Robert.** Petition of Mary Ann Dorsey of Wilmington solicits the Legislature to authorize her to hold property in her own right as she may hereafter acquire. Her husband is a confirmed drunkard and continually squanders the hard earned fruits other industry by which means she and her two children have frequently been reduced to extreme want. Her husband has often treated her in a cruel manner, and she has been obliged to separate herself from him. [On reverse:] "Granted." (GASR, Nov.-Dec. 1816, Box 3: folder "Petitions - Divorce and Alimony").

436. **Jean, Nancy and husband, Lemuel.** Memorial of Nancy Jean of Guilford County states she intermarried some years ago with Lemuel Jean, late of Stokes County "the parents on both sides being agreeable and well satisfied with the said match and both parties being in tolerable affluent circumstances." She lived with her husband for sometime and had several children, but the said Lemuel began to take advantage of "every kind of extravagance, viz. - gambling and drinking to very great excess" and had brought your petitioner and her little children to a state of indigence and disgrace. Prays for a law to secure to her what property she may hereafter acquire. 'Below.] Signatures of thirty-seven subscribers who are resident in the counties of Guilford, Rockingham, and Stokes and support said memorial. [On reverse:] "Granted." (GASR, Nov.-Dec. 1816, Box 3: folder "Petitions - Divorce and Alimony").

Divorces and Separations from Petitions to the North Carolina General Assembly from 1779

437. **Laspeyre, Harriet and husband, Bernard.** Memorial of Harriet Laspeyre of New Hanover County sheweth that she was married to Bernard Laspeyre, late of the Island of Hispaniola, in the year of 1795. Her friends caused to be secured to her the much greater part other little property by a marriage settlement bearing date [blank] of May 1795. Not many weeks passed after the marriage when your memorialist discovered "…that her property, trifling as it was, had been the primary object of his warmest affection." He would urge in the most pressing manner for her consent to sell the negroes secured to her by said settlement, and "…upon her refusal, he would fall into the most violent paroxysms of rage, and abuse her in the most virulent language the vulgarity of his mind could possibly suggest in language too gross and indecent to be repeated." At length your memorialist, worn down by his threats but hoping for kinder treatment, consented at three different times to his selling of three of the said negroes. She found that he made title to them. Her acquiescence in his demands had little effect but to expose her to new and aggravated insults by the said Bernard on her whole property. She was stripped of the right of every woman's claims, "…divested of her superintendence of her house, deprived of the authority of a mistress, her negroes forbidden to obey her orders under penalty of severe punishment and every attempt made to render her an object of detestation to her own children. The profits arising from the labor other slaves, which ought to have been appropriated to the support and education of her children, she had the extreme vexation to see wantonly lavished on his black and mulatto mistresses. Your memorialist, while subject to his authority, has suffered the most degrading and humiliating treatment, abused in the dirtiest language such as a v/ell bred man would blush to apply to the worst of servants, actually threatened with manual chastisement and frequently ordered to leave his house." The said Bernard has for a long time lived in the Town of Wilmington in open adultery with a negro wench, taken her into his house and permits her to exercise all the rights and authorities of a wife. Prays for an act to separate her from her said husband and to secure to her the residue of her little property and to what she may hereafter acquire. [Note on Jacket:] "Granted."
(GASR, Nov.-Dec. 1816, Box 3: folder "Petitions - Divorce and Alimony").

438. **Lumpkin, Polly (Winstead) and husband, William.** Petition of Polly Lumpkin sheweth that her husband, William Lumpkin, "…has absented himself for upwards of two years from his wife and nine children and since his absence the whole of his property has been sold for the payment of his debts. Prays a provision to secure to her such property as she may hereafter acquire." [On reverse:] "Granted."
(GASR, Nov.-Dec. 1816, Box 3: folder "Petitions - Divorce and Alimony").[42]

439. **Morris, Elisabeth and husband, John L.** Petition of Elisabeth Morris of Randolph County states she intermarried with John L. Morris of said county in 1805 and has had four children by him. Her husband spent his estate and absconded from that part of the state to parts unknown to her. When he left, he took away a part of his property even though several unsettled judgments and executions are on the balance of his property. Prays for a law to secure to her such property as she may hereafter acquire. [On reverse:] "Granted." (GASR, Nov.-Dec. 1816, Box 3: folder "Petitions - Divorce and Alimony").

440. **Murden, Mary and husband, Robert.** Petition of Mary Murden of Camden County that her husband, Robert Murden, has been deranged for nearly thirteen years and is not qualified to attend to any kind of business. Your petitioner has lived separate from him for nearly five years. Previous to said husband's derangement, he was intemperate, dissipated and extravagant in the highest degree, and he squandered away his entire estate, both real and personal. Your petitioner has acquired some small prop-

---
42   Marriage Bond of William Lumpkin and Polly Winstead, dated 5 February 1797, is filed in Person County, North Carolina, records at the North Carolina State Archives.

erty through her own industry since she has been separate from her said husband. She has three small children and prays for a law to secure to her any property she may hereafter acquire. Dated 2 November 1816. [On reverse:] "Granted." (GASR, Nov.-Dec. 1816, Box 3: folder "Petitions - Divorce and Alimony").

441. **Shaw, Polly (Smithson) and husband, Haley.** Petition of Polly Shaw of Randolph County before the Superior Court at Law of said county at March Term 1815: "[S]he has resided within this state ever since her birth and for many years past, in the County of Randolph…[In] the year 1807, she intermarried with Haley Shaw with whom she lived in much harmony for some time, when the said Haley, without any just cause or complaint against your petitioner, treated her with much coolness and neglect & formed Adulterous connexions in the neighborhood to the great disgrace of himself & discredit of his family." In the Spring of 1814, he compelled your petitioner to leave his home. Within five months thereafter, two base born children in the neighborhood were sworn to him, and he kept company with the mothers of these children in an open, shameful manner. At length, in the Spring of 1815, he formed a connexion with another woman with whom he traveled, as your petitioner is informed & believes, into the State of Virginia. He finally intermarried with the said woman and shortly thereafter, they returned together to live in his house. Your petitioner left this house and went to live with the family of her brother and of Davis Hicks. She has lost any hope of any reformation in her husband. Prays for a divorce and that she be given a share of the considerable estate of the said Haley Shaw. Dated 4 October 1815. Inventory of the property of Haley Shaw, 6 February 1816: 500 acres of land worth $500; two horses worth $100; one cow worth $10; two beds and furniture worth $30.

In suit of Polly Shaw vs. Haley Shaw, a jury find that a marriage was celebrated between Polly Shaw and Haley Shaw, that the defendant separated himself from the plaintiff and was living in adultery. The Court ordered that the petitioner, Polly Shaw, be divorced and separated from the bonds of matrimony, and that an account be taken of the real and personal estate of the defendant, Haley Shaw, and a report be made at the next court. (GASR, Nov.-Dec. 1816, Box 3: folder "Petitions - Divorce and Alimony").

Bill to establish and confirm the Jugment of the Superior Court of Law of Randolph County Divorcing Polly Shaw and her husband, Haley Shaw. Whereas it appears from a transcript legally authenticated that Polly Shaw of Randolph County filed a petition in the Office of the Superior Court of Law of said county contains allegations and charges against her husband, Haley Shaw, for adultery and praying for a divorce, and at last September Term of the Superior Court of Randolph County, the petition was heard and found true by a lawful jury, it is enacted by the General Assembly that the order of the Superior Court of Randolph County divorcing Polly Shaw from her said husband be established and confirmed. In Senate (23 December) and House of Commons (25 December), read third time, passed and ordered to be engrossed. (GASR, Nov.-Dec. 1816, Box 1: folder "SB 5 Dec.").[43]

442. **Todd, Solomon and wife, Milberry.** Petition of Solomon Todd of Wake County represents that his wife, Milberry, left his bed and board in the Year 1810 without just cause "and took up with a certain Henry Culpepper by whom she has had two children, and at this time continues with said Culpepper, leaving your petitioner in a disturbed condition - as the laws of the country forbid him intermarrying with any other woman. Under these circumstances he is free to acknowledge that he has improperly indulged himself with another female- That for this indulgence the Court of the County has fined him ninety dollars, which added to the cost amounts to one hundred and seventy dollars - which as a man

---

[43] Marriage Bond of Haley Shaw and Polly Smithson, dated 15 September 1807, Randolph County, North Carolina, is filed in Randolph County records at North Carolina State Archives.

of limited property, bears hard on him to pay. Your petitioner was advised to apply to the court to remit the fine, believing that if all the circumstances were known, that the court would have complied with his request - but that owing to the dispersed situation of the members of the court who assessed the fine, he has been unable to assemble them together - and no other justices by common practice of one court ever reverse a judgment except those who assess it. Prays that the General Assembly will grant him such relief." [On reverse:] "Indefinitely postponed." (GASR, Nov.-Dec. 1816, Box 3: folder "Petitions - Divorce and Alimony").

Deposition of Giles Underbill of Wake County and Micajah (€) Liles of Johnston County that during the Year 1810, Milberry Todd left the bed and board of her husband, Solomon Todd, taking some of the bedding and household furniture with her, declaring at the time that she did not intend to live with her said husband. The said Milberry took up with and lived with Henry Culpepper and has had two children since she left said Solomon Todd. When she left said Solomon, the said Culpepper assisted her in taking from said Todd's home. Micajah Liles says he heard the said Solomon solicit his wife Milberry to remain with him or to go back and remain at his house at the time of her leaving him, but she declared she would not..."that Culpepper was a better man than any of the Todd's." Deposed before William Boylan, J.P. of Wake County, North Carolina. (GASR, Nov.-Dec. 1816, Box 3: folder "Miscellaneous").

443. **Wolf, Christina and husband, Caleb.** Petition of Christima Wolf of Buncombe County sheweth she intermarried with Caleb Wolf in 1782 and had eleven children in the course of thirty-four years by him. She has performed every duty as a wife and mother, but she has experienced little affection from her husband except a brutal and violent conduct. Your petitioner, after suffering a series of wrongs and abuses until she is 50 years of age, is now deprived of a home and herself and children cast upon the world destitute of any earthly sustenance. The said Caleb has left them for several months past, and will probably never return, as he is in considerable debt. Prays for a law to secure to her such property as she may hereafter acquire. (GASR, Nov.-Dec. 1816, Box 3: folder "Petitions - Divorce and Alimony").

444. **Reference A.**
Committee of Propositions and Grievances to whom was referred the Petitions of Polly Lumpkin, Eunice Alford, Mary Ann Dorsey, Christian Wolfe, Mary Murden, Elizabeth Morris, Sarah Denson, and Nancy Jean severally prayed passage of a Law authorizing them to hold such property as they may hereafter acquire free from control of their husbands - recommend passage of the Bill herewith submitted.

Committee of Propositions and Grievances to whom was referred the Petitions following: Petition of Inhabitants of Haywood County; Petition of Inhabitants of New Hanover County in behalf of Michael Barry of said county; Petition of Harriet La Peyre of New Hanover County praying she may be secured from the claims of her husband, Bernard, to such property as she may hereafter acquire; Petition of George Blaze of Rowan.

(GASR, Nov.-Dec. 1816, Box 3: folder "JCR").

445. **Reference B.**
A Bill to secure the persons therein named such property as they may hereafter acquire:
>Polly Lumpkin of Granville, wife of William;
>Eunice Alford of Guilford, wife of Roy;
>Mary Ann Dorsey of Town of Wilmington, wife of Robert;
>Christinia Wolf of Buncombe, wife of Caleb;
>Mary Murden of Camden, wife of Robert;

1816 Session

  Elizabeth Morris of Randolph, wife of John L.;
  Sarah Denson of Moore, wife of Benjamin;
  Nancy Balance of Currituck, wife of Charles;
  Nancey Jean of Guilford, wife of Lemuel;
  Susanna Jones of Johnston, wife of Thomas; and
  Halnet Laspyere of New Hanover, wife of Bernard.
 In Senate (26 December) and House of Commons (27 December), read third time, passed, and ordered to be engrossed. (GASR, Nov.-Dec. 1816, Box 2: folder "SB 19 Dec").

446. **Reference C.**
 Laws of North Carolina, Nov.-Dec. 1816 Session. The persons listed on each line below, except those preceded by the letter "D" were entitled to hold, possess and enjoy in their sole right, all such estate, real or personal, as they may hereafter acquire by industry, purchase, gift or otherwise, in as full and ample manner as if they had not been married. The persons whose names are preceded by a "D" were granted full divorces from each other.

   Alford, Eunice of Guilford Co.; husband, Roy (p. 38)
   Balance, Nancy of Currituck Co.; husband, Charles (p. 42)
 D Bray, Hannah of Randolph Co.; husband, Solomon (p. 38)
   Chiles, Sarah; husband, Thomas of Anson Co. (p. 50)
 D Cole, Matthew of Richmond Co.; wife, Elizabeth (p. 51)
   Denson, Sarah of Moore Co.; husband, Benjamin (p. 42)
   Dorsey, Mary Ann of Wilmington; husband, Robert (p. 38)
   Jean, Nancy of Guilford Co.; husband, Lemuel (p. 42)
   Jones, Susanna of Johnston Co.; husband, Thomas (p. 42)
   Laspyere, Harriet of New Hanover Co.; husband, Bernard (p. 42)
   Lumpkin, Polly of Granville Co.; husband, William (p. 38)
   Morris, Elizabeth of Randolph Co.; husband, John L. (p. 42)
   Murden, Mary of Camden Co.; husband, Robert (p. 42)
 D Shaw, Polly of Randolph Co.; husband, Haley (p. 52)
   Wolf, Christina of Buncombe Co.; husband, Caleb (p. 42)

1817

447. **Barker, Mary and husband, Charles.** Petition of Mary Barker shewith that about two years ago she married Charles Barker, planter of Robeson County. "He continued with her a few days at her residence in Lumberton, then left her and went to his own former place of residence with another woman with whom he has continued to live." They have one child, and the woman is pregnant with a second. Your petitioner has no probability of a reconciliation and "sees with regret that the said Charles Barker has nearly...consumed his Estate." Prays that her circumstances be taken into consideration, and that she may be secured to have such property as she may hereafter acquire. Dated 1 December 1817. (GASR, Nov.-Dec. 1817, Box 3: folder "Petitions-Divorce and Alimony").

448. **Bass, Rebecca and husband, Drury.** Petition of Rebecca Bass of Northampton County states she intermarried with Drury Bass about fifteen years ago, lived with him for some time and had four children. The said Drury "never made any exertions to support your petitioner and her children..." but spent his days in idleness and took from your petitioner whatever she had acquired by her own industry and the benevolence of her friends. A few years ago, her said husband left your petitioner and went to the State of Georgia. He lately returned and seized what little property your petitioner had acquired during his absence. Prays for an act to secure to her such property as she may hereafter acquire and to manage it in her own name as if she had never been married. [On reverse:] "Granted." (GASR, Nov.-Dec. 1817, Box 3: folder "Petitions - Divorce and Alimony").

449. **Bynum, Mary and husband, Turner.** Petition of Mary Bynum of Northampton County states she intermarried with a certain Turner Bynum a number of years ago and lived with him until he had nearly exhausted his property by extravagance and dissipation. The intervention of your petitioner's friends has allowed some property to be settled on her. Her "husband has left her and now resides somewhere in the State of Louisiana." Prays for a law to secure to her such property as she may hereafter acquire and that she be authorized to enter into contracts and manage her property in her own name in the same manner as if her husband were dead. [On reverse:] "Granted." (GASR, Nov.-Dec. 1817, Box 3: folder "Petitions - Divorce and Alimony").

450. **Caddell, Polly L. and husband, William.** Petition of Polly L. Caddell of Richmond County states she 452 with one William Caddell. of Moore County about three years ago. She looked forward to enjoy as much conjugal felicity as usually results from matrimony, "and she was never wanting in her exertions in securing the affections of her husband and increasing their domestic happiness." However, your petitioner "soon found to her inexpressible mortification that her husband was destitute of that conjugal affection which was necessary to perpetuate her happiness - that he was abandoned to vicious habits which soon was evinced by ill treatment which she daily experienced from his hand, utterly derogatory to the character of a husband possessing a single spark of affection." At length, she was entirely abandoned by her husband, and the separation has continued for twelve months with no hope of recon-

ciliation. "Your petitioner has two children by her said husband solely dependent on tier daily exertions for their support." The youngest of her children was only two weeks old at the time of her husband's final separation. Prays for an act securing to her what property she may hereafter acquire by purchase, gift or devise free from the claims of her said husband. [On reverse:] "Granted." (GASR, Nov.-Dec. 1817, Box 3: folder "Petitions - Divorce and Alimony").

451. **Chambers, Elizabeth and husband, Thomas.**
    (a). Petition of Elizabeth Chambers of Montgomery County sheweth that in the year 1812 she intermarried with Thomas Chambers in Richmond County. Within a short time, the said Thomas evinced a disposition totally incompatible with his duty as a husband "and gave into habits of dissipation and vice, which led him to the commission of the crime of Horse stealing, and the said Thomas is now indebted to Executive clemency alone for his existence." Since said crime, she has never lived or cohabited with said Thomas, and there is no probability of a reconciliation. After the separation, she resided with her father who is willing to extend to her his parental bounty. Prays for a law to secure to her such estate as she may hereafter acquire. [On reverse:] "Granted." (GASR, Nov.-Dec. 1817, Box 3: folder "Petitions - Divorce and Alimony").
    (b). Certificate of Thomas (x) Chambers, dated 12 November 1817, Richmond County, North Carolina, states he was married in 1812 to Elizabeth Thompson, daughter of John Thompson of Montgomery County, North Carolina. Shortly after their marriage, said Thomas committed a crime, reference to which is in the records of the Superior Court of Richmond County. Since then, his wife and he have been entirely separated. "Neither do I expect to live with her the said Elizabeth...any longer. My wish and desire is to be entirely separated as man and wife by a Bill of Divorce...and should this not effectually answer the End intended,...my wish is that whatever estate my wife Elizabeth may hereafter acquire shall be to her own use...for which I freely and willingly relinquish all my right and interest to what she now has - or ever hereafter may acquire..." (GASR, Nov.-Dec. 1817, Box 3: folder "Petitions - Divorce and Alimony").

452. **Collins, Mary and husband, John.** Petition of Mary Collins of Orange County states she married John Collins on 23 June 1790.[44] For some years after the marriage, said husband behaved himself tolerably well, and they had a sufficiency of property. Gradually however the said John Collins indulged himself with intoxicating liquors, and he became negligent and inattentive in his affairs and ill-natured and evvel [sic] to your petitioner. He became a perfect slave to that habit, spent the whole of his property and frequently beat your petitioner in a barbarous manner without any cause. In November 1814, he threatened to put her to death with a large, open knife, and she fled to safety elsewhere. He continues to drink and fails to support his children. Your petitioner had seven children by her said husband, the eldest being only above fifteen years, and she has supported them ever since her separation from her husband. Prays that property she may hereafter acquire be secured to her and that she may be empowered to make contracts and enforce them as a single woman. [On reverse:] "Granted." (GASR, Nov.-Dec. 1817, Box 3: folder "Petitions - Divorce and Alimony").

453. **Corzine, John and wife, Mary.** Petition of John Corzine before Superior Court of Law, Cabarrus County, North Carolina, states that he intermarried in 1811 with a woman by the name of Mary Gib-

---

44   Marriage Bond of Orange County, North Carolina, lists John Collins and Polly Jackson dated 21 July 1797. Bondsman: Isaac Jackson.

son,[45] "who passed herself as a widow, but in fact...she was a single woman by name of Mary Robins and that previous to her marriage she had a child by her brother-in-law which facts were unknown to your petitioner at the time of the marriage..." The said Mary "has been guilty of the wicked, shameful and immoral crime of adultery at different times with different persons...[and] about one year since, his wife Mary eloped from his bed and board...[and] carried off with her much of the property of your petitioner." She continues to live in a state of adultery after she deserted the society of your petitioner. Requests a final and absolute divorce from the bonds of matrimony between your petitioner and his wife, Mary.

The said Mary Corzine was ordered to appear in court on the above charges, and a jury was impaneled to inquire into the allegations. At November Term 1817, said jury found for the plaintiff, and the Court decreed that the petitioner, John Corzine, be divorced from his said wife, Mary. (GASR, Nov.-Dec. 1817, Box 3: folder "Petitions Divorce and Alimony").

454. **East, Anna Maria and husband, Thomas.** Petition of Anna Maria East of Stokes County sheweth "that she some years since, intermarried with Thomas East, who at that time, was esteemed, a man of prudence and industry, possessed a handsome property, and for sometime after her union, continued to observe the duties which devolved upon him as husband and parent -." However the said Thomas at length disregarded such responsibilities and through dissipation, extravagance and imprudence entirely exhausted all resources in the support of your petitioner and their children. Prays that a law be passed which authorizes your petitioner to hold all property she may hereafter acquire free from the control of her said husband. Below are signatures of thirteen persons who subscribe to the statements above. [On reverse:] "Rejected." (GASR, Nov.-Dec. 1817, Box 3: folder "Petitions - Divorce and Alimony").

455. **Hassell, Mary and husband, Benjamin.** Petition of Mary Hassell of Bertie County states she married Benjamin Hassell and lived with him for some time in the utmost peace and harmony, and she has had one child. However, since that time, her said husband "has betaken to himself as a wife and companion, a negro woman, the slave & lawful property of your petitioner." To relieve herself from the odious embraces of a man so entirely destitute of all the finer feelings of sensibility and from one so much & deservedly stigmatized by every honest member of the communily, she has sought protection under the parental roof...and now remains. At the time of the marriage with said Hassell, her father is desirous of bestowing on her additional fruits of his earnings, provided it can be effectually secured from "the cruel & rapacious grasp of the monster." Prays for a law to secure to her the remnant of property remaining in her possession and all that she may hereafter acquire. [On reverse: "Granted as far as respects what she may hereafter acquire."] (GASR, Nov.-Dec. 1817, Box 3: folder "Petitions Divorce and Alimony").

456. **Johnson, Patsey and husband, John.** Petition of Patsey Johnson of Wake County, City of Raleigh, states she intermarried with John Johnson of this place about 25 years past and has had eight children. Her said husband conducted himself as a husband for some time, but for nine or ten years past, he has become; a common spendthrift and drunkard and has a violent tongue. He wasted what little property we had and for the past two years has abandoned your petitioner with three small children. Prays for a law to secure to her any property she may hereafter acquire. (GAS R. Nov.-Dec. 1817, Box 3: folder "Petitions - Divorce and Alimony").

---

45   Marriage Bond of Cabarrus County, North Carolina, lists John Corzine and Mary Gibson. dated 3 May 1810. Bondsman: Benjamin Robbin.

457. **Laspeyre, Bernard and wife, Harriet.** Memorial of Bernard Laspeyre of Sampson County sheweth that your memorialist has lately been apprised "that a Virulent and Infamous Libel, under the name of a Petition, had been presented to me Last General Assembly, subscribed Harriet Laspeyre, [and] your Memorialist procured himself a copy of that Long tissue of abominable calumnies. Though that obsecene Instrument is subscribed by your Memorialist's wife, it cannot be the production of that fallen Angel, once the ornament of her sex. Female depravity cannot as yet in this country have reached to that Summit, that a wife the mother of Six children, after having destroyed forever privately her husband's peace and happiness. Should have the imprudence, the hardihood to accuse him before the General Assembly of the State of Wrongs which in her Heart she knows to be utterly unfounded, and which had they been true, would have been presented long ago to a Superior Court which by an act passed in 1814, is the proper tribunal for redress. Your Memorialist is fully convinced that his wife never red that Instrument before she signed it, and that previous to the signing of it, some sporiferous potion had been given to her by the female with whom she now stays and who is constantly intoxicated herself."

"It would be irrelevant in the humble opinion of your memorialist to enter in this Petition a refutation of the unfounded charges brought against him in the Petition subscribed by his wife...Your Memorialist will only state what is now of Public Notoriety, that his wife, the Mother of six children by him, in a fit of Jealousy left his house and family in March 1807, was absent about a month, was taken back and forgiven, and treated afterwards, notwithstanding that faux pas, with as much tenderness and attention on account of her children...as before, tho she is the Proudest, haughtiest, the most Imperious and tyrranical woman existing, her female companion excepted...[A]bout four years ago, under pretence of going to see her Brother, then sick, your Memorialist's wife left his house and family, has refused to return, tho often urged by him...and continues to live in that State which is a flagrant violation of all civil and divine laws, and bids defiance to public opinion and marital authority, especially since by an act of the last General Assembly, it is believed by her that she has the same rights and privileges as if she was not feme coverft] and had never been married."

"Your memorialist has already experienced the dreadful consequences of that act by his wife, having threatened him publicly in the street to Pistol him, when he was urging her by the tenderest terms to return to your Memorialist's house and family, by having sent all his children out of state against his express direction, by inveigling from his services all his negros, which by a marriage settlement are under his sole control, and of which she could only dispose by testament at her death. Prays that in conformity with the spirit of the law passed in 1814, conferring on the Superior Court the right of granting divorces, alimony &c. that the act passed at the last session in favor of his wife be repealed." [On reverse:] "Rejected." (GASR, Nov.-Dec. 1817, Box 3: folder "Petitions Divorce and Alimony").

458. **Lewis, Mary and husband, William.** Petition of Mary Lewis [of New Hanover County] represents she intermarried in 1813 with one William Lewis, then a citizen of the town of Wilmington. They lived together in harmony for about eleven months, but then the said William ran away leaving his estate involved to a greater amount than it was worth and your petitioner with a helpless infant to maintain. Her said husband has now been gone for the space of three years and upwards and has never been heard from by your petitioner since his departure. She has been able to acquire a little property and hopes to add to it, but fears that her husband may return and deprive her and the helpless infant of it all. Prays for an act to secure to her her future earnings.

[Below:] Deposition of Junius C. Dunbibin that the above named William Lewis left this place more than two and one-half years ago and has never since returned or written to any of his family as he [the said Junius] believes. Dated 29 November 1817. [On reverse:] "Granted." (GASR, Nov.-Dec. 1817, Box 3: folder "Petitions - Divorce and Alimony").

Divorces and Separations from Petitions to the North Carolina General Assembly from 1779

459. **Maner, Sally and husband, Levi.** Petition of Sally Maner of Nash County states she intermarried with Levi Maner and lived with him agreeably for several years without any provocation on her part. In about the year 1801, said Levi left your petitioner "and flew tc the embraces of a lewd woman with whom he went off and your petitioner has never since seen him, but she has strong reasons for believing the said Levi in living in the state of Tennessee, where (by his confession to your petitioners neighbours) he married another woman." Sometime last Spring, said Levi was in the neighbourhood from which he ran away and requested a friend to seize what little property your petitioner may leave at her death and keep it for his own benefit. Prays for a law to secure to her such property as she may hereafter acquire. Dated December 1817. [On reverse:] "Rejected." (GASR, Nov.-Dec. 1817, Box 3: folder "Petitions - Divorce and Alimony").

460. **Mason, Ann and husband, William W.** Petition of Ann Mason [of Wake County] states "she is wife of William W. Mason, late of City of Raleigh, who from being a respectable tradesman hath become a Bankrupt fugitive…[H]er said husband was a tradesman of said city of apparent thriving circumstances…that she was fully impressed with the beliefs that he was in the way to provide respectably for your Petitioner & his children six in number…" In 1816, her said husband left his home without any apparent intention to return, taking with him all the money he could procure, leaving your petitioner entirely destitute. As soon as it was ascertained that her said husband had gone off. his creditors seized upon his property, but such property fell far short of paying his debts. Her said husband is now in confinement for his misconduct. She has visited him and believes that his misfortunes have impaired his reason. By exertions of honest industry she has managed to support herself and children but not to pay the debts of her husband. Prays for a law securing to her such property as she may hereafter acquire. [On reverse:] "Granted." (GASR, Nov.-Dec. 1817, Box 3: folder "Petitions - Divorce and Alimony").

461. **Miller, Salome and husband, Herrmon.** Petition of Salome Miller of Stokes County sheweth that "whereas her husband Herrmon Miller[46] by drinking spirituous liquors to an excess - so as to render him incapable of conducting his own affairs & disabled himself from taking care of his family - his children are growing up without education & he does in no manner provide for their support as he ought to do." Prays for an act securing to her such property as she may hereafter acquire by her own industry. [Below:] Signatures of fourteen persons who subscribe to the above statements as being true.] [On reverse:] "Granted." (GASR, Nov.-Dec. 1817, Box 3: folder "Petitions - Divorce and Alimony").

462. **Mullins, Nancy and husband, John.** Petition of Nancy Mullins [of Burke County] sheweth she intermarried with one John Mullins many years ago and lived in peace and pleasure for about seven years, when her said husband "took up with another woman & has not lived with your petitioner since." He "has used her with great severity & indifference, frequently taking her property from her & leaving her almost naked." Prays for an act to secure to her such estate as she may hereafter acquire. [On reverse:] "Granted." (GASR, Nov.-Dec. 1817, Box 3: folder "Petitions - Divorce and Alimony").

463. **Richardson, Sarah and husband, John.** Petition of Sarah Richardson of Randolph County represents she intermarried with John Richardson in 1798 or '99 and had one child by him. For the first few months she anticipated pleasures that would shortly be realized in her domestic circle from the affection and attachment of her said husband, "but she soon found out that pleasure with her was only an ideal. In the year 1801, your petitioner's husband absconded from this part of the world and took with him the

---

46   Marriage Bond of Stokes County, North Carolina, lists Harmon Miller and Salome Shouse, dated 10 September 1798. Bondsman: Frederick Shouse.

little property which they were in possession of and left your petitioner & child in a state of penurious indigence." She has accumulated some property which is liable (should he return) to his extravagance and waste. Prays for an act securing to her such property as she may hereafter acquire. [On reverse: "Prayer granted."] (GASR, Nov.-Dec. 1817, Box 3: folder "Petitions - Divorce and Alimony").

464. **Rutherford, Margaret and husband, James.** Petition of Margaret Rutherford of Buncombe County states she intermarried with one James Rutherford many years ago and "calculated to spend her days in the utmost harmony and peace." The pleasures she anticipated were fully realized for a time, but "at length her said husband appeared to prefer the paths of vice immorality to those of peace and domestic tranquillity, and this disposition...proved absolutely predominant, and your petitioner became entirely abandoned..." His dissipation led him to disregard the solemn ties of husband and wife, and all the property they possessed was squandered by his extravagance and waste. She has for sometime become solely dependent upon her friends and neighbors and upon her own industry for the support of herself and children.

Prays for an act to secure what property she may acquire from the demands of her husband or his creditors. [On reverse:] "Granted." (GASR, Nov.-Dec. 1817, Box 3: folder "Petitions - Divorce and Alimony").

465. **Singleton, Sarah and husband, Philip W.** Petition of Sarah Singleton of Caswell County sheweth that she was married to Philip Singleton[47] and had two children by him. For the past three years, her said husband has "left her without doing anything for her support." Prays for a law vesting in her the sole right and title of what property she may hereafter acquire by gift or otherwise. [On reverse:] "Rejected." (GASR, Nov.-Dec. 1817, Box 3: folder "Petitions - Divorce and Alimony").

466. **Smith, Mary and husband, William.** Petition of Mary Smith of Guilford County states that some years ago, her husband, William Smith, went away and left me and several small children after being involved in debt. The Sheriff has sold what property was owned by said William and his wife, most of which belonged to your petitioner before marriage. Her father died after said William departed and left a small piece of land to her by his will, but this property has been sold to satisfy her husband's debts. She is now left with her children in a deplorable condition. Prays relief to secure to her such property as she may hereafter acquire. Dated 1 October 1817. [Below:] Signatures of thirty-one persons subscribe to petition above.] [On reverse:] "Rejected." (GASR, Nov.-Dec. 1817, Box 3: folder "Petitions - Divorce and Alimony").

467. **Street, Charlotte and husband, John.** Petition of Charlotte Street of Hillsborough, Orange County, shews that her husband, John Street[48] has been reduced from circumstances of ease and comfort to entire poverty and is unable to support his family except by his manual labor. Owing to the extent of said husband's debts, her friends are unwilling to aid her except to furnish a shelter from the weather and daily food, for they fear that any property put in her possession would be iimnediately taken for his debts. Prays that she may be secured to such property as she may hereafter acquire. She has been assured that if such a law be passed, her friends would aid and assist her to get into business. [On reverse:] "Rejected." (GASR, Nov.-Dec. 1817, Box 3: folder "Petitions - Divorce and Alimony").

---

47 Marriage Bond of Person County, North Carolina, lists Philip W. Singleton and Salley Merret. Dated 2 November 1803. Bondsman: George Moton.

48 Marriage Bond of Orange County, North Carolina, lists John Street and Charlotte Harris, dated 10 December 1804. Bondsman: Henry Thomson.

Divorces and Separations from Petitions to the North Carolina General Assembly from 1779

468. **Reference A.**
Committee of Propositions and Grievances to whom was referred the following petitions, viz. - Petition of John Jarrett of Buncombe County; petition of James Allen of Buncombe County; petition of Charlotte Street of Hillsborough; petition of Ransom Harris of Randolph County; and petition of Robert Darlack of Currituck County — are of opinion that Legislative interference is not necessary and recommend the same be rejected. (GASR, Nov.-Dec. 1817, Box 2: folder "Joint Committee Reports").

469. **Reference B.**
Committee of Propositions and Grievances to whom was referred the petitions of Rebecca Bass, Ann Mason, Salome Miller, Mary Lewis, and Polly S. Cadell had same under consideration think them entitled to Legislative interference in their behalf. Recommend accompanying Bill entitled a bill "securing to the Femes Covert therein named all property they may hereafter acquire" be passed into law. [Below:] In Senate, 9 December 1817, read and concurred with. In House of Commons, 15 December 1817, not concurred in and same be indefinitely postponed.] (GASR, Nov.-Dec. 1817, Box 2: folder "Joint Committee Reports").

470. **Reference C.**
Committee of Propositions and Grievances to whom was referred the several petitions of Mary Bynam, Sarah Richardson, and Nancy Mullins, report they are of opinion that the same ought to be granted and recommend the accompanying bill be passed into law. [Below:] In House of Commons, 5 December 1817, and concurred with.] (GASR, Nov.-Dec. 1817, Box 2: folder "Joint Committee Reports").

471. **Reference D.**
A Bill to secure to persons therein named such property as they may hereafter acquire: Margaret Rutherford of Buncombe County, wife of John Rutherford; Elisabeth Chambers of Montgomery County, wife of Thomas Chambers; and Mary Hassell of Bertie County, wife of Benjamin Hassell. [On reverse: In Senate, 8 December 1817, read first time and passed; in House of Commons, 15 December 1817, read and indefinitely postponed.] (GASR, Nov.-Dec. 1817, Box 1: folder "Senate Bills, 8 Dec.").

472. **Reference E.**
A Bill securing to the femes covert therein named all property they may hereafter acquire: Rebecca Bass of Northampton County, wife of Drury Bass; Ann Mason of Wake County, wife of William W. Mason; Salome Miller of Stokes County, wife of Hermon Miller; Mary Lewis of New Hanover County, wife of William Lewis; and Polly L. Caddell of Richmond County, wife of William Caddell. [On reverse: In Senate, 9 December 1817, read first time and passed; in House of Commons, 15December 1817, read first time and indefinitely postponed.] (GASR, Nov.-Dec. 1817, Box 1: folder "Senate Bills, 9 Dec.").

473. **Reference F.**
Bill securing to the married women therein named the property they may hereafter acquire: Patsy Johnson of Wake County, wife of John Johnson; Mary Collins of Orange County, wife of John Collins. In Senate, 17 December, read first time and passed. In House, 16 December, read and postponed indefinitely. (GASR, Nov.-Dec. 1817, Box 1: folder "Senate Bill, 12 Dec.").

474. **Reference G.**

The order, decree and judgment of the Superior Court of Law of Cabarrus County divorcing John Corzine from his wife, Mary Corzine, is hereby established and confirmed by the General Assembly of North Carolina. In Senate and House, 22 December, read third time, passed, and ordered to be engrossed.

The order, decree and judgment of the Superior Court of Law of Mecklenburg County divorcing Richard Mason from his wife, Margaret Mason, is hereby established and confirmed by the General Assembly of North Carolina. In Senate and House, 22 December, read third time, passed and ordered to be engrossed.

(GASR, Nov.-Dec. 1817, Box 1: folder "Senate Bill, 13 Dec.").

475. **Reference H.**

Bill to secure to certain persons therein named such Estate as they may hereafter severally acquire: Mary Bynum, wife of Turner Bynum, late of Northampton County; Sarah Richardson, wife of John Richardson, late of Randolph County; and Nancy Mullins, wife of John Mullins, late of Burke County. In House, 15 December, and indefinitely postponed. Rejected. (GASR, Nov.-Dec. 1817, Box 1: folder "House Bill, 15 Dec.").

476. **Reference I.**

Laws of North Carolina, November-December 1817 Session. The persons listed below whose names are preceded by the letter "D" were granted full divorces from each other.

D   Corzine, John of Cabarrus County; wife, Mary, p. 41
D   Mason, Richard of Mecklenburg County; wife, Margaret, p. 57

1818-1819

477.   **Blackwell, Rachel and husband, Thomas.** Petition of Rachel Blackwell of Person County, North Carolina, sheweth that she married Thomas Blackwell of Halifax County, Virginia, in February 1815[49], but he left your petitioner in January 1818 after destroying what property your petitioner had at the time of marriage. He moved in Person County before he left your petitioner but has since returned to the State of Virginia. Your petitioner was left with two small children, and her said husband has provided no support for his family. Your petitioner has provided for this maintenance and prays that such property as she may acquire by her own labor be secured to her and not go to the discharge of the debts of her said husband. [On reverse:] In House of Commons, 14 December 1819, read and postponed indefinitely. (GASR, Nov.-Dec. 1819, Box 3: folder "Petitions - Alimony").

478.   **Chambers, Betsy and husband, Thomas.** Petition of Betsy Chambers [no Chambers and anticipated the enjoyment of a peaceful and happy life. Unfortunately, she soon discovered the unfeeling and cruel temper other said husband. In the course of idleness and vice which he pursued, the said Thomas soon wanted the property which was bestowed upon your petitioner at her marriage by a kind parent. At length, the said Thomas committed the crime of horse stealing, was indicted in the Superior Court of Richmond County, found guilty and sentenced to be hung. He was saved from the execution by the clemency of the Governor, but since that time, she and her child have been completely abandoned by her said husband. Prays for an act to secure to her such property as she may hereafter acquire by her own industry, by descent, or by gift from her relatives or friends. Dated 11 November 1818. [On reverse:] "Ordered that the prayer of the Petition be granted." (GASR, Nov.-Dec, 1818, Box 3: folder "Petitions - Alimony").

479.   **Elliott, Frances and husband, Thomas.** Petition of Frances Elliott of Randolph County sheweth that she intermarried with a certain Thomas Elliott of said county in 1818 and lived with him in perfect harmony for some time. However, her said husband was arrested and bound to make his appearance in court to answer the charge of committing fraud in the Post Office. He eloped from the county and removed about for eleven months, but returned and surrendered to Justice. He was tried, convicted and sentenced to remain in close confinement in the prison at Raleigh for three years. He was pardoned by the President of the United States after remaining in jail sometime and was discharged from confinement. During the confinement of her said husband, your petitioner at his request sold off his entire property and transmitted the money to him. This left your petitioner and her two children dependent on her friends for subsistence. The said Thomas left confinement and remained with your petitioner but a few days "then eloped with a woman of infamous character leaving your petitioner and her two children in the most distressed situation…" She is informed that he eloped to the State of Georgia, where he parted with her and removed to Alabama and there married a young woman of a respectable family. It

---

49   Marriage Bond of Person County, North Carolina, lists Thomas Blackwell and Rachel Link, dated 16 February 1815. Bondsman: Wilie Brooks.

was discovered that he had a wife living in this country, and he was arrested on a charge of bigamy and confined in jail. The father of the young lady he married has lately been in this county for the purpose of obtaining testimony of his marriage with your petitioner. Prays that a law be passed to secure to her such property as she may acquire by her own means or by descent. [Below:] Subscribed to by four persons. In House of Commons, 4 December 1819, read and postponed indefinitely. (GASR, Nov.- Dec. 1819, Box 3: folder "Petitions - Alimony").

480. **Hoffler, James and wife, Deborah**. Petition of James Hofflar of Gates County sheweth he intermarried in November 1802 with Deborah Outlaw, daughter of Jacob Outlaw.[50] In December, your petitioner discovered that "said Deborah was a Miscellany, unfaithful and incontinent to your petitioner…", and lie mildly rebuked her for her irregular behaviour. Unfortunately, this approach was to no avail, and his wife absconded from your petitioner and lived in open and notorious adultery with a certain John Lowance of New York…who was a married man. The said Lowance left her eventually and returned to New York, but said Deborah took up with a certain Solomon Bell of South Carolina, and she eloped with him to that state in 1802 or 1803, leaving your petitioner in a wretched state of misery and unhappiness. Further, the said Deborah has continued away from your petitioner and understands she lives in camps in the State of South Carolina and follows the soldiers from cantonment to cantonment and has become an incorrigible courtesan. Prays for a divorce from the bends of matrimony with the said Deborah.
A jury was impanelled and concluded that the above couple be divorced from the bonds of matrimony. The Superior Court of Law of Gates County decreed that such a divorce was adjudged subject to a review by the General Assembly of the State of North Carolina. (GASR, Nov.-Dec. 1818, Box 1: folder "Senate Bill, 18 Nov.").

481. **Langford, Delilah and husband, George.** Petition of Delilah Langford of Lincoln County states that her husband, George Langford, absconded from the State about four years ago leaving his wife and three small children to be supported by her labor and industry. The said George was heavily involved in debt, and his debtors have taken all the property he left with your petitioner. He recently sent a letter which states that he positively will never return to live with her again. Prays for a law to enable her to acquire property and to secure to her the property she has already acquired. [Below:] Signatures of six persons who have been acquainted with said Delilah Langford and support her petition. [On reverse:] "Ordered that: the prayer of the Petitioner be granted." (GASR, Nov.-Dec. 1818, Box 3: folder "Petitions - Alimony").

482. **McCeaughan, Phebe and husband, Hugh.**[51] Petition of twenty-six persons whose signatures appear at the end of the petition state that Phebe McCeaughan, wife of Hugh McCeaughan, is in moderate circumstances with a family of small children to raise and has been deserted by her husband for three years without any just cause on her part. We pray that a law be enacted to secure to her such property as she may hereafter acquire by her own industry, independent of the payment other husband's debts. [Below:] In House of Commons, 24 November 1819. Read and rejected. (GASR, Nov.-Dec. 1819, Box 3: folder "Petitions - Alimony").

---

50   Marriage Bond of Gates County, North Carolina, lists James Hofler and Deborah Outlaw, dated 22 September 1802. Bondsman: Willis Brown.

51   Marriage Bond of Rowan County, North Carolina, lists Hugh McKaughan and Phebe Pope, dated 25 March 1814. Bondsman: George Pope.

Divorces and Separations from Petitions to the North Carolina General Assembly from 1779

483. **Mooney, Hannah and husband, Daniel.** Petition of Hannah Mooney of Rutherford County states she has been married about ten years to Daniel Mooney[52], and her husband has not lived with her half the time. He "has been charged with every base and infamous actions which has often caused him to move his place of residence, and seldom continues more than a year in any one vicinity before he commits some misdemeanor that obliges him to evacuate the place." He has absented himself from her for periods of three months, six months and a year, and has returned each time to live with her once more, but always leaves her in a worse circumstance than when he returned. "I received a letter from him informing me that he never intended to come to this county again." Prays for an act to secure to her what little property she now has and such property as she may hereafter acquire. [Below:] Affidavit of Hugh Quin, Esq., who deposes that he believes the facts set forth in the above petition of Hannah Mooney. Dated 19 November 1818. [On reverse:] "Grant." (GASR, Nov.-Dec. 1818, Box 3: folder "Petitions - Alimony").

484. **Newkirk, Rebecca and husband, Alexander.** Petition of Rebecca Newkirk, wife of Alexander Newkirk of Duplin County[53] "sheweth that circumstances which in themselves are too painful for her to recount have driven her to this dernier report" in praying for a law securing to her such property as she may hereafter acquire. Though it wounds her very soul, she states that at the time of her said intermarriage she was in possession of good property in land and negroes, the whole of which has been sold to discharge her said husband's debts, leaving a great amount still unpaid and leaving your petitioner with three infant children reduced to poverty and wretchedness. Dated December 1819. [Below:] Signatures of nine supporters of this petition. [On reverse:] In Senate, 13 December, and referred to Committee of Propositions and Grievances. In House of Commons, 14 December, and postponed indefinitely. (GASR, Nov.-Dec. 1819, Box 3: folder "Petitions - Alimony").

485. **Richardson, Sarah and husband, John.** Memorial of Sarah Richardson of Randolph County states she intermarried with John Richardson in 1799. They lived together until 1801, when said husband left your memorialist and an infant child and has not returned. Prays for a law to secure to her such property as she may hereafter acquire. [On reverse:] "Granted". (GASR, Nov.-Dec. 1818, Box 3: folder "Petitions Alimony").

486. **Robinson, Jane B. and husband, William D.** Jane Robinson states she intermarried with William Robinson in 1816, both of them residing in Richmond County. She anticipated much conjugal happiness, but shortly after their marriage, she discovered that his affections were not placed on her alone, but that he lived in a state of promiscuous cohabitation with various women of loose and immoral habits. Her said husband exercised many acts of cruelty towards her and deserted her. She did not think her life could be safely trusted with him, and the indignities offered her by said husband rendered conditions intolerable while living with him. Prays for a divorce from matrimony and from bed and board.

A jury was impanelled in the case of Jane Robinson vs. Wm. D. Robinson at the September Term, 1818, of the Superior Court of Law for Richmond County. Allegations of various acts of adultery with white and black women and acts of cruelty towards the plaintiff were substantiated by evidence and found true; by a lawful jury. Whereupon it was ordered that the Petitioner, Jane B. Robinson, be divorced and separated from the bonds of matrimony entered into with the Defendant, William D. Rob-

---

52 Marriage Bond of Rutherford County, North Carolina, lists Daniel Mooney and Hannah McSwain, dated 30 April 1807. Bondsman: H. W. Kerr.

53 Marriage Bond of Duplin County, North Carolina, lists Alexander Newkirk and Rebecca Basden, dated 2 June 1811. Bondsman: William Southerland.

inson, which decree remains to be established by an Act of the General Assembly. (GASR, Nov.-Dec. 1818, Box 1: folder "House Bills, Nov. 24").

487. **Short, Jean and husband, Aaron; Short, Margaret and husband, James.** The petition of Margaret Short and [Jean] Short, both residents of Guilford County, states that about nineteen years ago, said Margaret married James Short, then of Guilford County, by whom she had five children. The said James, about nine years since, formed a connection with another woman and left the State, his place of residence unknown. The said [Jean] Short shows "that about nineteen years ago, she married Aaron Short and had four children. Seven years since that time, said Aaron formed an illicit connection with another woman and removed from the State. Your petitioners wish to accumulate a competent subsistence for the support of themselves and their families and hope to be secure in such property as they may hereafter acquire. They pray for a law giving them such security to save said property from the avarice and extravagance of men unworthy of affection and who have shown themselves unmindful of the obligation which as fathers they owed their families. [On reverse:] Certification by nine neighbors of the truth of the facts in said petition. In House of Commons, 22 November 1819, read and ordered to be postponed indefinitely. (GASR, Nov.-Dec. 1819, Box 3: folder "Petitions - Alimony").

488. **Spears, Margaret and husband, Elisha.** Petition of Margaret Spears of Cabarrus County claims that her husband, Elisha Spears, through neglect, dissipation, and habitual intoxication, has squandered all of his worldly substance, leaving your petitioner and children in a state of sufferance and has finally abandoned them. Prays for a law to secure such property as has accumulated or may hereafter accumulate by her own industry. [Below:] Signatures of four persons who support this petition. [On reverse:] "Granted". (GASR, Nov.-Dec. 1819, Box 3: folder "Petitions - Alimony").

489. **Stubbs, Elizabeth and husband John B.** Petition of Elizabeth Stubbs [no county designated] states she intermarried with John B. Stubbs, a mechanic from England in the year 1814. He was a stranger and native of a foreign country, but she was "induced to believe - from the partial and very limited acquaintance with him previous to their intermarriage - and from his own professions of a sincere and ardent attachment that her hopes of conjugal happiness rested upon strong probabilities - and that all their toils and troubles through life would be soothed and sweetened by the endearments of reciprocal affection…" Your petitioner soon discovered that her dreams were only delusions - and that he was sincere in nothing except in his vile purposes of crime and seduction. His daily practices were a continual repetition of offences, and he was capable of perpetrating anything from his "Petty Drunkard to the Midnight Assassin." The said John B. Stubbs formed a connection with Benjamin Gray, the notorious pickpocket and Bank Braker, "who was lately hung in Fayetteville." A letter dated 7 August 1817, signed Mary Stubbs, Manchester, England, authenticated that said John B. Stubbs had a wife, Mary Stubbs, resident there, and two daughters - Mary Ann and Charlotte.[54] Your petitioner states she is the only child of industrious and respectable parents who could provide a maintenance for herself and children provided they could be permitted to enjoy it. Prays for an act securing to her such property as she may hereafter acquire, free from claims of said John B. Stubbs. [Below:] Signatures of twelve persons who subscribe to above petition. [On reverse:] "Ordered that the prayer of the petnr be granted." (GASR, Nov.-Dec. 1818, Box 3: folder "Petitions -Alimony").

---

54 Copy of letter filed with these papers.

Divorces and Separations from Petitions to the North Carolina General Assembly from 1779

490.   **Taylor, Susannah and husband, Nathan.** Memorial of Susannah Taylor [of Guilford County, North Carolina] states she married Nathan Taylor about twelve years ago when she was very young and "contrary to the consent of her parents who were people in good circumstances and of good fame in the circle of their acquaintances." Said Nathan was a man without property, has spent all the product of his labor in drinking and has not lived with your memorialist for four or five years past. During this time she has lived with her father together with one of her children. This child is nine or ten years of age and has never walked a step in its life, being a cripple from its birth. Your memorialist and her father have kept said child from being a charge to the county and still wishes to do so. The father and mother of said memorialist are now dead, but a number of relatives would contribute towards her support. Prays for a law securing to her such property as she may hereafter acquire.

   [Below:] Signatures of thirteen subscribers support this memorial. [On reverse:] "Granted." (GASR, Nov.-Dec. 1818, Box 3: folder "Petitions - Alimony").

491.   **Warren, Elizabeth and husband, Samuel.** Petition of Elizabeth Warren states she married Samuel Warren[55], lived with him several years and has had two children by him. However, for the last ten years, he has neglected and abandoned your petitioner and refuses to live with or contribute to the support of her or her children. He has taken up with another woman with whom he has lived in adultery for several years. He left your petitioner and children in indigent circumstances, and she has by hard labour maintained them and accumulated some little stock and other necessarys to subsist upon. Prays for a law to secure to her such property as she may acquire since her husband's absence. [Below:] Signatures of four persons who subscribe to this petition.

   [Attached to above:] Depositions of Huldy (X) Lamb, Sarah (X) Burnet, and Joshua Norman before John Long, Justice of Peace of Randolph County, North Carolina, that Samuel Warren has not lived with his wife, Elizabeth of Chatham County, for nine or ten years. They believe the said Samuel left his wife with little to subsist upon without any provocation and has since lived with another woman for several years. Dated 22 November 1818. [On reverse:] "grant". (GASR, Nov.-Dec. 1818, Box 3: folder "Petitions - Alimony").

492.   **Reference A.**

   The Joint Committee to whom was referred the petitions of Charlotte Street, Delilah Langford, Betty Chambers, Elizabeth Stubbs, and Susannah Taylor praying passage of an act securing to them such property as they may hereafter acquire report that from the facts submitted, they are induced to believe these causes in all that deserve the interference of the Legislature provided it should be thought; that they possess the power of granting the wished for relief, which your committee from the best conception [?] they have been enabled to give to the subject, though…[interpretation is difficult in the handwriting]…they therefore recommend the passage of the Bill hereinafter reported. (GASR, Nov.-Dec. 1818, Box 4: folder "JCR Reports").

---

55   Marriage Bond of Randolph County, North Carolina, lists Samuel Warren and Elizabeth Laine, dated 13 May 1804. Bondsman: Jacob Staley.

1816 Session

493. **Reference B.**

The Committee of Propositions and Grievances to whom was referred the "Bill to establish and confirm the judgment of the Superior Court of Law of Richmond County divorcing Jane B. Robinson, wife of William D. Robinson, from the bonds of matrimony" and "A Bill to confirm the judgment of the Superior Court of Law of the County of Gates divorcing James Hoffler and his wife Deborah Hoffler from the bonds of matrimony" recommend the passage of the Bill herewith reported. In House of Commons (17 December 1818) and Senate (17 December 1818) - read third time, passed, and ordered to be engrossed. (GASR, Nov.-Dec. 1818, Box 1: folder "House Bills (Nov. 24)").

494. **Reference C.**

Laws of North Carolina, November-December 1818 Session, Chapter XXXVIII. The decrees of the Superior Court of Law of Richmond County, North Carolina, divorcing Jane B. Robinson from her husband, William D. Robinson, and of the Superior Court of Law of Gates County, North Carolina, divorcing James Hoffler from his wife, Deborah Hoffler, were affirmed.

1820-1822

495. **Barker, Mary and husband, Charles.** Petition of Mary Barker of Robeson County sheweth that she intermarried with one Charles Barker of said county about six years ago. A few weeks after the marriage, said Charles brought into his house to live with your petitioner - one Peggy McNamarra, a woman of ill fame with whom he had previously contracted an intimacy, which at the time of the marriage was unknown to your petitioner. The said Peggy has ever since resided with the said Charles by whom she has had several children. Consequently, your petitioner was compelled to separate from her said husband, and they both signed a mutual agreement in writing, and by virtue of said agreement, they have lived apart and separate for more than five years past. She has supported herself free and clear of any charge to her said husband, but the difficulty of collecting debts in her own name and enjoying property in her own right tends greatly to the injury of your petitioner. Prays for an act to secure her to such estate as she may hereafter acquire and to deal in her own name as though she had never been married to said Charles. (GASR, Nov. 1821-Jan. 1822, Box 4: folder "SCR").

    Report of the Committee of Propositions and Grievances to whom was referred the petition above, praying that a law be passed securing to the petitioner Mary Barker such property as she may hereafter acquire, that it appears by the statement of the gentleman introducing the problem that since the marriage, the said husband of the petitioner has been convicted several times on the charge of fornication by the Superior Court of Robeson County. The witnesses in the said trials gave evidence of such criminality on the part of the husband before any separation took place. The Committee recommends that the Legislature grant the prayer of the petitioner. [On reverse:] In Senate, 6 December 1821, read, and ordered to lie on the table. (GASR, Nov. 1821-Jan.1822, Box 4: folder "SCR").

496. **Bevins, Eliza and husband, Simeon.** Committee on Divorce and Alimony to whom was referred the petition of Eliza Bevins [petition not found] have said report under consideration. Apparently the petitioner, Eliza Bevins, married Simeon Bevins in the City of Charleston, South Carolina, on 10 November 1804. They lived together until November 1816, at which time they moved to Charlotte, Mecklenburg County, North Carolina. About this time, said Simeon left the petitioner for no apparent cause and went to the State of Kentucky where he now lives in a state of adultery according to a mutilated letter signed "S. Bevins." It also appears that the petitioner removed from Charlotte to Lincolnton where she has resided for four years and has sustained an irreproachable character for piety and virtue and has endeavoured to support herself and five children with great economy and industry. It is noted that the petitioner has ample means of obtaining a divorce under the Act of 1814 and subsequent amendments which give such powers to the Superior Courts of Law of this State. The Committee recommends rejection of the petition. (GASR, Nov.-Dec. 1820, Box 4: folder "JCR").

497. **Chadwick, Mary and husband. Wheeler.** Petition of Mary Chadwick of Guilford County states that her husband, Wheeler Chadwick, absconded from said county with the whole of his property in September 1820. Since that time, said property has been sold, leaving many of his debts yet unpaid and forc-

ing your petitioner to support herself and family by the labor of her own hands. Prays for a law to secure such property as she may hereafter acquire in her own name. [Below:] Signatures of twenty-one persons of Guilford County who support the petitioner. Dated 10 October 1820. [Enclosed:] Report of the Committee on the Judiciary to the above petition of Mary Chadwick "Recommend rejection." (GASR, Nov.-Dec. 1820, Box 4: folder "JCR").

498. **Conner, Henry Workman and wife, Catharine.** The Committee to whom was referred the bill for the divorce of Henry Workman Conner and his wife Catharine, are of opinion that said bill should be passed into law. The grounds on which legislative interference is sought are of a nature which do not admit of relief in the Courts of Justice. Every fact stated in the petition accompanying the bill appears to be fully proven.

[Enclosures:]

(a). Petition of Henry Workman Conner of Lincoln County sheweth he was married to Catherine Davidson, to whom he had been attached for many years, on 29 June 1820. About six months later, said Catherine was delivered of a child fathered by Charles D. Conner, the brother of your petitioner. It is painful to dwell on the subject, but the perpetrator of the act is the husband of a sister of your petitioner's wife and the father of several children by her. Though your petitioner has been irreparably injured by the conduct of his wife, he cannot but greatly blame her for the unutterable distress she has brought upon him, it is far from his feelings to speak harshly of her. He views her with an eye of sorrow rather than of anger. Prays for a law to dissolve the marriage contract with his wife.... It may be proper to inform the General Assembly that the child spoken of is dead, and that Catherine, the wife of your petitioner, has lived with her father since the child's birth.

(b). Marriage license of H. Workman Conner and Catharine Davidson, dated 26 June 1820, Iredell County, North Carolina. Witness: Robert Simonton, Clerk of Court.

(c). Letter from C. D. C. [Charles D. Conner] to his brother [H. W. Conner] strongly apologizing for his behavior and asking for forgiveness. Charles rationalized that he did not know that his brother and Catharine were going to be married. Dated 30 June 1820.

(d). Statement of Catherine Conner, dated 23 December 1820, that she was the mother of an infant whose father was Charles D. Conner.

(e). Note to Mrs. Catherine D. Conner from Henry W. Conner that he would petition the North Carolina General Assembly for a divorce of their bond of matrimony dated 8 November 1821. Attached to this notice is the deposition of Rev. James McKee, which supports the statements in the petition of Henry W. Conner above, dated 17 November 1821. (GASR, Nov. 1821-Jan. 1822, Box 4: folder "HCR (Miscellaneous)").

Bill for Divorce of Henry Workman Conner and his wife, Catharine. In Senate, 8 December 1821, read third time, passed, and ordered to be enrolled. (GASR, Nov. 1821-Jan. 1822, Box 1: folder "House Bill, 3 Dec.").

499. **Davis, Susan and husband, Willie O.** Memorial of Susan P. Davis of Franklin County represents that she intermarried with Willie O. Davis, late of Franklin County, in 1811 and had five children by him. In the year 1819, after dissipating his property and reducing your memorialist and his children to absolute want, poverty and distress, said husband abandoned her and his children and has gone to parts unknown, leaving a number of debts and demands outstanding and unpaid. Your memorialist has conducted herself as a faithful and affectionate wife from the time of their marriage and sought by every means in her power to reclaim him from habits of intemperance and dissipation. She has a reasonable expectation of being provided for in some measure by the bounty of her father, who had the means of

Divorces and Separations from Petitions to the North Carolina General Assembly from 1779

doing so. Prays for an act to secure to the separate case of your memorialist such property as she may hereafter acquire by gift, purchase or devise. [Below:] Signatures of nine persons residing in Franklin County who support the statements of the memorialist, Susan P. Davis. [On reverse:] In House of Commons, 28 November 1821. Read and ordered to be indefinitely postponed. (GASR, Nov. 1821 Jan. 1822, Box 4: folder "Petitions - Alimony").

500. **Howard, Drucilla and husband, John.** Petition of Drucilla Howard states that several years ago she had the misfortune to lose her first husband, Enoch Jeffers, who died leaving your petitioner in dependent and distressful circumstances. She had to depend on her own labor for subsistence and had acquired a few hundred dollars. Duringthe last Spring, it was her misfortune to become acquainted with one John Howard, whose decent appearance, respectful deportment and insinuating address inspired your petitioner with confidence in him and gained upon her affections. The said John Howard made proposals of marriage to your petitioner, and she acceded to them, their marriage being duly consummated.[56] She had been acquainted with her said husband but a short time before the marriage, but in a few days after the marriage, he absconded with all the money of your petitioner and such of her property as he could carry with him. He has never since returned, and your petitioner has learned that the said John Howard is a most accomplished swindler, and she had no reason to believe he will return. Prays for a law to enable her to hold such property as she shall hereafter acquire, free from any control of her husband. [Enclosed:] Report of the Committee of Propositions and Grievances to whom was referred the above petition of Drucilla Howard recommends the adoption of the following resolution - Resolved that it is inexpedient to grant the prayer of the petitioner. In Senate, 20 December 1820, read and concurred with. (GASR, Nov.-Dec. 1820, Box 4: folder "SCR - Privileges and Elections - Miscellaneous").

501. **MacDonald, Charlotte and husbands, Isaac MacDonald and Simon Sellers.** Petition of Charlotte (x) MacDonald, a poor, weak and distressed woman, born of parents who were in extreme low circumstances. Unfortunately, they have continued so ever since. At the age of eighteen years, your petitioner was lawfully married to Isaac MacDonald (Pilot) and bore for him six children, "two of whom it has pleased the Lord to take out of thy troublesome world." Said husband's disposition was very uneven, and he treated your petitioner "in a different manner from what he should all of which your Petitioner bore with fortitude until about four years ago, when he left me and children destitute of the means of support & went off in company with another man's wife." I was later informed that he never intended to return, and after many months "I was solicited to marry a man (then a widower)…Simon Sellers, whose circumstances were good & I not being aware of the enormity of the crime, consented & was married to him." About twelve months later, said Isaac MacDonald returned and prosecuted Mr. Sellers and recovered a considerable sum. Before payment was made, Mr. Sellers died, and his property was sacrificed to pay the judgment. MacDonald then solicited my return to him and said he would become a different man and treat me and the children well. Since I was in a destitute situation and unusually weak, I consented and returned to him. Shortly afterwards, Mr. MacDonald died, and I am now in a deplorable situation. Some considerable time ago, a writ from the Court issued against me (previous to MacDonald's death) to be brought to justice for a crime of which I was completely ignorant. The writ has not yet been served owing to my absence. Your petitioner and children are without any assistance except what little they obtain from an aged father, whose family is large and whose sole dependence is by farming on rented land. To add to my distress, my father unfortunately broke his arm a few weeks ago. Prays for relief by having

---

56   Marriage Bond of Wake County, North Carolina, lists Jno. Howard and Drucilla Jeffreys, dated 18 October 1819. Bondsman: Brinkley Lassit.

an act passed to have the suit dismissed. Dated 30 November 1821. (GASR, Nov. 1821-Jan. 1822, Box 4: folder "SCR - Prop. & Grievances Miscellaneous").

Report of the Select Committee to whom was referred the petition of Charlotte MacDonald are of opinion that the petitioner is entitled to legislative interferences and recommend the following Bill for her relief [bill is in another file as shown below]. (GASR, Nov. 1821-Jan. 1822, Box 4: folder "SCR -Prop. & Grievances Miscellaneous").

Bill for relief of Charlotte McDonald, late of County of New Hanover and widow of Isaac McDonald, late a pilot on the Cape Fear River. Immediately after the passage of this act, she is hereby discharged from any punishment to which she may be liable by reason of having intermarried with a certain Simon Sellers during the lifetime of said Isaac McDonald. In Senate, 11 December 1821, read third time and ordered to be engrossed. (GASR, Nov.-Dec. 1822, Box 2: folder "SB - 10 Dec.").

502. **McKaughan, Phebe and husband, Hugh.** Petition of Phebe McKaughan of Rowan County shows that your petitioner is the lawful wife of Hugh McKaughan who left this county on 11 November 1816 and has not returned. Shortly after said departure, the creditors of said Hugh seized and sold all his estate, which fell short of satisfying their demands, and your petitioner has been left destitute of any means of subsistence for herself and six small and helpless children. She has since had the misfortune to lose her father, George Pope, who died intestate. Creditors of said Hugh have levied attachments in the hands of Mary Pope, widow and administratrix of said George Pope, deceased, for the balance of their demands. Prays for a law to secure to her the residue of the estate of her said father George Pope's estate, which may remain due to her as a lawful heir and to also secure to her such property as she may hereafter acquire. [Below:] Signatures of thirty persons who say that said Phebe McKaughan is of good fame and family and support the above petition. (GASR, Nov.-Dec. 1820, Box 4: folder "Petitions - Alimony").

503. **Miller, Caleb and wife, Rachel.** Petition of Caleb Miller of Lincoln County sheweth he married Rachel Whitner in about April 1819 in Lincoln County.[57] In about October 1819, some six months later, said Rachel was delivered of a mulatto child. Your petitioner is "very little at home being out working at his trade." When he was at home, his said wife contrived to keep him from a full view of the child for a considerable time after its birth by having its face covered in a dark room. Your petitioner did not suspect anything until a rumor in the neighborhood reported that the child was colored. He found the child was of very dark color, but not being a judge, he called upon a practicing physician and a woman, whom he considered better judges than himself, to view the child, and they reported that it was a child of color. Upon being satisfied of this fact, he broke off all connection with said Rachel, procured a wagon, and took back all property he had received with her to her father's. Your petitioner filed a petition in Lincoln County Superior Court at April Term, 1820, praying to be divorced from said Rachel.

In September 1821, said Court declared that the petition does not come within the meaning of the Act of Assembly and is not a case upon which the Court could give the petitioner any relief. Your petitioner now prays that he may be divorced from said Rachel by act of the General Assembly. [Enclosed is the petition of Caleb Miller to the Lincoln County Superior Court, including several depositions and the subsequent ruling of said Court as explained above.]

The Committee of Propositions and Grievances to whom was referred the petition of Caleb Miller of Lincoln County report that the several depositions accompanying said petition satisfy your Committee that the petitioner intermarried in April 1819 with a certain Rachel Whitener, and that said Rachel

---

57 Marriage Bond of Lincoln County, North Carolina, lists Caleb Miller and Rachel Whitener, dated 24 April 1819. Bondsman: Jas. T. Alexander.

was delivered of a mulatto child in October of the same year; that as soon as the petitioner was assured of the colour of the child, he took his wife and all the property he received with her to her father's house and since that time has been entirely separated from her; that he duly notified her of his intention to petition this General Assembly for a divorce. Wherefore, your Committee believes that this case is entitled to legislative interference and recommend that the accompanying bill for the divorce of Caleb Miller and his wife Rachel be passed into law. [On reverse of bill:] In Senate, 15 December 1821, read first time and passed. In Senate, 17 December 1821, read second and third time, passed and ordered engrossed.

(GASR, Nov. 1821- Jan. 1822, Box 2: folder "SB, 15 Dec.").

504. **Patrick, John and wife, Sally.** True copy of a jury report at Superior Court of Law, April Term 1820, Craven County, North Carolina: We present that John Patrick of said county did on the [blank] day of October 1819, regardless of the solemnity of the holy estate for which matrimony was intended, did wantonly and not having the fear of God before his eyes, absolutely intermarry with a certain female child named Sally Rice under twelve years of age, to the great injury of the said Sally…and against the peace and dignity of the State.[58] [On reverse:] Resolved that the Judiciary Committee enquire into the expediency of making some provision that may secure infant female wards against being drawn into premature marriage by the interested views of unprincipled guardians.

True copy of a jury report at Superior Court of Law, April Term 1820, Craven County, North Carolina, that Elisha Patrick, one of the acting Justices of the Court aforesaid, did on [blank] day of October 1819 within the county aforesaid solemnize the rites of holy matrimony between John Patrick and Sally Rice, a female under the age of twelve years.

(GASR, Nov.-Dec. 1820, Box 4: folder "Miscellaneous").

505. **Pennington, Levice/Levisa/Louisa and husband, Ezekiel.** Petition of Levice Pennington of Burke County represents that she married one Ezekiel Pennington, who then resided near her father, Daniel England, on 6 April 1817. For some time previous to his marriage with your petitioner, said Pennington had been engaged in teaching an English school, and conducted himself with approbation, and had gained the esteem of the people in whose neighborhood he had lived near to Morganton. Your petitioner and her husband lived in harmony until 10 September 1817, when the said Ezekiel expressed his intention of going to Georgia to see his relations and did leave. In the next month of October, your petitioner received a letter from her said husband expressing his intention of returning soon to her. However, your petitioner has not received any further information from the said Ezekiel nor has any idea where he now lives. He left no visible property behind him and was indebted about two hundred dollars. Prays for a law to enable her to hold all such property as she may acquire. [Below:] Signatures of seventeen persons who support the above petition. (GASR, Nov. 1821-Jan. 1822, Box 4: folder "Petitions - Alimony").

Report of Committee of Propositions and Grievances to whom was referred the petition of Louisa Pennington, setting forth that she intermarried with Ezekiel Pennington of Burke County, who sometime afterwards abandoned her and has withdrawn himself and all assistance from her, and praying for a law to secure to her such property as she may hereafter acquire, recommend the passing into law the bill accompanying this report. (GASR, Nov. 1821-Jan. 1822, Box 4: folder "SCR - Prop. & Grievances, Miscellaneous").

---

58   Marriage Bond of Craven County, North Carolina, lists John Patrick, and Sally Rice, dated 27 October 1819. Bondsman: Isaac Patrick.

506. **Thomas, Temprance and husband, Richard.** Petition of Temprance Thomas of Haywood County sheweth that she was married to a young man named Richard Thomas in 1804. "[F]rom his deportment and conduct to her bid fare to make a kind, affectionate and faithful husband but also to the mortification of your petitioner this lasted but three months…" Under the pretense of trading or collecting money he bid her a friendly farewell, and she has never seen him since. Before he started on his journey, he contracted several debts, and no sooner than his creditors were informed of his elopement, they seized upon every cents worth of property your petitioner had made by her own industry. She had been raised an orphan, and her bedding and furniture were all she possessed. Six months after her husband left her, she had an infant son "without whereon to lay his head." With courage, study and working her land, she put her shoulder to the wheel and developed a surplus from her labor which went towards clothing, food and educating her fatherless child. She procured a station as clerk in astore for her son and hoped to use the money to procure a small tract of land. Prays that her situation be taken into consideration and that a law be passed to secure to her such property as she may hereafter acquire. [Enclosed:] Report on the above petition by the Committee on the Judiciary which recommends that the prayer of the petitioner be rejected for the same reason stated in their report on the petition of Harriot S. Strader. Such report and petition are not enclosed. (GASR, Nov.-Dec. 1820, Box 4: folder "SCR Claims, Militia Land").

507. **Reference A.**

Bill to secure to Levisa Pennington of Burke County, wife of Ezekiel Pennington, and Fanny Norman of Guilford County, wife of John Norman, such property as they may hereafter acquire. In Senate, 12 December 1820, read third time, amended, passed and ordered to be engrossed. In House of Commons, 13 December 1821, read first time and postponed indefinitely. (GASR, Nov. 1821-Jan. 1822, Box 2: folder "SB Dec. 11").

508. **Reference B.**

Laws of North Carolina, 1820. No divorces or separations were enacted.
Laws of North Carolina, 1821. No separations were enacted, but the following persons as preceded by the letter "D" were granted full divorces from 'sach other:
D   Conner, Henry Workman of Lincoln County; wife - Rachel, p. 67
D   Miller, Caleb of Lincoln County; wife - Rachel, p. 67

The following person was discharged from any punishment to which she may have been liable for marrying Simon Sellers during the lifetime of her first husband, Isaac McDonald:
McDonald, Charlotte, late of New Hanover County; widow of Isaac McDonald, p. 66

1822-1824

509.   **Barker, Elizabeth and husband, William.** Petition of Elizabeth (EB) Barker of Randolph County sheweth she intermarried with William Barker[59] of the same county in March 1820 and lived with him about ten months, hoping to continue in the enjoyments of his affections and the blessings of a married state. Alas, in consequence of his turbulent disposition and intemperance, her prospects were soon blasted, and she was forced to leave his bed and board and now lives on the hard earnings of industry and economy. Prays for a law to secure to her such property as she now has or may hereafter acquire. (GASR, Nov. 1823-Jan. 1824, Box 4: "SCR")

Certificate signed by eleven persons states that Elizabeth Barker has supported herself by honest industry and good economy since she was forced to leave her husband and has also supported a virtuous character. (GASR, Nov. 1823-Jan. 1824, Box 4: "SCR")

Deposition of Thomas Pugh of Randolph County states that the facts in the above petition of Elizabeth Barker were true and that her said husband told the deposer that he would not receive this wife anymore into his house but as a stranger. Dated 17 November 1823 before James Jones, Justice of Peace. (GASR, Nov. 1823-Jan. 1824, Box 4: "SCR")

Deposition of Frederick Brown of Randolph County states that the facts in the above petition of Elizabeth Barker are true, and that he heard the said William Barker say that his wife should never live another day with him. Dated 17 November 1823 before James Jones, Justice of Peace. (GASR, Nov. 1823-Jan. 1824, Box 4: "SCR")

Committee of Propositions and Grievances to whom was referred the petition of Elizabeth Barker of Randolph County states that "of the very few cases of the kind that could claim legislative interposition, this is not one of them." The Committee resolves that the prayer of the petitioner ought not be granted. [On reverse: In Senate, 27 November 1823, the report and resolution recommended to be adopted.] (GASR, Nov.1823-Jan. 1824, Box 4: "SCR")

510.   **Blackman, Annis and husband, Wyatt.** Petition of Annis Blackman of Sampson County represents she was married in March 1818 to Wyatt Blackman, who was considered sober, steady and industrious. Your petitioner hoped that such marriage would yield to her "and that of her unfortunate husband" much earthly comfort and happiness. However, about twelve months after said marriage, life together has been one of misery and sorrow. Said husband has become very intemperate and has wasted all the property he possessed. Your petitioner was compelled to return to her father's house to support herself and a little infant. Her husband had beat and abused her after frequent quarrels without any provocation on her part. Her life was threatened once by her said husband, but the timely interference of a friend prevented any further threat. The said Wyatt has now abandoned her and gone to the State of Alabama. Prays for a law to secure to her such property as she may hereafter acquire by her own indus-

---

59   Marriage Bond of Randolph County, North Carolina, lists William Barker and Elizabeth Barton, dated 22 February 1820. Bondsman: John Brower.

try and the charity or donations of her friends. [At bottom: Signatures of six persons who support the facts in the above petition.] (GASR, Nov. 1823-Jan. 1824, Box 3: "HCR")

Committee of Propositions and Grievances to whom was referred the above petition noted that the said Wyatt Blackman removed to the State of Alabama in the company of a harlot. The Committee recommended that the prayer of the petitioner be granted. [On reverse: In House of Commons, 20 December 1823, read and concurred with.] (GASR, Nov. 1823-Jan. 1824, Box 3: "HCR")

Bill securing to Annas Blackman of Sampson County any property, real or personal, which she may hereafter acquire, either by purchase, devise or descent, free and clear from any claim by her husband, Wyatt Blackman, or his creditors. In House of Commons, 22 December 1823, read third time, passed, and ordered to be engrossed. (GASR, Nov. 1823-Jan. 1824, Box 1: "HB 1 Dec.")

511. **Brewer, Sarah and husband, Daniel.** Deposition of Sarah (X) Brewer of Moore County states she intermarried with Daniel Brewer about 1807, and they lived together as man and wife for about thirteen years, during which time she had "as many as 8 children - six of which are now living…" On or about 27 December 1820, said Daniel abandoned her and these children, all of whom were small. At that time, said Daniel had spent and squandered nearly all his property. She has by her industry provided support for her children and herself and has acquired some small property, but threats against it have been made to pay for the debts of said Daniel. She is informed that her said husband is living in East Tennessee with a woman of loose and abandoned character, who he carried off with him. She has no hopes of said Daniel ever returning to her again. Prays for an act by which such property as she shall hereafter acquire be exempt from payment of the debts of said Daniel. (GASR, Nov. 1823-Jan. 1824, Box 3: "HCR")

Committee of Propositions and Grievances to whom was referred the petition of Sarah Brewer of Moore County report that there does not appear sufficient evidence to establish the allegations contained in the petition. [On reverse:] In House of Commons, 23 December 1823, read, and concurred with. (GASR, Nov. 1823-Jan. 1824, Box 3: "HCR")

512. **Gibson, Mildred and husband, John.** Petition of Mildred Gibson, wife of John Gibson of Stokes County, states she was legally married in January 1815[60] to the said John Gibson, who at the time was not rich, but was a man of moral and industrious habits. Alas, their flattering anticipations were dissipated by a lamentable change in the conduct of your petitioner's husband. Not three years had elapsed after the marriage that her husband became intemperate, profligate and indolent, and to crown all - turbulent and tyrannical to the last extreme. For the past two years, he has refused to live with your petitioner as a wife and has left her with three small children in extreme indigence. Your petitioner has acquired the means of subsistence by the labor of her own hands and the benevolence of her father. She has received visits by her husband, who utterly destroys and deprives her of everything he finds in her possession and says when her children are old enough to render him service, he will even deprive her of them. Your petitioner's father is disposed to make some provision for your petitioner and her infants, but is unable to do it effectually without the help of your Honorable body. Prays for an act vesting in her title to all such property as she earns by her own labor and the donations other father and friends. Witnesses: John Carson, James Carson. [On reverse:] Signatures of five subscribers to above petition, dated 16 November 1822. (GASR, Nov.-Dec. 1822, Box 4: "SCR - Claims, Miscel")

Committee of Propositions and Grievances to whom was referred the petition of Mildred Gibson report that it appears that the petitioner is the wife of John Gibson of Stokes County by whom she has

---

60 Marriage Bond of Stokes County, North Carolina, lists Jno. Gibson and Milly Young, dated 30 January 1815. Bondsman: Benja. Sanders.

had several children, that said husband does not discharge the obligation of husband and father, and that the petitioner is in great distress. Your Committee believes that John Gibson should have received notice [of this petition], a requisite which appears not to have been complied with. Your Committee therefore recommends that the prayer of the petitioner not be allowed. In Senate, 10 December 1822, read and concurred with. (GASR, Nov.-Dec. 1822, Box 4: "SCR Claims, Miscel.")

513. **Hampton, Sally and husband, James.** Petition of Salley Hampton, wife of James Hampton of Stokes County, states she was legally married on 7 October 1808[61] to said James Hampton who, at that time, was a man of considerable estate, both real and personal, and was esteemed "as a man of veracity, sobriety, morality, industry and good economy..." For several years after marriage, the most sanguine wishes and expectations of your petitioner and the friends of both were fulfilled in the conduct other husband. Unfortunately however for your petitioner and her husband, as well as for their forlorn family, "a lamentable revolution has taken place in his conduct and character within the last five or six years..." He has become intemperate, dissolute, profligate and depraved, and has spent the whole of an ample, independent estate composed of his own original property and property given to him by your petitioner's father. Your petitioner has had seven children by her said husband, all of whom are now living - the eldest is thirteen years and the youngest is twenty months. She receives not the smallest assistance to support these children, nor will he allow her friends to assist unless their donations are at his disposal. Your petitioner's father is a man of considerable estate, is now very old, and is desirous in his lifetime of making some provision for the relief of your petitioner and her children. Prays for an act vesting in her title to all such property acquired through her own labor, the assistance of her children, and the donations of her father and friends. Witnesses: Elisha Plummer, Thomas Flynt. [Below:] Signatures of twelve subscribers, dated 7 November 1822.] (GASR, Nov.-Dec. 1822, Box 4: "HCR - Misc.")

The Committee to whom was referred the petition of Sally Hampton is satisfied that the facts set forth in the petition are true, that owing to the revolution in the conduct of her husband, she and her family have been reduced from a state of affluence and respectability to a complete state of dependency and want. Nevertheless, your committee are of opinion that it would be impolitic to pass a law in conformity to the prayer of the petitioner. They therefore recommend the adoption of the following resolution: That it is inexpedient to grant the prayer of the petitioner. In House of Commons, 3 December 1822, read and concurred with. (GASR, Nov.-Dec. 1822, Box 4: "HCR - Misc.")

Petition of Sally (X) Hampton, dated 10 November 1823, states she was married in 1807, to James Hampton of same county, who at the time was known as sober, industrious and an honorable man, and whose fortune together with that of your petitioner under prudent and economical management was amply sufficient to keep the family independent and comfortable. Unfortunately, said husband John became intemperate shortly after the marriage, and by imprudent management has entirely exhausted the whole of the combined estate. Said husband is now not less intemperate, and frequently the small donations of your petitioner's friends are wrested to support his intemperance. Your petitioner has seven small children and finds herself unable to support them by the labor of her own hands. She has an aged father and other friends in "Easy" circumstances who are disposed to alleviate her distresses and to favor her with the means of support, provided such support is secured for the use and benefit of your petitioner and her children. Prays for an act to secure to her all such property as she may hereafter acquire by the donations of friends and the labor of their own hands. [Below:] Signatures of eighteen subscribers in

---

61   Marriage Bond of Stokes County, North Carolina, lists James Hampton and Sally Flynt, dated 29 September 1807. Bondsman: Richard Flynt.

support of the above petition who think it highly necessary that the prayer of the petitioner be granted, dated 11 November 1823.] (GASR, Nov. 1823 Jan. 1824, Box 4: "Petitions - Alimony")

514. **Hoggatt, Elizabeth and husband, Isaiah.** Petition of eighteen persons, including Geo. C. Mendenhall, Nathan Mendenhall and Richard Mendenhall, that Elizabeth Hoggatt, wife of Isaiah Hoggatt of Guilford County, has been dependent on her own exertions and the charity of her neighbors for me support of herself and five children. Her husband has been and is still greatly indebted. Property which she has acquired through her own industry is subject to be seized inpayment of her husband's debts. Her husband has not contributed in the least to the support of this family in several years, and for the past two years has entirely deserted them and resides in Rutherford County. The said Elizabeth is an industrious woman who is attentively engaged in the support of her family of small children. She has sustained a fair and unblemished reputation and was an affectionate wife. In no way did she contribute to his injury or embarrassment. The subscribers pray for an act to secure to said Elizabeth whatever property she may hereafter acquire by her own industry. The said Elizabeth Hoggatt has no near relatives in North Carolina, [undated]. (GASR, Nov. 1823-Jan. 1824, Box 1: "HB 23 Dec.")

The Committee of Propositions and Grievances to whom was referred the petition of Elizabeth Hoggatt report that said Elizabeth is the mother of six small children andentirely indebted to her own industry and the benevolence of her friends. Her husband is running in debt, has deserted his family, and has migrated to another state in company with a prostitute. This Committee recommends that the prayer of the petitioner be granted.

Bill to secure Elizabeth Hoggatt all such property she may hereafter obtain by purchase, gift or otherwise. In House of Commons, 26 December 1823, and in Senate, 27 December 1823, read second and third time, passed, and ordered to be enrolled.(GASR, Nov. 1823-Jan. 1824, Box 1: "HB 23 Dec.")

515. **Jernigan, Judith and husband, Ryan 0.** Bill to enable Judith Jernigan the wife of Ryan 0. Jernigan of Hertford County to hold and enjoy such property as she may hereafter acquire. [On reverse: In House of Commons, 10 December 1822, and referred to Committee of Propositions and Grievances.] (GASR, Nov.-Dec. 1822, Box 1:"HB 10 Dec")

Committee of Propositions and Grievances to whom was referred the above Bill report that the evidence before them supports the charge that the said Ryan 0.Jernigan is a man of loose, indiscreet and intemperate habits, and that his wife must be reduced to helplessness and want unless she be secured in the undisturbed enjoyment of such property as by her own efforts and those of her friends she may hereafter acquire. The Committee recommends passing of said Bill. [On reverse: In House of Commons, 16 December 1822, read, and resolved that this House do not concur therewith but that consideration thereof be indefinitely postponed.] (GASR, Nov.-Dec. 1822, Box 1: "HB 10 Dec.")

516. **Johnson, Jacob and wife, Hannah.** Petition of Jacob Johnson of Chatham County states that his wife, Hannah, has distinguished herself as an abandoned woman in point of morals and chastity by delivering a couloured child on 4 January 1822. Since that time, our conjugal embraces have entirely ceased. Prays for a divorce from said wife Hannah. Dated 27 November 1823. [Below:] Statement signed by seven subscribers who support the undisputed facts in the above petition.] (GASR, Nov. 1823-Jan. 1824, Box l: "HB 26 Dec.")

Committee of Propositions and Grievances to whom was referred the petition of Jacob Johnson report that Hannah, the wife of the petitioner, has separated herself from the conjugal embraces of her husband and has become the mother of a coloured bastard child. Recommend the prayer of the petitioner be granted. (GASR, Nov. 1823-Jan. 1824, Box l: "HB 26 Dec.")

Divorces and Separations from Petitions to the North Carolina General Assembly from 1779

Bill to divorce Jacob Johnson of Chatham County from his wife, Hannah. In House of Commons, 26 December 1823, and in Senate, 27 December 1823, read second and third time, passed, and ordered to be engrossed. (GASR, Nov. 1823-Jan. 1824, Box 1:"HB 26 Dec.")

517. **Neil, Mary and husband, Henry.** Bill to enable Mary Neil, wife of Henry Neil of Bertie County, to hold and enjoy such property as she may hereafter acquire. [On reverse:] In House of Commons, 11 December 1822, read and referred to Committee of Propositions and Grievances. (GASR, Nov.-Dec. 1822, Box 1: "HB 11 Dec.")

Committee of Propositions and Grievances to whom was referred the above Bill recommend the bill be indefinitely postponed. [On reverse:] In House of Commons, 30 December 1822, read and concurred with. (GASR, Nov.-Dec. 1822, Box 1: "HB 11 Dec.")

518. **Noomkaser, Daniel and wife, Catharine.** Bill to divorce Daniel Noomkaser of Davidson County from wife, Catharine. In House of Commons, 1 December 1823, read third time, passed, and ordered to be engrossed. (GASR, Nov. 1823-Jan. 1824, Box 1: "HB 1 Dec.")

519. **Pinnix, Sarah and husband, Trice.** Petition of Sarah Pinnix of Surry County states she married Trice Pinnix in 1807 and lived together until about two years past "when he took to find loose practices & finally went of[f] with another woman." Your petitioner understands that they live together as man and wife. Her said husband left much in debt, but little property, and seven small children to raise and maintain. His creditors have been taking her property from her as fast as she earns it and leaves her children and herself in a state of starvation. Prays for a law to secure to her all the property she now has in her possession or may acquire by her industry. [Below:] Certificate of Benedict Castavens that the statements in the above petition are correct, and that he has lived a near neighbor to the said Sarah Pinnix. Dated 8 November 1823. (GASR, Nov. 1823-Jan. 1824, Box 4: "SCR")

Committee of Propositions and Grievances to whom was referred the petition of Sarah Pinnix of Surry County report that the said Sarah was married to Trice Pinnix in 1807, that she sometime afterward removed with her said husband to South Carolina, and that they continued to live together until about two years ago, when the said Trice Pinnix took up with a loose woman of the neighborhood, went off with her, and left his wife Sarah Pinnix with seven small children to support. For several years before said Trice abandoned his wife, he had become very dissipated, had contracted many debts, and when it was known he had left, the whole of his property was seized and sold to pay his debts. Your committee submits the following resolution - that the prayer of the petitioner ought to be granted. [On reverse:] In Senate, 11 December 1823. The report read and the resolution adopted. (GASR, Nov. 1823-Jan. 1824, Box 4: "SCR")

520. **Price, Washington and wife, Susannah.** Petition of Thomas Price, the father, and of Washington Price, the son (a minor), sheweth that your petitioner Thomas has taken unwearied pains to procure for his said son the best means of instruction that his duty to a numerous family would allow him to employ. The youth availed himself of the advantages thus offered [which] would be expedient to complete at the University. During the time he remained there, more than a year, the youth was exemplary in his conduct, untainted in his morals and constant in his studies. But language cannot express...the agony which overwhelmed your petitioner when he received a few months since, the dreadful intelligence that the youth had been ensnared by the most subtle intrigues and deceived by the vilest arts, into a marriage with a common prostitute! He did indeed at that moment wish that he had never been born, or had been cut off before he was a father; and has ever since felt that every blessing of life is lost upon him, and

that the afflictions of age are doubled upon his head. Your petitioner further sheweth that he investigated upon the spot the means by which this conspiracy against his peace and his child's honor and prospects was consummated, and discovered in them such a tissue of artifice and baseness of depravity without example and wickedness without allay as would be incredible without the strong proof he is ready to furnish. He further shews that the youth very soon became convinced of the various stratagems of which he had been made the dupe and recovered from his delusion to a deep sense of shame at his own indiscretion and a profound feeling of disgust for the actors in the tragedy. Your petitioner prays (and in this, his son, now only nineteen years old, humbly and earnestly joins) that Washington Price may be divorced from Susannah Price, late Susannah Webb. Dated 9 December 1823. (GASR, Nov. 1823-Jan. 1824, Box 4: "Petitions - Alimony")

Papers in support of the above petition (GASR, Nov. 1823-Jan. 1824, Box 4: "Petitions - Alimony"): Affidavit of William Hillyard before Henry Thomson and Maurice Henderson, Justices of Peace for Orange County, states he has been acquainted with said Susannah Price for about three years, lived near her, and has good reason to believe from common report that said Susannah is a common prostitute, 4 December 1823.

Certificate of Joseph Caldwell of Chapel Hill, North Carolina, that he has occasionally heard of a woman by the name of Polly Webb as living a mile or two from Chapel Hill and that the Webb name has been usually connected with unchaste and infamous character. He sometimes has heard it said that Polly Webb was a woman of much art and cunning, 6 December 1823.

Certificate of A. Henderson in Raleigh, North Carolina, that he scarcely has personal acquaintance with either the mother or daughter ascribed to [Polly and Susannah Webb], but he has heard of their misconduct and abandoned principles and is induced to believe that both the mother and daughter are abandoned prostitutes.

Affidavit of Bryan Kittrell and Pleasant Kittrell of Orange County states that it is their belief from common reports that the said Susannah Price, now wife of Mr. Washington Price (late a student at the University of North Carolina) is a common prostitute, 4 December 1823.

Deposition of Jonathan Kittrell that the family of Susannah Price, formerly Susannah Webb, lived on the plantation of the deponent's father for a number of years, and the said deponent was well acquainted with said Susannah ever since she was seven years of age. He represents the character of said Susannah from common report as a common prostitute. He is also acquainted with Polly Webb, said mother of Susannah, and says that said Polly has had five or six base begotten children by a married man, and the said Susannah is also illegitimately begotten by another man.

[Depositions from William McCauley and Edmund R. Pitt, not abstracted here, are also in this file.]

Petition of Susan Price, dated 15 December 1823, states that since Thomas Price has reported that Washington Price was measurably forced to marry Susan Webb, said Susan thought it proper to relate the truth of the circumstances. Washington Price commenced courting Susan Webb in November 1822. In March 1823, he asked leave of her mother to marry her daughter Susan. She (the mother) objected, saying her daughter was too young, being scarcely fourteen. She also had another objection Price's father, being a man of considerable property and her daughter a poor girl should he marry her, perhaps his father might disinherit him. Price replied he did not think his father would have the least objection, for he had often heard him say he thought a parent ought to allow a child the privilege of making his own choice in a companion through life and further said that when his father married his mother, he did it quite contrary to the will of her parents. He also said that suppose his father should disinherit him, it would make no difference with him, for he was able and willing to work for his living as his father had done before him. He had rather marry a poor girl that he dearly loved and dwell with her in a cottage

Divorces and Separations from Petitions to the North Carolina General Assembly from 1779

than have possession of a King's palace with a girl he could not love. The mother of Susan Webb then talked with your petitioner privately, telling her by no means not to think of marrying Washington Price, fearing it would be; attended by bad consequences, he being under control of his father. But Susan Webb paid no attention to the solicitations of her Mother [and] said she preferred Price to any other person on earth. She then, though a girl of no property, had offers of gentlemen superior to Price as to property or principle, but Price appeared, very solicitous, and continued his visits to Susan, tho' often opposed by the family. In the month of September on Sunday evening, Washington Price and Susan Webb were sitting conversing together as usual, and the mother of Susan took her daughter by the hand and pulled her from said Price, saying that he should never have any more conversation with said Susan in her presence. Price protected Susan and tried to reason the case with her mother saying he would marry her daughter at the risk of his life. On the following Tuesday evening, Price took her from her mother. Mr. B. Kittrell, upon hearing that Price had stolen Susan Webb, went to her mother and asked if Washington Price and Susan had married.[62] The mother replied she did not know. Mr. Kittrell then replied that Susan had the worst end of the stuff, for Price was an idiot and further said he heard upwards of thirty students say they did not think Susan Webb would be such a fool as to marry Washington Price - fool is a key abrupt expression tho' I relate it as Mr. Kittrell expressed it. As the different sex often envy each other, Susan Price is one of those unhappy girls who have to bear these reproaches, which are groundless. Originated from malice and envy, a sure enemy is a dangerous monster who can defame the character of the most virtuous girl upon earth. Therefore, I hope gentlemen of the legislature you will maturely consider it and let not malicious inventions be carried into effect. Thomas Price took all advantages of Susan Price in secretly taking certificates and depositions of those that were her enemies.

If it is requested, Susan Price is able to bring certificates from her neighborhood establishing her character from respectable citizens. Prays that the legislature grant her time to obtain depositions to substantiate her character. (GASR, Nov. 1823-Jan. 1824, Box 4: "Petitions - Alimony")

Papers in support of the above petition and a second petition for Susannah Price by Mary G. Webb, "her next friend," dated 18 December 1823 (a printed petition not included in this article): Certificate of six persons "that Abdias P. Webb is now about leaving the parts adjacent to the neighborhood of Pittsboro, in which neighborhood he has taught school for nine years and has proved himself attentive to the instruction of youth, not only in advancing their education in spelling, reading, arithmetic, &c., but also particular to their morals; but not finding his schools sufficient to engage attention, we part with him with the greatest respect as a teacher…" Dated 23 November 1816. /s/ J. W. Bynum, Hastin Poe, Francis Tarrel, Stephen J. Petty, J. F. Poe, M. Bynum.

Deposition of Abdias P. Webb of Wake County, dated 20 December 1823, states he knows Susannah Price, formerly Webb, from her infancy. He does not believe she is a girl of evil or bad fame. That she is now between thirteen and fourteen years of age and that her deportment hath been upright, as chaste and free from vice as any young girl of her age in the neighborhood where she has been raised. Certificate that the subscribers are personally acquainted with Susan Price from her non-age, and that we have no just cause to believe but that she is a good, virtuous, well-behaved girl. Dated 20 December 1823. /s/ Isaiah Rigsbee and Nancy Rigsbee, his wife; John E. Rigsbee, Constable, and Phoebe Rigsbee, his wife; Geo. Oldham; Alien Oldham; Holloday Robert Oldham.

Deposition of John Hollowell of Chatham County, dated 22 December 1823 within a few miles of Chapel Hill, states he has been well acquainted with Susannah Price (late Webb) from her infancy and believes her to be a virtuous, good and industrious girl. Said Susannah lived for several years in the house of William Henry Merritt, Esq., a preacher or teacher of the Holy Gospel of God, and last Friday,

---

62   Marriage Bond of Orange County, North Carolina, lists Washington Price and Susan Webb, dated 2 October 1823. Bondsman: Holadey R. Oldham

he told this deponent - "that Thomas Price of Wake County, the father of Washington Price, applied to him three times to give a certificate of her [said Susannah] being a girl of bad character and loose and depraved morals" and prevailed upon him that he might get her divorced from his son Washington. Merritt refused to prepare such a certificate, stating to Mr. Price "that he thought she would make his son a good wife…as he knew nothing bad of the girl…" This deponent believes that the reports in circulation, prejudiced to her, are false and the results of malice, envy and ill will, and that in his opinion and belief, she is unjustly, falsely and maliciously slandered. Sworn before Nimrod Ragsdale, Justice of Peace.[63]
In House of Commons, 31 December 1823, read and rejected, and the Committee discharged.

521. **Skinner, Elizabeth and husband, Henry.** Memorial of Elizabeth Skinner of Edgecombe County sheweth she intermarried with one Henry Skinner about fifteen years past, bore him children, and endeavoured by industry and obedience to discharge her part of the marriage contract as a wife, mother and mistress of a family. Her regard for her husband, notwithstanding his misconduct, hoped that time would show him the error of his ways and produce a reformation. She was unwilling to make their domestic differences public, but his conduct became so outrageous that she was compelled to leave his house and seek the protection of her father. For the last seven years, his conduct towards her has been a continued series of "brutal barbarity," the details of which could "excite the indignation of every man of Honourable feeling." There is no hope of reformation. Prays for an act to secure to her any future acquisitions. Dated 28 November 1822. (GASR, Nov.-Dec. 1822, Box 4: "HCR - Misc.")

The Committee to whom was referred the memorial of Elizabeth Skinner, wife of Henry Skinner of Edgecombe County, praying a law to secure to her in her own right her future acquisitions, report that it appears that said Elizabeth has for a series of years been unjustly and cruelly treated by her husband, that she has lately been driven from her house and cannot return to the same, that he is a man of intemperate habits and is fast squandering his property, and that his wife, who appears to have conducted herself with propriety and to have foreborn complaint until now under the hope of a reformation in her husband, has no other prospect of exemption from poverty and wretchedness in the decline of life than protection in the undisturbed enjoyment of the fruits of her ownindustry. Recommend passing of a bill to grant her prayer. In House of Commons, 14 December 1822, read, and resolved that this House does not concur. (GASR, Nov.-Dec. 1822, Box 4: "HCR - Misc.")

522. **Vaughan, Elizabeth and husband, Peyton.** Petition of Elizabeth Vaughan of Warren County sheweth 517 intermarried with Peyton Vaughan of said county in1809.[64] Said Peyton has completely abandoned himself to intoxication and become unfit for business or governing a family. Your petitioner has had four children by said husband- one daughter and three sons, viz. - Martha Anne, Jno. Jeremiah, William Thomas and James Madison Vaughan. Since said Peyton has become so addicted to the habits of intemperance, he has used your petitioner in a cruel manner, unbecoming a husband or a man. He has repeatedly beaten her without provocation, and she has been compelled to bind him to the peace. Upon the first binding, when he made solicitation and fair promises of reform, your petitioner was induced not to appear against him. As soon as he was released, he again commenced the same course of conduct to her, which he had been in the habit of for several years, such as beating and threatening her life and the lives of their children. She was compelled to resort to the law of the country for protection and sought refuge with her children in the house of her father. Said Peyton has been in the habit of pursuing

---

63   On the reverse of the second petition of Susannah Price by "her next friend", Mary G. Webb, it is noted.
64   Marriage Bond of Warren County, North Carolina, lists Peyton Vaughan and Betsey Pegram, dated 20 April 1809. Bondsman: Ozbom Vaughan.

her, and upon occasion, broke down the door of her father's house, threatened his life and the lives of his family. This situation has repeated itself many times. Because of such ill treatment, your petitioner despairs of ever being able to live with her said husband, and is in constant dread of her life and those of her children. Prays for a law to secure to your petitioner custody and guardianship of her children, free from the molestation of her husband. If this prayer cannot be granted, your petitioner prays that at least she may have custody of her daughter and for a law securing to her such property as she may hereafter acquire. Dated 16 November 1822 before Thomas Paine, J.P. [Below:] Signatures of four subscribers who sincerely believe that the facts stated in the above petition are true and that from their knowledge, the petitioner's father, Gideon Pegram, the children could not be better disposed of than under the care of their mother and grandfather. (GASR, Nov.-Dec. 1822, Box 4: "SCR - Misc.")

The Committee of Propositions and Grievances to whom was referred the above petition report that without considering the policy of allowing pretensions set forth in the petition, your Committee is of opinion that inasmuch as the best rights of the husband are concerned in the question - he should have received notice this application would be made to the Legislature and which your Committee conceived would be in conformity to regulations heretofore adopted by the Legislature in such cases - such notice not being given - recommend that the prayer of the Petitioner be not allowed. (GASR, Nov.-Dec.1822, Box 4: "SCR - Misc.")

523. **Welborn, Jane and husband, John.** Petition of Jane Welborn of Randolph County sheweth she intermarried John Welborn of Guilford County [preceding two words crossed out] in 1776. Although he did not treat your petitioner well, she remained with him until 1793, when his abusive treatment and habits became so intolerable that your petitioner was compelled to separate herself from her husband and resort to her friends for protection and support, he having squandered away almost everything they had subsisted on. During their marriage, your petitioner had six children by her said husband, but by her own industry and the assistance of her friends, she has raised and educated them without any assistance from her said husband. Since the separation, he has been strolling about the country without being of much benefit to himself or anyone else, but when he has been sick or in distress, your petitioner rendered him every assistance and relief. Lately, her stepfather William Bell, bequeathed to her a lifetime right in a tract of land and the use of five negro slaves together with some other legacies for her support and maintenance during life. Prays for a law to secure to her such estate as she may hereafter acquire either by gift, descent or her own industry.[65] [On reverse:] In Senate, 21 November 1823, read, and referred to Committee of Propositions and Grievances. (GASR, Nov. 1823-Jan. 1824, Box 4: "Petitions - Alimony")

Bill to secure to Jane Welborne of Randolph County and Sarah Pinnix of Surry County the property they may hereafter acquire. In Senate, 12 and 26 December 1823, read third time, passed, and ordered to be engrossed. (GASR, Nov. 1823-Jan. 1824, Box 2: "SB 4 Dec.")

524. **White, John and wife, Tamar.** Petition of John White of Pasquotank County states he intermarried Tamar Meeds, a widow of Benjamin Meeds, lately deceased of the county aforesaid, about ten years ago.[66] He lived with her as his wife and supported and maintained her in the best style he was able to do. He had five children by her, two of which are living, the others dead. In April 1822, his wife was delivered of a coloured child, begotten by a negro slave that lived on his farm. After the discovery of this

---

65 This petition was subscribed to by four persons of Randolph County.
66 Marriage Bonds of Pasquotank County, North Carolina: Benjamin Meeds and Tamer Overman, dated 27 July 1804; Bondsman: John Lester. John White and Tamer Meeds, dated 24 December 1811; Bondsman: John Taylor.

coloured child, his said wife's relations carried her off to their home where she has remained ever since. He believes that because of this incident, he can no longer have any further relations with said wife and is determined to abandon her forever. Prays for a divorce.

[Attached to the above:] Notification to Mrs. Tamar White from John White that he will take depositions to prove the charges set forth in the above petition to the General Assembly on 14 September 1822 "at the store house belonging to Andrew Brother Sat New Biggin Creek in Pasquotank County." Dated 14 August 1822. (GASR, Nov.-Dec. 1822, Box 1: "HB 6 Dec")

Committee to whom was referred the petition of John White of Pasquotank County praying for a divorce from his wife. Tamer White, report that it appears that the petitioner has been married several years to his present wife, and by her has had five children, two of whom only are alive. During that time, he treated her with becoming tenderness and regard until April last, when she was delivered of a coloured child supposed to have been begotten by one of his own slaves. This statement by the petitioner has been substantiated by several depositions of persons well acquainted with and residing near the parties. A copy of the petition together with notice of the intention of the petitioner to present the same to the General Assembly was served on said Tamar White, his wife, in August last. Regarding matrimony as an institution as holy and sacred in the eye of heaven, as it is indispensable to the well-being and happiness of Man, your Committees are fully impressed with the conviction that its engagements should never be disturbed unless upon occasions the most urgent and important - but when a case like that before your Committee, involving circumstances at contemplation of which the heart of feeling and of sensibility must shudder, when a case like that is addressed to the sympathies and compassions, their instruction is enjoined by every feeling of humanity, by every principle of Justice, of honour, and of religion - the moral blight is deadly and irrevocable, a stain which human power cannot remove- Your Committee respectfully recommends the passing of the accompanying bill - "A Bill to Divorce John White of the County of Pasquotank from his wife Tamar." [On reverse: In House of Commons, 24 December 1822, read third time and passed.] (GASR, Nov.-Dec. 1822, Box 1: "HB6 Dec.")

525. **Wilkins, Elizabeth and husband, William.** Petition of Elizabeth (+) Wilkins of Burke County states she intermarried with one William Wilkins, and they lived together for four years, at which time her said husband abandoned her without any reason known to your petitioner, for she treated her husband with respect and affection. She further states: "…it is upwards of eleven years since the said William Wilkins left your petitioner and went to the Western Country as your petitioner has understood & believes…and it is about five years since she heard from the said William…" and heard that he had died, but is not sure if this report is true. Prays for a divorce from said husband. Dated 5 March 1823.

Depositions of George Hill and Thomas (?) Largent, dated 5 November 1823, state they were well acquainted with William Wilkins who intermarried with Elizabeth Hill, now Wilkins, and that the said William left his wife nearly eleven years ago and has never since been seen or heard in Burke County. The said Elizabeth conducted herself well while she lived with her said husband and treated him with every respect and affection. (GASR, Nov. 1823-Jan. 1824, Box 4: "SCR")

Committee of Propositions and Grievances to whom was referred the above petition beg leave to submit a Bill. (GASR, Nov. 1823-Jan. 1824, Box 4: "SCR") See Bill below.

Bill to divorce Elizabeth Wilkins of Burke County from her husband, William Wilkins. In Senate, 2 December 1823, engrossed and examined; in House of Commons, 23 December 1823, read third time, passed, and ordered to be enrolled. (GASR, Nov. 1823-Jan. 1824, Box 2: "SB 29 Nov.")

Divorces and Separations from Petitions to the North Carolina General Assembly from 1779

526. **Williams, Milley and husband, John.** Committee of Propositions and Grievances to whom was referred the "Bill to alter the names of Charles Alexander Williams & others and to legitimate them" report that more than twenty years ago John Williams of Granville County intermarried with Milley Hester of the same county, and they lived together several years. Afterwards, the said John Williams became debauched and drunken in his habits, connected himself with a loose and prostituted woman in the neighborhood and eventually eloped with her and took refuge in the State of Georgia, where he continued to live until between one or two years ago, when he died. After being abandoned by her said husband for several years, the said Milley Williams and William Barnes, being ignorant of the laws of the state, contracted a marriage, and the ceremony was actually performed.[67] In the belief that they were lawfully married, they have ever since lived together as man and wife in great harmony and comfort, having as issue the children whose names are contained in the Bill referred to us. The said William and Milly are honest and industrious and have acquired a handsome competency for the support of themselves and their children. Only lately have they been informed that the ceremony which they supposed was a good and valid marriage is null and void. The Committee recommends that the Bill referred to them be passed into law. [On reverse: In Senate, 3 December 1823, read and the Bill reported put on its passage.] (GASR, Nov. 1823-Jan. 1824, Box 4: "SCR")

527. **Reference A.**

The persons listed below with a prefix "D" were granted full divorces from the bonds of matrimony. All of the others with no prefix were secured in their estate and property acquired as if there had been no marriage. The wife was almost always the injured party in need of such security in the society of that time. The names below are found in the state-sponsored series. Laws of North Carolina, which were enacted in the year shown in the act found on the page number listed.

    Blackman, Annis of Sampson County from husband, Wyatt (1823, p. 95)
    Hampton, Sally from husband, James of Stokes County (1823, p. 95)
    Hoggott, Elizabeth of Guilford County, wife of Isaiah (1823, p. 94)
D   Johnson, Jacob of Chatham County from wife, Hannah (1823, p. 89)
D   Noomcaser, Daniel of Davidson County from wife, Catharine (1823, p. 89)
    Pinnix, Sarah of Surry County (1823, p. 95)
    Welborn, Jane of Randolph County (1823, pp. 94-95)
D   White, John of Pasquotank County from wife, Tamar (1822, p. 48)
D   Wilkins, Elizabeth of Burke County from husband, William (1823, p. 89)

---

67   Marriage Bond of Warren County, North Carolina, lists William Barnes and Milly Williams, dated 8 April 1810. Bondsman: John Ellington.

1824-1825

528. **Allen, Sarah and husband, William.**
(1).   Petition of Sarah Allen sheweth that her husband, William [H] Allen, late of Caswell County, has not made any exertions for the support of his family for the past two years and has been absent from ihem since 1 May 1824. Prays for an act to secure to her whatever she may acquire by her own industry or by inheritance. Dated 10 November 1824. [Below:] John McMullin certifies that the above statements are correct and that the said Sarah Allen has been left with seven children to support and provide for by her said husband.
(2).   Committee of Propositions and Grievances to whom was referred the petition of Sarah Allen of Caswell County have duly considered said petition and are of opinion that the prayer should be allowe'd.
(3). Bill to secure to Sarah Allen of Caswell County such property as she may hereafter acquire. [On reverse:] In Senate, 23 November 1824, read third time, passed and ordered to be engrossed. (GASR, Dec. 1824-Jan. 1825, Box 2: "SB 22 Nov.")

529. **Barber, John D. and wife, Mary.**
(1).   Petition of John D. Barber of Washington County states he married Mary Perry in 1811. He always treated her affectionately, but after three years, she left his house without cause "…and entered into the most abandoned scenes of feastitution [prostitution]…with black and white and it is fact that the line of conduct she has persued is too disgraceful to state…she has contracted a long time since a most hateful disease…she is a most uncommon drunkard and thief…" Prays for a law to dissolve the bonds of matrimony between him and the said Mary Barber. [Below:] Signaturesof thirteen subscribers.]
(2).   Accompanying above petition are separate depositions of William D. Harramond, Ezekiel H. Potter, and Ezekiel Hardison, all of Washington County, North Carolina, who say they have been well acquainted with Mary Barber, wife of John D. Barber, and since the year 1813, said Mary has lived in a state of adultery with three different persons and is considered one of the basest prostitutes and drunkards that can be found and is considered unfit for civilized society. The said John Barber treated her kindly while his said wife lived with him, and even after she left, he would receive and maintain her if she would abandon her course of life and return to him again.
(3).   Committee of Propositions and Grievances to whom was referred the petition of John D. Barber of Washington County report that the petitioner intermarried in 1811 with Mary Perry with whom he lived for three years contentedly and happy. At the end of that time, his said wife left his house without any known cause and has ever since been living in a lewd, unprincipled and disgraceful manner. She has abandoned all regard for her character and given herself to drunkenness, pilfering and incontinency. Recommend that application for relief be made to the Superior Court and recommend rejection on present petition. [On reverse:] In House of Commons, 24 November 1824, read, and concurred with. (GASR, Nov. 1824-Jan. 1825, Box 4:"HCR, Military Affairs - Miscellaneous" and Box 5:"Petitions - Divorce")

Divorces and Separations from Petitions to the North Carolina General Assembly from 1779

530. **Barker, Mary and husband, Charles.**
(1). Petition of Mary (VV^) Barker of Robeson County represents that in the year of 1816, she was "impressed with the delusive belief that happiness was not to be found in a State of Celibacy, that her situation in life would be rendered more comfortable and her happiness subserved by the Act; intermarried with Charles Barker her husband; that for a short time thereafter she deemed herself fortunate in the change; that she was in full fruition of all those expected pleasures & advantage which are the natural result of the married State; her companion was kind and indulgent, and your petitioner only looked forward for a continuation. But, alas, how soon were those delightful dreams of continued kindness and constancy dissipated. A Woman of loose morals supplanted me in the affections of my husband, and I was called upon to share with another those affections and attention to which I was exclusively entitled. This abandoned woman was brought to reside under the same roof with your petitioner, and the duty assigned her that of a menial servant, whilst the affection and attention of her husband was devoted to this adultress. Such conduct became insupportable and your petitioner was compelled to abandon her home, her husband and her promised happiness." Your petitioner further shews that she has never since resided with the said Charles, her husband, and he still lives with the said adultress. Several children have been the result of this unholy connection. Prays for an act to divorce her from the bonds of matrimony with said Charles Barker. Dated 8 December 1824.

(2). Committee on Divorce and Alimony to whom was referred the petition of Mary Barker of Robeson County recommend the passage of the accompanying Bill: A Bill to divorce Mary Barker of Robeson County from her husband, Charles Barker. [On reverse:] In Senate, 22 December 1824, read second and third time, passed and ordered to be engrossed. In House of Commons, 27 December 1824, read second time and postponed indefinitely.

(GASR, Nov. 1824-Jan. 1825, Box 3:"SB 22 Dec.")

531. **Barr, Isaac and wife, Elizabeth.**
(1). Petition of Isaac Barr. states he has resided in Stokes County for a long time and has several children by a former marriage. He raised them to maturity, and they are now reputable members of society. As a widower, he was in need of a housekeeper and took on a woman who happened to come to his house from another county, a stranger to him. Having conducted herself in an orderly way, he took her to be a woman of good fame and reputation, and made a proposition of marriage to her to which she consented, and they became man and wife.[68] He soon found that his new wife, Elizabeth Barr, was an artful woman who had taken him in and disturbed his quiet by lewd, lascivious conduct. She finally eloped from him without any cause to gratify her improper desires free from any restraint. She has now been about two years in some distant part of the country during which time she has led an adulterous life. She has lately married another man, arid your petitioner prays that he be granted a divorce from the bonds of matrimony with his now wife.

(2). The Committee on Divorce and Alimony to whom was referred the petition of Isaac Barr of Stokes County report there is no evidence produced to substantiate the petition and recommend rejection of the prayer of the petitioner. [On reverse:] In Senate, 8 December 1824, read and adopted.
(GASR, Nov. 1824-Jan. 1825, Box 4:"SCR: Claims - Finance")

---

68 Marriage Bond of Stokes County, North Carolina, lists Isaac Barr and Betsey Ader dated 14 August 1823. Bondsman: Andrew White.

1824-1825 Session

532. **Brame, Oliver and wife, Elizabeth.**

(1). Memorial of Oliver Brame of Warren County states that "on or about the twenty-fifth of December 1823, he unfortunately for his future prospects of happiness fell in company with a young woman of the county and state aforesaid by the name of Elizabeth Archer, that he was soon induced by the promises of his father in law and the allurements of her mother to court her..." On the 30th of the same month, Pie was married to the said Elizabeth.[69] At that time, he was about 20 years of age, inexperienced, intemperate and unguarded against the artifices of the family. Your memorialist protests that before his marriage, he had no personal connection with her, and that before the time above specified he had not even dreamed of courting her. On 20 February in the present year [1824], he discovered that his said wife was far advanced in pregnancy..."and that very soon after, he left her with a determination no more to claim her as his wife, and on the sixth day of June last as is stated in the accompanying affidavits, his said wife was delivered of a child." Prays for an act to divorce him from his said wife.

Documents accompanying above petition:

(a) Notice to Mrs. Elizabeth Brame from Oliver Brame, 19 October 1824, Warren County, North Carolina "...I shall petition the next general assembly of the State of North Carolina for a divorce and separation from you as my wife..."

(b) Depositions of Rebeckah (^) White, Nancy Burrow, Silvy (^) Duncum and Ruthy (x) Shearron of Warren County, North Carolina, taken at the storehouse of Henry Fitts on 30 October 1824 concerning petition of Oliver Brame to the General Assembly to obtain a divorce from his wife, Elizabeth:

(1). Rebeckah White sayeth she was at Mr. George Wortham's the day after Mrs.Brame, wife of Oliver, had her child, which was 7 June last; the child was born the sixth...I saw the child washed and dressed it. I am the mother of several children and am certain the child was born at the proper time. It is still living and sound and healthy.

(2). Nancy Burrow sayeth she was at Mrs. Wortham's the same day as Mrs. White was there and saw Mrs. Brame's child. I think it was and is now a fine child and born at the proper time. I heard Mrs. Brame, wife of Oliver, say the Thursday before her child was born that if she had her child in less than nine months from the time she married to Mr. Brame, she would not blame him for leaving her.

(3). Silva Duncan sayeth she was at Mrs. Wortham's the same day as Mrs. White was there, and afterwards Mrs. Wortham - the mother of Mrs. Brame was lamenting that her daughter had acted as she did. They both had always denied that said Mrs. Brame was with child before she married. Her mother blamed her and said to her that she must have known it. Her answer was — she did not know it. I have seen John Moseley with Mrs. Brame before she was married and thought they liked each other as well as I ever saw two young people, and it is a general report and belief in the neighborhood that the child is John Moseley's.

(4). Ruthey Shearrin sayeth that she saw Mrs. Brame about 7 weeks before she had her child, and she said to me if she was in the situation people said she was in, she would not blame Mr. Brame from leaving her. I heard Mrs. Wortham, the mother of Mrs. Brame, and Mrs. Brame herself say [after her husband left] that she was not with child the first time Mr. Brame left her and that she should not have been if she never saw him afterwards. She wished he had been at the devil before she saw him.

(2). Deposition of James W. Burrow of Warren County, North Carolina, at the storehouse of Henry Fitts, 2 November 1824: Mrs. Brame would not blame her husband for leaving her if her child

---

69 Marriage Bond of Warren County, North Carolina, lists Oliver Brame and Elizabeth Archer, dated 30 December 1823. Bondsman: Asa George.

Divorces and Separations from Petitions to the North Carolina General Assembly from 1779

was born in less than nine months of the marriage and also said that Mrs. Wortham said she heard that Oliver Brame offered to bet $500 that the child would be born in less than nine months. He also heard Mrs. Brame say that if Oliver Brame wished to be divorced, she was willing but that he should maintain the child.

(b).   Committee of Divorce and Alimony to whom was referred the petition of Oliver Brame of Warren County report that it appears that said Oliver Brame was married on or about 30 December 1823 to Elizabeth Archer. On 6 June 1824, said Elizabeth was delivered of a child, and it was generally believed in the neighborhood where said Oliver and Elizabeth resided, a man by the name of John Moseley was the father. Your committee "is not insensible to the unhappy situation of your petitioner, but from the evidence introduced by him…it appears that if said Oliver Brame had used that caution and circumspection which are necessary before entering into so solem engagement as the Bond of Matrimony, he could have avoided the misfortune of which he now complains." Recommend that the prayer of the petitioner be not allowed. [On reverse:] In Senate, 26 November 1824, read and recommend adoption.

(c).   Petition of John W. Moseley of Warren County states he has been informed that one Oliver Bream of said county has petitioned to be divorced from his wife Elizabeth upon a charge of said Elizabeth having an unlawful connection with some person before her marriage to him. Certain depositions accompanying said Oliver's petition allude to the fact that your petitioner is the one who has had this unlawful connection. "I do certify that I the said Moseley never had an unlawful connection with her the said Elizabeth Bream either before or since her marriage to the said Oliver Bream." Datsd 29 November 1824.

[Below:] (1).   Certificate of Robert R. Johnson, 29 November 1824, that he has been guardian to John W. Moseley for fifteen or more years; that he has at times conducted himself honorably and upright; and that he is a young man of good and fine character. Most of the last five years, he has been much in my company and it has afforded me a fair opportunity to judge his conduct as to some insinuation made by Oliver Brams about an intimacy between John W. Moseley and his wife Elizabeth Brame. I believe this entirely erroneous.

(2).   Certificate of Henry Foote, 27 November 1824, states he is near neighbor to George Wortham, father-in-law of Elizabeth Brame and have also been well acquainted with John W. Mosely for a number of years and that he always has conducted himself like a gentleman.

(3).   Deposition of George Wortham, 27 November 1824. Mr. John W. Moseley has often visited his house for the last four years and at all times he conducted himself entirely to my satisfaction. I am well convinced that he never was guilty of any improper conduct to Elizabeth Brame, wife of Oliver Brame.

(4).   Deposition of John King, 27 November 1824, that he is well acquainted with John W. Moseley, and he has often visited the house of Geo. Wortham, father-in-law of the wife of Oliver Brame. I believe that John W. Moseley to be too much of a gentleman to have been guilty of any improper act to said wife and I had a fair opportunity of judging.

(GASR, Nov. 1824- Jan. 1825, Box 4:"SCR, Claims - Finance" and Box 5:"Petitions - Divorce")

533.   **Bray, Hannah and husband, Jesse.**

(1).   Petition of Hannah (+) Bray of Camden County, wife of Jesse Bray, sheweth that her said husband left her about two years ago and reportedly is in the State of Tennessee where he has taken up with and married another woman. Some time previous to his leaving, he kept another woman in the house and treated your petitioner with great severity and indignity. When he left, he carried almost

1824-1825 Session

everything of value with him. Prays for a law to discharge your petitioner from the bonds of matrimony with her said husband.

(2). Committee on Divorce and Alimony to whom was referred the petition of Hannah Bray of Camden County recommend the passage of the accompanying bill: Bill to divorce Hannah Bray of Camden County from her husband, Jesse. [On reverse: In Senate, 22 December 1824, read second and third time, passed and ordered to be engrossed. In House of Commons, 27 December 1824, read and ordered to be postponed indefinitely.]

(GASR, Nov. 1824-Jan. 1825, Box 3:"SB 22 Dec.")

534. **Bullock, James and wife, Tabitha.**

(1). Petition of James Bullock of Martin County sheweth that he married Tabitha Pierce in 1808, and they lived peaceably as man and wife until November 1823, when said Tabitha left him without any known cause and went away with a certain William Harrel, formerly of said Martin County, but where said Harrel and Tabitha are now living is unknown. Your petitioner "fully expects that they are both living together somewhere in the western country as man and wife." His said wife left him with six small children which your petitioner had by his wife Tabitha. "She carried away with her one child, which made the seventh, and the youngest child that your petitioner had by his wife Tabitha, as he thought, but has been informed since she left…that the child she carried away was not his child but was the child of the said William Harrell." Prays for a law divorcing your petitioner from his said wife Tabitha. He is anxious to live with his children and keep house with them and raise them, which is bad to do without a woman to live with. Dated 10 November 1824. [On reverse:] Certificate of nine subscribers who state they are acquainted with both said James Bullock, who is a very poor man, and his wife Tabitha, who left said Bullock without any cause whatsoever on the part of her said husband. They believe that the said Bullock always used her as a loving wife, took care of her, and used her well up to the time of her leaving him.

(2). Committee on Divorce and Alimony to whom was referred the petition of James Bullock of Martin County recommend the passage of the accompanying bill: Bill to divorce James Bullock of Martin County from his wife Tabitha. In Senate, 22 December 1824, read second and third time, passed, and ordered to be engrossed. In House of Commons, 27 December 1824, read second time and postponed indefinitely.

(3). Committee of Propositions and Grievances to whom was referred the petition of James Bullock of Martin County report that your petitioner intermarried with Tabitha Pierce in 1808 with whom he lived until November 1823, at which time the said wife eloped with one William Harrell from Martin County and has not been heard from since that time. Recommend rejection of said petition. [On reverse: In House of Commons, 24 November 1824, read and concurred with.]

(GASR, Nov. 1824-Jan. 1825, Box 3:"SB 22 Dec." and Box 4:"HCR, Military Affairs - Miscellaneous")

535. **Bunn, Ann and husband, Nathaniel.**

(1). Petition of Ann Bunn sheweth she married a certain Nathaniel Bunn of the town of Fayetteville, North Carolina, in 1816. They lived together about two years, when for no cause known to your petitioner, he abandoned her, friendless and unprotected among strangers, to shift for herself in an unfriendly world. In such a forlorn and helpless condition, your petitioner has experienced the bufferings of adversity in their most afflicting character, and which are for her, too painful to recount. For the term of five years and more, your petitioner has been in this deplorable situation, never having once heard from her said husband, Nathaniel, or been able after the most extensive encuiries to ascertain whether he be dead, or whether he be in the United States. Pray for proceedings which will effect tlie earliest separation and divorcement of herself from the said husband. Dated 11 November 1824, Duplin County.

(2). Committee of Divorce and Alimony to whom was referred the petition of Ann Bunn of Duplin County recommend the passage of the accompanying bill: A Bill to divorce Ann Bunn of Duplin County from her husband, Nathaniel Bunn. [On reverse:] In Senate, 18 December 1824, read second and third time, passed, and ordered to be engrossed. In House of Commons, 27 December 1824, read second time and postponed indefinitely.

(GASR, Nov. 1824-Jan. 1825, Box 3: "SB 17 Dec.")

536. **Clark, Becca and husband, James.**

(1). Memorial of Becca Knott of Guilford County states she intermarried with James Clark about eleven years ago and lived with him about four years. He then took another woman, ran away, and left your memorialist with two small children after having spent what property was given tliem by her father, a man of independent property. Prays for a law to secure to her and her children all such property as she may hereafter acquire. [Below:] Signatures of eleven subscribers.

(2). Letter from Jno. Draughon and James Nelson of Greensboro, North Carolina, to Messrs. Jonathan Parker, William Unthank, and Major Neally "We hope you will use your influence to have the law alluded to within passed as the friends & connexions of the poor, indigent woman would aid her in making a living & acquiring property…but under present circumstances they fear…the unprincir ailed man would return from Tennessee & take it all away as he is very abandoned & hard hearted…"

(3). Committee on Divorce and Alimony to whom was referred the petition of Etecca Knott of Guilford County recommend the passage of the accompanying bill: A Bill to divorce Becca Clark of Guilford County from her husband, James Clark. [On reverse:] In Senate, 19 December 1824, read second and third time, passed and ordered to be engrossed. In House of Commons, 30 December 1824, read and ordered to be postponed indefinitely.

(GASR, Nov. 1824-Jan. 1825, Box 3:"SB 17 Dec.")

537. **Davis, Solomon and wife, Celia/Cecelia/Seleigh.**

(1). Petition of Solomon Davis of Carteret County states he married one Se eigh Douglass on 7 April 1817, lived with her about one year and enjoyed all the happiness in perfect peace and harmony. At the end of this time, said Seleigh absented herself from your petitioner and fled to Currituck County. In spite of all his effoits to reclaim her, she continues to reside in said county "and indulge in habit of the most grosses vises which your petitioner will not Repeat…" Prays that his case be takenunder consideration and grant him relief. Dated 3 November 1824.

(2). Deposition of Littlejohn Rich before Robert Cannon, one of the acting Justices of Peace for Wake County, states that Cecelia Davis, wife of Solomon Davis, has forthe last three years requested the deponent to endeavour to obtain a divorce for her from her said husband, Solomon, and further, the said Cecelia has refused to live with said Solomon for the last six years or thereabouts. Dated 25 November 1824.

(3). Committee on Divorce and Alimony to whom was referred the petition of Solomon Davis of Carteret County recommend the passing of the accompanying bill: A Bill to divorce Solomon Davis of Carteret County from his wife, Celia. [On reverse: In House of Commons, 27 December 1824, read second time and postponed indefinitely.] (GASR, Nov. 1824-Jan. 1825, Box 2:"SB 3 Dec.")

1824-1825 Session

538. **Fergerson, Elizabeth and husband, James.**

(1). Petition of Elizabeth Furgerson of Wilkes County "sheweth that sometime in the year 1814, she, being about the age of fourteen, became pleased with the asediuty and address of one William Furgerson, a man to whom she had been before unknown and as your Petitioner is informed and believes was a stranger and sojoumer in that part of the state, where she then and now, resides; Your petitioner further sheweth that she was induced and prevailed upon, to marry the said Furgarson - and your petitioner avers, that she did, and she believes she ever would have entertained that love and respect for her husband, which of right, ought to be given to him; but so far from returning her affection, he, without warning your petitioner and without any cause that she knows of, in two weeks wholy and entirely abandoned and separated himself from her, and from that time to this day she has not seen him..." When he left her, he pretended he was going on a journey to South Carolina to take possession of an estate which he owned there. He borrowed from your petitioner's father a considerable sum of money and clothes and valuable things from your petitioner. Prays for a law declaring that the bonds of matrimony be dissolved.

(2). Committee on Divorce and Alimony to whom was referred the petition of Elizabeth Fergerson of Wilkes County recommend the passage of the accompanying bill: A Bill to divorce Elizabeth Fergerson of Wilkes County from her husband, James Fergerson. [On reverse:] In House of Commons, 27 December 1824, read second time and postponed indefinitely. (GASR, Nov. 1824-Jan. 1825, Box 2:"SB 3 Dec.")

539. **Fry(e), Elizabeth and husband, Lewis.**

(1). Petition of Elizabeth Fry sheweth she became the wife of Lewis Fry in 1816. He was then a man of industry, sobriety and respectability. Unfortunately, your petitioner "is constrained to acknowledge that her husband (although she still retains for him the fondest affection) has become idle, extravagant and dissipated [and] has already squandered away an handsome estate..." He "continues to spend in prodigality and drunkenness even the small but hard earned pittance of her own labours; by which she vainly hoped to save herself and her five helpless children from want and misery." Prays for a law securing to her such property as she may hereafter acquire. [Below:] Signatures of seven subscribers.

(2). Committee of Propositions and Grievances to whom was referred the petition of Elizabeth Frye of Stokes County report that Elizabeth Frye, formerly Eilum, intermarried with Lewis Frye of Stokes County in the year 1816, at that time a sober discreet man possessed of & handsome property, which was increased by a snug advancement which she received of her parents on their marriage. Shortly afbr said marriage, her husband forgot the obligations he made to his wife and commenced a drinking habit in which he not only spent all he had but what total she brought to him and remained greatly in debt. It further appears to your committee that said Lewis Frye has by his wife five helpless children "who from the improvident conduct of their father are crying for bread." Recommend the accompanying bill be passed into law: Bill to secure to Elizabeth Frye Stokes County such property as she may hereafter acquire. [On reverse:] In Senate, 18 December 1824, read second and third time, passed and ordered to be engrossed. In House of Commons, 30 December 1824, read first time and postponed indefinitely. (GASR, Nov. 1824-Jan. 1825, Box 2:"SB 15 Dec.")

540. **Gurganus, Major and wife, Milley.**

(1). Petition of Mager Gurganus of Martin County sheweth that he married VIilley Atkinson of the same county on 6 April 1801, promising himself all the happiness that a virtuous mind could have anticipated from a married life. However, "to his inexpressible grief he too soon found that his fond hope of felicity was illusive that his wife instead of studying the happiness of her family gave herself up to all kinds of lewdness and intemperance inasmuch as she soon became a pest to the neighborhood where she lived-." Despite your petitioner's efforts to reclaim this partner of his affection, his endeavours have been treated with contempt, and she has constantly pursued her wicked course undl June 1820, when without any just cause, she quit your petitioner's bed and board and took up with a man as abandoned as herself. She moved with him "to the southward, leaving your petitioner and six children to mainta n, the youngest of which was an Infant at the breast." Prays for an act to divorce him from the bond of matrimony entered into with his wife Milley. [Below:] Signatures of over thirty-eight subscribers.

(2). Committee on Divorce and Alimony to whom was referred the petition of Major Gurganus of Martin County recommends the accompanying bill: Bill to divorce Major Gurganus of Martin County from his wife Milley. In Senate, 22 December 1824, read second and third time, passed and ordered to be engrossed. In House of Commons, 29 December 1824, read second time and rejected. (GASR, Nov. 1824-Jan. 1825, Box 3:"SB 22 Dec.")

541. **Hawkins, Mary and husband, James.**

(1). Petition of Mary Wilson of Buncombe County states that more than thirty years ago at a tender age, your petitioner (then Mary Forster) married James Hawkins of Buncombe County, "a man whose honest and honorable conduct in life, joined to the reputable character of his family connexion had deservedly acquired for him a respectable standing in society." She lived with him a year in utmost harmony, performing with affection and fidelity the various offices of a wife and mother. The fair character her then husband maintained for honesty and industry previous to and for sometime after the marriage underwent an inexplicable change of mind despite his being free from want and surrounded by kind relatives and friends. He commenced a system of pilfering which ultimately brought down on him the vengeance of the law. He became guilty of petit larceny and was publicly whipped at the District Court House. Not withstanding the misery and disgrace this unfortunate affair had upon her, she received him on his return from prison as the partner of her bosom, and confiding in the reality of his apparent penitence, strove to forget the crime and to love the author. Her exertions to reclaim him at that time proved abortive, and he at last concluded a catalogue of crimes with one (burglary) that compelled him "to fly his country and left her the miserable choice between following his desperate fortunes with her infant children or relying on the protection of her friends to separate forever from her husband." She pursued the latter case and obtained a Bill of Alimony. Unfortunately, she did not investigate the matter as strictly as prudence required and in the year 1802, she married John Wilson of this county with whom she has lived constantly and happily ever since. She raised a numerous family of children to honesty, industry and morality, most of whom are entirely ignorant of the stain attached to their birth,

Your petitioner further states that a prosecution has recently been commenced in the county against her present husband and herself for the crime of adultery. Prays for a special act to divorce her from James Hawkins. [Below:] Signatures of fifty-six citizens of Buncombe County who are well acquainted with the said Mary Wilson and join her most earnestly in her petition for a divorce.

(2). Committee of Propositions and Grievances to whom was referred the petition of Mary Wilson of Buncombe County recommend the passage of the accompanying bill: Bill to divorce Mary Wilson (formerly Mary Hawkins) of Buncombe County from her husband, James Hawkins. In House of Commons, 25 November 1824, read second and third time, passed and ordered to be engrossed. (GASR, Nov. 1824-Jan. 1825, Box 1:"HB 25 Nov.")

542. **Hendricks, Sarah and husband, George.**

(1). Petition of Sarah Hendricks that she was married to George Hendricks a few years ago and hoped to live in conjugal love and peace, but in a short time, "he fell to a bruisen your pertitioner and distroyed all here living and thertened here life for which she was compeld to Sweare the peace against him." Prays for a grant of relief. [Below:] Signatures of thirteen subscribers.

    (2).   Committee of Propositions and Grievances to whom was referred the petition of Sarah Hendricks of Ashe County report that the petitioner, Sarah Hendricks, intermarried with George Hendricks a few years ago, but in a short time, he became intemperate and began to abuse and mistreat the petitioner. His conduct became so outrageous and brutal that he even threatened her life. She was compelled to obtain a peace wairant against him, and he forsook her entirely, not being about for perhaps two years. It appears to be unknown where he is. Your Committee are of opinion that the case demands redress and recommend the accompanying bill be passed into law: Bill to secure Sarah Hendricks of Ashe County property as she may hereafter acquire. [On reverse:] In House of Commons, 30 December 1824, read first time and postponed indefinitely.
(GASR, Nov. 1824-Jan. 1825, Box 2:"SB 24 Nov.")

543.   **Jackson, Margaret and husband, Gabriel.**

    (1).   Petition of Margaret Jackson of Burke County states that her husband, Gabriel Jackson, left her with five children in low circumstances and in debt. She prays that the Assembly "grant me that security for Bread for my children and power to school them, and hold such property as it may hereafter acquire…" [Below:] "We the undersigned subscribers, knowing the unworthy, unnatural & ungenerous conduct of Gabriel Jackson towards his family; and his inclination for trading where and whenever he could get credit • making his known debts in this country and in Union District, South Carolina, and his probable debts during his four years rambling through South Carolina and Georgia, more than could be paid by a lifetime of hard service - and believing such a State of things had a tendency to discourage & paralyze exertion, and at a time with regard to the children that could never be redeemed do petition in behalf of Margaret Jackson that her prayer be granted." Signed by fourteen subscribers.

    (2).   Committee of Propositions and Grievances to whom was referred the Petition of Margaret Jackson of Burke County are of opinion that the Petition should be allowed and recommend that the accompanying bill be passed into law. [On reverse:] In House of Commons, 30 December 1824, read first time and postponed indefinitely. (GASR, Nov. 1824-Jan. 1825, Box 2:"SB 24 Nov.")

544.   **Keaton, John and wife, Susannah.**

    (1).   Petition of John Keaton of Pasquotank County states he was married in the year 1808 to Susannah Brothers[70] and lived in peace and harmony. In August 1812, being called upon by his country then engaged in a war with Great Britain, he enlisted under Capt. Lodowick Morgan of the Rifle Corps to serve during the War. He obtained an honorable discharge, returned in November 1815, and found to his unspeakable misery that his wife Susannah had taken up with another man by whom she had a child. The said Susannah has ever since continued to live separate and apart from your petitioner, indulging in her course of licentiousness.

    (2). Committee on Divorce and Alimony to whom was referred the petition of John Keaton of Pasquotank County recommends the passage of the accompanying bill: Bill to divorce John Keaton of Pasquotank County from his wife Susannah. In House of Commons, 29 December 1824, read second time and postponed indefinitely. (GASR, Nov. 1824-Jan. 1825, Box 2:"SB 8 Dec.")

---

70   Marriage Bond of Pasquotank County, North Carolina, lists John Keaton and Susannah Brothers, dated 11 October 1808. Bondsman: Silas Keaton.

Divorces and Separations from Petitions to the North Carolina General Assembly from 1779

545.   **Lane, Mary A. G. and husband, Joel H.**

(1).   Petition of Mary A. G. Lane requests a divorce from her husband, Joel H. Lane,[71] "whose conduct lately has been so obnoxious to me and indeed to honest and correct persons in civilized society." My brother will relate to you the circumstances that have reduced me to this sad dilemma. If proof be necessary, there is abundant to be had in Raleigh to establish the charges that will be disclosed to you without having reference to his late conduct in Franklin. My further wish is to lose the name also of the man who has brought such disgrace on my family and be hereafter known by the name of Mary A. G. Freeman.

(2).   Deposition of L. F. Perry states that on Friday morning, 17 December 1824, Joel H. Lane came to the store of Messrs. Howze and Yarbrough, Merchants of Louisburg, North Carolina, and after being in the counting room - being invited to partake of something to drink — he took a tumbler, left the counting room and went into the storeroom. This deponent, as Clerk of Messrs. Howze and Yarbrough, having business in the storeroom, entered the door to that room and, at the same time, heard the money drawer slide as if opened or in the act of being shut. The said Joel H. Lane was there alone in the storeroom. This deponent examined the drawer to see if any moneys were taken and discovered that between $20 and $80 had been taken there from, and while in the process of this examination, the said Joel H. Lane left the store. This deponent pursued the said Lane and requested him to return to the store, and the said Lane did so. Sworn before W. Moore, Justice of Peace of Franklin County, 27 December 1824.

(3).   Deposition of Henry Y. Howze, one of the partners of Howze and Yarbrough, states he was sent for at December Court week, 1824, by Mr. Lane F. Perry and was apprised that my money drawer had been robbed, and it was his opinion Joel H. Lane committed the robbery. The said Lane was then in the grocery room but left for the piazza in front of the store. Your deponent said in the presence of Mr. Lane that he would be searched, but since Lane expressed a wish to speak to me in private, we both went into the counting room. I believed that Mr. Lane was going to deliver tome the missing money, but he remained silent until I mentioned the robbery. He denied that he had taken anything but still appeared confused and uneasy. I requested Mr. Perry to seek Mr. Kelly, one of the Justices of Peace for the county, for the purpose of taking a search warrant against said Lane. I then returned to my counting room where said Lane had been left alone, and discovered something burning. I took my shovel and got the burning object out and discovered it to be the book in which I kept the small money belonging to the store. I then observed to the said Lane that I was satisfied he had committed the robbery. Sworn before W. Moore, J. P. for Franklin County, 27 December 1824.

(4).   The Committee of Divorce and Alimony to whom was referred the Bill to divorce Mary A. G. Lane of Franklin County from her husband, Joel H. Lane, report that Mary A. G. Lane and her husband, Joel H. Lane, are of families of the first respectability; that they were married about eight years ago; that the said Mary always manifested a most affectionate regard towards her husband; that the said Joel by intemperance and gambling became insolvent and for the last three years has given himself up entirely to intoxication and had made no exertion in an honest way to support his family. Notwithstanding this, his wife has always demeaned herself in the most affectionate uxorious manner towards him until the development of the following facts: During the last session of the Assembly, Joel H. Lane stole a gold watch and chain valued at $250 from a Mr. Savage of this place. In November last, said Lane purchased goods from Mr. Strong, merchant of Louisburg, and deposited the gold watch and chain for Mr. Strong to sell and pay himself, requesting that Strong not to let anyone know its origin, saying that Lane's brother had given the chain to his wife, and it was unpleasant for people to know that said Lane was compelled to sell the family jewelry. Mr. Savage found out about this scheme, obtained the watch

---

71   Marriage Bond of Warren County, North Carolina, lists Joel H. Lane and Mary A. G. Freeman, dated 4 January 1815. Bondsmen: John Snow and Stephen Davis.

and chain, and caused the said Joel to confess the theft of the watch. Later, it appears that the said Lane robbed a Mr. Howze, a merchant of Louisburg, of nearly $80. The said Lane is now a refugee from justice and is supposed to have left the country for Tennessee. Your committee is of opinion that this is one of the few cases in which legislative interference may justly take place to save an unfortunate female, and recommend the passage of the Bill referred to them.

(5). Bill to divorce Mary A. G. Lane of Franklin County from her husband, Joel H. Lane. [On reverse:] In Senate, 31 December 1824, read second time, and indefinitely postponed.

(GASR, Nov. 1824-Js-n. 1825, Box 3:"SB 28 Dec.")

546. **Lindsay, Violet W. and husband, Samuel W.**

(1). Petition of Violet W. Lindsay of Mecklenburg County states she was married on 16 March 1820 to Samuel W. Lindsay of the same county.[72] On or about 1 March 1822, the said Samuel went to Charleston, South Carolina, to make a sale of cotton and attend to other mercantile business, for such was his occupation. A few weeks aft'sr his departure, his creditors began to suspect he would not return, which suspicion has been unhappily verified. He has not returned. As a consequence, an attachment was immediately levied upon all our property. I had breakfast at home in the morning, but before noon, I had not anything left on which I could make my dinner. My corn, meat and stock of cattle, my poultry, and even a fine preserve were taken from me, and also the cradle of my infant daughter - a little over one year old - and the necessary accomodations of cleanliness for a child that age were taken from me. I then returned to my father's in Lincoln County where I now live with a proper bed and furniture together with an old cotton wheel. Prays that she may be secured in property that she may hereafter acquire. My friends believe that Mr. Lindsay will never return.

(2). Committee on Divorce and Alimony to whom was referred the petition of Violet W. Lindsay of Mecklenburg County recommend that the accompanying bill should be passed into law: Bill to divorce Violet W. Lindsay of Lincoln County from her husband, Samuel W. Lindsay. In House of Commons, 30 December 1824, read second and third time, passed and ordered to be enrolled.

(GASR, Nov. 1824-Jan. 1825, Box 2:"SB 8 Dec.")

547. **Mabry, Martha and husband, Kinchen.**

(1). Memorial of Martha (+) Mabry of Warren County sheweth she intermarried with Kinchen (+) Mabry of said county in 1822,[73] under the hope and belief of enjoying the comforts of matrimony. On the next day after said marriage, the said Kinchen left her after a most unaffectionate and unruly conduct without any cause known to your memorialist and remained absent for at least twelve months. Prior to the marriage, she had lived happily with the family other father, and after said Kinchen left, she supported herself by her own exertions and got into the house of a respectable neighbor and friend. The said Kinchen returned and by persuasion, induced her to leave and live with him. However, after two or three nights, he again left her homeless. He is an able young man, a pretty good carpenter, and capable of maintaining himself and a family, but continues to ramble about the country indulging in idleness and dissipation, contracting debts. Prays for a law to divorce your memorialist from her said husband. [Signed by both parties.]

---

72   Marriage Bond of Lincoln County, North Carolina, lists Samuel W. Lindsay and Vilet W. MacLean, dated 22 February 1820. Bondsman: Richard D. S. MacLean.

73   Marriage Bond of Warren County, North Carolina, lists Kinchen Mabry and Martha Riggans, dated 9 April 1822. Bondsman: Luke H. Paschall.

(2). Committee on Divorce and Alimony to whom was referred the petition of Martha Mabry of Warren County state that no evidence was produced to substantiate the facts set forth in the petition and recommend its rejection. [On reverse:] In Senate, 17 December 1824, and concurred in.

(GASR, Nov. 1824-Jan. 1825, Box 4:"SCR, Claims - Finance")

548. **Price, Washington and wife, Susanna.**

(1). Petition of Thomas Price, the father, and of Washington Price, the son - a minor, dated 21 November 1824.

(2). The Committee of Divorce and Alimony to whom was referred the Petition of his petition is an updated one submitted by the same parties, filed in GASR, Nov. 1823-Jan. 1824. It addresses the same subject and continues with considerable rhetoric. See this magazine, August 1999, pages 319-322. Thomas Price and Washington Price praying for an act to divorce the said Washington Price from his wife, Susanna, report that no evidence appears but what is contained in the petition itself. From the document alone, it seems that Washington Price, who was a student at the University at Chapel Hill, intermarried with one Susanna Webb. After the marriage, the petitioners say that they have good reason to believe she was not a girl of fair standing or reputable character and that undue means had been made use of by the mother of said Susanna in order to induce said Washington to enter into the marriage contract. However, there is no evidence. Recommend the petition not be allowed. In Senate, 26 November 1824, read, and resolution recommended adopted.

(GASR, Nov. 1824-Jan. 1825, Box 4:"SCR, Claims - Finance")

549. **Simpson, Priscilla and husband, James.**

(1). Committee of Propositions and Grievance to whom was referred "A Bill to secure to Priscilla Simpson of Duplin County, wife of James Simpson, such property as she may hereafter acquire" be rejected. [On reverse:] In House of Commons, 28 December 1824, read and concurred in.

(2). Bill to secure to Priscilla Simpson of Duplin County, wife of James Simpson such property as she may hereafter acquire. [On reverse:] Rejected agreeable to the report of the Committee of Propositions and Grievances.

(GASR, Nov. 1824-Jan. 1825, Box 1:"HB 16 Dec." and Box 4:"HCR, Military Affairs - Miscellaneous")

550. **Stamper, Martha and husband, John F.**

(1). Petition often persons shews that Martha DeJarnett of Surry County prays to be divorced from her husband "who called himself John F. Stamper & so to be allowed alimony." The reason she makes this application is because the superior courts of this state do not embrace her case. On 25 December 1821, she was married to said John F. Stamper, who stayed with her until 10 February following when he went on a pretended business about sixty or seventy miles and never returned. The said Martha is of respectable parentage and family and has always conducted herself with remarkable prudence and circumspection. The said Stamper had been in this section of the country for about ten months in the capacity of a Singing Master and expressed very genteel in his deportment. By his fair pretenses he deceived her and induced her to marry him, although a stranger. We pray she may be discharged from the bonds of matrimony and a law be made to secure to her such property as she may hereafter acquire, /s/ Jas. Parks, Henry G. Hampton, Jno. O. Parks, Daniel Hunt, Wm. C. Martin, R. H. Parks, T. Hampton, Obadiah Martin, Jno. Spencer, Daniel Cockerham.

1824-1825 Session

(2). Committee of Propositions and Grievances to whom was referred the Petition of Martha DeJarnett of Surry County summarize the above petition and recommend rejection. [On reverse:] In House of Commons, 24 November 1824, read, and concurred with.

(GASR, Nov. 1824-Jan. 1825, Box 4:"HCR, Military - Miscellaneous")

551. **Tomberaw/Tomberau/Tombereau, Lewis and wife, Nancy.**

(1). Petition of Lewis (+) Tombereau, dated 19 November 1824, states he is a native of France, a shoemaker by trade. He emigrated to the United States and settled himself near Williamston, Martin County, North Carolina, "where without a care beyond his lapstone, he worked at his trade with such assiduity and industry…that he was enabled to make both ends meet with comfort, which he hopes to do, and thereby to his last, eat the bread of Independence.

"To lighten the cares and sweeten the toils of life, he intermarried with a young woman of the neighborhood named Nancy Jolly to whom he became enamoured & to whom he was determined to stick as close as wax; and to exert the powers given to him by God and nature; to satisfy her desires, supply her wants, administer to her necessities, and provide for her support.

"Your petitioner feels himself compelled to state that his sunshine gleam of felicity was evanescent; and he too soon with heart rending horror found, that in indulging in the best passion incident to humanity, he linked his fortune with one of the most frail, lewd and depraved daughters of Eve, for without cause or provocation, she shortly after her said marriage withdrew herself from your petitioner and from the discharge of her conjugal duties. She forsook both his board and bed to cohabit with a certain mulatto barber named Roland Colanche, then living in Williamston, by whom she had a coloured child and became a public and notorious prostitute in the most unlimited sense of the word. She indulged in an unreserved and promiscuous intercourse with men of every colour, age, class, and description.

"Your petitioner is now settled in Raleigh in Wake County. His imperfect knowledge of the English language and the consequent difficulty of making himself understood, as well as a reluctance to make public what he thought disgraceful to him, he has brooded over his wrongs in agonizing silence. His poverty precludes the possibility of engaging a lawyer to file a petition for a divorce in a court of law. As your petitioner is able to substantiate the facts herein, he prays for a divorce from his said wife."

(2). Bill to divorce Lewis Tomberaw now of Wake County from his wife Nancy. [On reverse:] In Senate, 6 December 1824, read second and third time, passed and ordered to be engrossed.
(GASR, Nov. 1824-Jan. 1825, Box 2:"SB 3 Dec." and Box 5:"Petitions Divorce")

552. **White, Mariam and husband, John.**

(1). Petition of Mariam White of Pasquotank County shews she married John White in January 1820, but he has entirely abandoned her for the past three years and has utterly neglected to provide for the necessaries and conveniences of life. Requests that she be discharged from the bonds of matrimony. [Below:] Signatures of fourteen subscribers who support the above petition.

(2). Committee on Divorce and Alimony to whom was referred the petition of Mariam White of Pasquotank County report that no satisfactory evidence has been presented to said committee and recommend rejection of the prayer of the petitioner. [On reverse:] In Senate, 22 December 1824, read and agreed to. (GASR, Nov. 1824-Jan. 1825, Box 4:"SCR, Claims - Finance")

Divorces and Separations from Petitions to the North Carolina General Assembly from 1779

553. **Womack, Frances and husband. Henry.**
Committee on Divorce and Alimony to whom was referred the petition of Frances Womack of Person County praying to be divorced from her husband, Henry Womack, report that it appears that the petitioner was married to Henry Womack of Person County about ten years hence with whom she lived for several years and by whom she had two children. The character of said Henry previous to his marriage was fair and respected, but he has become a habitual drunkard for several years past, neglecting to provide even the necessaries for his family and treating his wife in a cruel and unfeeling manner, threatening in several instances her life. The said Frances has been compelled to leave her said husband and now lives with her sister. Recommend the passage of the bill herewith: Bill to divorce Frances Womack of Person County from her husband. Henry Womack. [On reverse:] In Senate, 31 December 1824, read first time and rejected.
(GASR, Nov. 1824-Jan. 1825, Box 3:"SB 31 Dec.")

554. **Reference A.**
The persons listed below are found in the state-sponsored series. Laws of North Carolina, which were enacted in the year shown with the page number following, All were granted full divorces from the bonds of matrimony.
Lindsay, Violet of Lincoln County from husband, Samuel. (1824, p. 93)
Tomberau, Lewis - now of Wake County, from wife. Nancy. (1824, p. 93)
Wilson, Mary (formerly Mary Hawkins) of Buncombe
County from husband, James. (1824, p. 93)

1825-1826

555. **Baldwin, William and wife, Ameilia.** Petition of William Baldwin states he was married to Ameilia Chism in February 1811 and expected to receive all those blessings, comforts and enjoyments that attend a married life. Not long after the rites of matrimony were solemnized, my beloved Ameilia, being freed from all restraint, threw off the mask of deception and appeared in her true character-an unfeeling being who attempted to take my life with poison but was detected. She then added insults accompanied by the most enormous threats that ever fell from the lips of any living being. She then left my bed and board on the 22nd day of June 1811 without any cause or provocation on my part and has never returned. I have only seen her once since that day. I went to her house to solicit her return to my house, but it availed nothing, for she added threats upon her insults and acted "more like a brute than a human being." She left this state for the western countries and has not returned for upwards of five years. Prays for a divorce from his said wife Ameilia. Your petitioner does not intend to sow the seeds of vice and immorality among the human family, for he is well aware of the obligations of the married state. The grievances set forth by your petitioner are nothing compared with others-"too meane to write, too Low to name, too wild to shout, too base to tame-was loudly harped and industriously pressed by her…" In the Fall of 1811, he was sued by his wife for separate maintenance -which was decided in behalf of your petitioner at October Term 1825. [Enclosed:] Depositions of Christopher Godwin and Edward Sampson with regard to William Baldwin and his said wife. Signed at Whitesides, Columbus County, North Carolina, 15 November 1826.

Committee on Divorce and Alimony to whom was referred the petition of William Baldwin report that the facts set forth in the depositions accompanying the same are not sufficiently substantiated to induce this committee to believe the petitioner is entitled to relief. Recommend the prayer of the petitioner be rejected. [On reverse:] In Senate, 2 December 1825, read and agreed into.

(GASR, Nov. 1825-Jan. 1826, Box 4: folder "SCR [Claims-Internal Improvements]").

556. **Barker, Mary and husband, Charles.** Petition of Mary (M) Barker of Robeson County states she intermarried with one Charles Barker[74] of the same county about ten or twelve years ago. Soon after her said marriage, she removed to the house of said Charles, where a short time later he introduced into his domicile "one Margaret McNamarra, a woman of ill fame with whom he bedded; and as your petitioner believes regularly cohabited as Satan prompted his inclination." Your petitioner was unable to bear the continued neglect of her husband, who treated her as a menial servant only. She was not admitted to his conjugal embraces, and his affections were entirely bestowed upon another in the face of the world. After a short period, she left her said husband and sought a maintenance for herself. Several years have elapsed since this separation, and her husband continues to keep the said Margaret McNamara, by whom he has had several children, in his house. A Bill of Indictment has been presented to the

---

74 Marriage Bond of Robeson County, North Carolina, lists Charles Barker and [name missing], [date missing], bondsman: II Brown. Marriage Bond of Cabarrus County, North Carolina, lists Charles Baker and Mary Baker, dated 18 March 1816; bondsman: Solomon Shinn.

said Charles by the Grand Inquest, and he is to be fined on conviction of adultery, but "disregarding the Sacred Laws of Jehovah and these mere mild admonitions of Our State Law…they continue to indulge themselves…" Your petitioner is unable to apply to a Court of Law for redress owing to her extreme poverty, for her exertions have only enabled her to procure a scanty subsistence. Her husband has now living several legitimate children by a former marriage but is notoriously insolvent. If your petitioner should survive her said husband, she may not only be deprived of her small property but left to such a subsistence from the provisions of the State's laws. Prays for a divorce from her said husband and to be secured in the property she has or may hereafter acquire. Your petitioner states she is now near the age of sixty years and has no desire of ever again entering into the marriage state. Sworn before Charles Moore, Justice of the Peace for Robeson County.

Committee on Divorce and Alimony to whom was referred the petition of Mary Baker praying to be divorced from her husband Charles reports that the said Charles Baker has been indicted, found guilty and sentenced by the Court to pay exemplary dam[ages] for living in open and notorious adultery. The petitioner appears from oral testimony to be old, poor and dependent, and the small earnings other industry have been taken from her by the creditors other husband. Your committee is satisfied that the petitioner has complete remedy under the statutes of this state passed in 1814, and it is unnecessary to grant the prayer of the petitioner. This committee asks to be discharged from further consideration of same. [On reverse:] In House of Commons, 24 December 1825, read and concurred with. (GASR, Nov. 1825-Jan. 1826, Box 4: folder "HCR [Divorce & Alimony-Internal Improvements]" and folder "Petitions [Divorce and Alimony]").

557. **Bevins, Eliza and husband, Simeon.** Petition of Eliza Bevins of Lincoln County, wife of Simeon Bevins, Esq., attorney at law, late of Mecklenburg County, North Carolina, now of the State of Kentucky, sheweth she married said Simeon in the City of Charleston, South Carolina, on 10 November 1804 as will appear from the certificate of the Reverend Israel Mounds, Minister of the Gospel, hereunto annexed.[75] Your petitioner and the said Simeon lived together until November 1816, having five children and then removing to and living in Charlotte, Mecklenburg County, North Carolina. In the said month of November, her husband was involved in debt and left your petitioner with her five children in a state of extreme poverty. He has never returned to her, and she is informed and believes that he married another woman several years ago with whom he lives in the State of Kentucky in a state of adultery. Said Simeon acknowledged this arrangement in a letter he wrote to your petitioner about two and one-half years ago. It was written in such insolent language that she threw it into a fire. One of her sons retrieved it, but much of it had been destroyed. It is hereunto annexed.[76] Your petitioner continued to reside in Mecklenburg County, North Carolina, for several years, but removed to Lincolnton, North Carolina, four years ago and presently lives there. She further states that her mother is yet living in Charleston, South Carolina, possessed of property of considerable value. After her mother's decease and agreeable to the last will and testament of the grandfather of your petitioner, said property will descend and be divided among the several children of her said mother, including your petitioner. Your petitioner fears that her said husband may then return, take possession of said property and dispose of the same without her consent. She has filed a petition in the Superior Court of Law of Lincoln County praying for a divorce from the said Simeon, but she has been unable to procure witnesses who could prove the fact of the second marriage of Simeon in Kentucky and his living in adultery. Prays for an act of divorce from the bonds of matrimony with said Simeon. [Enclosed:] Certificate signed by eleven residents of Lincolnton, North Carolina,

---

75   This certificate is not in this file.
76   It is not in this file.

who state that said Eliza Bevins has lived in said village for nearly four years and has an excellent moral character.

(GASR, Nov. 1825-Jan. 1826, Box 4: folder "Petitions-Divorce and Alimony").

558. **Bigham, Robert Jr. and wife Mary.** Petition of Robert Bigham, Jr., of Mecklenburg County states he intermarried with Mary Jackson in 1815,[77] and they had four children. For several years he had reason to suspect his said wife of incontinence and unfaithfulness to his bed, but proof was not sufficiently strong to produce a separation and thereby deprive his infant children of a mother. In August 1824, she deserted his bed in Ihe night, but he found her in bed with one John Hamilton in the embraces, and as he believes in a state of criminal intercourse. Since then, your petitioner has not had any intercourse with said wife and is well satisfied "from her own confession & other incontestable testimony that she kept up a criminal intercourse with one Archibald Esselmen for some time enticillent [antecedent ?] to their said separation, more especially when your Petitioner was absent on business..." Prays passage of an act annulling his marriage with said Mary. Dated 14 November 1825.

Petition of Robert Bigham, Sr., of Mecklenburg County states that sometime in the v/eek after the August Term of County Court, 1824, he carried on a conversation with the said Mary Barham at his house. She admitted she had been found in bed with John Hamilton under very suspicious circumstances by her husband, Robert, after she had left his bed. She hoped she had not offended past forgiveness and thought that if any of the friends of the parties would interfere, the matter could be accommodated between her and her husband. In consequence of the rupture that then took place between said Robert, Jr., and wife, said "Robert turned her off and gave publick notice for her not to be credited or accommodated on his acct. as he intended not to pay any debts other contracting from that time forward..." Your deponent further sayeth that sometime in the year 1818, said Mary Barham was put on trial before the Session of the Associate Congregation of Steel Creek of which congregation she was then a member on a charge of adultery with one Archabald Assellman. After a full examination of witnesses for and against her, the charge of adultery was fully proven against said Mary, and she then appealed to the Associate Presbytery of the Carolinas. After a full examination of the evidence and proceedings, the Presbytery confirmed the decision, and the said Mary was excommunicated and cut-off from said Church. [Below:] Deposition of Tho. J. Grier confirming the facts stated in the above petition.

The Committee on Divorce and Alimony to whom was referred the Petition of Robert Bigham of Mecklenburg County report that it further appears that Robert Bigham gave notice to the said Mary of his intention to petition this Legislature for divorce. Your Committee finds all the material facts sufficiently established, but in reviewing the course taken in similar circumstances, the Petitioner has a remedy under the statutes of the State, and therefore are of opinion that the prayer of the petitioner be rejected. In House of Commons, 16 December 1825, read and not concurred in.

House Bill, 23 December 1825. Robert Bigham, Jr., of Mecklenburg County is hereby divorced from his wife Mary and their marriage is annulled. In Senate, 23 December 1825, read first time and passed; in Senate, 2 January 1826, read second time and resolved that the Bill do not pass.

(GASR, Nov. 1825-Jan. 1826, Box 1: folder "HB 23 Dec." and Box 4: folder "HCR, Divorce & Alimony-Internal Improvements").

559. **Brickell, Elisabeth and husband, Samuel J.** Petition of Elisabeth Brickell of Halifax County sheweth that one Samuel Brickell came into her neighborhood in 1821 bringing with him a character distinguished for its piety and moral worth and there settled in an honest employment. After eighteen

---

77   Marriage Bond of Mecklenburg County, North Carolina, lists Robert Bigham and Polly Jackson, dated 4 January 1815; bondsman: John Porter.

months, said Samuel gained the esteem of his acquaintances, and your petitioner became his wife.[78] A few days after the marriage solemnization, said Samuel went to Petersburg, Virginia, and exhibited letters allegedly signed by James Hunter and James Moore that recommended him to several merchants there and promised security to said merchants for a large amount of goods to be purchased by said Samuel for his own use. Said Samuel was arrested on suspicion and brought to trial for the crime of forging said letters, was convicted and sentenced to serve five years in the Virginia Penitentiary, where he still remains. Your petitioner has been reared under the solicitous care, virtuous precepts and exemplary conduct of her reputable parents and has been taught to hold high all that gives excellence to character. Under such conviction, she found corresponding sentiments in said Samuel, but she has been sadly disappointed. Without any provision from her husband, nor prospect of happiness or reasonable anticipation in her relationship as a wife or expectation of enjoying life with a man rendered infamous for the remainder of his days, "…she looks forward with horror to the time she must…fall again under the domination of her disgraced husband and perform for him the duties arising from her relation." Prays for a dissolution of the bonds of marriage from said Samuel Brickell and restoration to her maiden name of Johnson. [Below:] Deposition signed by thirty-five subscribers who join in the prayer of the petitioner. Letter from the Superintendent of the Virginia Penitentiary, 11 October 1825, to Alfred W. Moore, Halifax County, North Carolina, states that Samuel J. Brickell is a convict now confined in this institution for five years. "…[A]ny female that has been so unfortunate to connect herself with such a man is realy to be pitied." At the time of his trial and connection, he had three names, viz.: Saml. J. Brickell alias Henry B. Johnson alias Bill Moore. He is a deep designing, incorrigible villain beyond all hopes of reclaim. [Enclosed:] Certificate of Tippoo S. Brownlow that "the keeper informed me that he [Samuel Brickle] could not be seen as he that morning given him fifteen stripes and had lock'd him up in his cell and on the following Monday he should give him the same chastisement and that he, the sd. Brickle was a very disorderly man." Dated 3 November 1825.

    Committee of Divorce and Alimony to whom was referred the petition of Elisabeth Brickell of Halifax County report that it appears that Samuel Brickell in the year 1821 manifested a great change from a dissolute young man to morality and religion. In 1822, he courted and married the petitioner, who was the daughter of a pious and reputable farmer. In a few days, perhaps not more than ten, he took his wife from Halifax to Northampton Court House, where he left her and proceeded to Petersburg, Virginia. While there, he presented a letter of credit to a merchant or merchants bearing the names of James Hunter and James Moore, merchants of Halifax. The letter authorized said Samuel to purchase large quantities of merchandise for his own use and purported to be security for whatever goods the said Samuel purchased.

    Brickell was arrested on suspicion of forgery, and by his own confession and the testimony of James Hunter and James Moore, was duly convicted of forgery and sentenced to five years imprisonment in the Virginia Penitentiary from 3 June 1823. Since that time, he has engaged in every species of irregularity, viz: setting fire to the buildings and destroying much thereof; forming plots to murder the keepers and make his escape. The Superintendent of the penitentiary states that Brickell still remains a most incorrigible villain. This committee is unanimous in the opinion that the prayer of the petitioner is just and ought to be granted and recommend the passage of the accompanying bill. [On reverse:] In Senate, 2 December 1825, read and the Bill put on its passage.

    SB 2 Dec. Elizabeth Brickell of Halifax County, formerly Elizabeth Johnson, is hereby divorced from her husband, Samuel Brickell, and her name is hereby altered to that of Elizabeth Johnson. In

---

78   Marriage bond of Halifax County, North Carolina, lists Samuel Brickell and Elizabeth Johnston, dated 16 July 1822; bondsman: William Browning.

Senate, 3 December 1825, and in House of Commons, 5 December 1825, read three times, passed and ordered to be engrossed.

(GASR, Nov. 1825-Jan. 1826, Box 2: folder "SB 2 Dec." and Box 4: folder "SCR, Claims—Internal Improvements.")

560. **Chambers, John and wife, Riney**. Petition of John Chambers of Haywood County states that about 1 February 1825, your petitioner became acquainted with a certain Theophilus ONeal and his family who had emigrated from Johnston County, North Carolina, to Haywood County. Your petitioner married his daughter, Riney, but about two weeks later, said Riney was delivered of a mulatto child, which was raised by a negro woman of the said Theophilus, the father-in-law of your petitioner. After being charged with this crime, the ONeal family confessed to it, and your petitioner carried his wife Riney to her father and has never lived with her since. Requests the marriage to be annulled. [Below:] Signatures of twenty-seven neighbors who support the above petition.

Committee on Divorce and Alimony to whom was referred the petition of John Chambers of Haywood County report that it appears it was common talk that Riney, the wife of John Chambers, had been delivered of a mulatto child previous to her removal. The said petitioner returned his wife to her parents and has had no fellowship with her since that time. Recommend the prayer of the petitioner be granted.

HB 6 Dec. John Chambers of Haywood County is hereby divorced from bonds of matrimony with his wife Riney. In Senate, 12 December 1825, read third time and ordered to be enrolled.

(GASR, Nov. 1825-Jan. 1826, Box 1: folder "HB 6 Dec." and Box 4: folder "HCR [Divorce & Alimony—Internal Improvements].")

561. **De La Chapel, Judith and husband, Gabriel.** Petition of Judith DeLa Chapel sheweth she married Gabriel Chapel in June 1824 with the hope of living in peace and harmony, but to her great mortification, she discovered within a few days after the marriage that the only object said Gabriel had in mind was the little property she possessed. He treated her in a very cruel and inhuman manner, and within three months said Gabriel sold the principal part of her property and abandoned her. He removed himself to foreign parts unknown to your petitioner, leaving her entirely destitute of support and dependent upon the charity of her friends and her own personal exertions. The said Gabriel left considerable debts unpaid. Prays for a divorce from the bonds of matrimony. [Below:] Signatures of twenty-eight subscribers.

[NOTE: Accompanying the above petition are depositions from H. Buchanan, Boswell Carr, Henry Allen, Martha Carr, and Daniel May which contain information similar to the following one:] William May of Anson County deposes that Gabriel DeLa Chappell said "he would ruin his wife Judith and break her up...[and] saw sd. Gabriel...drag his wife Judith out of the door and thertened with great violence to beat & abuse her..." Said Gabriel "came to his father's house & got a horse & brought back to his father's his wifes clothes & bed clothes and also sayeth that he brought two horses & a passel of cattle to his father's house and after he had destroyed all he could of the property, he went of[f] and left her..." Sworn on 8 November 1825 to Justice of the Peace, Charles Hinson.

The Committee who is taking consideration of the petition of Judith De La Chapel report that her said husband, Gabriel, threatened her life, and his conduct towards her was characterized by disrespect, cruelty and barbarity. However, much as your Committee deplores the situation of the petitioner, the obligations owed to the Legislature and the public demands upholding the Laws of the State. Recommend rejection of the prayer of the petitioner. In House of Commons, 6 December 1825, read and disagreed to.

Divorces and Separations from Petitions to the North Carolina General Assembly from 1779

HB 14 Dec. Judith De La Chapel of Anson County is hereby divorced from bonds of matrimony with her husband, Gabriel De La Chapel, late of Anson County. In Senate, 15 December 1825, read second and third time, passed, and ordered to be enrolled.

(GASR, Nov. 1825-Jan. 1826, Box 1: folder "HB 14 Dec." and Box 4: folder "HCR [Divorce & Alimony-Internal Improvements]".)

562. **Dickey, Rachel and husband, Moses**. Committee on Divorce and Alimony to whom was referred the Petition of Rachel Docleu of Orange County praying for a divorce report it appears the petitioner intermarried with her husband in February last, and both were raised in the same neighborhood and supposedly were well acquainted with each other. The petitioner claims that her said husband misused and abused her and left her last August. Upon the evidence submitted, your Committee does not feel justified in granting the prayer of the petitioner and recommend its rejection. [On reverse:] In Senate, 13 December 1825, read and agreed to.

(GASR, Nov. 1825-Jan. 1826, Box 4: folder "SCR [Claims-Internal Improvements]".]

563. **Ferguson, Elizabeth and husband, James.** Petition of Elizabeth Ferguson sheweth she intermarried with James Ferguson of Wilkes County on I July 1819, but said James absconded on 19 August of the same year without any cause on her part and has not been heard of by your petitioner since that time. Her father is still living and refuses to give her any property while she remains the ostensible wife of said James. Prays for a divorce from the bonds of matrimony with said James.

Committee on Divorce and Alimony to whom was referred the above petition report that the statements made by said Elizabeth Ferguson appear to be true, and although the petitioner is poor, she has always sustained the character of a prudent and upright woman. Your committee is of opinion that the petitioner's case merits the clemency of the Legislature and recommends passage of the accompanying bill: Elizabeth Ferguson of Wilkes County is hereby divorced from the bonds of matrimony with her husband James Ferguson. In Senate, 2 and 5 December 1825, read three times, passed and ordered to be engrossed. In House of Commons, 3 January 1826, read first time and rejected.

(GASR, Nov. 1825-Jan. 1826, Box 2: folder "SB 2 Dec.").

564. **Fields, Mary and husband, William.** Petition of Mary Fields of Ashe County states she was married to William Fields and lived with him several years in perfect peace and happiness. During said time she had six children, all of whom were small and helpless and required the steady industry of herself and husband to maintain them in a way of decent living. However, said husband tended towards habitual dissipation, and she endeavoured to persuade him to live a more sober and commendable life. Instead of reforming, he became more and more dissipated and eventually left your petitioner with her small children and little property to pay the debts he had contracted to maintain his habits. For two years, she did not know of his whereabouts but then received a letter from him in the State of Alabama. He said he expected to return in a few months. Your petitioner has awaited his arrival for more than five years since he wrote to her. She has not heard again from him during this time. Your petitioner is very poor and unable to pay the fees to obtain a divorce, but prays she may be divorced from her husband. [NOTE: Accompanying this petition are depositions from the following persons who support the statements of the petitioner: Joseph Doughter, Richard Gentry, Alien Berton, James Hathorne, John McMillan, Alexander B. McMillan, and David Edwards.]

Committee on Divorce and Alimony to whom was referred the petition of Mary Fields of Ashe County report that the statements of the petitioner appear to be true and recommends passage of the following bill: Mary Fields of Ashe County is hereby divorced from her husband, William Fields. In Sen-

ate, 19 and 22 December 1825, read three times, passed and ordered to be engrossed. In House of Commons, 24 December 1825, read first time and rejected.
(GASR, Nov. 1825-Jan. 1826, Box 2: folder "SB 19 Dec.")

565. **Fry, Elizabeth and husband, Lewis.** Petition of Elizabeth Fry states that in 1816 she became the wife of Lewis Fry, a man of industry, sobriety, respectability, and to all appearances had the most flattering prospects for a successful marriage. Unfortunately, she is constrained to acknowledge "…that her husband (altho she still retains for him the fondest affection) has become idle, extravagant and dissipated…" He has already squandered away a handsome estate and continues to spend in prodigality even the small but hard earned pittance of her own labors by which she vainly hoped to save herself and five helpless children from want and misery. Prays for a law to secure to her such property as she may hereafter acquire.
 Committee on Divorce and Alimony to whom was referred the Petition of Elizabeth Fry reports that from the facts set forth in the petition itself, which was the only evidence submitted to your committee, it is of opinion that the prayer of the petitioner be rejected. In Senate, 22 December 1825, read and agreed to.
(GASR, Nov. 1825-Jan. 1826, Box 4: folder "SCR [Claims-Internal Improvements]").

566. **Jackson, Margaret and husband, Gabriel.** Petition of Margaret Jackson of Burke County states that her husband, Gabriel Jackson, left her and six children homeless and in debt more than he could pay. I appeared before your body last year, the fourth year of his absence, praying to be secured to such property I might thereafter acquire. It was argued unconstitutional and of no avail if granted. I still thought he would return to his duty and be well received. He is now gone five years, and I have had no security for my industry "…and am ready to faint, impatient to be free, willing to do and suffer the Laws of our country - my liberation being of vital importance for my own happiness and the prosperity of my children." Prays for a divorce. [On reverse:] Signatures of seven subscribers in support of the petitioner.
 Committee on Divorce and Alimony to whom was referred the Petition of Margaret Jackson of Burke County note that the petitioner is supported by many respectable names as well as the testimony of the gentlemen representing the county, who concur in the truth of the facts set forth in the petition. Your committee believes the petitioner ought to be relieved and recommend passage of the accompanying bill. [On reverse:] In Senate, 14 December 1825, read and Bill put on passage.
(GASR, Nov. 1825-Jan. 1826, Box 4: folders "SCR [Claims-Internal Improvements]" and "Petitions [Divorce and Alimony]".)

567. **Lemar, Elizabeth and husband, James.** Petition of Elizabeth Lemar of Guilford County states she married James Lemar in 1808,[79] and they lived together until the year 1814, when said James sold his property and the property that was given to her by her father, even to her bed and all the household and kitchen furniture. He then left your petitioner with one small child at her breast at the mercy of her parents for protection and with whom she has lived ever since. Prays for a law to enjoy such property as she may hereafter acquire by her own industry or that her aged father may think proper to give her not subject to the disposition or debts of her husband. [Below:] Signatures often subscribers who support the petitioner.

---

79 Marriage Bond of Randolph County, North Carolina, lists James Lemar and Elizabeth Ozbourn, dated 29 September 1809; bondsman: Elijah Ward.

Divorces and Separations from Petitions to the North Carolina General Assembly from 1779

Committee on Divorce and Alimony to whom was referred the petition of Elizabeth Lemar of Guilford County report that the petitioner has it in her power to obtain all she asks and believe that any Legislative Act would be unnecessary and as tending to increase the number of petitioners to this legislature. Recommend rejection. [On reverse:] In House of Commons, 5 December 1825, read and concurred with.

(GASR, Nov. 1825-Jan. 1826, Box 4: folder "HCR [Divorce and Alimony-Internal Improvements]").

568.   **McCulley, Sarah and husband, John.** Petition of Sarah (X) McCulley of Orange County states she married John McCulley of the same county nearly thirty years ago.[80] About the year 1812, she was compelled to separate herself from the said John. "[H]is treatment was such as could not be expressed and much more born[e] by any human being…her life only being spared by the interferance of her friends…[S]he had when the separation took place five small children, all of which she kept and raised, and all attained to the age of maturity except one…" She was thrown on the world with nothing but her own hands and the benevolence of her friends to support herself and children, but was received into her aged father's family again. Prays for an act to secure to her any property she may hereafter acquire. [Below:] Signatures of forty-four persons who subscribe to the prayer of the petitioner.

Committee on Divorce and Alimony to whom was referred the petition of Sarah McCalley of Orange County recommend passage of the accompanying bill: SB 15 Dec.: A Bill to secure to Sarah McCalley of Orange County such property as she may hereafter acquire, separate from her husband. In Senate, 15 December 1825, read three times, passed and ordered to be engrossed. In House of Commons, 16 December 1825, read first time and rejected.

(GASR, Nov. 1825-Jan. 1826, Box 2: folder "SB 15 Dec." and Box 4: folder "Petitions [Divorce and Alimony]").

569.   **Mooneham, William and wife, Mary.** Petition of William (X) Mooneham of Wake County, laborer, sheweth that he was lawfully married "to the woman claiming to be his wife Mary Mooneham." The said Mary, who was the mother of several children by your petitioner, led "a loose, lewd and incontinent life, violating her marriage vows when opportunity served and inclination prompted. She indulged in a promiscuous, adulterous intercourse with all who offered that pleased her fancy, until finally one came who being wealthier than her other admirers cohabited with her for some time, and then took her off to Georgia where they live together in open adultery and have done so for years." Your petitioner is poor and unable to pay the costs of a suit. His lawyer obtained an order at the last Superior Court of Law for Wake County to prosecute for divorce without giving bond for the costs thereof, but the Clerk of said Court refused to issue the papers without immediate payment of the costs of such papers. Your petitioner has been unable to pay these costs. Prays to be divorced. [On reverse:] In House of Commons, 21 December 1825, read and postponed indefinitely.

(GASR, Nov. 1825- Jan. 1826, Box 4: folder "Petitions [Divorce and Alimony]").

570.   **Sharp, Susannah and husband, Thomas.** Petition of Susannah Sharp states she intermarried with one Thomas Sharp in Burke County about twelve or thirteen years ago[81] in hopes of enjoying the pleasures of a matrimonial life. She soon discovered she was sadly disappointed, for her husband soon

---

80   Marriage Bond of Orange County, North Carolina, lists John McCulley and Sarah Hurdle, dated 15 September 1797; bondsman: Andrew McCulley.

81   Marriage Bond of Burke County, North Carolina, lists Thomas Sharp and Susannah Endsley, dated 3 July 1813; bondsman: Charles (X) Brown.

began to treat her with coldness and ultimately with great harshness. Nevertheless, she continued to live with said Sharp for about two months, when he left her. After six months, he returned, and she received him in hopes he would treat her as a husband should. She was again disappointed, for he left her in about four months and went to the State of Tennessee. He returned after about twelve months and lived with your petitioner about five months, when she was informed that he had intermarried with another woman while in Tennessee. He then left your petitioner again and has since married a woman in Haywood County, North Carolina, whom he has since left and is now living with his father in Buncombe County. After being abandoned by her husband the third time, despairing of ever reclaiming him and being thrown friendless on the world without any means of maintaining herself and two infant children, your petitioner wandered from place to place for about three years. At the end of this wandering, she was received into the house of one William Winchester with whom she has continued to live ever since and by whom she has had four children. Your petitioner has been advised that in consequence of having lived with said Winchester, her case does not come within the jurisdiction of the Superior Courts in matters of divorce. Prays for consideration of her case and an act to divorce her from the bonds of matrimony with said Thomas Sharp. [Below:] Signatures of sixteen persons who subscribe to the prayer of the petitioner. Committee on Divorce and Alimony to whom was referred the petition of Susannah Sharp is of opinion that although the conduct of the petitioner has not been of the honest, upright kind, the conduct of her husband has been so much more improper and feel disposed to grant her relief. Recommend passage of the accompanying bill. [On reverse:] In Senate, 14 December 1825, read and bill put on its passage. (GASR, Nov. 1825-Jan. 1826, Box 4: folders "SCR [Claims-Internal Improvements]" and "Petitions [Divorce and Alimony]".)

571. **Smith, Gideon B. and wife, Eleanor.** HB, 12 Dec. 1825. Gideon B. Smith of City of Baltimore, Maryland, is hereby divorced from bonds of matrimony with his wife, Eleanor.[82] In Senate, 12 December 1825, read third time and ordered to be enrolled.
(GASR, Nov. 1825-Jan. 1826, Box 1: folder "HB, 12 Dec. 1825")

572. **Tindel, Susan(nah) and husband, James.** Petition of Susan Tindel, formerly Susanah Evans, sheweth she unfortunately married a young man by the name of James Tindel from the State of South Carolina. His flattering promises and the persuasions of a near relative induced her to enter into the banns of wedlock with him before having knowledge of his character and circumstances. Despite promises he made before and during my acceptance of marriage, he abandoned me within a very short time. This unfortunate circumstance took place about two years ago, and the last account I have heard is that he married another woman and is now living in the State of Tennessee. Prays for a divorce from said husband and to be placed in a situation "more agreeable to the human mind, being only a few months over eighteen years of age…I refer you to Gen'l. Love, who has been acquainted with myself and family ever since my Infancy, and also the other two gentlemen who represent Haywood County, which is the place of my nativity…" [Below:] "We tlie undersigned do hereby certify that we have been acquainted with Susannah Evins (alias) Tindel and with her father who is a Preacher of the Gospel…" Signed by twenty-three subscribers, including Jacob Evans and R. Love.

Committee on Divorce and Alimony to whom was referred the Petition of Susannah Tindel of Haywood County praying for a divorce report that the petitioner was married some years ago to a man from South Carolina by the name of James Tindel. At that time, she was very young and not capable of judging the propriety of this course but was induced by a relative to unite with this man in matrimony.

---

82 Marriage Bond of Wake County, North Carolina, lists Gideon B. Smith and Eleanor Sfanley, dated 20 January 1814; bondsman: Jos. Ross.

Divorces and Separations from Petitions to the North Carolina General Assembly from 1779

It appears to your committee that the petitioner has always sustained the character of a prudent, upright woman and is descended from respectable parents. Your committee believes the petitioner ought to be relieved and recommend the passage of the accompanying bill.

[On reverse:] In Senate, 14 December 1825, read, and bill put on passage. (GASR, Nov. 1825-Jan. 1826, Box 4: folders "SCR [Claims-Internal Improvements]" and "Petitions [Divorce and Alimony]".)

573. **Whitley, Jane and husband, Johnathan.** Petition of Jane Whitly of Mecklenburg County represents that she was married in 1812 to Johnathan Whitly[83] with whom she lived in harmony for six years and has three children, two of whom are now alive and dependent on her industry for their education and support. Delicacy prevents her from going into a detail of her circumstances but rests her case on the accompanying certificate from the hands of those who have long known her. Prays that the marriage contract with her husband be annulled.

Committee on Divorce and Alimony to whom was referred the Petition of Jane Whitley of Mecklenburg County report that a certificate which accompanied the petition was signed by several gentlemen and testifies to the good character and conduct of the petitioner. It further appears that the said Johnathan Whitly has entirely abandoned his wife and was heard of the last time in the City of New Orleans on his way to the Spanish Provinces. However, because it does not appear that any of the facts in the petition are legally proven, recommend the prayer of the petitioner be rejected.

[On reverse:] In House of Commons, 15 December 1825, read and laid on the table. (GASR, Nov. 1825-Jan. 1826, Box 4: folder "HCR [Divorce & Alimony-Internal Improvements]").

574. **Witherspon, Elizabeth and husband, David.** Petition of Elizabeth Witherspoon states she intermarried with one David Witherspoon of Wilkes County a number of years ago[84] and had nine children. However, said David reduced your petitioner to poverty and want by his misconduct and at length abandoned her and her children who must subsist on the charity of her friends. Prays for a law to secure to her such property as she may hereafter acquire. [Below:] Signatures of four persons who subscribe to the prayer of the petitioner.

Committee on Divorce and Alimony to whom was referred the petition of Elizabeth Witherspoon of Wilkes County praying for alimony report that the petitioner intermarried upwards of thirty years ago with one David Witherspoon in Wilkes County. Said David was at that time in possession of some property, which added to that received by the petitioner from her parents would with proper economy have been amply sufficient to have supported themselves and family in a decent and comfortable manner. It appears, however, that so far from enjoying that portion of human happiness which our nature invariable teaches us to believe is derived from the married state, the petitioner's whole life has been a continued scene of disappointment, misery and woe. Soon after said marriage, the said David commenced a course of dissipation and intemperance which finally resulted in the destruction of all the property they possessed and the total abandonment of the petitioner and her numerous family of children. The petitioner has from time to time accumulated small portions of property by her own industry, and if this could be secured from the hand other husband (who has resided the greatest part of his time in South Carolina), the petitioner and her children will be enabled to support themselves in a creditable manner. Recom-

---

83   Marriage Bond of Mecklenburg County, North Carolina, lists Jonathan R. Whitley and Jane Price, dated 23 August 1813; bondsman: B. W[ilson] Davidson.

84   Marriage Bond of Wilkes County, North Carolina, lists David Witherspoon and Elizabeth Gordon, dated 16 June 1791; bondsman: John Witherspoon.

mend passage of the accompanying bill. [On reverse:] In Senate, 2 December 1825, read and the bill put on its passage.

SB, 2 Dec. Elizabeth Witherspoon of Wilkes County is hereby entitled to enjoy in her sole right all such estate as she may hereafter acquire as if she had never been married to her husband, David Witherspoon. In Senate, 5 and 6 December 1825, read third time and ordered to be engrossed. In House of Commons, 3 January 1826, read three times, passed and ordered to be enrolled.

(GASR, Nov. 1825-Jan. 1826, Box 2: folder "SB, 2 Dec." and Box 4: folder "SCR [Claims—Internal Improvements]".)

575. **Womack, Frances and husband, Henry.** Petition of Frances Womack states she was married to one Henry Womack of Person County about eleven years ago.[85] She lived with him several years and had two children by him. At the time of the marriage, she had a comfortable and sufficient estate, and her husband also had some property. The said Henry was a sober, prudent and respectable man before and at the time of marriage, but for several years past, he has become a victim of vice and dissipation, neglecting to provide for your petitioner or family. He has spent all of his estate and all the property he received of your petitioner, and for sometime before their separation, has neglected to provide any support for his family, and for many years has lived on the charity of his father. She has conducted herself with prudence and kindness towards him, but from his continual intemperance, he has become cruel and desperate in his conduct towards her. She has been compelled to fly for her personal safety to the protection of one other sisters. She has not lived with said husband for more than five years. Prays for a divorce from her said husband.

Accompanying the above petition are the following depositions:

(a). Duncan Rose of Person County deposes that he is personally acquainted with Henry Womack and his wife, Frances, and that her conduct has been upright, chaste and moral. Her husband has made no provision for the support of his family, has spent all his property and that of his wife, and he is a habitual drunkard. The said Frances Womack had left him and taken protection of her sister, Mrs. Rebecky Williams with whom she has lived about four years. Dated 22 December 1824.

(b). [Depositions of John Wisdom, James McMurry, Sr., James Snipes, and John Bradshaw are similar in content to that of Duncan Rose above. In the deposition of Senna Jarrett, the following additional comment was made:] "…that she has seen said Henry draw his show knife and swear that he would murder her with it." He also "threw an iron at her from the fireplace" and "threw a gourd of powder in the fire for the purpose of destroying his wife."

Committee on Divorce and Alimony to whom was referred the petition of Frances Womack of Caswell County, praying to be divorced from her husband. Henry Womack, makes reference to the content of the petition and accompanying depositions but notes the committee is disappointed that said Henry Womack was not given notice of the petition of his wife nor the taking of the depositions. This committee cannot feel willing under all the circumstances of this case, from the irregularity of the affidavits being entirely ex parte, that what the committee members feel as men they would recommend as guardians of public trust and private confidence. The committee therefore recommends rejection of the prayer of the Petitioner.

(GASR, Nov. 1825-Jan. 1826, Box 4: folder "HCR [Divorce & Alimony-Internal Improvements]").

---

85 Marriage Bond of Person County, North Carolina, lists Henry Womack and [name missing], dated [day and month missing] 1813; bondsman: Solomon Paine.

Divorces and Separations from Petitions to the North Carolina General Assembly from 1779

576. **Wooters, Sarah and husband, John.** Petition of Sarah Wooters of Guilford County shews that she was in possession of two negroes, household furniture and an interest in land when she married John Wooters. Said John was in very humble circumstances at the time of the marriage, but he came into possession of said property and sold it a short time thereafter. He was not under any pressure of debt. He took the proceeds and left this state supposedly not to return. He has been gone for nearly three years, and his whereabouts are still unknown to your petitioner. Prays that property she may hereafter acquire be secured to her for separate use. [Below:] Subscribed to by the signatures of forty-six persons, including many Donnells.

Committee of Divorce and Alimony to whom was referred the petition of Sarah Wooters of Guilford County report that the statements of the petitioner appear to be true and recommend the passage of the following bill: Sarah Wooters of Guilford County, wife of John Wooters, is entitled to enjoy in her own right all such estate as she may hereafter acquire as if she had never been married to said John Wooters. In Senate 3, 5, and 6 December 1825, passed and ordered to be engrossed. In House of Commons, 3 January 1826, read and rejected.

(GASR, Nov. 1825-Jan. 1826, Box 2: folder "SB 3 Dec.").

577. **Reference A.**
Laws of North Carolina, 1825. The couples listed below with the prefix "D" were principals in an act providing complete divorces to each person. The couples with no prefix were principals in an act which entitled the female (heretofore i\feme covert) the right to hold, possess, and enjoy in her sole right, all such estate, real or personal, as she may hereafter acquire by industry, purchase, gift or otherwise, in as full and ample manner as if she had never been married (now becoming a feme sole Trader).
- D   Brickell, Elisabeth of Halifax Co.; husband, Samuel J., p. 74.
- D   Chambers, John of Haywood Co.; wife, Riney, p. 84.
- D   De La Chapel, Judith of Anson Co.; husband, Gabriel, p. 64.
- D   Smith, Gideon B. of Baltimore, Maryland; wife, Eleanor, p. 72.

578. **Reference B.**
Senate Bill, 14 December 1825. A Bill to divorce Susannah Tindel of Haywood County from her husband, James Tindel; Margaret Jackson of Burke County from her husband, Gabriel Jackson; and Susannah Sharpe from her husband, Thomas Sharpe. In Senate, 21 December 1825, engrossed and examined; in House of Commons, 21 December 1825, read first time and postponed indefinitely. (GASR, Nov. 1825-Jan. 1826, Box 2: folder "SB 14 Dec.")

1826-1827

579. **Barbee, Martha and husband, Willard.** Bill to secure to Martha Barbee of Wake County, wife of Willard Barbee,[86] all such estate, real or personal, as she may hereafter acquire as if she had never been married to said husband, free and clear from claims of said husband. [On reverse:] In Senate, 10 January 1827, read third time, passed and ordered to be engrossed. In House of Commons, 10 February 1827, read second time and rejected. (GASR, 28 Dec. 1826 - 10 Feb. 1827, Box 2: folder "SB 6 Jan.")

580. **Buckner, Polly and husband, Edward.** Petition of 106 citizens of Buncombe County prays that the North Carolina General Assembly grant a Bill of Divorce in favor of Polly Buckner from her husband, Edward Buckner. The undersigned citizens were acquainted with said Polly before she married said Edward and ever since the marriage. He has treated her in an inhuman and cruel way. She has conducted herself as a decent and prudent wife, but he absented himself and left her nothing on which she could subsist but the charity of her friends. Said Edward has been gone for six years.
Committee on Divorce and Alimony to whom was referred the petition of Polly Buckner recommend a divorce as the only alternative to the petitioner's situation. [On reverse:] In House of Commons, 7 February 1827, read and postponed indefinitely.
(GASR, 28 Dec. 1826 - 10 Feb. 1827, Box 4: folder "HCR (Agriculture - Divorce & Alimony)").

581. **Caldwell, Mary and husband, Andrew.** Committee on Divorce and Alimony to whom the petition of Mary Caldwell of Iredell County was referred report that the petitioner married Andrew Caldwell[87] of said county in 1808 and lived with him for eleven or twelve years. During this time, they had six children. About eight years ago, the said Andrew abandoned his wife and children and took up with a negro woman and continues to live and cohabit with her. The petitioner requests an act to secure to her any property she now has or may acquire in the future. The facts of the case present a strong appeal, but this committee believes her case comes within the provisions of existing laws giving jurisdiction to the superior courts of this state. It is inexpedient to grant the prayer of the petitioner, and it is the committee's opinion that the petitioner should apply at the tribunal of the court and not to the Legislature. [On reverse:] In House of Commons, 8 January 1827, read and concurred with.
(GASR, 28 Dec. 1826 - 10 Feb. 1827, Box 4: folder "HCR (Agriculture - Divorce & Alimony)").

582. **Chadwick, Nancy and husband, Jacob.** Petition of Nancy (+) Chadwick states she married Jacob Chadwick in 1809 in Buncombe County. Said Jacob moved from place to place, but made little effort to procure a living, and this caused the petitioner to gain support through her own efforts. She lived with said Jacob until she had seven children. He had frequently beat and abused her, and she greatly

---

86   Marriage Bond of Wake County, North Carolina, dated 27 September 1805, lists Willard Barbee and Patsey Harrard. Bondsman: James O'Bradly.

87   Marriage Bond of Lincoln County, North Carolina, dated 6 November 1807, lists Andrew Caldwell and Polly Wagener. Bondsman: William Little.

feared he would destroy her life. During her stay with him, "...there were two children laid to his charge by other women [and] afterwards the said Jacob took another woman in Blount County, Tennessee, and left her in the house with your petitioner and there beded with her as a wife and in the year 1821 he left your petitioner in Blount County & went off with the woman he thus kept & took with him all her children except one that your petitioner had at her Breast..." Your petitioner understands that the children he took with him are bounded out to strangers. When he left, he took almost all the property of your petitioner, and she had to travel on foot from Blount County to her father's house in Buncombe County -- about 110 miles and carry her child. She had no money and had to live on the courtesy of strangers. Prays for a divorce from the bonds of matrimony from her said husband and retain what property she has acquired since her separation from said Jacob. [Below:] Signatures of thirty-five subscribers who support the prayer of the petitioner.

Committee on Divorce and Alimony to whom was referred the petition of Nancy Chadwick of Buncombe County are of opinion that the petition be granted. [On reverse:] In House of Commons, 23 January 1827, read and laid on the table.

(GASR, 28 Dec. 1826 - 10 Feb. 1827, Box 4: folder "HCR (Agriculture - Divorce & Alimony)").

583. **Cox, Eliza Hope and husband, Longfield.** Petition of Eliza Hope Cox of Craven County sheweth that in the month of January 1808, your petitioner -- "then a very young girl but acting under the consent and approbation of her parents, intermarried with Captain Longfield Cox of said county and confidently hoped to find in the married state that happiness which it bestows on those who are united by affection as strongly as by law." In this hope, she has been most cruelly and injuriously disappointed. Scarcely three years passed after the marriage when her husband compelled her and her two infant children to find asylum and refuge under the roof of her father. Through the advice of her friends, she filed a Bill in Equity against her husband to compel him to afford her the means of subsistence without being a tax on the charity of others. This bill was nearly ready for a hearing in December 1812, but her husband appealed to her with expressions of regret for the past and promises of kindness for the future. He prevailed upon her to return to his house, recognize him as her husband, and dismiss the suit. In a few months thereafter, he abandoned her and took with him their only surviving child. He removed to a distant state not making the least provision for her support. Your petitioner understands that her said husband has visited Newbern, which was within seventy miles of her, for the purpose of executing a plan for a separation which had been agreed between him and her father. This plan settled to her separate use the sum of three thousand dollars and required a covenant from her father that she should never more prefer claims as a wife upon him or his estate. Your petitioner has been wantonly and cruelly banished from her husband for thirteen years and compelled through the affectionate feelings of her father to forego the rights and to be denied almost the name of a mother and wife. She has been encouraged to present her misfortunes before the Legislature and pray for an act divorcing her from those bonds of matrimony which bind her to a man who has repaid her fondness with hatred and her fidelity by desertion. [Below:] Signatures of twenty-one subscribers who unite with the petitioner in praying for relief.
(GASR, 28 Dec. 1826 - 10 Feb. 1827, Box 4: folder "HCR (Agriculture - Divorce & Alimony)").

584. **Dare, Elizabeth and husband, John.** Petition of Elizabeth Dare of Guilford County states she intermarried with one John Dare[88] in 1817 and lived in great harmony with him for four years. In the latter part of that period, he abandoned himself to drinking and gambling, and in a short time incurred debts which he was unable to pay. About the first of 1822 he left North Carolina and has not since

---

88   Marriage Bond of Guilford County, North Carolina, dated 29 September 1817, lists John Dare and Elizabeth Humphreys. Bondsman: Wm. T. Shields.

returned. She has not received a letter from him in more than three years past. She believed he has no intention of returning to his family. She has been informed that her husband was lately residing in Alabama and has abandoned himself to every species of vice. Your petitioner is a tailoress by profession and is barely able to procure a decent support for herself and her infant son. Prays that she be discharged from the bonds of matrimony with said John Dare. [Below:] Signatures of fifteen subscribers in support of this petition. (GASR, 28 Dec. 1826 - 10 Feb. 1827, Box 5: folder "Petitions (Divorce and Alimony)"). Committee on Divorce and Alimony to whom was referred the [petition of Elizabeth Dare of Guilford County]…believes her case to be worthy of legislative interference and recommend passage of the bill herewith reported. [On reverse:] In House of Commons, 18 January 1827, read and laid on the table.

(GASR, 28 Dec. 1826 - 10 Feb. 1827, Box 4: folder "HCR (Agriculture - Divorce & Alimony)").

585. **Dickey, Rachel and husband, Moses.** Petition of Rachel (x) Dickey states she was born in Orange County and still resides there. She was descended of respectable parents, and when about eighteen years of age, she intermarried with one Moses Dickey in February 1825 in the neighborhood. He was of fair character and about twenty-two years of age. "Your petitioner Indulged herself in the prospect of happyness in the continuation of love & Union for as much as nothing ever had transpired to create the most distant suspecion that he the sd. Moses Dickey would trate her amiss, but malencholy (for you - pertitioner to relate)…a few days after her Marriage [said Moses] began to misuse her and continued to do so and in such an inhuman Manner that your pertitioner was compeled to apply about the first of August 1825 for a peace warrant against the sd. Moses…" Soon afterwards, her said husband absconded and has not returned. Prays to be divorced from the bonds of matrimony with said Moses Dickey and prays also for a law to secure to her such property as she may hereafter acquire. Dated 20 October 1826. [Below:] Signatures of forty-three persons who "join in the prayer of the pertitioner and when Suffring female innocence is wounded with more than a two edged Sword we hope that you who alone can in a small degree repair the injury will be pleased to do so." Dated 20 October 1826.

Committee on Divorce and Alimony to whom was referred the Petition of Rachel Dickey of Orange County recommend the passage of the accompanying bill: A Bill to divorce Rachel Dickey from her husband Moses Dickey. [Below:] In Senate, 25 January 1827, and engrossed. In House of Commons, 29 January and 7 February 1827, read and postponed indefinitely.

(GASR, 28 Dec. 1826 - 10 Feb. 1827, Box 2: folder "SB 25 Jan.") (Also, GASR, 28 Dec. 1826 - 10 Feb. 1827, Box 2: folder "SB, 23 Jan.": Same bill as reported above, but it has only received Senate appraisal.)

586. **Dowling, Eliza S. and husband, Zacheus.** Petition of Eliza S. Dowling of Anson County states she intermarried to one Zacheus Dowling, a Methodist Circuit Rider, in November 1820. This marriage was contrary to the desires of my parents, who wanted him to desist. I was very young and hastily entered into contract, though with some degree of reluctance. Shortly after, I left my parents and wandered as an exile in distant parts, and within about nine months suffered most extremely–often in hunger, often left to find lodging, and still often the angry frowns of the man who I hoped to be my support in a strange land. I became afraid to travel with him, particularly so because of his threats (I had begged him to return me to my parents) that if the Devil got into him, he did not know what he should do. In August 1823, I got back to my parents very much reduced by sickness, and I have ever since remained there. Twelve months after my return, I lost my father by the hand of death. My mother and David Culbertson administered my father's estate, and they were legally notified by said Dowling that he intended to demand the share of the estate that was coming to me. Through the kindness of my friends, I applied to counsel on the case and was advised to try it in Equity. In the November 1826 Term at Charlotte, said

Dowling directed his agent to compromise by giving him one-third and making me pay costs. The case was decided accordingly. I have not seen said Dowling for upwards of five years, but he has endeavoured to deprive me of what small support I was entitled to from my father's estate. Request alimony and a divorce from the bonds of matrimony with said Zacheus.

    Bill of complaint of Eliza Dowling by her attorney, J. Wilson, to Court of Equity for County of Mecklenburg restates the facts of the above petition and also notes the following: Her father was Solomon Simons, and his widow was Mary Simons. He died seized of personal property worth $10,000. Eliza states that but for the marriage, she was entitled to one-seventh part of her father's estate.

    (GASR, 28 Dec. 1826 - 10 Feb. 1827, Box 5: folder "Petitions (Divorce and Alimony)").

    (Also, GASR, 28 Dec. 1826 - 10 Feb. 1827, Box 2: folder "SB 25 Jan.": Bill to divorce Eliza S. Dowling of Anson County from her husband, Zacheus Dowling. In Senate, 26 January 1827, read second time and ordered that the bill do not pass.)

587.   **Edney, Samuel J. and wife, Olivia.** Petition of Samuel J. Edney of Buncombe County sheweth the petitioner as a young man of respectable parentage and connections. His character has not been one to disappoint the hopes and expectations of his friends, and his prospects in life were flattering until a circumstance occurred about two years since which involved him in disgrace and misery. To the cold, calculating moralist, whose presence is rather the offspring of stoicism than sensibility, and who know not how to make due allowance for the frailities of man, or pardon those weaknesses which they have never felt, affairs of this kind are matters of little or no concern. But your petitioner trusts that in your honourable body there are but few, if any to be found who will not sympathize with him in his misfortunes, should even a rigid sense of duty forbid to extend the hand of relief to your petitioner. In a word to bring the facts of the case fairly before you–your petitioner was seduced in a moment of inebriety to intermarry with a young woman by the name of Olivia Elkins, whose beauty though the most fascinating was perhaps her greatest recommendation. The lapse of five months after the marriage made her the mother of an illegitimate child. Sometime previous to the birth, your petitioner committed her to the care and protection of her friends and relatives and has since that time had no other or further connexion with her. Prays relief by dissolving the marriage connexion thus unfortunately entered into. Dated 23 November 1826. [Below:] Statement signed by Olivia (+) Elkins that she is the person named in the above petition by Samuel J. Edney and admits the truth of most of the facts therein stated and joins with him in the prayer of the above petition, dated 27 November 1826. [Below:] Signatures of thirty-five subscribers in support of the prayer of the petitioner.

    Committee on Divorce and Alimony to whom was referred the Petition of Samuel J. Edney of Buncombe County recommend passing of accompanying bill.[89] (GASR, 28 Dec. 1826 - 10 Feb. 1827, Box 5: folder "SCR (Claims-Misc.)"). (Also, GASR, 28 Dec. 1826 - 10 Feb. 1827, Box 2: folder "SB 6 Jan.": Bill to divorce Samuel J. Edney of Buncombe County from his wife Olivia. [On reverse:] In Senate, 15 January 1827, read 2nd and 3d times, passed and ordered to be engrossed. In House of Commons, February 1827, read and rejected.)

588.   **Fields, Mary and husband, William.** Petition of Mary Fields of Ashe County states she was married to William Fields about seventeen years ago and lived with him in all the comfort and happiness of the life of wedlock for about five years. To her great misfortune, her husband took to the habits of drunkenness and would frequently gamble and spend what your petitioner received in gifts from her father and friends. He drank so much that he approached a state of insanity and went off and left your petitioner with five small children to maintain and little property to pay debts he contracted. Since then

---

89   Bill is in another file.

your petitioner has paid all his debts and maintained her children to this time. Her husband left her about seven years ago, and after two years, he wrote to his father that he was in the State of Alabama and intended shortly to return to his friends. He has not come nor been heard from since. Your petitioner has no hope he will return and has been advised that her case does not come under the Act of Assembly that makes provision to grant divorces in the Superior Court of Law. Prays she be granted a divorce from her husband, William Fields. [Below:] Deposition of George Bower and Richard Gentry before Jonathan Baker, J. P. of Ashe County, North Carolina, that they are acquainted with the petitioner, Mary Fields, and believe the contents of her petition to be true.

Committee on Divorce and Alimony to whom was referred the Petition of Mary Fields of Ashe County have reviewed said petition and are of the opinion that the petitioner merits legislative clemency and that her prayer ought to be granted. Recommend passage of the accompanying bill.[90] (GASR, 28 Dec. 1826 - 10 Feb. 1827, Box 2: folder "SB 19 Jan.")

(Also, GASR, 28 Dec. 1826 - 10 Feb. 1827, Box 2: folder "SB 8 Jan.": Bill to divorce Mary Fields of Ashe County from her husband, William Fields. In Senate, 9 and 18 January 1827, read three times, passed and ordered to be engrossed. In Commons, 7 February 1827, read 2nd time and postponed indefinitely.)

589. **Fugate, John and wife, Patsey.** Petition of John Fugate of Wilkes County states he was married to one Patsey Johnson on 8 May 1823, and on 8 July of the same year, she was delivered of a coloured child. At the time of the marriage, your petitioner had no knowledge that the said Patsey was pregnant, but when the facts came to his attention, he abandoned said Patsey and has had no connection with her since. Your petitioner is extremely poor and unable to make application to the Superior Court for relief. Prays for an act absolving him from the bonds of matrimony with the said Patsey. Dated 20 December 1826. [Below:] Signatures of sixteen subscribers who support the facts of the petitioner.

(GASR, 28 Dec. 1826 - 10 Feb. 1827, Box 4: folder "HCR (Agriculture - Divorce & Alimony)").

590. **Gibson, John and wife, Milly.** Petition of John Gibson of Stokes County states he was married to Milly Young in February 1814. However, in a very short time after the marriage, he was sadly convinced that his fondly anticipated hopes were to be destroyed. To his regret, she displayed a violent and ungovernable temper, assumed a disposition to involve him in debt, and finally succeeded in spending his estate. Within the space of three years after their marriage, she left his house and board without any apparent cause. He still had a tender affection for her and twice prevailed on her to return. However, after six years of marriage, she again left him and has refused ever to live with him again despite his repeated entreaties to return. She has for several years since acquired the character of a base and profligate woman. Prays for a divorce. [Below:] Signatures of fifty-one persons in support of the petitioner.

Committee on Divorce and Alimony to whom was referred the petition of John Gibson of Stokes County recommend the passing of the accompanying bill: Bill to divorce John Gibson of Stokes County from his wife, Milley. [On reverse:] In Senate, 19 January 1827, examined and engrossed. In House of Commons, 7 February 1827, read 2nd time and postponed indefinitely.

(GASR, 28 Dec. 1826 - 10 Feb. 1827, Box 2: folder "SB 17 Jan.")

591. **Green, Mary and husband, Allen.** Petition of Mary Green of Person County sheweth she was married to Allen Green on 14 February 1804,[91] lived with him in harmony until sometime in 1817, and

---

90 Said bill is in another file.
91 Marriage Bond of Person County, North Carolina, dated 9 February 1805, lists Allen Green and Polly Neeley. Bondsman: Edmond Dillhay.

became the mother of eight children. In the same year, "my mind was partially deranged and so continued for near three years." During these latter years, I was treated in a most cruel and outrageous manner more than twenty times and was beaten by said husband: "I was tyed with ropes at other times, I was Ironed and at Lenth he the said Green built a small hut about ten feet Square and confined me in chains for uppards of Four month and beat me Cruelly during my confinement and Frequently I remained in this condition for upwards of Twenty four hours without meat or drink. Some time in the course of 1820 I was again restored to my right mind and have so Continued…[D]uring the time of my mental derangement he the said Green took up with a Certain Martha Long and took her to his bed and board and does continue to this day to live in Addultry by whom he had had four children all of which time your petitioner was an out cast Living from House to house and on the Charity of my friends." About four years ago, her said husband was presented to the Grand Jury for living in adultery and fined $200 by Judge Paxton, but the fine was to be reduced to $25 if said Green separated from said Martha Long. Her husband failed to send said Martha away because of his infatuation, so he paid the higher fine. Your petitioner has rented land since coming into her right mind and has taken her three youngest children with her. Through her care and exertion, she owes nothing except twenty five pounds of her father's. Her said husband now threatens to dispossess her of her small pittance. She is poor and unable to pay the cost of a suit but prays for a law to divorce her from the bonds of matrimony and to change her name from Mary Green to Mary Nealy, her maiden name. [Below:] Signatures of three subscribers.

Committee on divorce and alimony to whom was referred the petition of Mary Green of Person County consider this case as one coming within the jurisdiction of the Superior courts and therefore recommend the rejection of the petition. [On reverse:] In House of Commons, 18 January 1827, read and concurred with.

(GASR, 28 Dec. 1826 - 10 Feb. 1827, Box 4: folder "HCR (Agriculture - Divorce & Alimony)").

592. **Hendrick, John J. and wife, Lucy.** Petition of John J. Hendrick and his wife, Lucy R. Hendrick (formerly Lucy Turner) of Granville County promotes their desire to be divorced, and said Lucy wants her name changed to its original form of Lucy Turner. Sworn before Anderson Paschall, J. P., on 2 January 1827 and witnessed by Charles R. Turner, Talithacume[92] Turner, Charles (x) Thoma[s]on, and Bevel (x) Ellington.

Committee on Divorce and Alimony to whom was referred the petition of John J. Hendrick and Lucy R. Hendrick report that no reason is furnished by the petitioners, nor has any evidence been submitted to show any justifiable grounds why their prayer should be granted. Recommend the same be rejected. [On reverse:] In Senate, 17 January 1827, read and concurred in.

(GASR, 28 Dec. 1826 - 10 Feb. 1827, Box 5: folder "SCR (Claims-Misc.)").

593. **House, Turner and wife, Patience.** Petition of Turner House of Pitt County sheweth that he intermarried with Patience Young many years ago and enjoyed in her society more than the usual comforts and blessings of a married life. His exertions to perpetuate this happiness were indefatigable, and he discharged the duties of an affectionate husband in every particular. Your petitioner and the said Patience were blessed during this time with those fondest pleadges, for they had born to them four promising children in whose society he believed both enjoyed the endearing pleasure of parents. This state of connubial bliss continued up to the year 1823, when the conduct of his wife was so strangely different and repulsive that his suspicions were awakened, and his mind yielded to the influence of cor-

---

92 Many given names are Biblical in origin, but this was not a personal name in its original context. It is taken from Mark 5:41: "And he [Jesus] took the damsel by the hand, and said unto her, Talitha cumi, which is, being interpreted, Damsel, I say unto thee, arise." (KJV)

roding jealously. He suspected that he had been supplanted in the affection of his wife by some object to him unknown. He was determined to conceal his feelings from his wife and the world and to grieve in silence. He believed that his forbearances would regain her love, and domestic harmony would be restored. But in these fond expectations, he was woefully disappointed, for his demeanor seemed to add to her alienation. Eventually she refused to admit your petitioner to her embraces and to a participation of all the rights of a husband. He was determined if possible to ascertain the cause for his suspicions and kept a strict watch on her conduct. To his great mortification he discovered her secretly enjoying the embraces of a slave, the property of your petitioner. What was before to him a terrestrial paradise was thus converted into a Hell. He has been informed and believes that she was guilty of a repetition of the same crime with the same person. Some time after this occurrence, your petitioner and the said Patience agreed to separate and entered into written deeds for that purpose. Your petitioner conveyed to said Patience the one-third part of his estate, and since that time, they have lived separate and apart. Prays for a divorce from said wife, Patience. Sworn to and subscribed before J. J. Brickell, J. P., 4 December 1826.

Deposition of Hillary Whitehurst of Pitt County that he is a near neighbor of Turner House and went to his house about eighteen months ago to make a pair of leading lines. He learned that Mr. House and his two eldest sons had gone to a neighbor, so he went into the house to get the instruments for making the lines. After entering one room, he saw through an open door of another room the wife of said Turner on the bed and a negro slave named Hardie, belonging to said Turner, on top of her in an act of adultery. This deponent being ashamed of the sight immediately turned around to the kitchen and sent a negro woman for the instruments. Mrs. House afterwards came to the door, but this deponent does not know whether she was aware of his discovery or not. Some weeks afterwards, this deponent was going to his brother's and while passing said Turner's house, he saw near the corner of the fence in a potato patch the same negro slave with Mrs. House engaged in the act of adultery. Sworn at Raleigh, 20 January 1827, before Wm. Peace, J. P. of Wake County.

The Committee on divorce and alimony to whom was referred the petition of Turner House have considered the same and report that the statements of the petitioner are well substantiated and recommend the accompanying bill be passed into law: that Turner House of the County of Pitt is hereby divorced from his wife Patience as if the rites of matrimony had never been solemnized. [On reverse:] In House of Commons, 22 January 1827, read and laid on the table. In House of Commons, 7 February 1827, read and postponed indefinitely.

(GASR, 28 Dec. 1826 - 10 Feb. 1827, Box 1: folder "HB 23 Jan.")

594. **Killion, Elizabeth and husband, David.** Petition of twenty-eight persons in favor of Elizabeth Killion of Lincoln County state they have been acquainted with Elizabeth Killion and her husband, David Killion, for a number of years and know they lived agreeably together until a few years past. Said David took up and co-habited with a base woman and supported her extravagantly until he exhausted his living support.

A separation took place between said David and Elizabeth, but he continued to cohabit with his concubine and caused embarrassment and impediments in the way of his wife's peace and happiness. She still appears to conduct herself prudently, and though in a very frail state of body by the infirmities incident to age, hardship and troubles, she is maneuvering to acquire a support by her own industry. Recommend a law to secure to her such property as she now has or may hereafter acquire. [Below:] Signatures of twenty-eight subscribers who support the petitioner.

Committee on Divorce and Alimony to whom was referred the petition of sundry persons in Lincoln County in favor of Elizabeth Killion are of opinion that the case is one of peculiar hardship and recommend the passage of the accompanying bill. [On reverse:] In Senate, 25 January 1827, read and agreed to.[93]

(GASR, 28 Dec. 1826 - 10 Feb. 1827, Box 5: folder "SCR (Claims-Misc.)").

(Also, GASR, 28 Dec. 1826 - 10 Feb. 1827, Box 2: folder "SB 25 Jan.": Bill to secure to Elizabeth Killion of Lincoln County such property as she may hereafter acquire. In Senate, 26 January 1827, read 2d time and ordered that the bill do not pass.)

595. **McKinne, Nancy and husband, Richard.** Petition of Nancy McKinne states she intermarried with one Richd. McKinne and lived with him nine or ten years, after which he left her without any known cause and without support. Prays for a divorce that she might strive to support herself and children.

(GASR, 28 Dec. 1826 - 10 Feb. 1827, Box 5: folder "Petitions (Divorce and Alimony)").

596. **McLilley, Mildred and husband, John.** Petition of Mildred (x) McLilley of Halifax County states that her husband, John McLilley,[94] has left her bed and board without any cause or provocation. He also left three children to maintain while he contracts debts for his own use and benefit. Requests a divorce or an act to secure hereafter her honest earnings. [Below:] Signatures of six subscribers in support of the petitioner. (GASR, 28 Dec. 1826 - 10 Feb. 1827, Box 5: folder "Petitions (Divorce and Alimony)").

Committee of Divorce and Alimony to whom was referred the petition of Mildred McLilley of Halifax County, wife of John McLilley, report that the husband of the petitioner has indulged himself in habits of intemperance and has entirely destroyed and squandered his property. He finally abandoned his wife and three children in a state of ruin and distress. The petitioner states she has paid many of her husband's debts, but that he is constantly contracting more. Recommend passage of the accompanying bill: To secure to Mildred McLilley of Halifax County such property as she may hereafter acquire. [On reverse:] In Senate, 19 January 1827, read 2nd and 3rd times, passed and ordered to be engrossed. In House of Commons, 10 February 1827, read and rejected. (GASR, 28 Dec. 1826 - 10 Feb. 1827, Box 2: folder "SB 18 Jan.")

597. **Mills, James W. and wife, Mary Ann.** Petition of James W. Mills of Mecklenburg County sheweth he intermarried with one Mary Ann Clemson, a resident of York District, South Carolina, on 3 June 1824. He entered into such a contract because of the pleasing prospect of happiness, both being young. "But strange to relate within a few days of our intermarriage my wife, without any grounds of complaint left my Bed & Board, and utterly refused, under any circumstances to Return. This strange and unaccountable conduct excited an enquiry into her motives…[and] it finally came to light that previous to our intermarriage, she was pregnant by a man of the name of Alexander Guyer, with whom I am informed she intended to Elope, and with whom she continually cohabitted." Under the protection of Guyer and under his wicked council, she threatened to kill me, either by poison or by the dagger. Your petitioner has resided in North Carolina for upwards of thirteen months past and now is a resident of said state and intends to continue therein. Prays that a Bill of divorce may be granted him.

(GASR, 28 Dec. 1826 - 10 Feb. 1827, Box 4: folder "HCR (Agriculture - Divorce & Alimony)").

---

93   Bill is in another file.
94   Marriage Bond of Halifax County, North Carolina, dated 25 May 1822, lists John McLilly and Milly Wallace. Bondsman: John Porter.

598. **Oakley, Nancy and husband, Stephen.** Petition of Nancy Oakley of Person County states she intermarried with one Stephen Oakley of the same county in March 1824. About three months later, said Stephen proposed to remove to Georgia and preemptorily ordered your petitioner to prepare to set out. She remonstrated and urged that they were unable to get there, having at that time but a single dollar to bear their expenses and no prospect of getting more. Said Stephen seized upon these remonstrances as a precedent to separate himself from your petitioner. He has not taken any care for the support of your petitioner since that time, but he has roamed about through the neighborhood without any fixed home and lived in habits of adultery. Your petitioner has been of chaste and unexceptionable character and has always been ready to live with said Stephen since this separation. Said Stephen persists on leaving nothing for your petitioner to hope for and has abandoned her to despair. She has given him notice by her agent that she was willing to live with him in obedience and use her utmost efforts for his comforts. He has turned a deaf ear to her reasonable proposals, so she endeavours to obtain a divorce from him. She is unable to advance the cost for such action but prays that her sufferings be recognized and that a law may be enacted to dissolve the bonds of matrimony with said Stephen. [Below:] Signatures of sixteen persons who subscribe to the prayer of the petitioner.

Committee on Divorce and Alimony to whom was referred the petition of Nancy Oakley of Person County believe this case is clearly provided for by the Law in the Superior Court and recommend the prayer of the petitioner should not be granted. [On reverse:] In Senate, 8 February 1827, read and agreed to.

(GASR, 28 Dec. 1826 - 10 Feb. 1827, Box 5: folder "SCR (Claims-Misc.)").

599. **Peck, Daniel and wife, Nancy "Ann".** Petition of Daniel Peck of the City of Raleigh, artisan, sheweth he intermarried with Nancy (alias Ann) Peck in 1795 in Henrico County, Virginia, where they continued to live for some years. Owing to discontent and other causes, your petitioner left said wife and a profitable establishment and removed to the City of Raleigh where he pursued his trade and art with profit. His said wife followed him, and they lived together in perfect harmony at times, but at other times, they were discontented, and said Nancy has withdrawn herself from his bed and board in direct contradiction to his wishes. She has continued to live separate for weeks and months at the homes of persons to which your petitioner has the most serious objections. On 17 May 1826, said Nancy absented herself from his bed and board and left his home and the county. Your petitioner has gone to see her and solicit her return to her home in a most tender and affectionate way and also to command her as it is might right to do so, but she positively refuses to do so. He earnestly solicits that he may be divorced from said wife. Dated 19 January 1827.

Committee of Divorce and Alimony to whom was referred the petition of Daniel Peck of Raleigh report it is inexpedient to grant the prayer of the petitioner and recommend its rejection. [On reverse:] In House of Commons, 1 February 1827, read and concurred with.

(GASR, 28 Dec. 1826 - 10 Feb. 1827, Box 4: folder "HCR (Agriculture - Divorce & Alimony)").

600. **Pope, Elijah and wife, Sally.** Petition of Elijah (x) Pope of Northampton County sheweth it has been about twenty years since his wife, Sally, to whom he had been married for several years and has [blank] children, had left his bed and board and has ever since remained absent from his house. As he believes, said Sally was enticed and seduced by the persuasions held out by one Barnabas Burns of said Northampton County. The said Burns is believed to have had three children by the said Sally as based on the following facts:

(1). He afforded maintenance and support to her and her children born after she lived apart and separate from your petitioner; and

Divorces and Separations from Petitions to the North Carolina General Assembly from 1779

(2). Said Burns made provisions for said Sally and her children in his last will and testament by providing for her during her life and devising his property to the children after her death. Since the death of said Burns, the said Sally still lives separate from your petitioner and continues to be supported by the provisions of said Burns' will. Inasmuch as your petitioner, who is now far advanced in life, may have it in his power to leave his own lawful children in a situation far from reproach and close his days in parity of life, your petitioner prays he may be divorced from the bonds of matrimony from this time and forever. [Below:] Signatures of seventy-seven subscribers in support of the petitioner and a certificate of Wm. Maget that he was "acting Magister in No.ampton County [when] Elijah Pope & Sary Parker applied to me to join them in wedlock & I done the same agreeable to Law." (GASR, 28 Dec. 1826 - 10 Feb. 1827, Box 5: folder "Petitions (Divorce and Alimony)").

Committee on Divorce and Alimony to whom was referred the petition of Elijah Pope of Northampton County report that about twenty years ago, said Elijah's wife, Sally, was seduced and misled by the allurements of one Barnabas Burns and abandoned his bed and board, her husband and children and has never returned to them. After her separation, she had several children supposedly by said Burns, for Burns has made provision for the support of these children and mother in his will. The petitioner further states that said Sally continues to live separately and apart from him and conducts herself in a manner highly disreputable to her family and disgraceful to herself. He says he is old and wishes to close his days in purity of life and leave his children free from reproach. He thinks this will be accomplished by a divorce from his wife Sally. Your Committee are of opinion that the provision of existing laws gives jurisdiction to the Superior Court and recommend it is inexpedient to grant the prayer of the petitioner. [On reverse:] In House of Commons, 8 January 1827, read and concurred with. (GASR, 28 Dec. 1826 - 10 Feb. 1827, Box 4: folder "HCR (Agriculture - Divorce & Alimony)").

601. **Robertson, Elizabeth and husband, Willis.** Petition of Elizabeth Robertson of Wake County claims she intermarried with a certain Willis Robertson[95] some years past and had several children. About ten years ago, her husband enlisted as a common soldier in the service of the United States, soon left this country and has never returned. At the time of his enlistment, he had entirely dissipated every species of property he possessed and left your petitioner and her little children dependent upon the charity of the world. Your petitioner has been able to support her family by her labor and industry and prays a law be passed for her relief to secure her property against any desire of her husband.
Committee of Divorce and Alimony to whom was referred the petition of Elizabeth Robertson of Wake County report that the said Willis Robertson, husband of the petitioner, returned to this country shortly after the close of the War of 1812 but remained a short time with your petitioner and family. He abandoned them after dissipating property he possessed. It is reported and believed that the said Willis is now married to or lives with another woman, and there is no expectation he will ever return to the petitioner and her family. Recommend the following bill be passed into law: Bill to secure to Elizabeth Robertson, wife of Willis Robertson of Wake County, such property as she may hereafter acquire. [On reverse:] In Senate, 22 January 1827, engrossed and examined. In House of Commons, 10 February 1827, read and rejected.
(GASR, 28 Dec. 1826 - 10 Feb. 1827, Box 2: folder "SB 18 Jan.")

602. **Rowland, Mary Eliza and husband, Alfred.** Petition of Mary Eliza Rowland of Robeson County represents she intermarried with Alfred Rowland of the same county in 1809.[96] At the time of the

---

95 Marriage Bond of Wake County, North Carolina, dated 8 November 1805, lists Willis Robertson and Elizabeth Bell. Bondsman: John Robertson.

96 Marriage Bond of Cumberland County, North Carolina, dated 20 May 1809, lists Alfred Rowland and Mary Clinton. Bondsman: K[enneth] Black.

marriage, said Alfred possessed a small estate encumbered by debt. Your petitioner possessed a considerable estate, but which by the marriage became the absolute property of said husband. In the year 1813, your petitioner inherited a large personal estate devised to her by the last will and testament of her mother, which indicated that the same should be secured to your petitioner and her heirs. However, owing to some legal technicality of expression, the intention of the will could not be sustained. Her husband's circumstances by unfortunate speculations or endorsements for others, or both, rendered the whole of her property thus acquired by her husband subject to the payment of his debts, and the same for that purpose has been sold, leaving your petitioner in a situation which before was unknown to him. By these means, your petitioner has been reduced to want. She has two small children wholly dependent on her for support and education. She also has many friends in affluent circumstances who would contribute to her if she could hold her own right in such property. Prays for an act to secure such property as she may hereafter acquire. Dated 29 January 1827.

Committee of Propositions and Grievances to whom was referred the Petition of Mary Eliza Rowland of Robeson County are of opinion after an inquiry into all the facts submitted that the case of the petitioner is one of extreme hardship and recommend the accompanying bill be passed into law: Bill to secure to Mary Eliza Rowland of Robeson County such property as she may hereafter acquire. In Senate, 7 February 1827, engrossed and examined. In House of Commons, 8 and 10 February 1827, read and postponed indefinitely.

(GASR, 28 Dec. 1826 - 10 Feb. 1827, Box 3: folder "SB 6 Feb.")

603. **Ruffin, Rebecca and husband, Grey.** Bill to secure to Rebecca Ruffin of Halifax County such property as she may hereafter acquire. In Senate, 20 and 22 January 1827, read 2nd and 3rd times, passed and ordered to be engrossed.

(GASR, 28 Dec. 1826 - 10 Feb. 1827, Box 2: folder "SB 20 Jan.")

604. **Smith, Gideon B. and wife, Eleanor.** Petition of Gideon B. Smith, a native of the State of New York, states he came to Raleigh in the year 1814 and became acquainted with a Mrs. Beard and her daughter, Eleanor. Said daughter sustained the character of being honest, virtuous and reputable, although mother and daughter were poor and moved in the humble walks of society. "Being himself young and inexperienced with no friend to advise him, he was soon entangled in the tacts of the artful and designing mother, and formed an attachment for Eleanor, which was consummated by their marriage.[97] The anticipations of an ardent young man were realized in the enjoyment of much comfort and happiness for a few months after his marriage…. These favorable prospects, however, were soon blighted, for in the course of a year, under the eye and influence of her mother, Eleanor became abandoned and faithless. Hoping that a change of place and a removal beyond the influence of her mother's contrivances and the reach of her criminal companions might produce a favorable change in the conduct of his wife, your petitioner moved to Wilmington in this State. Upon settling himself there, he immediately sent for his wife who refused to come to him, and although he urged every consideration in his power to induce her to accompany or follow him, it was all unavailing and your petitioner ascertained that she was in the actual keeping of a man then living in Raleigh with whom she lived as a mistress." In a strange place with no friend to sympathize with him in his distress, he became the victim of a disease and sickness, which for two or three years deprived him of reason. Depending upon his labour for a daily support may have proved fatal but for the charity of the citizens of Wilmington and the particular kindness of one by which he was carried back to his friends in New York. As he recovered, he made enquiries after his

---

97 Marriage Bond of Wake County, North Carolina, dated 20 January 1814, lists Gideon B. Smith and Eleanor Stanley. Bondsman: Jos. Ross.

Divorces and Separations from Petitions to the North Carolina General Assembly from 1779

wife and learned that she had left Raleigh with a Mr. Miller with whom she then lived in prostitution, had gone to Alabama and shortly afterwards he heard that she was dead. Too credulous in believing a report he so fondly hoped might be true, your petitioner was relieved from distress and entirely restored to his reason. He then settled in the City of Baltimore. His wounds were scarcely healed when he was urged to make a more minute and satisfactory enquiry about his wife. He learned that she was not dead but resided in Danville, Virginia, living as the wife of the man with whom she had left Raleigh. From Danville she came to Raleigh where she now lives. He would have gladly thrown a veil over the conduct of a woman he had vowed to love and honor had there been a prospect of reconciling her to the path of duty and honor. Although still poor and depending on his daily labour for support, he looked forward to brighter days which shall gladden his horizon, and to a standing in society both honorable and useful. Your petitioner looks to your honorable body as the only tribunal that can relieve him from a woman who has been living in open adultery for the last ten years of her life. Prays that he may be divorced from the bonds of matrimony with the said Eleanor. Dated November 1825.

    Committee on Divorce and Alimony to whom was referred the Petition of Gideon B. Smith, now of the City of Baltimore, report that the facts set forth in the petition and those from the evidence of respectable citizens of the City of Raleigh and Baltimore testifying to the good character, respectability and honorable deportment of the petitioner recommend the following bill.[98] (GASR, 28 Dec. 1826 - 10 Feb. 1827, Box 4: folder "HCR (Agriculture - Divorce & Alimony)").

605.   **Smith, Siddy and husband, Abner.** Petition of Siddy Smith of Wake County represents that sometime in the year 1805, she was married to Abner Smith,[99] and they lived together in peace and harmony for six or seven years and had one child. After that time, the said Abner became extremely dissipated, gave himself up to vice of almost every kind, and spent the whole of his property. Your petitioner continued to live with him and discharge the duties of a wife until about six years ago when said Abner took the only child of your petitioner and, as she was informed, went to the State of Alabama. The last account your petitioner had of him was about two years ago when she understood he had moved beyond the Mississippi. Prays for a law to secure to her such property as she may hereafter acquire. [Below:] Certificate signed by twelve persons who certify they were acquainted with Abner Smith, the husband of Siddy Smith, who was considered a man of bad character who was charged with several acts of a disgraceful and criminal kind in the neighborhood where he lived.

    Committee of Divorce and Alimony to whom was referred the petition of Siddy Smith, wife of Abner Smith, have substantiated the facts in said petition. In addition, said Abner was in the habit of beating and treating your petitioner inhumanly. At length he was arrested on a charge of having shot a man with an intent to commit murder and was committed to the Wake County jail. After he was discharged for lack of testimony to prove the fact, he spent all his property and absconded with the petitioner's only child to the State of Alabama. It is reported and believed he committed a murder in that State and fled beyond the Mississippi, not having been heard from since. Recommend that the accompanying bill be passed into law: Bill to secure to Siddy Smith of Wake County such estate as she may hereafter acquire. In Senate, 23 and 26 January 1827, read three times, passed and ordered engrossed. In House of Commons, 29 January and 10 February 1827, read and rejected.

    (GASR, 28 Dec. 1826 - 10 Feb. 1827, Box 2: folder "SB 23 Jan.")

---

98   Said bill is filed in GASR, Nov. 1825 - Jan. 1826, Box 1: folder "HB 12 Dec. 1825".
99   Marriage Bond of Wake County, North Carolina, dated 31 January 1805, lists Abner Smith and Siddy Busbee. Bondsman: Johnston Busbee.

1826-1827 Session

606. **Smith, William.** Committee of Divorce and Alimony to whom was referred the petition of William Smith of Hertford County report that the petitioner is a mulatoe of that class commonly called Negroes and recommend that the petitioner have leave to withdraw same. [On reverse:] In House of Commons, 22 January 1827, read, amended and concurred with.
 (GASR, 28 Dec. 1826 - 10 Feb. 1827, Box 4: folder "HCR (Agriculture - Divorce & Alimony)").

607. **Tindel, Susannah and husband, James.** Petition of Susanah Tindel of Haywood County sheweth she became acquainted with James Tindel, a native of South Carolina, in 1822, and he immediately commenced courting your petitioner. His conduct was of a sober, industrious young man, and through his persuasions and those of her friends, she married said James Tindell in the latter part of October 1822. Contrary to her expectations, her said husband commenced abusing and threatening the life of your petitioner about three weeks after the marriage. He said "that he only married her for the purpose of treating her in the above mentioned manner..." From this time, he also began to spend and convert what little property the father of your petitioner had given to her to his [said James] own use. The said James lived with your petitioner about four months "...and then swore he would never live with her anymore...got on his horse & left her from which time your petitioner has never seen him...but has understood that he lives in Kentucky with another woman." Your petitioner is entirely dependent on her connections and friends for support. The father of your petitioner is a very old man and has some property, but your petitioner will ever be deprived of enjoying such property unless she receives legislative interference. [Below:] Signatures of fourteen subscribers. (GASR, 28 Dec. 1826 - 10 Feb. 1827, Box 4: folder "HCR (Agriculture - Divorce & Alimony)").

608. **Turner, Mary and husband, Henry A.** Petition of Mary Turner, wife of Henry A. Turner, of Washington County sheweth she intermarried with said husband about March of 1817 with the anticipation of connubial happiness. Your petitioner's hopes were soon blighted, for in a short time after marriage, without cause on the part of your petitioner, the said Turner became peevish, fretful and perverse in temper towards her. Said husband did not have much property at the time of the marriage, and soon spent it in addition to that acquired by your petitioner. He had no house or home of his own, but by permission he alternately lived with his mother, the mother of your petitioner, and with your petitioner after marriage for about three years. In addition to his abuse and ill treatment, when your petitioner was far advanced in a state of pregnancy "he would frequently return home late at night after being absent eight to ten days on a drunken Frolic frequenting Houses of ill fame, and fire off a Pistol under the House to alarm your Petitioner without provocation and threaten to kill some person before day, and would go to bed with your Petitioner and put the Pistol under his head and thereby Kept your Petitioner under continual fear and trepidation, and after having one child by your Petitioner he left...[her] and child entirely to the mercy of their friends and the personal exertions of your Petitioner for support and swore he never would live with...[her] and remained absent for several months and afterwards he came back and promised future amendment in his conduct towards your Petitioner and desired to live with your Petitioner again. [She] assented with a hope that he would fulfill that promise, but in a short time your Petitioner was again disappointed and subjected to all the abuse, ill treatment and mortification which your Petitioner had before experienced from him and after having a second child by him he again left...[her] without provocation in the latter part of the year 1821 swearing he never would live with your Petitioner again..." Her said husband has ever since lived separate and apart from her, continually threatens to treat her ill, and withholds all manner of support. Prays for a law to secure to her all the property she may hereafter acquire. [Below:] Signatures of thirty-six subscribers who support the above petition.
 (GASR, 28 Dec. 1826 - 10 Feb. 1827, Box 5: folder "Petitions (Divorce & Alimony)").

Divorces and Separations from Petitions to the North Carolina General Assembly from 1779

(Also, GASR, 28 Dec. 1826 - 10 Feb. 1827, Box 2: folder "SB 19 Jan.": Bill to secure to Mary Turner, wife of Henry A. Turner, of Washington County such property as she may hereafter acquire. In House of Commons, 2 and 10 February 1827, read and rejected.)

609. **Waller, Mary and husband, Amos J.** Petition of Mary (x) Waller sheweth she intermarried with Amos J. Waller of Duplin County[100] about ten years ago. In the course of this period of time, they had no issue, and most of the time, the said Amos treated her with the greatest contempt and not as a faithful husband for the following reasons:

(1). spending and wasting her property;

(2). leaving her and following lewd women;

(3). absconding from your Petitioner about two years ago from this state and county and taking with him one of his lewd women;

(4). and wasting and spending all your petitioner's property that he had not wasted before. No person knows his whereabouts, and your petitioner is still harrassed by his creditors. Prays for an act to enable her to hold what property she now has and may hereafter acquire. Dated 26 November 1826, Duplin County, North Carolina. [Below:] Signatures of twenty-six subscribers who testify to the facts stated by the petitioner.

Committee on divorce and alimony to whom was referred the Petition of Mary Waller of Duplin County have taken into consideration said petition and declare additionally that the said Amos J. Waller has been absent for more than two years and not been heard of by your petitioner or friends. Her case is attended with mortifying circumstances of disappointment and that it forms a strong case for divorce. Your committee would feel no hesitation in making such a report if it had been demanded by the petitioner–but they have learned with much pleasure to themselves and credit to the petitioner that she is a pious and good woman and a member of the church–that she entertains some scruples of the moral propriety of being divorced–a contract too solemnly made to be broken–. Your committee are of opinion that the prair of the petitioner be granted and recommend passing of the Bill without amendment.

A Bill to secure to Mary Waller, wife of Amos J. Waller of Duplin County, such property as she may hereafter acquire. [On reverse:] In Senate, 19 and 20 January 1827, read three times, passed and ordered to be engrossed. In House of Commons, 10 February 1827, read and rejected.

(GASR, 28 Dec. 1826 - 10 Feb. 1827, Box 2: folder "SB 19 Jan.")

610. **Reference A.**

Laws of North Carolina, 1826 and 1827. The couples listed below with the prefix "D" were principals in acts providing complete divorces from bonds of matrimony. Those couples with the prefix "S" were principals in acts which entitled the female person the right to hold, possess and enjoy in her sole right, all such estate, real or personal, as she may thereafter acquire by industry, gift or otherwise, in as full and ample manner as if she had never been married.

1826

D Cox, Eliza Hope of Craven Co.; husband, Longfield, p. 76

D Dare, Eliza of Guilford Co.; husband, John, p. 76

D Fugate, John of Wilkes Co.; wife, Patsey, p. 76

---

100 Marriage Bond of Duplin County, North Carolina, dated 20 April 1815, lists Amos J. Waller and Mary Murray. Bondsman: Jas. Mallard.

S   Ruffin, Rebecca of Halifax Co.; husband, Grey, p. 79
D   Tindell, Susannah of Haywood Co.; husband, James, p. 76
1827
S   Rowland, Mary E. of Robeson Co.; husband, Alfred, p. 86

611. **Reference B.**
GASR, 28 Dec. 1826 - 10 Feb. 1827, Box 1: folder "HB 7 Feb.": House Bill, 7 February 1827. A Bill to divorce certain persons therein named: Eliza Hope Cox of Craven County from her husband, Longfield Cox; Susannah Tindell of Haywood County from her husband, James Tindell; Eliza Dare of Guilford County from her husband, John Dare; John Fugate of Wilkes County from his wife, Patsey Fugate. [On reverse:] In Senate, 9 February 1827, read three times, passed and ordered to be enrolled. In House of Commons, 8 and 9 February 1827, read three times, passed and ordered to be engrossed.

1827-1828

612. **Bardin, Jesse and wife, Ann Maria.**

(1). Petition of Jesse Bardin sheweth he had been in the habits of illicit intercourse with a certain Anna Bradbury, and the said Anna became pregnant and delivered a child. She averred that the child was his. He initially believed it was his child and intermarried with her immediately. In a few weeks, he was astonished and mortified that the child was a mulatto and the fruit of an adultery between her and a negro man. He prays for a divorce from his wife, Anna. [Below:] Signatures of nine subscribers who assert that all the facts in said petition are true. (GASR, Nov. 1827 - Jan. 1828, Box 2: folder "SB 13 Dec.")

(2). Petition of Ann Maria Barden states she was married to Jesse Barden in April last and lived with him about four months when she was compelled to leave his bed and board because of the ill treatment and threats made by said Jesse against her life. Your petitioner still entertains that affection for her husband but has learned that he intends to present a petition to your Honourable body for the purpose of obtaining a divorce from the bonds of matrimony which now exist between your petitioner and said Jesse. Your petitioner is informed that the principal ground assumed by her husband is that your petitioner had the misfortune to have a child born of which Jesse Barden is not the father. Such is the fact that your petitioner does not deny – the child was born one month and ten days before our marriage. Your petitioner is informed that said Jesse will state in his petition that said child was concealed from him until after their marriage was consummated, and that she induced him to believe he was the true father of her child -- the correctness of these statements your petitioner positively denies. She is able to establish the fact that said Jesse saw the child repeatedly before his marriage with your petitioner, and that he often professed perfect satisfaction when speaking on that subject. In fact, no effort was made at any time on the part of your petitioner to keep her child concealed from said Jesse, and it was always exhibited to him when he expressed a desire to see it. Your petitioner denies that she has ever tried to convince said Barden that he is the father of her child. The above statements of your petitioner can be established beyond doubt by some of the most respectable men in Wayne County. Prays that the Legislature will preserve inviolate the ties of matrimony that exist between your petitioner and Jesse Barden. Dated 5 December 1827. (GASR, Nov. 1827 - Jan. 1828, Box 5: folder "SCR (Claims-Military)").

(3). Committee on Divorce and Alimony to whom was referred the petition of Jesse Bardin of Wayne County praying to be divorced from his wife Ann has had the most satisfactory evidence of all the facts in the petition and recommend the prayer of the petitioner be granted and the accompanying bill be passed into law. [On reverse:] In Senate, 13 December 1827, read and bill put upon passage. (GASR, Nov. 1827 - Jan. 1828, Box 5: folder "SCR (Claims-Military)").

(4). Bill to divorce Jesse Bardin of Wayne County from his wife, Ann. In Senate, 13 [December] 1827, read three times, passed, and ordered to be engrossed. In House, 14 December 1827, read and postponed indefinitely. (GASR, Nov. 1827 - Jan. 1828, Box 2: folder "SB 13 [Dec.]").

613. **Beazley, Martha and husband, Edmund.** Petition of Martha Beazley, wife of Edmund Beazley, of Stokes County sheweth her said husband has by his misconduct wasted his estate and thereby brought his wife and children to poverty and want. Prays for a law to secure to her and her children what they obtain by their labor and honest industry. [Below:] Signatures of six subscribers in support of the petitioner. (GASR, Nov. 1827 - Jan. 1828, Box 4: folder "HCR (Agriculture-Internal Improvements)").

614. **Becknall, Jane and husband, Henry.**
    (1). Petition of thirty subscribers in support of Jane Becknal of Ashe County sheweth that Henry Becknal of Ashe County left his wife, Jane, and family about two years and eight months ago without any known cause, but leaving many unpaid debts and little or no property to pay same. His said wife is now past fifty-four years of age, and she has three children to maintain. Her husband was a drunkard and spendthrift, and she fears he is still contracting debts. Pray for an act to secure to her and her children what property she may hereafter acquire. (GASR, Nov. 1827 - Jan. 1828, Box 5: folder "SCR (Claims-Military)").
    (2). Committee on Divorce and Alimony to whom was referred the petition of sundry citizens of Ashe County recommend that the accompanying bill be passed into law. [On reverse:] In Senate, 1 January 1828, read and accompanying bill put on its passage. (GASR, Nov. 1827 - Jan. 1828, Box 5: folder "SCR (Claims-Military)").
    (3). Bill to secure Jane Becknall of Ashe County, wife of Henry Becknall, what property she may hereafter acquire. In Senate, 1 and 2 January 1828, read three times, passed, and ordered to be engrossed. In House of Commons, 2 January 1828, read three times, passed, and ordered to be enrolled. (GASR, Nov. 1827 - Jan. 1828, Box 3: folder "SB 1 Jan.")

615. **Bell, Rhoda and husband, Jeconias.**
    (1). Petition of Rhoda (+) Bell of Beaufort County sheweth she was married 9 January 1821 to Jeconias Bell of said county with whom she lived in peace and comparative happiness until Christmas of the same year. At that time, he was in a continued state of the most brutal intoxication and made several attempts on the life of your petitioner. He would have completed his diabolical and murderess intentions had he not been prevented by others. From Christmas 1821 to June 1825, said Jeconias, when drunk or sober and without provocation on her part, generally treated your petitioner with the most wanton indignity and unheard of barbarity. At length in the month of June as aforesaid, he left his wife and absented himself for more than two years, never informing her of his place of residence. She received a report that he was dead, but during the month of August last, said Jeconias returned to the neighborhood and took up with a Delia Bartlett, a girl of base notoriety. He remained in the vicinity about a fortnight (during which time your petitioner saw him once for about fifteen or twenty minutes). He went away and carried the said Delia with him. Prays for a divorce from the bonds of matrimony with said Jeconias. Dated 8 December 1827 at Pantego. (GASR, Nov. 1827 - Jan. 1828, Box 6: folder "Petitions (Divorce & Alimony)").
    (2). Deposition of Asa Simmons of Beaufort County confirmed the above petitioner's claim that her husband Jeconias became very abusive to his said wife about Christmas time in 1821 or 1822 and made several attempts on her life with different weapons. This deponent believes that Rhoda Bell's life would have been taken if it had not been prevented by this deponent and others. When Jeconias returned to the neighborhood after a two year absence, he took up at the house of a Mrs. Bartlett, a person of ill fame. This deponent heard from said Jeconias that he intended to take Mrs. Bartlett and her daughter, Delia, with him when he left and stated he would never stay with his wife another day. Dated 8 December 1827. (GASR, Nov. 1827 - Jan. 1828, Box 6: folder "Petitions (Divorce & Alimony)").

(3). Deposition of Thomas B. Winfield of Beaufort County confirms his observation of Jeconias Bell about Christmas of 1822 that said Bell was being intoxicated and abusive towards his wife. Dated 14 November 1827. (GASR, Nov. 1827 - Jan. 1828, Box 6: folder "Petitions (Divorce & Alimony)").

(4). Deposition of Joseph (+) Winfield of Beaufort County states he tended a crop with Jeconias Bell in 1823 or 1824 and frequently heard him use very abusive language to his wife Rhoda and wish her death. I saw him strike her but once. After an absence of a little more than two years from his wife, said Jeconias never went to see his wife but stayed with a Mrs. Bartlett, whose daughter, according to others, has gone away with Jeconias. Dated 14 November 1827. (GASR, Nov. 1827 - Jan. 1828, Box 6: folder "Petitions (Divorce & Alimony)").

616. **Bigham, Robert [Jr.] and wife, Mary "Polly."**
(1). Petition of Robert Bigham of Mecklenburg County represents he intermarried with Mary Jackson[101] sometime in 1815 and together had four children. They lived together until August 1824, when he separated himself from his wife because he detected her in an illicit intercourse with one Hamilton in the house of your petitioner. He also withdrew his children from the management of his wife and placed them under the protection of his female relations. Prays for a law to dissolve the bonds of matrimony between your petitioner and his said wife. (GASR, Nov. 1827 - Jan. 1828, Box 1: "HB 22 Dec.")

(2). Deposition of Thomas I/J Greer before Alex Greer, J.P. of Mecklenburg County, 25 November 1827: On 28 August 1824, he was at the house of Robert Bigham, Sr., and met Polly Bigham, wife of Robert Bigham, Jr. Said Polly acknowledged that her husband had caught her in bed with one John Hamilton in the house of her husband, drew her out of bed and discharged her from his bed and board. She also stated that if some friends would interpose to have the breech healed, she would endeavour to act more prudently for the future. Your deponent notes that said Robert Bigham, Jr., still continues to keep said Polly discharged and has not lived with said Polly since the incident. [Below:] Deposition of Robert Bigham, Sr., that said Robert Bigham, Jr., obstinately refuses any intercourse whatever with the said Polly Bigham as his wife. Dated 21 November 1827. (GASR, Nov. 1827 - Jan. 1828, Box 1: "HB 22 Dec.")

(3). Committee of Divorce and Alimony to whom was referred the petition of Robert Bigham, Jr., of Mecklenburg County recommend the accompanying bill: Bill to divorce Robert Bigham from his wife, Mary. [On reverse:] In House, 22 December, read first time and rejected. (GASR, Nov. 1827 - Jan. 1828, Box 1: "HB 22 Dec.")

617. **Brasher, Priscilla and husband, Nathan.**
(1). Memorial of Priscilla Brasher [of Guilford County], dated 25 November 1827, represents she intermarried with her husband, Nathan Brasher,[102] about eight years ago and lived together in peace and quietness until a few months ago. Her husband did not follow any honest occupation for the purpose of obtaining a living the greater part of this time, and this Fall ran away and left her with one little daughter to maintain and no property and support except her own labor. It is not expected he will again return and prays for a law to secure to her such property as she may hereafter acquire. /s/ Priscilla Brasher and John Draughon. [On reverse:] "Messrs. Jonathan Parker, John W. Moorehead & Francis L. Simpson – I hope you will use your influence to cause the law prayed within to pass in favor of my Sis-

---

101   Marriage Bond of Mecklenburg County, North Carolina, dated 4 January 1815, lists Robert Bigham and Polly Jackson. Bondsman: John Porter.

102   Marriage Bond of Guilford County, North Carolina, dated 23 September 1819, lists Nathan Brasher and Prescilla Hunt. Bondsman: Andrew Merideth.

ter In Law and you will lay me under great obligation. /s/ Andrew Merridith. N.B. She is the daughter of Thomas Hunt Senr. and a woman of unspotted character." (GASR, Nov. 1827 - Jan. 1828, Box 2: folder "SB 19 Dec.")

(2). Committee of Divorce and Alimony to whom was referred the petition of Priscilla Brasher recommend passage of the accompanying bill: A Bill to secure to Priscilla Brasher such property as she may hereafter acquire. In Senate, 19 and 21 December, read three times, passed, and engrossed; In House of Commons, 21 December, read first time and rejected. (GASR, Nov. 1827 - Jan. 1828, Box 2: folder "SB 19 Dec.")

618. **Burgess, Elizabeth and husband, James.**
(1). Petition of Elizabeth Burgess [no county or state mentioned] sheweth she married a certain James Burgess in March 1826 and lived with him for six or seven weeks "altho he never treated her as a wife not even to Eat the first meal of victuals with her in his own house…" He finally refused her support and ordered her off with severe threats. She did not feel safe and removed to her father's. Some time during the winter following, said James left this part of the country for some of the western states with the intention of living in a state of separation. Prays for a divorce from said husband. Dated November 1827. [Below:] Signatures of eleven supporters. (GASR, Nov. 1827 - Jan. 1828, Box 4: folder "HCR (Agriculture-Internal Improvements)").

(2). Committee of Divorce and Alimony to whom was referred the petition of Elizabeth Burgess report unfavorably to the prayer of the petitioner on the ground that the absence of the husband has been too short to warrant interference. [On reverse:] In House of Commons, 10 December, read and concurred with. (GASR, Nov. 1827 - Jan. 1828, Box 4: folder "HCR (Agriculture-Internal Improvements)").

619. **Bryan, Jonathan and wife, Ann Jane.** Petition of Jonathan Bryan of Wilmington, New Hanover County, North Carolina. On 1 January 1823, your petitioner was married to Ann Jane Anders. A very short time after said marriage, she left your petitioner's bed and board without just cause or his leave or consent, but expressly against his will and located herself in Bladen County, remaining absent between three and four weeks. During this time, your petitioner was confined with the bilious fever, and he sent his son to his said wife to tell her of his dangerous situation and the necessity of her returning home. She did so, but her conduct in administering the medicine prescribed by the attending physician, including the improper liquids poured into his drinks led your petitioner to believe that anything but his restoration to health was intended. Instead of dressing the blisters of his sickness according to the usual manner, he was compelled to think that her own method was a design for his death. Such was his conviction that he would not take any medicine from her hands nor permit her to drop his blisters. In December 1823, his said wife left his dwelling and remained absent nine or ten months. She returned home through the persuasion of a clergyman and raised an insurrection among your petitioner's servants, and when he interposed, he was thrown against a large bench and dangerously wounded by a Negro woman that formerly belonged to the said wife of the petitioner. The same said wife, Ann Jane, used many threats and encouraged the servants in the affray, so much so that your petitioner sent for an officer. One of the servants was taken to jail, and the said wife told your petitioner she would have him hung. In April 1824, the said Ann Jane, having drunk spirits very freely, used many threats, and your petitioner retired to his gunsmith's shop. In a few moments the "kook" [cook] appeared at the shop door and said- "Sir mind how you ate brakefast Mistress has thrown Somthing into the victuals[.] He went into the hall and throwed the Sweetning out [,] refused to drink the coffy made by her but nearly Lost his life by takeing a small piece of ham upon which ratsbain [ratsbane - arsenic trioxide] or som other poisonous droug had been thrown…" He was led to believe that the quantity was too great for the purpose intended, for

Divorces and Separations from Petitions to the North Carolina General Assembly from 1779

it was thrown up by a violent vomiting that followed. Your petitioner further states that the said Ann Jane at different times has threatened his life, has laid violent hands on his person twice, and has treated with cruelty the seven children he has had by a decent and former wife. Early in 1825, the said Ann Jane absconded the third time to Bladen County and remained absent for eleven months, during which time "she got herself with child and finding it would be diseased, she returned to Wilmington and took medicine and miscarried in the kitchen of your petitioner." In consequence of the same, her life was greatly endangered. As soon as her health would permit (about three or four weeks), she finally left her bed and board and has been absent one year and ten months. Your petitioner has not seen the said Ann Jane during this time, but she has been living with negros. Prays for a divorce from Ann Jane, his said wife. [On reverse are quotations from the Bible. Accompanying this petition are depositions from eight supporters of the petitioner.] (GASR, Nov. 1827 - Jan. 1828, Box 6: folder "Petitions (Divorce & Alimony)").

620. **Bryant, Mary and husband, Eli.**
(1). Petition of Mary Bryant of Haywood County states she became acquainted with Eli Bryant, a native of the State of Tennessee, in the Spring of 1810. After a short but constant courtship, they were married, and for twelve months it appeared that the morning sun of happiness would never set. However, in a few weeks after this time, said Eli made a pretense to go about thirty miles into Buncombe County to collect some money, but did not return for eighteen months. He excused the matter as well as he could, and we commenced living together again. After a few weeks, her husband said we must move to the State of Tennessee, and after some persuasion, we did move there. After living there some time, said Eli would frequently abuse your petitioner, and at length left her there in a strange land with no friends to administer to her necessities. Your petitioner procured money through her own industry and hired a man and horse to bring her home to her parents. However, the said Eli reappeared with his artful flattery, and through his persuasions and those of the friends of your petitioner, your petitioner and her husband made up the breach a third time. In about a month, the said Eli found an opportunity to steal what little property your petitioner had acquired and my infant child, the last relict of happiness which your petitioner had. She has not seen her husband nor her little babe, which was at her breast, for three years now. Requests consideration of her case and to pass an act to separate her from her said husband. [Below:] Signatures of seven subscribers. (GASR, Nov. 1827 - Jan. 1828, Box 1: folder "HB 10 Dec.")
(2). Committee of Divorce and Alimony to whom was referred the petition of Mary Bryant of Haywood County report favorably on the request of the petitioner and submit the accompanying bill: Bill to divorce Mary Bryant of Haywood County from her husband, Eli Bryant. In House, 10 December and 21 December, read two times and rejected. (GASR, Nov. 1827 - Jan. 1828, Box 1: folder "HB 10 Dec.")

621. **Carter, Jerry and wife, Polly.** Petition of Jerry Carter of Cabarrus County states he has been married to Polly Mires and has treated her with that honourable esteem due to a woman in the station of life to which his ability would permit. However, for some cause unknown to him, she has left his bed and board, lives with another man, and has been delivered of a child two years after leaving your petitioner. She has also behaved and conducted herself in such a manner that the laws of common decency forbid the prospect of a happy life. Prays to be "devourced" from his said wife. [Below:] Signatures of twenty subscribers. (GASR, Nov. 1827 - Jan. 1828, Box 4: folder "HCR (Agriculture-Internal Improvements)").

1827-1828 Session

622. **Crittenden, Christianna and husband, John.**

(1). Petition of Christianna Crittenden of Stokes County sheweth that her husband, John Crittenden, absconded from her bed and board about eight years ago without any just cause and has since intermarried (as your petitioner has been credibly informed) with another woman somewhere in the State of Tennessee, leaving your memorialist to the mercy of her friends and her own industry to maintain herself. Prays for an act to secure to her all such property as she may hereafter acquire. Dated 15 September 1827. [Below:] Signatures of eleven persons who say they have been acquainted with the petitioner, an elderly woman at this time, for a number of years past and recommend her prayer be granted. (GASR, Nov. 1827 - Jan. 1828, Box 5: folder "SCR (Claims-Military)").

(2). Committee on Divorce and Alimony to whom was referred the petition of Cristianna Crittenden of Stokes County report that the facts in the petition are true and recommend the prayer of the petitioner be allowed and the accompanying bill be passed. [On reverse:] In Senate, 4 December, read and bill put upon its passage. (GASR, Nov. 1827 - Jan. 1828, Box 5: folder "SCR (Claims-Military)").

(3). Bill to secure Christianna Crittenden of Stokes County, wife of John Crittenden, such property as she may hereafter acquire. In Senate, 4 December, read three times, passed, and ordered to be engrossed. In House, 7, 10, and 12 December, read three times, passed, and ordered to be engrossed. (GASR, Nov. 1827 - Jan. 1828, Box 2: folder "SB 4 Dec.")

623. **Culpeper, Elizabeth and husband, Charles.**

(1). Petition of Elizabeth Culpeper sheweth she intermarried with Charles Culpeper of Montgomery County sometime in 1825. Within a few months of the marriage, she "discovered his entire incapacity to provide for the support of a family owing as your petitioner believes to his indolence and want of exertion together with evident marks of alienation of mind which was discoverable to your Petitioner by frequent indications of a determination on his part to distroy his own life or the life of your petitioner." He remained in this situation a few months and left your petitioner without any means of support for the State of Tennessee where he remained nearly a year. He returned to the neighborhood of your petitioner and remained in the woods, apparently wishing to conceal himself from public notice. After some months, he went to the State of Georgia, as your petitioner is informed, where he has remained ever since. Your petitioner at the time of marriage was young and an orphan, having lost both father and mother. Her husband's family were respectable, and she was induced to marry him to procure the means of support. However, she was left in distress without any hope of reconciliation with her husband and dependent upon the charity of her friends and her own little exertions. Prays for a law to divorce her from her said husband. [Below:] Signatures of fifteen subscribers who support the above petition. (GASR, Nov. 1827 - Jan. 1828, Box 5: folder "SCR (Claims-Military)").

(2). Committee of Divorce and Alimony to whom was referred the petition of Elizabeth Culpeper respectfully report the accompanying bill. [On reverse:] In Senate, 22 December, read and bill put upon passage. (GASR, Nov. 1827 - Jan. 1828, Box 5: folder "SCR (Claims-Military)").

(3). Bill to divorce Elizabeth Culpeper of Montgomery County from her husband, Charles. In Senate, 22 December, read first time and passed; read second time and resolved that same shall not pass. (GASR, Nov. 1827 - Jan. 1828, Box 3: folder "SB 22 Dec.")

624. **Davis, Susan P. and husband, Wiley.** Petition of Susan P. Davis of Franklin County states she married Wiley O. Davis some fifteen or sixteen years ago and lived as man and wife for many years. Some seven or eight years ago, said Wiley took it into his head to abandon her and her four infant children which had been the fruit of their matrimony. As it was understood by his acquaintances, he went to New Orleans, but your petitioner has never heard from him. She was left in an abject and dependent

Divorces and Separations from Petitions to the North Carolina General Assembly from 1779

situation and has been compelled to labor for the support of her children and herself except for what she can obtain from her charitable friends. She has long since lost all hope that he, said husband, will ever return to his family. Prays for a divorce from said husband. (GASR, Nov. 1827 - Jan. 1828, Box 6: folder "Petitions (Divorce & Alimony)").

625.   **Dowling, Eliza and husband, Zacheus.** Committee on Divorce and Alimony to whom was referred the Petition of Eliza Dowling of Mecklenburg County praying to be divorced from her husband, Zacheus Dowling, report that said Eliza when quite young was prevailed upon by her husband, an itinerant preacher of the Methodist Society, to become his wife in opposition to the wishes of her parents and friends. She accompanied her husband in his calling and for nine months encountered hardship incident to the wandering life as well as the frowns, threats and ill treatment of her husband. She was afraid to remain with him and returned to her father in ill health in the Summer of 1821. Her husband, for the purpose of mortifying her feelings and making her a subject of public contempt, advertised her in the public Gazette stating he would not be accountable for any of her debts or contracts. After the death of the petitioner's father, said Zacheus gave notice to the administrators that he would claim all the estate to which he was entitled as husband of said Eliza. The petitioner believed the said Zacheus intended to deprive her of the means of subsistence and filed a petition at the November Session, 1826, of the Court of Equity which gave the said Eliza a divorce from bed and board, and $833 alimony, it being two-thirds of the amount to which she was entitled as a distributee in the estate of her deceased father. The said Zacheus, who received the remaining one-third of the settlement, continues to harass his said wife and has not made any efforts to reconcile with her for six years. Your committee recommends passage of the accompanying bill: A Bill to divorce Eliza Dowling from her husband Zacheus Dowling in as full and ample a manner as if they had never been joined. In Senate, 19 December, read third time, passed and bill put on its passage. In House of Commons, 21 December, read first time, and rejected. (GASR, Nov. 1827 - Jan. 1828, Box 2: folder "SB 19 Dec.")

626.   **Edney, Samuel J. and wife, Olivia.**
(1).   Petition of Samuel J. Edney of Buncombe County states that he is a young man of reputable parentage and connections and that his reputation, with the exception of a single affair, the particulars of which it is now necessary for him to detail, has not been such as to disappoint the hopes and expectations of his friends. He regrets to be compelled to speak thus of himself and still move to detail the history of an individual who is the cause of the misfortunes which at present overwhelm him. It is now nearly three years since your petitioner established himself as a merchant in this county at an age at which five persons are qualified to manage business transactions and in a settlement remote from the residence of his friends who might have watched over his course of life, and by proper advice, have secured a correct course of conduct. His success in business however was flattering, and his prospects in life in all respects as promising as could have been anticipated, until yielding to the allurements which are too apt to beguile the young and the thoughtless, he permitted himself to associate with a female by the name of Olivia Elkins whose beauty was the only recommendation she could have presented to one of riper years and maturer judgment. In a moment of inebriety however, this woman operating partly upon his fears and partly on his passions, seduced him into a marriage which has brought sorrow upon his friends and misery upon himself. The lapse of five months made her the mother of an illegitimate child sometime previous to which your petitioner committed her to the protection of her friends, since which time more than two years he has had no connexion with her. Her conduct since their separation has been anything else than that of a chaste and virtuous woman, and the day has gone by when a reconciliation could be hoped for. Under these circumstances your petitioner has been induced to spread the fact of his

case before the only tribunal clothed by the laws of the country with the powers to afford him relief by granting a divorce. [Below:] Signatures of thirty-two subscribers. (GASR, Nov. 1827 - Jan. 1828, Box 6: folder "Petitions (Divorce & Alimony)").

(2). Deposition of Andrew (x) Banks before James H. Poteet, J.P. of Buncombe County in October 1827, that the deponent has seen Olly Edney, wife of Saml. J. Edney, in bed with another man after night. (GASR, Nov. 1827 - Jan. 1828, Box 6: folder "Petitions (Divorce & Alimony)").

627. **Everitt, Winifred and husband, John.**

(1). Petition of Winifred (x) Everitt of Anson County sheweth she was legally married to John Everitt on or about 15 January 1818. On or about 20 September 1819, her said husband separated himself from her without visible cause or provocation, and in the Spring of 1821, he left this state and has not yet returned. She took all measures to conciliate and preserve the affections of said husband, but he did often abuse and ill treat her, and frequently threatened to kill her. Four or five times he actually assaulted and beat her to the great danger of her life. Notwithstanding those acts of violence, your petitioner continued to demean herself as a dutiful and obedient wife. She firmly believes a reconciliation impracticable as leading to a state of intolerable misery or wretchedness. Prays for a divorce from the bonds of matrimony between her and said husband. [Below:] Signatures of twelve subscribers who certify they have been acquainted with the petitioner since infancy, believe her to be a virtuous and honest woman, and hope the Legislature will grant her prayer. (GASR, Nov. 1827 - Jan. 1828, Box l, folder "HB 10 Dec.")

(2). Depositions of John Adams, Alexander Fields and Mrs. Edna Hailey before Hugh McKenzie, J.P., relate their eyewitness observations of said John Everitt, who cussed, beat and dragged his wife, Winifred, forcefully in their presence as he attempted to get her to go with him. (GASR, Nov. 1827 - Jan. 1828, Box l, folder "HB 10 Dec.")

(3). Committee of Divorce and Alimony to whom was referred the petition of Winifred Everitt recommend the passing of the accompanying bill: A Bill to divorce Winifred Everitt from her husband, John Everitt. In House, 10 and 12 December, read two times and rejected. (GASR, Nov. 1827 - Jan. 1828, Box l, folder "HB 10 Dec.")

628. **Faust, John and wife, Mary.** Petition of John Faust of Stokes County states he intermarried in 1815 with one Mary Corzine, then a widow, and had every reason to believe he was marrying a woman with whom he could spend his life in amity and comfort; that for aught he knew, she was everything that she seemed to be. He had not long been married to her before acts of unkindness, inhumanity, and even brutality characterized her conduct towards him as her husband. Most of the time since the marriage, your petitioner has been rendered wretched and miserable, for she has not been satisfied with heaping her abuse, curses and execrations upon him, but has declared her pReference F.or other men and has carried off most of the articles of personal property. She is now away from home, having separated herself from him. Her character now is extremely suspicious, for she appears to place others in as high a place in her affections as himself. His wife will not at all contribute to provide for their mutual support, but seems to do herself great pleasure in exercising as mistress of the premises, her authority in wasting and destroying everything that is accumulated by your petitioner. Your petitioner is in circumstances extremely indigent. He desires to spend the remainder of his days in peace with a degree of comfort, but he cannot do this while encumbered with a wife so perversely disposed. His life has become wholly intolerable. Prays for a law divorcing him from his said wife, Mary. [Below:] Signatures of some thirty-five subscribers in support of the petitioner. (GASR, Nov. 1827 - Jan. 1828, Box 4: folder "HCR (Agriculture-Internal Improvements)").

Divorces and Separations from Petitions to the North Carolina General Assembly from 1779

629. **Flowers, Sally and husband, Christopher.** Petition of Sally Flowers of Craven County states she was married in May 1822 to Christopher Flowers[103] of Craven County by whom she had one child and fondly hoped to have lived a life of harmony, but sometime in January 1823, the said Christopher deserted her without provocation and removed to Hyde County where he associated with another woman and has lived in defiance of all laws temporal and spiritual in a state of adultery with said woman. Prays that the bonds of matrimony between her and her said husband be absolved. [Below:] Signatures of eight subscribers in support of the petitioner. (GASR, Nov. 1827 - Jan. 1828, Box 6: folder "Petitions (Divorce & Alimony)").

630. **Gilmore, Amy and husband, Stephen.**
(1). Petition of Amy Gilmore states she intermarried with Stephen Gilmore[104] in 1818 and fondly hoped to spend her life in peace, harmony and conjugal affection. Shortly after the marriage, said Stephen removed your petitioner to the State of Georgia where they lived quietly for upwards of twelve months. Said Stephen gave himself up to habits of intoxication and became most cruel and abusive to your petitioner. He kept this up for something like four years, including beatings and whippings which made marks on her that she still carries to this day. Your petitioner further states that during the five to six years she lived with said husband, he several times shot at her with a gun, and more than once would have killed her but for providential interference. She has always been at a loss to know why she was mistreated and abused by said Stephen. She was advised by her friends in Georgia to leave him for her own security, and she did so and returned to her father's residence in Orange County, North Carolina, where she has resided the last four years. Your petitioner cannot brook the idea of ever living with said Stephen again inasmuch as she believes strongly that her life would be in danger. Prays for an act to divorce her from the said Stephen. Dated 6 December 1827. (GASR, Nov. 1827 - Jan. 1828, Box 6: folder "Petitions (Divorce & Alimony)").
(2). Certificate, dated 21 January 1823, Jasper County, Georgia: We certify that we have been acquainted with Mr. and Mrs. Gilmore ever since their residence in Georgia. We believe that Mrs. Gilmore was pure and chaste, and any charges alleged against her by the said Stephen Gilmore of a disrespectful nature are false, ungrounded and without the least evidence or suspicion. She is entitled to the attention and civility of all good people. Towards the latter part of 1821, Stephen Gilmore did wantonly abuse and treat her most inhumanely. /s/ Burt Crawford, Chas. McDowell, Allin Martin, Hugh H. Heard, Yearby Martin, Thomas Edmondson, George Crain, John S. Drew, John Heard. (GASR, Nov. 1827 - Jan. 1828, Box 6: folder "Petitions (Divorce & Alimony)").
(3). Deposition of Mary Pearson of Orange County, North Carolina, mother of Amy Gilmore (wife of Stephen Gilmore) and deposition of Joel A. Pearson, brother of said Amy Gilmore, both depositions dated 6 December 1827, provide the following information: Said Amy Gilmore came to her father's home in Orange County about four years ago, where she now resides. Your deponents saw her arms, neck and legs- which bore evidence of her having been severely whipped, and the said Amy said she had been beaten by Stephen Gilmore, her husband, before she left Georgia. (GASR, Nov. 1827 - Jan. 1828, Box 6: folder "Petitions (Divorce & Alimony)").

---

103 Marriage Bond of Craven County, North Carolina, dated 13 August 1822, lists Christopher Flowers and Sally Phipps. Bondsman: Robert (x) Phipps.

104 Marriage Bond of Wake County, North Carolina, dated 26 May 1818, lists Stephen Gilmore and Amy Pearson. Bondsman: Saml. Goodwin.

1827-1828 Session

631. **Hamblet, Rachel and husband, William.** Petition of Rachel Hamblet of Chatham County states she intermarried with William Hamblet,[105] a young man at that time of respectability and some property, some years past. They lived together happily for several years, but the said William became dissipated and spent all of his property as well as the property my father gave me. In addition, he has forsaken me entirely and taken up with a negro woman and been guilty of such other immoral conduct that no woman could live with him if he would permit her. These facts can be substantiated by a respectable member of your body. Prays for a divorce from the bonds of matrimony with said husband and a law to secure such property as I may hereafter acquire. Dated 28 November 1827. (GASR, Nov. 1827 - Jan. 1828, Box 6: folder "Petitions (Divorce & Alimony)").

632. **Holland, William and wife, Esther.**

(1). Committee of Divorce and Alimony to whom was referred the bill to divorce William Holland of Craven County from his wife Esther, together with a petition [not in this file] of said Holland praying for a divorce from his wife and a petition of many respectable citizens of said county [petition not in this file] praying that the prayer of said Holland may be granted, beg to report that said Holland intermarried with Esther Parsons, the widow of Nathan Parsons of Craven County on 7 February 1822. Prompted by affection, he hoped to obtain a companion who would share the enjoyment of life and soften its harshest trials. His circumstances were above mediocrity and free from embarassment, and she was the widow of a bankrupt. There was no striking disparity in their ages, and he believed his affection reciprocated on the part of his spouse. They lived in harmony until 22 August in the same year when, under pretense of visiting her relatives living in an adjoining county, she abandoned him. He has repeatedly entreated her to return, but she has turned a deaf ear to his prayers. She even refused to see him and avows her determination never to live with him. Your Committee joins with the respectable citizens from Craven County in recommending the case by legislative interposition and report the accompanying bill. [On reverse:] In Senate, 17 December, read, and accompanying bill put upon its passage. (GASR, Nov. 1827 - Jan. 1828, Box 5: folder "SCR (Claims-Military)").

(2). Bill to divorce William Holaand of Craven County from his wife, Esther. In Senate, 17 and 18 December, read three times and ordered to be engrossed. In House, 18 December, read first time and rejected. (GASR, Nov. 1827 - Jan. 1828, Box 2: folder "SB 26 Nov.")

633. **Ingram, Jennet and husband, Matthew.**

(1). Petition of Jennet Ingram of Montgomery County represents she married Matthew Ingram about nineteen years ago, but he gave himself up to intoxication and other vicious practices in a few months and frequently abused and "illy treated" your petitioner. By her own industry and laborious exertions, she provided her own subsistence, but his only care about it was to spend it in the indulgence of his own corrupt and immoral practices. Some fifteen or sixteen years ago, your petitioner applied by petition to the General Assembly to secure to her such property as she may thereafter acquire, and a law was passed to that effect to enable her to support herself and two children. If a law was passed to divorce her from the said Matthew, she and her children would be much better protected against the ill treatment of her said husband. Prays for the passage of such a law. Dated 15 October 1827. [Below:] Signatures of five persons who attest to the petitioner's good moral character and industry. (GASR, Nov. 1827 - Jan. 1828, Box 5: folder "SCR (Claims-Military)").

(2). The Committee of Divorce and Alimony to whom was referred the petition of Jennet Ingram of Montgomery County report that it cannot believe the case sufficiently aggravated to demand

---

105   Marriage Bond of Chatham County, North Carolina, dated 29 September 1812, lists W. Hamblet and Rachel Dismukes. Bondsman: Elisha Poe.

legislative interposition. In Senate, 19 December, read and concurred in. (GASR, Nov. 1827 - Jan. 1828, Box 5: folder "SCR (Claims-Military)").

634. **Justice, William.** Committee of Divorce and Alimony to whom was referred the petition of William Justice of Buncombe County praying to be divorced from his wife report unfavorably to the prayer of the petitioner. [On reverse:] The petition and attendant documents delivered to Mr. Allen of Buncombe on order of the House, 7 December. (GASR, Nov. 1827 - Jan. 1828, Box 4: folder "HCR (Agriculture-Internal Improvements)").

635. **Layfong, Mary and husband, Benedict.** Petition of Mary Layfong of Haywood County sheweth she intermarried in 1821 with one Benedict Layfong. For some time of the marriage, she was kept in continued fear of her life by said Benedict until he finally left her bed and has continued to live in a state of separation from her for six years. He has failed to maintain, comfort or assist her as he was bound to do, but threatens to marry some other person and leave her entirely. Prays to be granted a divorce from the bonds of matrimony. [Below:] Signatures of forty-two subscribers. (GASR, Nov. 1827 - Jan. 1828, Box 6: folder "Petitions (Divorce & Alimony)").

636. **McKaughan, Phebe and husband, Hugh.**
(1). Memorial of Phebe McKaughan of Guilford County states her husband, Hugh McKaughan, deserted her and six small children in 1816 and has not returned. All of the property left by said Hugh has been seized and sold to pay his debts. Your petitioner's father died since her husband's property was exhausted, but her legacy has been applied to the payment of her husband's debts, and she has been left with no means of subsistence except for her own labor and the benevolence of friends. Prays for an act to secure to her such property as she now has or may hereafter acquire. [Below:] Signatures of fifteen supporters, citizens of Davidson County "from whence Hugh McKaughan absconded some years ago," who say that the memorialist "is a woman of good carecter and family." (GASR, Nov. 1827 - Jan. 1828, Box 4: folder "HCR (Agriculture-Internal Improvements)").
(2). Committee on Divorce and Alimony to whom was referred the petition of Phebe McCaucohan of Guilford County report the accompanying bill [not in this file]. (GASR, Nov. 1827 - Jan. 1828, Box 4: folder "HCR (Agriculture-Internal Improvements)").
(3). Bill to secure to Phebe McKaughan of Guilford County such property as she may hereafter acquire. Wife of Hugh McKaughan of Guilford. In House of Commons, 30 November and 1 December, read three times, passed, and ordered to be engrossed. In Senate, 4 December, read three times, passed, and ordered to be enrolled. (GASR, Nov. 1827 - Jan. 1828, Box 1: folder "HB 30 Nov.")

637. **Mills, James W. and wife, Mary Ann.** Petition of James W. Mills states he married Mary Ann Clawson about 3 June 1824 in York District, South Carolina. Some fifteen days after the marriage, said Mary Ann eloped from the house of the petitioner's father, "where by reason of the declining years of his parents and their having no other children, he had brought her to reside, and went to the house of a single man to whom, as is generally believed, she bore a child about seven months after petitioner's marriage with her, which was not born prematurely; and with which, as your petitioner has since learned and believes, she was then pregnant." He has since sought her several times to return to a reconciled, though much injured husband, and proposed to take her to the west or any place she would choose for a residence. She not only refused to do so, but on the last occasion drew a knife from her bosom, and said that if he insisted on his right to make her return, she would cut his throat. Your petitioner, finding that she was immoveably opposed to return to him and wholly abandoned to her seducer (with whom she has oc-

casionally cohabited) has given up all hopes of regaining his marital rights. Prays for a divorce from his wife, Mary Ann Mills. Sworn on 29 May 1827 before Saml. Henderson, J. P. of Mecklenburg County, North Carolina. [Below:] Notice to Mrs. Mary Ann Mills by James W. Mills of his intention to proceed with a divorce and the oaths of five supporters of the petitioner. (GASR, Nov. 1827 - Jan. 1828, Box 6: folder "Petitions (Divorce & Alimony)").

638. **Mitchel, Hannah and husband, Robert.** Petition of Hannah Mitchel of Granville County states that her husband, Robert Mitchel,[106] who has reduced his family to absolute indigence and want, deserted them some twelve months ago and has settled himself in some remote back settlement of the United States without an apparent prospect of returning. The said husband left her with no means of supporting her family, which included several small children, but left many debts that may sweep off any little property she may be able to collect. Prays for a law to secure such property as she may hereafter acquire. Dated 10 December 1827. (GASR, Nov. 1827 - Jan. 1828, Box 4: folder "HCR (Agriculture-Internal Improvements)").

639. **Mixon, Mary and husband, Jeremiah.**
(1). Petition of Mary Mixon of Perquimans County states she was married in 1822 to a certain Jeremiah Mixon,[107] then of said county. Your petitioner discharged the duties of a wife, notwithstanding the ill usage she received from him and his bad conduct as a husband and father. The said Jeremiah left your petitioner with an infant sometime in the year 1824 (after his property had been sold from him, and he had taken the oath of an insolvent debtor) destitute of means for her support, and went to some other state in the union. Your petitioner has not had any direct information from him since that time, but has every reason to believe he now lives in a state of adultery with some woman unknown to your petitioner. Prays for a law to dissolve the bonds of matrimony with said Jeremiah to enable her to provide for the support and maintenance of herself and child. [Below:] Signatures of nine subscribers who bear testimony that the above petitioner is an honest, industrious and honorable woman. (GASR, Nov. 1827 - Jan. 1828, Box 5: folder "SCR (Claims-Military)").
(2). Committee of Divorce and Alimony to whom was referred the petition of Mary Mison of Perquimans County report the accompanying bill. [On reverse:] In Senate, 22 December, read and Bill put upon passage. (GASR, Nov. 1827 - Jan. 1828, Box 5: folder "SCR (Claims-Military)").
(3). Bill to divorce Mary Mixen of Perquimans County from her husband, Jeremiah. In Senate, 22 December, read first time and passed; read second time and resolved that the same shall not pass. (GASR, Nov. 1827 - Jan. 1828, Box 3: folder "SB 22 Dec.")

640. **Pitcher, John and wife, Lucy.** Petition of John Pitcher of Rockingham County states he married Lucy Thornhill with whom he lived many years. He hoped that she would be a good and affectionate wife, but in this he was disappointed, for her conduct was at times exceedingly disagreeable and ended in court. In the year 1821, she was charged with committing a felony and tried in Rockingham County court. Two of the jury did not consent to find her guilty, and she was permitted to escape a verdict of guilty for a felony and convicted of a trespass. Your petitioner thought it his duty under all circumstances to employ counsel to defend her upon that occasion, which he did, but your petitioner must acknowledge that though he had hoped before the trial that she was not guilty, the evidence was so clear and satis-

---

106 Marriage Bond of Granville County, North Carolina, dated 24 July 1817, lists Robert Mitchell and Hannah Russell. Bondsman: Thos. Mitchel.
107 Marriage Bond of Perquimans County, North Carolina, dated 17 June 1822, lists Jeremiah Mixon and Mary White. Bondsman: Wm. N. White.

Divorces and Separations from Petitions to the North Carolina General Assembly from 1779

factory that he could not but believe she was guilty of the offense she was charged with. A short time thereafter she left the home of your petitioner and has never since returned but at short intervals, and has continued to live an abandoned and vicious course of life, being often charged since of committing petty thefts of which he feels she is guilty. Prays for a divorce from the bonds of matrimony from said Lucy Pitcher. [Below:] Signatures of thirty-eight persons who support the petitioner. (GASR, Nov. 1827 - Jan. 1828, Box 6: folder "Petitions (Divorce & Alimony)").

641. **Powers, John and wife, Cynthia.** Petition of John Powers states he was married on 22 August 1824 to Cynthia Hammond, who appeared to possess all the virtues necessary to constitute happiness in the state of matrimony. Unfortunately, he discovered in a very short time that his said wife was abandoned in principle and engaged in every species of moral turpitude. In the course of twelve months after the marriage, she left him thirteen times, and despite his friendly persuasions to the contrary, she finally refused to live with him and has since had two children by other men. When living with him, she maliciously "bound him to the peace & used every means in her power to render him unhappy." Your petitioner has not seen her in two years and never intends to live with her again. Prays for a divorce. Dated 27 October 1827. [Below:] Signatures of twenty subscribers who recommend that the prayer of the petitioner be allowed. [108] (GASR, Nov. 1827 - Jan. 1828, Box 4: folder "HCR (Agriculture-Internal Improvements)").

642. **Price, Sarah and husband, Meridith.** Petition of Sarah Price of Caswell County prays for a law to secure to her and her children (free from the control of her husband, Meridith Price)[109] all such property as she shall hereafter acquire. Said husband has not made any provisions for the support of his wife and children for several years. He appears to have no other care or study on his mind than to haunt taverns and other places where he may procure spirits, totally neglecting even to see his family for months. If her husband had thousands of dollars, his thirst for spirits, his indolence and inattention to any kind of business would soon have squandered away this scene. [Below:] Signatures of eight persons who subscribe to the prayer of the petitioner. (GASR, Nov. 1827 - Jan. 1828, Box 6: folder "Petitions (Divorce & Alimony)").

643. **Price, Washington and wife, Susan.** Bill to divorce Washington Price of Wake County from his wife, Susan.[110] In Senate, 17 December 1827, read second time and ordered that same shall not pass. (GASR, Nov. 1827 - Jan. 1828, Box 2: folder "SB 17 Dec.")

644. **Pugh, Edward S. and wife, Lydia.**
   (1). Petition of Edward S. Pugh of Camden County sheweth that some time in November 1826, his wife Lydia left his bed and board and took up with one Tully Dozier, and has never since returned home. Previous to her elopement, she had been constantly in the practice of cohabiting with other men, particularly in the absence of your petitioner, who followed the sea for a livelihood. By her extravagance and dissipation, she squandered away everything your petitioner could earn by his labour. Her

---

108 County of residence of petitioner is not stated, but subscribers include: Daniel Welch, Bennet Hargroves, Fielden Davis, Taylor Westmoreland, and Jacob Salmons – all listed in the Census of 1820 for Stokes County, North Carolina.
109 Marriage Bond of Caswell County, North Carolina, dated 13 April 1819, lists Meridith Price and Sarah McDaniel. Bondsman: Thomas Penick.
110 Marriage Bond of Orange County, North Carolina, dated 2 October 1823, lists Washington Price and Susan Webb. Bondsman: Holadey R. Oldham.

ill humour, vicious habits and immoral conduct is such as to render it impossible for them ever to live together again as man and wife. Prays for a separation from the bonds of matrimony with said Lydia. (GASR, Nov. 1827 - Jan. 1828, Box 6: folder "Petitions (Divorce & Alimony)").

(2). Notice from Edwd. A. Pugh to Mrs. Lydia Pugh that he will take depositions from Silas and Jacob Forbes and others to accompany a petition to the next General Assembly praying for a divorce from the bonds of matrimony between said Lydia and Edward Pugh. (GASR, Nov. 1827 - Jan. 1828, Box 6: folder "Petitions (Divorce & Alimony)").

(3). Accompanying depositions to petition above:

(a) Deposition of Silas Forbes states that Tully Dozier and Lydia Pugh, wife of Edward S. Pugh, have taken up and cohabit together. (GASR, Nov. 1827 - Jan. 1828, Box 6: folder "Petitions (Divorce & Alimony)").

(b) Deposition of Abigail Forbes, wife of Jacob Forbes, deposes that the above deposition of Silas Forbes is true and that she has seen them in the act of adultery more than once in the woods and other places. The deponent heard the said Lydia Pugh say that her last child was Tully Dozier's. Said deponent was midwife at the time the child was born. (GASR, Nov. 1827 - Jan. 1828, Box 6: folder "Petitions (Divorce & Alimony)").

(c) Deposition of Jacob Forbes states that the deposition of Silas Forbes is true and that the deponent is a near neighbor to the said Pughs. In conversation with Lydia Pugh, she said she'd as soon have a live bear put his paw on her as her said husband put his hand on her, and that she would not live with him. (GASR, Nov. 1827 - Jan. 1828, Box 6: folder "Petitions (Divorce & Alimony)").

(d) Deposition of Britanna (x) Forbes states that the deposition of Silas Forbes is true and further says she saw said Tully Dozier run out of the house in a secret manner when the petitioner was coming home. (GASR, Nov. 1827 - Jan. 1828, Box 6: folder "Petitions (Divorce & Alimony)").

645. **Reed, Hugh and wife, Susannah.**

(1). Committee of Divorce and Alimony to whom was referred the petition of Hugh Reed of Burke County report that the petitioner when very young was married to Susan Johnson with whom he lived until she became the mother of four children. During this period, his feelings were incessantly tortured by the knowledge of her imprudent act [not explained] and insulted by the unblushing avowal of them on her part – that yielding to the solicitations of his wife and anxious for the welfare and character of his rising family, he removed in the year 1822 to Indiana. They had scarcely progressed in their journey when his cherished anticipation of reform in his consort [was] blasted by the…disposition she evinced of destroying his property and squandering his money…[A]fter their removal, she left him and associated herself with a family of disgraced reputation…one of whom she became pregnant. Further, it has been proven that said Hugh Reed is a man of sober, industrious habits and that said Susannah Johnson has always had the character of an imprudent and lewd woman…In tender consideration of all [these] aggravated circumstances, your Committee reports the accompanying bill. (GASR, Nov. 1827 - Jan. 1828, Box 1: folder "HB 10 Dec.")

(2). Bill to divorce Hugh Reed of Burke County from his wife, Susannah Reed. [On reverse:] In House, 10 and 31 December 1827, read two times and rejected. (GASR, Nov. 1827 - Jan. 1828, Box 1: folder "HB 10 Dec.")

646. **Roberts/Roberds, William and wife, Peggy.**

(1). Petition of William Roberds of Buncombe County states his wife, Peggy, has left his bed and board without any known cause and has absented herself from him for some eight to ten years. The greater part of that time has been living in adultery with another man. Prays for a divorce. [Below:]

Divorces and Separations from Petitions to the North Carolina General Assembly from 1779

Signatures of nineteen subscribers. (GASR, Nov. 1827 - Jan. 1828, Box 6: folder "Petitions (Divorce & Alimony)").

(2). Committee of Divorce and Alimony to whom was referred the petition of William Roberts of Buncombe County praying to be divorced from his wife, Peggy, report unfavorably to the prayer of the petitioner. [On reverse:] In House of Commons, 5 December, read and laid upon the table. (GASR, Nov. 1827 - Jan. 1828, Box 4: folder "HCR (Agriculture-Internal Improvements)").

647. **Rowland, Mary Eliza and husband, Alfred.**

(1). Petition of Mary Eliza Rowland, wife of Alfred Rowland of Robeson County, represents that she intermarried with said husband in 1809. At the time of marriage, she was possessed of a considerable paternal estate. In 1814, property of considerable value was devised to her by the Will of her mother to be secured to your petitioner and her children separate and apart from her husband. However, owing to some informality in drafting the instrument or want of legal technicality of expression, it was held that the property thus devised was not so secured as to protect it from the control of her husband or being subject to the payment of any debt which he contracted. At the time of her marriage and unknown to your petitioner, her husband was much involved in debt and possessed of little property. By endorsements for others, unfortunate speculation and the low price of property, the whole of her paternal and maternal estate has been sold to satisfy the claims of his creditors and your petitioner reduced to a state of dependence and want. She has two children tenderly reared and dependent upon his exertions for support, maintenance and education. She has many wealthy, influential relatives and friends where charitable feelings would go far to alleviate her conditions if by any means they could afford her relief without the same being subject to the claims of her husband's creditors. Prays for an act in her own name to secure to her any property she may acquire. Dated 5 December 1827. (GASR, Nov. 1827 - Jan. 1828, Box 2: folder "SB 11 Dec.")

(2). Committee of Propositions and Grievances to whom was referred the petition of Mary E. Rowland of Robeson County recommends the following bill: Bill to secure to Mary E. Rowland of Robeson County such property as she may hereafter acquire. In Senate, 11, 12, and 13 December 1827, read three times, passed, and ordered to be engrossed. In House, 19 and 24 December 1827, read three times, passed, and ordered to be enrolled. (GASR, Nov. 1827 - Jan. 1828, Box 2: folder "SB 11 Dec.")

648. **Salyear, John and wife, Elizabeth.**

(1). Petition of John Salyear shews he married Betsey Hassell[111] of Tyrrell County, North Carolina, in 1816 and lived with her until December 1825. Part of the time he lived in Tyrrell County, part in Currituck County, and lastly in the Town of Plymouth in Washington County, North Carolina. While he was out to sea pursuing his occupation, his said wife eloped "with one Henry Melvin, a man of mean character, and took with her such of your petitioner's property as she pleased on Board of the said Henry Melvin's vessel and started with him to Mobile." Your petitioner has heard nothing certain of them since. Prays for a divorce from his said wife. Dated 5 November 1827. (GASR, Nov. 1827 - Jan. 1828, Box 2: folder "SB 6 Dec.")

(2). Committee on Divorce and Alimony to whom was referred the petition of John Salyer recommend the prayer of the petitioner be granted and pass the accompanying bill. (GASR, Nov. 1827 - Jan. 1828, Box 2: folder "SB 6 Dec.")

---

111 Marriage Bond of Tyrrell County, North Carolina, dated 26 February 1817, lists John Salyer and Elizabeth Hassell. Bondsman: William Wynn.

1827-1828 Session

(3).   Bill to divorce John Salyear of Currituck County from his wife, Elizabeth. In Senate, 4, 7, and 8 December, read three times, passed, and ordered to be engrossed. In House, 8 and 10 December, read twice and rejected. (GASR, Nov. 1827 - Jan. 1828, Box 2: folder "SB 6 Dec.")

649.   **Sawyer, Keziah and husband, James.**

(1).   Petition of Keziah Sawyer of the town of New Bern sheweth she intermarried in the month of August 1813 with a certain James Sawyer,[112] "a native as she believes of one of the Eastern States – that the said Sawyer her husband was a seaman and usually employed as a mate, which occupation he followed for a livelihood…" Her said husband remained with her about 3½ years, during which time they lived in harmony, and your petitioner earnestly strove to do her duty as a faithful and affectionate wife. At the end of this period "her husband left her as she understood for the West Indies, and absented himself from her for more than three years, when he returned & remained with her about one day and left her again and has never since returned-." During the time he was absent, he never wrote to her nor contributed to her support. She is dependent upon her personal labor for her support. She recently became owner of a few hundred dollars worth of property and if deprived of it, would have to depend upon the charity of her friends or the humanity of strangers. In her present situation, she is exposed to the will of her husband who has cruelly deserted her. Even if he dies, her estate might be swept away by his next of kin, for they had no children. Prays that she is awarded a divorce or given security in what little property and future acquisitions she may obtain. [Below:] Signatures of thirty-four citizens of the town of New Bern who "state that the petitioner is a woman of unexceptionable and exemplary character and hope that her petition may be granted." (GASR, Nov. 1827 - Jan. 1828, Box 2: folder "SB 13 Dec.")

(2).   Committee on Divorce and Alimony to whom was referred the petition of Keziah Sawyer of Craven County are of opinion that the prayer of the petitioner be granted and the accompanying bill be passed into law: A Bill to divorce Keziah Sawyer of Craven County from her husband James Sawyer. In Senate, 13 and 14 December 1827, read three times, passed, and ordered to be engrossed. In House, 15 December 1827, read first time and rejected. (GASR, Nov. 1827 - Jan. 1828, Box 2: folder "SB 13 Dec.")

650.   **Simons, Eliza and husband, Zacheus**.

(1).   Petition of Eliza Simons, alias Dowling, of Mecklenburg County, dated 14 November 1827.[113] (GASR, Nov. 1827 - Jan. 1828, Box 6: folder "Petitions (Divorce & Alimony)").

(2).   Decree of Court of Equity in Case of Dowling vs. Simon's Admr's, November 1826, In Mecklenburg County: It is decreed that David Cuthbertson, the administrator, and Cloe Simons, now Dillon, the administratrix of Solomon Simons, dec'd., and Thomas P. Dillon, now the husband of said Cloe, as administrator in right of his wife, pay to the complainant in this suit, the sum of $416.50 subject to the costs, it being the one third distributive share of Eliza, the wife of the complainant, in & to the Estate of her father, the said Solomon Simons, and which by a compromise of the parties is decreed to be due and owing to the Complainant. It is further decreed that the costs on this Suit be paid out of the distributive share. [Below:] Further court decrees that said Eliza be divorced from said Zacheus Dowl-

---

112   Marriage Bond of Craven County, North Carolina, dated 20 August 1814, lists James Sawyer and Kesiah Chadwick. Bondsman: Jonathan Price.

113   This petition is similar to that of the same person in #911, Part 21 of this series. One main difference is that Eliza said in this petition that she returned to her father's house at the latter end of the summer of 1821 and her father died in the twelvemonth period after her return. The earlier petition of about December 1826 stated she "got back to my parents" in August 1823.

ing and a settlement of costs among all parties to this suit. (GASR, Nov. 1827 - Jan. 1828, Box 6: folder "Petitions (Divorce & Alimony)").

651. **Suddath, Susannah and husband, James.**

(1). Petition of Susanna Suddath of Caswell County sheweth she married James Suddath in May 1815 and lived together in peace and harmony for several years and became the mother of four children. In recent years, said husband has been in the habit of leaving home for months at a time, contracting debts and making little or nothing for his family's support. Eventually, everything was seized and taken away to pay his debts, and her said husband abandoned his family and went to some of the southern or western states. She has not seen him for twelve months, and when she last heard from him, he was in Georgia. He left her quite destitute of money and provisions, and she has been dependent upon her own exertions and the benevolence of friends for support. Unfortunately, even this small support is taken to pay his debts. Prays for an act to secure to her all property she may hereafter acquire. [Below:] Signatures of eleven supporters. (GASR, Nov. 1827 - Jan. 1828, Box 4: folder "HCR (Agriculture-Internal Improvements)").

(2). Committee of Divorce and Alimony to whom was referred the petition of Susan Suddath of Caswell County recommend passage of the accompanying bill. [Bill is not in this file.] (GASR, Nov. 1827 - Jan. 1828, Box 4: folder "HCR (Agriculture-Internal Improvements)").

(3). Bill to secure to Susannah Suddath of Caswell County, wife of James Suddath, such property as she may hereafter acquire. In House, 10 and 24 December, read three times, passed, and ordered to be engrossed. In Senate, 26 December, read three times, passed, and ordered to be enrolled. (GASR, Nov. 1827 - Jan. 1828, Box 1: folder "HB 10 Dec.")

652. **Taylor, William D. and wife, Nancy.**

(1). Committee of Divorce and Alimony to whom was referred the Petition of Wm. D. Taylor of Martin County praying for a divorce from his wife, Nancy, report that the petitioner intermarried with Nancy Monk of Martin County in April 1818 and lived in perfect harmony until some time in October 1819. Said Nancy left his bed and board at that time without cause or provocation, and although he has earnestly solicited her to return, she continues to live separate and apart from him. He has been cruelly disappointed, for it appears that said Nancy is now pregnant, and in a few weeks will deliver a child of which she avows he is not the father. His attempts to induce her to return have proved ineffectual, but he was still desirous of contributing to her comfort, and secured to her one-half of his personal estate and all the lands he received by her in marriage. However, a short time after such provisions were made for her, she "threw herself into the arms of a profligate paramour with whom she has been living in open adultery." At the time of his marriage, the said Wm. D. Taylor was in comfortable circumstances of a highly respectable family and connections. The desolate conduct of his wife has had an overwhelming effect upon the mind of this unfortunate young man as to drive him into habits of desperation and intemperance, and reduced him to a state of poverty and want. He is not able to pay the cost of legal proceedings of a divorce and throws himself on the mercy of the Legislature. With a hope that the granting of his prayer will be the means of reclaiming him from his evil habits, the Committee recommends the accompanying bill be passed into law. (GASR, Nov. 1827 - Jan. 1828, Box 2: folder "SB 11 Dec.")

(2). Bill which declares that William D. Taylor of Martin County is hereby divorced from the bonds of matrimony with his wife, Nancy. In Senate, 11 and 12 December 1827, read three times, passed, and ordered to be engrossed. In House, 19 December 1827, read first time and rejected. (GASR, Nov. 1827 - Jan. 1828, Box 2: folder "SB 11 Dec.")

1827-1828 Session

653. **Thompson, Julia Ann and husband, Thomas W.**

(1). Petition of Julia Ann Thompson of Carteret County states she was young and inexperienced when she was addressed by a certain Captain Thomas W. Thompson[114] "who came to her under the guise of a gentleman and a Christian, and with the assistance of other evil minded persons…prevailed…upon her to consent to a matrimonial connexion with him. For a few weeks only after her marriage, your petitioner was induced to believe that the appearances he assumed were real…[b]ut this deception soon after vanished…" His conduct since has been more like that of a demon than a man. He induced me to accompany him on a voyage to sea, and I consented to brave the dangers of the deep and went with him. Hardly had we arrived at Ocracoke, and his character developed in the most ungentlemanly conduct towards me. In one instance, we were invited to dine on board a vessel of which my uncle had charge. My said husband refused to go and insisted I go alone -- which I did with the assurance that he would be there for dinner. He came not, and after waiting until late, my Uncle conveyed me back to our vessel, where the said Capt. Thompson charged me with incontinency and illicit intercourse -- and that with the last man in the world to be suspected -- my Uncle. His subsequent conduct has been marked with abuse and acts of violence. On our arrival in the West Indies, we paid a visit to the family of a resident merchant, but after a short time, he excused himself for the purpose of going on board his vessel. After he left, the ladies proposed a walk and invited me along. I did so and attached myself to an elderly single lady. Upon leaving the house, two gentlemen joined our party and later appeared to be on intimate terms with the younger ladies. Capt. Thompson returned to the merchant's house, and not finding me, commenced a most violent and infamous abuse of me for walking in company with the two gentlemen. On my return, he hurried me on board our vessel, and commenced beating me with his coat and fists. After this unprovoked treatment, I was permitted to rest. Two American Captains came on board, and he related something of the affair to them, and threatened more severe treatment. They interceded for me, and he promised he would forgive me if I would go on deck, kneel before him, and ask his pardon. I knew it was in his power and dreaded that a refusal would bring about the most horrid conquesences, so I did kneel before him, but then asked for what offense I should entreat his pardon. He replied by naming "the walk." After returning to Beaufort in the dead of night, he seized me by the throat while in bed, and but for the speedy relief rendered by my family, I should have been murdered. For many days I wore the bruises produced by his hands. Soon after the affair, he told my mother that he frequently slept with a knife under his bed for the purpose of taking my life and afterwards his own. A few days afterwards, he came to the house where I reside and commenced the most unheard of abuse of myself and all the family, and demanded that I return to him all the wearing apparel he had given to me. I did so, and he swore he would never more have anything to do with me nor to live with me again. Prays that she be granted a divorce from said Capt. Thompson. (GASR, Nov. 1827 - Jan. 1828, Box 6: folder "Petitions (Divorce & Alimony)")

(2). Letter to Julia Ann Fuller from Thos. W. Thompson: "I have maid up my mind with my self never to see you again while I live – and have no risk you [k]no[w] what was the ca[u]s[e] first and last…and I will state the things in every paper I can in the uion…I all so shall get clare of you as soon as I can…I am very glad I have no children by you so that they [may never] be told of them things…I due not like to wast- so much good paper on so mean a spo[us]e as I think you to be…"[115] (GASR, Nov. 1827 - Jan. 1828, Box 6: folder "Petitions (Divorce & Alimony)")

(3). Deposition of Thomas Marshall, Sheriff of Carteret County, states he lived in the adjoining house where Thomas W. Thompson and his wife lived, and heard said Thompson make thousands of

---

114 Marriage Bond of Carteret County, North Carolina, dated 24 August 1826, lists Thomas W. Thompson and Julia Ann Fuller. Bondsman: John C. Manson.

115 This is a rambling, poorly constructed letter with numerous misspellings.

threats to his wife, Julia Ann. His ill treatment of her was almost perpetual day and night. One night in August, your deponent was aroused of his bed by the shrieks and cries of a woman in the house where Thompson lived. I called to my wife that Thompson was killing of his wife. My wife had a light and went over to ask what was the matter. Thompson said that his wife had a nightmare. The next morning I saw neck wounds on Mrs. Thompson which lasted for several days. On the 4th of November, said Thompson in a rage of anger brought all of his things out of his house and ordered his wife to give him everything he ever gave her. He even made her strip to her skin. The next day Thompson requested me to stay and make friends between him and his wife. I told him I should not interfere…that if his wife was the woman he stated she was, I thought no gentleman would live with her. He then told me that he did not charge her with inconstancy. I told him that he had. He then told me that he never had the least cause under the Heavens to treat her ill, and he looked upon himself as a Villain for the same. Being acquainted with Mrs. Julia Ann Thompson from her infancy, I think that she is an injured woman. She has for ever born[e] the character of a virtuous woman. Dated 24 November 1827. (GASR, Nov. 1827 - Jan. 1828, Box 6: folder "Petitions (Divorce & Alimony")

654. **Tilley, Sarah and husband, Edmund.**
(1). Memorial of Sarah Tilley states she married Edmund Tilley about 1794 and removed from Wilkes County, North Carolina, to South Carolina. The said Edmund Tilley for these past thirty years has lived an idle, dissolute and drunken life and taken no care for his family. This has caused a separation from said Tilley and your petitioner for the past six or seven years. Your petitioner was left destitute of reasonable subsistence until her father, advanced in age, brought her to his house in Wilkes County where she has remained for four years. She has just reasons to believe that her father, Jas./Jos. Fergerson, would settle on her some property at his death, provided it could not be liable to the devastation of her husband, who still resides in South Carolina. Prays for a law to secure to her what property she may hereafter acquire by her own industry or otherwise. [Below:] Signatures of nineteen subscribers. (GASR, Nov. 1827 - Jan. 1828, Box 2: folder "SB 5 Dec.")
(2). Committee on Divorce and Alimony to whom was referred the memorial of Sarah Tilley of Wilkes County recommend the accompanying Bill be passed into law: Bill to secure to Sarah Tilley of Wilkes County, wife of Edmund Tilley, such property as she may hereafter acquire. In Senate, 5 and 6 December 1827, read three times, passed, and ordered to be engrossed. In House, 7, 11, and 24 December 1827, read three times, passed, and ordered to be enrolled. (GASR, Nov. 1827 - Jan. 1828, Box 2: folder "SB 5 Dec.")

655. **Tuten, Thomas and wife, Elizabeth.**
(1). Petition of Thomas Tuten [no county listed, but probably Greene/Beaufort] sheweth he intermarried with his present wife, Elizabeth, sometime in September 1824 and flattered himself to spend the remainder of his days in peace and happiness. In the first six months, I thought that hope would be realized, but then found that hope elusive, for she began to be restless and dissatisfied for some unknown reason. From step to step she progressed in her violent disposition until she left my house and returned to the house of her relatives. Notwithstanding my kind solicitation to the contrary, during the time of her absence from home I paid her many visits and made cases of every persuasion in my power to get her to return home. She finally did come home, but I am sorry to say, her return was only to make deeper inroads to a heart already worn to a shadow by disappointed love. After remaining with me a few weeks, she again left with a full determination never to return. Upwards of eighteen months have now expired with no hopes of her return. Prays for a divorce. Dated 13 November 1827. (GASR, Nov. 1827 - Jan. 1828, Box 4: folder "HCR (Agriculture-Internal Improvements)").

(2). Deposition of Peter Dowty before Thomas Ellison, J.P. for Beaufort County, that he saw Elizabeth Tuten, wife of Thomas Tuten, some few days after her return to her husband the first time she left him. He enquired the reason she had for leaving her husband and if she did not treat him kindly. She said he always was very kind and attentive to her, that he treated her as kind as a child and that she never should have left him had it not been through the persuasion of her family…Dated 13 November 1827. (GASR, Nov. 1827 - Jan. 1828, Box 4: folder "HCR (Agriculture-Internal Improvements)").

656. **Wilson, Jane and husband, James.**
(1). Petition of Jane Wilson sheweth that her husband, James Wilson, eloped from this country in April 1824 and carried off with him the wife of Ned Webster with whom it was known he had lived in adulterous connexion for some years. Prior to this elopement, said James sold or otherwise disposed of all his property, most of which he acquired by his marriage with your petitioner. This act left your petitioner and three of her youngest children entirely destitute of the means of living except by their industry. Your petitioner has an aged and beloved aunt who possesses considerable property "and now tottering on the verge of eternity." Said aunt wishes to devise some of this property to your petitioner, provided a law is passed to secure to her such property as she may hereafter acquire. Will ever pray for such a law. [Below:] Signatures of twelve supporters. (GASR, Nov. l827 - Jan. 1828, Box 4: folder "HCR (Agriculture-Internal Improvements)").

(2). Committee of Divorce and Alimony to whom was referred the petition of Jane Wilson of Buncombe County report the accompanying bill. [Bill is not in this file.] (GASR, Nov. l827 - Jan. 1828, Box 4: folder "HCR (Agriculture-Internal Improvements)").

(3). Bill to secure to Jane Wilson of Buncombe County, wife of James Wilson, such property as she may hereafter acquire. In House, 5, 7, and 10 December read three times, passed, and ordered to be engrossed. In Senate, 11 and 13 December 1827, read three times, passed, and ordered to be enrolled. (GASR, Nov. 1827 - Jan. 1828, Box 1: folder "HB 5 Dec.")

657. **Reference A.**
Committee of Divorce and Alimony to whom was referred the petitions of John Faust, Jno. Pitcher, Martha Beasley, and numerous others praying to be divorced from their respective spouses report that believing from repeated decisions of the House that said prayers will not be granted pray to be discharged from further consideration of these. [On reverse:] In House of Commons, 3 January 1828, read and concurred in. (GASR, Nov. 1827 - Jan. 1828, Box 4: folder "HCR (Agriculture-Internal Improvements)").

658. **Reference B.**
Laws of North Carolina, 1827-1828
"Public Laws, Chapter XIX, p. 19. An Act giving the Superior Courts of Law exclusive jurisdiction in all cases of Divorce.

"Whereas the numerous applications for divorce and alimony, annually presented the General Assembly, consume a considerable portion of time in their examination, and consequently retard the investigation of more important subjects of legislation; and whereas such application might be adjudicated by other tribunals with much less expenditure to the State, and more impartial justice to individuals…the Superior Courts of Law shall have sole and original jurisdiction in all cases of application for divorce; and the said Courts are hereby authorized and empowered to divorce from bed and board, and from the bonds of matrimony, whenever they may be satisfied, upon due evidence presented of the justice of such application; any law, usage or custom to the contrary notwithstanding…Further…no defendant or

Divorces and Separations from Petitions to the North Carolina General Assembly from 1779

party offending, who shall be divorced from the bonds of matrimony...shall ever be permitted to marry again."

Because of the passage of the above law, no divorces were approved by the North Carolina General Assembly at this or future sessions. These matters became the jurisdiction of each of the Superior Courts of Law situated in each county.

However, the couples listed below were principals in acts which entitled the female member the right to hold, possess and enjoy in her sole right, all such estate, real or personal, as she may thereafter acquire by industry, gift or otherwise, in as full and ample manner as if she had never been married.

        Becknall, Jane of Ashe Co.; husband, Henry, p. 81
        Crittenden, Christiana of Stokes Co.; husband, John, p. 79
        McKaughon, Phebe of Guilford Co.; husband, James, p. 82
        Rowland, Mary E. of Robeson Co.; husband, Alfred, p. 85
        Suddath, Susannah of Caswell Co.; husband, James, p. 64
        Tilley, Sarah of Wilkes Co.; husband, James, p. 64
        Wilson, Jane of Buncombe Co.; husband, James, p. 87

659.   **Reference C.**

Committee of Divorce and Alimony to whom was referred the petitions of John Powers, Thomas Tuten, James W. Mills, and Jonathan Bryan report that having considered the aforegoing petitions and entertaining the same opinion of each founded on a point common to all, they beg leave to present their views in this condensed form.

Here follows reasoning of this committee in trying to come up with a fair analysis of each divorce case when located so far from the sources. The Superior Courts were pointed out as being in a far better position to determine the facts in each case of divorce because investigation would normally take place in "the bosom of the community in which they live where the characters of the parties are well known and the credibility of the testimony may be accurately estimated."

Your Committee must therefore protect any admission of the facts stated in the aforesaid petitions from the circumstances of their report being based upon another and separate point – they report unfavourably to the prayer of the petitioners. [On reverse:] In H. of Commons, 10 December 1827, read and concurred with. (GASR, Nov. 1827 - Jan. 1828, Box 4: folder "HCR (Agriculture-Internal Improvements)").[116]

---

116   As a result of the above recommendations, the Superior Courts of Law were given exclusive jurisdiction in all cases of divorce (above).

1828-1834

660. **Barber, William and wife, Mary.** P&GC to which was referred the petition of William Barber of Washington County praying to be divorced from his wife, Mary, report that it appears the wife of the petitioner, after having conducted herself with gross impropriety for sometime, has for the last twelve months separated herself from her husband and has led a life of the most brutal drunkenness and prostitution. In the Committee's opinion, these facts have only to be stated to the Superior Courts of the State to ensure a dissolution of the marriage, and so recommend a rejection of the accompanying bill: Bill to divorce William Barber of Washington County from his wife, Mary Barber. [On reverse: In House of Commons, 16 December 1833, read second time and indefinitely postponed.] (GASR, Nov. 1833-Jan. 1834, Box 1: folder "HB 6 Dec.")

661. **Blackwell, Rachel and husband, Thomas.**
(1). Petition of Rachel Bla[c]kwell of Person County states she intermarried with Thomas Blackwell sometime in 1814,[117] had two children by him, and lived with him for three years. Her said husband, through habits of intoxication and extravagance, spent the whole of your petitioner's estate and left her and her children to want. He then left her and removed to the State of Virginia. She has not seen said Thomas since June 1826, and he has not contributed one cent to the support of herself or her children in eleven years. Prays for a law to secure to her such property as she may hereafter acquire.
(2). P&GC to whom was referred the petition of Rachel Blackwell of Person County summarizes said petition and recommends passage of the accompanying bill: Bill to secure to Rachel Blackwell of Person County such property as she may hereafter acquire. [On reverse: In Senate, 17 December 1828, engrossed and examined. In House of Commons, 17 December 1828, read first time and rejected.] (GASR, Nov. 1828-Jan. 1829, Box 2: folder "SB 3 Dec.").

662. **Buckner, Polly and husband, Edward.** Bill to divorce Polly Buckner of Buncombe County from her husband, Edward Buckner, late of said county. [On reverse: In Senate, 5 December 1831, read second and third times, passed and ordered to be engrossed. In House, 5 December 1831, read first time, and on mention of Mr. Wyche, indefinitely postponed.] (GASR, Nov. 1831-Jan. 1832, Box 3: folder "SB 3 Dec.")
(1). Petition of Polly Buckner of Buncombe County states she is placed in a situation of extreme distress, misery and unhappiness. Having no other authority, she referred a petition for divorce to the Superior Court of Buncombe, and certain facts were submitted to a jury, and all were found in favor of your petitioner. The case was argued before Judge Martin, who claimed that his powers did not embrace her cause. Prays to the General Assembly to take her case under advisement and divorce her from the bonds of matrimony. [Below:] Signatures of some 130 subscribers who are acquainted with the petitioner and believe she is deserving of relief. They state she lived five years with her father after her

---

117 Marriage Bond of Person County, North Carolina, lists Thomas Blackwell and Rachel Link, dated 16 February 1815. Bondsman: Wilie Brooks.

Divorces and Separations from Petitions to the North Carolina General Assembly from 1779

husband fled for stealing a negro. The petitioner depends on her father, a poor man, for the support of herself and two children. It was reported that her husband was dead and by others, that he had been shot in Kentucky for stealing a horse.

(2). Certified true copy of proceedings at a Superior Court of Law held for Buncombe County in Asheville in April 1828 and 1829:

(a). Petition of Polly Buckner of Buncombe County sheweth she married Edward Buckner in December 1815, and they lived together for about five years during which time she had two children and was pregnant with a third. In 1820, said Edward left your petitioner, and shortly afterwards she heard that he had married another woman in Kentucky. Some four or five years later, he abandoned the second woman and returned to the neighborhood of your petitioner's father with whom she was living. Her said husband told her that he had behaved so bad that he could not insist on her living with him, and besides, he was so afraid of being detected for alleged crimes and being seen in the country. Your petitioner, in believing he had married another woman, had no confidence in him and did not desire to be reunited. He secretly left the country. Her brother, James Runion, who lived in Georgia, saw where her said husband had a blacksmith shop and lived under the name of Williams. He heard that said husband had been married twice and had stole the horse of his second wife. Your petitioner performed the duties of a faithful and affectionate wife when she lived with said husband, who left her for no excuse involving your petitioner, but because of his own unsettled disposition and habits of dishonest and immoral tendency. Prays for a divorce.

(b). Response of jury to whom the case was submitted: 1. Edward Buckner separated himself from his wife Polly and was living in adultery at the time of the petition. 2. Said Polly Buckner had knowledge of the above more than six months before the filing of the petition, and said Edward abandoned her without cause ten years ago. 3. Said Polly has herself been guilty of adultery and was so guilty before the filing of the petition, but such adulterous conduct was often the lapse of ten years from the time she was abandoned by her husband. The petition was disavowed with costs.

(3). Bill to divorce Polly Buckner from her husband, Edward Buckner. [On reverse: In Senate, 19 and 20 December 1832, read twice, passed and ordered to be engrossed. In House of Commons, 21 December 1832 and 8 January 1833, read three times, engrossed and ordered to be enrolled.]
(GASR, Nov. 1832- Jan. 1833, Box 2: folder "SB 19 Dec.")

663. **Burrow, Sarah and husband, Henry.**

(1). Petition of Sarah Burrow, wife of Henry Burrow of Davidson County, sheweth she intermarried in 1809[118] with her husband, who for several years appeared to be a careful, industrious man disposed to make a comfortable support for his family, which now consists of himself, your petitioner and six children. Unfortunately, your petitioner's husband has over the years destroyed his mental faculties through intemperance, especially for the past eight to ten years, and has involved himself in debt. This situation has deprived your petitioner and her children of the products of their honest industry which ought to be applied towards their subsistence. Prays for a law to secure to her such property as she may hereafter acquire, free from the claim of her said husband or his creditors. [Below:] Signatures of seventeen subscribers who support the statements and prayer of the petitioner.

(2). Committee to whom was referred the petition of Sarah Burrow report that by existing law, the Superior Courts of Law have jurisdiction to grant alimony in such cases. It would therefore be imprudent to grant the prayer of the petitioner. (GASR, Nov. 1831-Jan. 1832, Box 5: folder "HCR (Military-Miscellaneous)").

---

118   Marriage Bond of Cumberland County, North Carolina, lists Henry Burrow and Sally Wilson, dated 28 January 1809. Bondsman: John Smith.

1828-1834 Session

664. **Cabe, Mary B. and husband, Joseph.**

(1). Memorial of Mary Barbara Cabe, formerly Mary Barbara Smith, states she unfortunately intermarried on 20 May 1832 with a certain Joseph Cabe, a near neighbor to the father of your memorialist. In a very short time, said Joseph became very turbulent and disorderly and treated your memorialist with the utmost contempt, in every way degrading to the feeling of an affectionate wife and not affording the comforts of life. In your memorialist's view, he was constantly caressing his paramour, a young woman living in the same house with his widowed mother. This situation remained for some eight months, when said Joseph proposed a separation after refusing to sleep with your memorialist. In such circumstances, your memorialist returned to her father's house about two miles away, but still hoped for a friendly reconciliation. However, no prospects appeared, his utmost contempt continued, and he refused to speak when your memorialist took opportunities of seeing him, as when we accidentally met. Prays for a law to dissolve the rights of matrimony between said Joseph and your memorialist.

(2). Certificate of Robert Love that he has been acquainted with said memorialist from her birth; that she made frequent visits to his family; and that she has always been seen as a young lady of good and decent moral conduct.

(3). Certificate of David Bugg, Acting Justice of Haywood County, that he has been acquainted with said Barbary Kabe, the memorialist, from her birth and has never lived more than four miles distant from her father's house. She has been seen as a person of good moral character and demeanor. Dated 6 December 1833.

(4). Signatures of eighty-eight persons who support said memorialist. (GASR, Nov. 1833-Jan. 1834, Box 6: folder "Petitions (Divorce-Name change)"). Bill to divorce Mary B. CABE of Haywood County from her husband, Joseph Cabe. [On reverse: In House of Commons, 9 January 1834, read third time, passed and ordered to be engrossed.] (GASR, Nov. 1833-Jan. 1834, Box 1: folder "HB 8 Jan.") Published in N.C Laws Session 1834-1835, page 56.

665. **Collier, Frederick H. and wife, Lucretia.**

(1). Petition of Frederick H. Collier sheweth he was born and raised in Orange County, North Carolina, and resided there until about four years ago, when he removed to Randolph County where he now resides. On 19 February 1820, he intermarried with Lucretia W. Hunt,[119] a young woman of a respectable family in Orange County. She possessed and deserved as far as he then knew, a good reputation for chastity and propriety of conduct. Through marriage, he expected to enhance his happiness, but about two years later, a circumstance occurred which convinced your petitioner of his said wife's infidelity beyond the possibility of a doubt. He discovered that she had been frequently guilty of adultery, and before the marriage, kept up an illicit connection with a man who lived in the neighborhood. Upon this discovery, your petitioner separated himself from her and has never been reconciled with her. She has ever since lived in open prostitution and has born a child, the fruit of her guilt. The proof of such facts is contained in the annexed certified copy of record.[120] Your petitioner hoped to find relief by filing a petition in the Superior Court of Law for Orange County, praying for a divorce from the bonds of matrimony. The issues contained in the annexed copy of record were submitted to the jury, and the verdict is contained therein. However, the Court refused to dissolve the marriage as he had been led to believe, because he had endeavoured to reclaim his wife after he had reason to believe she had been guilty of improper conduct. Your petitioner notes that the statement from which the Court made that inference was inserted in the petition by mistake. He is ready to make oath that after he obtained knowledge of his

---

119 Marriage Bond of Orange County, North Carolina, lists Frederick Collier and Lucretia Hunt, dated 18 February 1824. Bondsman: Moses S. Pratt.

120 Said certified copy is not in this file.

wife's unchaste behavior, he has never cohabited nor been reconciled with her. He never made a statement or statements to any other person that was contrary to that which he now makes. He humbly prays that his marriage with his wife, Lucretia, be dissolved.

(2). Committee to whom was referred the petition of Frederick H. Collier praying to be divorced from his wife, Lucretia W., summarizes said petition and adds that the Superior Court of Orange County at the September Term of 1829 heard said case and declined to dissolve the marriage, but pronounced a decree of separation from bed and board only. Your committee is of opinion that the said Superior Court did not afford adequate relief, and therefore recommends passage of the accompanying bill: Be it enacted that the bonds of matrimony between Frederick H. Collier and his wife, Lucretia W., be dissolved. [On reverse: In House of Commons, 23 December, read first time, and on motion of Mr. Bynum was indefinitely postponed.]

(GASR, Nov. 1830-Jan. 1831, Box 2: folder "HB 20 Dec.")

666. **Dilliard, Frances H. and husband, Wil(l)ie.** Petition of Frances H. Dilliard, wife of Wilie M. Dilliard[121] and resident of Chapel Hill, Orange County, sheweth her situation requires the interposition of the Legislature to secure to her such property as she may by her honest industry thereafter acquire and may be devised to her by her father, Robert Campbell. Your petitioner's said husband is living within the limits of this state in dissolute habits, especially that of intemperance, and has contracted much debt which he is unable to pay, thereby subjecting your petitioner to the necessary support of herself and family. Her said husband has been absent from his family for about the last fifteen months. Prays she may be granted such relief as necessary. (GASR, Nov. 1828-Jan. 1829, Box 5: folder "Petitions (Divorce and Alimony; Name change)").

P&GC to whom was referred the petition of Frances H. Dilliard praying to be secured to such property as she may hereafter acquire report that her application is not substantiated by such evidence as would give it under any circumstances a claim to legislative interference. The committee recommends rejection of said petition. [On reverse: In House of Commons, 31 December 1828, read and concurred with.] (GASR, Nov. 1828-Jan. 1829, Box 5: folder "HCR")

667. **Garland, Cel(i)a and husband, James.** Petition of Cela Garland sheweth she intermarried sometime in 1824 with one James Garland of Greene County with whom she fondly hoped to have enjoyed all those blessings and comforts of the connubial state, but was soon disappointed that said husband had no other design than to get her little property for the purpose of spending to ensure his own ends. Further, he commenced a trove of practices on your petitioner by abusing and turning her out of doors, so now your petitioner is reduced to a state of indigence and is wholly dependent on the humanity of her friends for support. Prays for a law to secure to her such property as she may hereafter acquire. Dated 10 November 1828. [Below:] Signatures of eleven subscribers in support of the above petition.] Committee of Propositions and Grievances to whom was referred the petition of Cela Garland of Greene County report that said petitioner has received the most brutal and unfeeling treatment from her husband, James Garland, and has been driven from his house. Recommend adoption of the accompanying bill: Bill to secure to Celia Garland of Greene County such property as she may hereafter acquire. [On reverse: In House of Commons, 1 December 1828, read, and on motion of Mr. Pool, postponed indefinitely.]

(GASR, Nov. 1828-Jan. 1829, Box 1: folder "HB 28 Nov.")

---

121 Marriage Bond of Orange County, North Carolina, lists Willie Dilliard and Franky Campbell, dated 16 April 1809. Bondsman: Bolling Cox.

668. **Hauser, Susannah Mary and husband, Joseph.** Petition of Susannah Mary Hauser represents she intermarried with Joseph Hauser about seventeen years since and had by him six children. During the first years of their marriage, said husband was faithful in providing for his family, but within a few years, he passed into intemperance and entirely neglected your petitioner and children. He has done nothing for their support and has spent everything he has in drink, "leaving your petitioner to scuffle through the world poor and penniless while her hard earnings are torn from her by her husband and spent in dissipation or taken by officers to pay her debts…She is often in danger of her life, and lately he threatened to shoot her to prevent which her friends advised her to hand him to the peace-" Prays for a law in her behalf giving her such property as she may hereafter acquire. [Below:] Signatures of eleven subscribers.

P&GC, to whom was referred the above petition of Susannah Mary Hauser of Stokes County, summarizes said petition and recommends passage of the accompanying bill: Bill to secure to Susannah Mary Hauser of Stokes County such property as she may hereafter acquire. [On reverse: In Senate, 11 December 1828, engrossed and examined. In House of Commons, 27 December 1828, read and postponed indefinitely.

(GASR, Nov. 1828-Jan. 1829, Box 2: folder "SB 11 Dec.")

669. **Holland, William and wife, Esther.** Petition of William Holland of Craven County sheweth he intermarried with Esther Parsons, the widow of Nathan Parsons of said county, on 7 February 1822.[122] He entered into this union solely by affection and the hope to obtain a companion with whom to share enjoyments, discharge duties, and encounter the treats of life. His circumstances were above mediocrity and free from embarrassment, and she was "the widow of a bankrupt and without property." There was no striking disparity of years between himself and his companion. Their acquaintance was not of recent growth: his attachment to her was strong, and he was assured on her part it was returned. For a few short months, these hopes appeared to be realized. His said wife continued to reside with him until 22 August 1822. She occasionally expressed a wish to visit her relations in the adjoining county, and on that day, she went off on this alleged visit. Your petitioner's engagements did not permit him without inconvenience to accompany her, so he furnished her a servant, chair and a pair of horses. It was arranged that in ten days thereafter, your petitioner would come for her, and they would return home together. Anxious to rejoin her as soon as practicable and sure of receiving a cordial and affectionate welcome, your petitioner arrived at the place of meeting two days before the appointed time. To his surprise and astonishment, she refused to see him. By verbal messages and by letters, your petitioner has repeatedly entreated her to abandon this strange caprice and return to her husband and home. He has not been able to obtain but one interview with her, and that lasted long enough to assure him of her irrevocable determination never to go back to his house, never more to associate with him unless compelled to actual violence. Such violence your petitioner will not use. All means of persuasion have been exhausted, and after a separation of more than five years, there is not the faintest hope of a reunion. Your petitioner will not attempt to conciliate favor by insinuations against her from whom he seeks a legal separation. He has not treated her otherwise than a faithful and affectionate husband. Your petitioner is in law — a husband, but in fact without a wife. He is bound by the marriage contract to one who acknowledges not its obligations. He is compelled to support and maintain her who disclaims the performance of any domestic duty, and is responsible for her acts, although she renounces his authority. Through life he must be restrained to perpetual self denial because of claims which are contempted and despised, and at his death she is to be endowed as his widow who rejected him when living as her husband. Prays that his case be taken under

---

122 Marriage Bond of Craven County, North Carolina, lists William Holland and Esther Parsons, dated 7 January 1822. Bondsman: Elijah Clark.

Divorces and Separations from Petitions to the North Carolina General Assembly from 1779

consideration and grant him relief by an act to divorce him from the bonds of matrimony. [Below:] Signatures of ninety-three subscribers who are fully persuaded that the representations of the petitioner are true "and they write with him in praying that the relief be granted."
(GASR, Nov. 1830-Jan. 1831, Box 6: folder "Petitions (Divorce)").

670.   **James, Mary and husband, Gabriel.** Memorial of Mary James represents that an affected show of love and friendship for your memorialist from one Gabriel James, enforced by the most solemn pledges of the sincerity of his heart and the purity of his intentions, awakened in her feelings of regard which afterwards ripened into the purest love. From what your memorialist considered to be reciprocal love, founded upon the noblest friendship that exists among mortals, she was induced to form a marriage alliance with the said Gabriel James on 30 January 1817. But, fatal to the repose of your memorialist, and to her surprise and great confusion, before one month had rolled away, she saw that confidence she had reposed in him — abused and violated. Notwithstanding her attentions to please were unremitting, and her love for him indiminished, their matrimonial felicity was still incomplete. From a strange perversity of disposition on his part, he frequently treated her most insultingly, but such was the kindness of her dispositions and the meek forebearance of her nature, she was always ready to look over it and requiet him with her affections. Yet, clouds of oppression arose in quick succession. In this hour of adversity, when her mind was worn down by the cares, troubles and dangers which so heavily beset her — she derived consolation by hoping that her husband would yet leave off his bacchanalian riots and other obscene pleasures, establish himself in the road to happiness, and erect himself in the strict practice of all that is just, honorable and good. But, alas! Elusive hopes. Time has riveted him more closely to his vices, and rankling care has rooted out all domestic happiness from the bosom of your memorialist. Her said husband had now run tenfold deeper into every species of dissipation. Home had no allurements for him. He would spend whole nights and days at houses of ill fame, return home, reeling and tottering under the effects of habitual intoxication, and instigated by its pernicious influence, would take up his gun and shoot down any of the poultry or domestic animals that were in the yard, rending and breaking to pieces the household furniture. In the meantime, your memorialist could find safety only in retreat. In his calm and deliberate moments, he would threaten taking her life and provoke her to insult, causing his negroes to use insulting language to her & c. Your memorialist knew that she was in imminent hazard of losing her life and convinced that it was his determination to take it. She therefore went off to the house of her father to whom he had written - "to come and take her property, that he was going to move…" to effect which, a day of sale was appointed. Your memorialist was pursued by him to her father's house, which he waylaid for awhile.

Finding that his attempt was about to prove fruitless…he entered the house in the night time with a loaded pistol under his arm & cloak, determined to take her life if she could be found. The above account was the final separation, all of which happened a short time after marriage. Her said husband has left this state and has not been seen by her for nine years, nor does your memorialist know where he is, nor is there any correspondence kept up between them. In this odious contempt of every personal feeling, of public opinion, and of common humanity, did he thus unblushingly violate the most solemn pledge known among mortals? Instead of making a pillar for her soul in the kindness of his, and a support for its firmness to fill up the measure of his guilt, he gave her a thorny pillar for her kindness and disgrace for her tenderness. Begs to be divorced from the bounds of wedlock. Dated 24 November 1828, Duplin County. [Below:] Signatures of fifteen subscribers who say they have long known Mary James, who has an unimpeachable character and is entitled to the fullest credit in what she states.]

1828-1834 Session

Bill to divorce Mary James of Duplin County from her husband, Gabriel James. [On reverse:] In Senate, 12 December 1828, read first time and passed. In Senate, 13 December 1828, read second time and resolved that same shall not pass.

(GASR, Nov. 1828-Jan. 1829, Box 2: folder "SB 12 Dec.")

671. **Johnson, John and wife, Peggy.** Petition of John Johnson of Orange County sheweth he intermarried in 1816 with Peggy Barracks and lived a short time in perfect harmony. He was destitute of land of his own, but became partner in a farm with a free negro. During this time, his wife Peggy formed an attachment with said negro, and your petitioner was forced to abandon her. Since then, she has continued to live with said negro to the neglect of her husband. Prays for a divorce from said Peggy. Dated 3 November 1832. [Below:] Signatures of nine subscribers who state they believe the facts in the above petition.]

Petition of Peggy (+) Johnson states she intermarried with John Johnson on 20 May 1816, but lived a most disagreeable life, including receiving severe flagellation at his cruel hands and in imminent danger of her life in his drunken frolics. About two years ago, he left her and took most of the little property they had, leaving your petitioner destitute of anything to subsist upon. After she then acquired earnings of her own, they were seized to pay her husband's debts. Prays for a law to secure to her such property as she may acquire for her own benefit.

[Enclosed:] (1). Sworn statement of William Overman in Randolph County, North Carolina, 6 October 1832, states he was intimately acquainted with the manner of treatment that Peggy Johnson received from her husband, John Johnson. He knows that she was very much abused and believes the said John would have killed her had he not been prevented. Her husband kicked her in the face and attempted to throw a large piece of wood at her. He left her and took with him most of the property they had. They have been separated about three years.

[Enclosed:] (2). Certificate of Barbary (x) Buntin and Susanna (/) Buntin, 6 October 1832, that John Johnson and his wife Peggy have been separated three years, and he does not assist her in any way.

P&GC to whom was referred the petitions of John Johnson and his wife Peggy report that their complaints are cognizable in the Superior Court of Law and pray to be discharged from further consideration of this subject. [On reverse: In Senate, 27 November 1832, read and concurred in.]

(GASR, Nov. 1832-Jan. 1833, Box 5: folder "SCR (Prop. & Grievances-Miscel.)").

672. **Julin, Lucinda and husband, John.** Petition of Lucinda Julin sheweth she intermarried ten years ago with John Julin of Randolph County. She lived in harmony with said husband until the Spring of 1827, when, because of his association with men of profligate character, he wasted the whole of his property and contracted a number of debts which he was unable to pay. In the Fall of the same year, some criminal charges were alleged against him, and he fled, leaving his wife and family in a deplorable condition. The last time your petitioner heard from him was in the Spring of this year when he was on the southwestern frontier of the State of Georgia, marching on with the avowed intention of leaving this government, never more to return. Your petitioner has been left with four small children to maintain with no other means than her own labor. Prays for a law to secure to her whatever property she may hereafter acquire. Dated 5 November 1828. [On reverse: Signatures of thirty-four subscribers who say they have been acquainted with the petitioner since her intermarriage, and pray that her relief is granted.]

P&GC to whom was referred the petition of Lucinda Julin of Randolph County confirm the statements of the petitioner and additionally state that said John Julin undertook to perform some work in the eastern counties of this State. While engaged in this work, he gave himself up to habits of dissipa-

tion and intemperance until by gambling and other vicious practices, he involved himself deeply in debt. His creditors refused to let him return home before he discharged the demands they had against him. To relieve himself from his embarrassments, he forged a number of bonds and sold them to his creditors. After so doing, he called to take leave of the petitioner and fled to the western country, never to return. He should be prosecuted for the forgeries. Recommend the accompanying bill be passed into law: Bill to secure to Lucinda Julin of Randolph County such property as she may hereafter acquire. [On reverse: In Senate, 18 December 1828, engrossed and examined. In House of Commons, 18 December 1828, read first time and rejected.]
(GASR, Nov. 1828-Jan. 1829, Box 3: folder "SB 17 Dec.")

673. **Keith, Sarah Ann and husband, William.** Petition of Sarah "Sally" Ann Kieth of Plymouth [Washington County] represents she married William Kieth, then a resident of Bertie County, in 1818. At that time, said William stood fair in the community but had little or no property; your petitioner had property enough to have supported her in comfort under prudent circumspection. There was no marriage contract between them. A few years after the marriage, her said husband became insolvent, and all the property they had (except for so much of your petitioner's property as shall be mentioned later) was sold to pay his debts, including William's life estate in a 360 acre tract of land in Bertie County which descended to your petitioner upon the death of her father and sister: "that her estate in remainder in fee simple of the said land was not sold and still remains belonging to her..."[123] In 1828, her said husband left his home for a long journey and residence abroad for the avowed purpose of bettering his fortunes. He talked of going to Santa Fe in South America, but your petitioner has only received one letter from him, and that came from Lexington, perhaps in Kentucky. She understands he has written some four or five letters to others in Bertie County, and these were from somewhere in South America. None of the information she has received has indicated that he had abandoned her and their two young children, but there is also no information of his future intentions. She has not received any support from him, except for $10 sent to her two weeks after his departure, and her friends are in poor circumstances. Her husband did not leave because of any family dispute, and she is now only stating the facts, but not to reproach him. She has an opportunity to sell her estate in the aforesaid land, but cannot convey the title unless her husband joins in the execution and delivery of the deed. Your petitioner states her circumstances are embarrassed: she is in great adversity and oppressed by the difficulty in supporting and educating her children in the way they have been accustomed to enjoy. Prays for an act to enable her to sell her estate in the aforesaid land without the consent of her husband as if she were a feme sole and that the moneys arising from such sale be secured to her separate use apart from that of her husband. [Below:] Signatures of eight persons of Plymouth, North Carolina, who state they are acquainted with Mrs. Sarah Ann Kieth, that she is of fair and spotless character and good connections, that she has two small children, little or no property or income, and is in adverse circumstances. Dated 21 November 1833.] (GASR, Nov. 1833-Jan. 1834, Box 6: folder "Petitions (Divorce; name change)").

P&GC to which was referred the petition of Sarah Ann Keith summarizes the facts in the above petition and add that the petitioner is sustained by various gentlemen who speak of her in terms of high

---

123 Bertie County, North Carolina, Deed Books, T:212 (dated 12 February 1804) and HH:437 (dated 18 September 1849) describe this land and its owners: 150 acres on the north side of the Village [presumably Plymouth] Swamp that was sold by Blake B. Wiggins to Mary Jernagan, widow of Arthur Jernagan, decd., and to Patsey and Sally Jernagan, daughters of said Arthur Jernagan, decd.; and 200 acres adjoining this 150-acre tract which descended to Sarah Ann (Jernagan) Keith upon the death of her father, Arthur Jernagan, decd. Both tracts were later occupied and cultivated by one Huested Reynolds after the death of said Arthur Jernagan, decd.

circumstances. The committee recommends passage of the accompanying bill. [See next paragraph.] (GASR, Nov. 1832-Jan. 1833, Box 5: folder "HCR")

Bill states it appears that William Keeth hath abandoned his wife, Sarah Ann Keeth, and his children and has gone into a foreign state; that said Sarah Ann is seized of an estate in her own right in Bertie County, and she is in very needy circumstances with no means to support herself and her children. She cannot sell same unless she is a feme sole. Therefore, said Sarah Ann Keeth, notwithstanding her coverture, shall have full power and authority to sell any lands as though she were a feme sole. She shall hereafter hold and possess all property which she may acquire, free from claims of her said husband. [On reverse: In House of Commons, 31 December 1833, read third time, passed and ordered to be engrossed. In Senate, 8 January 1834, read third time, passed and ordered to be enrolled.] (GASR, Nov. 1833- Jan. 1834, Box 2: folder "HB 18 Dec."]

674. **Lawrence, Martha and husband, Arthur.** Petition of Martha Lawrence of Edgecombe County sheweth she intermarried in 1828 with Arthur Lawrence.[124] At that time, your petitioner was both young and inexperienced (being then but 16 years of age) and was easily deceived by the flattering and false representations of her lover. He represented himself to have lived in the County of Hertford, a man of property and respectable connections. Upon being carried by her husband to his county, she found he had neither property or character, and though his parents were respectable, they had from his bad conduct entirely discarded him. Your petitioner was then brought back to her father's [Moses Baker], and though she would most willingly have toiled through life with the said Lawrence, not withstanding his want of fortune, she could ill respect a man who had deceived her and was in the daily habit of telling her the most bare faced falsehoods. Still, she submitted to her fate in satirical grief and endeavoured in every respect to fulfill her duties as a wife faithfully and to the utmost of her ability. Nonetheless, said Arthur Lawrence, without cause or provocation, secretly absconded, leaving your petitioner entirely dependent on her father and ignorant of the cause of his flight as well as the place of his destination. The said Lawrence has now been absent near six years and as she learns, the courts of law afford her no relief. She prays for an act divorcing her from the bonds of matrimony from her said husband.

P&GC to whom was referred the petition of Martha Lawrence report that the facts in the petition are not of such a character as to authorize the interference of the Legislature and ask to be discharged from further consideration of the subject. [On reverse: "Concurred in."]

(GASR, Nov. 1833-Jan. 1834, Box 5: folder "HCR (Private Bills-Miscel.)").

675. **MacEachern/McEachern, Mary and husband, Malcom.** Petition of Mary (+) MacEachern [of Robeson County] states that about "fourteen years ago her wedded Husband, Malcom MacEachern, left his Home, as he then stated on a Tour to the State of Georgia with a promise of a short return…leaving your Petitioner with their first Born child, then about two years of age, & herself then in a state of forward Pregnancy - those two children she has with Occonemy this far maintained-." Further, she is credibly informed, and such information she has every evidence to believe, that said husband is now married to another woman in the State of Georgia. Prays for an act to secure to her all property she may hereafter acquire. [Below:] Signatures of nine subscribers, neighbors to the petitioner.]

P&GC to whom was referred the petition of Mary McEachern of Robeson County recommend passage of the accompanying bill: A Bill to secure to Mary McEachern of Robeson County such property as she may hereafter acquire. [On reverse: In Senate, 11 December 1828, engrossed and examined.

---

124 Marriage Bond of Edgecombe County, North Carolina, lists Arthur Lawrence and Martha Baker, dated 17 April 1828. Bondsman: Henry Austin.

In House of Commons, 27 December 1828, read and postponed indefinitely.] (GASR, Nov. 1828-Jan. 1829, Box 2: folder "SB 5 Dec.")

676. **Orrin, Mary L. and husband, William.** Petition of Mary L. Orrin of Rockingham County states that her husband, William Orrin,[125] left her in August 1831 pretending he was going out to sell some produce, but has not returned. She has been left with four children and the debts of her husband, whose creditors have seized his property and sold every article. Prays for a law to secure to her all the property she may hereafter acquire. [Below:] Signatures of eleven subscribers, dated 20 November 1833.]

P&GC reports that this case is provided for in the Act of Assembly of 1828 and recommend rejection of petition and alimony. [On reverse: "Concurred in."]

(GASR, Nov. 1833-Jan. 1834, Box 5: folder "HCR (Private Bills-Miscel.)").

677. **Patrick, Martha W. and husband, William.** Petition of Martha W. Patrick of Greensboro, Guilford County, sheweth that sometime in 1821, the rites of matrimony were celebrated between herself and one William Patrick,[126] since which time they have lived together and had two children, both now living. Said husband has become the victim of intemperance, idleness and negligence, and has become greatly involved in debt. A large amount of his property and hers before marriage has been consumed in debt to the extent that such property has been taken away by creditors, and several of them still have unsatisfied claims. Her said husband is now entirely destitute of any means of maintenance of his family. Such support will in the future devolve entirely upon herself, which she finds will be attended with great difficulty and embarrassment unless she is able to be granted relief. Prays that she may be entitled to hold in her sole right any estate which she may hereafter acquire by industry, purchase or gift, and be authorized to prosecute and defend such in her own name as if she had never been married to said William Patrick. P&GC to whom was referred the petition of Martha W. Patrick of Guilford County recommends passage of the accompanying bill: Bill to secure to Martha W. Patrick such property as she may hereafter acquire. [On reverse: In Senate, 15 December, read second and third time, passed and ordered to be engrossed. In House of Commons, 17 December, read and rejected.]

(GASR, Nov. 1829-Jan. 1830, Box 3: folder "SB 9 Dec.")

678. **Read/reed, Jacob and wife, Franky.** Petition of Jacob Read sheweth he married Franky Williams in the year 1821, expecting to spend the remainder of his life in peace and harmony and to provide for his companion the duties of a husband and father of a family. They lived together for two years, most of which time was in a disagreeable manner, she being very indolent and not providing decent clothing for herself. She had one child while we lived together and one other in the ten years since she quit my bed and board. It is likely she will never return. Prays for a divorce from said wife. Dated 30 October 1833. [Below:] Signatures of twelve subscribers.

P&GC to whom was referred the petition of Jacob Reed of Buncombe County unanimously agree that this case is one provided for by the Act of 1827 and therefore report against the prayer of the petitioner. [On reverse: In Senate, 30 November 1833, read and concurred in.]

(GASR, Nov. 1833-Jan. 1834, Box 6: folder "SCR (Propositions and Grievances-Miscellaneous)").

---

125   Marriage Bond of Rockingham County, North Carolina, lists William Orrin and Mary Joyce, dated 17 October 1819. Bondsman: William Fewell.

126   Marriage Bond of Guilford County, North Carolina, lists William Patrick and Martha W. Dick, dated 12 December 1821. Bondsman: Saml. Scott.

679. **Read, Polly and husband, Elias.** Petition of Polly Read sheweth she intermarried with Elias Read some four or five years ago,[127] by which said Elias acquired from your petitioner a very large personal estate consisting mostly of negro slaves. Soon after said marriage, instead of the kind and affectionate treatment which she might expect as the wife of Elias, her husband began to exhibit dissatisfaction with your petitioner. After telling her that although she was his wife, he had no regard for her and never had any, but had married her alone for the property she brought to him. After heaping every insult and indignity possible upon her by his language, he banished her from his house and placed her in his negro quarter, where she was deprived of all the conveniences and necessaries of life beyond a base sufficiency to support her existence. Her provisions were measured out to her in the same way as if she had been a field laborer. His ill treatment was accompanied by acts of violence and threats of continued maltreatment, and this induced her to separate herself from him for her own safety. Said Elias has sold or otherwise disposed of all his real estate with the declared object of leaving your petitioner destitute. Further, he has removed all the negro slaves beyond the limits of this state, including himself, and has declared that he will never return during the life of your petitioner. She is now destitute and still subject to the legal control of her husband, but at the same time cast off by him and in fear of his return. Prays for a dissolution of the tie which binds her to her husband. [Below:] Signatures of thirty-three subscribers who support the prayer of the petitioner.] (GASR, Nov. 1832-Jan. 1833, Box 6: folder "Petitions (Divorce)").

Bill to dissolve the bonds of matrimony between Mary Read and her husband, Elias Read. [On reverse: In Senate, 11 December 1833, read third time, passed and ordered to be engrossed. In House of Commons, 9 January 1834, read third time, passed and ordered to be enrolled.] (GASR, Nov. 1833-Jan. 1834, Box 3: folder "SB 31 Dec.")

680. **Roberts, John and wife, Agness.** Petition of John Roberts of Buncombe County represents he intermarried with Agness Lea of Cocke County, Tennessee, in December 1822 and lived with her for about three years, after which she left his home, and they have lived separate ever since. A short time previous to the separation, he had strong reasons to believe his said wife was inconstant to him, and at the time of this parting, he "caught her in the woods with a certain Anderson North, who was the person he had suspected of having illicit intercourse with his said wife previously." She has lived in Tennessee the last seven years and has had a child by a certain John Woods as she alleges. Your petitioner is advised that since the cause of the divorce originated in Tennessee, he is not entitled to the divorce laws of the State of North Carolina and has no mode of relief except that granted to him by your Honorable Body. Prays for a divorce from the bonds of matrimony with the said Agness.

P&GC to whom was referred the petition of John Roberts recommend the passage of the accompanying bill: Bill to divorce John Roberts and his wife, Agness. [On reverse: In Senate, 26 and 27 November 1832, read first and second time, passed and ordered to be engrossed. In House of Commons, 29 November 1832, read first and second time, and on motion of Mr. Outlaw, indefinitely postponed.]

(GASR, Nov. 1832-Jan. 1833, Box 2: folder "SB 26 Nov.")

681. **Singleton, Kesiah and husband, Christopher.** P&GC to whom was referred the bill to secure to Kesiah Singleton of Burke County such property as she may hereafter acquire, report that Christopher Singleton of Burke County abandoned his wife and family some ten or twelve years since and has not yet returned. He left his wife and two children with little means of support. He was involved in debt

---

127   Marriage Bond of Halifax County, North Carolina, lists Elias Read and Mary Pritchett, dated 25 October 1828. Bondsman: John H. Throw.

when he left, but since that time, his wife has lived a prudent and industrious life and supported his children by her honest labor and industry. Recommend passage of said bill. (GASR, Nov. 1833-Jan. 1834, Box 6: folder "SCR (Propositions and Grievances - Miscellaneous)").

Bill to entitle Kesiah Singleton, wife of Christopher Singleton, of Burke County to hold, possess and enjoy any estate, real or personal, which she may hereafter acquire as if she had never been married. [On reverse: In Senate, 18 December 1833, engrossed and examined. In House of Commons, 8 January 1834, read third time, passed and ordered to be engrossed.] (GASR, Nov. 1833-Jan. 1834, Box 3: folder "SB 12 Dec.")

682. **Sloan, John and wife, Elizabeth.** Select committee to whom was referred a Bill to divorce John Sloan of Mecklenburg County from his wife, Elizabeth,[128] reports that it appears said Elizabeth possesses as diabolical a temper as woman ever possessed. Her conduct towards her husband is outrageous and disgraceful in the extreme, such as to render it utterly impossible for any man to live in peace and happiness with her. It further does not appear to your Committee that said Elizabeth has any just cause for thus treating her husband. It appears that said John Sloan is a man of good temper and has always treated her with forebearance. From the testimony, said Elizabeth has been incontinent to her husband, but not in such manner as to authorize the Superior Courts to divorce him under the existing laws on that subject. Your Committee recommends the passage of the accompanying bill without amendment: Bill to divorce John Sloan from Elizabeth Sloan. [On reverse: In Senate, 2 January, engrossed and examined. In House of Commons, 5 January, reconsidered on motion of Mr. Wheeler and postponed indefinitely.] (GASR, Nov. 1829-Jan. 1830, Box 3: folder "SB 23 Dec.")

683. **Smith, Rebecca Ann and husband, Richard.** P&GC to whom was referred the Bill to divorce Rebecca Ann Smith of Columbus County from her husband, Richard Smith, report that this case was cognizable in the Superior Court and request this Committee be discharged from further consideration of this Bill. [On reverse: In Senate, 20 December 1832, and concurred in.] (GASR, Nov. 1832-Jan. 1833, Box 5: folder "SCR (Propositions & Grievances - Miscellaneous)").

Bill to divorce Rebecca Ann Smith of Columbus County from her husband, Richard Smith. [On reverse: In Senate, 20 December 1832, reported from Committee without amendment, read second time and resolved that same shall not pass.] (GASR, Nov. 1832-Jan. 1833, Box 2: folder "SB 26 Nov.")

684. **Smith, Selah and husband, [not listed].** P&GC to whom was referred the petition of Selah Smith of Montgomery County praying for a law to allow her to acquire and hold property independent of her husband report that the Act of 1827, amended in 1828, gave the power of giving alimony was vested in the Superior Courts of this state. (GASR, Nov. 1831-Jan. 1832, Box 5: folder "HCR (Military-Miscellaneous)").

685. **Sorrels, Nancy and husband, William.** Petition of Nancy Sorrels of Burke County represents she was married to William Sorrels in said county about 23 or 24 years ago and lived with him nearly ever since in said county. She conducted herself as an affectionate, kind, industrious, prudent and virtuous wife, and they have had ten children, eight of whom are now living with your petitioner and said husband. The said William is much given to intemperance and stays out from home drinking. When he can get credit, he purchases liquor in that way, and when he cannot get credit, he will sell his clothes off his back to purchase spirits. Said husband spends so much of his time away from home that he makes

---

128   Marriage Bond of Mecklenburg County, North Carolina, lists John Sloan and Elizabeth Elliott, dated 8 January 1821. Bondsman: Robert McCombs.

no provision for the support of either the children or herself, so she is compelled to work to raise provisions for the family besides spinning for their clothing. Frequently, after raising grain to bread the family and raising pork and fattening it, all has been taken to satisfy debts contracted by her husband for liquor purchases. She has never seen her husband in debt one cent which he had to pay. Your petitioner is now advanced in life and not so able to work as heretofore. Prays for a law securing to her whatever property she may hereafter acquire. [Below:] Signatures of fifteen subscribers who support the petitioner.] P&GC to whom was referred the Petition of Nancy Sorrels of Burke County summarizes the content of the petition above and recommend passage of the accompanying bill: Bill to secure to Nancy Sorrels of Burke County such property as she may hereafter acquire. [On reverse: In House of Commons, 28 November 1828, read first time and passed.]

(GASR, Nov. 1828-Jan. 1829, Box 1: folder "HB 24 Nov.")

686. **Speight, Sally and husband, William W. D**. Bill for relief of Sally Speight of Greene County. Said Sally Speight will be entitled, upon her coming of age of 21 years, to a legacy of $1,000 under the Will of her deceased father, and whereas William W. D. Speight, husband of aforesaid Sally, has fled from the county having an amount of outstanding debts more than sufficient to cover the aforesaid legacy: be it enacted that the whole of the aforesaid legacy, whenever it becomes payable, shall be paid to said Sally Speight free from control of her said husband or any of his creditors. [No action listed.]

P&GC to whom was recommitted the petition of Sally Speight have reconsidered same, and report that the case of the petitioner is embraced in the Acts of 1814 and 1828, and consequently, it is inexpedient for this Legislature to interfere in her behalf. [On reverse: In House of Commons, 5 December 1829, read and concurred in.]

(GASR, Nov. 1829-Jan. 1830, Box 1: folder "HB 30 Nov.")

687. **Stevenson, Gatsey and husband, Silas.** Petition of Gatsey Stephenson [signed Stevenson] of Lenoir County sheweth she intermarried with Silas Stephenson of Craven County "at an early period after her arrival at a suitable age." All her talents and abilities were honestly devoted to the attainment of her determination that nothing should be left undone on her part to contribute to their mutual happiness and prosperity. Your memorialist regrets to state that she soon discovered that all her efforts were in vain. Her husband was unfortunately addicted to habits of intemperance, which became more frequent as time moved on. Her honor, peace of mind, and personal safety demanded she should quit his society, and after a few years of marriage, she took shelter under the roof of her father. She remained there for the next twelve or eighteen months and received overtures from her husband to return, for he promised to change and alleged that he had abandoned the use of ardent spirits. Your memorialist was induced to return in hopes that a change had actually taken place in his habits and disposition towards her. However, she was doomed to disappointment soon after her return. Despairing of any favorable change in his conduct, she again left his home and went to her father's. Your memorialist is the mother of four children, all of whom she brought away with her, and [she] has personally furnished the support necessary for their maintenance without the aid of her husband. She left five negro slaves in her husband's possession, they being a part of the filial portion which she brought to him, including valuable stock and a plantation worth $1,000-2,000 at that time. Your memorialist took little property with her when she left except her wearing apparel and a few articles of furniture. A short time after her last separation, her husband took into his house a profligate woman named Polly Heath and is now living in adulterous intercourse. He has procured title to the plantation to the said Polly, who now claims it under a pretended purchase from a trustee to whom it had been conveyed for the benefit of a creditor. Your memorialist is thus cast upon the world utterly destitute without friends to assist her except an aged mother (her father being now dead)

and with several of her children claiming a large share of her time and attention. Prays for a law to secure to her such property as she may hereafter acquire. [Below:] Signatures of twenty-three subscribers in support of the petitioner.]

    P&GC to whom was referred the petition of Gatsey Stephens, wife of Silas Stephens, report that said petition states that said Silas is both a drunkard and a spendthrift. This case is therefore provided for by an Act of Assembly passed in 1828. The Committee therefore asks to be discharged from further consideration of the subject.

    [On reverse: Concurred in and Committee discharged.] (GASR, Nov. 1833-Jan. 1834, Box 5: folder "HCR (Private Bills - Miscellaneous)").

688.   **Tutner, Mary and husband, Henry.** Committee on Divorce and Alimony to whom was referred the petition of Mary Turner of Washington County, wife of Henry Turner, report that the petitioner intermarried with Henry A. Turner in 1817. A short time after the marriage, said Henry became peevish, fretful and perverse in temper, dissipation and habitually a drunkard. As a result, his wife and child have been reduced to penury and went without a home and without property except the clothes they wear and the support acquired by the petitioner's labor and the assistance given her by her friends. This couple has lived together about three years and were without a home, but resided alternately with the mother of the petitioner and that of the said Henry. The petitioner's husband left her and the child without any provocation on her part. He came back promising an amendment in his conduct, but she was soon subjected to his abuse and ill treatment again. After having a second child, her said husband finally abandoned her in the latter part of 1821 and has failed to support the petitioner and surviving child. Recommend the prayer of the petitioner to be secured to such property as she may hereafter acquire be passed into law.[129]

(GASR, Nov. 1833-Jan. 1834, Box 5: folder "SCR (Claims - Judiciary)").

689.   **Viverett, Ann Eliza and husband, Micajah.** Petition of Ann Eliza Armstrong represents she has been placed in a situation as delicate and novel as it is to her painful and embarrassing. She is advised there is no tribunal in the State competent to her relief, save only your honorable body upon whom she is induced to throw herself under the confident hope that she is not to ask in vain. Your petitioner represents that she is now but 17 years of age, residing in the County of Edgecombe where she was born and has been raised. About twelve months ago, she was addressed by a man by the name of Wilkins and another by the name of Viverett. She gave preference to the former, and was at that time disposed to have married him, but her parents, though not favorable to the latter, were most decidedly opposed to the former. In this delicate situation, she was greatly perplexed as to the proper course to pursue. To marry Wilkins, she should encounter the displeasure of kind and indulgent parents, and to marry Viverett, she should doom herself to misery and unhappiness. She would most willingly have given up them both, but her parents, under the fear that she might marry Wilkins, insisted upon her marrying Viverett. In this painful dilemma, she resolved to relieve the fears of her parents, and at an evil hour, under a misapprehension as to consequence, consented to pass through the marriage ceremony, provided no license should be had.[130] This she did with the view of quieting the apprehension of her parents for the moment, intending if she could become reconciled to Viverett, to have the license afterwards obtained and the marriage consummated. Viverett was accordingly sent for by her father, the ceremony performed by a magistrate, and she gave her silent assent with the mental reservation that as she was not at heart, so she was not in fact a married woman. She refused her consent to have the license taken out or in any way

---

129   No further action listed.
130   Marriage Bond of Edgecombe County, North Carolina, lists Micajah Viverett and Ann Eliza Armstrong, dated 30 January 1833. Bondsman: James Viver[e]t.

to be treated as the wife of Viverett, still thinking that without a license, the marriage was a nullity. She found too, that so far from being reconciled to the man (she cannot tarnish the second man by calling him husband), her aversion daily increased. His awkward efforts to please only seemed to render him the more obnoxious. Nor could she reconcile it to her feelings to unite herself to a man who had so little spirit of independence as to ask the hand of one whom he must have known despised him. For such is the peculiar cant of the female character that whilst she loves with ardor, she hates with bitterness — and now so it is, may it please your honorable body, your petitioner learns our laws recognize the marriage state as but a civil contract, and therefore binding whenever the assent has been given, whatever the motives or feelings which may have prompted it. Although your petitioner did not give her free and voluntary assent to the engagement, she unfortunately did manage to render the marriage valid in law. The circumstances of the case do not furnish grounds for her to appeal to the judicial tribunals in the country, and your honorable body can alone cut the Gordian knot and restore her once more to her maiden privileges and independence. Your petitioner therefore prays your honorable body to pass an act divorcing her from the said Viverett, not with the view of her to marry another against the will of her parents (for this she pledges herself not to do), but to relieve her from the power of a man whom she can neither love or respect, and to quiet the self-reproaches of her unhappy parents. She makes this appeal to you as the only power who can relieve her present unfortunate condition. /s/ Ann Eliza Armstrong. (GASR, Nov. 1833-Jan. 1834, Box 6: folder "Petitions (Divorce; name change)").

Certificate of Gray (x) Armstrong, father of Ann Eliza Armstrong, alias Viverett, states that the facts set forth in the petition of said Ann Eliza are to the best of my knowledge and belief correctly stated. My daughter, as aforesaid, at no time entertained for the individual to whom she has been married, those feelings of respect and affection without which marriage instead of a blessing becomes a curse — and that she was induced to marry him to gratify my own and her mother's wishes. The present situation of my daughter is unhappy in the extreme. She refuses to receive Viverett as her husband, and from her great aversion for him, I am assured she will not do so at any future time. Deeply regretting that I should have been at all instrumental in inflicting such misery on my child, I unite with her in praying the Legislature to divorce her from the said Micajah Viverett. (GASR, Nov. 1833-Jan. 1834, Box 6: folder "Petitions (Divorce; name change)").

Statement of Benjamin Wilkerson, Justice of Peace for Edgecombe County, dated 10 September 1833. He was called upon by Gray Armstrong last January to marry his daughter, Ann Eliza, to Micajah Viverett. Said [Armstrong] stated he "had gotten his daughter to agree to the marriage but was fearful if it was delayed, she might change her mind & the License would be gotten afterwards…" As the request came from the father of the girl, I consented to perform the ceremony, not knowing of my difficulty. I accordingly married them & the license was obtained a few days afterwards. I learned the next day that the girl refused to bed and cohabit with the man and from my knowledge of what has taken place, I have cause to believe they never have bedded and cohabited as man and wife. She is a girl of fair and irreproachable character. (GASR, Nov. 1833-Jan. 1834, Box 6: folder "Miscellaneous")

P&GC to whom was referred the bill to divorce Ann Eliza Viverett of Edgecombe County from her husband, Micajah Viverett, recommend the passage of the accompanying bill. [See below.] (GASR, Nov. 1833-Jan. 1834, Box 6: folder "SCR (Propositions & Grievances - Miscellaneous)").

Bill to divorce Ann Eliza Viverett, who was Ann Eliza Armstrong, of Edgecombe County from her husband, Micajah Viverett, and that she be restored to the privileges of a feme sole. [On reverse: In House of Commons, 26 November 1833, read three times, passed and ordered to be engrossed. In Senate, 3 December 1833, read three times and ordered to be engrossed.] (GASR, Nov. 1833-Jan. 1834, Box 1: folder "HB 25 Nov.")

Divorces and Separations from Petitions to the North Carolina General Assembly from 1779

690. **Wooters, Sarah and husband, John.** Petition of Sarah Wooters of Guilford County states she was in the possession of a handsome estate left partly by her father, and in 1820, married a young man by the name of John Wooters.[131] After living together about two years, he sold my two negroes and all the property I had except a bed and "close" under the pretense of moving to the western country. He collected the money and notes and left me to see the country and purchase land. He now has been absent near six years, and it has been told to me by good authority that he married a second time since he left the country. Prays for an act that the property hereafter acquired by me to be secured to me so he cannot take it from me. [Below:] Signatures of seventeen subscribers in support of the petitioner.]

P&GC to whom was referred the Petition of Sarah Wooters of Guilford County summarize the contents of said petition and recommend passage of the following bill: Bill to secure to Sarah Wooters of Guilford County such property as she may hereafter acquire. [On reverse: In Senate, 6 December 1828, engrossed and examined. In House of Commons, 6 December 1828, read first time and passed; read second time and rejected.]

(GASR, Nov. 1828-Jan. 1829, Box 2: folder "SB 25 Nov.")

691. **Reference A.**
Laws of North Carolina, November 1828 through November 1833 (selected):
Session of November 1828, page 25: The Superior Courts of Law shall have jurisdiction of all applications for alimony, as well as of those for divorce and alimony.

Session of November 1829, page 27: An Act giving femes covert the right of suing and being sued. "When any married woman shall file her petition in any of the Superior Courts of Law of this State, praying that alimony may be decreed to her, and that such property as she may thereafter acquire may be also secured to her, the Judges of said Courts may, if they think proper, decree that the petitioner may sue and be sued in her own name without joining the name of her husband…in the same manner as if the petitioner was a feme sole."

Session of November 1833. The following persons were either given a divorce (prefix "D") or given security of property thereafter acquired (prefix "S):
- S   p. 155 - Keeth, Sarah Ann, wife of William Keeth, of Washington County.
- D   p. 156 - Read, Mary from husband, Elias Read, of Halifax County [?].
- S   p. 155 - Singleton, Kesiah of Burke County, wife of Christopher Singleton.
- D   p. 154 - Viverett, Ann Eliza, who was Ann Eliza Armstrong of Edgecombe County, from husband, Micajah Viverett.

---

131   Marriage Bond of Guilford County, North Carolina, lists John Wooters and Sally Aydelott, dated 25 December 1820. Bondsman: Eli Brewer.

1834-1835

692. **Ambrose, Peter and wife, Thirza/Thurza/Theresa.**

(1). Petition of Peter Ambrose of Onslow County sheweth he married one Thurza Hatch, widow of Durant Hatch (former resident of Onslow County), on 8 July 1830.[132] After the marriage ceremony, they returned to the petitioner's house from her brother's where the marriage had been celebrated. For a short term, they lived together as well as could be hoped in perfect harmony and affection. After a few months, this life was interrupted by the said Theresa becoming anxious for the petitioner to break up his establishment where he was so comfortably off, sell out, remove to the west, and hurry out of the State in order to accompany her brother and sister, who with their families intended to remove. Your petitioner explained to her the impracticability of such a scheme — that he was comfortably off, had good lands and slaves to cultivate it, and every inducement to remain where he was — that if she had mentioned such a thing before their marriage, he could and would have promptly informed her it was out of the question. He hoped she would give up such an idea. From that time, his wife became dissatisfied, and although she continued to live with him, she teased him on the subject. He finally told her he would not at this time of life break up and move from the county where they had both been born and raised to go to an unknown and distant country. She became disagreeable of her duty as a wife, and under some frivolous pretense went away from her home and stayed at her sister's for a time. Your petitioner, to his chagrin and disappointment, received a letter from her, informing him of her intention not to return, and demanded her clothes. Your petitioner was mortified at this, as he had treated her with all the kindness and affection which was his duty to do. He sent her clothes according to her request in hopes she would see her folly in the course of conduct she had adopted. A few days after, she returned with her sister's husband and stayed about six months, apparently contented, but she soon began to open the old subject of removal. On his reiterating his determination to stay where he was, she left your petitioner about the first of October 1830 and has never returned. She removed to Craven County for a time, where she resided with her brother, and finally on 15 March 1832, she left this State for Tennessee with her brother and sister, where she has ever since resided. She has expressed her determination never to return to North Carolina. Your petitioner has applied to the Superior Court of Law for this county for a divorce without effect. He has thus made application to your body, hoping for a remedy to this case by passing an act for his relief. He prays for a divorce from his said wife. [Below:] Signatures of twenty-two subscribers in support of the petitioner.

(2). P&GC to whom was referred the petition of Peter Ambrose of Onslow County summarized said petition and recommended legislative interference "to unloose the petitioner from his painful and unpleasant situation" by passing the accompanying bill: Peter Ambrose of Onslow County is hereby declared to be divorced from his wife, Thirza Ambrose, who was Thirza Hatch previous to this intermar-

---

132 Marriage Bond of Onslow County lists Peter Ambrose and Thursy Hatch, dated 7 July 1830. Bondsman: Wms. Humphrey.

Divorces and Separations from Petitions to the North Carolina General Assembly from 1779

riage. [On reverse:] In House of Commons, 1 December 1834, engrossed and examined; in Senate, 3 December 1834, read second and third times, passed, and ordered to be enrolled.

(GASR, Nov. 1834-Jan. 1835, Box 1: folder "HB 26 Nov.")

693. **Brownrigg, Theresy/Theresa and husband, Henry.**

(1). Petition of Theresey [signed Theresea] Brownrigg of Wayne County, who states she was born in Pitt County. On 31 October 1811, she intermarried with one Henry Brownrigg, who was then, and is believed now, to be a citizen of Edgecombe County. She demeaned herself in all respects towards her said husband as a dutiful and affectionate wife, ministering to his wants, and using all her efforts to promote his happiness. Unfortunately, said Henry became addicted to habits of intemperance, and by his inattention and intoxication, soon expended his own property as well as that which he acquired from your petitioner. About ten years ago, the whole of his property was sold, and your petitioner was left destitute and dependent on her friends. Her husband has become a habitual drunkard and spendthrift, and he has long since wasted all his substance to the impoverishment of his family. Your petitioner has continued to reside with a friend in Wayne County, but her husband has never once visited her nor provided for her support. Prays for a law which allows her such property as she may hereafter acquire.

(2). P&GC to whom was referred the petition of Theresea Brownrigg of Wayne County report that it appears the petitioner was raised in Pitt County of respectable parents, and hoping to enjoy the comforts of a married life, she intermarried with one Doctor Henry Brownrigg of Edgecombe County. Said Henry removed himself and family to the town of Waynesborough in Wayne County and became addicted to habits of intemperance. He soon expended his own property and that acquired by his wife.

Passage of the accompanying bill is recommended: That Theresy Brownrigg of Wayne County, wife of Henry Brownrigg, be entitled to hold any estate, real or personal, which she may hereafter acquire by industry, purchase, gift or otherwise. [On reverse:] In Senate, 1 December 1834, engrossed and examined; in House of Commons, 3 December 1834, read third time, passed, and ordered to be enrolled.

(GASR, Nov. 1834-Jan. 1835, Box 3: folder "SB 29 Nov.")

694. **Cabe, Mary Barbara and husband, Joseph.**

(1). Petition of Barbara Cabe, formerly Barbara Smith, states she married one Joseph Cabe on 20 May 1832 and hoped to end her days in a prosperous and happy life. However, within one month after the wedding, said Joseph began to maltreat and abuse your petitioner. He seemingly associated himself with a certain Anne Bugg, then living in the same house with said Joseph and his mother. Said Anne had been deserted by her husband, Henry Bugg, but within two months after your petitioner's marriage and within her view, it was a common thing for her said husband, Joseph, and the said Ann "to be Huging and kissing each other, and be sitting or lyeing in her lap." During some eight or nine months your petitioner remained in the house with her said husband, it was common practice for said Joseph to get up out of the bed from your petitioner and go to some other bed out of her view but in the same house where resided said Anne. Her said husband continued to abuse and maltreat your petitioner and compelled her to go to her father's home and remain there, a distance of three to four miles. She informed the said Joseph that if he removed from the house of his mother, where also lived the said Anne, your petitioner would willingly live with him again and forgive the past injury. He refused this offer and would not speak to her about this problem. Your petitioner humbly beseeches your honorable body to release her from wedlock with the said Joseph by passing a law to divorce them. /s/ Barbery Cabe. [Below:] (a) Certificate of Robert Love of Haywood County stating he has been acquainted with the said Barbara, formerly Barbara Smith, from the day of her birth, "she having been born within two & half miles of where I was then or now residing, and whose father, Colo. Jacob Smith, has never resided

1834-1835 Session

out of this county from the day of her birth…" I have always considered her to be a very virtuous and prudent woman. (b) Signatures of eighty-nine subscribers who support the prayer of the petitioner.

(2). P&GC to which was referred the petition of Mary B. Cabe summarizes it and recommends passage of the accompanying bill: Bill to divorce Mary B. Cabe of Haywood County from her husband, Joseph Cabe, and that she be restored to the privileges of a feme sole. [On reverse:] In Senate, 10 December 1834, engrossed and examined; in House of Commons, 16 December 1834, read three times, passed and ordered to be enrolled.

(GASR, Nov. 1834-Jan. 1835, Box 3: folder "SB 27 Nov.")

695. **Cobb, Ellena and husband, John.**

(1). Petition of Ellena M. Cobb of Burke County states she intermarried with John Cobb of Hamburg, South Carolina on the last of January 1832. The said John Cobb came to Morganton [Burke County, North Carolina] when your petitioner resided with her father, and addressed her on the subject of matrimony. He represented himself as highly respectable and of good standing in the town where he resided. He also claimed considerable celebrity as a physician, having a large and extensive practice which was very profitable, and that he owned and was in possession of one or two valuable plantations and some fifteen negroes. Your petitioner further charges that said John Cobb travelled "in very handsome stile with a carriage, two fine horses and a servant and dressed in a gentul and fashionable manner, and as far as your petitioner knew, conducted himself soberly and in every appearance as a gentleman." A few days after the marriage took place, they set out from her father's for Hamburg, the residence of said John Cobb. They had not travelled more than two days, when he began to drink to excess all the way to Hamburg. He was constantly intoxicated and incapable of doing anything. He became a constant source of deep and heart rending mortification and regret, and it required her whole attention to take care of him. Upon their arrival in Hamburg, she ascertained that he had no home of his own but resided with his widowed mother. He had no land, no negroes and did not possess one particle of property. The carriage, horses and servant were hired or borrowed. As far as she could learn, he was without credit, had no practice as a physician, and was entirely ignorant of the profession according to his acquaintances. Your petitioner found that all of his representations to be largely false, fraudulent and deceitful. After they arrived in Hamburg, he continued to drink to excess, and became incapable of attending to any kind of business. As soon as he arose in the morning, he would go off and get drunk, return home and throw himself down on the floor and sleep. When he awoke, he would abuse his aged mother, and in a short time would return to the tipling shops. He associated with no persons of respectability. He seemed to have lost all respect for his own character, his family, and your petitioner. She did not spend one hour at any time with him when he was sober — from the time she went to Hamburg until she left him. She left his mother's house in May 1832 and went to the residence of a friend in Hamburg, where she remained until her father sent for her, and has remained with her father ever since. (GASR, Nov. 1834-Jan. 1835, Box 5: folder "Petitions [Divorce]")

(2). Letter from Thos. J. Bouchell, Wilkesboro, North Carolina, 14 December 1834 to William J. Alexander, Raleigh, North Carolina: I presume that a petition for divorce for my unfortunate sister, Ellena, has arrived in Raleigh to the care of Mr. Ship or Mr. Carson. The case is a hard one, and I am advised it is without remedy in the Courts of Justice, and she has been advised to apply by petition to the Legislature. I fondly think you could have some weight with the Committee to whom the matter will probably be referenced. "It is that yet in the bloom of youth, that tyed to a vagabond who even within the first three months of marriage should deny to her even the common necessaries of life and but for a few dollars of pin money given her by her father with which she bought from meal to meal what supported her existance, must have absolutely starved among strangers…[F]ortunately a philanthropic Lady,

263

Divorces and Separations from Petitions to the North Carolina General Assembly from 1779

Mrs. Stark, of Hamburg, discovered her pitiable situation and acted the part of a friend by informing her relations of her situation and acted the part of a mother to her untill the arrival of her friends — It may be proper to state that as soon as Mrs. Stark had Ellena under her own roof, although a perfect stranger to her, she caused Ellena to break off all communication at once with the drunken vagabond — and immediately informed us of her situation. The conduct of this estimable lady requires no comment…this is the man who represented to her that he was wealthy, that he had a large practice as a physician, who came to see her with a borrowed servant[,] carriage and horses and urged under some pretext a hasty marriage[,] all of which to her sorrow proved utterly false…I only ask you to imagine a sister of yours thus duped[,] deceived and deluded, and all her prospects in life utterly blasted, and your fraternal feelings will excuse me the interest I take in this matter…"

(3).   Bill to divorce Ellena M. Cobb of Burke County from her husband John Cobb. [On reverse:] In House of Commons, 16 December 1834, read three times, passed and ordered to be engrossed; in Senate, 2 January 1835, read third time, passed and ordered to be enrolled. (GASR, Nov. 1834-Jan. 1835, Box 2: folder "HB 16 Dec.")

696.   **Durham, Susan and husband, Archibald.**
(1).   Petition of Susan Durham, formerly Susan Mitchell of Burke County, sheweth she married James Sherley in December 1822[133] and with whom she lived happily until 16 May 1829, at which time he departed this life intestate, leaving three children surviving — two daughters and a son — and a small personal estate, which through the kind office of a friend and relation, Mr. James Jeffreys of Caswell County, was secured to her and her children. In September 1830, she married Archibald Durham[134] and lived in utmost harmony. In January 1831, they removed from Caswell to Burke County, where they continued to reside until February 1832, when said Archibald became involved beyond his means of paying and absconded without the knowledge of your petitioner to parts beyond the limits of this State. He left her entirely dependent upon her industry and the kindness of friends for the support and maintenance of herself and family, consisting of an only daughter by him and her three children before mentioned by her first husband. The little property left by her first husband was brought to Burke from Caswell, but it has been seized and sold by the creditors of her second husband when he abandoned her. Your petitioner's immediate relations are poor, and although they interfered in her behalf to make known that the property had not been divided among your petitioner and his children by her first husband, they did not feel able to encounter the expense and trouble of law suits to recover said property from the purchasers. Your petitioner further believes that said Archibald Durham has lost all the affection he ever entertained for her and his child, and has never once written her since he deserted. She is informed by a respectable source that he was in Wilcox County, Alabama a few weeks ago, passing himself off as a single man and paying his addresses to a young lady with a view to marriage. Distressing as is the condition of your petitioner, thus deserted in her utmost need with a family of four small children, and three of them daughters thrown upon her hands penniless and in want and without any prospect of a reunion which could give her the slightest hope of happiness or aid on her afflictions, she is advised that the Courts of Law have not the power to grant her any other aid than a divorce from bed and board. She therefore prays your honorable body to grant her a divorce from the bonds of matrimony and permit her to assume the name of her first husband, to wit — that of Susan Sherley.

---

133   Marriage Bond of Person County, North Carolina, lists James Shirley and Susan Michell, dated 17 December 1822. Bondsman: Thomas Winstead.

134   Marriage Bond of Caswell County, North Carolina, lists Archibald Durham and Susan P. Shirley, dated 29 September 1830. Bondsman: William Barr.

(2). Letter from Arch. Durham to William Taylor and Mary Taylor, Sr., dated 8 May 1832: "I am in good health hoping these few lines may reach you all in the same. When I left your house, I thought to return by the first of May, but I have not done so. I went to Nashville & there staid a few days and then to Franklin & there staid 12 days & then to Columbia and there staid a short time and then Uncle dorman Taylor's and there staid 8 or 10 days and back to columbia & there spent a short time and then started west again…[to] Brown's ferry on the Tenn. river…there crossing came within one minuet of being cast away in a storm…it was the most alarming seen I ever saw, then the next my mare leaped off the top a bridge into a river with me on her back but she made her way out to the bank with me safe…then I had to swim on orther streams the same day but went on to lexington…there staid all knight — from there to Jackson where I am know…Dr. Sir I have seen some the most beautifull country in the world down on the big legs[?] and in this sizion[?] there is the most dredfull country in the world…Jackson is a handsome place[,] the most of my time has been pleasurefull[.]

I was invited home with a gentleman not long since & he went out to rob some beegums there…found something near 100 stands[.] There was eating…smacking Sweet lips. I found all well at Uncle dorman s[.] I have not been to Uncle Johns yet —, I expect to go on down in Alabama before I return[.] I will be at your house sometime in the summer[.] 4 days ago I met up with one of my county men who was Just on from there a given me all the news in that sesion[?] I see some of my acquantance every day[.] Sir I am now a hundred miles west of Nashville[.] I wish to go down about 300 miles futher which will land me about Memfrys on the Mississippi[.] there I shall be at a friend s house from Caswell. Dr Sir I have passed through the land whare milk & honey flows & I am fat & sacy & can maid the Mississippi[,] Swim the Ohio[,] fite like a tiger[,] clime like a catamount and if that wont do I will come back among your cedars again & drink some of my father dukes brand & see how that will do. So I must conclud my letter by describing…cincear friend…"

(3). Letter from Albert Yerger, Pulaski, Tennessee, 24 July 1832 to Mrs. Susan P. Durham, Nashville, Tennessee: "Madam, your favour of the 15th July was duly rec'd. and I would sooner have answered it, but Mr. Nye to whom you referred me for information was absent from home. I of course had to await his return before I could hear anything — I have just seen Mr. Nye…he says he does not know of any person by the name of Durham and that no such person has been [here]…that he knew Mr. Nye has not been to Florence since last September…"

(4). P&GC to which was referred the petition of Susan Durham summarizes the facts in said petition and are of the opinion that the accompanying bill be passed: That Susan P. Durham of Burke County is hereby divorced from her husband, Archibald Durham. [On reverse:] In Senate, 6 December 1834, read second and third times, passed and ordered to be engrossed; in House of Commons, 16 December 1834, read second and third times, passed and ordered to be enrolled.

(GASR, Nov. 1834-Jan. 1835, Box 3: folder "SB 29 Nov.")

697. **Edwards, Rachal and husband, Edmund.**

(1). Petition of Rachal Edwards, "now a citizen of Yancy County," states that at the October Session of the Superior Court for Buncombe County in 1830, a decree of divorce was made on the application of her then husband, Edmund Edwards. Your petitioner has lived unmarried since that time, being forbidden by the laws of the State of North Carolina from remarrying. Your petitioner prays that she may have the privilege once again entering the marriage state. She writes that a sense of her former imprudence is so deeply felt (however much it may have been palliated by circumstances with which it is not needful to trouble your honorable body) as to secure a faithful obedience to marriage vows should she again take them. It will doubtless occur to your body that marriage is the natural state of woman. — her helplessness points it out, and the divine sanction is upon it. It will be recollected that it is human to err — she humbly asks for one frail moment — be cut off from all the privileges of her sex, all the sweet charities and dignities of domestic life, when perhaps by a keen sense of what she has lost, she is more than ever able to appreciate the advantages of her condition. Your honorable body will pardon this attempt at argument, and your wisdom will doubtless suggest other and better reasons for complying with this request of a penitent and defenceless woman. Dated 7 November 1834. [Below:] Signatures of eighteen subscribers who state they are well acquainted with Rachal Edwards, and compliance with her petition would be a good policy, as the rigor of the law being enforced in her case may be productive of more evil than good.

(2). P&GC to whom was referred the petition of Rachel Edwards of Yancy County report that said Rachel, having once joined in the bonds of matrimony, and by her own acts and imprudent conduct caused the separation, and the decree of the Court by which she is now forbidden to enjoy the privileges of her sex and restrained from the marriage state — are reasons of themselves sufficient to form an impression unfavorable to the petitioner. It is true that it is set forth from a respectable source that withholding from her the privilege asked for may be productive of more evil than good. Your Committee however, although they feel some sympathy for her situation, and knowing the rejection of her request may lead to acts which are contrary to the laws of God and man, yet they are of the opinion that perhaps these evils would not be so great as to place her in the possession of again deceiving another person and probably committing those heinous offenses, already enumerated, as formerly for which she was placed in her present situation. Your Committee prays to be discharged from the further consideration of the subject.

(GASR, Nov. 1834-Jan. 1835, Box 5: folder "SCR")

698.   **Ep(p)es, Mary T. and husband, Peter.**
(1).   Petition of Mary T. Epes of Warren County, dated 26 November 1834, states she was unfortunately married on 24 July 1821 to one Peter Epes of Nottoway County, Virginia at the house of Edward Chambers (who at that time was wedded to my Aunt, who had adopted me for her daughter) in Lunenburg County, Virginia. I lived with said Peter for five years, and in 1825, we moved to Warren County, North Carolina. He soon squandered what property I had and what his father had loaned him. He was in "habits of Illicit Commerce with Common women, which modesty, refused to investigate at that time." In 1828, he went to Tennessee, and after staying nine months, returned the same year and pretended he had been to make provision for myself and three helpless infant daughters — but did not. After loitering several months at his father's in Virginia, he came back to North Carolina and borrowed my brother's horse to go to Tennessee a second time to make provision for his family (as he said). He left my father's house on 14 March 1829, and after his arrival in Tennessee, he wrote to me and my sister in 1830 that he had gotten a house and furniture, sixty head of hogs, and everything to "House Keeping." He was then in the "employ of Col. Richard C. Napier and could support his family and lay up $600 per annum…I doubted the truth of his statement, and at my instance prevailed on my father to introduce himself in a letter to Col. Napier and ask for the facts…" [See Col. Napier's letter below.] In March 1835, it will be six years since he has gone off, and last July of 1834, it will be eight years that myself and helpless infants have been on the charity of my parents. I have every reason to believe that said husband Peter has been living in habits of adultery with one Betsy Alexander and others in Dickson County, Tennessee, as may be seen by reference to letters from James Rucks, Esqr., Counsel at Law, Nashville, Tennessee, and Benj. Kelly of Stewart County, Tennessee. The information from Mr. Kelly was not sought nor asked for. Your petitioner was advised to apply to the Superior Court for a divorce by her counsel. She made some efforts to do this, but found herself unable to give her said husband the notice required by law to bring him before the Honorable Court, because last August he left that section

of the country, and it is not known where your petitioner must now apply. References as to the general character of your petitioner are enclosed for persons in Warren, Granville and Franklin Counties. Your petitioner hopes that you will dispose of her case favorably. [Below:] Signatures of thirty subscribers who recommend the petitioner's prayer be granted and a separate certificate signed by six other subscribers.

(2). Extract of letter from Peter Epes in Davidson County, Tennessee, to his wife, Mary T. Epes, dated 9 October 1830: Yours of 15 September has come to hand, the contents of which have been deliberated on for the last 48 hours. Perhaps, Mary, you are unapprised agreeable to the laws of this state — two years separation of man and wife will allow either or both to marry again. I never expect to be in Virginia or North Carolina again.

(3). Extract of letter from Peter Epes, Turnbull Forge, Davidson County, Tennessee, 14 March 1831, to Eliza G. Sale [sister of Mary T. EPES]: Dear Eliza…Yours bearing date of 22 January is now before me. My final determination is for me & her to never to pester each other again, not even with a letter. I have determined this course but never have communicated it to any of my relations until about 10 days since — I then wrote to Brother Thomas and informed him of it. I then determined to take up with a girl who at that time lived at the works. I was intimate with her for two months. Her parents then removed to Illinois. She was desirous to remain with me, but on mature reflection, I determined to make her go, and got off promising her that I would follow her in a few days and go with her to Illinois.

(4). Letter from R. C. Napier, Nashville [Tennessee], 8 May 1831, to Rev. Anthony Sale, Ellisville, Warren County, North Carolina: Yours of 18 March is before me, and a journey to Orleans and Saint Lewis prevented me from giving you an answer. I feel it is my duty, having children of my own, to answer you candidly. Sometime last July or August, from the high opinion which I then entered of Capt. Epps, I indorsed for him for $525 in the Bank. About two weeks after he got the money, heard he was in jail in Lebanon, Wilson County [Tennessee]. I then pursued him and had to advance a further sum of $214 to take him out [of jail], as he promised to return home with me and then stay until I was paid, as he said he would write his brother in Virginia, who would certainly forward me the money…which money has never been received. Out of the $739 which I paid for him, I received from him $345 in cash which he had with him when I took him from the jail. I also got from him three pistols which I allowed him $20 and a mare at $80, making it all $445, which is all that I ever received. Some weeks after I took him to my works, there was a vacancy for an overseer at my forge on Turnbull where I sent him at one dollar per day. Since he has been with me, he has conducted well, sober, industrious and attentive to business as to his friends. He now appears steady, and it would not be right for me to venture an opinion. I hope you keep it to yourself and let no other person know what I have stated, as he might do me considerable damage if it should reach him before I could know anything about it — living at a distance from my works.

(5). Letter from Benjamin Kelly, Brunson's, Tennessee, 11 August 1833 to Rev. Anthony Sale, Ellisville, Warren County, North Carolina: I am in moderate health and found all my family well on my return home from your county. On my road home I spent a day with Simon Green whom I found 17 miles southeast of Nashville…Peter Epps in May last was living in Dickson County where he has been for the last three years…I was informed that he was concerned in a small distillery…There was an expectation of his marrying Miss Betsy Alexander, whose company he had sought during his residence there; spent his money to maintain her whole family on her account. She is not considered in her neighborhood a respectable woman. He resolved last Fall to go to New Orleans about the time he left the employment of Col. Napier but afterwards declined and commenced the Distillery in the neighborhood and so much for Mr. Epps.

Divorces and Separations from Petitions to the North Carolina General Assembly from 1779

    (6).   Letter from James Rucks, Nashville, Tennessee, 3 April 1833 to Rev. Anthony Sale, Ellisville, Nutbush, Warren County, North Carolina: Col. Napier has an iron store in this town and upon enquiring of his young men, I find Mr. Epes is regarded as a man of very loose morals. They say he lives in Dickson County, & it is understood he keeps a woman named Alexander — a daughter of Joe Alexander & refer us to Thomas & Green Sears & Mark Gower for proof. I am at a loss to advise you about getting depositions unless we employ a young man of this town…it would cost $20 to employ any one competent to do it with accuracy…My father & mother are still living & in good health — so are my Aunt Brodie & Aunt Taylour.

    (7).   P&GC to whom was referred the petition of Mary T. Eppes of Warren County summarize the facts in the petition and state it is of opinion that the prayer of the petitioner be granted and recommend passage of the following bill to divorce Mary T. Eppes from her husband, Peter Eppes. [On reverse:] In Senate, 12 December 1834, read second and third time, passed and ordered to be engrossed; in House of Commons, 16 December 1834, read second and third time, passed and ordered to be enrolled.

    (GASR, Nov. 1834-Jan. 1835, Box 3: folder "SB 4 Dec.")

699.   **Flowers, Sally and husband, Christopher.**

    (1).   Petition of Sally (X) Flowers of Craven County sheweth she intermarried with Christopher Flowers many years ago.[135] The said Christopher withdrew his affections from her due to intemperance and other evil habits, and for the last seven years has abandoned her and lived in parts of the country unknown to your petitioner. Her only support is derived from the fruits of her own labor. She has no reason to hope said Christopher will ever return to his family and understands that he associates with women of loose character. Prays for a divorce from said husband. [Below:] Signatures of six subscribers in support of the prayer of the petitioner.

    (2).   P&GC to whom was referred the petition of Salley Flowers of Craven County recommend passage of the following bill: Bill to divorce Sally Flowers of Craven County from her husband, Christopher Flowers. [On reverse:] In House of Commons, 12 and 13 December 1834, read second and third time, passed, engrossed and examined; in Senate, 24 December 1834, read third time, and on motion of Mr. Wyche, ordered to lie on the table.

    (GASR, Nov. 1834-Jan. 1835, Box 1: folder "HB 6 Dec.")

700.   **Harvey, William and wife, Sophia.** Bill to divorce William Harvey of Beaufort County from Sophia, his wife. Before this act is in force, said William Harvey shall execute a bond with good securities to be judged by the County Court at Beaufort in the sum of $10,000, made payable to the Clerk of said county conditioned that said Harvey shall annually pay from and after 1 June 1835 the sum of $400 for the support and maintenance of said Sophia during the term of her natural life. [On reverse:] In House of Commons, 22 December 1834, engrossed and examined; in Senate, 22 December 1834, read first time, and on motion of Mr. McCormick, resolved that same be postponed indefinitely. (GASR, Nov. 1834-Jan. 1835, Box 1: folder "HB 6 Dec.")

701.   **Hendrick, Lucy R. and husband, John.**

    (1).   Petition of Lucy T. Hendrick of Granville County sheweth at the tender age of thirteen years, she married John Hendrick, then of Warren County, in March 1824.[136] Said husband, unknown to

---

135   Marriage Bond of Craven County, North Carolina, lists Christopher Flowers and Sally Phipps, dated 13 August 1822. Bondsman: Robert (X) Phipps.

136   Marriage Bond of Granville County, North Carolina, lists John Hendrick and Lucy R. Turner, dated 21 March 1825. Bondsman: Muses Neal.

her at the time, was a man of exceedingly loose and immoral habits, and so violent in temper that your petitioner did not consider herself safe from his reach even after she left him. He voiced many threats of personal violence, including an attempt to throw her in a mill pond, and this compelled her to bind him in a bond of five hundred dollars to prevent him from doing personal harm. He openly doubted the fidelity of his wife, your petitioner, and even accused her of incest with her own father and brother. After living with him for five months, his conduct was generally brutal [and] she was compelled to fly to her father for protection. Since the separation, her said husband has removed to the State of Virginia without affording her any sustenance or protection. Your petitioner is poor and may also say friendless, as her friends are unable to afford her any efficient aid. She has sustained an irreproachable character since she left her husband. In your wisdom, you have given power to the Superior Courts to grant divorces, but your petitioner for want of means is unable to carry the case before the Court, and respectfully requests that her case be taken into consideration and a divorce granted to her from her husband, John Hendrick.

(2). Statement of Jos. W. Hawkins of Warren County notes that several years ago, Charles W. Turner lived with him as an overseer. His wife sustained an excellent character, and their daughters (amongst whom was Lucy R. Turner) were in good standing and reputed for industry and virtuous deportment.

(3). Certificate signed by fifteen subscribers testify that from long acquaintance, Mrs. Lucy Hendrake, the unfortunate wife of John Hendrake, is a very reputable lady. She should not be holden any longer by the bonds of matrimony to said Hendrake, "he having left her without cause, he being of the Vilest of men as having paid any attention to his wife for Nine Years last past —"

(4). Bond of $500 to prevent John Hendrick from inflicting harm on his wife, Lucy R. Hendrick. Dated 5 September 1825.

(5). P&GC to whom was referred the petition of Lucy R. Hendrick report that the application of the petitioner is not one which in the opinion of your Committee entitles him to the releaf preyed for…your Committee therefore pray to be discharged from the further consideration of the subject…[On reverse:] "Committee discharged."

(GASR, Nov. 1834-Jan. 1835, Box 5: folder "Petitions [Divorce]")

702. **Jennings, Sidney M. and husband, Richard D.**

(1). Petition of Sidney M. Jennings sheweth she married Richard D. Jennings in Newbern [Craven County] in September 1826[137] and resided there until October 1828, when they removed to Nashville, Tennessee, where they lived until November 1831. From that time, said husband has not contributed in any manner to her support and has not been heard from in two years. She has had two children by said Richard depending upon her for support, although the youngest child died in September 1833. Her friends in Nashville made up a contribution in October 1833 for the purpose of returning her to her parents and relatives in North Carolina, and this enabled her to reach Chapel Hill, Orange County, in November 1833, where she now resides in the family of her brother-in-law, Isaac C. Partridge. When she was living in Nashville with her husband, he frequently beat and otherwise ill-treated her. He was almost wholly given up to intoxication and frequently took her ear rings to purchase liquor. At present, she has one child about seven years old, and this child and your petitioner are dependent upon her own exertions for support. Prays that the bonds of matrimony existing between said Richard D. Jennings and herself be forever dissolved. Dated 8 December 1834. [Below:] Deposition of Isaac C. Partridge that the statements in the above petition are entirely true. The signatures of eleven subscribers support this statement.

---

137 Marriage Bond of Craven County, North Carolina, lists Richd. Jennings and Sidney Mitchell, dated 27 September 1826. Bondsman: Spence P. Willis.

Divorces and Separations from Petitions to the North Carolina General Assembly from 1779

(2). Deposition of Mrs. Elizabeth Akroyd before Hardy Whitfield, J. P. of Craven County, North Carolina, 4 December 1834, that she lived in Nashville, Tennessee, when Richard D. Jennings and his wife Sidney lived there and was well acquainted with them. The statements made by the petitioner are true. Mrs. Jennings is a smart, industrious woman who works for her living.

(3). P&GC to whom was referred the petition of Sidney Jennings think it inexpedient to legislate upon the subject and pray to be discharged from further consideration of it. [On reverse:] Committee discharged.

(GASR, Nov. 1834-Jan. 1835, Box 5: folder "HCR")

703. **Overbey, Susannah and husband, William.**

(1). Petition of Susannah Overbey of Stokes County sheweth that her husband, William Overbey, has absconded from her bed and board and has remained absent for five months without any just cause, leaving her to take care of five children. For several years prior to his leaving, he was in the habit of spending most of what he made by his labour at tipling houses or taverns for spirituous liquors which he dearly loved. Prays for an act to secure to her and her children all such property she may hereafter acquire by her own industry or by legacy. Dated 6 November 1834. [Below:] Signatures of eleven subscribers in support of the petitioner.

(2). P&GC to whom was referred the petition of Susannah Overbey report that the claims of the petitioner are not such a connection as entitles them to legislative action. Pray to be discharged from further consideration of the subject. [On reverse:] Committee discharged.

(GASR, Nov. 1834-Jan. 1835, Box 5: folder "HCR")

704. **Parks, Catharine and husband, Gabriel.** P&GC to whom was referred the petition of Catharine Parks of Buncombe County report that it appears that said Catharine intermarried with Gabriel Parks about the year 1818, and they continued to live together for seven or eight years in peace and happiness. In the year 1826, they removed to Georgia, where they lived in a happy and agreeable manner for about a year, when the petitioner returned to her mother's home in Buncombe County in a pregnant condition, to remain there until she gave birth. Her said husband accompanied her part of the way, but left her on pretence of urgent business to return to Georgia. This event led her to believe the reports made to her were true — "that he had been guilty of elicit intercourse with another woman." After she arrived in Buncombe County, she was informed that said Gabriel had been charged with being the father of an illegitimate child by one Polly McAffee. Since that time, said Catharine has indignantly renounced the society and embraces of her said husband and lived separate and apart from him. She has stated that she treated him with tenderness and affection when living with him, but a short time after leaving Georgia, her husband wrote to her "that he never intended to live with her again but would endeavour to procure a divorce from her if he could." Accompanying the petition was a Certificate of J. Roberts, Clerk of the Superior Court of Law for Buncombe County, stating that Judge Strange refused to grant a divorce to said petitioner at the 1834 Spring Term on grounds that the separation was set forth to have taken place in the State of Georgia. Your committee believes that the prayer of the petitioner should be granted and report the following bill: Bill to divorce Catharine Parks of Buncombe County, North Carolina, from her husband, Gabriel Parks. [On reverse:] In Senate, 13 December 1834, engrossed and examined; in House of Commons, 19 December 1834, read second and third time, and on motion of Mr. Outlaw, "Post[poned] Indef[initely]."

(GASR, Nov. 1834-Jan. 1835, Box 3: folder "SB 12 Dec.")

705. **Potter, Isabella A. and husband, Robert.**
(1). Petition of Isabella A. Potter of Granville County states she married as a very young woman in 1828 to one Robert Potter of the same county.[138] She conducted herself as a chaste and dutiful wife, and at the expiration of about nine months, she bore him a child. She was shocked when her husband entertained the foulest and most injurious suspicions of the chastity of your petitioner. Afterwards, for the period of about two years, in which your petitioner bore him another child, she was the victim of his unceasing suspicions towards her. If such suspicions had been confined to her husband, unfounded as they were, she could have continued to bear with them in silence in a life of meekness and submission. However, said Robert, through acts of malignity published them to the world — acts which are of a character so revolting that your petitioner from self respect forbears to state the particulars, but believes they are known to every individual of your body.[139] Said Robert has continued to degrade your petitioner by a refinement in cruelty, an intensity of selfishness one can hardly conceive, and with a view to his own advancement. He has even attempted to fix upon their children a stigma of illegitimacy. The conduct of her husband has rendered it impossible to live under the same roof with him. Prays for a divorce.

(2). P&GC to whom was referred the petition of Isabella A. Potter of Granville County are of opinion that most of the Legislature know the truth of the peculiarities of this case and deem it not necessary to enumerate them, and believe the prayer of the petitioner should be granted.

(3). Bill to divorce Isabella A. Potter from her husband, Robert Potter, both of the County of Granville. In Senate, 9 December 1834, read three times, passed and ordered to be engrossed; in House of Commons, 11 December 1834, read three times, passed and ordered to be enrolled.

(GASR, Nov. 1834-Jan. 1835, Box 3: folder "SB 10 Dec.")

706. **Reid, Lucy T. and husband, Thomas M. D.**
(1). Petition of Lucy T. Reid sheweth she intermarried with Thomas M. D. Reid in 1828[140] at the tender age of nineteen years. Before marriage, he resided at a distance from your petitioner, but by his address and plausible manners, he won her affections but deceived her as to his character and standing. After the marriage, she lived with her said husband for some time, but he became cruel in his behavior towards her and spent all the estate your petitioner had inherited from her father and became bankrupt and insolvent. Her sense of duty to herself and family constrained your petitioner to endure these wrongs in silence. He soon adopted the scheme of coercing your petitioner's mother, a widow, to convey her property to him. His conduct came to the knowledge of her brother, and said brother and a near relative from Alabama came to your petitioner's house and took her to her mother's house a few miles away. She went for protection from her husband, not to abandon him. In reaction, the said Thomas insinuated to the neighbors that she had been dishonored by prostituting herself to the lust of said relative, and this falsehood led to her determination to never return to her husband. The said Thomas M. D. Reid then sought to procure a continuance of an indictment against him pending in Moore County Court for forgery by claiming a necessity to return to Wake County before the trial, because he was afraid that

---

138 Marriage Bond of Granville County, North Carolina, lists Robert Potter and Isabella A. Taylor, dated 9 April 1828. Bondsman: Step. K. Sneed.
139 See the misadventures of said Robert Potter in 1831 in GASR, Nov. 1834-Jan. 1835, Box 6: folder "Contested Election - Robert Potter." Also see this magazine, 7 (1981):96, 97.
140 Marriage Bond of Cumberland County, North Carolina, lists Thomas M. D. Reid and Elizabeth Shaw, dated 31 December 1818. Bondsman: Archibald Monk. [Note: This is probably an earlier marriage intent of said Thomas M. D. Reid.]

your petitioner meant to elope with her relative, who was then in this State. This excuse was made to strangers in open court. Her said husband has lately professed to be religious and has exhorted others to the duties of repentance and godliness, but he is now indicted for forgery in Chatham Superior Court, and these professions were never made before he was indicted. She humbly hopes he may be indeed penitent, but because of his former deceits, she cannot be reconciled to the belief that his professions are sincere. She and her children and family have been so outraged by this villainous scandal upon her honor, that reconciliation is impossible. Accompanying this petition is an agreement made on 14 November 1833 between said husband and her mother and herself which cannot be carried into effect without the aid of your honorable body. Your petitioner shews that she does not care one straw about the mode of giving her relief. She does not care about being divorced unless that is the only mode of securing to her protection against said Reid's control and the enjoyment of such property as her relations will give for the comfort and support of your petitioner, and which she may acquire by her own industry. Dated 20 December 1834, Wake County.

(2). Articles of Agreement between Thomas M. D. Reid, Lucy T. Reid, and Elizabeth A. Phillips — all of Wake County, North Carolina, that a separation should take place between said Thomas M. D. and said Lucy T.; that said Thomas M. D. relinquishes to said Lucy and their two children, Thomas and Martha, equally in regard to his interest in any estate; that said Lucy T. surrenders any claim which she may be entitled in land as the wife of said Thomas; and said Elizabeth A. Phillips agrees to bond the said children named and said Lucy T. without charge to said Thomas.

(3). Certificate signed by three subscribers who were acquainted with William Phillips, decd., father of Mrs. Lucy T. Read, and said Mrs. Lucy, and they were respectable neighbors.

(4). Statements of three subscribers of the petitioner that they have been acquainted with Miss Lucy T. Phillips, now Mrs. Lucy T. Reid, that her character is without blemish, and that her father and mother were among most respectable citizens. Dated 20 December 1834, Wake Forest, North Carolina.

(5). P&GC to whom was referred the petition of Lucy T. Reid of Wake County states their opinion that it is inexpedient to legislate upon the subject at this time and pray to be discharged from consideration of the subject. [On reverse:] "Com discharged."

(GASR, Nov. 1834-Jan. 1835, Box 5: folder "Petitions [Divorce]")

707. **Sheets, Cyntha and husband, Solomon.**
(1). Petition of Cyntha Sheets prays to be divorced from her husband Sollomon Sheets. She was married to him about four years since, and he left her after one week and has never given her any assistance since then. His whereabouts are unknown, and she is unable to pay the expenses of getting a divorce in court.

(2). P&GC to whom was referred the petition of Cyntha Sheets of Buncombe County summarizes the above petition and report that the prayer of the petitioner ought not be granted and request to be discharged from its further consideration. [On reverse:] Read and concurred in.

(GASR, Nov. 1834-Jan. 1835, Box 5: folder "SCR")

708. **Starnes, Elizabeth and husband, John.** P&GC to whom was referred the petition of Elizabeth M. Starnes of Macon County praying to be divorced from her husband, John Starnes, report that they intermarried in 1832,[141] and after a few months, the said John abused his said wife "in a way that would be painfull to your Committee to detail." They lived together until they had one child, but the abuse continued, and a separation became absolutely necessary for the safety of the petitioner. The said husband

---

141 Marriage Bond of Macon County, North Carolina, lists John Starnes and Elizabeth Cockrm (dau. of Wm.), dated 10 August 1832. Bondsman: W(allace) W. Dobson.

became infatuated with jealousy and accused the petitioner of having illicit connection with her father's negro boy. It appears to your Committee that the said John Starnes is a man of wicked and desperate disposition. He is a jealous, cruel and ungrateful man, whereas the petitioner is a virtuous, industrious and obedient wife. It is the opinion of this committee that the petitioner should be granted a divorce. (GASR, Nov. 1834-Jan. 1835, Box 5: folder "HCR")

Bill to divorce Elizabeth Starnes, who was Elizabeth Cockerham of Macon County, from her husband, John Starnes, and that she be restored to the privileges of a feme sole as if she had never been married. [On reverse:] In House of Commons, 6 December 1834, read third time, passed and ordered to be engrossed; in Senate, 2 January 1835, read second time and resolved that same shall not pass. (GASR, Nov. 1834 Jan. 1835, Box 1: folder "HB 26 Nov.")

709. **Whitchard[142], Willoughby and wife, Tripheny.** P&GC to whom was referred the petition of Willoughby Whitchard of Pitt County praying for a divorce from his wife, Tripheny, state that the petitioner intermarried with Tripheny House in 1822, and they lived together for eighteen months. At the expiration of that time, said Tripheny went with her father, John Williams, to Crawford County, Georgia, where said Williams then resided. An understanding was made that Willoughby's said wife would return in about two months, and the petitioner travelled to Georgia to bring her back. However, the said Williams told said Willoughby that his said wife, Tripheny, would live with him no more. Your petitioner remained in that neighborhood for one month endeavouring to reconcile matters, but was unable even to procure an interview with her. It appears that the said Tripheny is still living in Georgia with her father. The committee is of the opinion that this case comes under the powers of the Superior Court for divorces and ask to be discharged for its further consideration. [On reverse:] Concurred in.

(GASR, Nov. 1834-Jan. 1835, Box 5: folder "SCR")

710. **Reference A.**
Laws of North Carolina, Session of 1834-1835

An Act Concerning Divorces. From and after the passage of this act, Courts of Equity shall have concurrent jurisdiction with the Superior Courts of Law in granting divorces either from bed and board or the bonds of matrimony.

The following persons were either granted a divorce (prefix D) or security of property thereafter acquired (prefix S):

- D Ambrose, Peter of Onslow County from wife, Thirza Ambrose - p. 17
- S Brownrigg, Theresa of Wayne County, wife of Henry Brownrigg - p. 17
- D Cabe, Mary of Haywood County from husband, Joseph Cabe - p. 17
- D Cobb, Ellena of Burke County from husband, John Cobb - p.17
- D Durham, Susan P. of Burke County from husband, Archibald Durham, and said Susan P. Durham to be hereafter known by name of Susan P. Shirley - p. 17
- D Eppes, Mary T. of Warren County from husband, Peter Eppes - p. 17
- D Potter, Isabella A. of Granville County from husband, Robert Potter - p. 17

---

142 This surname Whitchard has the more common spelling of Whichard.

Divorces and Separations from Petitions to the North Carolina General Assembly from 1779

711. **Reference B.**
Laws of North Carolina, Session of November 1835
The following persons were granted a divorce (prefix D) — [partial list]:
- D Parks, Catharine of Buncombe County from husband, Gabriel Parks
- D Starnes, Elizabeth M. (who was Elizabeth Cockerron) of Macon County from husband, John Starnes

1835

712. **Anderson, Mary and husband, Charles.**

(1). Petition of Mary (+) Anderson of Haywood County states she married Charles Anderson on 27 December 1834 on Tuesday night and lived in perfect peace and harmony until the Sunday following, when he set out for Buncombe County and has never returned. He was engaged to marry another woman, but the truth of his having married me broke the match. His intention leaves me in the situation of spending my days as an abandoned wretch. I believe that your honorable body cannot hesitate to place me in a proper sphere of life by making me a free dealer and entered separate from the man of whom it was my misfortune to marry.

(2). Petition of twenty-two citizens of Haywood County asks the General Assembly to take into consideration the situation of Mary Anderson, who is of respectable parentage and has ever conducted herself in a becoming manner, observing the strictest rules of morality and living a virtuous life. She is a daughter of Jeremiah Stillwell, a respectable man and a good citizen. A man by the name of Charles Anderson (an entire stranger) of mature age came into the neighborhood, paid his addresses to said Mary, and they were joined together as man and wife on Tuesday night, but [he] left the following Sunday without any cause on the part of said Mary. Something like six years has elapsed, and he does not show any willingness to alleviate her cares or distresses. He has since been heard of in the county of Buncombe and lately of his living in the State of Georgia. Said Mary was of an unripe age (being about 17 years old) and too easily overcome by the flattery of [a] man of the same detestable character of Charles Anderson. Your petitioners feel duty bound to state that from the conduct of the man, he intended to impose fraud upon said Mary, and that she, at an age which is too common of the female sex, abandoned a state of celibacy to embark into the connubial blessings of life and plunged herself into wretchedness and misery. Pray that your honorable body grant said Mary a divorce. [On reverse:] Statement of Samuel Gibson, J. P. of Haywood County, who supports the petition of said Mary Anderson.

(3). P&GC to whom it was referred the petition of Mary Anderson of Haywood County states that it feels very anxious to relieve Mrs. Anderson from her husband, but her claims have not been sufficiently made [apparent] to your committee, and they therefore ask leave to be discharged from further consideration of the subject. [On reverse:] "discharged."

(GASR, Nov.-Dec. 1835, Box 6: folder "HCR, folder 2.")

713. **Bennett, Equilla S. and husband, John C.**

(1). Petition of Equilla S. Bennett of Pitt County sheweth she was born in Hyde County, North Carolina, but a few years ago removed to Greenville, Pitt County, where she established herself as a milliner. She succeeded in acquiring a sufficiency to support herself decently and comfortably. Soon after her removal to Greenville, she became acquainted with one John C. Bennett who also then resided in Greenville. He paid his addresses to her, and hoping to share with him a reasonable portion of this world's comforts and to procure that aid and protection she needed, she consented to become his wife. They were married on 20 October 1831. Soon after this date, her said husband became addicted to

Divorces and Separations from Petitions to the North Carolina General Assembly from 1779

habits of intemperance, dissipation and gambling, and so far from aiding her in obtaining a support and maintenance for themselves, he soon became a tax and burden to her. Your petitioner was still hopeful that the kindness of a dutiful and affectionate wife would reclaim him from the course of life into which he had fallen, but her efforts proved entirely unavailing. On 29 February 1833, her said husband opened the trunk where your petitioner had secreted what little money she had saved with a false key and took possession of the whole of it. That night, without informing your petitioner, he abandoned her by leaving Greenville and making her dependent on her own exertions and the charity of her friends. As soon as his absence was ascertained, attachments were levied on what little property she had remaining and sold to satisfy his debts. The said Bennett has never returned nor written a single line to apprise her of his address, but she understands he first went to his native Baltimore, then to Tennessee, where she supposes he now resides, and where she has been informed he has intermarried. Prays for a divorce. (GASR, Nov.-Dec. 1835, Box 5: folder "HCR [folder 1]")

  (2). Statement signed by thirty-three subscribers depict Equilla S. Bennett of Greenville as a chaste and virtuous woman and incapable of making false statements. They hope she may be granted her prayer. (GASR, Nov.-Dec. 1835, Box 5: folder "HCR [folder 1]")

  (3). P&GC to whom was referred the petition of Equilla S. Bennett of Pitt County recommend passage of the accompanying bill [not enclosed]. (GASR, Nov.-Dec. 1835, Box 5: folder "HCR Folder 1")

  Bill that Equilla S. Bennet of Pitt County be divorced from her husband, John C. Bennet. [On reverse:] In House of Commons, 5 December 1835, engrossed and examined; in Senate, 7 December 1835, read third time, passed and ordered to be enrolled. (GASR, Nov.-Dec. 1835, Box 1: folder "HB 23-27 Nov.")

714. **Calvert/Colvert, Lucy and husband, Thomas.**

  (1). Petition of Lucy Calvert of Granville County represents she is the daughter of the late Benjamin Blount of Southampton County, Virginia, and was married on 9 June 1825 to George B. Edmunds of Northampton County, North Carolina. After the expiration of 8-9 months, "she was afflicted by the melancholy bereavement of a husband with whom she had lived without the slightest interruption of their mutual happiness by his death which occurred in February 1826." Being still quite young, she was married after the lapse of a little more than two years to Thomas Calvert of Southampton, Virginia. Said Thomas "was a member of a highly respectable family of the Lower of Norfolk, and having exhibited nothing objectionable in his character and habits of life…her matrimonial connexions with him took place by the consent and approbation of her friends." At the time of this second marriage, she was possessed of an independent estate, the title of which said Thomas acquired by marriage. He commenced selling off this estate to discharge his debts and to supply the demands of his current wasteful extravagance. In about two years he was totally insolvent. In 1830, her said husband was absent for about five months with a cargo of flour to South America. Your petitioner was left in the family of his sister in Nansemond County, Virginia. On his return, he remained with your petitioner less than one week and went to Norfolk for the alleged purpose of seeking employment as a merchant, assuring your petitioner he would return the next day. He did not return, and your petitioner has not seen him since. From Norfolk he wrote a letter stating he was going to Petersburg to contract for the carrying of mail from Petersburg to Washington City. In the course of a few weeks, she received another letter from him, dated Savannah, Georgia, and instructing her to send his clothes boxed up to Norfolk and to route them on to New York. He followed up this letter with another, dated 15 October 1830, that repeated the instructions previously stated, and adding that he was going to sea and would return in three or four months. She has not received any communication from him since that time, and became dependent upon her friends for subsistence, and then moved to Granville County, North Carolina, to live with the family of her sister, Mrs. Ridley. Some months later, she learned that her said husband returned for the last time to Southampton County, Virginia, where he found a trunk of your petitioner's wearing apparel, which she had left in the possession of his sister. He sold the contents of the trunk and put the miserable pittance in his own pocket. He did not visit here or evince the slightest regard for her in any manner. She would have had the charity that her husband was dead, but she occasionally had intelligence of his existence and his unprofitable wanderings and doubtless dissipated course of life. She recently heard that he is again married, but she cannot vouch for the report. Her husband has been absent for upwards of five years. Prays for a law to dissolve the bonds of matrimony between her and her said husband, Thomas Calvert. [Below:] (a) Certificate of Thos. D. Ridley, dated 6 November 1835, that he has known Mrs. Lucy Calvert for many years and is intimately acquainted with the history of her connection with her husband, Thomas Calvert, and that the circumstances stated in her petition are true in every instance. (b) Statement of Thomas L. W. Mott, Rector of St. Stephens Church in Oxford [North Carolina], Jasper Hicks and John C. TAYLOR that they are neighbors and acquaintances of Mrs. CALVERT, that she has maintained a standing and reputation above reproach, and they justly appreciate the extreme hardship of her condition resulting from the ill treatment of her husband, and believe she has a high claim on the liberality of the Legislature. (GASR, Nov.-Dec. 1835, Box 6: folder "HCR [folder 2]")

(2). P&GC to whom was referred the petition of Lucy CALVERT report that it is unnecessary to enter into a detailed statement of this case, but believe the claims of the petitioner are strong and call upon the Legislature to redress such grievances. A Bill to do this is respectfully submitted. (GASR, Nov.-Dec. 1835, Box 6: folder "HCR [folder 2]")

Bill that Lucy Colvert of Granville County be separated and divorced from her husband, Thomas Colvert. [On reverse:] In House of Commons, 14 December 1835, engrossed and examined; in Senate, 15 December 1835, read three times, passed and ordered to be enrolled. (GASR, Nov.-Dec. 1835, Box 1: folder "HB [28 Nov. - 1 Dec.]"

715. Cheatham, Isaac and wife, Sally.

(1). Petition of Isaac Cheatham sheweth that on 9 April 1834, he intermarried with Sally Eads, daughter of William Eads, and hoped and expected to live in the enjoyment of all those pleasures which flow from the connubial state. In the Fall of that year, his said wife's father and mother concluded that they would remove to the State of Indiana and insisted on your petitioner and his wife to accompany them. At that time, your petitioner was indebted within the County of Stokes (where he had married his wife and where he has lived ever since) to an amount far beyond his ability to pay at that time. He objected to going on that ground, promising that as soon as he could pay off his debts, he and his wife would follow them. They advised him to go off and leave his debits unpaid, which he refused to do, remarking that if he was poor, he wished to be honest — they then advised him to start off before them and that they would bring his wife — this he refused to do. They then suggested to him to set in to work with some person as if he intended to pay his debts, let them go off with his wife, and for him to follow them, leaving his debts unpaid, to all of which he objected, preferring to act the part of an honest man. Your petitioner represents that so soon as his wife found that he could not be prevailed upon to run away and leave his debt unpaid, which was some time early in October 1834, she left him and went to live with her father, where she has lived ever since. Your petitioner sent for her, requesting her to come and see him in order that they might try to live together again, but instead of coming, she sent him such of his clothes as were in her possession, and requested the messenger to inform him that she had no business with him. On all occasions, she has refused to live with him and says she never will unless he will act so dishonestly as to runaway without paying his debts. She now threatens to leave the State for the

State of Indiana. Prays for a law to divorce him from said wife. [Below:] Signatures of sixty-four subscribers who say they are well acquainted with the petitioner and his wife, Sally, and confirm the facts set forth in the petition as true.

(2).   Notice from Isaac Cheatham, 15 September 1835, to Mrs. Sally Cheatham that he would present a petition to the North Carolina General Assembly to be divorced from said Sally.

(3).   P&GC to which was referred the Petition of Isaac Cheatham of Stokes County state that there does not exist any cause of divorce in any tribunal in the State, the main allegation of the Petitioner being that his wife wishes to remove to Indiana whilst he is not willing to remove and that there is no charge of incontinency or want of fidelity on the part of his wife, the sum and substance of the Petition being a recitation of a dispute between the Petitioner and his wife with which the Legislature having nothing to do — the Committee ask to be discharged from the further consideration of the subject. [On reverse:] Committee discharged.

(GASR, Nov.-Dec. 1835, Box 6: folder "HCR [folder 2]")

716.   **Cloud, Frances and husband, Jonathan.**

(1).   Petition of Frances Cloud of Chatham County sheweth she intermarried with one Jonathan Cloud many years ago and resided with him until she became the mother of five children. About five years ago, her said husband ran away from this State and deserted your petitioner and her helpless family, leaving them entirely dependent upon the charity of their friends and their own feeble exertions for support and maintenance. She has had no certain information of his whereabouts or even of his existence since his desertion. Prays for a law to divorce her from her said husband. (GASR, Nov.-Dec. 1835, Box 6: folder "HCR [folder 2]")

(2).   Committee of P&GC to whom was referred the above petition report that the facts set forth in the petition are true and recommend passage of the accompanying bill [not in this file]. (GASR, Nov.-Dec. 1835, Box 6: folder "HCR [folder 2]")

Bill that Frances Cloud of Chatham County is hereby severed and divorced from her husband, Jonathan Cloud. [On reverse:] In House of Commons, 14 December 1835, engrossed and examined; in Senate, 15 December 1835, read three times, passed and ordered to be enrolled. (GASR, Nov.-Dec. 1835, Box 1: folder "HB 2-3 Dec.")

717.   **Edwards, Rachel and husband, Edmund.**

(1).   Petition of twenty-eight citizens of Yancey County who address grievances of Rachel Edwards that her husband is divorced and married to another woman, and the said Rachel should also be allowed to divorce her said husband in the name of justice and equality of right. (GASR, Nov.-Dec. 1835, Box 6: folder "Senate Committee Reports")

(2).   P&GC to whom was referred the petition above recommend the following bill [not enclosed in this file]. (GASR, Nov.-Dec. 1835, Box 6: folder "Senate Committee Reports")
Bill to restore Rachel Edwards to all the rights and privileges of a feme sole as if she had never been married to Edmund Edwards. [On reverse:] In Senate, 3 December 1835, engrossed and examined; in House of Commons, 4 and 16 December 1835, read three times, passed and ordered to be enrolled.

(GASR, Nov.-Dec. 1835, Box 3: folder "SB 28 Nov. - 4 Dec.")

718.   **Gillespie, Henry T. and wife, Judith.**

(1).   Petition of Henry T. Gillespie sheweth he was married to a Miss Judith Askew during the month of January 1831 at a tender age, and lived with her for some time. He would have continued to live with her if she had conducted properly, "…but circumstances of a nature corresponding with her conduct since our seperation drove me to the necesity of taking her to her parents. It is so painfull to me to advert to these circumstances that I will only refur you to the Deposition of L. Burnet Esqr. who proves clearly that her conduct has been such as would forever prevent me from receiving her again." Prays for a divorce.

(2). Deposition of L. Berry Burnett before James G. England, J. P. for Burke County, 4 December 1835, states that the deponent knows Mrs. Judith P. Gillaspie, formerly Miss Judith P. Askew, and that she had been separated from her husband, H. T. Gillaspie, for three or four years. The deponent was "at her farther's sometime in the last summer 1835 and I saw a child they her parrents told me that She had the child since she was separated." The two separated persons live about seventy miles from each other, and H. T. Gillaspie has not visited his wife anytime since their separation.

(3). Committee on Private Bills to whom was referred the petition of Henry T. Gillaspie report that the petitioner is entitled to favorable action and recommend the following bill be passed into law: That Henry T. Gillaspie of Burke County be divorced from his wife, Judith P. Gillaspie. [On reverse:] In House of Commons, 19 December 1835, read two times and rejected.

(GASR, Nov.-Dec. 1835, Box 2: folder "HB 18-22 Dec.")

719. **Hall, Tempe and husband, Thomas.**

(1). Petition of Tempe (X) Hall of Wake County sheweth she intermarried with one Thomas Hall about sixteen years since.[143] Within two weeks thereafter, he commenced drinking to excess and began to ill-treat and abuse her, frequently beating her most unmercifully and driving her from home. At the same time, he became jealous of her and accused her of incontinence without the slightest shadow of a cause. Also, said Thomas had a child sworn to him in the City of Raleigh with whom he was accustomed to cohabit. Notwithstanding these unpleasant circumstances, your petitioner has lived with said Thomas about fifteen years, during the whole of which time, he has continued to drink and abuse her as above stated. But about 12 months since, as will appear from the accompanying certificates, after having squandered their means of living in the most abandoned company, said Thomas drove your petitioner from his bed and board and had never since taken any care of her. She applied for work and was fortunate enough to be received in several respectable families where she could have supported herself but for the relentless persecution of her husband, who followed her from place to place, assailing her character and threatening to kill her. These visits from him became so annoying to those in whose houses she had sought protection and employment, that they were compelled in regard to their own quiet to dismiss your petitioner from their service. Your petitioner is in very delicate health, but with her needle could support herself very comfortably could she be secure from the persecutions of her husband. Your petitioner further represents that she has had but one child since her marriage — a son now about fourteen years of age — and that she has no one who is able to provide for her in her forlorn situation. Prays for an act to be divorced from said husband.

(2). Statements of J. P. Devereux, William Roles, Cyrus Whitaker, Burrill Perry, D. L. Barringer and Weston R. Oles attest to the statements of the above Tempe Hall.

(3). P&GC to whom was referred the petition of Tempe Hall summarizes said petition and state that said Thomas Hall has commenced an adulterous affair with another woman in Raleigh. The Committee recommends the passage of the following bill: That Tempe Hall of Wake County be separated and divorced from her husband, Thomas Hall. [On reverse:] In House of Commons, 15 December

---

143 Marriage Bond of Franklin County, North Carolina, lists Thomas Hall and Temperance Wall, dated 15 May 1820. Bondsman: Lewis (X) Harrison.

1835, read second and third times, passed and ordered to be engrossed; in Senate, 21 December 1835, read second and third times, passed and ordered to be enrolled.

(GASR, Nov.-Dec. 1835, Box 2: folder "HB 15-17 Dec.")

720. **Hardin, Edmund and wife, Cynthia.**

(1). Petition of Edmund Hardin of Rutherford County states he intermarried with Cynthia Gage about 1822 and lived in peace and harmony until sometime in the summer of 1833, when a certain man began to frequent my house very commonly. I discovered an increasing intimacy between this man and my wife, and I forbade him coming to my house. From that time to the present, said Cynthia has frequently left my house without the smallest provocation from me, sometimes staying longer, sometimes shorter in time and returning again. Every argument and persuasion your petitioner could make has failed to produce the desired effect of causing said Cynthia to stay home and act the part of a prudent woman. At this time, your petitioner believes (for good reasons) that said wife is living in adultery, not only with the man who first seduced her, but with others. Prays for a divorce from said Cynthia. Dated 6 November 1835. [On reverse:] Signatures of twelve subscribers who certify that the contents of the above petition are true and that the petitioner should be granted a divorce.

(2). P&GC to whom was referred the petition of Edmund Hardin of Rutherford County report that the only complaint set out by the petitioner is that his wife was guilty of an adulterous intercourse with another man. Your committee ascertains the fact to be that the petitioner's wife was neglected by the petitioner for the sole purpose of compelling her to resort to another chamber than that of her husband's for redress of an outrage committed upon her feeling by the petitioner. This breech then of the marriage vow being a matter of necessity with the wife of the petitioner occasioned [?] by the act of the husband and the wife still being anxious to live with him are disposed to compel the unfaithful husband to accuse his spouse again…[?] Your committee [?] ask leave to be discharged from the further consideration of the subject.

(GASR, Nov.-Dec. 1835, Box 6: folder "HCR [folder 2]")

721. **Hines, William and wife, Elizabeth.**

(1). Petition of William Hines of Wayne County states he was united in the bonds of matrimony to Elizabeth Graddy in January 1825.[144] He well hoped to derive happiness and comfort, but soon after their marriage his said wife became very perverse and contrary, refusing to your petitioner the rights and privileges of a husband. She would often absent herself from his bed and board for several weeks and carried with her the property of your petitioner, which she pretended to claim as her own. When at his home, she utterly neglected to attend to the well management of the kitchen household affairs and other duties incident to a married woman. She continued to conduct herself in this manner, and in early 1832, left his bed and board and removed herself to the State of Kentucky where she now resides. A few days past he received a letter from the said Elizabeth couched in the most insulting manner by declaring that she would not go back with him if he came there for her and would not live with him. She gave a strong intimation of an intention to marry again. Prays for a divorce. Sworn to before James Griswold, J. P., 4 December 1835. [Below:] Deposition of Dennis S. Glisson that the facts in the above petition are true. Dated 4 December 1835. (GASR, Nov.-Dec. 1835, Box 5: folder "HCR - [Folder 1]")

---

144 Marriage Bond of Duplin County, North Carolina, lists William Hines and Elizabeth Graddy, dated 22 September 1825. Bondsman: H. Kornegy.

(2). Committee on Private Bills to whom was referred the Petition of William Hines of Wayne County summarizes the above petition and recommends passage of an accompanying bill [not enclosed]. (GASR, Nov.-Dec. 1835, Box 5: folder "HCR - [Folder 1]")

Bill to divorce William Hines from his wife, Elizabeth. [On reverse:] In House of Commons, 14 December 1835 and in Senate, 15 December 1835; read three times, passed and ordered to be enrolled. (GASR, Nov.-Dec. 1835, Box 2: folder "HB 1011 Dec.")

722. **Hunt, Margaret and husband, William.**

(1). Petition of eight citizens of Cumberland County state that William Hunt of said county "is an intemperate Spendthrift and that Margaret Hunt," his wife, and children are likely to be deprived of the necessaries of life through the intemperate habit and extravagances of said William. Pray for relief of said Margaret by securing to her such property as she may hereafter acquire.

(2). P&GC to whom was referred the petition of Margaret Hunt of Cumberland County state that the facts disclosed in the petition present a clear case for the interference of the Court of Justice and therefore ask leave to be discharged from further consideration of the subject. Dated 12 December 1835. [On reverse:] Committee discharged.

(GASR, Nov.-Dec. 1835, Box 6: folder "HCR - [folder 2]")

723. **Judd, Jefferson and wife, Mary.**

(1). Petition of Jefferson Judd of Moore County sheweth he intermarried about three years ago with his now wife, Mary, and they lived together for two years in utmost harmony, when his said wife informed him to his utter astonishment that she could not place her affections on him, for they were placed on another man, and she would prefer leaving your petitioner. A short time thereafter, she quitted his bed and board and refused to return. Your petitioner states he has no cause of complaint against his said wife, except she refuses to live with him. He does not in the least suspect her virtue or charity. Your petitioner prays for a divorce.

(2). Examination of Jennet McDougald and Alexander McDougald of Cumberland County regarding Jefferson Judd and his wife, Mary, of Moore County on 24 November 1835 is enclosed in this group of papers. The answers to questions posed to the examinees reveal no new information except the following: Question to Jennet McDougald — Did you ever hear said wife, Mary, assign any reason for leaving Mr. Judd? Ans. I never did hear her give any good reason at all except this — "I heard Mary [say] she had been a good wife for Mr. Judd & that she thought it was not Right in the sight of God that she should be Mr. Judd's wife, for she thought she ought to be the wife of another man and named the man who is living in this neighborhood."

(3). P&GC to whom was referred the petition of Jefferson Judd of Moore County report that "the material fait disclosed to your committee…was that he and his wife intermarried about three years since…that they lived together about two years without any interruption of their joint affection…but about one year since the wife of the petitioner informed him that she was dissatisfyed to live longer with him as her affection was placed upon another man in the neighbourhood and upon this information the[y] separated…Your Committee is not disposed to interfeear with that solom matrimonial connexion existing between the parties and ask leave to be discharged from the further consideration of the subjects." [On reverse:] "Com discharged."

(GASR, Nov.-Dec. 1835, Box 6: folder "HCR [folder 2]")

Divorces and Separations from Petitions to the North Carolina General Assembly from 1779

724. **Lynan, Malinda and husband, Aretus.** Bill to divorce Malinda Lynan, wife of Aretus Lynan of Buncombe County. [On reverse:] In H. of Commons, 19 December 1835, read two times and rejected. "Leave granted to withdraw petition." (GASR, Nov.-Dec. 1835, Box 2: folder "HB 18-22 Dec.")

725. **Massey, Margaret and husband, John H.**

(1). Petition of Margaret Massey, formerly Margaret Vail of Edenton, sheweth that about two years ago, she married one John H. Massey.[145] He had come to Edenton about three months before from the District of Columbia to carry on the business of a tailor. He acquired the confidence of many citizens in Edenton and gained the affections of your petitioner, not dreaming he was going to act the part of a hypocrite and a scoundrel. Soon after their marriage, he became lazy and totally inattentive to his business, dissipating and frolicking away his time. His support of herself and of her aged and widowed mother with whom she lived devolved in great measure upon her own exertions and industry. About six months after their marriage, he was detected stealing a gold lever watch, and because of this and other base conduct, he left Edenton, deserted his wife and went to Virginia, District of Columbia and to parts unknown. This happened about twelve months ago. Your petitioner has been informed that he has been roving and wandering about the country out of this State, has been courting again, and is actually engaged to marry another woman at Port Royal, Virginia. It is utterly out of the question for him ever to return to the State of North Carolina, and more particularly, to the town of Edenton. He is looked upon there as odious and detestable by her numerous friends and relatives. He dares not to show his face there. Prays for a law to divorce her from her said husband, John H. Massey. (GASR, Nov.-Dec. 1835, Box 5: folder "HCR [folder 1]")

(2). Committee on Private Bills to whom was referred the petition of Margaret Massey of Chowan County report that the facts in the petition are substantially correct and recommend passage of the accompanying bill into law [bill is not in this file]. (GASR, Nov.-Dec. 1835, Box 5: folder "HCR [folder 1]")

Bill to divorce Margaret Massey of Chowan County from her husband, John H. Massey. [On reverse:] In House of Commons, 14 December 1835, engrossed and examined; in Senate, 15 December 1835, read three times, passed and ordered to be enrolled. (GASR, Nov.-Dec. 1835, Box 2: folder "HB 10-11 Dec.")

726. **McCaw, Elizabeth H. and husband, William B.**

(1). Petition of Elizabeth McCaw of Salisbury, North Carolina, states she married W. B. McCaw in 1831.[146] Not long after their marriage, he became habitually and grossly intemperate. I understand that he was addicted to lewd and improper conduct with other women and was in the habit of inflicting violence upon her person and offering her other indignities. Her condition became so intolerable that an affectionate father came and took her to his own house in 1833 and she has resided with him in the town of Salisbury from that time. Her said husband is a citizen of South Carolina and at their marriage was possessed of a handsome property, all of which she believes he has wasted and conveyed away. Said McCaw continues to grow worse in his lewdness and intemperance. He contributes nothing to the support of your petitioner or their infant child, and has warned all persons by a public advertise-

---

145 Marriage bond of Chowan County, North Carolina, lists John H. Massey and Margaret Vail, dated 15 July 1835. Bondsman: Nathan Massey.
146 Marriage bond of Rowan County, North Carolina, lists William B. McCaw and Elizabeth H. Slaughter, dated 10 February 1831. Bondsman: George W. Williams.

ment not to give her credit. Prays for a divorce from the bonds of matrimony. (GASR, Nov.-Dec. 1835, Box 6: folder "Senate Committee Reports")

(2). Copy of a deed recorded in York District, South Carolina, 23 July 1835: [Abstract] I, William B. McCaw of said District, having been forsaken by my wife, Elizabeth McCaw, who has withdrawn herself from my society without any just cause, and in consideration of the natural love and affection which I bear towards the object of my bounty hereinafter named and for the consideration of one dollar to me paid by my mother, Mrs. Nancy McCaw, have conveyed to said Nancy all my right in the Estate of my father, the late Robert McCaw of said District, being one-third part which has not yet been recovered from my guardian. The said Nancy McCaw shall permit me to receive the annual dividends of said estate during my natural life, and after my death, said Nancy shall pay to Mary McCaw, the sole child of myself and my present wife, Elizabeth McCaw, the sum of $1,000 as her full share of my estate if she survives and the age of twenty-one years or marriage, whichever may first occur. The remainder of my estate shall be held in trust for other children, whom I may leave living, at the time of my death to share and share alike exclusive of said Mary. If any of these children (exclusive of said Mary) die before arriving at the age of twenty-one years, and unmarried, then the estate in trust (exclusive of said Mary) is for the use of the survivors who shall arrive at the age of twenty-one years. If all the said children (exclusive of said Mary) should die before the age of twenty-one years and unmarried, then the said Nancy should hold the estate hereby granted over and above the said one thousand dollars in trust for the use of my brothers, John and Robert McCaw. If the said Mary should die before arriving at the age of twenty-one years, and unmarried, then said Nancy McCaw shall hold the said one thousand dollars in trust for my brother, Robert McCaw. (GASR, Nov.-Dec. 1835, Box 6: folder "Senate Committee Reports")

(3). Deposition of Thomas J. Holton of Mecklenburg County, North Carolina, 16 November 1835, that the following notice sent to him by William B. McCaw of Yorkville, South Carolina, appeared in the Miners & Farmers Journal, dated 4 March 1833: "My wife Elizabeth having this day left my bed and board without any just and reasonable cause, this is to forwarn all persons from trading with her on my account, as I will not pay any debts she may contract. [/s/ W. B. McCaw]." The said W. B. McCaw was then Editor and proprietor of said paper. (GASR, Nov.-Dec. 1835, Box 6: folder "Senate Committee Reports")

(4). Notice to W. B. McCaw from Elizabeth H. McCaw, dated 4 September 1835, Salisbury, North Carolina: "I am driven to the painful alternative of applying to the next Legislature of No. Carolina…for a divorce…between you and myself." (GASR, Nov.-Dec. 1835, Box 6: folder "Senate Committee Reports")

(5). Depositions from Thomas Hugson, J. M. Martin, and Nathaniel Macon Foulks that Wm. B. McCaw treated his wife with violence and that he was a habitual drunkard. Dated 13 November 1835. (GASR, Nov.-Dec. 1835, Box 6: folder "Senate Committee Reports")

(6). P&GC to whom was referred the petition of Mrs. Elizabeth McCaw of Salisbury, North Carolina, find the following facts: The petitioner relied upon the advice of her friends and married the said William B. McCaw in 1831. Fatal experience soon after their removal to South Carolina convinced her that she had been deceived in these representations. Her husband treated her with cold indifference and occasional brutality, but she remained with him for near 18 months after the birth of their child in hopes there might be some alternative to applying to a tribunal for redress. The separation took place in 1833 under most afflicting circumstances. Reference I.s made to the deposition of said Wm. B. McCaw's estate in York District which left nothing to his said wife. Your committee advises that the prayer of the petitioner be granted and recommend adoption of the following bill [not enclosed in this file]. (GASR, Nov.-Dec. 1835, Box 6: folder "Senate Committee Reports")

Divorces and Separations from Petitions to the North Carolina General Assembly from 1779

Bill to divorce Elizabeth H. McCaw of Rowan County from her husband, William B. McCaw. [On reverse:] In Senate, 30 November 1835, engrossed and examined; in House of Commons, 30 November and 12 December 1835, read three times, passed and ordered to be enrolled. (GASR, Nov.-Dec. 1835, Box 3: folder "SB 28 Nov.-4 Dec.")

727. **Morgan, William B. and wife, Polly.**

(1). Petition of William B. Morgan of Macon County represents he was married to one Polly Queen of same county about November 1832.[147] She lived with your petitioner about 3-4 months and then separated herself from him and took the greatest part of the things she brought with her. Shortly afterwards in his absence from home, said Polly "broke into his house, broke the lock of his chest and took off all his property she could cary on two horses…" Since then, she has lived in an unchaste and whorish way with other men. Her character is infamous, and she stands indicted in the Superior Court of Haywood. She has fled with her mother and father from the laws of this State and are fugitive from justice. Before she became infamous, he did all he could to reclaim her and induce her to live with him as a good wife, but all to no purpose, for she became abandoned and has gone off to South Carolina with her parents and is living there with another man as he is informed. Prays for a divorce. (GASR, Nov.-Dec. 1835, Box 2: folder "HB 15-17 Dec.")

(2). Statements of Wm. Roane and Silas McDowell relate the infamous character of Polly Queens, wife of William Morgan. Statement signed by thirty-five subscribers support the prayer of the petitioner in requesting a divorce from his wife, Polly, and notes that she "is a lewd woman who has disgraced herself in the counties of Haywood and Macon & has run off for stealing…and is now out of the jurisdiction of this State. He William Morgan is an industrious blacksmith" and has worked in both Macon and Haywood counties, being peaceable and orderly in his behavior. His said wife belongs to a family of bad character. Her father and mother ran away from Court after a Bill of Indictment found against them for stealing iron. (GASR, Nov.-Dec. 1835, Box 2: folder "HB 15-17 Dec.")

(3). P&GC to whom was referred the petition of Wm. B. Morgan summarizes said petition and are of opinion that the prayer of the petitioner should be granted. The following bill is reported: That William B. Morgan of Macon County be divorced from his wife, Polly Morgan. [On reverse:] In Senate, 16 December 1835, engrossed and examined; in House of Commons, 22 December 1835, read three times, passed and ordered to be enrolled. (GASR, Nov.-Dec. 1835, Box 2: folder "HB 15-17 Dec.")

Bill as above with same results. (GASR, Nov.-Dec. 1835, Box 3: folder "SB 512 Dec.")

728. **Muse, Margaret and husband, Thomas W.**

(1). Petition of Margaret Muse of Moore County sheweth she intermarried five years ago with Thomas W. Muse, and they lived together some few months in full enjoyment of all the blessings and comforts arising from a conjugal life. To her utter astonishment her said husband left her without any cause whatsoever giving no notice of his intentions. He was gone some six or eight months to parts unknown to your petitioner, and returned penniless. He lived with your petitioner a short time, became desperate in his habits and temper (frequently inflicted cruelties and privations on your petitioner without any reason) and finally left her and ran away to the western country. The last your petitioner heard of him was in Kentucky. He has been absent from her about four years and prays for a divorce.

(2). P&GC to whom was referred the petition of Margaret Muse summarizes said petition and notes that the petitioner has resided in the family of her father, a respectable citizen, since the departure of her husband. The Committee recommends passage of the following bill: Bill to divorce Margaret

---

147   Marriage bond of Macon County, North Carolina, lists William B. Morgan and Mary Queen, dated 3 February 1833. Bondsman: Ruddy Morgan.

Muse of Moore County from her husband, Thomas W. Muse. [On reverse:] In Senate, 10 December 1835, read second time and resolved the same shall not pass.
(GASR, Nov.-Dec. 1835, Box 3: folder "SB 5-12 Dec.")

729. **Nelson, Esther E. and husband, Josephus.**
(1).	Depositions from Oliver Sidney, Daniel Tolson, Bartholomew Paul, John Neale, and Mary Brew — all of whom say that Josephus Nelson was disposed to intemperance and became a habitual drunkard. He abused his wife on several occasions and threatened to kill her, resulting in her running off to the protection of her neighbors. Esther Nelson was considered to be an affectionate wife and treated her husband with kindness.[148] Dated 16 and 17 October 1835. Taken in Craven County.
(2).	Bill to divorce Esther E. Nelson of Craven County from her husband, Josephus. [On reverse:] In House of Commons, 18 December 1835, read three times, passed and ordered to be engrossed; in Senate, 19 December 1835, read three times, passed and ordered to be enrolled.
(GASR, Nov.-Dec. 1835, Box 2: folder "HB 15-17 Dec.")

730. **Parks, Catharine and husband, Gabriel.**
(1).	Petition of Catharine Parks of Buncombe County sheweth she intermarried with Gabriel Parks about the year 1818 and enjoyed uninterrupted peace and happiness for the next seven or eight years. About the year 1826, she removed to the State of Georgia with her husband. (GASR, Nov.-Dec. 1835, Box 6: folder "SCR")
(2).	Petition of 105 citizens of Buncombe and Haywood counties, dated 27 October 1835, request that Catharine Parks be given a divorce from her husband, Gabriel L. Parks. This couple removed to Habersham County, Georgia, but said Catharine returned to North Carolina while her husband went to Missouri. (GASR, Nov.-Dec. 1835, Box 6: folder "SCR")
(3).	P&GC to whom was referred the petition of Catharine Parks of Buncombe County recommend passage of the accompanying bill [see bill in next paragraph]. (GASR, Nov.-Dec. 1835, Box 6: folder "SCR")
Bill to divorce Catharine Parks of Buncombe County from her husband, Gabriel Parks. [On reverse:] In Senate, 28 November 1835, read second and third times, passed and ordered to be engrossed; in House of Commons, 30 November and 12 December 1835, read three times, passed and ordered to be enrolled. (GASR, Nov.-Dec. 1835, Box 3: folder "SB 28 Nov. - 4 Dec.")

731. **Partin, Green T. and wife, Mary.**
(1).	Petition of Green T. Partin of Orange County sheweth that for some years he has reason to believe that his wife Mary[149] was unchaste, but in the absence of any direct evidence, he continued to live with her until 8 November, when he caught a man in his wife's room in his night dress which fully satisfied him of the baseness of his wife. Your petitioner is aware that his case is cognizable by the courts, "…but the difficulty which presents itself is that the adulterer has ran away and that he cannot make any positive proof except by his own oath." Prays for a divorce. Sworn to on 15 December 1835. (GASR, Nov.-Dec. 1835, Box 6: folder "Petitions")

---

148   Marriage bond of Craven County, North Carolina, lists Josephus Nelson and Esther E. Nelson, dated 13 March 1830. Bondsman: Oliver Sidney.
149   Marriage bond of Orange County, North Carolina, lists Green Partin and Mary Jinkins, dated 3 March 1830. Bondsman: A. Blackwood.

Divorces and Separations from Petitions to the North Carolina General Assembly from 1779

(2). Five depositions relating to the above are enclosed. (GASR, Nov.-Dec. 1835, Box 6: folder "Petitions") P&GC to whom was referred the Petition of Green T. Partin report that the wife of the petitioner had conducted herself in such a manner as to excite many suspicions as to her chastity in the mind of her husband and the minds of her neighbors. In the absence of proof of her infidelity, the petitioner continued to reside with her until 8 November. On the night of the day aforesaid, he surprised her in bed with a young gentleman of the village which left him no doubt as to her business, and he separated from her. Recommend passage of the accompanying bill: That Green T. Partin of Orange County is hereby divorced from his wife, Mary. [On reverse:] In House of Commons, 17 December 1835, read first time and passed; on 18 December 1835, read two times and rejected. (GASR, Nov.-Dec. 1835, Box 2: folder "HB 15-17 Dec.")

732. **Perkins, Pharoah and wife, Susan.** P&GC to whom was referred a bill to divorce Susan Perkins report that no evidence is before your committee to satisfy them of the propriety of passing the bill referred to them, and therefore ask leave to be discharged from future consideration of the subject. [On reverse:] In House of Commons, 10 December 1835, read second time and bill rejected. (GASR, Nov.-Dec. 1835, Box 1: folder "HB [2-3 Dec.]")

733. **Powell, William M. and wife, Mariah A.** Bill to divorce William A. Powell of Halifax County from his wife Mariah A. Powell.[150] In House of Commons, 18 December 1835; on motion of Mr. Graham, postponed indefinitely. (GASR, Nov.-Dec. 1835, Box 2: folder "HB 15-17 Dec.")

734. **Roberts, Thomas and wife, Martha.**
(1). Petition of Thomas Roberts of Orange County states he intermarried with Martha Bledsoe of Granville County, widow of Washington Bledsoe, in 1828[151] and lived with her in peace and harmony until 18 March 1835, when she told him she did not intend to live with him any longer, that he was not man enough for her, and she loved another man better than she did him. She took her clothes and went off to the house of one John Vaughan and put herself under the protection of his son, Samuel Vaughan, who made many threats against your petitioner in case he should attempt to disturb them. Shortly afterwards, they went off together over the mountains in Virginia, where they are now living together as he is informed and believes. Your petitioner and said wife have had no children and prays for such relief as may seem proper. [Below:] Thomas Roberts was born and raised in Orange County near the Granville line, and in all respects is a good citizen. Signed by thirty-six subscribers.
(2). Committee reports that the facts set forth in the above petition are substantially true and recommend passage of the accompanying bill: That Thomas Roberts of Orange County be divorced from his wife, Martha. [On reverse:] In House of Commons, 18 December 1835, read three times, passed and ordered to be engrossed; in Senate, 19 December 1835, read three times, passed and ordered to be enrolled.
(GASR, Nov.-Dec. 1835, Box 2: folder "HB 15-17 Dec.")

---

150 Marriage bond of Warren County, North Carolina, lists William M. Powell and Maria Johnston, dated 10 November 1823. Bondsman: George Cawthorn.
151 Marriage bond of Granville County, North Carolina, lists Thomas Roberts and Martha Bledsoe, dated 12 July 1828. Bondsman: Moses Wheeler.

1835 Session

735. **Silva, Elizabeth and husband, David.**

(1). The following petitioners of Macon County represent that David Silva left his wife, Elizabeth, about seven years ago without any known cause. Her name before marriage was Elizabeth Duckworth, and she has always conducted herself uprightly and as a prudent and virtuous woman. The said David left this State with another woman reportedly for the State of Illinois and has not been heard from for the last four years. Said Elizabeth is a very industrious woman, but her said husband did not live with her more than about six weeks. They had no children as a result of this marriage. Pray for a dissolution of said marriage. [Below:] Depositions of Drury Weeks, William Morrow, Elias M. Kilpatrick, Joseph Marr and Jas. Truit, who give oath before Isaac Truit, J. P. of Macon County, for the facts stated above. (GASR, Nov.-Dec. 1835, Box 6: folder "HCR [folder 2]")

(2). P&GC to whom was referred the petition of Elizabeth Silva report that Elizabeth Silva intermarried with David Silva about the year 1828 and lived with him for about six weeks, when said David removed to Illinois with a woman of bad character.

Recommend passage of the accompanying bill [not in file]. Dated 31 November 1835.

(GASR, Nov.-Dec. 1835, Box 6: folder "HCR [folder 2]")

Bill that Elizabeth Silva of Macon County, who was wife of David Silva, be separated and divorced from said husband, David. [On reverse:] In House of Commons, 14 December 1835, engrossed and examined; in Senate, 15 December 1835, read third time, passed and ordered to be enrolled. (GASR, Nov.-Dec. 1835, Box 1: folder "HB [28 Nov. - 1 Dec."])

736. **Spear/Speer, Margaret P. and husband, Alexander.**

(1). Petition of Margaret P. Speer of Long Creek, North Carolina, 6 December 1835, states she unfortunately joined herself in matrimony with Alexd. Speer in 1831 and lived with him in New Hanover County for nearly one year, during which time said Alexander did not behave towards her as a good husband, but committed many bad and wicked acts. Your petitioner treated him with every sort of kindness and affection. He then removed your petitioner to Currituck County and resided near Poplar Branch. During her stay in Currituck County, said husband used very abusive language and threats towards her, and frequently shoved her with violence. She was afraid of receiving personal injury in one of his fits. In November 1833, said Alexander permitted your petitioner to visit her family and promised to come to your petitioner a short time afterwards, a promise he never kept. Your petitioner has heard, and believes, said Alexander Speer left Currituck County for South America, and has not been heard of since. Prays that the bonds of matrimony with said Speer "be loosed."

(2). Certificate from Long Creek, North Carolina, 6 December 1835, and signed by three subscribers [members of the North Carolina Legislature] certify that all the allegations in the above petition of Margaret P. Speer are perfectly true and worthy of consideration.

(3). P&GC to whom was referred the petition of Mrs. Margaret P. Spear report that the petitioner is a female in good standing in society of one of the best families in New Hanover County and against whose moral character and chastity, suspicion has never breathed a murmur. A year after their marriage, they removed to Currituck County until November 1833, during which time they had two children. It appears that the said Margaret then left Currituck with her children on a visit to her family with the full consent of her husband, who promised to come after her at a certain time. She wrote him frequently, urging him to come for her, but he never condescended to answer, but swearing, as your committee is informed, that she, children and property were with her friends, where they might stay and be damned; that never would [he] go after her and never intended living with her again. Recommend passage of the accompanying bill: that Margaret P. Spear, who was Margaret P. Williams of New Hanover County, be declared divorced from her husband, Alexander SPEAR. [On reverse:] In Senate, 11 December 1835, engrossed and examined; in House of Commons, 12 and 18 December 1835, read three times, passed and ordered to be enrolled.

(GASR, Nov.-Dec. 1835, Box 3: folder "SB 5-12 Dec.")

737. **Starnes, Elizabeth and husband, John.**

(1). Memorial of Elizabeth M. Cockraham, "your hand Maid," sheweth "she intermarried with a man by the name of John Starnes in the year 1832.[152] Her prospects at that time were flattering, but she lived but a short time in harmony with him, for he commenced a course of abuse to her. Within three months after the marriage, with a hope of better times, they removed to Georgia, but he became more abusive, accused her of incontinence and restricted her in every privilege. All of this was without any provocation or cause in the slightest degree. Your memorialist, in all her conduct with her husband, has behaved herself as a loving and obedient wife and has acted with others in a chaste and virtuous manner. She "…would further observe (and which was certainly too much for her to bear) he accused your memorialist with intimacy with her father's negro boy. And finally a separation took place, and Mr. Starnes is gone I know not where. Your memorialist is therefore left an injured and disconsolate woman, and still further, [h]e has left a small daughter, the child of your Memorialist, which she has now to scuffle with, and which with the existence of her friends she has no fears of being able to do." The danger of her husband returning and taking from your memorialist any property that her friends may give her, or that she may have the fortune to acquire, renders her situation more difficult and forbids her friends from doing what they otherwise would do. Prays such relief as you in your wisdom may think proper — either a separation from the bonds of matrimony or the authority to hold all such property as she may hereafter acquire.

(2). Certificate of William Cockraham, 9 October 1834, states that John Starnes from the State of Tennessee came into Macon County, North Carolina, in 1831, a stranger, but an industrious mechanic. In August 1832, he married my daughter, Elizabeth M. Cockraham. Three months after their marriage, while living at my house, Starnes exhibited signs of conviction, for almost every day he took a Bible into a retired place, as I thought to read. This conduct continued some time, when in 1833 — Starnes and his wife moved from my house into the State of Georgia, and in the Fall of that year, they separated from each other. Soon after, Starnes in company with the Rev. Mr. Posey, came to my house (my daughter having returned home) in order to effect a reconciliation with his wife, as he said, when for the first time I was led fully into the causes of their separation. Mr. Starnes acknowledged to me and his wife in the presence of Mr. Posey, that he had not only accused her wrongfully, but had treated her ill. When they had lived at my house, he had often pretended to be under conviction for Sin, for no other purpose than to watch her under an impression that she loved some other better than him. At the time when he took a Bible and retired to read, as we had thought, it was only to watch her and my negro man. He stated that she had uniformly treated him well and behaved in every particular as an affectionate wife, and that the whole of his jealousy and harsh conduct originated in his own base and depraved heart. In her whole conduct, he did believe her not only innocent, but in every respect, a chaste and virtuous woman. To all of this, his wife replied that he had made such acknowledgement to her before, that she had done all for him that an honest woman could do, and that she had often told him that if his treatment to her ever became public or to the ears of her father and mother, she could not again have the courage to live with him.

---

152 Marriage bond of Macon County, North Carolina, lists John Starnes and Elizabeth Cockram (daughter of William), dated 10 August 1832. Bondsman: W. Wallace.

(3).	Certificate of Humphrey Posey, 8 October 1834, relates similar information as given by William Cockraham (above) and ends with — "it appeared that she (his wife) had suffered so much from him that she could not think of ever putting herself into his power any more, he therefore went away."

(4).	Statement signed by sixty subscribers, "citizens of Macon and Haywood Counties, who are acquainted with Elizabeth Starnes long before and since her intermarriage with John Starnes" unhesitatingly say she has ever supported a virtuous, honest and industrious character. Dated 11 October 1834.

(5).	P&GC to whom was referred the memorial of Elizabeth M. Starnes summarizes the information in the memorial and recommends passage of the following bill: That Elizabeth M. Starnes, who was Elizabeth M. Cockerham of Macon County, is hereby declared divorced from her husband, John Starnes. [On reverse:] In Senate, 11 December 1835, read three times, passed and ordered to be engrossed; in House of Commons, 12 and 18 December 1835, read three times, passed and ordered to be enrolled.

(GASR, Nov.-Dec. 1835, Box 3: folder "SB 5-12 Dec.")

738.	**Walls, Mahala and husband, James.**

(1).	Petition of Mahala (+) Walls of Haywood County states she intermarried with James Walls in April 1832,[153] and they lived together on the best of terms. Said Mahala treated her said husband as a wife should treat her husband — that she loved and obeyed him, "that he used hir and treated hir kindly that they lived togeather and done well untill the said James Walls tookit into his head without any case to leave your petitioner and in the month of August 1833 he left your petitioner without ever saying anything about it…without any difference of the small ist kind ever hapening…on the friendlyest terms…he the said James Walls haz been gone from this State ever since." She has never heard from her said husband except a flying report that he was dead and "dyd" in Georgia. Your petitioner has one child "by hir said husband and that she haz been chast " during his absence and when they lived together. She has a bad way of making a livelihood for the maintenance of herself and child, and relies on the world for a support of his character. Prays for a divorce. [Below:] Signatures of fifty-three subscribers in support of petitioner. (GASR, Nov.-Dec. 1835, Box 5: folder "HCR - folder 1").

(2).	Committee on Private Bills to whom was referred the petition of Mahala Walls of Haywood County summarizes the contents of the said petition and adds that it is their opinion that said James Walls had a wife living in some portion of the Union at the time of his marriage with the petitioner. This being a case not cognizable by the Courts, your Committee asks leave to introduce the accompanying bill and recommends its passage into law. [See bill in next paragraph.] (GASR, Nov.-Dec. 1835, Box 5: folder "HCR - folder 1").

Bill to divorce Mahala Walls from her husband, James Walls. [On reverse:] In House of Commons, 14 December 1835, engrossed and examined; in Senate, 15 December 1835, read three times, passed and ordered to be engrossed. (GASR, Nov.-Dec. 1835, Box 2: folder "HB [4-9 Dec.]")

739.	**White, Thomas and wife, Mahala.**

(1).	Petition of Thomas White of Craven County sheweth he was united in the bonds of matrimony with Mahali Holland of said county in July 1824,[154] and lived with her for several years without any extraordinary interruption of their domestic peace until about the year 1829 or 1830. At that time,

---

153	Marriage bond of Haywood County, North Carolina, lists James Wall and Mahaly Cooper (daughter of Nancy), dated 29 March 1832. Bondsman: George (X) Cooper.

154	Marriage bond of Craven County, North Carolina, lists Thomas White and Mahala Holland, dated 27 June 1824. Bondsman: Lewis White.

the said Mahali grievously wronged your petitioner, but he was prevailed upon by the solicitations of her friends and family, and professions of penitence from said Mahali to forgive her and continue to live with her. About the year 1831, your petitioner removed to Cove Creek in said county, where he had reason to fear that said Mahali did not regard him with that love and respect with which a wife would regard a husband, but being a poor man and having had three children by his said wife, he felt unable to break up his household and disperse his family. In Cove Creek, he made an engagement with a reputable citizen to superintend his turpentine boxes, and this required his absence from home nearly all day. During these absences from home and while engaged in laboring for the support of said Mahali, she commenced an adulterous intercourse with a man who kept a school in the neighbourhood and continued the same until she became shameless in her prostitution. Your petitioner will not disgust your Honourable body by the details, which became the subject of conversation in the neighbourhood to the great mortification and affliction of your petitioner. He begs leave to refer to the testimony on oath heretofore annexed. Prays he may be granted speedy relief by a dissolution of the bonds of matrimony with a woman who has dishonored the name of wife. Dated 10 November 1835.

(2). Statement of Mahala (X) White, dated 3 September 1835: With feelings of regret and mortification, I do confess that in the month of June last, Mr. Robert L. Parnell kept a school near the Plantation of Thomas White, my husband, and that during that time and diverse times…the said Parnell seduced me from my allegiance to my said husband. At various times from June to August 1835, I admitted said Parnell to use the freedoms and privileges of a husband with me by cohabitation, and this act continued until discovered by my husband, since which time he has made me an alien to his bed and affections. I make this confession, which is true, freely and voluntarily in hopes my said husband may remember that a free confession of guilt is the first step to repentance and amendment — and may be thereby moved to restore me to his affections…and also that he may attach the principal blame to the said Robert L. Parnell by whom I was seduced to injure my said husband.

(3). Note to Mrs. Mahali White, 12 September 1835: Madam — I propose to apply to the next General Assembly for a divorce from you on account of your criminal intercourse with Rob't. L. Parnell, and I intend to take testimony relating to your conduct on the 18th and 19th days of this month at the home of Richard Richardson on Cove Creek in Craven County. /s/ Thomas White.

(4). Depositions of Jane (+) Heath, William Prescott, and Mrs. Gatsy (X) Richardson are in this file regarding the alleged liaison between Mahala White and Robert L. Parnell, dated 19 September 1835.

(5). Deposition of Joseph Rhem, dated 18 November 1835, states that Thomas White treated his wife in a cruel manner and beat her with a whip.

(6). Deposition of Mrs. Mahala (+) White, dated 24 November 1835: Her husband has used her in a manner in which he ought not to; that he whipped this deponent several times. He often whipped her in anger, and when the deponent had her last child, he used her mighty bad. The deponent did not remember why her husband first whipped her, but said that her husband beat her because he suspected her of having improper intercourse with Owen Lockhart, and such an offense was not committed. She stated she has never had any illicit intercourse with any men.

(7). P&GC to whom was referred the petition of Thomas White of Craven County summarizes the contents of said White's petition, submits the following bill to the House of Commons, and asks to be discharged from further consideration of the subject: Bill that declares Thomas White of Craven County to be divorced from his wife, Mahala White. [On reverse:] In House of Commons, 28 November 1835, read third time, passed and ordered to be engrossed; in Senate, 16 December 1835, read second time and resolved that the same shall not pass.

(GASR, Nov.-Dec. 1835, Box 1: folder "HB 25-27 Nov.")

740. **Reference A.**
Laws of North Carolina, Session of Nov. 1835
The following persons were granted a divorce from each other as if they had never been married:
  Bennet, Equilla S. of Pitt Co. from husband, John C. Bennet
  Cloud, Frances of Chatham Co. from husband, Jonathan Cloud
  Colvert, Lucy of Granville Co. from husband, Thomas Colvert
  Hall, Tempe of Wake Co. from husband, Thomas Hall
  Hines, William of Wayne Co. from wife, Elizabeth
  Massey, Margaret of Chowan Co. from husband, John H. Massey
  McCaw, Elizabeth H. from husband, William B. McCaw
  Morgan, William B. of Macon Co. from wife, Polly Morgan, (Polly Queen)
  Nelson, Esther E. of Craven Co. from husband, Josephus
  Parks, Catharine of Buncombe Co. from husband, Gabriel Parks
  Roberts, Thomas of Orange Co. from wife, Martha
  Silva, Elizabeth of Macon Co. from husband, David Silva
  Spear, Margaret P., (Williams) of New Hanover Co. from husband, Alexander Spear
  Starnes, Elizabeth M., (Elizabeth Cockerran) of Macon Co. from husband, John Starnes
  Walls, Mahala of Haywood Co. from husband, James Walls

1787, 1836-1837

741. **Garrett, James and wife, Mary.** Petition of James Garrett and Mary, his wife, late Mary Hofler. In October 1772, your petitioners, at that time - James of 17 years and Mary of 14 years, were intermarried with the concurrence of their parents agreeable to the rites and ceremonies of the Church of England. Soon after there arose a variety of quarrels and disputes between them which gradually grew into a mutual disgust and inveterate hatred. In this miserable state, they continued to live together for three long years. As their reason approached to a state of maturity, they discovered that their tempers were so dissimilar and discordant that they must never hope to taste that comfort and happiness in wedlock which is only the lot of congenial minds formed to promote the mutual happiness of each other. They did agree to live separate and apart, which at that time they did. Your petitioner, James, being unable to endure the solitude of a single life, prevailed upon another woman to marry him while his former wife was still alive. As a consequence, he was involved in a most expensive and dangerous prosecution of bigamy and polygamy. He was relieved of this by the death of his second wife. After expending large sums of money in his defense and suffering much trouble and vexation, he has since lived a most uncomfortable and solitary life, exposed to all the inconveniences of celibacy and deprived of all those blessings which arrive from a happy union of kindred souls, Your petitioner, Mary, has languished in a situation equally solitary and uncomfortable from the time she parted with your petitioner, James. They pray for an act to dissolve their marriage. [On reverse:] In Senate, 20 November 1787, read and ordered to be put to the House of Commons; in House of Commons, 21 November 1787, read and rejected. (From: General Assembly Session Records, Nov. - Dec. 1787, Box 1: folder "Joint Papers: Petitions - rejected or tabled," in North Carolina State Archives, Raleigh NC)

INDEX

The Index is listed in alphabetical order by last name and then first name. The number with which a name is listed is the entry number under which the name is found, not the page number.

A

Abbets, Samuel 123
Abbot, Rebecca 336, 337
Abbot, William 336, 337
Abercrombie, Anne 95
Abercrombie, Robert 95
Abrams, Penelope 77
Adams, John 242, 627
Adams, Penelope 242
Adams, Robert 298
Adams, Sally 298, 327, 328
Ader, Betsey 531
Akroyd, Mrs Elizabeth 702
Alderson, John 90
Alexander, Aaron 314
Alexander, Adam 122
Alexander, Augustus 122
Alexander, Azariah 96
Alexander, Betsy 698
Alexander, Cassandra 122, 314
Alexander, Catharine 338, 381
Alexander, Esther 332
Alexander, Fanny 96
Alexander, George 122
Alexander, Isaac 286
Alexander, Jane 122
Alexander, Jas T 503
Alexander, Joe 698
Alexander, John 238
Alexander, Marshall T 122
Alexander, Mary 238
Alexander, Ms 698
Alexander, Paris 122
Alexander, William 338, 381
Alexander, William J 695
Alexander, Zeb 122
Alford, Eunice 444, 445, 446, 428
Alford, Roy 428, 446
Alfred 610
Allen, Elizabeth 77
Allen, Henry 561
Allen, James 468
Allen, Mr 634
Allen, Sarah 528

Allen, William [H] 528
Alley, Elisabeth 239
Alley, John 239
Allison, Andrew 78
Allison, Jane 78
Allison, Jean 78
Allison, Theoph 78
Allowance, John 185
Alston, Col Thomas 258
Ambrose, Peter 692, 710
Ambrose, Thirza 692, 710
Anders, Ann Jane 619
Anderson, Charles 712
Anderson, Charlotte 97
Anderson, George 97
Anderson, Mary 712
Ansley, Joseph 332
Archer, Elizabeth 532
Armstrong, Ann Eliza 691
Armstrong, Archibald 98
Armstrong, Eliza 689
Armstrong, Elizabeth 240
Armstrong, Gray 689
Armstrong, Martha 98
Armstrong, Martin 240, 241
Arnold, Elizabeth 327, 328
Arnold, Robert 166
Arnold, William 327, 328
Asa, George 532
Askew, Judith 718
Askew, Tabitha 356
Assellman, Archabald 558
Atkinson, Villey 540
Austin, Henry 674
Avery, Col W 372
Avery, Polly Mira 372
Avery, Waightstill 195, 363, 372

B

Badger, Nathaniel 99
Badger, Temperance 99
Bailey, Mr 12
Bailey, Polly 346
Baker, Jonathan 588

Baker, Mary 674
Baker, Moses 674
Bal(l)ance, Nancy 381, 329, 429, 445, 446
Balance, Charles 381
Baldwin, Ameilia 555
Baldwin, William 555
Ball, Mourning 100
Ball, Spencer 100
Ball, Thomas 360
Ballance, Charles 329, 429
Ballard, James 52
Ballard, Nancy 52
Ballard, Wiley 52
Banks, Alsey 340, 382
Banks, Andrew 626
Banks, John 350
Banks, William 340, 382
Banner, Charles 300
Barbee, Martha 579
Barbee, Willard 579
Barber, John D 529
Barber, Mary 529, 660
Barber, William 660
Bardin, Ann Maria 612
Bardin, Jesse 612
Barham, Mary 558
Barker, Charles 430, 447, 495, 530, 556
Barker, Elizabeth 509
Barker, John 101
Barker, Liney 101
Barker, Mary 430, 447, 495, 530, 556
Barker, William 509
Barnes, William 526
Barr, Elizabeth 531
Barr, Isaac 531
Barr, William 696
Barracks, Peggy 671
Barringer, D L 719
Barringer, Elizabeth 103
Barringer, P 279
Barry, Michael 444
Bartlett, Delia 615

Index

Bartlett, Mrs 615
Barton, Elizabeth 509
Barton, William 94
Basden, Rebecca 484
Bass, Benjamin 329, 341, 381, 382, 383
Bass, Drury 448, 472
Bass, Rebecca 448, 469, 472
Bass, Susanna 329
Bass, Susannah 341, 381, 382, 383
Bass, Uriah 368
Battee, Nancy 113
Battel, Nancy 152
Beard, Eleanor 604
Beard, Elizabeth 378
Beard, Jno 378
Beard, Margaret 378
Beard, Mrs 604
Beasley, Martha 657
Beaty, Betsey Sally 114
Beazley, Edmund 613
Beazley, Martha 613
Beckham, Martha 342
Beckham, Patty 381, 382
Beckham, Zachariah 342, 381, 382
Becknall, Henry 614, 658
Becknall, Jane 614, 658
Beedle, John 145
Beedle, Nancy 145
Beeson, Elizabeth 79, 102
Beesonn, Azael 102
Bell, Elizabeth 601
Bell, Jeconias 615
Bell, Miles 242
Bell, Penelope 242
Bell, Rhoda 615
Bell, Ruth 1
Bell, Samuel 343, 381
Bell, Sarah 343, 381
Bell, Solomon 480
Bell, William 1, 523
Benedict, Mr 519
Bennet, Equilla S 740
Bennet, James 285
Bennet, John C 713, 740
Bennett, Equilla S 713
Bennett, John C 713, 740
Bennett, Mark 239
Benton, Polley 344, 381
Benton, Polly 381
Benton, Thomas 344, 381
Berton, Alien 564
Betts, Elizabeth 103
Betz, Elizabeth 103
Betz, George 103
Bevins, Eliza 496, 557
Bevins, Simeon 496
Bezzell, Elizabeth 270, 292, 293, 297, 299, 328
Bezzell, Isaac 270, 297, 299, 328
Blackwell, Jemima 328
Biggs, Reverend Amariah 303
Bigham, Mary 558, 616
Bigham, Polly 616
Bigham, Robert 616

Bigham, Robert Jr 558, 616
Bigham, Robert Sr 558
Bitting, Anthony 80
Bitting, Ursilla 80
Bittle, Achsa 71
Bittle, Agatha 71
Bittle, Esther 71
Bittle, Joseph 71
Bittle, Parthena 71
Bizzell, Elizabeth 270, 292, 299
Bizzell, Isaac 222, 270, 292, 299
Bizzell, William 368
Black, Betsey 110, 148
Black, Elizabeth 148, 175
Black, Frederick 175
Black, Kenneth 602
Blackman, Annas 510
Blackman, Annis 510, 527
Blackman, Barzillai Jr 104
Blackman, Druzillai 104
Blackman, William 299
Blackman, Wyatt 510, 527
Blackwell, Jemima 300, 327
Blackwell, Rachel 477, 661
Blackwell, Robert 300
Blackwell, Thomas 477, 661
Blackwood, A 731
Blalock, David 206
Blalock, John 64
Blalock, Nancy 206
Blance, Charles 445, 446
Blaze, George 444
Bledsoe, Elizabeth 105
Bledsoe, Isaac 105
Bledsoe, Martha 734
Bledsoe, Washington 734
Blelock, David 206
Blelock, Nancy 206
Bloom, Patsy 297
Bloom, Lewis 297
Blount, Benjamin 714
Blount, Lucy 714
Bodenhamer, Mr 12
Bond, Jemima 146
Bond, John 233
Bond, Rebecca 345, 381
Bond, Samuel 345, 381
Bond, Southey 356
Bond, Thomas 146
Bostick, Ezra 2
Bostick, Mary 34
Bostick, Nathaniel 34
Bostick, Sarah 2
Bouchell, Thos J 695
Boucher, Ann 176
Boucher, Thomas 176
Bowen, Avis 387
Bower, George 588
Bowers, Barnabas 3
Bowers, Mary 3
Bowman, Elizabeth 366
Bowman, William 366
Boyce, Isaac 384
Boyce, Nancy 384

Boyet, Ethelred 299
Boyet, James 299
Boylan, William 323, 442
Bracewell, Isaac 147, 207, 243, 271, 293
Bracewell, Nancy 147, 207, 243, 271
Brackett, Bett 164
Braddy, Bailey Richard 382
Braddy, Polly 346, 382
Braddy, Richard 346
Bradford, Elizabeth 250
Bradshaw, John 575
Brady, Love 385, 426
Brady, Mills 385, 426
Brame, Elizabeth 532
Brame, Oliver 532
Brandon, Mr Richd 279
Branson, Thomas H 396
Brasher, Nathan 617
Brasher, Priscilla 617
Braswell, John 244
Braswell, Robin 4
Braswell, Sarah 244
Bray, David 241
Bray, Hannah 431, 446, 533
Bray, Jesse 533
Bray, Solomon 431, 446
Brehon, J G 176
Brew, Mary 729
Brewer, Daniel 511
Brewer, Jane 174
Brewer, Sarah 511
Brickell, Elisabeth 559, 577
Brickell, J 593
Brickell, Samuel J 559, 577
Bright, James 398
Bright, Jane 245
Bright, Richard 245
Brightman, Joseph 347, 382
Brightman, Margaret 347, 382
Brinks, Nancy 108
Brink, William 108
Brinson, Elizabeth 106
Brinson, John 106
Brite, Jane 245
Brite, Richard 245
Brooks, Jesse 182
Brooks, Wilie 661
Brookshire, Manring 415
Brother, Andrew 524
Brothers, Susannah 544
Brower, John 509
Brown, Ann 348, 382
Brown, Bond V 35, 246, 301
Brown, Bonville 107
Brown, Charles 570
Brown, Frederick 509
Brown, Henry 323
Brown, Mary 3
Brown, Peter 3
Brown, Solomon Shinn 556
Brown, Susanna 246
Brown, Susannah 107, 301

Index

Brown, Uncle Johns 696
Brown, William 348, 382
Brown, Willis 480
Brownlow, Tippo S 559
Brownrigg, Henry 693, 710
Brownrigg, Theresa 693
Brownrigg, Theresa 693, 710
Brownrigg, Theresy 693
Brucks, Nancy 108
Brucks, William 108
Bryan, Ann Jane 619
Bryan, Eleanor 272
Bryan, Jonathan 619, 659
Bryan, Nathaniel 272, 296
Bryan, Nelly 272
Bryant, Eli 620
Bryant, Mary 620
Bryon, Eleanor 296
Buchanan, H 561
Buckner, Edward 580, 662
Buckner, Polly 580, 662
Bugg, Anne 694
Bugg, David 664
Bugg, Henry 694
Buie, Donald 109
Buie, Margaret 109
Bullock, Benjamin 305
Bullock, James 534
Bullock, Micajah 305
Bullock, Tabitha 534
Bun, Barnaba 169
Bunch, Eleanor 20
Bunch, Thomas 20
Bunn, Ann 535
Bunn, Barnaba 226
Bunn, Nathaniel 535
Buntin, Barbary 671
Buntin, Susanna 671
Burgess, Elizabeth 618
Burgess, James 618
Burket, Elisabeth 42
Burnet, L 718
Burnet, Sarah 491
Burnett, Berry 363, 718
Burnett, L Berry 718
Burns, Barnabas 600
Burrow, Henry 663
Burrow, James W 532
Burrow, Nancy 532
Burrow, Sarah 663
Busbee, Johnston 605
Busbee, Siddy 605
Butler, Ann 349, 382
Butler, Ann L 382
Butler, Henry L 5
Butler, Mr 9
Butler, Reuben 349, 382
Butler, Teresa 5, 9
Buzzell, Elizabeth 299
Byars, Drusilla 208
Byars, Joseph 110
Byars, Nathan 208
Byars, Thomas 110
Byers, Drusilla 208

Byers, Nathan 208
Bynam, Mary 470
Bynum, J W 520
Bynum, James 215
Bynum, Luke 215
Bynum, M 215, 520
Bynum, Mary 449, 475
Bynum, Mr 665
Bynum, Tapley 215
Bynum, Turner 449, 475
Bynum, Wm 215
Byron, Joshua 35
Byrum, Amelia 36
Byrum, James 6, 36

C

Cabe, Joseph 664, 710, 694
Cabe, Mary 710
Cabe, Mary B 664
Cabe, Mary Barbara 694
Caddell, Polly L 450, 472
Caddell, William 450, 472
Cadell, Polly S 469
Cain, Elisha 177
Cain, Elizabeth 433
Cain, Rebecca 177, 209
Caldwell, Andrew 581
Caldwell, Betsy 110
Caldwell, Elizabeth 148
Caldwell, James 110, 148
Caldwell, Joseph 520
Caldwell, Mary 581
Caldwell, Thomas G 110
Caldwell, Thomas Given/Gavins 148
Caldwell, William 110
Calvert, Lucy 714
Calvert, Thomas 714
Campbell, Archibald 81
Campbell, Elizabeth 81
Campbell, Robert 666
Canaday, Richard 242
Candler, Rhoday 37
Candler, Zachariah 37
Capehart, John 273, 297
Capehart, Rosan(n)a 273, 297
Carmack, Polly 398
Carmer, James 285
Carpenter, Joseph 178
Carpenter, Sally 178
Carr, Boswell 561
Carr, Martha 561
Carrick, Anne 111
Carrick, John 111
Carruth, John 114
Carson, James 512
Carson, John 512
Carson, Mr 695
Carter, Benjamin 7
Carter, Elizabeth 7
Carter, Jerry 621
Carter, Polly 621
Carven, Sarah 297
Carven, Thomas 297

Casey, William 38
Caskeden, Mary 223
Cathey, Archd 110
Cathey, Archibald 148
Cawthorn, George 733
Cazey, William 38
Cazey, Catharine 38
Cenlee, Absalom 335
Chadwick, Jacob 582
Chadwick, Kesiah 649
Chadwick, Mary 497
Chadwick, Nancy 582
Chadwick, Wheeler 497
Chambers, Betsy 478, 492
Chambers, Edward 698
Chambers, Elisabeth 471
Chambers, Elizabeth 451
Chambers, John 560, 577
Chambers, Riney 560, 577
Chambers, Thomas 451, 471, 478
Chapel, Gabriel Chapel 561
Chappell, Ruth 210
Chappell, Solomon 210
Chappell, Winefred 163
Cheatham, Isaac 715
Cheatham, Sally 715
Cherry, Jesse 129
Chesher, Mary 272
Chester, William P 388
Chevers, Andrew 149
Chevers, Molly 149
Chiles, Sarah 432, 446
Chiles, Thomas 432
Chiles, Thomas 432, 446
Chism, Amelia 555
Christopher, Nancy 336, 337
Christopher, Simon 336, 337
Chunn, Samuel 333
Clark, Becca 536
Clark, Elijah 669
Clark, James 536
Clark, John 286
Clark, Lucy 386, 426
Clark, Rebeccah 247
Clark, William 247
Clark, William Henry 426
Clawson, Mary Ann 597, 637
Clinton, Mary 602
Cloud, Frances 716, 740
Cloud, Jonathan 716, 740
Coakeley, Sarah 39
Coakley, Benjamin 39
Cobb, Ellena 695, 710
Cobb, John 695, 710
Coble, John 335
Cockerham, Daniel 550
Cockerran, Elizabeth 711, 740
Cockraham, Elizabeth M 737
Cockraham, William 737
Cockrm, Elizabeth 708
Cockrm, Wm 708
Coffin, Hannah 248
Coffin, William 248
Cokely, Sarah 39

Index

Colanche, Roland 551
Cole, Aggy 433
Cole, Elizabeth 433, 446
Cole, Matthew 433, 446
Collier, Frederick H 665
Collier, Lucretia 665
Collins, Avis 387
Collins, Benjamin 387
Collins, Elizabeth 150
Collins, Isaac 150
Collins, John 452, 473
Collins, Mary 452, 473
Collins, Penelope 303, 330
Colvert, Lucy 714
Colvert, Lucy 740
Colvert, Thomas 714
Colvert, Thomas 740
Colyear, John 388, 426, 427
Colyear, Polly 388, 426, 427
Comer, Mary 84
Conner, Catharine 498
Conner, Catherine D 498
Conner, Charles D 498
Conner, Henry 110
Conner, Henry Workman 498, 508
Conner, James 110, 148
Cooper, George 738
Cooper, Mahaly 738
Cooper, Nancy 738
Corpening, Albert 195
Corzine, John 453, 474, 476
Corzine, Mary 453, 474, 476, 628
Courtner, Barbara 335
Coval, Jacob 336, 337
Coval, Mary 336, 337
Cowan, David 406
Cowan, Isaac 82
Cowan, Sarah 82
Cox, Bolling 666
Cox, Eliza Hope 583, 610, 611
Cox, Longfield 583, 610, 611
Cox, Marther 404
Cox, Patsey 404
Cox, Rachel 355
Craig, James 249
Craig, Nancy 249
Crain, George 630
Craner, Hannah 188
Craner, Moses, Jr 188
Cratch, John 77
Cratch, Mary 77
Crawford, Burt 630
Creecy, Joseph S 223
Creecy, Lemuel 16
Critchfield, John 241
Crittenden, Christiana 622, 658
Crittenden, John 622, 658
Crockett, Luc(e)y 211
Crockett, William 211
Crossland, Alexander 350, 382
Crossland, Catharine 382
Crossland, Catherine 350
Crossroads, Alexander 350
Crow, Isaac 299

Crowder, Elijah 274, 292, 297
Crowder, Mary 274, 292, 294, 297
Crutchfield, Eusebius 250
Crutchfield, Lidea 250
Cruthis, Susanna 334
Crywell, Martha 98
Culbertson, David 586
Culpeper, Charles 623
Culpeper, Elizabeth 623
Culpepper, Henry 442
Cumming, Jean 142
Curtis, Benjamin 350
Custus, Mary 223
Cuthbertson, David 650

D

Daniel, Drury 302
Daniel, Orpah 302, 327, 328
Daniel, Robert T 323
Dannell, David 179
Dannell, Susanna 179
Darden, John 368
Dare, Eliza 610, 611
Dare, Elizabeth 584
Dare, John 584, 610, 611
Darlack, Robert 468
Daugherty, James 279
Davenport, Nancy 332
Davenport, William 303
Davidson, B Wilson 573
Davidson, Catherine 498
Davidson, Ephm 110
Davidson, Rebeckah 77
Davidson, Rebekah 60
Davidson, William 406
Davis, Baxter 151
Davis, Cecelia 537
Davis, Celia 537
Davis, Downing D 303, 330
Davis, Eady 275, 292, 294, 297
Davis, Edward Patrick 212
Davis, Elizabeth 212, 299
Davis, Elizabeth P 212
Davis, Faithey 407
Davis, Fielden 641
Davis, Henry 299
Davis, Isaac 5
Davis, James A 330
Davis, Jane 77
Davis, Lewis 275, 297
Davis, Lucretia 151
Davis, Mildred 276, 292, 294, 297
Davis, Penelope 303, 330
Davis, Peter A 176
Davis, Richard Child 8
Davis, Sarah 8
Davis, Seleigh 537
Davis, Solomon 537
Davis, Stephen 176, 545
Davis, Susan 499
Davis, Susan P 499, 624
Davis, Teresa 5, 9
Davis, Wiley J 389

Davis, Wiley O 624
Davis, William 276, 292, 297
Davis, Willie O 499
Dawson, Bersheba 233
De La Chapel, Gabriel 577
De La Chapel, Judith 561, 577
De Loach, John 251
De Loach, Nancy 251
Deavon, Elizabeth 112
Deavon, John 112
Deavor, Elizabeth 112
Deavor, John 112
Deens, Dempsey 299
Deens, Dorety 299
Deeton, Nancy 351, 382
Deeton, Thomas 351, 382
DeJarrett, Martha 550
Dennis, Francis 113, 152, 180
Dennis, Nancy 113, 152
Dennis, Sarah 180
Denson, Benjamin 434, 445, 446
Denson, Sarah 434, 444, 445, 446
Dever, Elizabeth 352
Dever, John 352
Devereux, J P 719
Dick, Catharina 10
Dick, John 10
Dick, Joseph 10
Dick, Martha W 677
Dickey, Mary 336, 337
Dickey, Moses 562, 585
Dickey, Rachel 562, 585
Dickey, Zachariah 336, 337
Dickins, Robert 64
Dickson, Alex 11
Dickson, Elizabeth 11
Dickson, Robert 289
Dickson, Sarah 262
Dillard, Henry 174
Dillhay, Edmond 591
Dilliard, Frances H 666
Dilliard, Wil(l)ie 666
Dilliard, Wilie M 666
Dillingham, Betsey Sally 114
Dillingham, Vechel 114
Dillon, Cloe 650
Dillon, Jenny 336, 337
Dillon, Leven 336
Dillon, Levin 337
Dillon, Thomas P 650
Dills, William 12
Dismukes, Rachel 631
Doak, Susannah 115
Dobson, Anna 363
Dobson, Joseph 363
Dobson, Sally 26
Dobson, W(allace) W 708
Docleu, Rachel 562
Dodd, Lydia 153
Dodd, Robert 153
Dollar, Patience 213
Dollar, William 213
Donnells, Sarah 576

Index

Dorsey, Mary Ann 435, 444, 445, 446
Dorsey, Robert 435, 445, 446
Doty, Leml 331
Doublin, Mrs Davice 398
Dough, Ambrose N 252
Dough, Barbara 252
Doughter, Joseph 564
Douglass, Littlejohn 537
Dowd, Conner 13
Dowd, Mary 13
Dowday, Eliza 390, 426
Dowday, John 390, 426
Dowdy, Eliza 427
Dowdy, James 91
Dowdy, John 427
Dowdy, Mary 91
Dowling, Eliza 625, 650
Dowling, Eliza S 586
Dowling, Zacheus 586, 625, 650
Dowty, Peter 655
Dozier, Sarah 370
Dozier, Tully 644
Draughon, Jno 536
Draughon, John 617
Drew, John S 630
Drumas, Drusilla 328
Duckworth, Elizabeth 735
Dudley, Christopher, Jr 304, 328
Dudley, Leah 328
Dudley, Lean 304
Duke, Hardaman 305
Duke, Hardiman 305
Duke, Mary 305
Dumas, Amos 328
Dunagan, James 391
Dunagan, Nancy 391
Dunbar, Teresa 9
Dunbibin, Junius C 458
Duncum, Silvy Silva 532
Dunn, Francis 206
Durham, Archibald 696, 710
Durham, Susan 696
Durham, Susan P 710
Durrell, Catherine 350
Duskin, Michael, Jr 323
Duty, Rebeccah 154
Duty, Russell 154

E

Eads, Sally 715
Eads, William 715
Eady, Lewis 292
East, Anna Maria 454
East, Thomas 454
Easton, Samuel 40, 83
Easton, Zilphia 40, 83
Eaves, Martin 350
Edington, Mr 279
Edmondson, Thomas 630
Edmunds, George B 714
Edmunds, Lucy 714
Edney, Olivia 587, 626
Edney, Olly 626

Edney, Samuel J 587, 626
Edwards, David 564
Edwards, Edmund 697, 717
Edwards, Edward 219
Edwards, Lucy 297
Edwards, Mary 299
Edwards, Michael 297
Edwards, Rachal 697
Edwards, Rachel 717
Edwards, Thomas 299
Eisenhauer, Mary 116
Eisenhauer, Nicholas 116
Eium, Elizabeth 539
Elkins, Olivia 587, 626
Eller, Jacob 155
Eller, Mary 155
Ellington, Bevel 592
Ellington, John 526
Ellington, Stephen 215
Elliott, Frances 479
Elliott, Thomas 479
Ellison, Thomas 655
Ellrod, Barbara 117
Ellrod, Jeremiah 117
Elrod, A C Barbara 84
Elrod, Jeremiah 84
Emerson, Reuben 110
Emery, Jinny 353
Emery, Stephen 353
Emmery, Jinny 382
Emmery, Stephen 382
Endsley, Susannah 570
England, Daniel 505
England, James G 718
England, Levice 505
England, Levisa 505
England, Louisa 505
Eppes, Mary T 698, 710
Eppes, Peter 698, 710
Erwin, Andrew 221
Erwin, William W 195
Etherage, David 91
Etheridge, Davis 91
Eunice, Roy 445
Eure, Selah 385
Evans, Anna 41
Evans, Anne 77
Evans, Jacobs 572
Evans, Major 60
Evans, Susanah 572
Evans, Zachariah 41
Everitt, John 627
Everitt, Winifred 627
Evins, Susannah 572

F

Fabre, Elizabeth 118, 156
Fabre, Peter, Jr 118, 156
Falkener, Wake 176
Falkener, Wm 176
Fannigan, John 214
Fannigan, Trecy 214
Fannigan, Tricey 214

Fargerson, Joel, Jr 392
Farr, Robert 181
Farr, Susanna 181
Farrar, John 215
Farrar, Milly 215
Farress, Mary 90
Farris, Mary 90
Farrow, John 42 119, 182
Farrow, Rebecca 182
Farrow, Rebekah 42, 119
Faust, John 628, 657
Faust, Mary 628
Fender, Elizabeth
Fender, Elizabeth 307
Fender, Elizabeth 327
Fergerson, Elizabeth 538
Fergerson, James 538
Fergerson, Jas 654
Fergerson, Jos 654
Fergerson, Sarah 654
Ferguson, Elizabeth 563
Ferguson, James 563
Ferguson, Joel 392, 427
Ferguson, Malcolm 14, 43
Ferguson, Mary 43
Ferguson, Mary G 392, 427
Ferrill, Susannah 179
Fesler, Adam 306
Fesler, Judith 306
Fessenden, Benja 285
Fewell, William 676
Field, Jeremiah 393, 426, 427
Field, Peggy 393, 426, 427
Fields, Alexander 627
Fields, Mary 564, 588
Fields, William 564, 588
Finder, Elizabeth 307
Fitts, Henry 532
Fitzgerald, Nancy 308, 327, 328
Fitzgerald, Thomas 308
Flanakin, John 214
Flinn, Hannah 234
Flowers, Christopher 629, 699
Flowers, Sally 629, 699
Flynt, Richard 513
Flynt, Sally 513
Flynt, Thomas 513
Fogleman, Henry 319
Fohey, Margaret 90
Fohey, Mrs 90
Fomey, Peter 114
Foote, Henry 532
Forbes, Abigail 644
Forbes, Britanna 644
Forbes, Jacob 644
Forbes, Silas 644
Ford, James 44
Ford, Susanna 44
Forester, Dinah 310
Forester, Samuel 310
Forge, Turnbull 698
Forseth, America 309
Forseth, John 309
Forsett, America 309

297

Index

Forsett, John 309
Forster, Dinah 310
Forster, Mary 541
Forster, Samuel 310
Forsyth, Benjn 306
Foster, Asa 216
Foster, Dinah 310
Foster, Sall(e)y 216
Foster, Samuel 310
Foulks, Nathaniel Macon 726
Foulson, Rebekah 119, 182
Foust, Peter 401
Fox, Jacob 335
Frazier, Elizabeth 85
Frederick, Peter 299
Freedle, Esther 157
Freedle, John 157
Freeman, Mary A G 545
French, Willm 331
Fry, Elizabeth 539, 565
Fry, Lewis 539, 565
Fugate, John 589, 610, 611
Fugate, Patsey 589, 610, 611
Ful(l)wood, Betsey 331
Fulenwider, Jno 114
Fullar, Brittain 166
Fullar, Gilly 166
Fuller, Julia Ann 653
Fuller, Sylvester K 358
Fullwood, Andrew 331, 337
Fullwood, Eliza 331, 337
Fulwood, Betsy 293
Furgeson, Joel 426
Furgeson, Mary G 426

G

Gage, Cynthia 720
Ganey, Druzillai 104
Ganey, William 104
Garland, Cel(i)a 667
Garland, Cela 667
Garland, James 667
Garrett, Easter 311
Garrett, Esther 45
Garrett, James 741
Garrett, John 311
Garrett, Mary 741
Garrett, William 45
Gentry, Richard 564, 588
George, Asa 532
Gibbs, Rachel 138
Gibson, John 512, 590
Gibson, Mary 453
Gibson, Mildred 512
Gibson, Milly 590
Gibson, Samuel 712
Gillaspie, Judith P 718
Gillespie, Henry T 718
Gillespie, Judith 718
Gilmore, Amy 630
Gilmore, Stephen 630
Gilmour, Charity 354, 382
Gilmour, Stephen 354, 382

Glisson, Dennis S 721
Gloster, Thos B 176
Godwin, Christopher 555
Goodwin, Saml 630
Gordon, Alexander 350
Gordon, Elizabeth 574
Gotten, Henry 71
Gower, Mark 698
Graddy, Elizabeth 721
Graham, Mr 733
Granby, William 343
Grandy, Solomon 91
Grant, Catherine 77
Grantham, Rachel 355, 381
Grantham, William 355, 381
Gray, Alexander 334
Gray, Benjamin 489
Gray, Elizabeth 352
Green, Allen 591
Green, Mary 591
Green, Thomas 122
Greene, Silas 323
Greenwood, Morris 113, 152
Greenwood, Nancy 113, 152
Greer, Alex 616
Greer, Thomas I/J 616
Gregory, Edmond 394, 426
Gregory, Edmund 217, 427
Gregory, Elizabeth 46, 85
Gregory, Mary 217, 394, 426, 427
Gregory, William 46, 85
Grey, Elizabeth 112
Grice, Charles 343
Grier, Tho J 558
Griffin, John 152
Griffin, Martin 285
Griffis, Catharin 225
Grissum, Nancy 158
Grissum, Thomas 158
Griswold, James 427
Griswold, Mary 427
Griswould, James 395, 426
Griswould, Mary 395, 426
Guion, Thomas 93
Gunter, Anne 218
Gunter, Hanna 218
Gunter, Jesse 218
Gurganus, Mager 540
Gurganus, Major 540
Gurganus, Milley 540
Guthrie, Zilphia 83
Guyer, Alexander 597
Guymon, Sarah 219

H

Hackett, Alley 396, 426, 427
Hackett, Thomas 426, 427
Hadly, Easter 311
Hagins, Nancy 322
Hailey, Edna 627
Haley, Salley 216
Hall, Capt Thomas 156
Hall, Jno 176

Hall, Levi 15
Hall, Priscilla 15
Hall, Sally 253
Hall, Tempe 719, 740
Hall, Temperance 719
Hall, Thomas 719, 740
Hall, Willoby 253
Hall, Willoughby 253
Hamblet, Rachel 631
Hamblet, William 631
Hamilton, Col John 223
Hamilton, John 223, 558
Hamilton, Mr 616
Hamilton, Robert 333
Hammond, Cynthia 641
Hammonds, Doctor 312
Hammonds, James 312
Hammonds, Mary 312, 327, 328
Hampton, Henry G 550
Hampton, James 513, 527
Hampton, John 513
Hampton, Sally 513, 527
Hampton, T 550
Hancock, Joseph 356, 381
Hancock, Tabitha 356, 381
Hancock, Thomas 356
Haney, Timothy 2
Hanna, Polly 110, 148
Hannah, Nancy 397, 426, 427
Hannah, Robert, Jr 397, 426, 427
Hardin, Cynthia 720
Hardin, Edmund 720
Hardison, Ezekiel 303, 330, 529
Hare, Marmaduke 16
Hare, Rachel 16
Hargett, Fredk 152
Hargroves, Bennet 641
Harman, Zach 215
Harramond, William D 529
Harrard, Patsey 579
Harrel, William 534
Harrel, Zilpha 222
Harris, Amelia 86, 120
Harris, Charlotte 467
Harris, John 286
Harris, Lamender 284
Harris, Nailicy 183
Harris, Nancy 183
Harris, Peggy 86
Harris, Ransom 468
Harris, Robert 241
Harris, William 120, 183
Harrison, Lewis 719
Harvey, Charles W 385
Harvey, Sophia 700
Harvey, William 700
Hass, Sarey 160
Hassell, Benjamin 455, 471
Hassell, Betsey 648
Hassell, Elizabeth 648
Hassell, Mary 455, 471
Hatch, Durant 692
Hatch, Henry 357, 382
Hatch, Polly 357, 382

Index

Hatch, Thirza 692
Hatch, Thursy 692
Hatch, Thurza 692
Hatcher, Margaret 313, 327
Hatcher, Mary 328
Hatcher, Thomas 313
Hatfield, Elizabeth 285
Hathorne, James 564
Hauser, Joseph 668
Hauser, Susannah Mary 668
Hawkins, James 47, 77, 541
Hawkins, Jos W 701
Hawkins, Mary 47, 77, 541, 554
Hawley, Sarah 39
Hawley, William 39
Haynes, Herbert 215
Heard, Hugh H 630
Heard, John 630
Heath, Jane 739
Heath, John 398
Heath, Polly 687
Heath, Rachel 398
Henderson, James 363
Henderson, Maurice 520
Henderson, Saml 637
Hendley, William 34
Hendrake, John 701
Hendrake, Mrs Lucy 701
Hendrexson, John 257
Hendrexson, Josiah 257
Hendrexson, Samuel 257
Hendrick, John 701
Hendrick, John J 592
Hendrick, Lucy R 592, 701
Hendricks, George 542
Hendricks, Sarah 542
Henry, William 386
Herring, Frederick 277, 292, 297
Herring, Susanna 292, 294
Herring, Susanna(h) 277, 297
Hess, Catharina 128
Hess, John 128
Hester, Milley 526
Heuster, John 254
Heuster, Rebecca 254
Hiatt, Anna 363
Hiatt, Seth 363
Hicks, Davis 441
Hicks, James 64
Hicks, Jasper 714
Higbie, David 358, 382
Higbie, Thisbe J 358, 382
Hiland, Henry 195
Hill, Aaron 77
Hill, Bennitt 104
Hill, Elizabeth 232, 525
Hill, George 525
Hill, Isaac 48
Hill, John 303
Hill, Mary 48
Hill, Moses 232
Hill, Nancy 124, 184
Hill, Nathaniel 330
Hill, Patsey 77

Hill, Seth 184
Hillyard, William 520
Hines, Elizabeth 721, 740
Hines, William 721, 740
Hinkle, Hanah 359
Hinkle, Hannah 382
Hinkle, Jacob 359, 382
Hinkle, Michael 322
Hinslars 279
Hinsley, Miss Peggy 279
Hinson, Charles 561
Hinson, Delilah 121
Hinson, Joshua 121
Hobbs, Nehemiah 399, 426, 427
Hobbs, Sarah 399, 426, 427
Hoffler, Deborah 87, 360, 381, 480, 493, 494
Hoffler, Garrett 360
Hoffler, James 87, 360, 381, 480, 493, 494
Hoffler, William 360
Hofler, Deborah 159
Hofler, James 159
Hofler, Mary 741
Hoggatt, Elizabeth 514
Hoggatt, Isaiah 514
Hoggott, Elizabeth 527
Hoggott, Isaiah 527
Holdsonback, R 64
Holland, Esther 632 669
Holland, James 361, 382
Holland, Mahala 739
Holland, Mahali 739
Holland, Milley 361
Holland, Milly 382
Holland, William 632, 669
Holloday, Robert 520
Hollowell, John 520
Holten, Lovy 58
Holton, Thomas J 726
Holtzclaw, Nathan 278, 292, 297
Holtzclaw, Susanna 294
Holtzclaw, Susannah 278, 292, 297
Hooker, Stephen R 223
Horney, Lydia 362
Horney, Manlove 362
Horse, Sarah 160
Horse, Simon 160
Horton, William 215
Hosea, Christian 336, 337
Hosea, Hugh 336, 337
Hosea, Penelope 49, 77
Hosea, Seth 49
House, Patience 593
House, Patience J 593
House, Tripheny 709
House, Turner 593
Houser, Catherine 17
Houser, Henry 17
Houston, Cassandra 122, 314
Houston, James 122, 314
Howard, Drucilla 500
Howard, John 500
Howze, Mr 545

Hoze, Henry Y 545
Hubble, Daniel 379
Hudson, Eleanor 279, 293, 297
Hudson, Ellen 279
Hudson, Jacob 279, 297
Hughes, Francis 88, 161
Hughes, John 130
Hughes, Lydia 88, 161
Hugson, Thomas 726
Huldy, Lamb 491
Hulsenback, Agatha 64
Humphrey, Wms 692
Humphreys, Eleanor 257
Humphreys, Elizabeth 584
Humphreys, Finus 50
Humphreys, Milley 50, 77
Humphreys, Spencer 50, 77
Hunt, Daniel 550
Hunt, Lucretia W 665
Hunt, Margaret 722
Hunt, Martha 400, 426, 427
Hunt, Prescilla 617
Hunt, Thomas, Senr 617
Hunt, William 400, 426, 427, 722
Hunter, James 559
Hurdle, Sarah 568
Huster, John 254
Huster, Rebecca 254
Hyatt, Anna 336, 337, 363, 382
Hyatt, Hezekiah 363
Hyatt, Seth 336, 337, 363, 382
Hyman, Thos 285

I

Ingram, Jennet 315, 327, 328, 633
Ingram, Matthew 315, 633
Ingrim, Rhody 373
Irwin, Francis 406

J

Jackson, America 309
Jackson, Gabriel 543, 566, 578
Jackson, Margaret 543, 566, 578
Jackson, Mary 368, 558, 616
Jackson, Polly 616
James, Gabriel 670
James, George 280, 292, 297
James, Mary 670
James, Nancy 280, 292, 294, 297
Jarratt, Killian 363
Jarrett, John 468
Jarrett, Senna 575
Jean, Lemuel 436, 445, 446
Jean, Nancey 445
Jean, Nancy 436, 444, 446
Jeffers, Enoch 500
Jeffreys, Drucilla 500
Jeffreys, James 696
Jennett, Christain 42
Jennings, John 53
Jennings, Richard D 702
Jennings, Sidney M 702

Index

Jernagan, Arthur 673
Jernagan, Mary 673
Jernagan, Patsey 673
Jernagan, Sally 673
Jernagan, Sarah Ann 673
Jernigan, Judith 515
Jernigan, Ryan 0 515
Jinkins, Mary 731
Johns(t)on, John L D 123
Johns(t)on, Sarah 123
Johnson, Elizabeth 559
Johnson, Hannah 516, 527
Johnson, Henry B 559
Johnson, Jacob 51, 516, 527
Johnson, John 456, 473, 671
Johnson, M Duke 176
Johnson, Moses 401, 426, 427
Johnson, Nancy 255
Johnson, Patsey 456, 589
Johnson, Patsy 473
Johnson, Peggy 671
Johnson, Polly 401, 426, 427
Johnson, Rachel 51
Johnson, Ro R 176
Johnson, Robert R 532
Johnson, Susan 645
Johnson, Thomas 255
Johnson, William 181
Johnston, Maria 733
Johnston, Rachel 77
Jolly, Nancy 551
Jones, Alexander 364, 382
Jones, David 285
Jones, Esther 285
Jones, Fowler 220
Jones, James 509
Jones, Mary H 364, 382
Jones, Nathaniel 28, 95
Jones, Reddick 190
Jones, Robt H 176
Jones, Solomon 285
Jones, Susanna 445, 446
Jones, Thomas 445, 446
Jones, William 190
Jonston, Joel 52
Jonston, Mary 52
Jordan, George 402, 426, 427
Jordan, Sarah 402, 426, 427
Jordin, George 402
Jordin, Sarah 402, 426
Joyce, Mary 676
Judd, Jefferson 723
Judd, Mary 723
Julin, John 672
Julin, Lucinda 672
Justice, William 634

K

Kabe, Barbary 664
Kearns, Susanna 246
Keaton, Elizabeth 53
Keaton, J 53
Keaton, John 544

Keaton, Silas 544
Keaton, Susannah 544
Keen, Amelia 6, 36
Keeth, Sarah Ann 691
Keeth, William 691
Keith, Sarah Ann 673
Keith, William 673
Kelly, Benj 698
Kelly, Benjamin 698
Kelly, Mr 545
Kennedy, Jacob 368
Kerns, Susannah 301
Kerr, H W 483
Kerr, Sarah 219
Kerr, William 219
Kieth, Sally 673
Kieth, Sarah Ann 673
Killion, David 594
Killion, Elizabeth 594
Kilpatrick, Elias M 735
Kincaid, James 195
King, Elizabeth 299
King, John 532
Kitrell, Jonathan 520
Kittrell, A Bryan 520
Kittrell, Pleasant 520
Kitts, Oliver 176
Knight, Lewis 125
Knight, Murfree 54, 124
Knight, Nancy 54, 124
Knight, Priscilla 125
Knott, Becca 536
Komegay, Jacob 368
Kornegy, H 721

L

La Peyre, Bernard 444
La Peyre, Harriet 444
Laine, Elizabeth Laine, 491
Lamb, Eaton 350
Landreth, Rachel 336, 337
Landreth, Thomas 336, 337
Lane, Joel H 545
Lane, Martha 186, 256
Lane, Mary A G 545
Lane, William 186, 256
Langford, Delilah 481, 492
Langford, George 481
Largent, Thomas 525
Laspeyre, Bernard 437, 457
Laspeyre, Harriet 437, 457
Laspyere, Bernard 445, 446
Laspyere, Hal-net 445
Laspyere, Harriet 446
Lassit, Brinkley 500
Lassiter, Polley 104
Lawrence, Arthur 674
Lawrence, Martha 674
Lawwell, Elizabeth 55, 77
Lawwell, Samuel 55, 77
Laxton, Meador 327
Laxton, Nancy 327
Layfong, Benedict 635

Layfong, Mary 635
Lea, Agness 680
Leck, Catharina 126
Lee, Elizabeth 127
Lee, Jesse 127
Lee, Nancy 147
Lee, Simpson 333
Legget, Elizabeth 105
Leigh, Benjamin 403, 427
Leigh, Sarah 403, 426, 427
Lemar, Elizabeth 567
Lemar, James 567
Leroy, Hellen 90
Leroy, L S 90
Lester, John 524
Lewis, Aaron 162
Lewis, Benjamin 309
Lewis, Mary 458, 469, 472
Lewis, Patsey 404, 426, 427
Lewis, Patsy 426
Lewis, Sophia 162
Lewis, Stephen 404, 426, 427
Lewis, William 458, 472
Liles, Micajah 442
Limbaugh, Catharina 128
Limbaugh, Christian 128
Lindsay, Samuel W 546
Lindsay, Violet 554
Lindsay, Violet W 546
Lindsey, Samuel 554
Link, Rachel 661
Little, William 581
Lockhart, Owen 739
Long, John 491
Long, Martha 591
Loughbridge, John 350
Love, Gen'l 572
Love, R 572
Love, Robert 664, 694
Low, Eve 292, 297
Low, Nancy 207, 243, 271
Low, Thomas 292, 297
Lowance, John 159, 360, 480
Lowe, Eve 281, 294
Lowe, Thomas 281
Loyd, Mary 394
Lumpkin, Polly 438, 444, 445, 446
Lumpkin, William 438, 445, 446
Lunceford, Abraham 257
Lunceford, Eleanor 257
Lunsford, Abraham 257
Lunsford, Abram 257
Lunsford, Eleanor 257
Lunsford, William 257
Lynan, Aretus 724
Lynan, Malinda 724
Lyndon, Josiah 415

M

Mabry, Kinchen 547
Mabry, Martha 547
MacDonald, Charlotte 501
MacDonald, Isaac 501

Index

MacEachern, Malcom 675
MacEachern, Mary 675
Machen, Mary 405
Machen, Thomas W 405
MacLean, Violet W 546
Maget, Wm 600
Maks, Peggy 381
Mallard, Jas 609
Maner, Levi 459
Maner, Sally 459
Manier, Ann B 187
Manier, Anne B 187
Manier, Daniel J 187
Manlove, George 188
Manlove, Hannah 188
Manning, Eli 129, 163
Manning, Winefred 163
Manning, Winnefred 129
Manson, John C 653
Manton, Ann 218
Marly, J 401
Marr, Joseph 735
Marsh, Daniel 90
Marshall, Thomas 653
Martin, Allin 630
Martin, J M 726
Martin, Jesse 164
Martin, Jessi 164
Martin, Judge 662
Martin, Obadiah 550
Martin, Sally 164
Martin, Wm C 550
Martin, Yearby 630
Mask, John D 365, 381
Mask, Patsey 241
Mask, Peggy 365
Mason, Ann 460, 469, 472
Mason, Hannah 56
Mason, Margaret 406, 474, 476
Mason, Richard 56, 406, 474, 476
Mason, William W 460, 472
Massey, Adkins 332, 337
Massey, John H 725, 740
Massey, Levina 332, 337
Massey, Margaret 725, 740
Massey, Nathan 725
Massey, Olive 189
Massey, Samuel 189
Massingale, Daniel 58
Morgan, James 59
Massongill, Amey 57
Massongill, James 57
Mathews, Nancy 206
Mathis, James 268
Matox, Mary 52
Matthews, Mabel 190
Matthews, Reddick 190
May, Daniel 561
May, William 561
McAffee, Polly 704
McCaul, Capt 128
McCauley, William 520
McCaw, Elizabeth H 726, 740
McCaw, John 726

McCaw, Mary 726
McCaw, Nancy 726
McCaw, Robert 726
McCaw, William B 726, 740
McCeaughan, Hugh 482
McCeaughan, Phebe 482
McClure, John 89
McClure, Rachel 89
McComb, Robert 406
McCormick, Mr 700
McCulley, Andrew 568
McCulley, John 568
McCulley, Sarah 568
McCulloh, John 122
McDaniel, Sarah 642
McDonald, Charlotte 508
McDonald, Isaac 508
McDougald, Alexander 723
McDougald, Jennet 723
McDowell, Chas 630
McDowell, Dr Alexander 272
McDowell, Silas 727
McGonnigold, Eli 292, 297
McGonnigold, Rachel 292, 297
McKaughan, Hugh 502, 636
McKaughan, Phebe 502, 636
McKaughon, James 658
McKaughon, Phebe 658
McKee, Rev James 498
McKenzie, Hugh 627
McKinley, James 165
McKinley, Sarah 165
McKinne, Bama 299
McKinne, Nancy 327, 595
McKinne, Richard 595
McKinney, George 316, 336
McKinney, Nancy 316
McKinnie, George 337
McKinnie, Nancy 336, 337
McKinsey, Elizabeth 366
McKinsey, James 366
McKinsie, Elizabeth 382
McKinsie, James 366
McKinsie, James 382
McLilley, John 596
McLilley, Mildred 596
McMillan, Alexander B 564
McMillan, Jno 92
McMillan, John 564
McMullin, John 528
McMurry, James Sr 575
McNamarra, Margaret 556
McNamarra, Peggy 495
McNaughton, Barbara 297
McNaughton, Neill 297
McPherson, Elizabeth 366
McQuestion, Susanna 382
McQuestion, William 382
McQuistion, Susanna 381
McQuistion, William 381
McSwain, Hannah 483
Mease, Martin 335
Meeds, Benjamin 524
Meeds, Elizabeth 53

Meeds, Tamar 524
Meeds, Tamer 524
Meek, Jean 413
Melton, Jemima 225
Melvin, Henry 648
Mendenhall, Geo C 514
Mendenhall, Nathan 514
Mendenhall, Richard 514
Merideth, Andrew 617
Merit, Benjamin 239
Merit, John 239
Merret, Salley 465
Merridith, Andrew 617
Merritt, William Henry 520
Mewir, Margaret 69
Meyers, Mary 116
Meyers, Michael 116
Mhoon, John 129
Micajah Allen 77
Midgett, Barbara 252
Midyett, Sarah 42
Miers, Jacob 220
Miers, Sally 220
Miles, Eleanor 317, 327, 328
Miles, Thomas 317
Millar, Alfred 166
Millar, Gilly 166
Millar, James 166
Millar, John 166
Millar, Martin 166
Millar, Peter 166
Miller, Caleb 503, 508
Miller, Haman 166
Miller, Herman 415
Miller, Hermon 472
Miller, Herrmon 461
Miller, James 415
Miller, Mr 604
Miller, Rachel 503, 508
Miller, Salome 461, 469, 472
Miller, William B 368
Mills, Ambrose 111
Mills, Anne 111
Mills, James W 597, 637, 659
Mills, Mary Ann 597, 637
Mires, Polly 621
Mison, Mary 639
Misters, Jno B 279
Mitchel, Hannah 638
Mitchel, Robert 638
Mitchel, Thos 638
Mitchell, Faithey 407
Mitchell, James G 407
Mitchell, Sidney 702
Mitchell, Susan 696
Mixon, Jeremiah 639
Mixon, Mary 639
Monk, Archibald 706
Monk, Nancy 652
Mooneham, Mary 569
Mooneham, William 569
Mooney, Daniel 483
Mooney, Hannah 483
Moore, Alfred W 559

Index

Moore, Bill 559
Moore, Charles 556
Moore, James 559
Moore, John 52
Keaton, Patrick 53
Moore, John 58
Moore, Lovy 58
Moore, Sally 195
Moore, W 545
Moorehead, John W 617
Mordecai, Jacob 176
Moreign, Mary 130
Moreign, Thomas 130
Morgan, Benjamin 191
Morgan, Capt Lodowick 544
Morgan, Joseph 93
Morgan, Mary 191
Morgan, Polly 727, 740
Morgan, Rebeckah 59
Morrice, Rebekah 60
Morgan, Ruddy 727
Morgan, William B 727, 740
Morine, Thomas 130
Morrice, John G 60
Morris, Elisabeth 439, 444, 445, 446
Morris, John G 77
Morris, John L 439, 445, 446
Morris, Rebeckah 77
Morrison, Archibald 192
Morrison, Capt Alexander 122
Morrison, Elizabeth 192
Morrow, Elizabeth 259, 282, 333
Morrow, William 735
Moseley, John 532
Moseley, John W 532
Moton, George 465
Mott, Thomas L W 714
Mound, Reverend Israel 557
Muir, Margaret 69
Mullins, John 462, 475
Mullins, Nancy 462, 470, 475
Muray, Samuel, Jr 168
Murden, David 258
Murden, David 258
Murden, Mary 440, 444, 445, 446
Murden, Robert 440, 445, 446
Murdin, David 258
Murdin, Frances 258
Murphey, Alexander 380
Murphy William 363
Murphy, James 372
Murray, Archibald 167
Murray, Delilah 167
Murray, Elizabeth 168, 259, 282, 333, 337
Murray, Mary 609
Murray, Samuel Jr 193, 259, 282, 293, 333, 337
Murry, Elizabeth 221
Murry, Samuel, Jr 221
Muse, Margaret 728
Muse, Thomas W 728
Musgrave, Micajah 222, 299
Musgrave, Zilpah 222, 299

Musgrove, Micajah 270
Mustgrave, Micajah 222
Mustgrave, Zilpha 222
Muvir, Margaret 69

N

Napier, Col Richard C 698
Napier, R C 698
Naylor, John 18
Naylor, Matilda 18
Neal, Muses 701
Neale, John 729
Neally, Major 536
Nease, Betty 335
Nease, John 335
Neeley, Polly 591
Neeley, Thos 317
Neese, William 335
Neil, Henry 517
Neil, Mary 517
Neilly, Elsey 367, 382
Neilly, William 367, 382
Nelson, Esther E 729, 740
Nelson, James 536
Nelson, Josephus 729, 740
Newberry, Elizabeth 272
Newkirk, Alexander 484
Newkirk, Rebecca 484
Noomcaser, Catharine 527
Noomcaser, Daniel 527
Noomkaser, Catharine 518
Noomkaser, Daniel 518
Norcom, Abner 223
Norcom, Dr James 223
Norcom, Jno 223
Norcom, John Hamilton 223
Norcom, Mary 223
Norfleet, Benjamin 86, 131, 194
Norfleet, Peggy 131, 194
Norlee, Peggy 86
Norman, Fanny 508
Norman, John 508
Norman, Joshua 491
Norris, Lotty 323
Norris, Peyton 203
North, Anderson 680
Nye, Mr 696

O

O'Bradley, James 579
O'Briant, Jane 224
O'Briant, William 224
O'Bryant, Jane 224
O'Bryant, William 224
O'Neal, Riney 560
O'Neal, Theophilus 560
O'Neal, William 42
O'Neel, William 182
O'Quin, John 368
O'Quin, Mary 368
Oakley, Nancy 598
Oakley, Stephen 598

Oates, Col Jethro 299
Odel, Caleb 372
Odom, Amelia 120
Oel, Catherine 260
Oel, Peter F 260
Ogle, Hiram 195
Ogle, Sally 195
Oldham, Alien 520
Oldham, Geo 520
Oldham, Holadey R 643
Oles, Weston R 719
Oliphant, Ann 33
Oliphant, Sarah 33
Oliphant, William 33
Orrin, Mary L 676
Orrin, William 676
Outlaw, David 185
Outlaw, Deborah 87, 159, 185, 360, 480
Outlaw, Debory 159
Outlaw, George 185
Outlaw, Jacob 159, 185, 360, 480
Outlaw, James 185
Outlaw, John 360
Overbey, Susannah 703
Overbey, William 703
Overman, Tamer 524
Overman, William 671
Owen, Aaron 241
Owins, Jane 318
Ozbourn, Elizabeth 567

P

Paine, Solomon 575
Paine, Thomas 522
Pannal, Martha 283, 294, 297
Pannal, William 283, 297
Parker, Jonathan 536, 617
Parker, Sally 600
Parkes, Sarah 169
Parks, Catharine 704, 711, 730, 740
Parks, Gabriel 704, 711, 730, 740
Parks, Gabriel L 730
Parks, Jas 550
Parks, Jno O 550
Parks, Mr 279
Parks, R H 550
Parks, Sarah 226
Parnell, Mr Robert L 739
Parratt, James 5
Parrish, Claborn 305
Parsons, Esther 632, 669
Parsons, Nathan 632, 669
Partin, Green T 731
Partin, Mary 731
Partridge, Isaac C 702
Paschall, Anderson 592
Pasteur, Martha 256
Pastieur, Martha 186
Patrick, Elisha 504
Patrick, Isaac 504
Patrick, John 504
Patrick, Martha W 677

Index

Patrick, Sally 504
Patrick, William 677
Patterson, Daniel 19
Patton, Joseph 408
Patton, Patsey 408
Paul, Bartholomew 729
Paxton, Judge 591
Peace, William 203, 593
Peal, Jesse 285
Pearson, Amy 630
Pearson, Joel A 630
Pearson, Mary 630
Peck, Ann 599
Peck, Daniel 599
Peck, Nancy 599
Pegram, Betsy 522
Pegram, Gideon 522
Penick, Thomas 642
Pennington, Ezekiel 505, 508
Pennington, Levice 505
Pennington, Levisa 505
Pennington, Levisa 507
Pennington, Louisa 505
Perkins, Jesse 379
Perkins, Pharoah 732
Perkins, Susan 732
Perry, Burrill 719
Perry, Daniel 382
Perry, David 371, 381, 409
Perry, Eleanor 20
Perry, Elizabeth 369, 381
Perry, Jacob 370, 381
Perry, John 20
Perry, L F 545
Perry, Lane F 545
Perry, Mary 529
Perry, Nancy 371, 381, 382, 409
Perry, Reuben 369
Perry, Sarah 370, 381
Perry, Willis 370
Person, Patsey 408
Persons, Landry 195
Persons, Mr Charles 372
Petty, Stephen J 520
Philemon, James 336, 337
Philemon, Nancy 337
Philips, Deborah 332
Philips, Susanna 334
Philips, Susannah 337
Philips, Willis 334, 337
Phillips, Elizabeth 265
Phillips, Elizabeth A 706
Phillips, Lucy 706
Phillips, Polly 388
Phillips, William 706
Philmon, Nancy 336
Phipps, Robert 629, 699
Phipps, Sally 629, 699
Pierce, Tabitha 534
Pinnix, Sarah 523, 519, 527
Pinnix, Trice 519
Pipkin, Mark 299
Pipkin, Sareigh 299
Pirant, Joshua 107

Pit(t)man, Mary 225
Pitcher, Jno 657
Pitcher, John 640
Pitcher, Lucy 640
Pitt, Edmund R 520
Pittman, Robert 225
Plummer, Elisha 513
Plummer, Kemp 176
Poe, Elisha 631
Poe, Hastin 520
Poe, J F 520
Pool, Mr 667
Poor, Caleb 336, 337, 372, 382
Poor, Polly Mira 336, 337, 372, 382
Pope, Elijah 169, 196, 226, 600
Pope, George 482, 502
Pope, Mary 502
Pope, Phebe 482, 502
Pope, Saley 226
Pope, Sally 600
Pope, Sarah 169, 196, 226
Porter, Daniel 373
Porter, James 406
Porter, John 596, 616
Porter, Rhody 373
Posey, Humphrey 737
Posey, Rev Mr 737
Poteet, James H 626
Potter, Archibald 284, 293
Potter, Ezekiel H 529
Potter, Isabella A 705, 710
Potter, Lemender 284
Potter, Robert 705, 710
Potts, Jonth 110
Powell, Benjamin 34
Powell, Calley 4
Powell, Elizabeth 410, 426, 427
Powell, John 410, 426, 427
Powell, Mariah A 733
Powell, Nancy 21
Powell, Nathan 21
Powell, William M 733
Powers, Cynthia 641
Powers, John 641, 659
Powers, Lucy 411, 426, 427
Powers, Rodham 411, 427
Pratt, Moses S 665
Pratt, Susanna 181
Pratt, William, Sr 181
Prescott, William 739
Price, Jane 573
Price, Jonathan 649
Price, Meridith 642
Price, Sarah 642
Price, Susan 520, 643
Price, Susanna 548
Price, Susannah 520
Price, Thomas 520, 548
Price, Washington 520, 548, 643
Prince, Oliver 215
Pritchett, Mary 679
Prutt, Willis 344
Pugh, Edward S 644
Pugh, James 412, 426, 427

Pugh, Lydia 644
Pugh, Rebecca 412, 426, 427
Pugh, Thomas 509
Pugh, Thomas Whitmell 58
Pyron, Joshua 301

Q

Queen, Mary 727
Queen, Polly 727, 740
Query, Susanna 61
Query, William 61
Quin, Hugh 483

R

Ragland, Mrs 212
Ragsdale, Nimrod 520
Rainey, Eleanor 317
Rains, Nancy 132
Randall, Jane 328
Randall, Jean 327
Randell, Jean 318
Randell, Thornton 318
Randol, George 318
Randol, Jean 318
Randol, Thornton 318
Rankin, Jean 413
Rankin, Samuel 413
Ray, Hannah 431
Ray, Ursilla 80
Read, Elias 679, 691
Read, Franky 678
Read, Jacob 678
Read, Mary 679, 691
Read, Philip 333
Read, Polly 679
Record, David 62
Record, Mary 62, 401
Record, Polly 401
Redding, Jane 170
Redding, Reham 170
Reed, Franky 678
Reed, Hugh 645
Reed, Jacob 678
Reed, Susannah 645
Reid, Lucy T 706
Reid, Martha 706
Reid, Thomas 706
Rencher, John G 95
Rencher, John P 95
Reynolds, Keith Huested 673
Rhem, Joseph 739
Rhodes, Alston 150
Rhodes, Arnold 90, 150
Rhodes, Benjamin 95
Rhodes, Capt Arnold 90
Rhodes, Euphan A 90
Rhodes, Uphan 90
Rice, Abigail 22
Rice, John 22
Rice, Sally 504
Riceson, Isaiah 215
Rich, Robert Cannon, 537

Index

Richardson, Amos 272
Richardson, John 374, 463, 475, 485
Richardson, Mrs Gatsy 739
Richardson, Richard 739
Richardson, Sarah 374, 463, 470, 475, 485
Riddle, Harmon 414, 426, 427
Riddle, Susanna, 427
Riddle, Susannah 414, 426
Ridley, Mrs 714
Ridley, Thos D 714
Riggans, Martha 547
Rigsbee, Isaiah 520
Rigsbee, John E 520
Rigsbee, Nancy 520
Rigsbee, Phoebe 520
Riley, Patsy 375, 415
Riley, Peter 375, 415
Riley, Rhodus 415
Roan, Matthew 63
Roan, Peggy 63, 77
Roane, Jesse 416, 426, 427
Roane, Margaret 416, 426, 427
Roane, Wm 727
Robards, William 305
Robbin, Benjamin 453
Robbins, Joseph 415
Roberds, Peggy 646
Roberds, William 646
Roberths, Thomas 381
Roberts, Agness 680
Roberts, Col 409
Roberts, J 704
Roberts, Jno 242
Roberts, John 680
Roberts, Martha 734, 740
Roberts, Peggy 646
Roberts, Phoebe 376, 381
Roberts, Rev George 64
Roberts, Thomas 376, 734, 740
Roberts, William 646
Robertson, Elizabeth 601
Robertson, Eve 335
Robertson, James 335
Robertson, John 601
Robertson, Lovey 173
Robertson, Willis 601
Robins, Mary 453
Robinson, Arthur 34
Robinson, Jane B 486, 493, 494
Robinson, Judah 27
Robinson, Nathaniel 335
Robinson, Robert 406
Robinson, William B 350
Robinson, William D 486, 493, 494
Rodgers, Agatha 64
Rodgers, Samuel 64
Rogers, Benajah 227
Rogers, Mr Alien 203
Rogers, Sarah 227
Rogers, Thos 238
Rolenson, Thomas 182
Roles, William 719
Rolinson, Christopher 182

Rolinson, Thomas 42
Rose, Duncan 575
Ross, Jos 571, 604
Rothhaas, Amy 133
Rothhaus, Ann 133
Rothhaus, Balser 133
Rowe, Mary 405
Rowland, Alexander 232
Rowland, Alfred 602, 647, 658
Rowland, Mary E 610, 658
Rowland, Mary Eliza 602, 647
Roygers, Agatha 64
Roygers, Samuel 64
Rucks, James 698
Ruffin, Grey 603, 610
Ruffin, Rebecca 603, 610
Ruffin, W 176
Runion, James 662
Runion, Polly 662
Russel, Martha 336
Russel, Mr 279
Russell, Aaron 65, 77
Russell, Hannah 638
Russell, Leziah 77
Russell, Lizea 65
Russell, Martha 337
Russell, Samuel 401
Russell, William 336, 337
Rutherford, James 464
Rutherford, John 471
Rutherford, Margaret 464, 471
Ryler, Peter 415
Ryley, Patsy 415

S

Sadler, Averelles 197
Sadler, Averiller 197
Sadler, William 197
Sale, Eliza G 698
Sale, Rev Anthony 698
Salisbury, Polly 198
Salisbury, Willis 198
Salmons, Jacob 641
Salyear, Elizabeth 648
Salyear, John 648
Sampson, Edward 555
Sanders, Amey 57
Sanders, Benja 512
Sanders, Lemuel 23
Sanders, Martha 336, 337
Sanders, Philip 242
Sanders, Sabra 23
Sanders, Tilman 336
Sanders, Tilmand 337
Savage, Jesse 385
Savage, Mr 545
Sawyer, Dinah 67, 77, 91, 134, 171
Sawyer, Frederick B 223
Sawyer, James 649
Sawyer, Keziah 649
Sawyer, Willis 67, 77, 91, 134, 171
Scott, Mary 238
Scott, Saml 677

Searingam, John 334
Sears, Green 698
Sears, John 156
Sears, Love 385
Sears, Thomas 698
Sears, William 385
Seats, Josiah 172
Seats, Mary 172
Seehon, Joseph 135
Seehon, Mary 135
Self, Lucey 228
Sellers, Simon 501
Sellers, Simon 508
Sessums, James 199
Sessums, Susannah 199
Sexton, Nancy 328
Sexton, Thomas 328
Shackelford, Richard 166
Shaddy, Jacob 335
Sharp, Henry 299
Sharp, Hzziah 299
Sharp, Susannah 570
Sharp, Thomas 570
Sharpe, Susannah 578
Sharpe, Thomas 578
Shaver, Fanny 24
Shaver, George 24
Shaw, Elizabeth 706
Shaw, Ha(i)ley 417
Shaw, Haley 441, 446
Shaw, Mathew 330
Shaw, Polly 417, 441, 446
Shearrin, Ruthey 532
Shearron, Ruthy 532
Sheaver, Fanny 24
Sheaver, George 24
Sheets, Cyntha 707
Sheets, Solomon 707
Sheppard, Josiah 410
Sherley, James 696
Shields, Wm T 584
Ship, Mr 695
Shirley, Susan P 696, 710
Shof(f)ner, Sarah 335
Shoffner, Michael 335
Shoffner, Michael Jr 337
Shoffner, Sarah 337
Shofner, Michael 319
Shofner, Michael, Sr 335
Shofner, Sarah 319
Shoftner, Michael 293
Short, Aaron 487
Short, Dinah 310
Short, James 487
Short, Jean 487
Short, Margaret 487
Shouse, Frederick 461
Shouse, Salome 461
Sideney, Oliver 729
Silva, David 735, 740
Silva, Elizabeth 735, 740
Simeon, Eliza 557
Simmons, Asa 615

Index

Simmons, Daniel 398
Simmons, Eliza 625
Simons, Cloe 650
Simons, Eliza 586, 650
Simons, Mary 586
Simons, Solomon 586, 650
Simons, Zacheus 650
Simonton, Robert 498
Simpson, Francis L 617
Simpson, James 549
Simpson, Priscilla 549
Simpson, Sally 261
Simpson, Samuel 156
Simpson, Solomon 261
Singletary, Nelly 272
Singleton, Christopher 681, 691
Singleton, Kesiah 681, 691
Singleton, Philip W 465
Singleton, Sarah 465
Skidmore, Ann 200
Skinner, Elizabeth 521
Skinner, Henry 521
Slaughter, Elizabeth H 726
Sloan, Elizabeth 682
Sloan, John 682
Slocumb, Ezekiel 299
Smart, Francis B 122
Smart, Geo W 122
Smelley, Frances 25
Smelley, Francis 25
Smelley, John 25
Smith, Abner 605
Smith, Alex 262
Smith, Alexander 92, 229, 262
Smith, Barbara 694
Smith, Benj 152
Smith, Colo Jacob 694
Smith, Eleanor 571, 577
Smith, Eleanor 604
Smith, Elizabeth 136
Smith, Gideon B 571, 577, 604
Smith, John 663
Smith, Joseph 136
Smith, Mary 466
Smith, Mary Barbara 664
Smith, Nancy 363
Smith, Nancy 363
Smith, Polley 335
Smith, Rebecca Ann 683
Smith, Richard 683
Smith, Sally 26
Smith, Sarah 92, 262, 319, 335
Smith, Selah 684
Smith, Siddy 605
Smith, Thomas 26, 335
Smith, William 466, 606
Smithson, Polly 441
Smithwick, Baldy 285
Smithwick, Edmund 263, 285, 293
Smithwick, Edmund, Sr 285
Smithwick, Mary 285
Sneed, Step K 705
Snider, Barnet 379
Snider, Catharine 379

Snider, John 379
Sniper, Thos 215
Snipes, Delia 230
Snipes, Dilly 230
Snipes, James 575
Snipes, John 230
Snow, John 176, 545
Sorrels, Nancy 685
Sorrels, William 685
Southerland, William 484
Sowell, Mr 7
Spear, Alexander 736
Spear, Alexander 740
Spear, Margaret P 736
Spear, Margaret P 740
Spears, Absalom 418, 426, 427
Spears, Elisha 488
Spears, Margaret 488
Spears, Sally 418, 426, 427
Speer, Alexander 736
Speer, Margaret P 736
Speight, Sally 686
Speight, William W D 686
Spell, Celia 68, 93
Spell, John 68, 93
Spencer, Jno 550
St Lawrence, Elisabeth 66, 77
St Lawrence, Patrick 66
Staley, Eve 231
Staley, Jacob 231, 491
Stallcup, William 363
Stamper, John F 550
Stamper, Martha 550
Stanaland, Thomas 27
Stanfield, Sarah 166
Stanley, Eleanor 571, 604
Stark, Mrs 695
Starling, Bersheba 233
Starling, Stephen 233
Starnes, Elizabeth 708, 737
Starnes, Elizabeth M 711, 740
Starnes, John 708, 711
Starnes, John 737, 740
Starr, Henry 69
Starr, Margaret 69
Steel, Colen 415
Steele, Robert J 34
Steiner, Ann 133
Stephens, Ebenezer 232
Stephens, Ebenezer 264, 320
Stephens, Elizabeth 137, 264, 320
Stephens, Elizabeth 332
Stephenson, Gatsey 687
Stephney, Elizabeth 265
Stephney, William 265
Sterling, Bersheba 233
Sterling, Stephen 233
Stevens, Ebenezer 232
Stevens, Elizabeth 232
Stevenson, Gatsey 687
Stevenson, Silas 687
Steward, Sarah 82
Stewart, Lovey 173
Stewart, Sally 286

Stewart, Thomas 173
Stillwell, Jeremiah 712
Stillwell, Mary 712
Stokes, David 201
Stokes, General Mumford 128
Stokes, Nancy 201
Stone, Ann 333
Stone, Rheuben 333
Stone, Susannah 333
Strader, Harriot S 506
Strange, Judge 704
Street, Charlotte 467, 468, 492
Street, John 467
Strickland, Elizabeth 433
Strong, Mr 545
Stubbs, Charlotte 489
Stubbs, Elizabeth 489, 492
Stubbs, John B 489
Stubbs, Mary 489
Stubbs, Mary Ann 489
Suddath, Benjamin 416
Suddath, James 651, 658
Suddath, Susan 651
Suddath, Susannah 651, 658
Sugg, Joshua 22
Sumerset, Hannah 234
Sumerset, Simon 234
Summerlin, Mary 225
Sumner, Elizabeth 70
Sumner, James B 70
Sutherland, Mordecai 95
Sutton, Elizabeth 285
Sutton, Hannah 321, 327, 328
Sutton, John 321

T

Tapley, Robert 419, 426, 427
Tapley, Tempy 419, 426, 427
Tarrel, Francis 520
Taylor, Alfred 327, 328
Taylor, Isabella A 705
Taylor, John 138, 524
Taylor, John C 714
Taylor, Mary Sr 696
Taylor, Nancy 652
Taylor, Nathan 490
Taylor, Rachel 138
Taylor, Sarah 327, 328
Taylor, Susannah 490, 492
Taylor, Teresy 214
Taylor, Uncle Dorman 696
Taylor, William 696
Taylor, William D 652
Teague, Isaac 335
Teague, John 335
Teague, Joseph 335
Tender, Elizabeth 328
Tender, John 307
Thodes, Mrs Euphan Alston 90
Thomas, Anna 420, 426, 427
Thomas, Charles 28
Thomas, Charles Alien 174
Thomas, Elizabeth 377, 382

Index

Thomas, James 420, 426, 427
Thomas, Jane 174
Thomas, Jenny Jarrit 28
Thomas, John Sr 333
Thomas, Levina 235
Thomas, Levinah 202
Thomas, Lewis 202, 235
Thomas, Richard 506
Thomas, Temprance 506
Thomas, William 377, 382
Thomason, Charles 592
Thompson, Ann 29
Thompson, Elizabeth 451
Thompson, James 331
Thompson, John 451
Thompson, Julia Ann 653
Thompson, Thomas W 653
Thompson, William 29
Thomson, Henry 467, 520
Thornhill, Lucy 640
Thornton, Heroad 104
Throw, John H 679
Thweatt, William 350
Tillery, Ann 94
Tillery, George 94
Tilley, Edmund 654
Tilley, James 658
Tilley, Sarah 654, 658
Tindel, James 572, 578, 607
Tindel, Susannah 572, 607
Tindell, James 610, 611
Tindell, Susannah 578, 610, 611
Tinker, Capt Edward 156
Tinker, Elizabeth 156
Todd, Jane 78
Todd, Milberry 442
Todd, Solomon 442
Todd, Thomas 78
Todd, Thomas the Younger 78
Toffler, Deborah 185
Toffler, James 185
Tois, Benjamin 427
Tolson, Daniel 729
Tolson, Rebekah 42
Tomberau, Lewis 551
Tomberau, Lewis 554
Tomberau, Nancy 551
Tomberau, Nancy 554
Tomberaw, Lewis 551
Tomberaw, Nancy 551
Tombereau, Lewis 551
Tombereau, Nancy 551
Torence, Elizabeth 30
Torence, Thomas 30
Tores, Benjamin 378, 381, 382, 421, 426, 427
Tores, Elizabeth 378, 381, 382, 421, 426
Toris [Tores], Elizabeth 427
Townsend, Sally 286
Townsend, Thomas 286, 293
Truit, Isaac 735
Truit, Jas 735
Tucker, Aaron 322
Tucker, Nancy 322
Turnage, Martha 74
Turner, Charles R 592
Turner, Charles W 701
Turner, Henry A 608
Turner, Lucy 592
Turner, Lucy R 701
Turner, Mary 608
Turner, Talithacume 592
Tuten, Elizabeth 655
Tuten, Thomas 655, 659
Tutner, Henry 688
Tutner, Mary 688

U

Underbill, Giles 442
Unthank, William 536
Upton, Dinah 171
Upton, Willis 171
Utley, Mary 287, 291
Utley, Polly 203, 266, 323, 328
Utley, Wm 323
Utley, Young 203, 266, 287, 291, 323, 328

V

Vail, Margaret 725
Vannoy, Nathaniel 422
Vannoy, Nathaniel, Jr 426, 427
Vannoy, Sarah 422
Vannoy, Sarah 426, 427
Vannoy, Sary 422
Vaughan, Elizabeth 522
Vaughan, James Madison 522
Vaughan, Jno Jeremiah 522
Vaughan, John 734
Vaughan, Martha Anne 522
Vaughan, Ozbom 522
Vaughan, Peyton 522
Vaughan, Samuel 734
Vaughan, William Thomas 522
Venables, J 219
Vervell, Daniel 139, 236
Vervell, Mary 139, 236
Vining, Peggy 365
Vivere, James 689
Viverett, Ann Eliza 689, 691
Viverett, Micajah 689, 691
Vogler, Barbara 117

W

Wade, Patsy 375, 415
Wagener, Polly 581
Waldron, John 336, 337
Waldron, Nancy 336, 337
Walker, Amos J 609
Walker, Betsey 292, 294
Walker, Betsy 288, 297
Walker, Elizabeth 140, 288
Walker, James 305
Walker, Joseph 140, 288, 292, 297
Walker, Margaret 406
Walker, Mary 285
Walker, Mr 285
Wallace, Milly 596
Wallace, W 737
Waller, Mary 609
Wallis, Mary 305
Walls, James 738, 740
Walls, Mahala 738, 740
Walters, Nancy 225
Ward, Catharine 379
Ward, Elijah 567
Ward, Frederick 379
Ward, Joshua 423, 426, 427
Ward, R 331
Ward, Silvia 423
Ward, Sylvia 426, 427
Warmoth, Betsy 237
Warmoth, James 237
Warren, Elizabeth 335, 491
Warren, Mary 267
Warren, Samuel 491
Warren, William 267
Watkins, Samuel 433
Watson, Mr William 398
Watson, Nancey 398
Watson, Sinthy 398
Webb, Abdias P 520
Webb, Mary G 520
Webb, Polly 520
Webb, Susan 520, 643
Webb, Susanna 548
Webb, Susannah 520
Webster, Ned 656
Weeks, Drury 735
Welborn, Jane 523, 527
Welborn, John 523
Welch, Daniel 641
Wells, Fanny 380, 382
Wells, John 380, 382
Wells, Nathaniel 73
West, Rachel 141
West, William 141
Westcott, John 252
Westmoreland, Taylor 641
Weston, Benjamin 324
Weston, Elizabeth 324, 327, 328
Wheeler, Moses 734
Wheeler, Thos 114
Whichard, Tripheny 709
Whichard, Willoughby 709
Whidbee, Mayor 182
Whidbee, Robert 31
Whidbee, Sarah 31
Whitaker, Cyrus 719
Whitchard, Tripheny 709
Whitchard, Willoughby 709
White, Achsa 71
White, Agatha 71
White, Andrew 531
White, Ann 71
White, John 524, 527, 552
White, Joseph 71
White, Lewis 739
White, Mahala 739

306

Index

White, Mariam 552
White, Mary 639
White, Nancy 384
White, Parthena 71
White, Rebeckah 532
White, Tamar 524, 527
White, Thomas 71, 739
White, William 58
White, Wm N 639
Whitehurst, Hillary 593
Whitener, Rachel 503
Whitesenhunt, Henry 427
Whitesenhunt, Holland 426
Whitesenhunt, Holland 427
Whitfield, Hardy 702
Whitherspoon, David 574
Whitley, Jane 573
Whitley, Johnathan 573
Whitley, Jonathan R 573
Whitsenhunt, Henry 424, 426
Whitsenhunt, Holland 424, 426
Whitworth, Elizabeth 72, 77
Whitworth, John 72
Wiggins, Blake B 673
Wilfong, Elizabeth 204
Wilfong, Jacob 204
Wilkerson, Benjamin 689
Wilkins, Eliza 689
Wilkins, Elizabeth 525, 527
Wilkins, William 525, 527
Wilkinson, Barbara 289, 292, 294, 295, 297
Wilkinson, Elisabeth 33
Wilkinson, John 289, 292, 297
Willey, Hillery 385
Williams, Ann L 325, 327, 328
Williams, Ashkenaz 215
Williams, B 73
Williams, Charles Alexander 526
Williams, Edward 662
Williams, Franky 678
Williams, George W 726
Williams, James 325
Williams, John 205, 526, 709
Williams, Joseph 215
Williams, Margaret P 740
Williams, Milley 205, 526
Williams, Milly 526
Williams, Rebecky 575
Williams, Tripheny 709
Willis, Spence P 702
Wills, Mildred 73
Wills, Nathaniel 73
Wilson, General 257
Wilson, J 586
Wilson, James 156
Wilson, James 554, 656, 658
Wilson, Jane 658
Wilson, John 541
Wilson, Mary 541, 554
Wilson, Sarah 663
Winchester, William 570
Winders, John 74
Winders, Martha 74

Winfield, Joseph 615
Winfield, Thomas B 615
Wingate, Arthur 75
Wingate, Dorcas 75
Winkler, Francis 321
Winkler, Hannah 321
Winstead, Polly 438
Winstead, Thomas 696
Wisdom, John 575
Witherspon, Elizabeth 574
Witherspoon, John 574
Withrow, James 32
Withrow, Sydney 32
Witty, Ezekiel, 142
Witty, Jean 142
Wolf, Caleb 443, 445, 446
Wolf, Christina 443, 446
Wolf, Christinia 445
Wolfe, Christian 444
Womack, Frances 553, 575
Womack, Henry 553, 575
Wood, Ann 33
Wood, Elisabeth 268
Wood, Joseph 33
Wood, Sarah 33
Wood, William 33
Wood, William, Sr 268
Woodard, Mary 287
Woodward, Mary 323
Woodward, Polly 203, 323
Woodward, Richard 323
Woodward, Richd 323
Woodyard, Polly 144
Woodyard, William 144
Woogard, Polly 143
Woogard, William 143
Wooters, John 576, 690
Wooters, Sarah 576, 690
Workman, Rachel 508
Wormoth, Betsy 237
Wormoth, James 237
Wortham, Charles 425, 426, 427
Wortham, Elizabeth P 425, 426, 427
Wortham, George 532
Wray, Susanna 329
Wray, Susannah 341
Wren, Howell 290, 292, 297
Wren, Sarah 290, 292, 294, 297
Wright, Isaac 272
Wright, Polley 344, 381
Wyche, Mr 662, 699
Wynn, William 648

Y

Yarborough, Philis 326, 328
Yarborough, Philliss 327
Yarborough, William 326, 327, 328
Yarbrough, Mr 545
Yarrell, Mary 327, 328
Yarrell, Matthew 327, 328
Yates, Drusilla 433
Yerger, Albert 696
Young, Milly 512, 590

Young, Nathaniel 76
Young, Tabitha 76
Younger, John 269
Younger, Rebecca 269

www.ingramcontent.com/pod-product-compliance
Lightning Source LLC
Chambersburg PA
CBHW080423230426
43662CB00015B/2200